THE PARTING OF FRIENDS

The Parting of Friends

The Wilberforces and Henry Manning

David Newsome

William B. Eerdmans Publishing Company
Grand Rapids, Michigan

Gracewing.

In Memory of
DR OCTAVIA WILBERFORCE

First published 1966 in the U.K. by John Murray
under the title *The Parting of Friends:*
A Study of the Wilberforces and Henry Manning

This edition published 1993 jointly
in the United States by Wm. B. Eerdmans Publishing Co.
255 Jefferson Ave. S.E., Grand Rapids, Michigan 49503
and in the U.K. by Gracewing
2 Southern Ave., Leominster, HR6 0QF

Printed in the United States of America

Library of Congress Cataloging-in-Publication Data

Newsome, David, 1929-
The parting of friends: the Wilberforces and Henry Manning / David Newsome.
p.   cm.
Originally published: London: Murray, 1966.
Includes bibliographical references and index.
Eerdmans ISBN 0-8028-3714-X
Gracewing ISBN 0 85244 176 2
1. Manning, Henry, 1808-1892 — Friends and associates. 2. Wilberforce, Robert Isaac,
1802-1857. 3. Wilberforce, Samuel, 1805-1873. 4. Wilberforce, Henry, 1807- 1873.
5. Wilberforce family. 6. Converts, Catholic — England — Biography. 7. Cardinals —
England — Biography. 8. Oxford movement. I. Title.
BX4705.M3N4   1993
274.2'081'0922 — dc20
[B]   93-6749
                                            CIP

CONTENTS

Contents

ILLUSTRATIONS

Unless otherwise acknowledged the photographs are reproduced from Samuel Wilberforce's albums by courtesy of the Principal, Cuddesdon College, Oxford.

FOREWORD

The Parting of Friends is one of that small handful of books which stay firmly etched in my memory many years after a first reading. I know others who share this experience, and it is not difficult to see why.

David Newsome writes beautifully, and here he succeeds in giving us the Wilberforces and Henry Manning to the life. He does so with a gentle detachment which is the more persuasive since every page demonstrates his intimate understanding of the friends whose parting he describes.

He also shows vividly how the interplay of theological ideas, religious beliefs and private emotions can sometimes lead to profound personal and public consequences. His story reminds us how religious loyalties test the strongest personal ties, strengthening some, fracturing others. *The Parting of Friends* is a narrative masterpiece, and the issue it addresses has lost none of its impact even in a more secularized age. Its republication is timely, and warmly to be welcomed.

THE RIGHT REVEREND ROBERT RUNCIE
Former Archbishop of Canterbury

PREFACE

This book has two main themes. The first (which supplies its title) is the unfolding of the intensely human drama in which a group of brilliant young men, bound together by ties of close kinship and united in their resolve to achieve great and common objectives, became so deeply involved in the religious controversies of their time that each in turn was confronted with the necessity of making a decisive personal choice between the claims of love and duty. The second is a study of the various influences at work within the Anglican Church during the first half of the nineteenth century which threw traditional party allegiances into such a state of turmoil that these claims of duty became peculiarly difficult to define. It has long been observed that many of the most active supporters of the Oxford Movement were those who had been brought up in the Evangelical tradition; and that those who underwent one conversion were liable to undergo another and to end their spiritual wanderings in the Church of Rome. But the phenomenon has never been adequately explained; and to observe the Evangelical origins of Anglo-Catholicism without such explanation is to present an incomplete picture of two of the most significant forces in the religious history of the nineteenth century.

This must be my apology for adding yet another item to the vast published literature on the history of the Oxford Movement. It is well-worn territory, but only because the confines of the Movement have been too narrowly drawn, too much reverence having been shown to the authority of Newman in the *Apologia* and to R. W. Church's early masterpiece on – to use his own sub-title – the 'Twelve Years 1833–1845'. All the major characters of this narrative were outside Oxford during these twelve years. Most of them were Evangelicals who became Anglo-Catholics, and finally Roman Catholics. Since they were all more or less touched by the spirit of Oxford churchmanship during the decade prior to 1833, and all in their different ways attempted in the years after 1845 to mend the breaches made by the secession of Newman to the Roman Church, their story has a special relevance to the genesis and development of Tractarian ideas quite apart from the fact that it has never yet been written.

ix

Preface

The innumerable histories and special studies of the Oxford Movement have been curiously fettered to the same set of original sources, chiefly the Newman Papers at the Birmingham Oratory and the enormous collection of Tractarian papers at Pusey House. Invaluable as these collections are, they cannot supply the answer to all the questions which should be raised. If the Oxford Movement was something more than the teaching of its principals, then the papers of those who were profoundly influenced by their teaching, and who came in time to undertake the re-statement of the Tractarian position in the years after 1845, must be of equal value. These papers are still largely in private hands. It has been my endeavour over the last four years to trace as many as have survived and to discover the story they have to tell.

Indeed this book has changed its shape several times as new sources came to light. It all began with a visit to Dr Octavia Wilberforce at Henfield in Sussex in the spring of 1961, when she was kind enough to show me her fine collection of the private papers of her grandfather, Samuel Wilberforce. Most of his episcopal and diocesan papers had already been lodged in the Bodleian Library at Oxford, but she had kept at home the more personal correspondence – chiefly the letters from his father, the papers of the Sargent family and the remarkably full correspondence which he maintained with his brother-in-law, Henry Manning. Further enquiries unearthed more treasures: at Catterick, the family papers preserved by Mr C. E. Wrangham – a very large collection of Wilberforce papers, including the most valuable source of all, the seven hundred or so letters which passed between Samuel Wilberforce and his brother Robert; at Harrogate, in the possession of Mrs Judith Sandwith, many of Henry Wilberforce's family papers; in Kensington, only recently discovered by Miss Irene Wilberforce, a very large album containing Robert Wilberforce's most personal papers, including the correspondence with Newman, Pusey and Gladstone.

The generosity of the Abbé Alphonse Chapeau at St Mary of the Angels, Bayswater, in allowing me to use the extensive Wilberforce collection in the Manning archives, and of Father Payne at Ushaw in letting me take microfilm enlargements of the most intimate correspondence of Manning with Henry and Mary Wilberforce; the friendly encouragement of Father Stephen Dessain at the Birmingham Oratory, of Father Donald Allchin at Pusey House and of the late Rev. Charles Linnell, whom I met twice while he was working on the catalogue of the Keble Papers; and the last-minute discovery of the missing G. D. Ryder Papers, in the possession of Sir George Clutton at the British Embassy in Warsaw (very kindly dispatched by the owner to me, so that I could work on them in England); all these kindnesses enabled me to gain a far more complete picture of my subjects than I could originally have hoped and also to extend the range of my principal characters.

My debts of gratitude are legion. What one cherishes above all are the acts of personal kindness which one has no right to expect. I have received these in abundance from so many members of the Wilberforce family; and I shall always remember with affection the generous hospitality of Mr and Mrs Wrangham at their lovely house in Yorkshire, the cheerful interest of Mrs Scott at Backsettown, the fund of personal reminiscences supplied by Mrs Winkworth (who could recall several meetings, when a young girl, with Cardinal Manning) and the many very valuable conversations which I have enjoyed with other scholars working in the same field. I have especially appreciated the detached appraisals which I have been able to gain from several American and continental scholars who have visited me to discuss their own work and to exchange information about sources. Many of them, in reading this book, will recognise ideas which they implanted in my mind – Professor Robert Smith of the University of Oregon helped to throw light on the financial background of the Wilberforce family; Dr A. Härdelin, Librarian of Uppsala University, did much to clarify my ideas about Robert Wilberforce's rôle as a sacramental theologian. I have also learnt much from discussions with Father Chapeau, whose great work on Manning will shortly appear in English translation, with Professor Torben Christensen from Copenhagen and with Father Marvin R. O'Connell of the College of St Thomas, Minnesota.

I should like to add my thanks to Mr E. O. Tancock for assistance in preparing my typescript for the press; and to Professor Owen Chadwick, Canon Charles Smyth, the late Mr B. Goulding Brown and Dr G. D. Evans, who all read the typescript and made many useful suggestions and corrections.

One unhappy circumstance must be recorded: the death in December 1963 of Dr Octavia Wilberforce. But for her this book would never have been written, and unfortunately she did not live to see any portion of it in typescript. She was a thorough Wilberforce, not unlike her grandfather in appearance. Among her many interests, her delight and pride in her family history was perhaps closest to her heart. To her memory this book is dedicated. I hope she would have liked it.

Preface

Grateful acknowledgments should also be made to Edward Arnold & Company, Macmillan & Company, Messrs. Burns & Oates and the Oxford University Press, for permission to quote extracts from their publications; to the Provost and Fellows of Oriel College, Oxford, and to the Warden and Fellows of Keble College, Oxford, for permission to publish extracts from papers in their possession. I must also thank the Principal of Cuddesdon College for permission to reproduce a large number of photographs from an album belonging to Samuel Wilberforce which is one of the most prized possessions of Cuddesdon. Finally, I must express my indebtedness to the managers of the Bethune-Baker Fund, who were kind enough to make me a grant to cover the expenses of copyright fees.

Emmanuel College
Cambridge

DAVID NEWSOME

'We see the band of friends, cheerful, united, sanguine, starting together on life's path. Pass sixty years, we check the list, to find a scattered remnant of survivors, telling sadly of havoc wrought in their train by the storms of life, themselves too often alienated at its close. But the record of their deeds survives.'

(From William Tuckwell, *Reminiscences of Oxford* (1900), 85)

'God alone foresees what may be the lot of us four brothers, whether death, or the tiding undercurrents of life shall separate; or whether we shall be an exception to the sad destiny which splits up early confidences, and intimacies . . . and narrows them to a rare correspondence, and a rarer intercourse.'

(Henry Edward Manning to Samuel Wilberforce, 4 July 1836)

'Oh when I think of our name – what is expected from us and what religious advantages we have had – I tremble.'

(Elizabeth Wilberforce to her brother Robert, 11 October 1823)

'It is a wonder to me to see grown men misinterpret, and ill-treat each other like offended children. I believe that both of us have been in a school too real to fall into such a weakness. Alas that we should be as we are – but with our convictions, alas still more if we were otherwise. Between those who have given their life and themselves as we I trust have given ours to serve Truth and God, no Judge below Him can interpose. And for His award we are, I hope, waiting in mutual forbearance and affection.'

(Henry Edward Manning to Samuel Wilberforce, 9 August 1852)

'The glory of our beloved little church is departed. The heavens weeping over us, and the trees dropping round us, seem acted parables of our thoughts.'

(Samuel Wilberforce to Richard Cavendish, 10 June 1851)

xiii

THE CRISIS OF EVANGELICALISM

1. *The Beginning and the End*

Among Samuel Wilberforce's private papers may be found several of his poems. They have little claim to be considered great poetry. Many of them are only essays in versification, the pastime of an idle hour, like the poem which he wrote for Bishop Sumner, while visiting Sark with him in 1839, expressing their thoughts arising from the contemplation of a solitary rock dashed by a stormy sea. Some are jaunty, comic verses written from school to his favourite brother Robert, showing – if nothing else – some ingenuity as a rhymester. But occasionally we pass from the trivia of the commonplace-book into higher realms. There is the moving poem on the death of his young wife Emily, written eight years after his loss, when the wound was aching as painfully as ever, 'too tender and too perfect to admit of one word of comment', as Henry Manning described it to Henry Wilberforce when the poem was discovered after Samuel's death in 1873.[1]

A sonnet written in Milan in September 1851 and addressed to Robert Wilberforce is not an especially beautiful piece, but it tells an interesting story; and since the poem supplies the theme of this book and also the emotional accompaniment without which the theme would be insipid and lifeless, it is reproduced here rather as a text on which the remainder of the book may be taken as a commentary.

> Oh Brother! thrice beloved, who from those years
> When, as with common heart we lived, and shared
> Childhood's keen griefs and joys, hast ever bared
> Thy breast to every storm of woes and fears
> Which beat on me, and often with thy tears
> Hast staunched mine; who in dark days hast dared
> All questions to explore—Since it has fared
> So sadly with our house that careless ears
> Of passers-by with the wide severance ring
> Of four who at one altar vowed to serve –
> How closer to thy faithful love I cling;
> How pray we two may yet endure, with nerve

Strung as of iron, and beneath the wing
Of this our Mother Church hold fast and never swerve.[2]

What Samuel appears to be describing is the fall of the house of Wilberforce; how, while the world mused over the collapse of the mighty, only Robert and he remained to fulfil the aspirations of their father and to maintain the connection between their family name and devoted service to the Church of England. So Samuel prayed for strength and resolution, little knowing, as it happened, that worse was still to come.

The facts, in brief, are these. William Wilberforce, the Great Emancipator, had six children – two girls, Barbara and Elizabeth, and four sons, William, Robert Isaac, Samuel and Henry. From their infancy these children grew up with the eyes of the world upon them. This is hardly surprising. In the first place, their father – in his own lifetime – was acknowledged to be a saint. He was the revered leader of that group of Evangelical philanthropists, later to be nicknamed 'The Clapham Sect', pledged to drive vice out of London society, slavery off the face of the earth, and – among a hundred other laudable objects – to render the enthusiasm of the more rugged pioneers of the Evangelical revival acceptable to the Established Church. Secondly, their father believed that his prime responsibility under God – ranking more highly than his political services to the nation and his championship of great public causes – was to transmit to his children that principle of vital godliness which had been the inspiration of his own life. He therefore renounced his seat as M.P. for Yorkshire, the public position which had enabled him to become the major spokesman in the House of Commons on all social issues, in order to devote his time more fully to the education and spiritual welfare of his children.

This was common knowledge. Equally well known was the atmosphere of piety and Christian joyousness which pervaded the Wilberforce household. If we sometimes wonder how it was that family prayers came to be conventional practice in middle-class homes during the Victorian period, and how it was that the moral revolution of the nineteenth century came to be regarded as something which essentially began at *home*, we may find the answer in part to lie in the new standard of family ethics exemplified in the households of the Thorntons, the Macaulays, the Stephens, and the Wilberforces – wealthy and influential people who were in a position to spread their notions of the duties of Christian stewardship far and wide, and whose system of domestic worship therefore rapidly became the model for others in a similar social *milieu*, and thence for the classes beneath them.

What, then, might they become – these children of the saints, themselves trained in saintliness? No wonder men observed them! William Wilberforce himself, however, wished no more for them than that they should mature to Christian manhood through the light of God's grace and devote themselves to pious and useful occupations. By the time of his death, in July 1833, he saw his eldest son William set upon a disastrous course. Removed from Cambridge for dissipation in 1819, he became involved in a ruinous farming enterprise, in which he speculated heavily with his father's money and lost a large part of the family fortune. Robert, Samuel and Henry certainly promised better. They all gained Firsts at Oriel College, Oxford, and all subsequently took Anglican orders. They married into clerical families, Robert marrying Agnes Wrangham, the daughter of the Archdeacon of Cleveland and of the East Riding, Samuel and Henry both marrying daughters of John Sargent, Rector of Lavington and Graffham in Sussex.

With their marriages to Emily and Mary Sargent, Samuel and Henry united with the purest Evangelical stock, for John Sargent was the disciple of Charles Simeon and had been an intimate friend of Henry Martyn, whose biography he was later to write. The union of the Wilberforce and Sargent families was also to bring into their circle two other young Evangelical clergymen – Henry Edward Manning, who married Caroline Sargent, and George Dudley Ryder, who married Sophia, the youngest of the Sargent girls. Manning and Ryder belonged to exactly the same world as the Wilberforces. Manning's father had been a wealthy West India merchant and a Director of the Bank of England with some tenuous connections with the Clapham Sect. Ryder's father was Henry Ryder, Bishop of Gloucester and later Bishop of Lichfield and Coventry, the first, and for some time the only, Evangelical bishop on the bench. Both Manning and Ryder had been contemporaries of one or other of the Wilberforce boys at Oxford.

Of this group, the three Wilberforces and Henry Manning stand out as especially united in their aims and affections. Ryder tended rather to go his own way, possibly because he did not enjoy the proximity to Lavington which Manning, who became John Sargent's successor in the living, possessed; or it could be that an impression of aloofness is given from the dearth of his letters in the extant sources. Brother William, of course, can hardly be counted a member of this circle, although he flits across the pages of this narrative from time to time, always somewhat elusive in his gaffes and misdemeanours, always a considerable embarrassment to his brothers and their families when he threatened them with a visit or wrote to solicit their aid.

The group was held together by a double bond of kinship. In the first place, there was the personal bond of blood relationship; and secondly what one might call the spiritual bond – the unity of aim and action in their religious ideals. They had all inherited the Evangelical tradition; they had all learnt respect for religious decorum and the authority of the Established Church from their Oxford days; they were all touched to a greater or lesser extent by that militant restatement of Church principles and apostolical tradition which emanated from Oxford in the *Tracts for the Times*; they all became clergymen in country parishes, where they encountered similar problems and responded in similar ways. Finally, there was common to all of them an intensity of evangelical zeal which was demonstrated, in their individual lives, by the constant battle which they waged against the enticements of worldliness, and, in their respective ministries, by their pastoral energies in propagating the faith and in inducing holy living.

This unity of aim and action is most noticeable in the 1830's. In the following decade, however, it was shattered beyond repair. The personal bond was ultimately weakened by bereavement. They were all to suffer. Henry Manning and Robert Wilberforce both lost their wives in the 1830's; Emily, Samuel's wife, died in 1841; Sophia Ryder died in 1850; and Henry Wilberforce was to be chastened by the loss of four children between 1841 and 1853. At first the feeling of common loss brought the brothers together more intimately than ever, but thereafter it was primarily the spiritual affinity which united them as a group, and when wide divergences appeared in their understanding of the needs of the Church and the best ways of fulfilling these needs, there was really little left, except enduring affection, to prevent complete dissolution. When Samuel in 1851 lamented the 'wide severance' which attracted the 'careless ears of passers-by' he was referring to the sensational outcome of their gradual estrangement – the reception into the Roman Catholic Church of his brother Henry (with Mary his wife) in 1850, and of Henry Manning in 1851. George Dudley Ryder and Sophia had preceded the others to Rome in 1846; and in 1854 Robert himself put an end to a torment of indecision and took the same step.

How this came about will be seen later. The answer, of course, can be found only by going beyond this small inner group of intimates into that larger circle of common friends whose opinions, writings and actions

4

impinged – in some cases directly, in others only rather remotely – upon the four main characters. It is no small part of this tragedy that each member of this inner circle was forced, through the pressure of events, into the dilemma of having to decide in which direction he would allow himself to be pulled by rival tensions, knowing that, whatever the outcome, he would be faced with estrangement and misrepresentation.

As early as 1836, Manning prayed that it might never be so. He wrote to Samuel:

> God alone foresees what may be the lot of us four brothers, whether death, or the tiding undercurrents of life shall separate; or whether we shall be an exception, to the sad destiny which splits up early confidences, and intimacies . . . and narrows them to a rare correspondence, and a rarer intercourse. This seems now cold, and shocking, and to be impossible – and yet it is most true of brothers by blood, even the most affectionate – after the natural heads of the family are gone, and the faggot is broken up for want of a binder.[3]

It is almost as if he had a premonition of the wreck that was to come.

II. *Evangelicalism and Church Order*

Why did so many of the converts to Rome come from the ranks of the Evangelicals? The answer is not a simple one, since it necessarily involves some consideration of the religious background of the period. Before embarking upon the full story of this strange journey an attempt must be made to describe the anxieties which beset so many churchmen at that time, in order to explain why the heirs of the great Evangelical pioneers were dissatisfied with their heritage, and how they came to a clearer perception of the spiritual needs of their times as being supplied through – and only through – the corporate authority of the Church.

In the first place, the decades which followed the close of the Napoleonic wars were a period of great unsettlement and alarm. There was an intense consciousness of a rapid movement forward in every department of human activity, not only in speculation and learning, but also – perhaps more frightening – in technology and in the ability of man to conquer nature and thereby to increase the material comforts of life. This was a generation of men who were living through the greatest industrial revolution hitherto experienced in the history of the world, who had just witnessed the most terrifying political cataclysm in France, and who saw all around them the

5

signs of intellectual ferment, the cracking of the very fabric of society, a new and purposeful onslaught on hallowed institutions. As the pace of life was increased (and who could doubt the fact of movement in the early railway age?), so the motion of mankind towards the fulfilment of its destiny was immeasurably accelerated. This might mean progress – or it could mean ruin. On this men were divided. The followers of Jeremy Bentham, the Utilitarians, believed that they stood on the threshold of a new era which, in its achievement of widescale social amelioration and a sweeping programme of informed legislation, would infuse into every organ of government a new efficiency, and create a just and prosperous state. The enemies of the Benthamites – and among them were the vast majority of churchmen – linked the new philosophy to the new materialism, and linked both to the 'principles of the Revolution' which had brought disaster upon France. In short, the whole ethos of the times was dynamic. Expressions of fear and hope, often curiously intermingled, were common to reformer and reactionary. All were fired by a sense of urgency. Something must be done *now*, or else the opportunity will be irretrievably lost. Tomorrow may be too late.

What exactly did they fear? The sinister forays of ill-led and ill-bred labourers – the horror of the 'Swing Riots' – certainly. Samuel Wilberforce buried the family plate in his garden and mounted guard over the deeds[1]; the Reform Bill – 'I almost tremble for the consequences', William Wilberforce wrote to Samuel in March 1831.[2] 'Henceforth no government will be able to command what the mob may choose to resist', wrote an Evangelical friend to Robert Wilberforce later in the same year.[3] Rationalism and latitudinarianism – 'We live in a novel era', J. H. Newman wrote to his mother in March 1829, '. . . Men have hitherto depended on others, and especially on the clergy, for religious truth; now each man attempts to judge for himself. . . . The talent of the day is against the Church.'[4] Samuel Wilberforce, in 1835, expressed to his friend Charles Anderson his utter detestation of 'the march of mind and of rail-roads'.[5]

More generally, however, it was the whole spirit of the age which they deplored. 'The world is gone mad', James Stephen wrote to his wife in the early 1830's. 'It is useless to enquire what is to happen, but it is difficult not to apprehend much and most formidable calamity on the earth. I find all folks hereabouts full of the dread of wars and tumults. It can do no good, and give no pleasure to think on the subject.'[6]

The same note is sounded in a letter of Samuel to his brother Robert in January 1835: 'There is a spirit of discontent and mad restlessness poured out upon the land which is to work our over-throw as a nation. The only way to have tolerable peace is to be conscious of having in our station honestly withstood it.'[7] He denied, in a letter to Charles Anderson, that he always took the part of Toryism:

> ... but for modern liberalism I abhor it. I think it is the Devil's creed: a heartless steam-engine, unchristian, low, sensual, utilitarian creed which would put down all that is really great and high and noble; all old remembrances and customs; merely to set up what is low, and multiply such miserable comforts as going very fast through the air on a rail-road – and for this purpose it would overturn the Church, that is Christianity; and worship the very Devil if his horns were gold and his tail were a steam engine. I hate the breaking down the character of the old English country gentleman. I think it one of the finest characters in the world . . . doing more good than all the vile bushels of *Useful Knowledge* which have turned the heads of all the half-learned tinkers in the Universe.[8]

The sense of impending catastrophe may be felt in the writings and sermons of churchmen of every party during this time. It provided the impulse to the Oxford Movement, most particularly in its early stages. It was in 1833, on his way home from Sicily, that Newman was inspired to write his most beautiful hymn, beginning with the words 'Lead, kindly light, *amid the encircling gloom*.' The mood expressed is precisely that of the Evangelical H. F. Lyte's famous hymn 'Abide with me' (written in the next decade), with the mournful note of 'Change and decay in all around I see', and the prayer which follows – 'O Thou who changest not, abide with me.'

The Church was assailed from all sides; but where were the defenders to be found? It is reasonable to assume that they would come from the ranks of those who had led the religious revival which, coincident with the rise of the forces of secularism and utilitarianism in the period during and immediately after the Napoleonic wars, was already making its impact on both the Established Church and the country at large. This revival had been a triumph for the Evangelicals. Its origins lie in the mid-eighteenth century, when spontaneously and without any obvious interconnection (save the common reaction to a commonly-felt defect in the spirituality of the time), pietistic movements and ministries, some inspired by Wesley or Whitefield, others owing nothing whatever to their teaching, emerged as little oases of gospel-preaching and 'enthusiasm' amid the arid latitudinarian wastes. Much was lost by the separation of the Methodists, yet – with the writings of Thomas Scott and Joseph Milner, the ministries of men like John Newton, Henry Venn and his son John, and the continuous

7

campaign to win souls and to train gospel preachers waged in Cambridge by Isaac Milner, Charles Simeon and William Farish – the Evangelical forces within the Established Church had rallied, and by the turn of the century were supplying the most vital source of spiritual renovation in the Church, even though their party was not numerically strong.

Opinions of the relative strength and weakness of Evangelicalism in the early part of the nineteenth century are disconcertingly inconsistent. On the one hand, Gladstone firmly maintained, in a critique of Lecky, that the Evangelicals were never, properly speaking, dominant within the Anglican Church, save in the profound influence which they exercised on 'the general tone and tendency of the preaching of the clergy' in the period following the first phase of the Oxford Movement.[9] They were at their lowest ebb in the second and third decades of the century, when they numbered scarcely an eighth of the clergy. On the other hand, Newman, James Stephen and other contemporaries were describing Evangelicalism as the 'fashionable' party in the 1830's and spoke of the former days of the Milners, the Venns and the Clapham Sect as a golden age before corruption and declension set in.[10] It is possible that Gladstone gave less than their due to those – like the Venns, the Milners and Wilberforce – who had, in their different ways, been the true party architects, chiefly because, although he had been brought up an Evangelical by his mother,[11] he had encountered very few distinctively Evangelical strongholds in the circle in which he subsequently moved. Eton certainly could not be described as such, although J. B. Sumner had been a master there, and Simeon was one of her alumni. Oxford, apart from St Edmund Hall, which counted little, a sprinkling of earnest souls at Wadham and the stentorian Bulteel at St Ebbe's, was overwhelmingly weighted on the side of the opposite tradition.[12] If Gladstone had looked for gospel preachers in London, further at least than the parishes west of Temple Bar,[13] he could have found that they were not without influence in the capital, especially through the medium of the proprietary chapels. They were weakly represented in both the S.P.G. and the S.P.C.K. (the two societies in which Gladstone took chief interest), but they were immensely strong in the C.M.S. and the Bible Society, and countless other organisations which they had themselves founded and caused to be multiplied in hundreds of auxiliaries and branches all over the country.[14]

The strength of early nineteenth-century Evangelicalism cannot be gauged by the number of professed Evangelical clergy or by the meagre representation of the party among the higher ranks of the Church.

8

One must look rather to the extraordinary proliferation of philanthropic and missionary societies; to the mounting circulation of the *Cheap Repository* tracts; to the astounding demonstration of pertinacity, solidarity and inspired leadership afforded by the successful campaign for the abolition of the slave trade; and, finally, to the influence of a small number of very remarkable men. Of these William Wilberforce was perhaps the most important, partly because his influence was chiefly exercised upon the upper class of society, whose support was clearly necessary if gospel-preaching and the profession of 'seriousness' were to be freed from the taint of sedition and dissent; and partly because in his *Practical View*, published in 1797, he was able to stir the consciences of thousands who were confronted for the first time by a frank exposure of the shallowness and deceitfulness of professing a Christianity which was purely nominal and wholly untouched by the leaven of a living faith. At Cambridge Charles Simeon was no less a force among the undergraduates than Newman was to be at Oxford. Henry Martyn, who died at Tokat in 1812, was the first Evangelical saint and martyr. Daniel Wilson, theologian and forceful preacher, became Bishop of Calcutta. C. R. Sumner, who gained an Evangelical foothold at court as chaplain to George IV, became Bishop of Winchester and did more than any other man to instruct Samuel Wilberforce in the ways and means of exercising that direct and personal control over his diocese which was to make his episcopate so significant in the history of the Church. In short, they were a powerful and well-organised group.

Yet manifestly all was not well with the party in the 1820's and perhaps the two decades thereafter. The great figures of the golden age were passing from the scene. William Wilberforce died in 1833 and Charles Simeon in 1836. If Daniel Wilson and C. R. Sumner still had their best years in front of them, their influence did not greatly transcend the limits of their dioceses, and there was no conspicuous group of wealthy and dedicated men to take the place of the Clapham Sect. Some historians – notably Mr Ford K. Brown – have suggested that this succession problem did not greatly matter. After all, the seeds had been sown; respectability had been won; the moral transformation of England was under way. 'In anything that vitally concerned England, it [sc. the party] had done its work.'[15]

This is questionable. The Evangelical party lost its greatest leaders, and failed to secure the services of those who should have been their natural successors (the sons of Wilberforce, Ryder and others) at the precise moment when the battle between Church and State, and between Christianity and infidelity, looked to be at its fiercest. The situation cried out for effective leadership, so that any party which championed the cause of the Church against secular interference and adopted the appropriate militant tone would be likely to attract large numbers – especially of the young men, ardent for a crusade – to fight under its banner. And if the Evangelicals themselves failed to issue this challenge, then they would inevitably lose the initiative and, at the same time, the allegiance of many of those who had been groomed to carry on their fathers' work.

Actually the predicament was not as clear-cut as this. The period after 1820 was for Evangelicals, both within and without the Establishment, a time of acute crisis. A growing rift can be discerned between the older and more responsible group of Evangelicals, whose organ was the *Christian Observer*, and whose major spokesmen were Simeon, Daniel Wilson and the members of the Clapham Sect, and the younger, more fiery elements who were attracted towards Edward Irving and Henry Drummond, and whose viewpoint was represented in the *Evangelical Magazine* and the *Morning Watch*. The older generation had fought a long battle against unbridled enthusiasm, and had learnt from early days 'that, although the Kingdom of Heaven is indeed taken by violence, it is not to be held by indiscipline'.[16]

This was more than politic counsel – the price which Evangelicals had to pay for acceptance by the Established Church. It was fundamental to the teaching of the Venns, Simeon and Daniel Wilson.[17] They called for sobriety and 'regularity' because adhesion to the Scriptures, the Anglican liturgy and the formularies of the Church were a safeguard against that individualism and peculiarity, which could so easily degenerate into self-indulgence, spiritual vanity and antinomianism. They possessed the true passion for souls which is the *sine qua non* of Evangelicalism, but they were well aware of the deceitfulness of emotions and were keen to point out that as good a way to preserve a sound scriptural basis was to abide by the rulings of the Church. 'I really do not know what to call myself', John Venn once said, 'except a Church of England man: for indeed I think the Church of England in her liturgy, articles and homilies speaks more in unison with the Scriptures than any systematic writer I know.'[18]

It was therefore with the gravest concern that the Evangelicals of the *Christian Observer* school viewed the excesses of Edward Irving and others in the 1820's. They detected a new and disturbing spirit abroad – the note of adventism in Evangelical preaching, a fresh insistence on personal conversion as the true sign of God's grace, unpleasant manifestations of spiritual pride. It first came home to them as they observed the changed character of the annual May Meetings – the occasion of a great concourse of Evangelicals in London to attend the annual meetings of their various societies. They deplored the way in which 'ranters' were capturing the platform, indulging in play-acting and rowdyism. As Marianne Thornton commented, after a particularly ludicrous display of histrionics by Edward Irving, the scene had been 'very amusing to some good people who do not go to plays, but seriously speaking it is sad to see such tricks played before high Heaven'.[19]

James Stephen felt the same. He never really outgrew his distaste for the narrow and bigoted successors of his father's generation. 'Oh where are the people who are at once really religious, and really cultivated in heart and in understanding?' he exclaimed in a letter to his wife in 1845, 'the people with whom we could associate as our fathers used to associate with each other. No "Clapham Sect" nowadays . . .'[20]

When we recollect the grim forebodings which haunted the minds of churchmen during this decade, it is not surprising to find the apocalyptic strain becoming more prominent in Evangelical preaching. As the shadows lengthened, the earlier note of optimism gradually passed away. It survived with Simeon who could still say, as late as 1824, 'glorious times are fast approaching'[21]; and with William Wilberforce who revealed to William Jay in 1833, the last year of his life: 'I am not among the croakers. I think real religion is spreading: and I am persuaded, will increasingly spread, till the earth is filled with the knowledge of the Lord, as the waters cover the sea.'[22]

But the 'noisy professors' (as the turbulent element came to be called) were full of revelations and prophecies, and elated their disciples with the prospect of the imminence of the Second Coming. Simeon's comment on all this is revealing: 'They are led aside . . . from a doctrine which humbles, elevates, refines the soul . . . to a doctrine which fills only with vain conceits, intoxicates the imagination, alienates the brethren from each other, and by *being unduly urged upon the minds of humble Christians*, is doing the devil's work by wholesale.'[23]

The apocalyptic strain was not peculiar to the left wing of the Evangelical party, and may be found also in the writings of the Tractarians themselves.[24] Nevertheless it goes far to explain why – as Simeon put it – the brethren were alienated from each other, and why many of the *Christian Observer* school came to insist even more vehemently on the

11

virtues of church order, or – if one may so express it – the claims of the Law rather than the privileges of the Gospel. As Dr Walsh has pointed out, the moderate Calvinists had always been anxious to stress 'the terrors of the Law', as 'a kind of homiletic blow-lamp by which the preachers tried deliberately to burn through the layers of pride and self-deception to the hearts of the people'.[25] He draws our attention to the consciously defensive note in the sermons of the *Christian Observer* group, who had been mindful from the first of the perilous antinomianism implicit in the teaching of William Romaine. By the 1820's their anxiety had become so intense that occasionally they seem to use the language of the High Churchmen. An interesting example is Newman himself.

The first volume of *Parochial Sermons*, published in 1834, contains sermons delivered between the years 1825 and 1833, a period which covers Newman's transition from Evangelicalism into Tractarianism. Yet the volume is a unity, and the language of the earlier sermons is not markedly different from that of the later. Some of the severest injunctions on the attainment of sanctification come in the two sermons, delivered respectively in August 1826 and June 1825, on 'Holiness necessary for future blessedness' and 'Secret Faults'.[26] 'The whole history of redemption ... attests the necessity of holiness in order to salvation' appears on the very first page. Although in the same sermon Newman admits that good works have nothing of merit in them and that 'they are the means, under God's grace, of strengthening and showing forth that holy principle which God implants in the heart and without which (as the text tells us) we cannot see Him',[27] he asserts most forcefully that the first step towards possessing God's grace is 'being obedient in outward deeds'. Men 'have ever to learn to practise good works, as the means of changing their hearts, which is the end'.[28] This is entirely the language of Daniel Wilson in his sermon before the University of Oxford in 1810, when he affirmed 'that a right disposition of heart was essential to the attainment of just sentiments in religion, that obedience was the path to knowledge'.[29] And when Newman inveighed against complacency in his sermon on 'Secret Faults', with the reminder that 'to be at ease is to be unsafe',[30] his words were not offensive to Evangelicals of the Simeon stamp who were themselves accusing the followers of Edward Irving of exactly this fault.

There is, however, a difference between saying that Evangelicals, in resisting the pretensions of their pentecostal wing, sometimes adopted the language and sentiments of High Churchmen, and declaring that, in their distaste for the current trend of Evangelical preaching, they actually *became* High Churchmen. This is a complete misreading of the situation, of which Mr Ford K. Brown – in his recent study of the Evangelicals entitled *Fathers of the Victorians* – is guilty, for he goes so far as to suggest that William Wilberforce in his old age abandoned the Evangelicalism of his early days and was converted to the High Church school.[31] The truth is that Wilberforce was as firmly Evangelical in the last year of his life as he was when he first saw the light of God's grace when studying Doddridge's *Rise and Progress of Religion in the Soul* in the autumn of 1784. His final conversation with the dissenter William Jay in 1833 is sufficient to demonstrate this. He expressed himself glad that Jay had not altered in his religious views over the years, and that he had 'kept to the common, plain and important truths, in which all Christians are nearly agreed'. He concluded: 'I hope you will never leave the good old ways.'[32]

The point which Mr Brown misses is that William Wilberforce, whom he represents quite erroneously as a man committed entirely to promoting the interests of a single religious party, abhorred the very name of party as applied to religion even more decidedly than he disliked embroiling himself in the concerns of political parties. 'There is a danger', he wrote to Samuel in 1826, 'lest a party spirit should creep in with its usual effects and evils. Against this, therefore, we should be ever on the watch.'[33]

Daniel Wilson, on the other hand, was much less afraid of party spirit and was even prepared to encourage it. But he was a stalwart defender of the Church. Henry Wilberforce, in a letter to his brother Robert, gives us a picture of him in 1832 presiding at a great clerical breakfast:

> There was including about 16 ladies and as many laics about 60, the Bishop* presided. He asked Mr Pratt to expound and pray: then Mr Cunningham to explode . . . : then he summed up the whole with a Charge chiefly addressed to the *young*, warning them against the dangers of the day – against taking up new notions, instead of the good *old* notions of the great men of former times, e.g. Cecil, Newton, H. Martyn, Scott etc. Then he cautioned them to keep to the Church! Then he told them there was a hydra lately sprung up – a number of young men who were afraid of *party* and *party spirit*. He very well observed that this was a snare of the Devil, and a being ashamed of the Cross, for that when *he* was a young man he had never felt afraid of party spirit.[34]

Ever since Dr Yngve Brilioth, the Swedish scholar, brought to his study of the English religious scene in the first half of the nineteenth

---

* Daniel Wilson was then Bishop of Calcutta.

century the detached approach of a foreign observer, we have been able to see more clearly the affinities between Evangelicalism and Tractarianism, which the bitter polemic of the mid-Victorian age had tended to obscure, and to realise that Gladstone was in error when he stated that the Evangelicals 'joined . . . with the other world, in utterly condemning the Tractarian movement from the first'.[35] It is not only that sections of all parties were beginning to see that the advance of materialism and the passion for reform on all fronts might resolve itself into a battle between Church and State, and that Christians everywhere were therefore compelled to think of the means of resisting this challenge in institutional terms. The alliance had tighter bonds than this. In many ways the Tractarians appeared – in the early stages of the Oxford Movement – to be the continuators of the Evangelicals.[36] Robert Wilberforce asserted this himself in 1851, when in a charge to the clergy of his archdeaconry, he recalled those early days. 'During the first quarter of the century', he wrote, 'men were roused from slumber and wakened to earnestness; the next period gave them an external object on which to expend the zeal that had been enkindled. For it must be observed . . . that these movements, though distinct, were not repugnant. On the contrary, persons who had been most influenced by the one, often entered most readily into the other. . . . So then the second movement was a sort of consequence of the first.'[37]

At this stage it was not at all clear that sacramentalism, and all that followed from high sacramental teaching, might become a dividing factor. After all, the Evangelicals were pioneers in recalling Christians to the importance of the sacraments and in encouraging the practice of frequent communion.[38] The tightest knot which bound the Evangelicals and the Tractarians together, however, in these early years was the common pursuit of holiness. 'Holiness rather than peace' – the dictum of the Calvinist Thomas Scott – was the inspiration of the Evangelical revival. Newman admitted, in later life, that his yearning for unworldliness dated from his reading of Thomas Scott ('to whom, humanly speaking, I almost owe my soul') and that he used his maxim almost as a proverb.[39]

Appreciation of John Keble's religious poetry, admiration for Newman's sermons, and a sense of the common endeavour in urging upon a worldly generation the virtues and duties of holiness, could all go together with a distaste for the teaching and principles of the traditional High Church party. The Tractarians seemed most truly the heirs of the Evangelicals when one compared their teaching and sentiments with the traditional tenets of the old High Church school. They were certainly not 'high and dry'; they were far from being 'Church and King'. Indeed with the furore over the Reform Bill, few High Churchmen felt disposed to cleave to the traditional alliance.[40] In the 1830's the champion of the Royal Supremacy and the essential unity of Church and State was the latitudinarian Thomas Arnold, whose views[41] were as abhorrent to the Tractarians as they were to the Evangelicals.

No wonder there was confusion in the ranks. If the older generation of Evangelicals could see little to fear in the first numbers of the Oxford Tracts (Bishop Sumner, it is said, heartily approved of them),[42] then the younger members of the same circle, who were themselves at Oxford at the headquarters of the movement of resistance against the pretensions of the State, were not likely to feel any qualms in accepting the invitation of Newman, Froude and Keble to come over to help them. When they looked at the aggressively Evangelical response to present dangers – at the wild excesses and futile prophecies of the 'noisy professors' – they were repelled. What, then, should they do? Robert Wilberforce put this question to an Evangelical friend in 1831 and received an interesting answer. His friend, T. W. Carr, began by quoting the *Christian Year*.

> Don't Keble's lines continually haunt your mind? [he wrote],
>
> > 'Think not of rest – though dreams be sweet
> > Start up and ply your heavenward feet.
> > Is not God's oath upon your head
> > Ne'er to sink back on slothful bed?
> > Never again your loins untie
> > Nor let your torches waste and die,
> > Till, *when the shadows thickest fall*
> > Ye hear your Master's midnight call.'[43]
>
> That time I cannot but apprehend is now upon us. The shadows over our land appear to get blacker and blacker – as I travel along on the coach and hear the anticipations of men well versed in the commercial affairs of the country – the murmurs of all ranks – the threatenings – the gnashing of teeth against the Church and clergy – as I have done this week past, it is impossible not to foresee dangers. ... As for the beloved Church of England I believe the Saints of God will rally round her when stripped of all her worldly decorations and that she is still destined to be the Thermopylae where the only effectual stand shall be made against the last inundation of lawless power.[44]

The advice was quite plain: the Church must protest, and all her loyal sons must join her in the fight.

Introduction : The Crisis of Evangelicalism

III. *Dramatis Personae*

The protest came, as the world knows, from Oxford. And those who had for years looked for effective leadership in troublous times were predisposed to follow the direction of men who could offer both a practical programme of action and a spirit of exuberant confidence. Once swept up in the movement, under a leader who had no sympathy for the halfhearted, few had either the strength of mind or the inclination to refrain from becoming totally committed.* Some, indeed, found themselves so inspired by the new understanding of sanctity which they gained from a study of the early Church, that they came in time to look for the realisation of the ideal in a place which formerly they had shunned as forbidden territory. They came to study the devotional practices of the Church of Rome. When the sanguine period was over – when infidelity seemed to grow worse, and when their ideals seemed only to provoke opposition from the very powers whose authority they had attempted to enhance – then some, in despair, came to believe that the Roman Church alone possessed the true marks of sanctity and the effective authority to withstand the progress of secularism. Indeed, by 1840, Newman could write to his sister:

> I begin to have serious apprehensions lest any religious body is strong enough to withstand the league of evil but the Roman Church. At the end of the first millenary it withstood the fury of Satan, and now the end of a second is drawing on. It has *tried* strength; . . . we on the other hand have never been tried and come out of trial without practical concessions. I cannot see that we *can* receive the assault of the foe. We are divided among ourselves, like the Jews in their siege. So that it seems to me as if there were coming on a great encounter between infidelity and Rome and that we should be smashed between them.[1]

If an Evangelical could become a Tractarian because he believed that the Oxford leaders alone could supply the direction to resist the attack of secular foes, then it is but an extension of the same principle for a disillusioned Tractarian to seek refuge in the Church of Rome.

This is a simplification of the dilemma faced by the principal characters in this book. That each of them responded in his own individual way was due in part to the different influences to which he was exposed and also

* Even Keble found this, as his remark to Isaac Williams in 1859 shows – 'I was fairly carried off my legs by the sanguine views they held.' G. Prevost (editor), *The Autobiography of Isaac Williams* (1892), 118 n.

16

to differences in temperament and character. Robert Wilberforce was guided rather by his head, Henry Wilberforce by his heart. Both, however, were alike in having no ambitious temptations to self-advancement, and in preferring to be led rather than to lead. Henry was always wild and volatile, small and charming like his father, anxious to love and to be loved. He was given to extravagant enthusiasms, and once enraptured could not rest to prove his devotion to a friend or his allegiance to a cause. Uncertainty left him helpless and inert.

Robert, on the other hand, was slow and stolid by comparison – shy, reserved and scholarly, much more a Spooner (his mother's family) than a Wilberforce. He was less devoted than Samuel to his father, less ardent in his love for Keble than either Froude or Isaac Williams[2]; and he regarded Newman as a colleague, never a master. He was conscientious to a degree, spending months in Germany studying the language while loathing the inhabitants, forcing himself to preach on mission tours because Samuel and Henry Manning had won such victories for Christ thereby, but knowing in his heart that he was ineffective on the platform and that every minute of public utterance was a torment. Of all the brothers, Robert possessed by far the most impressive equipment as a scholar, yet even in this realm he could scarcely conceal a slight timidity.

Samuel Wilberforce and Henry Manning, one sometimes feels, were in their natural gifts a little too close for comfort. Both were essentially public men, adept in all the public arts, clearly intended by nature to take the lead. Neither ever acknowledged any man to be his master; both fought a constant battle against the lure of worldly ambitions. Here, however, the resemblance ends. If public men can be divided into two categories, those who say more than they mean and those who say less, Samuel Wilberforce belonged to the first* and Henry Manning to the second.†️ Samuel had inherited all his father's social charm and oratorical gifts. He was also intensely emotional, with an eager, urgent disposition; and while he strove to keep his emotions in check in public, some portion of the pent-up power and sentiment always escaped to leave a lasting impression of warmth and energy – in a word, of humanity – upon any company with whom he mixed. His letters suggest this too. His writing

* Gladstone upbraided Samuel for 'a habit of too free comments or remarks'. Wilberforce MSS. G. 168.

†️ Newman constantly complained that Manning's words did not prepare him for his deeds. See especially E. S. Purcell, *Life of Cardinal Manning* (1896), II. 306; W. Ward, *Life of John Henry Cardinal Newman* (1912), II. 182.

could never keep pace with his thoughts. Restraint would gradually slip, punctuation was forgotten; in the end, his emotions would triumph in a mighty torrent of words.

Manning was wholly different. Warmth and tenderness he had in plenty, but his emotions were in public so completely disciplined, his mind so apparently cool, his speech so measured, fluent and apt (while being always spontaneous) that men were less conscious of their kinship with him than they were of their own inadequacies. A perfect public manner, allied to a tall, commanding presence and an impression of high idealism and great austerity, gave to Manning an extraordinary power over both individuals and assemblies. It was a power which he retained to the end of his life.

The temperaments of the two men differed in other respects which may go far to explain the parting of their ways. Samuel, although of able intellect, was not really a scholar. He had phenomenal powers of personal influence; he was a masterly organiser and administrator. But above all he possessed a practical mind, capable of discerning the pitfalls of idealism, and sufficiently flexible to be able to demarcate the line where extremes could meet. Manning, on the other hand, was a scholar without a scholar's disposition; that is to say, there was a pragmatic element in his scholarship. He sought the answer to his problems through dispassionate study, but once he believed that the answer had been found, he closed his mind entirely to further argument. He was, in fact, an idealist; and – throughout his priesthood – was preoccupied with two great ideals, the attainment of personal sanctity and the effective assertion of the infallible authority of the Church. While, in his Anglican career, he showed the ability to compromise, in his Catholic career he gained at last the power and the opportunity to cast off the fetters of moderation, and to work for the realisation of his ends with a tenacity which, if sometimes emulated by others, has rarely been rewarded with such conspicuous success.

In the pages that follow, the dramatic events of the ecclesiastical history of England in the first half of the nineteenth century are viewed through the eyes of four different men, thrown together partly by the accident of birth and partly by the initial unanimity in objective which seemed to seal their friendship for all time. That, as it turned out, was a delusion. The most striking feature of their correspondence is, without a doubt, the unfolding of the personal tragedy wherein this bond of friendship was severed. At the same time, since none of the major figures of this group was himself a principal in either the Evangelical revival or the Oxford

Movement, though affected deeply by both, this study may serve to shed more light, albeit over a limited area, on the relationship between the two great forces which were to re-vitalise and to re-shape the Anglican Church. For, as Dr Brilioth has written, to explore further into the history of the interaction of these two enduring influences, 'it would be necessary to go far outside the limited circle of the principal actors, to the lives of many, university men, country clergy, and laity as well, who felt the tension between the two poles'.[3]

Chapter 1

THE CRADLE OF EVANGELICALISM

1. *Family Alliances and Barbara Spooner*

The children of William Wilberforce never knew their father as a young man. He was, after all, in his thirty-eighth year when in 1797 he married Barbara Ann Spooner, the eldest daughter of Isaac Spooner of Elmden Hall, near Coventry, and had already become a national figure. He had been Member for Yorkshire for thirteen years. His youthful intimacy with William Pitt – when they had played faro into the night at Brooks's and Goosetree's and paid court to Mrs Crewe and Mrs Siddons – had years ago passed into a more sober, if no less affectionate, friendship; ever since, in fact, William had first felt the call of 'true' religion in the winter of 1784. He was already the acknowledged champion of the reformation of public manners and the abolition of the slave trade.

His marriage was immediately fruitful. A son, William, was born in 1798, followed by two girls, Barbara and Elizabeth, in 1799 and 1801, and by Robert Isaac in 1802. Samuel was born three years later, and Henry, the last child, followed in 1807, when the country was still resounding with the cheers and acclamations which greeted the successful conclusion of the abolitionist cause in March of that year.

Wilberforce had long ago given up his house at Wimbledon which he had inherited from his uncle, where Pitt had so often stayed with him to take the country air and to breakfast off peas and strawberries[1]; and he had for some years before his marriage been living with Henry Thornton at Battersea Rise in Clapham. Marriage meant, however, finding a home of his own again and, since he had no wish to abandon the colony of imposing villas and mansions which ringed the Common, so redolent of mercantile wealth and solid respectability, William looked no further than the house next door. For ten years the Wilberforces lived at Broomfield and all the children were born there. In 1807, William was beginning to find the calls upon his charity so considerable that he felt it wrong to keep up two establishments (for he also owned a property in Palace Yard, where he stayed during parliamentary sessions), and he therefore decided to move the family nearer to Westminster. In 1808 they settled in Kensington Gore, next door to James Stephen at 42, Hyde Park Gate.

> The Kensington of those days [Leslie Stephen subsequently recalled] was still distinctly separate from London. A high wall divided Kensington Gardens from the Hounslow Road; there were still deer in the gardens, cavalry barracks close to Queen's Gate, and a turnpike at the top of the Gloucester Road. The land upon which South Kensington has since arisen was a region of market gardens, where in our childhood we strolled with our nurse along genuine country lanes.[2]

At the house in Kensington Gore the children spent their formative years. Of their previous home at Clapham, only William and Robert could have retained any memories. Yet in a certain sense Clapham was to all of them their spiritual home. If the wealth of the Wilberforces had been made in Yorkshire, the reputation and the influence of William himself had been gained at Clapham which had been for some twenty years the power-house of the Evangelical revival, where, together with his like-minded friends and neighbours, he had launched the projects and created the organisation which were to convert Evangelicalism into a national force.

It was a strange setting for a great religious movement – Battersea Rise, the vast three-storeyed Queen Anne house with thirty-four bedrooms, its enormous garden of sloping lawns, ancient elms and massive tulip trees, and its beautiful oval library designed by William Pitt. The saints regularly assembled here; at first sight, rather cosy saints, but nevertheless a real religious community which, if it took no vows, yet recognised its obligations. The first of these was bounty. Six-sevenths of Henry Thornton's annual income, as a bachelor, was spent on charity, and at least one-third when he became the head of a large household. William Wilberforce gave away nearly as much himself, if more spontaneous in his bounty and less painstaking with his accounts. Their works of mercy and of mission were all sustained by a life of regular prayer; and while they permitted themselves to display a grandiose exterior in their style and mode of living, they never sought to advertise their countless acts of self-denial or the severe schedule of devotional exercises which they imposed upon themselves as a voluntary act.

This was the ethos of the religious life at Clapham; and wherever the members of the Clapham Sect dispersed – for their life as a group was relatively short – that spirit accompanied them. To return to the Common, to visit Battersea Rise again – as the Wilberforce children frequently did – was essentially a homecoming. And so it remained for them even after

1815, when the great house passed to Sir Robert Inglis, who became the guardian of the nine Thornton children on their parents' death. The redoubtable Marianne was there, Henry Thornton's eldest daughter, aged eighteen in 1815, the caustic chronicler of all their doings. There were for the older of the children memories of the fabulous children's parties, with puppet shows written by Hannah More and narrated by the head of the household, demonstrations of the mysteries of galvanism, charades and plays (in one of which William Wilberforce junior was cast as the Pope, lost his head in his dialogue with Bonaparte – acted by Tom Macaulay – and duly forgot his lines), and, at the close of the festivities, supper in the dining-room and a magic lantern show.[3]

Another notable feature of the Clapham Sect was its homogeneity. Not only were most of its members exceedingly wealthy, but they had also acquired or inherited fortunes recently made, often enough by similar means. This goes far to explain the common social background, the influences and prejudices which they shared, and the way in which their families came to intermingle, to inter-marry, and finally to produce, in the next generation, an immensely influential group, related by blood and united by cultural and religious ties, which came in time to constitute what Lord Annan has described as 'the intellectual aristocracy' of mid-Victorian England. 'Philanthropy was the magnet which drew them together', he writes.[4] In fact other circumstances had already worked to form them into an influential group before the magnet of philanthropy was applied. Clearly, propinquity of residence was one; and it is more significant still that inter-marriage had been taking place before any of the families had moved to Clapham, that most of them were Tories in politics and, besides their other work and interests, were either M.P.s (like William Wilberforce, Henry Thornton, Charles Grant and James Stephen) or had been associated in some way or other with political and administrative posts (Lord Teignmouth as Governor-General of India, Zachary Macaulay as Governor of Sierra Leone).

The wealth of the Wilberforces came from merchant adventuring in the Baltic trade. William's father (Robert) and his grandfather (William) had both been Russia merchants in Hull. In the middle of the previous century the families of the Wilberforces and the Smiths came to be united both by marriage (Abel Smith the banker* married the sister of Elizabeth Bird,

---

* Smith's bank was first established at Nottingham by Thomas Smith in 1658, Abel Smith II established the bank of Smith, Payne and Smith in London, and branches at Lincoln and Hull. These are the banks which came in time to be formed into the National Provincial Bank.

William Wilberforce's mother) and by commercial partnership with the establishment of the firm of Wilberforce and Smith, Baltic merchants, in 1784. Through this family connection with the Smiths and the Birds, the Wilberforces came also to be related to both the Mannings and the Sumners. William Manning (also a merchant, in the West India trade), the father of the future Cardinal, married Elizabeth Smith, the sister of Robert Smith, first Baron Carrington.* Robert Wilberforce's sister, Judith, married John Bird, a London alderman, whose daughter Hannah was the mother of both John Bird Sumner, later Archbishop of Canterbury, and C. R. Sumner, Bishop of Winchester. Thus the children of William Wilberforce were second cousins to the Sumners.

The Thorntons too were Baltic merchants in Hull. They were doubly related to the Wilberforces through the marriage of William Wilberforce (the Emancipator's grandfather) to a daughter of John Thornton early in the previous century; and, later, through the marriage of William Wilberforce's uncle to a grand-daughter of the same John Thornton. This Mrs Wilberforce was therefore aunt to both William Wilberforce and Henry Thornton. The Thorntons were united to another merchant family of Hull by the marriage of Henry Thornton to Marianne Sykes, the daughter of Joseph Sykes, in whose business the Wilberforces and the Smiths bought an interest in 1784.[5]

The prosperity of all these families rose throughout the eighteenth century with the steady expansion of Hull into one of the four leading ports of the country.† To cope with the rise in the volume of the Baltic trade—due to increased imports of iron, copper, hemp, flax and muscovy linen—a dry basin and new quays were constructed in 1774 and two new docks opened in 1799 and 1809.[6] Both William Wilberforce and Henry Thornton abandoned any direct participation in the affairs of their trading firms. Henry Thornton became a partner in the London banking house of Down, Free and Thornton in 1784. William Wilberforce, while inheriting his father's share in the family business, remained a sleeping partner only, and although he possessed land in Yorkshire (in the Tranby area) he ceased to live there after 1780.

---

* Elizabeth Manning (*née* Smith) died in 1789, leaving two daughters, Elizabeth and Mary. William Manning married again in 1792. By his second wife (Mary Hunter) he had four sons and four daughters. Henry Edward Manning was the youngest son of this second marriage. Mary Smith (Elizabeth Manning's niece) married John Sargent, Rector of Lavington and Graffham.

† Ranking after London, Liverpool and Newcastle.

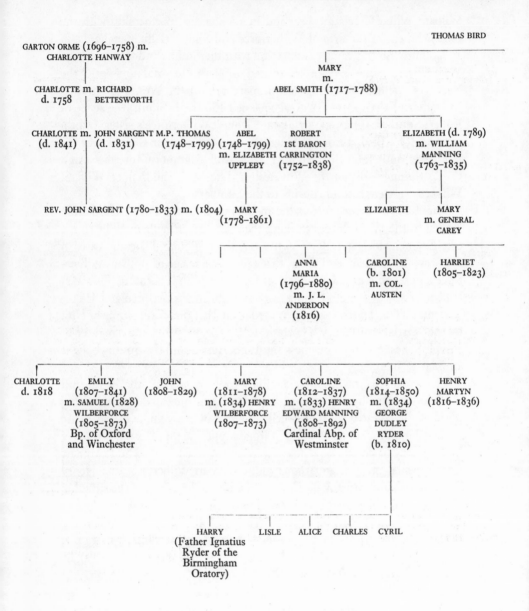

FAMILIES OF WILBERFORCE, SARGENT, SUMNER, MANNING AND SMITH

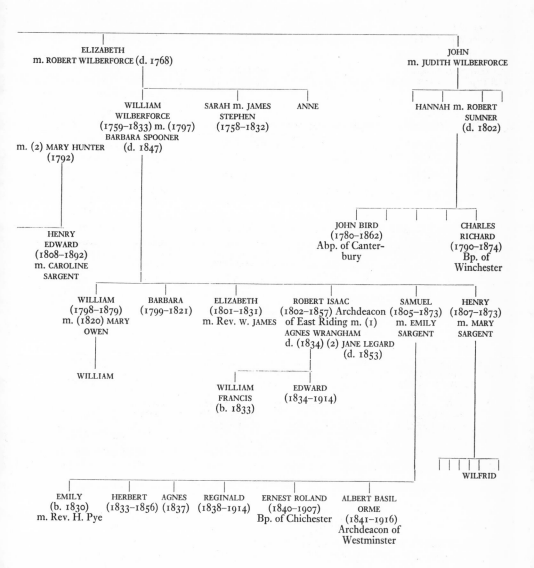

The wealth of the Stephens had certainly been newly acquired, if not founded on mercantile interests. James Stephen had made his money at the Bar, having inherited nothing from his father who had started life as a supercargo and ended it in debt. He began his practice in the West Indies, was assisted financially by his elder brother, who had inherited money from an uncle, and largely through his own ability as a lawyer and his natural eloquence he established a successful practice in England, becoming a Member of Parliament and a Master in Chancery. He was brought into the Clapham group partly through his abhorrence of the cruelties inflicted on slaves (which he had witnessed with his own eyes while living in the West Indies) and partly because he had become a relation of the Wilberforces by his marriage in 1800 to William's sister Sarah. His son James – Sir James Stephen of the Colonial Office – married the daughter of John Venn in 1814, thus creating a further marital link within the Clapham Sect.

William Wilberforce went outside this circle in choosing Barbara Spooner for his wife: not entirely outside, for Isaac Spooner, Barbara's father, was a Birmingham banker (or merchant) and Lord Calthorpe, a cousin of the Spooners, was a supporter of the anti-slavery compaign.[7] It is clear, too, that the Spooners were strong Evangelicals. William Spooner, Barbara's younger brother, became Archdeacon of Coventry and Rector of Elmden, and Wilberforce's description of him as 'so truly good a man that it must be useful to anyone to be his associate'[8] suggests an allusion to Evangelical principles. The childhood of Catharine Spooner, William's daughter, who married Archibald Campbell Tait, later Archbishop of Canterbury, has been lovingly described by the Archbishop himself in his memoir of his wife and eldest son, where a fine picture is drawn of a tender and sheltered Evangelical upbringing.[9] Of Barbara's own distinctive brand of effusive piety, much will be seen hereafter.

Marianne Thornton thought that William had married beneath him, and disliked Barbara intensely.

> He fell in love very suddenly with a Miss Barbara Spooner, the only religious member of a worldly family [her angry pen spat out inaccurately], and she confided to Mr Wilberforce all her persecutions and difficulties. She was extremely handsome and in some ways very clever, but very deficient in common sense, a woman with narrow views and selfish aims, that is if selfishness can be so called when it took the shape of idolatry of her husband, and thinking everything in the world ought to give way to what she thought expedient for him. Instead of helping him forward in the great works which it appeared Providence had given him to do, she always considered she was harshly used when he left her side, and instead

of making his home attractive to the crowds of superior people that he invited, her love of economy made her anything but a hospitable hostess. Yet the oddity and queerness of the scenes that went on there often made up, especially to young people, for all other deficiencies.[10]

Although she did less than justice to the Spooners as a family, Marianne erred only by exaggeration. Certainly Barbara was a very trying woman. She fussed too much. She fussed over William, worried about his manifold engagements, made herself ill with anxiety until she had succeeded in forcing him to retire from public life. She fussed over her own health – her teeth,[11] or her depressions,[12] or her 'gouty stomach',[13] or her rheumatism, or her collective aches and pains which she described as 'rheumatic gout'.[14] She was a bad patient, apt to become hysterical, prone to seeking out fantastic remedies and cures. She fussed over money; became peevishly anxious whenever they had to travel, and was always ready with grim forebodings or a morbid tale of sudden disaster to cheer them on their way. She fussed over her children – over their clothes, and the state of their bowels, sought their confidences and mused mournfully over the temptations to sexual sins.[15]

In short, Barbara Wilberforce was an over-anxious parent. She was also at heart a very kindly soul who tried her best to be a companion to her husband, and to understand the various enthusiasms of her children. But she could never quite relax. In her moments of ease, a sudden pang of alarm would grip her which must be assuaged on the instant by an anxious question. Nowhere did this anxiety show itself more markedly and repeatedly than in affairs of the spirit. Barbara's chief – and most proper – concern was the spiritual health of her charges. She had been brought up to believe (and William agreed entirely with her in this) that no letter was complete without some expression of a religious sentiment. Unfortunately she was apt to let herself be carried away in her zeal to do her duty, so that her letters to her children, as often as not, while starting with some definite object to communicate and some sense of restraint, would gradually degenerate into frantic sermons, full of urgent moralisms and ready texts. Nor did this sermonising abate as the children grew older. If anything, it grew worse.

Thus to Samuel, aged nineteen, recently arrived at Oxford, Barbara wrote:

> I am anxious ... to know whether you have any cough, any hoarseness, any pain in your chest, any Rheumatism about you – Pray write very particularly to satisfy a mother's anxiety and remember that November

pours his surly looks upon us tomorrow. . . . Have you got your great coat yet? . . . Dearest Samuel, I am still far more anxious about your better part and when I pray for you, think of all the horrid temptations that surround a young man like you – pleasant to your young companions, and just at the age to be most in danger from simple compliance and the snares of the Evil One and his miserable agents which line too often at night all the paths of every Town and City. Oh, think of peace of mind – of safety and comfort – think of your God and Saviour who died for you – think of your parents at home – remember, dear Boy, the horror of disease, of early corruption, of death in an unpardoned state, of the want of the light of that Countenance which only can confer happiness – that favor which is better than Life – and fly from all manner of evil.

Trust not in your own strength, remember our subtle, our crafty Enemy ever on the watch to allure and to destroy; and may God give you grace to overcome every temptation and preserve you from falling and present you *at length* washed in the Redeemer's blood, faultless before the Throne. May you be enabled so to walk during this *sejour* at Oxford as to preserve *peace of mind* and grow in *grace and spirituality of Soul* – then you will find the joy of the Lord your strength and be satisfied. Tomorrow I hope you will have a blessed Sunday and may every one be a day of rest and refreshment and strengthening to your soul. I like much that Saturday night hymn in the Olney collection –

> 'Safely thro' another week
> God has brought us on our way'

Do you know it. Farewell . . . .[16]

All the Wilberforce children regularly received letters like this when they were away from home. Another of Barbara's lengthy spiritual transports, this time to Robert (aged twenty-one) at Oxford, was written while she was waiting in a carriage for William to emerge from a committee meeting of the Bible Society:

. . . I cannot say that your dear Father is quite well tho' only I hope unhinged in his stomach by a little mismanagement in dining too late on Saturday [she began auspiciously, proceeding to describe some visits which they had lately been paying].

We went in the evening . . . to see a beautiful place of Mr Rowlands who married a Miss Maitland, sister to the one who lived with Mr H. Thornton's family as Governess; a remarkably elegant pleasing woman Mrs Rowlands is and they are of a very good family in Scotland tho' several of them thro' their father's misfortunes have been obliged to go out as Governesses. Mr Rowlands is in the Law and manages all Lord Abergavenney's Fortune and we might have seen the place (tho' not the castle because My Lord was there) had we known all about it in time. We much enjoyed the beauties we saw and the driving about etc. etc. – but the best

28

of it is that Mrs Rowlands is a truly pious excellent Woman and thro' her means Mr R. seems becoming so and has taken a very great liking to Mr Spragg and comes whenever he thinks he may leave his Parish Church to hear him. . . .

I trust Samuel's health is much benefited of late and I never saw Henry look so well. Of course we all feel very anxious about dear Samuel's line of conduct at Oxford and the formation of his future character which so much depends on the course he runs there. May a gracious God shield him from the many dangers of his trying tuition, for the Universities are sadly trying, and grant that he may not only preserve his moral character – preserve his mind from taints of evil and give himself to his studies as a duty and with needful fervour – but also keep up his hitherto intended line of life, the Church, and grow more and more spiritual and fitter therefore for the Sacred Office. Let him have your earnest prayers, dearest Robert, for these blessings and in all your thoughts for him, all your advice to him, every friend you may introduce him to, every project you form for him at Oxford, and I rejoice to see your kind desire of acting like an elder brother to him, bear this great thing in mind, for much indeed does your father desire to see him an excellent Clergyman. It will go very near his heart in the way of grief and sorrow and perhaps shorten his days if Samuel does not choose that profession and prove worthy of being admitted to it. He has I think many excellent preparations for that state.

Oh, pray earnestly for him that he may grow more and more fit, may ultimately glorify God in that most honourable line, may be delivered from everything that would impede him in fitting himself for it and devoting himself to do it and while my dear Robert is thus praying for his Brother may he be watered himself. May the one thing he most needs and feels he most needs be granted to him – more and more of that Spirit which is promised to all that ask and may he feel that to be carnally minded is death but to be spiritually minded is Life and Peace and earnestly seek after that spiritual mindedness which is the gift of God in answer to earnest prayer, thro' Christ Jesus our Lord and which alone can prove him a real Xtian, give him peace and joy in any circumstances, in any course of life and Occupation of this poor, mortal state which conscience may dictate to him to follow. And Robert do not let your present situation [he was studying at Southrop with John Keble] prove hurtful to your best interests while it is aiding your attainments – I fear lest the spiritual, the evangelical, the biblical growth of your mind should be hurt either from too much attention being drawn to learning and not time enough taken daily for God and religion – or from your company being not quite of the kind I wish as most desirable for you and most wanted by your best interests at present, or by your Sunday advantages being low and not truly evangelical and spiritual.

By this time William had come out of the Bible Society meeting and the carriage had moved on. But Barbara was not yet done.

Dearest Robert, I began this letter as mentioned and am finishing it at

Downing Street, Mrs W's old lodging where Mrs Balche has been kind enough to provide us a dinner between your Father's being at the Bible Society and going to the House this – as I hope – last time this year. Weigh well, dear Robert, what I have written and let me beg you to think much respecting spirituality of mind and to be very earnest in prayer for this great blessing – to be renewed in the Spirit of your mind, to be assimilated to the Image of your Saviour's mind to follow him, to enjoy conversation with God thro' Christ, to walk with God in holy obedience and faith – to have a mind raised above the world, your affections set on things above as Scripture says, and to have your life hid with Xt. in God – this is the privilege and duty of a Xtian.

Have I not already quoted that Text to be carnally minded is death but to be spiritually minded is Life and Peace. Let me beg you to be very particular about a morning time for reading and devotion and about Sunday – let Sunday be sacred and not merely used for the ceremonies of the Church but a portion, my dearest Robert, be solemnly set apart for private devotion and reading the Scriptures and may these exercises be more blessed to your Soul and Christ be made known to you in them as He was to His Disciples in breaking bread. The blessing of the most High be on my beloved Robert thro' our Lord Jesus Christ, the Mediator of the New Covenant. Amen.[17]

This letter, as good an example of 'ranting' as one could find, is important in its way. The Wilberforce children saw much of the pure gold of Evangelicalism in their own household, but they also encountered the dross. In reading this letter we see the force of what was to become a common criticism of Evangelicalism in the next decade – how its preachers became 'nervously afraid of departing from the consecrated phrases of its school, and in the perpetual iteration of them . . . lost hold of the meaning they may once have had'.[18] Or, as James Stephen expressed it in a letter to Samuel Wilberforce, deprecating the soulless monotony of Evangelical tub-thumping: their 'endless revolution through a narrow orbit, from which all variety of subject and illustration is superstitiously excluded – the head giddy with the eternal recurrence of certain threadbare dogmata'.[19] No wonder the preaching of Keble and Newman seemed attractive after this!

II. *The Wilberforce Household*

Marianne Thornton had written of 'the oddity and the queerness of the scenes' which might enliven visitors to the Wilberforce *ménage*. This was certainly so. Of course, life on the Common itself could supply some pretty odd sights: you never quite knew whom you would meet – strange outcasts come to solicit charity; the occasional emancipated slave; Zachary Macaulay's little train of coal-black African boys, brought from Sierra Leone to be civilised and saved. But in William's house at Kensington Gore, such, and even stranger, scenes might be witnessed daily in the smaller space of a single residence.

The household itself was weird. Mrs Wilberforce was not, as might be imagined, a very efficient housekeeper, not being 'strong eno'', as William apologised to Isaac Milner, when that corpulent and raucous divine was in one of his more demanding moods, 'to meddle much in domestic matters'.[1] William himself did not notice how imperfectly his material needs were supplied. Such matters were indeed 'things indifferent'. As Marianne observed, every home in which the Wilberforces lived was 'thronged with servants who are all lame or impotent or blind, or kept from charity; an ex-secretary kept because he is grateful, and his wife because she nursed poor Barbara, and an old butler who they wish would not stay but then he is so attached, and his wife who was a cook but now she is so infirm. All this is rather as it should be however for one rather likes to see him so completely in character and would willingly sit in despair of getting one's plate changed at dinner and hear a chorus of bells all day which nobody answers for the sake of seeing Mr Wilberforce in his element'.[2]

William Wilberforce was one of those rare people who could be scintillating both on the public platform (after all, he was as an orator in Parliament reputed to be the peer of Burke, Pitt and Fox) and in an intimate group. He was happiest when surrounded by his family; he was happy with his servants too, because it gave him pleasure that he had helped them when no other help was theirs. There was within him a vein of sheer gold – a warmth of feeling and lightness of heart which captivated an audience, confounded his critics, and made even the most vehement radical or the most austere orthodox clergyman admit, after meeting him, that he had been utterly disarmed by his encounter with a man who expressed so fully in his own life and character the true spirit of Christian joy and living faith. Their surprise is understandable, for William, if he was a master of the spoken word, was quite incapable of transmitting this vivaciousness and joyousness to his writings. The success of *A Practical View* is explained by its timely appearance and its evident earnestness and sincerity. But it fails completely to convey the personality of the writer. The same may be said of his letters. Many of them are lively; but the didactic, serious note is dominant, most especially in his letters to his children. A writer who would attempt to portray William's character – in particular the mutual love and happy relation which existed between the father and his children – and who is forced to rely upon William's family letters as his main source of evidence, is faced with a peculiarly difficult task. The letters, in both tone and substance, are often only a little less censorious and trite than Barbara's epistolary sermons. There was very much more to the man than is shown of him in these.

There is, for instance, the man who paid so little attention to his own material comforts that he did not notice the inefficiency and the absurdities of his servants. Probably the children failed to notice these things too – at least, when they were young – for children have a habit of thinking that the normal is what goes on at home. They must, however, have been aware that there was more coming and going in their household, and their visitors more exotic, than one would expect to find in the average home. For day in and day out the strangest assortment of visitors would make their way to the house in Kensington Gore. There would be statesmen and ex-slaves, dissenting ministers and bishops, peers of the realm and ex-convicts; and William had time for them all. Often his peace would be broken by the arrival of some unexpected caller who would try to solicit his aid – it might be pecuniary or as patron of some particular project – and William would listen with patience as the hours ticked by. 'Such incidents are salutary', he wrote to his daughter Elizabeth. 'They accustom us to bear with cheerfulness the little vexatious interruptions which people sometimes bear with less equanimity than more serious grievances'.[3]

On a quiet day, when there was no call to attend Parliament, and no committee meetings of societies to speak at, the routine would be something like this: William would rise at seven. On this he was punctilious, and all the children were brought up to recognise that late rising was an indulgence not to be countenanced. 'There was scarcely anything else equally injurious', Samuel reported him as saying. He would point out '. . . that God frequently made self-indulgence its own punishment, and that a decline in religion generally began in this way as it led to a hurrying over of the morning devotions; that he had seen many instances of it, when from lying in bed late private prayers had been neglected and the soul had always suffered in consequence.'[4]

These morning devotions, after rising, would last for about an hour. He would then dress while one of the children read to him for some three-quarters of an hour. Breakfast would be served at nine, and the rest of the morning would be spent in dealing with the post. Dinner would be taken with the whole of the family in the middle of the day. Depending on the season of the year, he would take a two-hour walk in either the afternoon or early evening, usually with the children if they were at home. The remainder of the period would be spent in reading, studying or writing. At eight in the evening, he would spend another hour in devotions, which would be followed by family prayers, supper and bed.[5]

We have two descriptions of the Wilberforce family prayers. The first comes in the third volume of the Farington Diary (19 July 1806), describing prayers at Broomfield. We may take it that the same procedure was adopted at Kensington Gore.

> About a quarter before 10 o'clock, the family assembled to prayers, which were read by Wilberforce in the dining-room. As we passed from the drawing room I saw all the servants standing in regular order, the woemen ranged in a line against the wall and the men the same. There were 7 woemen and 6 men. When the whole were collected in the dining room, all knelt down each against a chair or sopha, and Wilberforce knelt at a table in the middle of the room, and after a little pause began to read a prayer, which he did very slowly in a low, solemnly awful voice. This was followed by 2 other prayers and the grace. It occupied about 10 minutes, and had the best effect as to the manner of it.
>
> After prayers were over, a long table covered with cold meat, tarts, etc. was drawn to a sopha on which sat Mrs Wilberforce and Miss Hewit. Wilberforce had boiled milk and bread, and tasted a little brandy and water which at night He said agrees better with Him than wine.[6]

When Marianne Thornton came to describe the devotions at the Wilberforce's to her sister Henrietta, she was writing of a later period – 1828. The family were then living at Highwood, where a short session of morning prayers had been introduced.

> The scene at prayers is a most curious one [she wrote]. There is a bell which rings when Mr W. begins to dress; another when he finishes dressing; upon which Mr Barningham begins to play a hymn upon the organ and to sing a solo, and by degrees the family come down to the entrance hall where the psalmody goes on; first one joins in and then another; Lizzy calling out 'Don't go near dear Mama, she sings so dreadfully out of tune, dear', and William 'Don't look at Papa, he does make such dreadful faces.' So he does, waving his arms about, and occasionally pulling the leaves off the geraniums and smelling them, singing out louder and louder in a tone of hilarity: 'Trust Him, praise Him, trust Him, praise Him, praise Him ever more.' Sometimes he exclaims 'Astonishing! How very affecting! Only think of Abraham, a fine old man, just a kind of man one should

naturally pull off one's hat to, with long grey hairs, and looking like an old aloe – but you don't know what an aloe is perhaps: it's a tree – no a plant which flowers . . . ' and he wanders off into a dissertation about plants and flowers.[7]

The morning and evening readings were probably what the children chiefly remembered in after years. William, whose eyesight was never good and deteriorated to near blindness by the end of his life, always preferred to be read to rather than to read himself. When the children were at home they all attended these readings. At these moments, he was at his gayest and his mind was most active. He 'would pour forth all his stores', Samuel wrote, 'gathering around him book after book to illustrate, question, or confirm the immediate subject of the evening.'[8] For spiritual edification his favourite books were Doddridge's *Rise and Progress of Religion in the Soul* (that 'super-excellent book'[9]) and Owen on *Spiritual Mindedness* ('eminently useful'[10]). He enjoyed the novels of Walter Scott, but was at pains to warn his children against their seductive attraction. It pained him 'that a man of such evidently superior talents should not seem to have directed one thought towards doing good but mainly towards gaining money. He had . . . better be the author of *The Shepherd of Salisbury Plain* than of all these novels.'[11] He also had a taste for Hume, Smollett and Gibbon. Cowper was his favourite poet.[12]

During these readings, and on their walks and talks, he would expatiate freely on these and other books, and would comment on the political questions of the hour. He would speak of his political colleagues – how Pitt was the wittiest man he had ever met, and how Fox was the most pitiable, because he had never had 'the smallest advantage of a religious nature',[13] and how Sheridan was the most ingenious in devising means of eluding his creditors. On one occasion Sheridan encountered a horse-dealer, to whom he owed a great deal of money, and was somewhat put out.

> The man came and pressed him to pay him his bill. Mr Sh. could not escape because the dealer was on horseback and himself on foot. So he said to him, 'Well, it is very true I should have paid you before – but come home now and I will give you a draught on my banker for the amount.' On his way home he looked at the horse the dealer was on and said: 'a very pretty little thing that: I think it would just suit me. I have been looking out for one for Mrs Sheridan: pray let me see him trot: one cannot altogether judge by a walk.' The man trotted on to show his paces, and Sheridan turning down the first alley made the best of his way out of the dealer's reach.[14]

It is a rare thing indeed for William's sense of gaiety, so often alluded to by his contemporaries, to show itself in his manuscript remains; and when it does, it may appear to a more sophisticated generation faintly juvenile. One of his anecdotes, however, is certainly worth recording; for this was the type of story, especially when narrated by William, which would dissolve his audience into tears.

> I remember my dear mother telling me a story something like this – There was a lady who was rather proud of her son: she called him to her (he was quite young) to say his alphabet to show the company how well he could do it. He got very well through A, but stuck at B; she said to him, 'What is that, my dear, that flies about and stings naughty boys who tease it?', He thought a minute and then replied 'wasp'. She said, 'No not quite right, my dear – BEE. Well, what's the next? – What is it I do with my eyes?' 'Squint', replied the boy (which she did), after a moment's thought. You may be sure she never endeavoured to exhibit him again.[15]

It was a happy home. Even that notorious torment for the Evangelical young – Sunday at home – was strikingly free from the rigidity and severity which became more fashionable in the middle years of the century.[16] It had its ritual, but also its lighter moments. William was very nervous lest his children should come to associate religious observance with austerity and gloom. He wrote in his diary in 1813, on the death of a friend, that he suspected that 'poor C. N. . . . was overdosed with religion, and that of an offensive kind, while young. It is an awful instance, and well deserves the study of all parents; they should labour to render religion as congenial as possible. . . .'[17]

And so it was in his own home. One of the most lasting impressions that a visitor would gain from a call at Wilberforce's house was that it was a place of merriment and laughter. James Stephen, who as a neighbour was likely to know, chose this particular facet of William's character – his simple unaffected joy in the company of his children – to portray his personality in his famous essay on the Clapham Sect. Wherever they went as a family, the merriment followed. There would be grave deliberations of the saints at Battersea Rise, Wilberforce not yet arrived. Shouts of delight from the garden would herald his approach, and then in he would burst, a laughing boy clinging to each hand.[18] On another occasion, when the pressure of work was affecting his spirits, and he was closeted with a visitor in the study at Hyde Park Gate, their converse was interrupted with a sudden burst of voices upstairs. '"There", he said. "How can I be worried by such trifles, when I have such constant remembrances of God's goodness to me?" It was his children playing overhead with a noisy glee which would have jarred upon the feelings of almost any one besides himself.'[19]

When he could, he joined in their games. In 1810 he was confined to a sofa under doctor's orders after playing cricket with them, in which he received a painful blow on the foot from a ball[20]; in 1812 we hear of him 'running races with them' in the garden[21]; and, in 1815, playing blind man's buff at a Twelfth Night party.[22] There were frequent excursions to places of interest; to the British Museum 'to see the great fish, and the toy shops'[23]; 'to see some jugglers'[24]; picnic parties at 'Caesar's Camp and the cherry orchards'[25]; a visit to Stowe, 'a work to wonder at'. 'We were still in the land of poetry', wrote John Bowdler, about this visit 'and of music too, for Mr Wilberforce made the shades resound to his voice, singing like a blackbird wherever he went. He always has the spirits of a boy, but here "not little Sam himself can beat him, though he does his best".'[26]

Sometimes the anxious Barbara took part in their games as well. The earliest surviving letter of the children is one from Samuel to his brother William, written in January 1810 from Kensington Gore:

> Dear brother William. We are very well. We hope you are quite well again. I wish you were here. Papa is coming home. Papa and Mama are very well. Brothers and sisters are not quite well. I hope you will soon come home. B.E.R.H.* all send their love to you. Yesterday Mama played with us in the Gallery at Puss in ye Corner. Was it not fine. We have found your Bandelour and a small loadstone and we mean to send them. Farewell. Sam Wilberforce. His mark.[27]

As a family they travelled more than most. As often as they could they escaped from London to find the country, the mountains and the sea. Most frequently they went to the Lake District or to Bath where William took the waters. In 1808 they took their holidays at Eastbourne; in 1809 they stayed at a quiet parsonage near Newport Pagnell to spend a 'Cowperizing summer'[28]; in 1810 they went to Hurstmonceux, near Battle, to stay at a country house lent to them by a friend. In 1812 they were at Sandgate, where the children looked with awe at the coastline of Martello towers, erected to defy Bonaparte, and peered anxiously across the Channel to the French coast for signs of imminent invasion.[29] In 1815 they went to Brighton, which even then resembled 'Piccadilly by the sea-side',[30] where they subsequently stayed often. The family were at Lowestoft in 1816, and

* Barbara, Elizabeth, Robert, Henry.

took a special fancy to Earlham,[31] and at Weymouth in 1820, a quick change of plan to escape the intolerable heat of Bath.[32]

1821 was a year of sadness for it brought the first bereavement in the family – the death of Barbara, the eldest daughter. The house in Kensington Gore was sold and thereafter they were on the move for five years before they settled in permanent quarters. They took a year's tenancy at Marden Park, in Surrey, while William pondered over the time and place of his retirement. In 1823 they went to live at Barmouth, pleasantly near to mountain country ('Any one whom I love at all, I seem to love better in a land of mountains', William wrote)[33]; and when they ascended Snowdon, Samuel was taken ill at the top. During 1825 they lived at Uxbridge. Then William decided to retire ('Thank God, the Die is cast',[34] wrote the importunate Barbara, triumphant at last), and permitted himself the luxury of buying a large country house with an estate at Highwood Hill near Mill Hill. 'I shall be a little Zeminda there', he wrote excitedly to Thomas Gisborne, '140 acres of land, cottages of my own, etc.'[35] In fact he had grown worried at the effect on his children of this peripatetic existence. Samuel especially had complained of a 'feeling of desolateness', a year after leaving Kensington Gore.

> I do not deny that your remarks were very natural [William replied]. Yet any human situation has its advantages as well as its evils. And if the want of a home deprive us of the many and great pleasures which arise out of the relations and associations . . . with which it is connected, yet there is an advantage, and of a very high order, in our not having this well-known anchoring ground, if I may so term it. We are less likely to lose the consciousness of our true condition in this life; less likely to forget that while sailing in the ocean of life we are always exposed to the buffeting of the billows, nay, more, to the rock and the quicksand.[36]

At last William felt that he owed it to his children to listen to their entreaties. So queer old Knowles the butler, and the half-blind secretary, and the various servants – the deaf, the mute and the halt – made what was thought to be their last move. William himself would have wished to end his days there. Here were green fields and gardens in plenty.

> Who that ever joined him . . . cannot see him as he walked round his garden at Highwood? Now in animated and ever playful conversation, and then drawing from his copious pockets (to contain Dalrymple's State Papers was their standard measure) some favourite volume or other; a Psalter, a Horace, a Shakespeare, a Cowper, and reading, and reciting, or 'refreshing' passages; and then catching at long-stored flower-leaves as the wind blew them from the pages, or standing before a favourite

gum cistus to repair the loss. Then he could point out the harmony of the tints, the beauty of the pencilling, the perfection of the colouring, and run up all into those ascriptions of praise to the Almighty which were ever welling forth from his grateful heart.[37]

It was tragedy to have to see him leave. But the time came when he had to expose himself once more 'to the buffeting of the billows'. He had trusted his eldest son with the large part of his fortune, and unfortunately his own poor financial sense was magnified a hundredfold in his first-born. He and Barbara were forced to put Highwood to let in 1831 and to spend the last two years of their lives as lodgers in the houses of one or other of their married sons. William felt the loss deeply, but he never showed his sadness. There was not a word of recrimination for the prodigal son. Robert built his father a special garden walk at East Farleigh, and there William would wander, his small body stooping, towards the end, but his spirits as buoyant as ever. He could not make out the flowers so well, as his eyesight gradually failed, but he was still a rewarding companion: tender, kind, and thankful – talking no less than in the old days, ever 'drawing out of his treasury things old and new.'[38]

III. *The Children at School*

William had no high opinion of the public schools and was determined not to send any of his sons to one. The decision was made as early as 1807 when he had a long conversation with his young friend John Bowdler on the subject. 'Much talk about education', he recorded in his diary. 'He agreed that public school inadmissable, from its probable effects on eternal state.'[1] Some years later he had cause to visit Harrow (in 1812) and was very favourably impressed with what he saw there,[2] but this did not make him reconsider his decision. William, the eldest son, was therefore put into the hands of private tutors until the age of twelve; and Robert likewise until his ninth year, when both boys were sent away to a private school. No details of this early schooling have survived save a memorandum, dated 1810, which consists of directions to each of them instructing them on their proper behaviour to each other while away from home. Each set of precepts was headed 'Hints for my dear Robert [or William], to be often read over, with self-examination.'

William was warned against being bossy to his younger brother; he was bidden, when tempted, to conjure up a picture of Robert as a baby in the unlikely hope that he would be at once suffused with a countervailing tenderness. Robert was instructed to guard against the temptation of resenting William's overbearing manner and sulking at his 'raillery'. 'An elder brother has a right to some influence from being such. See 1 Peter, v. 5.' Both were reminded that 'it is not sufficient not to be unkind to your brother; you must be positively kind to all, and how much more then to a brother!'[3]

Robert was subsequently sent to a small private school at Nuneham Courtenay, near Oxford, run by the Rev. E. G. Marsh. Samuel joined him there in 1817, having spent a year as a pupil of the Rev. S. Langston near Hastings. The earliest of Robert's letters to survive is addressed from Nuneham to Samuel, written probably sometime in 1816:

> Dear Sam. I am much obliged to you for having written to me so often as you have done this time and I hope whenever anything remarkable happens you will let me know of it. For instance I hope you will tell me as soon as you know the school to which you go and when you go and so forth. In the book which Mr. Rolleston gave me called Bacon's Essays at the end there is a curious collection of proverbs and apothegms. I will give you two rather odd instances of them. Some scolars going out to catch rabbits took one scolar with them who was rather silly but they all told him if he saw any rabbits not to speak for fear he should frighten them – but as soon as he saw them he called out in Latin that he saw a great many rabbits upon which they immediately ran away. When the other scolars asked him why he spoke and frightened the rabbits, he said Why who would have thought that the rabbits could understand Latin. Another story is that a man went to play before the window of a lady whom he wanted to marry but she threw stones at him; whereupon a person said to him that his playing must be most excellent since stones came about him as they did about Orpheus. I have got another good story to tell you if I receive a good letter from you in the meantime. I remain, your affectionate brother, Robert Wilber-force.[4]

Robert remained at Mr Marsh's establishment until he matriculated at Oriel in February 1820. Samuel's sojourn there was very short. According to Tom Mozley (admittedly, a very doubtful source), he so disliked the place that he determined at all costs to contrive to be expelled. When a violent quarrel with his tutor failed to produce the desired result, he 'thereupon . . . ran into the road before the cottage, then traversed by a score or two of London coaches a day, threw himself flat on the ground, in the very track of the coaches, and announced his intention of remaining there till he was sent home'.[5] Marsh was compelled to give in. At any rate, at the beginning of 1819 Samuel became the pupil of the Rev. George

39

Hodson, who was then chaplain to a Mr Lewis Way at Stanstead Park near Emsworth in Sussex. This was an obvious choice. Lewis Way was a close friend of the family and Mrs Hodson was related to the Wilberforces through being a niece of James Stephen. The Evangelical upbringing was further strengthened by the close association between the Hodsons and the Sargents, who lived not far from Stanstead and were regular visitors to the house.

It is not easy either to discover the details or to recapture the atmosphere of the small private schools, of which in the first half of the nineteenth century there were legion. Some undoubtedly were atrocious – like the school at Streatham, kept by a Welsh clergyman called Davies, where Manning received his first schooling.[6] Thomas Arnold, who himself kept a small private school at Laleham before becoming headmaster of Rugby, believed that of all systems of education, that offered by the large private school was 'the worst possible'. When he came to consider the education of his own children, he observed that 'the choice lies between public schools, and an education whose character may be strictly private and domestic'.[7] The schools to which William Wilberforce sent his sons were really of this last category – schools, very like Laleham in pattern, where a few pupils lived together in the house of a clergyman, were trained primarily in the classics with the sons of the family and became part of the domestic circle. George Hodson, as chaplain to Lewis Way, acted as tutor to his son Albert Way, and it was an arrangement agreeable to all parties that he should collect together a number of other pupils so that the education of the son of the house should be stimulated by competition and emulation. For the same reason John Sargent, who educated his sons privately at home, was eager to take Henry Wilberforce into the house to become the schoolfellow and playmate of his children. It is not possible to say how many pupils George Hodson was taking at this period, although we know that both James Thomason, a future Indian civil servant, and Henry Hoare, who was later to be closely associated with Samuel in their joint efforts to promote the revival of Convocation, were pupils at Stanstead at this time.[8] When Hodson obtained a curacy at Maisemore, near Gloucester, in 1820, he took his pupils with him, including Samuel, who remained there until 1822. In that year he went with his younger brother Henry to F. R. Spragge's establishment at Little Bounds in Bidborough, near Tonbridge, to obtain more formal coaching for the university.

The occasional family letter affords us a glimpse of private-school life and the sort of enthusiasm which it engendered. When Samuel left Mr

Marsh for Mr Hodson, Robert wrote to him (in February 1819) to ply him with questions in the appropriate elder-brother manner:

> Dear Sam, I have been intending to write to you for some time, but I thought that it would be better to wait till you were somewhat settled. In the first place I beg that you will not show my letters to anyone. I intend to finish this letter as soon as I can but I do not know how soon I shall be able. I have got several fishing lines, and hooks of different kinds, which I intend to send you on the first opportunity. I will also send you two pegtops, which I have got here, but I do not know how soon it will be. I wish you to tell me how you like Mr Hodson's, how much business you do there, what time you get up, and go to bed, what games you play at, and how you like your companions. Now I do not want you to write me a short letter, in a great hurry, but I wish you would take your time, to write me a good one.
>
> I have got a bow since you were here, which is not quite finished. I bought a peice of yew, which George Watts has been fashioning. I have made arrows, out of deal wood, with peices of iron wire in the end, and I have got a quiver of basket work. Since your going I have found many new walks, because I have explored the country more. . . . Tell me what books you read, and how long, when you begin and when you leave off.[9]

Robert was in his seventeenth year when he wrote this letter, manifestly very much more the letter of a boy than of a young man. If the incitement to robustness in the public schools had not yet developed into the cult of manliness, which was to grip all the public schools in the second half of the nineteenth century, it seems likely that the private school system of education tended to permit boys to be children longer than was possible in the rougher atmosphere of Eton, Winchester or Westminster (or indeed any of the great 'seven'), where boys were forced to curb their individualism and to assert manly airs, if only to escape the favourite charge of being a 'sawney', and were confronted with the responsibilities of self-government at a relatively early age.[10] There is no doubt that when the Wilberforce boys came up to Oxford, they were at first conscious that their manners were naive, their background very sheltered and their scholarship somewhat blunt in comparison with the self-assurance, refinement and worldly wisdom displayed by the products of Eton, Winchester and Harrow.

In common, however, with most aspirants to higher learning, they liked to write to each other in verse – although, even here, their command of the medium seems to lack the polish and elegance of a Charles Wordsworth or a Francis Doyle. When Samuel had passed from Maisemore to Little Bounds, he wrote to Robert, then at Oxford, a poem of great length, seeking *inter alia* assistance with his Latin:

41

> And now be kind enough to look
> In Livy's history: third book
>   And chapter forty five
> And tell me how I may translate
> The first four sentences: where great
>   Obscurities arrive.

He concludes, at length:

> Believe me now my Robert dear,
> What I myself will subscribe here,
>   Your brother fond and true.
> May heaven thine onward progress bless
> And give thee peace and happiness
>   So prays S.W.[11]

Barbara, their mother, clucked anxiously in the background, noting the progress of her sons, but intervening regularly to warn them against the fearful pitfalls of adolescence and the dire consequences which would attend the slightest indiscretion in supplying their bodily needs. Samuel had taken up skating.

> I rejoice to receive so good an account of you [wrote his mother], and am quite glad you have so enjoyed your skating for I think air and exercise so particularly good for you . . . I only hope you will not go to skate when the ice is not strong enough to hold you for that would indeed be very dangerous.[12]

Samuel had been suffering from heartburn.

> You cannot think [Barbara wrote] how very fearful I shall be of your eating almonds and raisins: there are not two worse things for you in the world. They will perhaps affect you as you may remember the Spanish chestnuts did at Barham Court. The Raisins are particularly clogging to the bowels and will cause you to want more medicine than otherwise. The almonds are indigestible and all such kind of things as nutts, etc., are especially bad for you. Will you let me know what you want them for – whether for eating or giving away. . . .[13]

Barbara was anxious lest Samuel should acquire expensive tastes in clothing while he was away at school:

> It will be very bad indeed for you when you are older and as I hope you will turn out to be a good pious Clergyman you will see that in that state of life you will not be able to afford much in Clothes and I hope it will be your endeavour to restrain yourself now in every expense not absolutely needful that you may please your God and Saviour who says it is more blessed to give than to receive.

I have spoken to Lord Rocksavage about your dog. I told him how earnestly you were longing for it and wanting it in hot weather to teach it to go into the water – and he assures me he does not know of any yet born which you can have and has promised me that on Fanny's next accouchement he will order one of the greatest beauties reserved for you. . . .[14]

After the death of their eldest daughter, Barbara became even more anxious to have regular news of her children's welfare.

Dear Samuel [she wrote in 1822], It seems very long since we heard from you, and one day your dear Father remarked how seldom he heard from his sons when once they left him to go to their places of destination. . . . I am sure you will wish to comfort us as much as you can by letting us hear from you pretty often.

May dearest Samuel tell us any kind of particular respecting yourself and your Situation, your studies, companions, and everything that relates to your health, comfort and improvement. I wish also very much to know how your hand is and whether you have received the full use of your fingers and can write well and with ease in spite of the burn. I mean as well and with as much ease as before. Pray be very particular in answering my enquiries.

Dearest Samuel. I wish I could peep at you to-night and see how you are and have a little talk with you – but that is impossible. I hope however as it is Saturday night, you may be preparing for tomorrow and am going to offer up my petition for you which is a work not of Saturday only but of every day in the week morning and night. I hope you will have a happy and blessed Sunday tomorrow and find much refreshment to your Soul. When you write, find time to let me know how you spend your Sunday, that at the different hours of the day I may think of you and of your various employments, and perhaps we might contrive a time to meet together at the Throne of Grace. Oh, dearest Samuel, endeavour to make your parents happy and to be a Crown of Rejoicing to them.

She brooded a little over the Day of Judgment: 'Oh that in that awful day the great God may spare all our Six as a Man spareth his own Son that serveth him – but that so it must be they must fear Him and think on His name and perhaps they may also speak often together on such subjects as those which relate to the momentous concerns of Eternity. See the last chapter of Malachi . . .'.[15]

The letters of the various children at this stage of their lives are too few in number to enable us to write with any confidence of their growth in character. When Robert first looked through the family papers (as he started work on his father's biography), he was struck by the quaintness of their early efforts at letter-writing. 'Mine have a rigid formality', he wrote to Samuel, 'which now looks to me inexpressibly ludicrous. Perhaps this may do the same for some other reason twelve years hence. Yours are more lively and less constrained. It seems Marsh had managed to correct my two main faults of being too communicative and eager in my manner. Henry's are untidy but affectionate and thoughtful. . . . You seem to have written much more than the rest of us.'[16]

The somewhat stilted and reserved manner of Robert's letters, however, shows us the man in embryo: shy, self-effacing, scholarly; a man too preoccupied with his work to spare time for small talk and who was to begin writing a book on the first day of his honeymoon.[17] Even as a boy he found his mother's anxious injunctions and trite conversation very wearisome. He admitted to Samuel some years later: 'It hurts and galls me to be forced to talk about other things when I don't care about them. In this way, my dear mother, without at all meaning it, used often to try me exceedingly.'[18]

William, the eldest, appears to have been a difficult child – and in his subsequent career ran true to form. He is pictured as being moody (Mrs Wilberforce once complained of 'his usual grumbling style'[19]), apathetic in his religious life,[20] disinclined to study.[21] His father, in 1822, attributed his failings to his fear of solitariness and his refusal to discipline himself in self-examination.

> Use yourself, my dearest Samuel [he wrote], to take now and then a solitary walk, and in it to indulge in . . . spiritual meditations. The disposition to do this will gradually become a habit, and a habit of unspeakable value. I have long considered it as a great misfortune, or rather I should say, as having been very injurious to your brother William, that he never courted solitude in his walks, or indeed at any time.[22]

As for Henry, his father's chief fears were that he might become 'volatile and bird-witted',[23] not a bad description of the faults of the man whose brothers were constantly scolding him for being scatter-brained and impetuous. 'For you, my dear boy', his father wrote to him in 1823, 'I am anxiously musing whether you have been endeavouring to get the better of that habit, for which there are many almost nicknames but scarcely any serious one; the habit I mean of appearing engaged in any given occupation of mind while your thoughts are in reality wandering to other objects. There is also another particular which you ought always to bear in mind – I mean the disposition not to practice self-denial habitually.'[24]

We possess a clearer picture of Samuel. Even as a boy he displayed something of that liveliness and charm, combined with a masterfulness of

44

manner, which were later to be the qualities which most men remembered. This early inclination to take the lead and to lay down the law made both his parents and his teachers fear a want of meekness in his character and a tendency towards arrogance. In 1817 his mother wrote to rebuke him for his behaviour in the holidays.

> My dear Sam, I meant to write you a long letter to-day but if I do I must quite give up my ride so I will write but little and send another letter very soon. . . . My dear Samuel, while you were at home you got dissipated, thought too little of God and gave much too little time to prayer and reading the Scriptures. You also got into a bad state of mind in some respects – too much selfwill, self-pleasing, and showed often unkindness to Henry and improper ways of speaking to me and to the servants. Now all these things displease God and grieve the Spirit and when one who is at all in God's favour does anything that grieves the Spirit, He withdraws *for a time* and the person becomes very miserable. Your being unhappy is therefore *so far* a good sign, but do not *rest* in that state – for it is not a good sign when any one remains long in it. Endeavour by repentance and sorrow of heart for past Sin and earnest prayer to regain the favour of God and to move His pity towards you thro' Christ. . . . You will find many beautiful and comforting promises in Isaiah – read aloud with *prayer* the 14 chapters of Hosea – the 103 and 130 Psalms. In the prayer book in the Service for Ash Wednesday called the Commination Service are some beautiful passages: it comes soon after 'Burial of the Dead'. There is the 51st Psalm in it and the lesson before is beautiful and all the prayers after it are beautiful and suited to the frame of mind you mention.[25]

A fragment of a school report, undated, finds like faults to deplore, and is more to the point:

> You will be glad to hear that he has passed the half-yearly examinations in a highly creditable manner, and his proficiency in Classics, Mathematics and collateral subjects is, I think, very satisfactory, considering his years, and shews that he has been very diligent and attentive. . . .
>
> I wish I could say everything that you would wish to hear on points of character and disposition. I must however in faithfulness observe that his *temper* needs much subjugation and softening. I have too often had to remark an overbearing and wayward disposition among his companions – and occasionally, a considerable want of meekness and modesty towards his elders. I *fear* that his mind is less under the influence of religious feeling and principle than it was when he was younger. . . .[26]

This must have been hard for William to bear. If he rejoiced in the academic distinctions won by his sons, these were nothing compared to the attainment of high religious principles. And of all his sons, he expected the most from Samuel, with whom he developed the closest intimacy and on whom he lavished his greatest gifts.

45

IV. *Joyousness and Seriousness*

Of course William loved all his children; but for Lizzy, his second daughter who died aged 31 in 1832, and for Samuel, his third son, his letters seem to show a special tenderness, as if he saw in them some peculiar grace which God had been pleased to bestow on them to fulfil some appointed task. Louisa Noel, the dearest friend of Samuel's wife Emily, described the scene at Brighstone when William and Barbara, in their old age, came to live there – one of those unconscious vignettes, so precious to the historian, which with a stroke of the pen suddenly bring the characters to life: 'The dear Father is walking about the room with Croker's Boswell's *Life of Johnson* in his hand, hunting for some passage. Samuel is sitting on the *other* sofa with Lord E. Fitzgerald in his hand laughing at something the dear Mother has said about the cholera which he says is a "striking remark". The Mother is laughing too at being laughed at. The dear Father every minute coming in with "My poor B." and "dear old heart". How he loves Samuel!' [1]

It was a love perfectly reciprocated. Of all the calumnies which Samuel Wilberforce was to have to endure in his lifetime (and by which his posterity has sometimes misrepresented him), none was more unjust than the imputation that he showed disrespect for his father's memory by making a mockery of the lessons which he had learned from him as a child. To generations not unacquainted with the image of the diffident father and the surly son, the relationship revealed by the letters which passed between William and Samuel Wilberforce may seem quaint or even repulsive. The point, however, must be forcefully made that in the heyday of the Evangelical revival, the relationship between father and son was viewed very differently. The six hundred or so letters which William wrote to Samuel may be preserved to-day rather as oddities, but there can be no doubt that Samuel treasured them as the most precious relics of one whose teaching he cherished more intensely than that of any other man.

In 1823, when Robert was twenty and Samuel only seventeen, both boys began to compile notebooks about their father's sayings and doings. It is probable that by this time they had both realised that they were to be entrusted with writing the official biography which William's fame and distinction would demand. Both notebooks contain copies of letters of various dates to different correspondents, and both record biographical details, especially relating to William's early life, which appear – in part, at least – to have been dictated by their father. Robert's notebook, although bulkier than Samuel's, is less interesting: the main portion is devoted to copies of letters (some in William's own hand) which were subsequently printed either in the *Life of William Wilberforce*, published in 1838, or in the two-volume collection of *Correspondence*, published two years later. Samuel's notebook, inscribed 'Fragments of his Father's Conversation', is much more lively and revealing. This book, together with the large collection of letters written to Samuel between 1814 and 1833, provides an exceptionally vivid picture of the Evangelical influence at work in that sphere – the family circle – where its impact was most keenly felt.

By far the greatest part of the material deals with moral behaviour. The children were told, first of all, that there was a world of difference between professing Christianity and acting up to what one had professed. Time and time again the Evangelicals would stress that there were two kinds of Christian – the *nominal* Christian and the 'truly religious' or 'real' Christian, a distinction which gained currency with the publication of Joseph Milner's *Church History*,[2] which appeared in stages during the 1790's and the following decade, and with Wilberforce's own *Practical View*. While this distinction was soon recognised as stock Evangelical phraseology – and indeed its acceptance rapidly became a sort of party shibboleth – it was not regarded by all Evangelicals in the same light. Some undoubtedly interpreted it in a Calvinist sense, distinguishing between the truly elect, predestined to salvation, transformed by God's grace and equipped with the God-given attribute of *perseverantia* to attain the fullness which would be theirs, and those outside God's favour, who had no righteousness imputed to them and whose acts were therefore worthless. The majority, however – sometimes described as 'moderate Calvinists', a name which they tended to disown [3] – found this unacceptable. William Wilberforce, for instance, would have none of it. 'The Methodists, you know,' he said to Samuel on one occasion, 'do not believe in predestination and final perseverance, but they go a great deal on the feeling at the moment that you are accepted and in short become a Christian. . . . We know that religion does not consist in the assurance of our salvation; so have written all our *sound* divines – Baxter, Doddridge and all; and so infer the apostles for they do not pray for that as the most necessary thing for their converts.'[4]

On another occasion Samuel commented in his diary on a discussion which he had had with his father on the teaching of the Calvinist Romaine: 'Father reading some of Romaine in the evening exclaimed "Oh how unlike is this to the Scripture! He writes as if he had sat at the Council Board with the Almighty!" He then mentioned Mr Newton's having told him that more of Romaine's people had become Antinomians than any other he knew.'[5]

Although Wilberforce, in company with Simeon, Daniel Wilson, John Venn and others, was suspicious of claims of sudden conversion – the expectation that one could pass from being a nominal Christian or a sinner into a state of grace in one brief blinding flash – he believed that justification involved a conversion or transformation which left a very noticeable mark upon the recipient. He objected very strongly to the supposition that all baptised Christians were necessarily children of God. Regeneration may take place in baptism, but the privilege was forfeited through sin, and thereafter the sinner must look with faith unto Christ for His justifying grace. He upbraided Robert in 1828 for preaching too much in the orthodox style, assuming that his congregation consisted entirely of 'real' Christians – 'children of God etc. who needed (to use our Saviour's figure in John xiii) only to have their feet washed'.

He continued:

> Whatever may be the right doctrinal opinion as to baptismal regeneration, all really orthodox men will grant, I presume, that as people grow up they may lose that privilege of being children of God which we trust they who were baptised in their infancy did enjoy, and would have reaped the benefit of it had they died before, by the gradual development of their mental powers, they became moral agents capable of responsibility. And if so, should not their particular sins of disposition, temper, or conduct be used rather to convince them of their being in a sinful state, and as therefore requiring the converting grace of God, than as merely wanting a little reformation?[6]

Men are indeed 'moral agents capable of responsibility'; sin can be washed away only by true repentance.

> Even the most decided Predestinarians I have ever known have acknowledged that the invitations of God were made to all without exception, and that it was man's own fault that they did not accept these invitations. Again, does it not appear undeniably from one end of Scripture to the other that men's perishing, where they do perish, is always represented as their own bringing on?[7]

While good works could never be held to a man's account – he must put his trust wholly in Christ – they may yet be taken as evidence of the justified state. One must therefore look for the signs. The first thing to look for would be – and here Wilberforce resorted to stock Evangelical language – 'the great change'. When Samuel was nine years old, William wrote to him:

> You must take great pains to prove to me that you are nine not in years only, but in head and heart and mind. Above all, my dearest Samuel, I am anxious to see decisive marks of your having begun to undergo the *great change*. I come again and again to look to see if it really be begun, just as a gardener walks up again and again to examine his fruit trees and see if his peaches are set; if they are swelling and becoming larger, finally if they are becoming ripe and rosy. I would willingly walk barefoot from this place to Sandgate to see a clear proof of the *great change* being begun in my dear Samuel at the end of my journey.[8]

How did one recognise 'the great change'? Outward piety, religious earnestness, most especially 'becoming serious', were the hallmarks of a converted man. This seriousness is a difficult quality to define. It certainly did not entail either gravity of manner or the cultivation of ostentatious austerities. One of the qualities of seriousness, for instance, was the evident possession of the spirit of Christian joyousness. William Wilberforce once told Samuel that he should address a preacher of the 'high and dry' school thus:

> It is a very curious thing, sir, and I should like to know how you would explain it, that we always find in the Bible the reception of the Gospel seemed to produce joy. Thus the apostles continually impress it 'rejoice evermore', 'rejoice in the Lord always and again I say rejoice', 'righteousness and peace and joy in the Holy Ghost'. Then again in example we find joy always one of the features of the gospel. 'There was great joy in that city', when Philip preached the gospel to the Ethiopean eunuch he went on his way *rejoicing*: again the disciples eat their meat in *gladness* and singleness of heart. Now it is singular to think that if the gospel is, as it certainly is, a code of strict morality, and men are thus obliged to perform its dictates that its reception should have produced *joy*![9]

Austerities, if they were good for the soul, had rather be practised in private. Few people knew that it was sometimes William's habit to insert a little pebble in his shoe to serve as a constant reminder that his mind should be set on heavenly things.[10] Fanaticism was quite proper if directed away from oneself towards evangelisation or the rousing of the public conscience. 'If to be feelingly alive to all the sufferings of my fellow-creatures', William once said in a speech to the House of Commons, 'and to be warmed with the desire of relieving their distresses, is to be a fanatic, I am one of the most incurable fanatics ever permitted to be at large.'[11]

To be serious, then, did not mean to renounce the world, but rather to

49

conquer it. One must be *in* the world, but not *of* it. Thus, while he wished that his sons might take orders, William strongly disapproved of the notion that 'religious' people should feel their conversion to be a clear vocation to the ministry. 'He thought it a great pity,' Samuel wrote, 'that officers in the army and navy should upon becoming religious quit that line of life in which they had been engaged and enter into the Church. He said it was quite contrary to St Paul's injunctions who commanded Christians to glorify God in the stations in which they were placed by providence'.[12]

Yet, with all their distaste for ostentatious unworldliness, the Evangelicals believed firmly that appearances counted a great deal. To hide the light of one's seriousness under a bushel was unscriptural. Sometimes we get the impression from William's letters that he was enjoining his children not only to be prayerful but also to be *seen* to be prayerful. 'Henry and Robert have a sad habit', he wrote to Samuel in 1823, 'of appearing, if not of being, inattentive at church. The former I have known turn half or even quite round and stare (I use the word designedly) into the opposite pew. . . . I trust I need not endeavour to enforce on you that it is a practice to be watched against with the utmost care. It is not only a crime in ourselves, but it is a great stumbling-block of offence to others.'[13]

Earnestness in prayer (and sometimes the length of one's prayers) were taken as a sure test of seriousness. William once told Samuel about his doubts as to the genuine seriousness of an accomplished Evangelical preacher, Martin Madan, whom he had heard very often in his youth.

> He then seemed a most exemplary Christian, but . . . in his later years there was a lamentable declension. He [William] . . . had asked the old Mr Venn, whether he had observed anything at the time when Mr Madan appeared most religious, which might lead him to think all was not well at the bottom. He replied 'Yes'. That when he had travelled with him through Yorkshire in the little inns where they stopped for the night, the partitions were often so slight between the rooms that they heard in one whatever was done in the other. That on these occasions, he observed that Mr Madan gave a very short time to prayer, and that he had expressed to him his surprise that he was able with such short spiritual exercises to keep up anything of the life of religion in his soul.[14]

There were, of course, many other ways of using one's seriousness to impress others. While one should mix freely in society, one should always be ready to seize upon any opportunity offered to engage in 'serious' conversation. Similarly in writing letters, one should always try to introduce the expression of some religious sentiment for the edification of the reader.[15] A mark of special affection – indeed a recognition of the

Barbara and William Wilberforce
from a pair of pastels by John Russell

Henry Manning, *c.* 1840, by George Richmond

Samuel Wilberforce, aged twenty-nine,
by George Richmond

'seriousness' of one's correspondent – was the readiness to reprove or censure any defect which one might have observed in the other's conduct of religious duties. Zachary Macaulay, G. W. E. Russell tells us, would carry this out to disconcerting lengths.[16] William constantly impressed the point upon his children.[17] Barbara, as we know, needed little encouragement.

Again, one must always be ready to recognise and to demonstrate to others the glory of God's work in nature, to espy the miraculous in the commonplace, to sing little praises in the most natural way:

> How wonderful an ordination of providence is it [said William to his children at the sea-side], that the sand should be placed as the boundary to the roaring sea. 'Who placed the *sand* for a bound to the sea by a perpetual decree etc.' Here we see the power of omnipotence: had counsel been asked of man, he would have said: 'place the granite rock, the adamant bar to restrain the swelling ocean.' But no, God places the *sand*, that which would seem the weakest of barriers, that which is proverbial for instability, as the bound to the sea which it cannot pass over.[18]

To glorify God's creation daily was a fundamental duty. Conversely, anything that distracted the mind from heavenly thoughts, save in the discharge of one's normal occupation, or when it was politic to conform to the habits of society, was regrettable and to be avoided. To turn for pleasure to the theatre or to dancing and profane singing was irreverent and – because of its own seductive charms – positively injurious. This attitude is admirably illustrated in a letter written in 1823 to Lady Catharine Grahame who had asked William's advice on the propriety of her daughter singing at private parties:

> Mr Wilberforce desires me to state [wrote his amanuensis] that he sees nothing *criminal* in singing songs the words of which contain no sentiments improper for a Christian to utter. It must undoubtedly be our wish that they whom we most dearly love, should always have it in their view to please their God and Saviour, but this does not require us to be always speaking the sentiments or language of religion. Nature requires relaxation, and also we should conform where we can do it innocently to the manners and habits of mankind at large, that we may produce in them a favourable impression of our principles and motives, and if these considerations would justify our adopting any particular mode of recreation the desire to comply with a father's wish must be a still more powerful incitement. But I need not say to you, my dear Lady C, that it is to be wished that the religious end in view – the desire to please God and to benefit our friends – should as it were hallow and sanctify recreations which in worldly people may proceed merely from a love of applause or from thoughtless good

51

humour. I confess I think the songs to be sung should be selected with some caution. . . .[19]

A 'real' Christian was 'serious'; a nominal Christian was not. One had constantly to be on the watch to preserve this seriousness by choosing serious friends and by shunning the society of the worldly save in so far as was necessary to foster their best interests. Seriousness required strict self-discipline. It was the little acts of self-denial and moral courage which really counted. Take swearing, or giving way to peevish expressions, for instance:

> Nothing could be more contrary to the very spirit of Christianity [William would say]; these were almost the only opportunities we had of taking up our Cross daily and following Christ. . . . Many persons spoke of going to the stake or to the block for Christianity while they knew they could not be called upon to do it, and . . . yet these very people could not govern their temper in the little transactions of life. . . . These people were guilty of the grossest self-deception.[20]

In the same vein he wrote to Lizzy:

> One of the main differences as I must before have said to you between real Christians and nominal, consists in the cases in which they respectively apply religious principles. Even nominal Christians apply them on great occasions; real Xtians apply them on small, that is on all, and thus a habit is formed.[21]

This was the kernel of William's Evangelicalism. One might not therefore expect from him an undue regard for the exclusiveness of the Church and of ecclesiastical authority. The Church consisted of real Christians and nominal Christians. Real Christians were to be found as much without as within the Establishment. He told Samuel on one occasion that 'the differences between Churchmen and dissenters . . . were in his eyes of very small consequence. They were but the scaffolding, . . . when the building was complete no one would ask what sort of scaffolding it had been . . . He nowhere found in Scripture that it would be asked at the last day "Were you Churchman or dissenter?" but "What were your works?" '[22]

There is no doubt that on this issue his children found his teaching very puzzling. He would insist on respect for the authority of the Church, defend episcopacy, deprecate any violation of the Church's liturgy and formularies and try to ensure that those of his sons who showed an inclination to take holy orders should be protected from any influence which might cause them to indulge in irregularities. Yet in his heart William knew that seriousness was the vital attribute; Church membership was,

by comparison, a 'thing indifferent'. As Dr Best has so felicitously expressed it – the more respectable Evangelicals felt the value of the Established Church 'in much the same way that St Paul had felt the value of the
rule of Roman law. It helped no one to heaven, but it hedged the brink of
hell'.[23] William's defence of episcopacy was of this order. Dr Walsh has
observed that the Evangelicals had no charismatic conception of the
episcopal office. It was a useful form of government, but by no means
indispensable to the existence of the Church.[24] William Wilberforce defended bishops not because they were the successors of the apostles, but
because they represented an exalted rank in the Church, thus allowing
eminent men a proper status within the ministry and enabling them to
speak with an authority which might win respect from other eminent men.

Speaking of 'the Scotch nobility', William is reported by Samuel to have
said: 'They were in general far behind ours in morality and religion and
he traced it chiefly to their having no regular church establishment. For
that as they had no bishops or other dignitaries of the church whom they
might consider as of equal rank with themselves, they looked down upon
the clergy as on an inferior class of persons.'[25]

This raises, however, another interesting feature of William's parental
teaching which, when one encounters it divorced from the context of his
other teaching and from the person of the instructor, gives the impression
of a somewhat worldly concern for social rank and honour, curiously
unbecoming in a man who was so widely acknowledged as a saint. In his
letters to his children, and especially to Samuel, there is one recurrent
theme: the children must acquire useful friends; they must cultivate the
society of worthy men. 'Useful' and 'worthy' are both words which can
have a spiritual connotation, and doubtless William often used them in this
sense; at the same time he could not have been unaware of the advantage
which would accrue to his children if these worthy men were also members
of the best society and in a position to offer material assistance when the
occasion required.

> My dear Samuel [he wrote on 26 October 1822], . . . I assure you one of my
> chief motives now for paying visits is to cultivate the friendship of worthy
> People who I trust will be kind to my dear children when I am no more. I
> hope you and the rest will never act so as to be unworthy of the Connec-
> tions I have formed which I must say are the very *Élite* of the kingdom,
> if I may use the expression.[26]

In his next letter, he went further:

> How thankful ought we to be, to be enabled thus to select for our Associates

53

the *best* families in so many different counties, best I trust in the true sense of the word. Some of them indeed Men of rank and fortune. But still more, men of real worth. Persons too who I am sure will always receive you with kindness for my sake. I often look up with gratitude to the Giver of all good, for the favour with Men, which it would be affectation not to confess, where it is not improper to mention such things, that He has graciously given me, chiefly in the view of its ensuring for my children the friendly regard and personal kindnesses of many good people after I shall be laid low in the Grave.

I could have made them acquainted with great people, but I have always avoided it from a conviction that such connections would tend neither to their temporal comfort in the long run, nor to the advancement of the Eternal Interests. But it is most gratifying to me to reflect that they will be known to some of the very best people in the kingdom and to good people of other countries also.

. . . How rich will our portion appear when compared with that of so many of our fellow creatures. It used, when I was a bachelor especially and when I often spent my Sundays alone, to be my frequent Sunday habit to number up my blessings, and I assure you it is a most useful practice, e.g. that I have been born in Great Britain, in such a Century, such a part of it, such a Rank in life, such a Class and Character of Parents, then my personal privileges. But I have no time to-day for the long Enumeration . . .[27]

A letter written to Samuel just before he went up to Oxford is more generally known. It is worth some study because it contains not only the fullest expression of William's hopes for his children but also the key to an understanding of his own life's work. He had just effected the introduction of 'an excellent man' (a Mr Wilson of Castletown) to the Archbishop of Dublin and had stated that the making of such introductions was 'in conformity to a principle I hold to be of first-rate importance'. He continued:

It is a principle on which for many years I have acted. It is that of bringing together all Men who are like-minded, and who may probably at some time or other combine and concert for the public good. Never omit any opportunity, my dear Samuel, of getting acquainted with any good man or any useful man (of course I mean that this usefulness, in any one line, should not be countervailed by any qualities of an opposite Nature, from which defilement might be contracted). More perhaps depends on the selection of acquaintances than on any other Circumstance in life, except I mean of course still more close and intimate Unions. Acquaintances, indeed, are the raw Materials, from which are manufactured friends, wives, husbands etc. I wish it may please God to give you an Opportunity of having some good ones to chuse out of, on your first settling at Oxford.

But at least beware and form no acquaintance with loose or vicious men. ... O my dearest Boy, *Aim high*. Don't be satisfied with being hopeful, still less with being merely 'not vicious'. Strive to be a Christian, in the highest sense of that term. How little do you know to what Services Providence may call you. If when I was at your age, anyone had pointed to me and said, that youth will in a few years (not above seven or eight) be Member for the first county in England, it would have been deemed the speech of a madman! But I can truly say I had as much rather see you a Daniel Wilson, or a Buchanan, as Eternity is beyond any given portion of time in the estimate of a reasonable being.

There is one particular in your composition which you must watch closely, lest it greatly injure your advance in the Christian life. I mean the dread of ridicule, and, as incurring it, the fear of singularity. Singularity for its own sake, I grant is worse than folly; so thought St Paul also. But we shall find it next to impossible to face it when it is our duty to do so, unless we diligently cultivate the habit of judgment and feeling, by which alone we shall be able ... to withstand it when Duty requires.[28]

Only the most superficial reading can make of this letter an exhortation to procure the means of social advancement. William was only too well aware of the advantages of rank; the greatest advantage of all being the undeniable truth that the higher you rise the greater the opportunity you enjoy of doing far-reaching and lasting good. Even so, rank was not everything. It was better to be singular than sociable, to eschew all temporal ambitions in favour of spiritual objectives. No doubt he was sometimes perfectionist in the demands which he made of his sons, and he certainly took a not unnatural pride in their achievements, but both his expectations and his delight in their fulfilment were chiefly excited by the prospect of the spiritual work to which his sons were thereby committed and by the blessings which would accrue to them in their faithful discharge of their responsibilities.

Indeed, the recent suggestion that William Wilberforce was a snob, who 'never believed that true religion is incompatible with the characteristic good qualities of the upper classes or felt at home with the assured vessels, the rough old Calvinists' with their 'rigid, hard and mannerless pedantry',[29] is one of those dangerous half-truths, which conceal a fundamental misunderstanding both of the personality concerned and of the age in which he lived, by presenting with undue prominence a single facet of a character whose true motives and feelings are unintelligible if not viewed as a whole. In an intensely class-conscious age, William was mindful of his rank in society. He did, indeed, abhor the radicalism and subversive tendencies of some of the Methodist or dissenting preaching. He was wholly out of sympathy with the resuscitation of dissenter-like qualities among the Evangelicals in the 1820's, mainly because his own life's work had been to prove to those of his own class that enthusiasm was not necessarily synonymous with licence or defiance of traditional authority, and that Evangelicalism was not purely – as it seemed to be in the hands of the Wesleys – a gospel for the poor, but rather contained the means of salvation for all classes, and, if it could be made to permeate the Establishment, for the nation as a whole. This did not lead Wilberforce either to despise the uncouth or to flatter gentility. If he believed that the existing social system was God-given and that poor people were intended to be poor, his feeling of compassion for the under-dog was no less warm and sincere for all that. He felt nothing but shame for those who looked 'down with a species of contempt on those of lower birth than themselves. He said it was quite contrary to the precepts of scripture to, "condescend to men of low estate". The Greek, he said, was particularly strong, being literally "be borne about with".' [30]

His sons may have felt differently. They did not share their father's affection for dissenters, for 'honest Butterworth' and the bucolic Dr Coke. [31] This was a quaintness and indulgence which they found difficult to understand. They were also far more conscious than their father of the vulgarity and brash enthusiasm which seemed to them to typify the low-class 'religious' men at Oxford. This sentiment, however, they did not learn at home. When they went up to Oxford in the 1820's they breathed a different air; and for the first time in their lives they encountered bewildering influences and alien traditions. This was to mark a new epoch in their lives.

Chapter 2

THE BASTION OF ORTHODOXY

1. *Choosing a University*

Why did William Wilberforce choose to send three of his sons to Oxford? On all counts Cambridge seemed the obvious choice. He himself had been educated there – at St John's; all his closest friends in the university world were Cambridge men. Besides that, Cambridge in the early nineteenth century was the recognised breeding-ground of Evangelicals, the university of Simeon, the Milners and the Venns. Oxford, by contrast, had little to attract an Evangelical. If it had been the university of the two Wesleys and George Whitefield, it subsequently had shown nothing but contempt towards their spiritual children. The gospel torch still burnt faintly at St Edmund Hall, the college of Isaac Crouch and Daniel Wilson where the small nucleus of Oxford Evangelicals was gathered, but William appears to have ignored its claims. Not less surprising than his choice of university was his choice of college. He sent his sons to Oriel, the chief representative of the rival tradition, dedicated to the cause of Church and King. It was as if a Whig had preferred the Carlton Club to the Reform.

His own memories of Cambridge may well have influenced his judgment. Looking back on the folly of his youth, he told Samuel that the dons and his undergraduate companions at St John's had done him nothing but harm. They had gone out of their way 'to make me idle and dissipated', flattering him on his ability to do well without effort, reminding him that with his wealth he had no need to 'fag', all of which was 'poison to a mind constituted as mine was'.[1] He wrote to a friend in 1822: 'You cannot but remember, what I can never review but with humiliation and shame, the course I ran at College', lamenting that he had never found one true, pious friend who had been bold enough to arrest his degradation into indolence, dissipation and gambling by reminding him of 'the fate of the unprofitable servant'.[2] Subsequent visits to Cambridge – to Isaac Milner or to talk with Simeon – did not cause him to change his opinion of the low nature of Cambridge society. In 1788, while staying with the Milners, he was introduced to a young man from Trinity Hall, whom he described in his diary as 'a forward, vulgar and ignorant youth', and his general impression of the undergraduates of St John's was that they lacked 'the refined feelings and elevated principles which become a studious and sequestered life'.[3] In the following year, after dining at St John's, he wrote in his diary, 'How vain and foolish is the general run of conversation here! – more so than in London.'[4]

The poor spirit of Cambridge was confirmed by the disastrous career of his eldest son, William. From incidental references, chiefly in Wilberforce's diary, we may trace the main outlines of this unhappy episode. In July 1817 Wilberforce secured entrance for William at Trinity College, Cambridge, and he appears to have gone into residence at the end of that year.[5] Very soon he acquired expensive tastes. In January 1819, the diary records 'Wm. buying another horse for 60 guineas and not behaving well about it tho' I most honourably to him. . . . Alas poor Wm. sad work – I must draw in my expenditure some way or another.'[6] Shortly afterwards William's affairs took on a more serious aspect. On 15 March his father recorded in his diary, 'A letter from H. Venn to-day strongly of opinion poor William should be taken from College. I fear rightly, on the ground that he won't read and therefore will be licentious and corrupted in mind as well as practice.'[7] Apparently Wilberforce intervened to take strong action, for in an undated letter to Lady Sparrow he described the effects of his rebuke. 'He took it all with good-humoured submission. I took away his horse. I stopped his allowance and yet he owned he could not say I had used him harshly, or that he could have expected anything different. . . . He is now reading and going on well in all respects.'[8]

The diary entry for 28 March 1819 is rather more explicit:

> But the *grand* grief and shame is this sad business of poor Wm. His crime this last time has every aggravation. At the very moment of Blundell's body lying in his Rooms and his funeral to be the next day. To have been led into conviviality on a Sunday eve, to have been so drunk as to be beastly in a piously disposed friend's room and to have refused the hint of 2 friends, . . . and Venn to spend the Sunday evening with him, alleging he wished to be alone; God grant this may have been at the time answered sincerely. Alas, alas! Yet I cannot abandon my trust in the promises of God.[9]

Whatever young William may have done – and the passage suggests a fair catalogue of offences, including debauchery, drunkenness, hypocrisy and untruthfulness – it was adjudged sufficiently heinous to warrant his removal from Cambridge. Wilberforce wrote the 'decisive' letter on 31 March.[10] Later in the same year every effort was made to get William safely married and established in some profession where he would be carefully supervised. It was considered advisable to set him to study law in the City, where Wilberforce's friend John Owen, secretary of the Bible Society, could keep an eye on him:[11] and on 19 January 1820 William married Owen's daughter, Mary. Shortly afterwards he persuaded his father to let him embark upon the business enterprise which was to drain the Wilberforce fortune nearly dry in the course of the next ten years. As a classic demonstration of the rake's progress, this story might have been taken from the pages of a Victorian melodrama.

As an explanation of Wilberforce's motives for sending his three younger sons to Oxford, however, it will not suffice. It does not explain why he chose Oriel in preference to St Edmund Hall; nor does it take into account the significant fact that before his eldest son was matriculated at Trinity, he had previously been entered, as it happened without avail, for a vacancy at Oriel. As early as March 1817 Wilberforce's diary recorded that the 'present plan is to wait in hope of William's getting into Oriel by some unexpected vacancy',[12] and to Lady Sparrow in July of the same year he had written: 'after long hesitation in the hope of getting William into Oriel, he is at last admitted of Trinity, Cant.'.[13]

It is perhaps significant that Wilberforce had chosen in 1816 an Oxford man to serve as private tutor to his eldest son. This was a Mr Matthew Rolleston, described in the diary as 'a Tutor of one of the first colleges in Oxford, a man of genius, polite literature, much admired . . . a manly simple character, apparently of solid piety'.[14] It would be natural enough for Wilberforce to consult this tutor, for whom he had such a high regard, on the question of university education. Rolleston, however, was not an Oriel man. He was a fellow of University College, having graduated in 1808 and been chosen as Select Preacher to the University in 1815.[15] What advice Rolleston may have given can only be conjecture, but it is at least possible that his allegiance to his own college did not blind him to the fact that Oriel's rising academic reputation was rapidly enhancing its claim to be the first college in the University. More satisfactory evidence may be found in R. G. Livingstone's reminiscences of Edward Hawkins, printed in Dean Burgon's *Lives of Twelve Good Men*. In 1815 Wilberforce and Hawkins chanced to meet on the stage-coach travelling between London and Oxford. William was on his way to Nuneham Courtenay to visit E. G. Marsh with a view to sending Robert to study at his school. Hawkins, subsequently Provost of Oriel, was then Tutor at the college. They had a long and friendly conversation, concluding with the mutual resolution to call on each other whenever opportunity permitted. 'This was the Provost's first introduction', wrote Livingstone. 'He called on his new acquaintance in London, and from that time till his death, enjoyed a considerable degree of intimacy with him. . . . I suspect that it was the conversation between London and Nuneham, and the friendly intercourse which ensued, which eventually determined his, Wilberforce's, choice of a college at Oxford for three of his sons.' [16] Actually Livingstone exaggerated the degree of intimacy between the two men. In 1828, when Hawkins was elected to the Provostship, William wrote to congratulate him, recalling their earlier acquaintance, while regretting that it had never been allowed to ripen into a friendship. [17] Hawkins came to stay with the Wilberforces later in that year, a prospect to which William looked forward with much pleasure. 'Your society', he wrote, 'is a gratification we can enjoy so seldom that you ought not to stint us to a mere scrap of it.' [18] It is clear, however, that William thought sufficiently highly of Hawkins to entrust his sons to his care.

Other factors have to be taken into account. William was not only profoundly uneasy at the manifest profligacy of certain undergraduate circles at Cambridge; he was also perturbed at the tendency to indiscipline and irregularity which he discerned in Cambridge Evangelicalism. There might be more true religion at Cambridge – indeed, he admitted as much to Samuel in 1823. [19] On the other hand, there was the danger that enthusiasm might run to seed; and at Oxford, where signs of a nascent pietism could be detected, the traditional decorum and respect for authority might prove a salutary antidote to the excessive individualism which pietism tends to breed. This, at least, is what Hannah More felt in 1818 when she wrote anxiously to Marianne Thornton about the trials and temptations which awaited young Henry Thornton who was just embarking on his Cambridge career.

> I pray God [she wrote] to preserve dear Henry from the contagious atmosphere of Cambridge. . . . Much will be expected from him, his example must give the tone to the young men who have not had the advantage of such parents. . . . I am much changed with respect to the two universities. I used greatly to prefer Cambridge, but this Summer I have had so much intercourse with men of talents and piety from Oxford that I believe not only that the general discipline there is much stricter but in two or three colleges religion is in more esteem. It behoves such youths as Henry Thornton and Tom Macaulay to raise the depressed standard of religion and morals by their exalted principles and exemplary conduct. [20]

For the same reason, William wrote to a friend in 1821: 'If you have sons who are likely to distinguish themselves, and wish them to go into the Church, I would advise you to send them to Oxford',[21] thinking especially of the distinctive Oxford qualities which he once defined for Samuel's benefit as 'more respect to appearances, more decorum amongst the irreligious part'.[22]

After all, William had no reason to suppose that the religious influences of home and of school would be erased or even diluted by contact with the ecclesiastical atmosphere of Oxford. He was, it seems, perceptive enough to appreciate that if his children were to make the impact upon the Anglican Church which he felt was in their power, they must at some stage be released from the sheltered Evangelical environment in which all their boyhood had been spent, thus to acquire that veneration for the Establishment which was the traditional gift of Oxford to her sons. The function of a university was to complete a man's formal education. This meant, at least in part, the correcting of excesses in one direction by a better acquaintance with the corresponding excesses in the opposite direction. To make precisely this point, William wrote to his friend William Gray in December 1830:

> It is curious to observe the effects of the Oxford system in producing on the minds of young men a strong propensity to what may be termed Tory principles. From myself and the general tenour of our family and social circle, it might have been supposed that my children, though averse to party, would be inclined to adopt Liberal or, so far as would be consistent with party, Whig principles, but all my three Oxonians are strong friends to High Church and King doctrines. The effects I myself have witnessed would certainly induce me, had I to decide on the University to which any young protégé of mine should go, were he by natural temper or any other causes too prone to excess on the Tory side, I should decidedly send him to Cambridge, Trinity; were the opposite the case he should be fixed at Oriel, Oxford.[23]

All reservations apart, this is an astonishing letter. Many of William's contemporaries would have been startled to hear him suggest that if he had any political affiliations, his sympathies tended towards the Whigs. And his Evangelical friends might have felt abashed at his manifest unconcern over his sons' affections for the tenets of the school of 'Church and King'. The truth is that William's good nature and amused indifference to party, whether political or ecclesiastical, had always protected him from intransigence and – in his later years – enabled him to understand that a younger generation often wishes to clothe old truths in garments which it rashly supposes to be new. He did not worry for his sons on that account.

When he trembled, he trembled for their morals, knowing only too well the fearful temptations to dissoluteness and immorality to which they must necessarily be exposed.

He lived long enough to see the furies and fantasies which heralded the century's fourth decade. What he could not have foreseen was the breaking of old alliances, the militant anti-Protestantism which controversy was to bring to the surface, the revolution which was to cause all religious parties to shift their ground. He could never have supposed that those who brought these things about would be the friends and associates of his own sons, and that they in their turn would become inextricably involved in the battles which were to come. 'Above all their literary acquirements', he wrote thankfully in January 1831, 'I value their having . . . passed through the fiery trial of an university . . . without injury.'[24] That chapter, he fondly imagined, was closed. Mercifully, he was never to know otherwise.

II. *The Oxford Renaissance*

The first of the Wilberforces to go to Oxford was Robert, who matriculated at Oriel in February 1820. He was joined there by Samuel in 1823 and by Henry in 1826, in which year Robert was elected a Fellow of the College. Their Oxford careers, therefore, spanned the whole of the third decade of the century. Samuel was the first to leave (in 1827); Robert remained until the autumn of 1831; and Henry, who stayed at Oxford for several years after taking his degree, saw the first numbers of the *Tracts for the Times* launched before he decided to follow his brothers into holy orders and to seek a curacy.

The many surviving memoirs of this period of Oxford history agree on one important point: they all represent this decade, or more precisely the period from about 1825 to 1835, as Oxford's golden age. It was certainly a time of peculiar buoyancy and zest. It was not the first time in history that a period of intellectual and cultural florescence has heralded a great religious movement, that Renaissance has preceded Reformation. The Tractarians themselves were wont to see their work as a second Reformation, a re-breaking of the limbs so badly set three hundred years before,[1] and it is hardly fanciful to describe the previous decade as a renaissance, fostering a spirit and devising techniques which, when translated to the religious sphere, were to have cataclysmic effects.

It might indeed be argued that Oxford could never have been the effective centre of such a religious movement, nor could its leaders have wielded the influence which they did, had not the University previously experienced an intellectual revival and imbued its sons with a veneration for ancient learning ('in antiquis est scientia' was, after all, as much the maxim of the Tractarians with their deep regard for patristic sources as it had been of the earlier humanists and reformers) and trained the ablest of them in the art of logic, that discipline in which the Oriel Fellows of the 1820's particularly excelled.[2] *Humani nil alienum*, the Abbé Bremond tells us, was the 'fundamental doctrine of humanism'.[3] Amid the doubts and fears of the twenties and thirties the same note of jubilant individualism asserts itself. On his return from Sicily, Newman's spirits were quickened by the realisation of the boundless potentiality of individual effort. *Humani nil alienum:* 'Deliverance is wrought, not by the many, but by the few, not by bodies but by persons.'[4] In just such a mood of buoyant self-confidence did he and his friends echo the words of Achilles returning to the fray: 'You shall know the difference, now that I am back again.'[5]

A recent biographer of Dean Church has observed the same phenomenon. 'It almost seems', he writes, 'that there was something electrical in the academic atmosphere during those twenty years which ended so dramatically with the cloudburst of 1845.'[6] When we try to be more precise, we find ourselves – perhaps unconsciously – recalling images from the period of the *quattrocento*. We notice the cult of personality – the intense hero-worship, the passionate friendships and fierce enmities, the sense of the worth-whileness of everything one sees and does, the amassing of personal relics and memoranda with one eye on self-improvement and the other on the verdict of posterity; the sense of living in an age of Titans, the glorification of scholastic achievements, honoured the more if accompanied by other graces. Was there ever a finer description of *l'uomo universale* than Francis Doyle's moving encomium on young Henry Denison, 'a sort of Admirable Crichton among his contemporaries',[7] or William Tuckwell's rhapsodic eulogy on Charles Wordsworth – tutor to the finest brains in Oxford, 'the best scholar, cricketer, oar, skater, racquets-player, dancer, pugilist, of his day'?[8]

Then we have that matchless description of Oxford in the 1830's drawn by the masterly hand of R. W. Church, who had lived both in Italy and Oxford and whose heart was torn between these two great loves – the Oxford of his youth and the Italy of his fertile historical imagination, an Oxford which was never the same once Newman had departed, an Italy linked forever in his mind to the glorious name of Dante.[9] To him the affinities between the two societies, Tractarian Oxford and late medieval Florence, were plain. Both were small, proud and jealous communities; both could boast of a quaint and ill-working polity; both were liable to sudden fits of *stasis*, in which all the pent-up forces of frustration, irritation and factious animosity, the more intense for being parochial, would be released in passionate conflict. And Church had lived through such a conflict – bitter contests which, as he himself put it, 'for a time turned Oxford into a kind of image of what Florence was in the days of Savonarola, with its nicknames, Puseyites and Neomaniacs, and High and Dry, counterparts to the Piagnoni and Arrabbiati, of the older strife'.[10]

Of course Oxford had had her conflicts in the past, and had traditionally engendered a fierce loyalty among her sons. Nevertheless the men who came up to Oxford in the 1820's and 1830's, while temperamentally disposed – like all men – to romanticise the springtime of their lives, seem both to have given more, by their energies and attainments, to the corporate life and ethos of the University and to have taken away a larger share of her nostalgic spoils.

In those days Oxford had never seemed prettier, William Tuckwell tells us, looking back from the end of the century:

> The approach ... by the Henley Road was the most beautiful in the world. Soon after passing Littlemore you came in sight of, and did not lose again, the sweet city with its dreaming spires, driven along a road now crowded and obscured with dwellings, open then to cornfields on the right, to uninclosed meadows on the left, with an unbroken view of the long line of towers, rising out of foliage less high and veiling than after sixty more years of growth to-day. At once, without suburban interval, you entered the finest quarter of the town, rolling under Magdalen Tower, and past the Magdalen elms, then in full unmutilated luxuriance, till the exquisite curves of the High Street opened on you, as you drew up at the Angel, or passed on to the Mitre and the Star.[11]

Oxford a few decades later was, by comparison, drab. It had little of the wit and merriment of former times,[12] when the academic eccentrics, of which there were legion, were grotesque in their eccentricity, and the brilliant men could boast of a brilliance unsurpassed.

> Never in the history of the University [writes Tuckwell as he takes us into the thirties] has a decade opened and progressed amid a group so brilliant. In 1830 we have Gladstone, Liddell, Charles Wordsworth, Hope, T. Acland, Manning, Church, Halford Vaughan, William Adams, Walter Hamilton, Lords Dalhousie, Elgin, Lincoln, Canning, to take names almost at random. Nor was this dawn of golden times confined to Oxford; at

Cambridge in the very same year gathered a not less rare group of *conjurati fratres*: Spedding, Thompson, Brookfield, Trench, Tennyson, Monckton Milnes, Charles Buller, Merivale, Arthur Hallam.[13]

Doubtless we see them now, from over a century's distance, a good deal arger than life; but contemporary chroniclers found it equally difficult to resist superlatives. In what other terms could one describe John Keble's academic career, or Gladstone's First Class in the schools ('the best that had been gained for many years')[14] or that Homeric debate in the Oxford Union when Manning and Francis Doyle on their home ground battled with Hallam, Sunderland and Monckton Milnes from Cambridge on the relative merits of Byron and Shelley[15]; or the singular achievement of J. B. Mozley, who in the Oriel Fellowship Examination, when candidates were permitted to write on the essay paper for the whole of the day till the light failed, sat motionless until dusk and then, flinging himself down on the floor to catch the light from the dying embers of the fire, wrote an essay of ten lines – the prize essay, in fact, for 'the ten lines were such as no other man in Oxford could have written'.[16]

This was an impressive generation, but an academic revolution had enabled it to be so. In the space of some twenty years the whole ethos of Oxford was transformed by a new respect for learning. It may be illustrated by the changed attitude towards the 'scholars' as opposed to the gentlemen commoners. Mark Pattison noted the difference between his own generation and that of his father: 'In 1808, it seems, the position of a scholar had been quite different from what it had become in 1833. In my father's time the "scholars" were not regarded as gentlemen. They did not associate with the commoners, but lived among themselves, or with the bible-clerks. They were nicknamed "charity boys". In twenty-five years this had quite changed. The scholar's gown, from being the badge of an inferior order, had become a coveted distinction.'[17] This change of attitude may have happened earlier than Pattison supposed. In 1818, when Newman became a scholar of Trinity, he was overcome with shyness when he first donned his scholar's gown, though inwardly he was nearly bursting with pride at the distinction.[18] When four years later he received news of his election to an Oriel Fellowship, he was too excited to be shy, dashing through the streets of Oxford, ignoring the bows of the tradesmen as he passed, while the bells of the three towers of Trinity pealed out the triumph for the whole of Oxford to hear.

Well might he run. Oriel by the 1820's was the first college in Oxford. Copleston was then Provost, and about him he had gathered a group of

Fellows remarkable not only for their own distinction but also for their ability to recognise distinction in others and to draw them into their society. Arnold, it is true, had disappeared into the country to launch a small private school; Keble had ceased to be resident after 1823 when he left Oxford for a curacy at Southrop in Gloucestershire. The most prominent of the others, however, formed a group whose natural heterogeneity is at least implicit in the label commonly accorded them – the Noetics, perhaps best rendered by the term 'free thinkers'. Contemporaries admired or feared their dialectic and penchant for logic; posterity, for lack of literary remains, looks to the aptest, while yet most rebellious, of Whately's pupils – Newman himself – for the evidence of what they had to teach: liberal principles and distrust of dogma, precepts which Newman rejected as temperamentally unsuited to him, and a training in the weapons of disputation, which he was to turn to devastating use.

The most formidable figure was Richard Whately, portly, unruly and voracious, hammering out disturbing truths on the anvils of young, impressionable minds* – a tough and tireless iconoclast in Tory Oxford, soon to be translated, as Archbishop of Dublin, to a far less congenial theatre of war. Edward Hawkins, more respectful but no less persuasive, a man of incisive speech and engaging candour, was another soon to be called to high office, though sadly soured thereby. Renn Dickson Hampden, out of Oxford in the early 1820's, was also of their number: a modernist before his time, a gentle, diffident man though courageous in adversity, the least militant of an aggressive group, whom fate had impishly selected to earn the greatest notoriety and the most bitter opprobrium. The strangest of the group was Joseph Blanco White – not a Fellow, but an honorary member of the Oriel Common Room – the renegade Roman priest from Spain, who had fled to England and taken Anglican orders, and who stayed long enough in Oxford to become a devotee of Whately and a useful informant on Roman devotions for those who had never seen a breviary and yet damned Rome as Antichrist.

The older Fellows found in Blanco White a kindred spirit, and so eager were they to learn from him that Liddon maintained that 'it is not too much to say that he is the real founder of the modern latitudinarian school in the English Church'.[19] Hampden certainly first learnt from him to distrust all theological systems, and there is some substance in the common allegation that behind Hampden's Bampton Lectures of 1832 lay the

---

* Whately commonly referred to his pupils as his 'anvils'.

66

Sir Charles Anderson

W. E. Gladstone

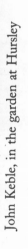

John Keble, in the garden at Hursley

fertile, enquiring mind of this sad, unusual man.[20] The younger Fellows, who joined this latitudinarian group in the 1820's, were equally fascinated though perhaps for different reasons. And it was these younger men, clearing in successive years the intimidating hurdle of the fellowship examination, who earned for Oriel a national fame and who became, incidentally, the tutors, friends and colleagues of William Wilberforce's three sons: in 1822, John Henry Newman; in 1823 Edward Bouverie Pusey and Edward Churton; in 1826 Richard Hurrell Froude and Robert Wilberforce himself. The undergraduates of these years (totalling about 76 in any one year) were a lively and distinguished set. Chief among the friends of Robert and Samuel Wilberforce were three gentlemen commoners, Sir George Prevost, Charles Anderson and Patrick Boyle; and amongst the commoners, the two Froude brothers (Hurrell and Robert), Henry Ryder (the eldest son of the Bishop of Lichfield) and Edward Denison. In the later twenties the men who were more nearly Henry Wilberforce's contemporaries were George Dudley Ryder, Frederic Rogers (later Lord Blachford), S. F. Wood (the brother of Lord Halifax) and Tom Mozley.

Oriel was acknowledged as the great college for 'reading men' in the 1820's, possessing also a reputation for gentility which its chief rival for academic honours – Balliol – was deemed to lack. But the time was fast approaching when Oriel would give way to Balliol. Mark Pattison dates the transition precisely with the three years 1830 to 1832, following the virtual dismissal by the new Provost, Hawkins, of the three Oriel tutors – Newman, Froude and Robert Wilberforce – in 1830.[21] No college could stand the loss of three such men within a single year; and, in the meantime, Balliol under the mastership of Jenkyns and, a little later, with W. G. Ward and A. C. Tait as tutors, was piling talent upon talent. Arnold sent his best pupils there – his own son, Matthew, Arthur Stanley and A. H. Clough; and in the same decade scholarships were won by Benjamin Jowett, E. M. Goulburn, Sir Stafford Northcote and Frederick Temple.[22] In the late 1820's, when Herman Merivale was tutor and Frederick Oakeley, Frank Newman and George Moberly were Fellows, the undergraduates were less notable, with the exception of Henry Edward Manning who came into residence in 1827. Christ Church, however, provided an extraordinary crop of talented undergraduates during the twenties and early thirties – E. B. Pusey, Charles Wordsworth, James Hope, Walter Hamilton, Henry Denison, W. E. Gladstone, T. D. Acland, Charles Canning, W. G. Ward and Francis Doyle.

These names are mentioned for two reasons. In the first place they give substance to the contention that Oxford during this period was peculiarly rich in talent at a time when academic prestige was rising and competition for university prizes and college fellowships became intense. Secondly, the talent, by being spread over a number of colleges, was likely to transcend the limits of college society just because these societies provided too small a sphere within which such talents might operate. In short, what we are seeing during these two decades is a new consciousness of the University as an entity in itself, which meant a gradual lessening of the parochial character of college life. Sir Geoffrey Faber has written of Oxford in the early nineteenth century that 'the colleges were everything in those days, the University almost nothing'.[23] This is true only of the turn of the century. By the 1820's the barriers were down and the University was acquiring for the first time in its history a distinct corporate ethos. This can be seen in several ways. One obvious way was the common quest of all reading men for an effective private tutor. This was how Manning and Gladstone came to meet as pupils of Charles Wordsworth of Christ Church.[24] A new vogue for vacation reading-parties brought together the better men of several colleges. In this way, Isaac Williams of Trinity discovered kindred spirits in Robert Wilberforce and Hurrell Froude when they came together to study with John Keble in the Long Vacation of 1823. Samuel Wilberforce's set – nicknamed the Bethel Union (because the members showed sufficient religious principle to eschew all party connections on Sundays) – consisted of a number of Oriel men, augmented by three or four like-minded friends from other colleges.[25] Charles Wordsworth was the centre of a prominent Christ Church group – nicknamed 'the Tribes' – but his circle of close friends included nine from other colleges, from Trinity, Magdalen, Balliol, University, Worcester, Oriel and New College.[26]

One of the reasons for this phenomenon was the beginning of athletic societies within the University which brought together men from all the colleges. It is significant that the first cricket match between Oxford and Cambridge was played at Lord's in 1827 and that the first boat race between the two universities was rowed at Henley in the following year (Charles Wordsworth, true to his reputation as the 'universal man', taking part in both contests).[27] Even more significant, however, was the rise of the Oxford Union, founded as the Attic Society in 1823. It established itself at once as the meeting-place of the reading men with high political aspirations. Manning, we are told, after his maiden speech in March 1829, became famous throughout the University overnight.[28] Samuel and Henry Wilberforce both in their turn became Presidents of the Union, an honour enjoyed within the first decade of its foundation by Manning, Gladstone, Sidney Herbert, Lord Lincoln, Roundell Palmer, W. G. Ward, Edward Cardwell and A. C. Tait.

The term 'renaissance' as applied to this exhilarating period of Oxford history is not, then, inappropriate. In the exuberance of the 1820's few could have anticipated the religious movement of which it was the herald. Some – like Mark Pattison – deplored the change which Tractarianism was to effect, describing the next decade as a 'nightmare', a suspension of 'all science, humane letters, and the first strivings of intellectual freedom which had moved in the bosom of Oriel'. He too saw the analogy with the sixteenth century – 'nascent humanism was submerged beneath the rising tide of theological passion'.[29] Samuel Wilberforce, on the other hand, visiting Oxford in 1836, was impressed by the change for the better. The one drawback of his undergraduate days had been the markedly secular tone. 'How different Oxford was in our time', he wrote to Charles Anderson. 'There was something so miserably low in old Tyler[30] – and such a want of that high tone and intellect and morality which they have now found.'[31] Gladstone felt the same. Oxford had given him little to nourish the soul.[32]

For the Church, however, and for those, like the Wilberforce brothers, who were to make the Church their career, these years were crucial. The intellectual revival in Oxford and Cambridge was bound to have a salutary effect upon the Church at a time when there were no theological colleges or seminaries and when a parson received no more spiritual and intellectual training than what the universities could provide. Spiritually this might amount to very little – compulsory attendance at college chapel, examinations on the content of sermons. On the other hand, the resuscitation of learning and the livelier competition within the universities meant a better-educated clergy and, partly because of the rising prestige of the universities as a result of their awakening from sleep, a further advance of the clergy generally in the social scale, an acceleration of a process which really has its beginnings in the eighteenth century.[33] In a sense, all the professional classes found themselves on a rising market in this period. They were acquiring organisation, recognised qualifications, professional solidarity; so that doctors, lawyers, architects and civil engineers, to mention a few, all came to occupy a higher social status than had been accorded to them in the previous century. The academic professions (virtually entirely clerical) were peculiarly favoured just because they were most closely related to the universities which then, as never before, were seen to provide something which could be obtained hardly anywhere else – the education of a gentleman.

'The nineteenth-century ideal of a resident gentleman in holy orders in every parish', writes Charles Smyth, ' . . . was, because of this element of class-consciousness, subtly different from the determination of King James I "to have a resident Moyses in everye parish".'[34] The men who came down from Oxford and Cambridge in the early years of the nineteenth century – especially those who had gained First Classes in the Schools or who had enjoyed the acclaim of their contemporaries for their triumphs in the Union – did not regard themselves as 'painful preachers'. They were rather scholars and gentlemen, endowed with a natural authority to direct their parishes (which one day would be exchanged for a diocese) rather as a headmaster runs his school. They were expected – and were usually very ready – to pronounce authoritatively on all the questions of the hour. The particular education which they had enjoyed, and the adulation of their companions which success had commanded, gave to men like Samuel Wilberforce and Henry Manning a masterful self-confidence, coupled perhaps with a perilous sense of omniscience, which explains their readiness to assume the leadership of any society in which they were placed and also their quick response to queries and doubts addressed to them by others who lacked their incisiveness and assurance. Only if we appreciate this shall we understand Samuel's prompt and pontifical judgments on *Essays and Reviews* and on the researches of Charles Darwin; or Manning's readiness to allow himself to be adjudged 'a forward piece' by English Catholics when he joined the Roman communion. 'That is what I have always been to them', he once said in his old age to his young Anglican friend J. E. C. Bodley:

> 'A forward piece'. He then began to count on his long, emaciated fingers: 'I had been captain of the Harrow eleven; I had got my first at Balliol; I was the leader in debate at the Oxford Union; I had been a Fellow of Merton, and Archdeacon of Chichester – and all they could say of me was that I was "a forward piece".'

They were not to know. They had never encountered the *genius loci* of Oxford. What was Matthew Arnold's *The Scholar-Gipsy* to them? 'Only Oxford men like you and me can understand that.' Then again to Bodley, 'Nobody here understands Oxford, none of them have quite understood me. . . . It was always so from the first.'[35]

III. *Robert Wilberforce and John Keble*

The arrival of the Wilberforces at Oriel caused something of a stir, Tom Mozley tells us. They were expected to be more Evangelical than they were, and the sad fate of the young William Colquhoun was recalled – 'a fair and promising lad' from a good Evangelical home, who spent a solitary two terms contemplating the stars (always facing East) before home-sickness drove him from the heathen camp.[1] Robert, who formed the advance party, was certainly solitary and studious in his ways, and being then, as ever afterwards, utterly without ambition,[2] he ignored the advice of his friends who felt he should aspire to high society, and contented himself with improving his scholarship which, by all accounts, lacked the polish and assurance which those who had enjoyed a public school education had painfully but surely acquired. 'Robert's industry', Mozley writes, 'enabled him to surmount any difficulties, and he was his own teacher.'[3] At any rate, he made sufficient impression on his examiners to obtain First Classes in both classics and mathematics, so that it was an obvious decision for him to remain at Oxford after taking his B.A. to study for an Oriel Fellowship.

The sources are virtually silent on Robert's undergraduate career. The occasional letter from home has survived, couched in terms of gentle admonition. His father seemed concerned at Robert's careless way of keeping accounts, though he was very generous in sending him advances.[4] The close association with John Keble which began in the summer of 1823 provoked a few anxious letters, showing less concern over the possible influence of Keble's churchmanship than over Robert's manifest predilection for donnish pursuits. Even his sister Lizzy could not forbear a lengthy letter which reveals a curious mixture of the playful and the pious:

> My dear brother. I am really ashamed of the time I have been here without writing to you. But the truth is on my *side* this *neglect was not intentional.* Indeed I sisterly began a letter the Saturday after I arrived but Henry first came in to warm his feet in the sun in my room and to have a coze and then Mama insisted on his reading 'the useful and interesting annual' with her. So in my resolution I verified that assertion of Cowper's – 'vain and irresolute is man', tho' I ought to say woman – tho' I secretly observe that the very Lords of the Creation partake of this frailty. Tho' really when Sam told me you were become so very scholastic as to forget your English I was really afraid that you would not be able at all to decipher my scrawl: none of our family having ever learnt to write being proved by

experience. . . . But nonsense apart, the first thing that presents itself to my mind is dearest Sam. You cannot think how exceedingly anxious I am about him. He haunts me day and night. His passions are so much more energetic than yours. . . . He will be more led in his opinions and habits than ever you would be from the acquaintances he keeps. Oh then what importance it is that he should live with decidedly religious men.

My dear Robert, I know you will forgive me if I say that I think Oxford has had this bad effect upon you, that it has lead you too much to bury religion in your own bosom, not enough to see the distinction between the Christian and the amiable and good man of the world, that their grand design in life should be different. . . . I sometimes wish you and dear Sam, where there is real piety, were more disposed to get over manner and not as I fear to prefer a man for his elegant and gentlemanlike manners to one who has more piety. Not that I would wish you at all to keep company below yourselves for I think that has a very prejudicial effect on people and prejudices others against religion, but that in some instances you should get over a disagreeable manner for the sake of religion. Oh when I think of our name – what is expected from us and what religious advantages we have had – I tremble. . . .[5]

Mrs Wilberforce certainly trembled. If only Robert and Samuel would seek 'truly religious men' to be their companions and friends; if only they would realise that Greek and Latin must always take second place and that nothing could be more profitable than 'serious conversation'. That Keble and his group could supply this, she was very doubtful. In 1824 she took heart from the fact that Robert decided to go abroad and chose for his companion John Venn, the son of the Evangelical Rector of Clapham. If they took 'sweet counsel together', this has not been recorded in any of Robert's letters. Indeed his visit to Munich during this grand tour, according to Tom Mozley, awakened in him an interest in medieval religion and devotions which doubtless was transmitted to Hurrell Froude. He was deeply affected by the sight of Cologne Cathedral and with the examples of medieval religious art which he found in the galleries of Munich. Later, his rooms in Oriel – in the corner of the Quad looking into Magpie Lane – were decorated with tinted lithographs of medieval paintings, an unusual sight in the 1820's, though soon to become fashionable.[6] Robert also visited Paris with John Venn, and disliked it intensely – almost as much as he disliked the French. 'I cannot speak French', he wrote to Samuel, 'and the stupid dogs cannot understand English, which is a great bore. Paris is certainly a very entertaining place, but as dirty as sin in wet weather and there being no footpath, it is monstrous hard to get out of the way of the carriages.'[7]

Lizzy understood her brothers through and through. The trouble was that both Robert and Samuel found the Evangelical set utterly unprepossessing. Samuel explained his difficulties quite frankly to his father soon after he came into residence:

> At Oriel there are not perhaps above two or three men whom you can call really religious, a great proportion of moral, hopeful, *good sort* of men, and on the other hand men occasionally perhaps actually immoral but who would not obtrude their actions and dispositions on their acquaintances if *they* were differently disposed. . . . Robert's acquaintance is certainly very large: to a great part of this I should be naturally introduced. Would you have me not become at all *acquainted* with any of those not positively good or merely to just know them and thus keeping within the laws of civility? . . . Again the men generally who are most religious belong (I believe) to Wadham or St Edmund Hall and are very very low by birth and equally vulgar in manners, feelings and conduct. Would you have me form acquaintances with these? . . .[8]

The Keble group was, by comparison, very much more exciting, although Robert, who was one of the first to take advantage of Keble's offer of free lodgings for Long Vacation reading-parties at Southrop Parsonage in 1823, was at the start somewhat disturbed by his encounter with the man whose academic brilliance had caused his examiners to shake their heads in wonderment and who had overwhelmed Newman with such a feeling of awe that, on their first introduction, he had nearly sunk through the floor with the consciousness of his own unworthiness. For the first time in his life Robert came face to face with a real High Churchman. He was genuinely perplexed. As exemplars of the religious character, his father and John Keble were clearly utterly different. Both possessed great personal charm, it was true; both were humble men who could combine a serious disposition with playfulness of manner. But what could one make of Keble's extraordinary reticence on all matters of the spirit? Shortly after Robert had joined Froude and Isaac Williams at Southrop, he confessed his uneasiness to the others: 'What a strange person Keble is,' he said, 'there is Law's *Serious Call*; instead of leaving it about to do people good, I see he reads it and puts it out of the way, hiding it in a drawer.'[9]

Only gradually did the secret of Keble's power come home to him – the meaning of the apparent spiritual aloofness which had earned for his party in the Church the popular nickname of 'High and Dry'. The first, and most obvious, explanation was that Keble's reticence was entirely in tune with the rest of his character; it was all part of that deeply humble nature which hesitated to obtrude itself upon others precisely because he was so acutely conscious of his own unworthiness and inadequacy. To appear better than you are was to him sheer hypocrisy; so, too, was the opposite attribute, that of appearing *worse*, as Keble once admitted when teasing Henry Ryder for too complete a *volte-face* from the Evangelicalism of his youth.[10] This indeed was his own temptation. As an undergraduate he would stow away his books when a companion approached in case he should be thought too ostentatiously academic.[11] Later, he shrank with genuine horror from the self-revelation of which he felt himself guilty in publishing *The Christian Year*. The phenomenal success of these verses pained him deeply. Froude's taunt of 'methodism'[12] had touched a tender spot. He feared lest some discerning eye should pierce the studious sobriety of his expressions and detect a vein of spiritual pride.

But indeed this reticence went far, far deeper. It was firmly embedded within the religious tradition in which Keble had been brought up. His father was equally averse from outpourings of the spirit. His letters are entirely free from the pious effusions and earnest imprecations which the Wilberforces were brought up to recognise as the mark of true 'serious-ness' and the proper content of communications between 'real' Christians.[13] High Churchmen considered that the facile bandying of biblical texts was a debasing of scriptural truths into meaningless clichés: the endless recitation of pious injunctions could so easily degenerate into cant. Most repugnant, however, was the profanation of the most sacred doctrines of Christ's Passion; as Newman was to put it, the 'commonplace, mechanical way . . . in which the great doctrine of His sacred death and the benefit of His bloodshedding is thrown to and fro, at best as if a spell or charm, which would surely convert men'.[14]

It was not so much the fervid emotionalism of Evangelicalism which Keble and others of his school distrusted; it was rather the form in which this emotionalism was expressed. After all, Keble and Newman were children of their age and were outspoken in their rejection of the cold rationalism and the lack of spirituality which seemed to them to typify the religion of the eighteenth century, the 'low-minded school of Burnet and Hoadly' which 'robbed the Church of all her more beautiful charac-teristics'.[15] In the age of Romanticism it was far easier to be high than it was to be dry. Keble's emotions were no less strong for being chastened and restrained; and in his silent adoration of the holy mysteries, his rever-ential tenderness in speaking of Christ and His saving works, his awe and trepidation in expressing the ideal of sanctity and purity to which the Church had borne witness throughout all ages through the trials and victories of her saints – and never so tried, nor yet so victorious as in the earliest centuries of her life – he made an appeal to the hearts of countless men and women in his day, all of them more or less touched by a spirit – in part romantic, in part pietistic – which yearned for warmth in worship, mystery in doctrine, and discipline in the conduct of the Christian life. Herein lay the attraction of the verses of *The Christian Year*, published in 1827. He 'woke up in the hearts of thousands', as Newman wrote long afterwards, 'a new music, the music of a school, long unknown in England'. He forbore to analyse 'the effect of religious teaching, so deep, so pure, so beautiful'.[16]

Modern critics have challenged the music of Keble's verses (he was in fact tone deaf),[17] and Keble would himself have disclaimed originality. His poetry was the most perfect expression of his theology which was itself rooted in the writings of the Caroline divines, and drawn by them from the early Church Fathers. The nature of this theology came to be more fully understood with the publication of Newman's study on *The Arians in the Fourth Century* in 1833, which – of all his writings – was most nearly in accord with Keble's teaching and also most pertinent in its demonstration of the true content of Tractarianism.[18] Through *The Christian Year*, Newman's work on *The Arians* and, finally, the two tracts of Isaac Williams on 'Reserve in Communicating Religious Knowledge', the patristic method of disclosing sacred doctrine (for which there was ample scriptural authority, as Williams was at pains to show) was recovered and revealed as a fundamental tenet of Tractarian theology. In the early Church, the principle of reserve was developed into a regular system, described as the *Disciplina Arcani*, the discipline of the secret, whereby the catechumens were gradually educated in the mysteries of the faith, the level of instruction being determined according to the worthiness and capacity of the recipient. In the words of Justin Martyr: 'Knowledge is not safe without a true life.'[19] Keble illustrated the teaching by recalling the words of Hippolytus:

> Take care that these things be not delivered to unbelieving and blasphemous tongues. . . . But impart them to serious and faithful men, who wish to live holily and justly with fear. For it is not without a purpose that the blessed Paul in his exhortation to Timothy says . . . 'keep the deposit committed to thee', and again, 'what thou hast heard from me by many exhortations, commit these to faithful men, etc.' If therefore that blessed Saint delivered these truths which were easily accessible to all, with religious caution, seeing by the Spirit that all have not faith; how much

75

more shall we be in danger, if, at random and without distinction, we impart the oracles of God to profane and unworthy men?[20]

We are now at the very bedrock of the High Church tradition, as understood by John Keble. From this come his veneration of apostolic tradition and his firm belief in the necessity of a teaching Church, and, with these, his understanding of the divine nature of episcopal authority, through the apostolic succession, and his high sacramentalism. Hence, too, his preoccupation with purity and sanctity, for 'the pure in heart see God', 'without holiness no man shall see the Lord'. The message of *The Christian Year* and the teaching of his sermons were barely distinguishable. Walter Lock has observed that to Keble 'poetry and religion are at one, and they demand one and the same temper of mind'. He continues: 'Poetry, like religion, hides its deepest truths and reveals them only to the pure in heart, to those who love them enough to press into their secrets. Thus poetry rises almost to the dignity of a Sacrament, with its outward visible words and inward spiritual truth?[21]

This is not the sum of Keble's teaching; but it may serve to indicate how much he differed both from the peculiar tendencies of Evangelical teaching and from the standpoint of the 'High and Dry' school. His poetic sense, his yearning for the mysterious and his awareness of the co-existence of the natural and the supernatural bound him emotionally to the age of George Herbert, his spiritual precursor. And yet this conservatism, although intense, was very different from that of many of his contemporaries in that he sought not to preserve the Establishment as it then was but rather to restore to the Church those principles of the apostolic age which, in part through the negligence of the Reformers and in part through the evils of Erastianism, had been submerged and forgotten to the detriment of true spirituality.

> Is there not a hope [he asked] that by resolute self-denial and strict and calm fidelity to our ordination vows, we may not only aid in preserving that which remains but also may help to revive in some measure, in this or some other portion of the Christian world, more of the system and spirit of the apostolic age? New truths, in the proper sense of the word, we neither can nor wish to arrive at. But the monuments of antiquity may disclose to our devout perusal much that will be to this age new, because it has been mislaid or forgotten, and we may attain to a light and clearness, which we now dream not of, in our comprehension of the faith and the discipline of Christ.[22]

IV. *Relations with Pusey and Hawkins*

All this took some time for Robert Wilberforce to assimilate and comprehend. Indeed, when the reading party of 1823 broke up, he was still
far from being a disciple. What had been to Isaac Williams and Froude
the turning point of their lives had been for him merely a useful opportunity to gain fresh advice on his work in convivial company and pleasant
surroundings. He sought Keble's company for a different reason from
the others. As Williams recalled, 'each of us was always delighted to walk
with him, Wilberforce to gain instruction for the schools, and the rest of
us for love's sake'.[1] It is significant that after Robert had achieved his
double First later in the same year, he apparently had no wish to join the
others at Southrop in the following summer. The group which assembled
for the reading-party of 1824 included Froude, Williams, Herbert Cornish,
George Prevost and Henry Ryder. Robert was away on his grand tour
with John Venn.

In the two years which elapsed between taking his B.A. and submitting
himself for the Oriel Fellowship examination, Robert seems to have passed
through a period of tension and depression. He was involved in an
unhappy love affair, which nearly carried him on the rebound to seek
oblivion as a missionary. Mrs Wilberforce confided her anxieties to Samuel
in February 1825:

> Dear Robert's case has been much trial to us all. I cannot but lament and
> deplore that such a mind as his should meet with so severe a trial just at
> the setting out in Life but if you see him do not talk to him about it. He
> now wishes to forget her and the less he is talked to about it the more likely
> he is to forget the distressing subject. I only wish that She would speedily
> make it impossible if indeed it is never to be. But I feel sure that dear
> Robert is indeed a servant of the Most High God who ruleth all things in
> heaven and earth and will order everything for good for his servants.
> Therefore tho' such feelings at present are not 'joyous but grievous' yet
> afterwards they will yield to him the peaceable fruits of righteousness.
>
> His mind seems now strongly to turn to some missionary undertaking,
> but he does not wish this at all mentioned or hinted at because, young as
> he is, he may change or see some reason to give up entirely the plan. It is
> a plan very distressing to my feelings – but I feel another ground of appre-
> hension besides any feelings of my own. I fear lest he should be mistaken
> about himself and lest it should not be a true missionary spirit, but rather
> a want of stimulus in common life and common exertions, not unlikely to
> take place in a mind like his after all the stimulating effects of Oxford
> studies. . . . He may turn from every thing in common life as too vapid

77

and insipid and sigh like Alexander for other worlds to conquer. You may well hint something of this kind to him. It may put him on self-examination, for this is not a missionary spirit.[2]

Robert recovered from the blow to his pride. He submerged himself in his books, and in the following year (1826) secured his immediate ambition by gaining an Oriel Fellowship. Thereafter he came into almost daily contact with Newman and Froude, and his acquaintance with Keble developed into a close and intimate friendship. Pusey he knew less well. At the time of his election and during the greater part of 1823 Pusey was away in Germany studying oriental languages and investigating the work of Schleiermacher, Neander, Tholuck and Freytag, theologians and commentators whose writings were taking Protestant Germany by storm but had hardly as yet aroused the merest flicker of interest in England.

At first Robert felt inclined to follow Pusey into this field. Soon after his election he was in correspondence with him to ask his advice about the initial problems which he would encounter in the study of Arabic. He supposed that he, too, would have to study in Germany. Pusey promised – in reply – to provide him with letters of introduction to Lücke, Freytag and Sach, professors at Göttingen and Bonn who had all been influenced by Schleiermacher.[3] Robert's enthusiasm had sprung from the same source as Pusey's own – Dr Lloyd, Regius Professor of Divinity, a scholar whose painstaking exegesis and meticulous precision left their mark on all the brilliant pupils who came to study under him in the 1820's. He was one of the few biblical scholars in England who perceived that the advance of theological study would be stunted without a clearer understanding of the techniques of German 'critical' scholarship. That Oxford was lamentably ill-equipped at this time to follow the German lead (even if it had been disposed to do so) was manifest from the fact that only two persons in the whole of the University were capable of reading German – Cardwell, Principal of St Alban Hall, and Mill of Magdalen College.[4]

Robert's first problem, then, was to master the German tongue; then to study Hebrew and Arabic. Pusey tried to dissuade him from embarking upon Arabic:

> For a theologian the Arabic literature as far as it is yet known possesses little which is interesting. Mohammedanism is the only problem which can be resolved by his knowledge of the language, with which he is even distantly concerned. . . . I do not on the whole repent of my undertaking; when wearied by it, I opened my Hebrew bible and in the assistance which

my knowledge of Arabic gave me, I found myself recompensed. You, from your study of mathematics, your stronger memory and from beginning it younger, will find the task easier; but I question whether you will find it compatible with the continuous reading of the fathers and reformers which you proposed, and (division of labour being necessary) whether after having given so much time as would be necessary to it, you would not think it more expedient to make subjects connected with those languages and the O.T. the chief object of literary exertion. Before I close, I must venture to turn your attention to Syriac and Chaldee: they are both very easy languages, lie much nearer to Hebrew (tho' they do not yield so large a produce for its illustration as Arabic) and their literature is for a theologian much more interesting.[5]

Robert delayed for a while before taking the decisive step. He had recently taken deacon's orders (he was to be ordained priest in the following year) and was in two minds whether he ought not to abandon his researches for pastoral work. While he was in Cambridge during the summer of 1827, following a suggestion from Pusey that he ought to consult the Cambridge orientalists (Dr Wait and Dr Lee), he received an offer from Lord Calthorpe of the curacy of East Waltham, which he eventually decided to decline.[6] He was on the point of leaving for Germany in the winter when he heard news of Edward Copleston's elevation to the bishopric of Llandaff, an event which created a vacancy in the provostship of Oriel. He therefore stayed for the election, found himself on the spot when a vacant tutorship became available and duly accepted it. The intended visit to Germany did not take place until the summer of 1831, by which time Robert's enthusiasms had been diverted into other channels.

During these years his religious opinions were in a state of flux. At one moment he would find himself defending the 'Peculiars' against Froude's jibes; at the next he was trying to persuade Samuel of the errors of solifidianism.

Robert and I have daily arguments as usual [Froude wrote to Samuel in March 1828] in which as usual I make an ass of myself, talking loud and never listening to what he has to say, being carried away by an irresistable instigation, directly as I get a glimpse however distant of anti-Kebleanism. It is a melancholy discovery to find oneself such a goose.[7]

Robert was amused, however, to find that when he was staying at Cambridge to study Hebrew, he was looked upon as dangerously High Church. He thought that Froude should know. 'At Cambridge', he wrote, 'I was a regular Church and King man from having been looked upon by you with suspicion when at Oxford.' He knew, at least, that Froude would join him in deprecating the low tone of Cambridge religious life.

There seems a strong spirit of infidelity in the debating society there, where Voltaire was eulogised the other day as 'an excellent man'. The disposition of the masters of arts seems much more fair and liberal in the encouragement of learning and talent in the University than it is with us. They have no fellowships to which men are elected by interest. Such a thing would be quite scouted. At the same time there does not seem to be a due attention paid to moral character, and a bad dog is rather encouraged than not. I was surprised to see how stupid and useless many of the fellows were, notwithstanding they had got their situations by fair and open election. This certainly rather confirms your hypothesis about close fellowships.[8]

The most accurate description of Robert's state of mind in 1827 may be found in a series of letters which he wrote to Samuel, criticising the Calvinist teaching of the popular preacher Malan, whom Samuel had encountered at Geneva and had engaged in discussion on the subjects of election and reprobation.[9] Robert had no taste for the 'hell-fire' approach. He warned Samuel that the effects of Malan's preaching had been 'that he had made the heart of the righteous sad, whom the Lord hath not made sad, while into those, for whom anxiety would be desirable, he had infused confidence'. He continued:

> This tendency of his doctrines I would never use as a proof of their falsehood. . . . but I think the effect which it ought to have is to make every person who receives these notions very cautious how he allows them to take hold of his own mind. . . . I don't think you are likely to become a Malanite, except his notions are true, and then I hope we both may. But I see people in general want this caution exceedingly. Thus I heard of a lady . . . who when she had seen very little I believe of Mr M. wrote in her prayer-book *Rejouis te, mon âme, tu est sauvé, sauvé, sauvé*.

Robert then turned to his own difficulties on the doctrine of justification by faith alone:

> It seems to depend mainly upon the meaning of the word faith, as laid down in Scripture, for which I never could get a definition to my mind. It is obvious that it cannot mean a belief of the truth of the record, for the devils also believe and tremble, nor do I think the case is mended if it be said it means that you believe that Christ came to save you, for what could be the meaning of exhortations to a change of heart and of character as needful to salvation, if all that be required is only that you should believe that Xt came to save a certain body of persons, of whom you are one.

Such a way of thinking would involve 'the highest Calvinism'. Robert was inclined to take 'I believe in the Lord Jesus Christ' as meaning 'I believe him to be a mediator needful for the lost state in which I find myself, and desirable for the holy state he holds out to me. This would include what Hooker calls faith of assurance, as well as faith of evidence.'[10]

In his next letter, written on 23 August 1827, Robert wrote more boldly on the necessity of works, having satisfied himself that Samuel agreed with him that a mental impression could not be a certain proof of conversion. He took his stand on St John's First Epistle General, chapter II, verse 3.* 'It is clearly implied here that a man must examine himself whether he is in the faith and that the way to examine himself is to see whether he keeps his commandments.' Again, he was firmly convinced 'that a man will not be saved independently of his own desire, that if he longs for salvation with a humble heart, that will be done for him which it is impossible he should ever do for himself. . . . But if this longing for assistance is required at first, is it not required afterwards?' This led Robert to a consideration of the doctrine of final perseverance, against which – again leaning on Hooker – he distinguished between having a full moral conviction of the continuing assistance of God in preventing the lapse of a regenerated Christian and the Calvinist certainty of the gift of perseverance, based on the text 'My sheep hear my voice, neither shall any man pluck them out of my hand'.[11]

Samuel annotated Robert's letter with contradictory texts,[12] concluding with the injunction to the Philippians 'For it is God which worketh in you both to will and to do of his good pleasure'. Robert was not discountenanced. He upbraided Samuel for citing separate and unrelated texts instead of satisfying himself 'about the general tenor of Scripture' and dispatched for his edification a volume of Hooker and a copy of *The Christian Year*.

> I only hope [he wrote] that the more we both study the glorious truths of the Gospel the more the prayers of Keble's hymn may be verified –
>
> > 'More than Thy seers we know –
> > O teach our love to grow
> > Up to Thy heavenly light,
> > And reap what Thou hast sown.' [13]

With the publication of *The Christian Year*, Robert began to declare his admiration for Keble unreservedly. He wrote to Samuel in July 1827:

> Keble's hymns are at last come out. They are singularly beautiful. They are not the least likely to be popular, and they require to be well known and closely studied in order to be liked, and in many parts I find them extremely obscure, tho' certainly [with] the few I have studied (for I have only had

* 'And hereby we do know that we know him, if we keep his commandments.'

the book a few days) I find this fault diminishes. They are thoroughly Keblean, and will I should think be of great use in diffusing ... a chastened and spiritual frame of mind. I don't think that I ever saw hymns more likely to do good. They are not like sweet wine, nice at first but soon cloying, but have a wholesome dryness, which will make them keep for ever. In short they are worth your hastening home to read.[14]

In a letter to Froude in the following month, his excitement was even more intense:

Nothing that has come out for this last hundred years can bear a moment's comparison ... The effect of poetry I never felt so strongly in perusing any other work. It is usual to find brilliant ideas suggested which you never had before. But Keble seems to make his poems out of the common perceptions of all mankind, only without his aid they are portions of gigantic forms which you find it impossible to develope; he takes them, 'et vera incessu patuit Dea' ... I am exceedingly glad that we are no longer doomed to see

> 'thankless silence seal
> Lips that might half heaven reveal'.[15]

In the autumn of 1827 the provostship of Oriel fell vacant, and the Fellows were confronted with an unusually difficult decision. Whately was out of the running since he had accepted the post of Principal of St Alban Hall two years earlier; the two most likely candidates seemed to be Edward Hawkins and John Keble. Robert was very slow to commit himself. Pusey and Newman both wrote to him to persuade him to cast his vote for Hawkins, suggesting that Robert was putting his personal feelings before the best interests of the College.[16]

There was truth in this. Robert wrote to Froude in great perplexity on 27 December:

I am afraid you have understood me as more decidedly pledged to support the great man whom I wish elected, than I feel I can be. On every account, both as relates to himself, and as relates to me, I should *like* to see the greatest of Oriel fellows at the head of the College, but that awkward accompaniment of my pleasure and pain principle, I mean its weak brother of approbation and disapprobation keeps continually asking me, whether Hawkins would not be the fittest person.

The duties which a Provost has to discharge seem to be two, one that in the College, the other towards the University. I can't help thinking this last a very essential part of his employments. Now I have no idea that Keble would engage in the task of cleansing that Augean stable – the meeting of Heads. The sharpness which their insensibility requires he never would assume, the tone of authority which alone they would respect he never would persuade himself he was entitled to. Now in all the part of the Provost's

Lavington House

Emily Wilberforce, shortly after her marriage, by Richmond

office I feel convinced that Hawkins, being a better man of business, will be more useful. On the other hand I have a kind of feeling that Keble will infuse his spirit wherever he is known, and if every one had his spirit what would there be left to desiderate?[17]

What were Keble's own opinions of the matter? Mrs Battiscombe, in a recent biography, has suggested that despite his humility and preference for a quiet life, he was convinced of his ability to undertake the office and would certainly have accepted an offer if made by a solid majority of the Fellows.[18] She has also expressed her own belief that Pusey and Newman badly underrated Keble's firmness and his capacity for guiding the College through stormy issues.[19] Actually Keble took Robert entirely into his confidence and, in an extremely revealing letter written on 31 December 1827, he explained his reluctance to allow a contest to take place. This letter shows also that Robert had decided to ignore Pusey's and Newman's advice and to join Froude in pressing Keble's claims.

> I can never forget your kindness [Keble wrote], and that of several others, but particularly yours and Froude's, in thinking of me as you did: and you will readily believe that on many accounts it would be very pleasant to me to be elected Provost: nor do I think myself particularly incompetent to the office. Yet on the whole matter, comparing my circumstances with those of Hawkins, public and private, I am convinced that it is best for me to decline being nominated at all. You know pretty well how I am engaged here, and though that would not be an absolute bar to one's accepting an eligible preferment or employment under any circumstances whatever, it must come in with great force, when the thing lies between two, to determine which had better have it: supposing both to be absolutely eligible men. And as far as matter of *taste* goes, you are pretty well aware that I should prefer something more independent and countrified. . . . Not but that Oriel is indeed a great prize: too great for any one who is not yet a good way above the ordinary temptations of wealth and honour. I am writing oddly and ramblingly, I know, but when we meet, I shall I dare say be able to convince you that it is anything but insensibility to my friend's partial kindness which has led me to do as I have done. I must add that my Father and all around me quite approve of what I am doing. It is most probable indeed, at least I think so, that if we had come to a decision – the majority would have determined it in the same way.[20]

That, it would seem, was that. In fact nearly three weeks of negotiations followed.* Robert refused to take Keble's word as final. As soon as he received this letter, he wrote to Froude to say that Keble's arguments

---

* The election actually took place in the third week of January. Compare Mrs Battiscombe (*op. cit.*, 119) who is in error when she states that Hawkins was elected before the New Year.

ought not to be taken too seriously. His attitude was typical of his generous nature; and, besides that, 'his situation at Fairford is not one which he is long likely to occupy'.[21] On 3 January he wrote to Hawkins to tell him that he had decided to vote against him.[22]

Keble, however, refused to go back on his decision, and the way was made easy for Hawkins at the last. The Fellows in caps and gowns ranged themselves in two lines around the closed College gates with Newman as Dean at their head, awaiting the arrival of the Provost-elect who would knock on the gate to demand possession of his new kingdom. None could have known that the elegant and dignified figure who would soon be in their midst would reign over them for forty-six years and would prove to be – as Dean Church later described him – 'the ablest and most hurtful opponent' of the religious spirit which John Keble had done so much to foster.[23] The drama of the occasion was softened by an absurd incident. Tuckwell describes it:

> A knock was heard, and Newman, the Dean, asked 'Quis adest?' 'Please Sir, it's me' was the half audible response: the gate was opened, and through the double line of expectant Fellows marched, buckbasket in hand, the College washerwoman. Once more the gate was closed: soon came three peremptory knocks: and to the invocation 'Quis adest?' pealed the answer, 'Edwardus Hawkins, Hujusce Collegii Praepositus.'[24]

v. *The Three Oriel Tutors*

For the next three years Newman, Froude and Robert Wilberforce worked together as tutors of Oriel. At first Robert found the diversion from Hebrew to the classics rather trying.

> I have done fearfully little as yet [he wrote to Froude in August 1828]. I have but been gnawing at the corners of some Greek plays . . . and lamenting my fearful ignorance of the principles on which they are constructed. It really sometimes makes me start all over to think how little I know on the subjects I lecture about. And whereas I had anticipated being perfectly at home in the thing in about 6 months, I have a much stronger sense than ever how much I have to do. Besides this I have had upon my hands the preparation for Burton, and have read about half Prideaux's Connection. Do you know the Poetics well? I am intending if I can get them up to take my Rhetoric class thro' part of them next term, and I want to compare my opinions about the thing with yours.[1]

At home some uneasiness was expressed at Robert's donnishness.

William wrote to Samuel in March 1829 that he was a little fearful about 'the tutor of Oriel. For though I doubt not the solidity of his religious character, yet I fear his situation is far from favourable to the growth in grace.'[2] All Robert's friends, however, were made very welcome at Highwood. Pusey was certainly introduced to the family,[3] and subsequently asked Robert if he would persuade his father to breathe his name in the Duke of Wellington's ear in connection with the vacancy in the Regius Professorship of Hebrew on the death of Professor Nicoll.[4] Keble stayed at Highwood for short periods in 1829 and 1830 and made a favourable impression.[5] It was Robert's special wish, however, to bring John Keble and John Sargent, the saintly Evangelical Rector of Lavington, together. He wrote to Samuel in 1830: 'J. Sargent would be a most excellent man to get to meet Keble. You remember the favourable opinion formed about him by Archdeacon Froude. I don't think tho' that Keble will much alter his notions about a class of men from seeing an individual. It will merely show him that many persons are not properly to be referred to that class who go by its name.'[6]

The desired meeting nearly took place. When Keble came to stay at Highwood in March 1830, John Sargent had spent the previous week with the Wilberforces. He wrote to his wife Mary to tell her that he had to stay longer than intended but would leave before Keble arrived:

> It will not surprise nor I hope much vex you to learn that I stay here on Sunday. Amongst various reasons, Sam's *nose* is one. He is engaged to preach next Sunday but the state of that organ renders it doubtful and he wished much to have me at hand in case of necessity. Mrs Wilberforce has conveyed him this morning to Mr G. Babington, who is to inspect the works and report upon them – poor fellow, it makes him very uncomfortable. To run away the very day the author of the Christian Year arrives would be *odd* and yet perhaps *wise*. I am no poet and am one of those unfortunate men whom the divines of Mr Keble's school deem heretical and schismatical. Robert would be *tenter-hooked* lest I should say something that Keble would oppose – or lest he should say something that I should oppose, and in the meantime his *expectations* would be as bad as the reality. I confess I should like to see the sweet singer in our Israel.[7]

Newman, too, was a guest of the Wilberforces on at least two occasions. He stayed at Highwood in October 1827 for a short while with two others of his family, including his mother. On 18 October he wrote of his delight in meeting the great Emancipator for the first time – 'it is seldom indeed we may hope to see such simplicity and unaffected humility, in one who has been so long moving in the intrigues of public life and the circles of private flattery'.[8] In December of the same year he returned to Highwood for another week while suffering from acute headaches, induced by overwork, for which he was put in the hands of the Wilberforce family doctor, Mr Babington, who remained his medical advisor until 1856.[9] During the following year, spent intermittently in convalescence at Brighton, he became a near neighbour of William, the eldest son of the family, who was staying there with his wife and infant son for the remedial benefits of the ozone.[10] Again, the evidence suggests that the relations between Newman and William Wilberforce were entirely cordial. When Henry became Newman's pupil at Oriel, William was pleased at the arrangement and wrote to thank Newman for his favourable reports. On one such report he observed: 'The pleasure it gives me is much enhanced by my high respect for the principles, the judgement and the means of information of the individual by whom that favourable opinion was expressed. Allow me . . . to express my Hopes that whenever we may have the opportunity of cultivating each other's personal acquaintance and friendship, you will allow us to embrace it.'[11]

Robert saw a great deal of Newman at this time. Many years later, when they had drifted apart, he wrote rather wistfully to him to express his wish 'that I could take a walk with you every day as we used to do in years back, that I might confer with you on 100 points which daily arise in the course of my reading'.[12] In July 1828, just after taking orders, he turned to Newman for advice on preaching. 'I feel', Newman replied, ' . . . that I am not worthy to suggest anything to anyone. What am I among the thousands in Israel? . . . I cannot doubt you are perfectly safe under our Lord's teaching, waiting on him day by day.'[13] In the next year, Newman wrote to ask Robert if he would become one of his curates at St Mary's, an invitation which, after some thought, he declined.[14]

An earlier proposal of a rather different kind had, however, found him enthusiastic. This was a plan initiated by Blanco White to establish a symposium in which a small number of correspondents would from time to time discuss provocative theological questions, their letters being circulated to all the members of the group, who might respond, as the spirit moved them, to any challenge thrown down. Blanco White sketched out his idea to Newman in February 1828:

> Three or four friends might unite for the purpose of writing to each other upon subjects, moral and religious, requiring more thought than research. Any one of these should be at liberty to start a subject, addressing himself to whomsoever he liked. The letter should be handed round to all the party;

and every one might, if he pleased, answer it as if it had been originally addressed to each.

He preferred this personal approach to a simple circular because

> I find that the character, the ethos of what I say or write depends, in a considerable degree, on that of the person or persons I address. So it must happen to every one who has not acquired disputatious habits; for in such cases the person addressed has a kind of *inverse* influence.

Correspondence should be confidential.

> The average of candour is very low even in the most enlightened public, especially on the subjects which we shall have to discuss. Most of the best and ablest men I know are deficient in what I should call *intellectual* toleration, in religious matters. It seems to me that few men (especially Divines, who have been brought up with little or no free communication of thought with others) have any notion of the infinite variety of intellect which exists in mankind. Accustomed to consider their intellectual habits, as being very near the *natural* standard, whatever deviates from the line of these habits, assumes for them the character of perverseness. Hence the *odium theologicum*; a passion which though greatly subdued by the still growing results of the Reformation, has at this day more vigorous and deeper roots than are allowed to appear in the usual course of life. Divines, however, are not satisfied with *conformity*, or *orthodoxy* in results; they demand for the most part, conformity and orthodoxy of arguments. It is this spirit which has consecrated the most questionable proofs of many an unquestionable Christian truth, and which in the eyes of unbelievers gives to Christianity the character of a mighty edifice, borne by an unsound foundation, and made up of the most heterogeneous materials.

Here is the true spirit of Noeticism, expressed in the words of its true founder – the spirit of bold, though respectful, enquiry, calculated to invigorate a moribund theology and to alleviate the acerbity of religious disputation – which was to be spurned and all but stifled by the excessive dogmatism of those to whom it made its first appeal and who came to brand as scepticism an approach to religious enquiry which was, in its first manifestation, only too conscious of the futility of adopting an unreverential and querulous tone.

Blanco White knew the fears in the minds of his contemporaries:

> Are we then intending to pull it [Christianity] to pieces in the spirit of German rationalism? God forbid! On the contrary I will tell you without disguise, that in proposing this association, I feel under considerable alarm, lest for want of that humility which my intellectual wanderings make my own peculiar duty, I should become a snare to any one of you. Under this salutary fear therefore I propose to write, and as I trust that I shall never

take up the pen without imploring the Divine assistance, I may hope that without compromising the interests of Truth, I shall set the example, which becomes my age and circumstances – that of modest caution, arising from the experience of my weakness.[15]

Newman responded with alacrity. He sent Blanco's letter to both Robert Wilberforce and Hurrell Froude and was pleased to report to its author that they liked the proposal; 'thus we shall, I hope, have an agreeable party of four'. In the same letter he plunged at once into religious controversy. The subject which he chose for discussion was one which to students of Newman will come as no surprise: it was none other than the problem of the relationship between Faith and Reason – the posing of the questions, what are the limits of the intellect in its search for evidences of Christianity and what is the connection between moral disposition and assent to religious truth? This was a field of theological enquiry which Newman first encountered in the writings of Bishop Butler and which he himself was to explore in the series of sermons preached before the University of Oxford between 1826 and 1843 and again in what was to be his fullest exposition of the theme, *The Grammar of Assent*, published in 1870. The peculiar interest of this correspondence with Blanco White is two-fold. In the first place, it is one of the earliest expositions by Newman, albeit very brief, of his notion that in matters of faith, words and intellect are inferior to feelings and moral disposition. It is true that Newman had already delivered his first University Sermon on the subject of 'The Philosophical Temper', in which he argued *inter alia* that 'to be in earnest in seeking the truth is an indispensable requisite for finding it'.[16] In his letter to Blanco White he is taking a position which looks forward to the great sermon on 'Faith and Reason, contrasted as Habits of Mind' delivered to the University on the feast of the Epiphany 1839, where faith is spoken of as a moral principle and his hearers are warned against the indifferentism of 'the schools of the world',[17] that 'error, the common and fatal error, of the world, to think itself a judge of Religious Truth without preparation of heart'.[18]

So he wrote to Blanco White on 1 March 1828, agreeing with him especially 'in feeling the incommensurability . . . of the human mind'.

We all look at things with our own eyes [he continued] – and invest the whole face of nature with colors of our own. Each mind pursues its own course and is actuated in that course by ten thousand indescribable incommunicable feelings and imaginings. It would be comparatively easy to enumerate the various external impulses which determine the capricious motion of a floating feather or web, and to express in an algebraical formula the line it describes – so mysterious are the paths of thought. Nay, I might even be tempted to say that on no single point do any two individuals agree – no single object do their minds view from the same spot and in the same light. And this will of course hold good in religious matters. Necessary as it is, that we should all hold the same truths (as we wd. be saved) still each of us holds them in his own way; and differs from his nearest and most loved friends either in the relative importance he gives to them, or in the connected view he takes of them, as in his perception of the particular consequences arising from them.

Accordingly I trust I shall always be very slow to quarrel with persons differing from me in matters of *opinion*. For *words* are not *feelings* – nor is intellect ἦθος. Intellect seems to be but the attendant and servant of right moral feeling in this our weak and dark state of being, defending it when attacked, accounting for it, and explaining it in a poor way to others. It supplies a medium of communication between mind and mind – yet only to a certain extent – and when we think we can detect honest principle, purity of heart and a single eye, it is irrational to delay the recognition of these real excellences till we have settled subordinate points, to exalt what are but means into an end, and make expressed opinions and formal statements an objection to our *believing* in the existence of moral feelings in others which by the exercise of common sense we may actually see.

I have Froude's authority for thus lowering the intellectual powers into the handmaid of our moral nature. But I doubt whether he or Wilberforce will think it safe to proceed to the lengths to which I expatiate. . . . Let me then challenge W or F to give me some account of the connexion of speculative error with bad ἦθος – e.g. *in what is a consistent Socinian a worse man than an orthodox believer? I* think him to be worse, but I wish my mind clear on the subject.[19]

The second point of interest in this correspondence now emerges. Blanco White so thoroughly agreed with Newman – at least at this stage of his spiritual development – that his reply reads like a continuation and elaboration of his correspondent's views. It comes almost as a shock (their handwriting was not dissimilar) to find the initials 'J.B.W.' at the letter's end.

Every one who has experienced any change or improvement under Christian influence [he wrote], is (I believe) aware that the part of himself which has been affected is his *moral* feeling. Even the most intellectual persons will generally find that their reasoning faculties have a very indirect power on their moral feelings. From these considerations I am inclined to believe that the supernatural influence of Divine grace is exerted chiefly on that faculty of our mind through which we seem to partake of reason in something like the shape of instinct: in a word, that conversion and moral improvement is what the Scriptures describe by the expressive metaphor of creating in us a new heart. . . .[20]

It would be interesting to know what Robert had to say on this. Unfortunately the remainder of the correspondence, which must have contained something from his pen, has not survived. All we can safely say is that these letters reveal the nature of the theological discussions in which the three Oriel tutors were from time to time involved.[21]

Robert's intimacy with Newman and Froude became closer with the appearance, in 1826, of his brother Henry on the Oriel scene. Henry became Newman's pupil, and very soon his favourite pupil. Quite naturally the two families of Wilberforce and Newman were brought closer together by this relationship; and since the Newman family circle in 1826 consisted not only of John and his two brothers, Charles and Francis, but also of three unmarried sisters aged respectively 22 (Harriett), 18 (Jemima) and 17 (Mary), the regular visits of two eligible bachelor brothers might reasonably have led to a union of the two families.

At least the Newman girls themselves seem to have thought so, if Mr Sean O'Faolain's reading of ambiguous initials and pet names in their diaries and letters is correct.[22] Ever since the death of their father in somewhat straitened circumstances in 1824, the Newman family had lived a very unsettled existence, boarding with relations, staying with friends, or keeping house for one or other of the sons in Eastern Terrace, Brighton, or in the tiny house at Strand-on-the-Green in which one of their aunts had established a small finishing school for young ladies. The Newman girls, high-spirited creatures all three, flitted from place to place, singly or as a trio, as circumstances or convenient invitations permitted.

Often enough during 1826 and 1827 they found themselves at Ulcombe, a small village near Maidstone, where Newman would occasionally take duty during vacation for his friend Samuel Rickards, a former Fellow of Oriel who had become Rector of Ulcombe in 1822. From time to time a party of Oriel men, Fellows or undergraduates, would be there too to enjoy the genial domesticity of a household with a brace of young children, a charming hostess who would make her guests write verses on flowers in her visitors' book, and – in the centre of them all – Samuel Rickards himself, a gentle, affectionate man who would treat his most intimate friends to a display of one of his proudest accomplishments, reading character from handwriting.[23] The Wilberforces and the Newman sisters certainly met at Ulcombe, probably in the summer of 1827. Harriett and Jemima were both staying there in July of that year[24]; Newman and Robert Wilberforce were there in September, and Mrs Rickards, in a letter to Harriett dated 12 September 1827, described the party there in terms which suggest that Harriett and Robert were already well acquainted.[25] Two weeks later came an invitation to the Newman family to spend some days at Highwood.[26]

There is nothing in Robert's papers to support Mr O'Faolain's contention that Robert and Henry were regarded by the Newmans as prospective suitors; not a hint of romance after the sad experience of 1825[27] until Robert's first description of his meeting with Agnes Wrangham in 1830. The letters of the Newman sisters, however, abound with affectionate references which show without doubt that Harriett and Jemima were both very conscious of the eligibility of Robert and Henry and were teased for being so by their younger sister Mary.'That nice little Henry Wilberforce, what a nice fellow he is,' Mary wrote to Jemima in October 1827. 'Has Mama told you of his absurd impudence last Friday! I like them all better and better, and R.W. with all his quietness and gentleness, he is as bad as H.W. and worse because *he* is honest. H.W. says "I am impudent, I am a torment", and he is so. R.W. says "I am gentlemanly and timid", and he is – impudent and tormenting. . . .'[28]

This impudence appears to have been a plot, hatched by Rickards and Newman, to alarm the two elder sisters into exposing their true affections for the Wilberforces by allowing the rumour to circulate that they were all set for imminent departure to Botany Bay as missionaries. This arose from the news that Lord Winchelsea, Rickards's patron, was likely to be appointed Governor of New South Wales and that he was thinking of suggesting the name of the Rector of Ulcombe as his bishop. Doubtless he would not have gone alone. He would need a suffragan – Newman, perhaps? He would certainly find an appointment for Robert Wilberforce, who would equally certainly accept with some reluctance. Thus the rumour was embroidered; and the girls had shown their consternation.[29]

During the next summer (1828) the Newmans had the loan of a cottage at Nuneham Courtenay, and there they encountered the Wilberforce brothers again. Henry was now the most favoured. Robert seems to have wearied of the badinage and the well-meant endeavours of his friends to secure him an alliance. As early as August 1827 he had written to Samuel to express his distaste for indulging in tiresome 'small talk' with young ladies[30]; and after his experience at Ulcombe he felt that he had had a fortunate escape. Commenting to Samuel on the election of George

Cornish to a Fellowship at Exeter College, he wrote in November 1827: 'I esteem [him] the most lucky man I know, inasmuch as he was just on the point of being married a little while ago, and now has managed to get off that and get a fellowship into the bargain. Was it not luck?'[31]

At any rate, when Newman wrote to his mother about the proposed holiday at Nuneham Courtenay, he made no mention of Robert. Henry was dangled as the bait. 'I am led to think you must not wait for the letting of the house before you come here, and I will tell you why. H.W. will be coming.'[32] On the few occasions when Harriett and Jemima met Robert he appears to have been cold and aloof.[33] Harriett transferred her affections to Henry, leaving Robert for Jemima. In the following year, she wrote to her aunt: 'We had a call yesterday from your favourite, Robert Wilberforce. He dined with us lately, else we have seen him only for morning calls. Henry is my little friend who is no Don and never will be.' In the same letter she added: 'You must enquire of Jem for R.'[34]

Both girls were to be disappointed. Henry, at this stage of his life at any rate, was a fickle creature, 'falling in and out of love', as Newman himself commented.[35] Poor Jemima deluded herself into thinking that Robert was in love with her, while being too shy to profess it. When she heard the news of his engagement to Agnes Wrangham in the spring of 1832 she thought that she had been jilted, and Harriett wrote a fierce letter to comfort her bruised heart. He was marrying Agnes for money, she thought. 'If this is his motive for change of plan how unhappy he must sometimes feel.' And again: 'Oh, Jemima, I almost despise him.'[36] Thereafter their attentions were turned to the two Mozley brothers, a more successful venture, for Harriett was married to Tom Mozley and Jemima to John in the course of 1836.

Robert's visits to Ulcombe and Nuneham Courtenay were not merely social occasions. Primarily he went there to read, to study and to talk. A visit to the Newmans at Brighton in the summer of 1828 was the occasion of a long talk with his fellow tutor on the current system of college tuition. Both Robert and Newman were troubled by arrangements as they then stood. In the first place they disapproved of the practice of allowing freshmen to come into residence at different times during the academic year, preferring them to come up in a body at the beginning of the year so that they could form a separate class in which the teaching could be geared to their needs.[37] Secondly, they were uneasy at the conventional notion of a tutor's function. He was little more than a college lecturer who had a general responsibility for maintaining college discipline.

Was the undertaking of such a work, both Newman and Robert asked themselves, compatible with their solemn ordination vows? Newman had no doubts on this: tutors of colleges were men in orders; accordingly they should treat their office as if it were, in part at least, a pastoral cure. This is how he had interpreted his function from the date of his appointment to a tutorship in 1826. Robert and he now proposed that tutors, while retaining their duties as lecturers, should also have the special charge of a limited number of pupils whose academic and moral supervision should be the tutor's first responsibility. This would at once put an end to the system whereby 'reading men' sought their own individual coaches, whom they would pay privately for special tuition, and it would allow the pastoral nature of a tutorship to receive formal recognition.

Newman, in his autobiographical memoir, gives the impression that these proposals were made on his own initiative[38]; and Miss Meriol Trevor, in her recent biography, goes further in saying that 'the new system was entirely Newman's'.[39] This is open to question. As early as the summer of 1828 (the proposals of Newman were drafted during the autumn) Robert Wilberforce had tackled Hawkins, the new Provost, on these very points. In a letter written to Hawkins in 1830 he recalled the occasion:

> You may remember that two years ago I complained to you (it was at Highwood one Sunday in returning from Church) of the irregular way in which instruction was given in College on certain subjects. This I said I had felt, and heard complained of, as an Undergraduate, and found it impossible as a tutor, under the existing system, to obviate. Another point which I felt, tho' I do not remember mentioning it, was the disadvantage of addressing moral instruction to indiscriminate classes. You then directed my attention to the connection between each tutor and his private pupils as obviating this objection. I have ever since had that system more in view than before, and since my Colleagues, by acting upon it themselves, have felt it in their power to do so, I have certainly found it a remedy to every thing that I complained of.[40]

It would appear, then, that Robert's approach to Hawkins was made before any steps had been taken by Newman, and that Hawkins, by himself pointing to the advantage of the moral instruction of a tutor's individual pupils, was not initially opposed to this conception of a tutor's function. Dornford and Froude, the other two tutors, certainly followed the lead given by Robert and Newman.

Hawkins's subsequent objections arose from fear of favouritism. Although he was himself a firm disciplinarian, he suspected that the tutors were discriminating in favour of the 'reading men' against the gentlemen commoners, who, because of their wealth and status, often enough considered themselves exempt from the chore of reading for honours. He did not intervene, however, at first, although it was always in his power to suppress the activities of Newman and the others, exercising his authority as Provost by refusing to allocate any pupils to the tutors. He chose to wait upon events.

In fact he did not wait long. In 1829 the University was split into rival factions, Newman and Hawkins taking opposite sides, over the issue of Catholic Emancipation.[41] That this event was a turning-point in Newman's life is well known; it marked the final breach with Whately and the Noetics; henceforth he was ranged with Keble and Froude amongst the extreme conservatives. Keble emerged from comparative obscurity and prepared himself for battle because he felt that Peel as University Member had betrayed his trust by championing a measure in the Commons which he had been elected to resist. Newman's hostility, however, went very much deeper. Although he counted himself as one of Keble's disciples, he had never fully taken to heart his master's teaching on the Church of Rome as 'an erring sister'[42]; if he had been weaned from his Evangelical notion that Rome was Antichrist, he still believed that she was 'bound up with the cause of Antichrist'.[43] To him the ejection of Peel from his university seat was crucial: it represented the triumph of Church over State; it marked the downfall of the latitudinarians. The fierce enthusiasm of his letters home ('We have achieved a glorious victory. It is the first public event I have been concerned in. . . . We have proved the independence of the Church and of Oxford'), the taunts at his rivals, among them Whately and Blanco White ('Their insolence has been intolerable; not that we have done more than laugh at it'[44]), reveal that he was at last conscious of his ability to stand on his own feet; he could afford to spurn those who had once been his teachers.

Robert Wilberforce held back from all this. Like his father,[45] he perceived the expediency of Catholic Emancipation and refused to associate himself with the general outcry against Peel. This did not mean that he was sympathetic towards the Whately group or that he was feeble and timid in his defence of the rights of the Church. He viewed with horror the collapse of the clerical régime of Charles X of France in August 1830 and the triumph of the Duke of Orleans, although he felt that the French king (recently arrived in England as an exile) had hopelessly mismanaged his *coup d'état* to replace Louis Philippe by his grandson Henry. 'Have you seen anything of poor Charles?,' he wrote to Samuel on 26 August 'I should fear there was no chance of King Henry's . . . being ever restored. It is easier losing crowns than recovering them. I cannot but think that if Charles had held out more, he might have done something. . . . A man must be a fool to make a *coup d'état* and then run when it is *being* struck.'[46]

Robert's refusal to support Newman and Keble on the issue of Peel's re-election did not save him from the wrath to come. Hawkins, vexed beyond measure by the triumph of the Church party in securing the election of Sir Robert Inglis, was not easily thwarted. He hit back at Newman by demanding that the tutorial reforms of the previous year should be rescinded, threatening to assign no pupils to the tutors who defied him. Newman and Froude ignored the request; their senior, Joseph Dornford, gave way. Robert asked for time to think the matter over. As always he was very slow to commit himself. At last, in September 1830, during a short holiday on the Continent, he decided to follow the example of his friends. He wrote to Hawkins: 'I can sincerely say that all the reflexion I have been able to give to the subject has but the more convinced me that I . . . should be unable to carry on the tuition in a manner beneficial to my pupils and therefore satisfactory to myself except on the system I have heretofore pursued.'[47]

Wilfrid Ward was wont to point to the loss of the tutorship as the turning-point in Newman's career: 'Had he been absorbed by his Oriel tutorship we should never have had the work on *The Arians of the Fourth Century*, with its really remarkable historical generalisations on the genesis and *rationale* of creeds and dogmatic formulae; and it is doubtful if the Oxford Movement, as history knows it, would ever have come into existence.'[48]

For Robert the event was hardly less important. For some years he had been considering leaving Oxford for pastoral work. His chief reasons for remaining at Oriel were to guide his brother Henry through the Schools and to satisfy the pastoral urge in his capacity as a tutor. In December 1830 Henry secured his degree, with a First in classics and a Second in mathematics. Hawkins had already effectively blocked any supply of new pupils. What should hold him now?

There was another very good reason why he should leave Oxford. During 1830 the unhappy fact was pressed upon the Wilberforces that their family fortune was gone, squandered by the reckless speculation of the eldest son and heir. Highwood was to be put to let; a new home had to be found for the ageing William and Barbara. Robert, deprived of his income as a tutor, was obliged to find a living, preferably a wealthy one, with a house large enough to accommodate his father and mother. He could also think seriously about finding himself a wife.

While his father and John Sargent used their influence with higher powers, Robert decided – in the summer of 1831 – to fulfil his original intention of visiting Germany, where he could pursue the linguistic studies which had been interrupted by his appointment to the tutorship in 1828. Although he did not vacate his fellowship until 1833, his Oxford career was effectively at an end.

VI. *Samuel Wilberforce at Oxford*

Samuel Wilberforce, as an undergraduate, moved in a different circle from that of his elder brother. Keble was to him merely a name, and a name with which he was so ill acquainted that – as late as 1827 – he misspelled it 'Keeble' in a letter to Robert and was sternly taken to task.[1] One might suppose that this was calculated ignorance and that Samuel, anxious to preserve his religious upbringing from any alien influence, was playing the role of the dutiful son, were it not for the fact that his father actually regretted Samuel's indifference to the opportunities offered by the vacation reading-parties at Southrop. 'I have been for some days thinking of writing to you,' William observed to Samuel in August 1824, 'in consequence of my having heard that your friend Ryder and Sir George Prevost were reading classics with Mr Keble. Could you not have been allowed to make it a triumvirate? Much as I value classical scholarship, I prize still more highly the superior benefit to be derived from associating with such good young men as I trust the two gentlemen are.'[2]

With Newman he had little more than a formal acquaintance. He was, after all, an undergraduate at Oriel before the reformed tutorial system and therefore met Newman only in the chapel and lecture-room; and Newman was not the type of man (in the first years of his fellowship, at any rate) to seek intimacies with undergraduates until his outward shyness and diffidence had been penetrated by a direct approach from the other party.[3] Samuel, many years later, wrote to Robert to describe a conversation with Newman in 1838: 'He was what he has *always* been to me exactly: i.e. kind and courteous and *distant*. I never felt to know him the least and I have my own solution for it, but too long for writing.'[4]

Newman's account of his relationship with Samuel is even more frigid. 'I never was intimate or familiar with Samuel Wilberforce, though I had known him almost from the first day when he came up as a freshman to Oriel in October 1823. But he was drawn towards me by the friendship which his brother had formed with me.'[5] In the early 1830's he was more forthright in stating his opinions of Samuel in private letters to friends. 'Samuel Wilberforce', he once complained, 'is so far from anything higher than a dish of skimmed milk that we can hope nothing from him.' And again, he described him as the man 'whom Froude and I have stigmatized as a humbug for many years'.[6]

It is sad – though in the light of subsequent events significant – that they did not know each other better. Samuel expressed his own regret to Newman himself. 'I wish', he wrote in 1834, 'that ... you would ... allow me to repair one of my great Oxford faults – that of neglecting the endeavour to obtain a more intimate acquaintance with you.'[7]

We may doubt, however, whether their views would have been in any way different. They had really very little in common. In temperament, tastes and accomplishments, Samuel was everything that Newman was not: a social charmer, a great platform speaker, a superb improviser. He had no wish to become any man's disciple; the cult of 'Newmania' made no sense to him at all. Indeed his letters to Hurrell Froude in the late 1820's go far to supply the explanation of the enigmatic reference, cited earlier, to his 'own solution' of the fundamental estrangement between them: his affections were fully committed before ever he met John Henry Newman. The desire to eschew a compromising intimacy with the opposite sex, the passion to give oneself utterly to the Church by aspiring to the highest ideal of sanctity which required the living of virgin and celibate lives – that cast of mind which rendered to all those who subscribed to this view of religious duty a sort of inner understanding of each other's trials and temptations, and created therefore a peculiar bond of intimacy between them – were all utterly incomprehensible to Samuel, not because his character was secular and unspiritual nor because he had a passion for virility such as possessed the robust and simple mind of Charles Kingsley, but because his vision of a saint was much more like the father whom he knew and loved than an anchorite of the ancient Church or a monk of the Middle Ages. At the time of his first encounter with Newman, Samuel was already deeply in love. This may explain, incidentally, why he seldom accompanied his brothers to Ulcombe; and why, when the Newman sisters *did* meet him, they thought he was grumpy and gave himself airs.*

There is no doubt that Samuel had a taste for grand society. His mother trembled at the report of his attending wine parties. She warned him to 'avoid too much company and keep from much intercourse with worldly and careless tho' polished young men. . . . I wish you might have one pious friend to whom you could speak openly – take sweet counsel together and walk to the House of God as friends.'[8]

A great deal of Samuel's social life was spent in the circle of the newly-established Union Society. In those days, apparently, he was famed for supporting liberal causes, attacking borough patrons, defending Charles James Fox, supporting Catholic Emancipation and censuring the Union with Ireland.[9] This Whiggish ardour was soon to cool.

He was fond of regular exercise – chiefly riding. Many of his afternoons during term were spent at Bullingdon Green, then a wide open common, amusing himself and astounding his companions by displaying his considerable prowess at hurdle-jumping (he once for a wager took ten hurdles in the space of a hundred yards).[10] On other days he would join a pack of harriers with Charles Anderson, or explore the countryside in search of insect life. His contemporaries would mock him for this particular pastime, Frederick Oakeley threatening to send him through the post an 'enormous death's head Moth' which he had found lurking in his bed[11]; it was clearly an enduring enthusiasm, for Robert sent him from Germany in 1831 a gift of particularly fine insect tongs.[12]

Those who encountered Samuel's tempestuous energy in later life would find it hard to believe that both his family and he himself supposed his besetting sin to be indolence.

> I sometimes doubt [Samuel wrote to Robert in 1830] whether I do now possess powers of application strong enough to make me fit for anything. But I must not yield to this ruinous belief – the surest excuse of hardened indolence. When I see though all that is to be acquired – in history – in Philosophy – in Moral Science – to put me even upon a par with those whom I should long to surpass, I almost despair and resolve to set up for 'an honest man', to know something about turnips and perhaps sometime or other preside at a turnpike meeting. You will help me from this my idleness if any friendly shoulder can.[13]

Actually his academic work as an undergraduate, if unsupported by the

---

* D. Mozley, *Newman Family Letters*, 97. In a letter dated 31 December 1840, Harriett told Jemima how unpopular Samuel was with the lower orders in the Isle of Wight.

C. R. Sumner, Bishop of Winchester

Mrs John Sargent, as a widow

deep learning which Robert acquired, was of a high order. His vacations were usually spent in sharpening his scholarship. In 1824, for instance, he was at Rottingdean working with a tutor called Otley.

> I read tolerably hard here [he reported to Robert] – having got through now 5 plays of Sophocles, 2 Aeschylus and some *very* little Thucydides, written divers essays for Otley, some in tongue vernacular, some in language Latin ... I am quite confirmed in my preference to Euripedes over Sophocles by reading Sophocles through. I quite hate the generality of Sophocles and it has not even I think those redeeming beauties which to my mind render Euripedes so *comparatively* attractive.[14]

Robert adjudged some of Samuel's 'themes' to be so good that, as a tutor, he asked his brother to send him a batch of them to act as models for his pupils.[15]

Samuel took his Schools in the winter of 1826, much discomforted by a streaming cold. 'I have now pretty nearly got through my classical examination,' he wrote to his father, 'and I do not believe myself that I have much or indeed any chance of a first; but I hope I have done my duty and not disgraced you or my other friends. I have been a good deal impeded in the schools by a very bad cold which I caught the first day of my examinations and which made my head very thick and stupid. Sunday and Monday I was in bed all day and dosing.'[16] When the results were published he was placed in the First class in mathematics and in the Second for his classics, 'no bad things', as Charles Anderson wrote in his letter of congratulation, 'though I will say, without flattery, not the full reward you ought to have had'.[17]

Charles Anderson fulfilled most nearly Mrs Wilberforce's desideratum of the 'one pious friend', with whom Samuel was to have sweet and regular converse. He was the son of a Lincolnshire baronet, whom he later succeeded, with a considerable estate at Lea, near Bawtrey. He came to Oriel as a gentleman commoner, and the friendship which he immediately formed with Samuel was to last their lifetime, strengthened in later years by his marriage to Emma Foljambe, an intimate friend of Robert's first wife, Agnes Wrangham. Not at all the gentleman commoner of university fiction, he was sober, unsophisticated and commendably 'serious'; in all respects thoroughly good for Samuel, if not quite the ideal companion whom Barbara had conjured up in her mind. He was not, for instance, given to effusions. On their walks and talks, Samuel usually did the talking. When they travelled the Continent together, if Samuel was in the mood to muse, an afternoon's expedition might pass in almost total silence.[18] When Anderson was moved to speak he was usually refreshingly down to earth.

All through the early days of their friendship Samuel was hopelessly in love. Charles Anderson was not. He would break through Samuel's reveries and get him to work, or to come out riding, or to notch up another victory at the Union. Very typical of him was his reception of the news of Henry Ryder's engagement to Cornelia Cornish in 1826:

> I am quite surprised to hear of Ryder's matrimonial engagement. I am sorry to hear she is taller than him but hope she will prove all he wishes tho' between ourselves I have no great idea of *wild poetical simplicity*. I had rather have a woman who could make a good pie or pudding and help me to eat it with a jolly radiant visage at the bottom of the table. I have however not fixed upon any one yet but hope something will turn up before long that will suit.[19]

Samuel's love-sickness went back to 1821 when, as a schoolboy of sixteen, he first set eyes on Emily Sargent, then a girl of only fourteen. He met her at Marden Park when John Sargent brought all his family over to see the Wilberforces. Looking back many years later he was to describe this event as the beginning of 'my great life dream'.[20] Whether this love was immediately reciprocated we cannot say. Certainly later in the same year he confided in his father and received his approval of the future match. William felt that it would be to Samuel's eventual advantage in his university career to have the 'great security of a strong virtuous attachment',[21] which was perhaps a more sober and appropriate way of making the point than Barbara's frantic letters about the early death which lay in wait for those who fell to the blandishments of Oxford whores.

They hoped to marry as soon as possible after Samuel had taken his degree; but the parents on both sides adjudged them to be too young. Samuel must first settle the question of his future career. The most likely course was that he should take orders. At first, however, it was felt that he should try to emulate Robert and compete for a fellowship. In November 1826 he tried his hand at Balliol in the company of George Moberly, Francis Newman and Frederick Oakeley. He received a letter from Oakeley shortly before the contest:

> You may be well assured, that, as far as I myself am concerned, I should consider my chance greatly improved by your withdrawal from the contest. The nice thing would be for both of us to succeed, but that I fear is very unlikely and I am inclined to think that success would lose its charm to either of us in proportion as it conveyed the idea of victory over the other.[22]

In fact neither was successful, Moberly and Francis Newman securing the prize. Oakeley was elected Chaplain Fellow in the next year. Samuel then thought of studying for the stiffer test demanded for joining the Oriel 'colony'.[23] In February 1827, with his plans still unsettled, he tried again to win John Sargent to his side, so that at least his engagement to Emily could be announced. He first asked his mother's advice and received a typical reply:

> Dear Samuel, I feel much interested for you and long to hear all particulars of your visit that you can properly and with comfort communicate to a Mother. Only write 'Private' on it and that will do, and I will keep it to myself, except any communication to your Father. Only let your Prayers be earnest for direction from on high and a blessing, and if you should be successful, do not be in a hurry. You are both too young and 3 or 4 years will do no one any harm to wait. Remember Jacob's 14 years of hard service . . .[24]

Nothing was settled by his visit to Lavington. He therefore resolved to go abroad for a long holiday in the company of Charles Anderson. They had originally planned to take another Evangelical friend with them – H. F. Lyte, the hymnographer of later fame – but he was taken ill shortly after their departure and had to return home. The two friends, sometimes by themselves, sometimes in the company of other acquaintances (like the Prevosts), whom they met at different stages of the 'grand tour', took the conventional route – the Rhine cities, Switzerland, Northern Italy, through Germany again into Holland and Belgium, and finally (after a visit to the battlefield of Waterloo) into France for a three-week sojourn in Paris. They looked at incomparable scenery and drew sketches, visited art galleries and tried to express the moral effects on their minds of what they had seen, they communed – like Wordsworth – with nature on the mountain-tops. But above all they made for the cathedrals and the churches, observing not only the buildings and the ornaments but also the form, content and ethos of the worship conducted therein.

Samuel's letters and diaries over this period form a most revealing commentary on his religious development. He was still a convinced Evangelical, as his correspondence with Robert on his conversations with the Calvinist Malan at Geneva clearly shows. At the same time, his letters to Hurrell Froude suggest that he was trying to understand the enthusiasms for 'apostolical' views and Catholic sentiments which many of his Oriel contemporaries were deriving from Keble. These letters are the best available evidence of Samuel's relations with Froude, which were closer in 1827 than at any other period, although even then their kinship seems but slight in comparison with the difference of opinion and mis-understandings which their various exchanges revealed. Samuel never really understood Froude. He would write to him in a playful, bantering style, perhaps in the hope that he might provoke in response some of the wit which others gave him credit for. 'They talk of Froude's fun', Samuel once complained, 'but somehow I cannot be in a room alone with him for ten minutes without feeling so intensely melancholy that I do not know what to do with myself.'[25]

The strain of melancholy, however, was not absent from Samuel's own letters. Writing to Froude in March 1827, when all his plans for the future seemed hopelessly unsettled, he confessed:

> I am quite come to the opinion that we never should expect to be *happy* in life: and that a sort of negative state of peace is the highest good in point of comfort to which we can attain: and so high a one that it seems almost unattainable. Also to live like a cabbage in a garden – and a cabbage too with its leaves so rotten as to be unfit for cutting, is at present my condition; whether I shall ever be so transplanted and grafted as to become useful and therefore peaceful I quite dread to think. *At present* I anticipate taking orders in about 2 years – have no particular prospect of a curacy – and for some things should most exceedingly like to join the colony. Do you think it would be feasible? ... I wish I could have been more settled in cubic measure – more experienced – more informed, or rather less ignorant before entering into the Church than I could hope to be in two years. ... I wish very much indeed that I could enjoy the great pleasure and (even to me possibly) advantage of knowing Keeble [sic]. But fate seems to forbid it.[26]

Froude replied a week later to warn Samuel 'against leaning on a bruised reed; or to use another metaphor against looking on my sullied mirror for a reflection of Kebleanism'. His sense of the distance between himself and Keble had been heightened by a conversation which he had had with the great man only the previous evening:

> Unfortunately he is so much engaged that I can see but little of him. Yet that little suffices to refresh my fading memory of his greatness, and to bring before me the immeasurable interval which separates him from his fellow wanderers on earth. There is a sort of deep richness in his observations, which gives a resting place to one's dreary feelings, and helps one to see things through an enchanted atmosphere.

He continued the letter on the following day:

> We have just parted company in common room, where I have had much fun with Oakeley. Keble was there but it was too mixed a company for

enjoyment, so I was content to amuse myself, and O. was benevolent enough to supply me with materials. . . . I will advise you to go into some bookseller's shop to buy George Herbert; a new edition of his came out last year so that it must be easily procurable and I think you would, as I have done in part, gradually forget the odd language and versification in the very great genius which peeps through it. Keble says he thinks they were written to suit in some degree the silly taste of the time just as many of the things we see in Shakespeare and that the same allowance which we so easily make for the one may by those who choose be extended to the other.

Froude was particularly delighted with *The Country Parson*: 'Among the ideas which it has instilled into me, it has made me determine to learn medicine, which in a parson is quite different from in a doctor; as you will not fail to perceive from a most delicious chapter in G.H.'[27]

Samuel's reply, in July 1827, contained a lengthy description of his travels on the Continent. He then turned to Oxford affairs, joining Froude in poking fun at Frederick Oakeley:

By the way, I heard that our little splendid friend has got the Theological as well as the English Essay.[28] It is really a pity for what will he do next year – he will have nothing to be in a fever about, and out of a fever I should think at that time of year he can hardly exist: at least if with him habit is a second nature.

Pray do write and tell me all you can about yourself and others. Are you going to be tutor next term? Has Copleston eaten his 5th of November sermon sufficiently? What are your plans for the summer etc.? How was it that when I was at Oxford last time I hardly saw you at all? I think being here sometimes would render your friend (of I forget where) less uneasy as to your turning Catholic. The abuses of the religion meet one's eyes more than its excellencies, for some such I believe there still remain. We saw yesterday, for instance, as often before, stuck up on a cross by the roadside that the Bishop gave 40 days indulgence to every one who would repeat before it an ave, a pater, and an act of confession. I was talking to our guide who is a very sharp intelligent man about the priests. I asked what they preached about. He said 'Oh, faith in Christ, the Virgin Mary and God.' I asked him how they were told to pray to the Virgin by the Curé: whether to ask her to pray for them. He said, 'Oh no – just in the same way as to God – and then she will take us to Paradise.' But I shall stop. . . .[29]

Samuel wrote again in October from Brussels; at least he began a letter, then broke off and returned to it a month later, after he had arrived back in England and paid a second visit to Lavington to secure – at last – John Sargent's permission for his engagement to Emily. In this letter, he touched upon the fundamental difference between himself and Froude –

most particularly their understanding of the vocation for holy orders and the nature of the religious life, on which Samuel had to express his bewilderment at the way in which Newman and Froude were extolling the virtues of virginity as a quality of self-denial most necessary for those who would aspire to true 'apostolical' sanctity.

He began in a jocular vein:

> What have you been doing all the summer? Reading principally, I suppose, since you have abandoned the Noetick school. Have you made many marine excursions down your beautiful river? I hear that you have taken the tutorship. Really it is almost worth while to come up again for a fortnight for the sake of belonging to one of your classes, and seeing you assume the Don and reprove any *very gross* behaviour. Did Oakeley visit you this summer? I have been reading lately a good deal of Paschal – and am most exceedingly delighted with it. I think you don't read French: really it is worth your while to acquire it for the sake of reading it. He is so *grate*. Besides you as an almost Roman Catholic would like him better than I should. I am longing for Keeble's hymns or whatever they are called. The taste I have had of them in some extracts George and my brother have sent me has made me very much desire to get the work itself.

The letter broke off here. When he resumed in November, his mood had changed.

> It is not from having forgotten it my dear Froude that this letter has so long remained unfinished, but from my being utterly dissatisfied with what I had written and equally hopeless of writing anything better. . . . But how shall I tell you what will shew my practical dissent from those doctrines of yours with respect to Matrimony, which I have often combated in argument with you. The only plea I think of is, that I am in high company since the great Pusey is similarly situated,* at least so Isaac tells me. However, dear Froude, I do not wish my friends to confirm the truth of the rumour which is spread about me. and therefore while I tell them I do not wish them to tell others. Indeed had I not always held the *doctrine* which you know I did, I am sure I should have practised as I have now done, when I met such a one as I have found, but then I should have expected the condemnation which I am told you now pronounce upon me when I have only acted up to what I before justified; and which therefore I beg to assure you I think perfectly uncalled for. However my wrath will only lead me to express the wish which I earnestly feel that I may one day have my revenge upon you when you are in a like situation. . . . Tell me how *you* are, why you are so fierce against me. . . . To tell the truth one reason of my writing to tell you of my engagement is that I hear Robert says that it is dread of you which keeps me from Oxford. This I think I cannot better refute than by writing directly to yourself.[30]

* Pusey's engagement to Maria Barker became generally known in November 1827.

Although he met Froude for a brief moment in the following spring, he had to wait until April 1828 for a reply. After a conversation with Henry, Froude had felt overcome with guilt at 'having talked against you so long...' (as he admitted to Samuel). 'I certainly am very often provoked at you [he continued], and sometimes can hardly fancy that there can be any subject of common interest to both of us; but since I saw you I have learned to put less confidence in my fancies, having in the course of the last year experienced a good deal of drilling – and your last letter has brought home to me the consciousness that there are yet many things for us to talk about.'[31]

He would have felt even more provoked if he had seen Samuel's pencilled comments in the margin of this letter. It appears from these that at the time of his receiving Froude's letter Samuel had just had the chastening experience of his first lovers' tiff. In every available space of the notepaper, anguished protestations of undying love were scribbled – 'Did you not say "do you still suspect?" All I mean is my Emily to beg you not to be vexed with me for suspecting you when I only feared that how, when I could not tell you what I feel, I had hurt you. Oh pray my sweetest love be as usual and believe how fondly and excessively I love you.' – 'Won't you my own love write me a little note to tell me all you *did* and *do* feel?'

Whatever the quarrel had been, it soon blew over. Plans for the marriage were now in hand. Samuel had firmly resolved to take orders; unfortunately the Sargents insisted that he should be settled in a curacy before they would fix the date of the wedding. William Wilberforce intervened on his behalf. He pointed out that it would be highly undesirable for Samuel to proceed to ordination with his mind preoccupied with the personal matter of his impending marriage. The earliest date for his reception into the diaconate being Christmas 1828, the marriage should take place in the summer of that year. He offered to help the young couple financially for the few months before Samuel's taking a curacy, and reminded John Sargent that he could count on the benevolence of other influential friends – especially Bishop Sumner, who would gladly ensure that Samuel received 'a liberal competency'.[32] The Sargents gave way and the wedding was fixed for June 1828.

Charles Simeon was asked to officiate: an obvious choice for the uniting of the son and the daughter of two of the most respected Evangelical families in the land. Apart from his dislike of the ill-mannered 'Peculiars' of St Edmund Hall and a growing attachment to the writing of the Caroline divines, Samuel Wilberforce had felt no call to question the tradition in which he had been reared. His letters to Charles Anderson during this period, in so far as they touched upon religious subjects, reveal quite clearly his respect for inherited doctrines, quickened by that strong pietistic impulse which seemed to grip, more or less keenly, almost all his Oxford contemporaries, whether they were 'serious' or 'apostolical'. In March 1827 we find Samuel advising Anderson to read *A Practical View* for his spiritual edification. 'I hope I may profit by it', Charles duly replied.[33] They expressed their mutual delight at the signs which they discerned of a new reforming and pastoral spirit amongst the Bench of Bishops. Of Kaye's work at Lincoln, Anderson wrote to Samuel: 'He intends to force residence and not allow a Curate to hold more than two churches on any plea and also to enforce double duty for the evening service. . . . By the bye we hail the second Sumner's elevation to Chester instead of G. Wellesley. The Bench of Bishops will soon be what they ought to be.'[34]

In August 1828, he treated Samuel to a discourse on Providence – a subject very dear to Evangelical hearts. It was occasioned by a fearful accident which his father had witnessed on Loch Lomond, when a boat carrying twenty people had overturned in water seventy fathoms deep:

> The shrieks of the women of whom there were several they describe as dreadful. Some of the men swam to shore but from there being so many doubtless they clung to each other, at any rate 11 are drowned. Miss Noyon saw one poor woman go down with her hands clasped above her head. Thus another awful lesson was read to us on the uncertainty of life, and the horrors of being called suddenly and unprepared to render up our souls before God. How mysterious are the ways of Providence, how past man's understanding. . . . The surviving spectators are answerable if they regard not the warning and do not turn to Him who is alone able to prepare them for an equally certain tho' not perhaps equally sudden call.[35]

A long letter which he wrote to Samuel in February 1829 exactly captures the mood of their religious discussions and the mingled hopes and fears of these years:

> My dear Sam, I was very glad to hear from you. . . . I will not omit to read Butler's *Analogy*. Among other things that I have lately read I have been much pleased with the Life of Fletcher, Vicar of Madeley. It is a perfect picture of a good Country Clergyman. I quite agree with you as to the mistake which some people make in fancying that 'renouncing the world' is equivalent to leading a Christian life. Yet on the other hand I think great circumspection in mixing with the World, is necessary to a young be-

ginner, so soon are we led away by its fashions etc. I know by myself that I have often returned from parties so occupied by worldly thoughts that I have not known how to compose myself to Prayer. However I am not going to preach Seclusion. Prayer and reading the Holy Scriptures daily are the most necessary of all duties, I am quite convinced and I intend to force myself to do both and tho' I may feel myself cold and heartless, yet I do believe, aid will in time be given. Perseverance is commanded and the Spirit of Faith and Grace will be given.

He then turned to the contemplation of political events:

I can't make up my mind as to the advantage of Catholic Emancipation for either way I think the prospect a very gloomy one for Ireland. I think there will never be any peace there, till some kind of government is formed so as to induce the gentry to reside on their estates. In short I begin to croak: 'that we are all going down hill' – . . . The extreme luxury and expense of the Higher Classes and the expensive and also cheap shops with slight capitals, the consequent expense of the Middling Classes, the increase generally of betting, gaming etc. among all classes, which I believe is not a false statement, I think very bad signs, and I sometimes think we shall live to see some great blow up. If that should be the case and the latter days really coming we shall find Religion our only prop. I have not become a 'prophet' but if the Apostles talked of Our Lord's coming as *near*, after 1829 years have passed we must be *nearer still*, which seems to me a strong reason why we should be preparing, and looking for it, keeping our lamps burning against the hour which no one knows but the Father. Blessed is he that waiteth.[36]

This note was heard often enough in the 1820's and 1830's, the period which witnessed the frantic prophecies of an Edward Irving and the morbid introspections of a Hurrell Froude. If there is a touch of Irving in Charles Anderson's letter, there is also – in other letters which passed between the two friends – an echo of the tribulations recorded in Froude's *Remains*.

My dearest Charles [Samuel wrote in February 1832], let us both aim at more holiness of life, more of the real life of spiritual religion in our souls, that in the evil day we may be able to stand.[37] [Normally he recommended devotional reading – especially Leighton.] Read a letter every day. You may miss (as I do) the Calvinistic parts which we both I believe dislike, but there is a holiness, an eminent spirituality, which makes reading a little, meditating and praying over it of especial use in helping us to maintain a spiritual state of mind. It is like conversing with an angel for a while.[38]

But little acts of self-denial were useful too. Some years later, Charles Anderson wrote to Samuel to remind him of their decision on one occasion to make self-denial a test of religious feeling. For a while they struggled hard to support each other in their resolution. All went well until they attended together a sumptuous dinner-party in London. Gradually the strain became unbearable, so that each began rather to resent the presence of the other. At last a course was served – as Charles Anderson recorded – at which 'we exchanged looks across the table as the double temptation was consecutively offered and yielded to'.[39] It was a dish of turbot and lobster sauce.

VII. *Henry Wilberforce and J. H. Newman*

When Henry came up to Oriel at Michaelmas 1826, Samuel was on the point of taking his Schools and Robert was already a Fellow. Both his brothers were well-known figures in the college and, not unnaturally, the arrival of Henry was awaited with eager curiosity. The first impression was not entirely favourable. Hurrell Froude thought him 'a silly fellow; certainly he is very forward and obtrusive'.[1] Some – especially Tom Mozley – chuckled at stories of Henry's diffident but determined truthfulness, for, like his brothers, he had none of the glibness and urbanity of the public school man, and his secluded upbringing in an atmosphere of evangelical domesticity had ill-prepared him for the conventions and courtesies of Oxford social life. There was a story which Mozley gleefully related that on one occasion Henry received an invitation to a wine party from an acquaintance whose society he particularly wished to shun. He could not tell a lie or fabricate an excuse, so he simply refused the invitation without explanation.

> The very morning after the wine party, upon entering the covered passage leading from the square of the Radcliffe to the Schools' quad, he encountered the disappointed host entering the passage from the quad. They were *vis à vis* and there was no escape. They came to a dead stand with their eyes fixed on one another. The other man waited for an explanation, and Henry had none to offer. Something, however, was expected, and there was nothing but the bare fact. He delivered it in naked form. ' – – – I did not go to your wine party yesterday.' The man waited for the reason why, and said nothing. Henry, after a pause, could only repeat, 'I did not go to your wine party yesterday.' After another pause of helplessness on one side and vain expectation on the other, he repeated a third time, 'I did not go to your wine party yesterday'; which said, both pursued their respective courses, and, it is needless to say, never recognised one another again.[2]

John Henry Newman, who as a young man might have found himself in just such a predicament and who therefore always had a certain sympathy for those who were gauche or tongue-tied, especially when this shyness concealed acute intelligence and intellectual power, found Henry from the first quite irresistible.

> I well recollect my first sight of him [he wrote many years later, when called upon to supply his obituary], on his presenting himself before the tutors of his college – when the lectures had to be arranged for the Term, and his place in them, as a Freshman, determined. He was small and timid, shrinking from notice, with a bright face and intelligent eyes. Partly from his name, partly from his appearance, I was at once drawn towards him; and as he subsequently told me, he felt a corresponding desire to know me; and, in a little time, though I was not formally his college tutor, and only had relations with him as with other undergraduates in my lecture room, we became very intimate.[3]

Henry was in many ways the most attractive of all the Wilberforce brothers. He had none of Samuel's striking good looks and lacked the forcefulness and determination which were to carry the other to high office in the Church. Despite his clumsiness and notorious untidiness ('as fine an Apostolical within as ragged a brute without',[4] Robert once wrote of him) Henry was an engaging and lively companion – always eager and good-humoured, ardent in his prosecution of a cause while impetuous and volatile in the causes which he often chose to prosecute. He could be a fine, impassioned speaker and delighted in making an impression; on the other hand, he was not unduly vexed by hostility or reproof and could be (so his brothers thought) infuriatingly carefree. 'Anxiety is not my natural tendency',[5] he confessed disarmingly to Robert in 1833.

None of the family expected Henry to distinguish himself academically at Oxford. His father thought he had no staying power: he was too 'scatter-brained', always mislaying things – his cap and gown,[6] a sermon lent to him by Newman.[7] When the time came for him to go down, he discovered that most of his plate, half his linen, a prize essay in draft and a small desk table, which he had supposed was still in his room, had all mysteriously disappeared.[8] Robert Wilberforce was commissioned to be his taskmaster. In this capacity, he received from George Dudley Ryder, one of Henry's most intimate friends, a promise not to lead him astray:

> I should naturally wish to see more of Henry than you are inclined to allow me [he wrote], yet if he thinks it worth his while to read for honours at all, it is certainly worth his while to do so steadily – and to use all honourable

means to insure success. I will therefore promise neither to entice to nor to
acquiesce in any idleness to which he may be inclined to yield. I shall be
the less likely to break this promise as I come up with the full intention of
reading myself – for though I must own I am but an idle dog, yet when it
comes to upwards of two months of such a course, my appetite for it is not
a little cloyed.[9]

Even after Henry had taken his Schools and was working for a prize
essay the family saw little improvement in his character. Robert wrote
quite crossly to Samuel in April 1831:

I am glad Henry is at last going to you. I am sorry to say that I don't
think him much mended after so long a series of remonstrances in the
articles of determination of character. There is no getting him to do anything at the time. I feel this the more from the extreme annoyance I feel
just at present because after taking immense pains to make him finish his
essay, he has put it off so that he will have far less chance than he might have
had. . . . It is a very trying thing when you are anxious about an object of
this kind, and see it lost by the dawdling of another person.[10]

Newman, however, had a very high opinion of his intellectual capacity.
For a portion of four consecutive long vacations Henry studied with him
privately – at Hampstead in 1827, at Nuneham in 1828, at Horsepath in
1829, and at Oxford in 1830. Newman especially saluted his 'singularly
quick apprehension', his 'clear head' and 'largeness and sobriety of mind',[11]
and told Robert in 1828 that his reading power was similar to his own.
'He cannot read fast – I cannot myself – yet I read, as perfectly as maybe,
what I read – and that is his case.'[12] Unfortunately William Wilberforce
seemed reluctant to concede that his youngest son was deserving of
success; this was one of the few points on which Henry felt genuinely
aggrieved. He did extremely well in the Schools, securing as good a degree
as Samuel – a First in classics and a Second in mathematics – and he
understandably expected his father to show his pleasure at this result.
On the contrary, William was nettled that he had not done better. In a
letter to Robert in December 1830 Henry relieved his feelings:

I own that I have felt my disappointment more than I expected since I
see the effect it has had on my father who obviously considers my degree
in the light of a trial to be submitted to. I know very well that this is not the
case, but it is provoking that he should think so, as to please him was one
of my chief reasons in wishing for university honours. It is almost amusing
to see how *utterly* incredulous he is as to the fact of my having deserved
my mathematics. When I explained it to him, he said 'Do you think so?'
with his incredulous look and afterwards remarked that tho' glad I had
got what was thought most of at Oxford, yet he almost wished I had got

my mathematics as being more useful to the mind. I replied that I did not think *success* necessary to make them useful – and that I was notoriously a better mathematician than Anstree – Oh, no! (he) said – I cannot think that because *he succeeded*, showing that either he did not believe or did not *understand* the explanation that I gave him.[13]

Perhaps William became too much of a perfectionist in his old age; or possibly he thought that praise would go to Henry's head. None of his other children ever complained that their achievements were allowed to pass unrecognised. In a letter written in June 1831, after failure to obtain a university prize, Henry expressed his chagrin to Robert with some bitterness:

I am much vexed at these repeated failures when I see how they grieve you and when I think how success would have delighted both you and my father. The latter does not seem grieved by these events, for the very low idea which he has of all of us in point of ability prevents him from being disappointed. I am vexed however to think that no one thing that I have done in the university has given him pleasure, for the degree was *to him* tho' certainly not to me, a disappointment.[14]

After all, he, again like Samuel, had been President of the Union, in the richest period of its history, the other Presidents of his year being Manning and W. E. Gladstone. It was at the Union that he first met his future brother-in-law, although they did not at this stage become close friends. The first mention of Manning in his letters to his brothers occurs in a letter of 2 May 1832 when he deplores the folly of the Oriel Fellows in allowing Manning of Balliol and Hamilton of Christ Church (the future Bishop of Salisbury) to secure fellowships at Merton.[15] In his undergraduate days his closest friends were George Dudley Ryder (also to become his brother-in-law), Frederic Rogers, Tom Mozley, S. F. Wood and – outside Oriel – John Rogers of Balliol and Sir Thomas Acland of Christ Church. He never knew Gladstone well, and had but a slight acquaintance with the man whose star was rising in the Union just after he himself ceased to attend: William George Ward, who once addressed to him the remark which could only have been uttered by the man who was to become Oxford's notorious, though strangely engaging, *enfant terrible* – 'Intellect is a wretched gift, my dear Henry. Absolutely worthless. Now my intellect is in some respects almost infinite, and yet I don't value it a bit.'[16]

Henry Wilberforce was no W. G. Ward, but they nevertheless shared certain characteristics. They were both clumsy and indifferent to their physical appearance; they were both impetuous, querulous and excitable in argument, while usually maintaining their good humour. They were both untroubled by ambitious dreams. This makes Henry's success at the Union even more extraordinary. At first he amused everybody by laughing so uproariously at his own jokes that the point of his stories was frequently lost.[17] Francis Doyle ascribed his success to his voice – 'the wonderful Wilberforce voice, so remarkable for its melody and power'.[18] Newman pointed to his 'sense of humour and power of repartee which makes a man brilliant in conversation and formidable to opponents', recalling one particular debate in his presidential term, when the meeting was thrown into confusion by the sudden appearance of a drunkard who attempted to make an incoherent and nonsensical speech. 'It seemed hopeless to restore order', he wrote, 'when the President arose, and looking around on the members, simply asked, "Has the noble Lord no friends here?" These words had their effect at once. . . . The offender was removed, and the debate proceeded'.[19]

Of all Henry's Oxford friendships, his attachment to Newman became in time the most intimate. Isaac Williams described it as something approaching 'idolatrous veneration' and recalled how Samuel, in later years, would petulantly remind his friends that he had 'often told Henry that he was not himself when with Newman. He loses himself and his own mind.'[20] Within a few months of their first formal introduction, Henry wrote to Newman to thank him for all his kindness, 'which has indeed, I can say without affectation, been to me that of an elder brother'. When he heard that Golightly had been often in Newman's company during the summer of 1827, he wrote: 'I am quite jealous of Golightly, that he should be making ground in your acquaintance, while I am deprived of the advantage which, however, I prize, I believe, as much as he can.'[21]

Newman was equally captivated. Time and time again he would surrender to the temptation of putting work aside to listen to his 'nonsensical chat'.[22] When Henry was about, patristic studies were thrust aside. 'Henry and I rode over and dined at Neate's', Newman wrote to Robert in September 1828. 'Indeed I have become an indefatigable equestrian – as has your brother. In consequence of our rides, I find the Fathers make marvellously little progress.'[23]

Henry was given to intense emotional attachments. According to Tom Mozley, he was at first reckoned a 'ladies' man', in consequence of his not having been to a public school and his having lived so long in the company of the pretty daughters of John Sargent.[24] In his first year, however, he was teased remorselessly for his affection for a dreamy, elegant youth called John Rogers (of Balliol). They were, Mozley writes, 'Damon and Pythias'. During a raid on Henry's rooms, a list was discovered containing the names of all those whom Henry intended to invite to a series of wine parties, and it was observed with delight that one name (concealed cryptically by the designation 'Number 14' – obviously John Rogers) appeared in every list. From that moment, of course, John Rogers was universally referred to by that label, to Henry's extreme annoyance and embarrassment.[25] Henry's feeling towards Newman was simple hero-worship. He spoke of him affectionately as Neander.[26] On one occasion he dated a letter to Robert 'Newman's birthday'.[27] In moments of idle reflection he would imitate Newman's signature, doodling over his papers, or would reproduce one of his master's favourite aphorisms – 'Humble men persecuted'.[28] All the time that Newman was away, during his second tour of Sicily in 1833, Henry was nervous and upset. When Newman failed to return on the appointed date, he wrote to Robert to say that he was 'in the state my mother would be in if she cared as much for him as I do'.[29]

Newman was fully aware of all this. Looking back on that Sicilian tour and reading through the account of the desperate illness which he had contracted there, he thought – seven years later – to add some finishing touches. Then he mused:

> What am I writing it for? . . . Whom have I, whom can I have, who would take an interest in it? I was going to say, I only have found one who ever took that sort of affectionate interest in me as to be pleased with such details – and that is H. Wilberforce, and what shall I ever see of him? [Henry was married by this time] This is the sort of interest a wife takes, and none but she – it is a woman's interest – and that interest, so be it, shall never be taken in me. Never, so be it, will I be other than God has found me. All my habits for years, my tendencies, are towards celibacy. I could not take that interest in this world which marriage requires.[30]

Can one wonder, then, that Newman took Henry into his closest confidence, addressed him in his letters as 'Charissime', the title given only to a chosen few, and – after Hurrell Froude's death in 1836 – thought first of him as the person to whom he should communicate his doubts as to his ability to refute Wiseman's attacks on the Anglican position, his first inkling that the Church of England might be in schism? Indeed, it could be argued that Henry's close intimacy with Newman had a more profound effect upon his subsequent life and development than any other factor. The clearest proof of this is, of course, the decisive influence which his friendship with Newman was to have on his own conversion to the Roman Church in 1850. Earlier than this, however, Newman's advice was sought and taken over another fateful decision. Should Henry take orders or try his hand at the Bar?

His first plan, after taking his degree, had been to sit for an Oriel fellowship; but in spite of Robert's cramming,[31] he was defeated in the contest by C. P. Eden, a former Bible Clerk of the College. Henry thereupon resolved to enter his name at Lincoln's Inn, and in the summer of 1831 took a few months' holiday in Switzerland with his brother William (who had fled the country with his family to escape the most importunate of his creditors) in the hope that a rest and a change of scene might help him to come to a final decision. William reported on Henry's state to Robert, approving the step which he had taken with regard to Lincoln's Inn. 'I think he will do well', he wrote, 'but he must learn sometime or other to treat with less roughness the prejudices and opinions of others than he does at present. It is a lesson he will learn at the Bar.'[32] He had been much amused at their mother's anxiety over Henry's welfare in foreign lands. 'My mother's short postscript', he told Robert in August 1831, 'gives a certain proof that she is much more comfortable, for after saying that he [their father] is better, it goes on in a strain of lamentations and fears about old Henry which is perfectly amusing really speaking of him as if totally unable to take care of himself and as liable to loss as if a mere parcel without the means either of voluntary locomotion or of speaking or writing.'[33]

Henry wrote to Robert in October from Geneva to say that he was still undecided about the future: 'I cannot *make up my mind* that it is my *duty* to go to the bar and I am *sure* that I cannot do it without a considerable measure of inclination.'[34]

In February 1832 Henry received a long letter from Newman.

> Now as to Law and Church [he wrote]. It is certainly a most difficult thing to give an opinion; and I do not like to say anything. However it is my opinion, such as it is, that you would have a greater field of usefulness in the Church than in the Law – You are *sure* of usefulness, more or less in the former – and a bird in the hand etc. In the Law you cannot do religious good *by it* till your name is known and then *if you* continue practice, it is only *your name* that does good, for time you have none. As things are, I am sceptical of the great good of going into Parliament – doubtless every additional religious voice there is a good – but the question is whether you would do *more* good than you might reasonable expect *ultimately* in the Church.

If you say that, should the Church require defenders, it is better they should be laymen than clerics, I scruple – it is better indeed for *them*, but worse for the Church. Surely, however it may show their sincerity, it shows greater strength in the Church to put forth *her own* peculiar servants as champions – at least in an age when promotion is not the necessary reward of standing in the breach. I think this is too much forgotten. If a lawyer's life be a martyrdom, it is good to be such – but put it quietly to yourself, whether you dare aspire to a martyrdom? Is it not so? You have not (whatever be the cause) disciplined yourself yet for hot temptation. What right have you to thrust yourself into it? Can I recollect (I hope I do you injustice) one instance in which you have exhibited that self mastery which gives me hope you will act the Elijah in a tide of corruption?

I wish you would resolve on making yourself a divine or scholar (i.e. compatible as it is with clerical employments). They say you have a competency. When I spoke of Mr Rose, I suppose you observed I spoke of his Magazine now forthcoming, and since I began myself to write in such at 20, it seems no great compliment to another to consider him at 23 old enough for such employments. You mistake me, if you think I consider clergymen, as such, should not marry. I only think there should be among the clergy enough unmarried to give a character of strength to the whole – and that therefore everyone should ask himself whether he is called to the celibate. I think Hebrew would hardly suit you – yet if you thought of it earnestly, should rejoice as at a vigorous measure. I wish you would take a curacy in this neighbourhood. . . .[35]

Henry returned to Oxford for a while to prepare himself for the English and Theological Essay prizes. By the summer of 1832 he had definitely resolved to prepare for orders. He must, of course, seek a title; and here he was assisted by John Sargent. Henry had known the Sargent family intimately for many years. As a little boy he had been deeply attached to the eldest of the five daughters – Charlotte, who died in 1818 while still only a girl.[36] In the days when he had been tutored at Graffham Rectory, he and young Harry Sargent were inseparable. They had played together as boys, and so they continued in later life. Samuel observed to Robert in 1831 that there was always horseplay when the two found themselves together under the same roof and that a recent visit by Henry to Lavington had been no exception. 'Henry and Harry have just had a battle on the sofa in the Library and the former grew so savage that we were obliged to separate them. They fight upon all occasions, every hour, and Grandmama declares she must leave the house if it continues. . . .'[37]

Since John Sargent in 1832 was in need of a curate to serve the tiny church of Upwaltham, a hamlet about two miles from his house, it was not surprising that he put the proposition to Henry. Henry hesitated before accepting. Newman was against it. Caroline, Mary and Sophia were, after all, still unmarried and might prove something of a distraction to a young curate still undecided about his vocation to the celibate state. Also the feminine atmosphere would be positively harmful.

> I fear the ladies of the house will make you idle [Newman wrote]. You will be lounging and idling with them all day. There is this mischief attends all familiar society between us and the fair sex. We cannot talk without being idle, but ladies are employing their fingers in a thousand ways while they encourage idleness in us.[38]

Henry expressed his quandary to Robert in November 1832:

> As to Lavington I do not find my mind so far settled that I can comfort-ably take orders at Christmas. Such being the case I consider it a point of duty not to let myself be hurried into doing so by the temptation which Mr Sar.'s offer holds out. I therefore wrote on Tuesday evening to decline it saying at the same time what my reason was, so that he must see how glad I should be to take it if he could wait till Easter. I had thought that possibly they might take a *locum tenens* till Easter, and it occurred to me that *Manning* would be a very fit man if he would accept it. I sounded him (of course I could do no more without authority from Mr Sar.) and I am sure that he will gladly take it from Christmas to Easter. I think there is no doubt that Mr Sargent would like this and there is no difficulty about it as he is to be ordained at Christmas *upon his fellowship* and therefore will be quite at liberty . . . .
>
> I certainly feel the dangers you mention as to a residence at Lavington. They are serious, especially *one of them*. The second, I mean that I have lived there as a child, does not apply with much force because I shall not if I go there have to preach (as a general rule) at Lavington or Graffham, but only to read prayers, and at Upwaltham I am not known at all. . . . One objection I mean that it would be better for *me* to act more inde-pendently than I should do with a resident Rector to whom I looked up much would not really signify if I did not keep the situation long, which neither party contemplates, and at Waltham I should be always acting very much on my own foundation.[39]

It is a pity that Henry did not say more about Robert's objection and that Robert's previous letter has not survived. Clearly Henry was already troubled at the prospect of serving an Evangelical rector, whom he greatly admired, at a time when his own views were becoming increasingly 'apos-tolical'. At least Newman could advise him no further for a little while. He was busy making ready for his foreign tour in the company of Hurrell Froude. By the time of his return (the following Easter) the situation had somewhat changed. Manning went to Lavington as Henry proposed and by Easter was engaged to Caroline Sargent. His stay became more permanent than anyone had envisaged. Henry was therefore obliged to think again and to seek a title elsewhere.

Chapter 3

FAMILY AFFAIRS

1. *Lavington and the Sargents*

Henry Manning, in his early days as a Roman Catholic, often felt homesick. He would sometimes grieve for old friends, and although he would assure himself that the past was better dead and buried, there was a part of his mind which persistently refused to respond. He was haunted by the memory of old familiar scenes. From Rome, in 1852, he wrote a short anguished letter to his penitent Mary Wilberforce who – herself a Sargent – would understand. 'I am afraid it is a weakness of mine', he said, 'to remember the past, but it rises up to me like the background of some old sacred picture where even earth looks like Paradise. Lavington in 1833. The Hill and the Friday evening lecture at Graffham, and Upwaltham Church. ... The Downs seem to me only less beautiful than heaven.'[1]

He had lived there for seventeen years. Yet those who have seen Lavington only once may cherish a memory of unspoiled beauty and perfect seclusion which time cannot dim. For an estranged member of the family, like young Wilfrid Wilberforce, one of Henry's sons who had been brought up a Roman Catholic, to go to Lavington as he did in 1873 to attend the funeral of his uncle, the Bishop of Winchester, and to see the setting of his mother's childhood days was an experience almost too precious to record. His family history seemed to be written into every inch of the springy downland turf which he trod as the cortège moved slowly to the tiny graveyard at the back of Lavington church. There he saw Samuel laid to rest beside three other family graves – those of Emily Wilberforce, of whom Wilfrid had no memory save what his mother had told him of her beauty and the torment which the Bishop had endured at her early death; Caroline Manning, the lovely wife of the future Cardinal who died only four years after her marriage; and young Herbert Wilberforce, Samuel's eldest and favourite son who, as a lieutenant in the Royal Navy, died at the age of twenty-three from an illness contracted in the Crimea.

When Wilfrid came to describe the scene to his mother it was the beauty and tranquillity of Lavington that he chiefly remembered. It had been a hot summer day in late July. 'It is curious', he wrote, 'that the sunshine, especially in the country, never strikes one as a breach of *mourning*. It is wonderfully bright and cheerful, yet it never seems *garish*, and we were glad of so much brightness, though our hearts were heavy enough. . . . I think nothing can excel the loveliness of the Sussex downs with their white chalk peeping out, on a fine July morning.'[2]

The Sargents had lived at Lavington since 1778. In the two preceding centuries the great Elizabethan mansion with its vast estate had been owned first by the Garton family, from whom it had passed by marriage to a Peterborough family, the Ormes, in the middle of the seventeenth century. The third of this line, Garton Orme, M.P. for Arundel between 1741 and 1747 – painted by Highmore as an innocent little boy dressed in blue, seated at a spinet – was, in fact, the family's evil genius. In the first place, it was rumoured that he murdered his first wife (Charlotte Hanway) by putting her down a well, so that he could be free to marry the daughter (Anne La Fitte) of the local rector. And indeed, when Manning came in 1845 to supervise the moving of the family coffins during the restoration of Lavington Church, he caused one of them to be opened because of its excessive weight and found it to be full of stones.[3] Secondly, Garton Orme had been a gambler, and in order to pay his debts sold at least half the estate and a large portion of the family treasures.

Orme's third misdeed was to have brought a curse upon the family, pronounced under a willow tree on the Graffham road by the outraged father of a local girl whom he had seduced. The exact form of the curse is not known, but it was generally believed to have involved a malediction upon the male line of the family, a supposition which gained currency from the undoubted fact that after Garton Orme's death no son ever succeeded to the Lavington estate until 1873. There was a certain spot at the new boundary of the estate, which marked the limit of Garton Orme's sale of the property, where the eldest son of the family was supposed to spit to free himself from the taint of his ancestor's sins. Samuel was sufficiently affected by the legend to make it the subject of one of his more lugubrious cautionary tales in his *Note Book of a Country Clergyman*, published in 1833, entitled 'The Hall', a melancholy chronicle of deaths in unspeakable agony visited upon the innocent victims of an affronted beldam who had cursed the house of St Aubyn under an oak tree.*

Garton Orme's only daughter, Charlotte, married in 1751 into the

* See footnote on p. 120.

Sussex family of Bettesworth. There was one daughter of this marriage, also called Charlotte, who became sole heiress on her mother's death in 1758. Twenty years later she married John Sargent, the son of a director of the Bank of England. These were the parents of the Rev. John Sargent and the grandparents of the four beautiful girls who allied with the Wilberforces, the Mannings and the Ryders. They were both still alive, living in Lavington House, at the time of Samuel's marriage to Emily in 1828. By this time the old Elizabethan house had been entirely rebuilt in the Georgian style. John Sargent the elder, who had served for a short while in the Ordnance Office and the Treasury, died in 1831. His widow (referred to in the family letters as 'old Mrs Sargent' or 'Grandmama') survived him for ten years, outliving also her son John and five of her grandchildren. The Lavington inheritance passed via Emily Wilberforce (the eldest surviving granddaughter) to her husband Samuel in 1841. John Sargent, Rector of Lavington, never therefore succeeded to his father's property, residing until his death in 1833 at Graffham Rectory.

John Sargent had been Rector of Graffham since 1805 and of the adjoining parish of Lavington since 1813. Educated at Eton and King's, where he came under the guiding influence of Charles Simeon and formed a strong attachment to Henry Martyn, he soon became convinced of his vocation to enter the ministry. Unfortunately his father disapproved and pressed him to enter the legal profession, Simeon advising his pupil to accept his lot with meekness. 'You are *certain*', he said, 'that you are acting according to your duty in obeying the wishes of your father: whereas I could not say so in the other case.'[4] His father soon realised his mistake, and his mother provided him with a title for orders by presenting him to the family living.

In 1804 he married Mary Smith, the only daughter of Abel Smith the banker (the niece, therefore, of Lord Carrington and of Elizabeth Smith, the first wife of William Manning). Her father and William Wilberforce were first cousins, and indeed William had known Mary well since her

---

* S. Wilberforce, *The Note Book of a Country Clergyman* (1833), 196, where the curse is given as follows:

> 'Though many a year this oak hath past:
> But the light'ning shall rift its head at last:
> Gladsome and gay is the summer's day:
> But the night shall come, and its beauty decay:
> And the name of St Aubyn shall pass away.'

childhood.* It was quite natural that she should turn to him for his advice on her proposed marriage to John Sargent. William consulted Lord Carrington about the financial position and calculated that the young couple would have an income of about £1,000 a year, which 'when all which is hereafter to come to you both shall have fallen in' would increase to about £2,200. It was reckoned that the Lavington estate 'with the wood' would be worth £50,000 and that Abel Smith's estate, which Mary would inherit, would be about £20,000.

> Now remember, my dear Mary [William wrote], that a fortune is great or small according to anyone's situation in life. If I lived with my wife quietly in the country (Oh I wish I did! and how much more does she! ...) if I were for instance Vicar of Graffham – O how I wish I were! – ... I should be as affluent as I now am with half my present fortune. I believe I could go further than this – really a clergyman with £1000 p.a. is not a necessitous man ... I don't suppose you would wish, nor I am sure would your friends wish, that you should make a brilliant figure at Lewes Races, or bring down the newest fashions to Graffham, after studying them in your own assemblies in Portman Square. Still, I confess frankly that I wish you had more – much more – and why? Because, my dear Mary, I think so highly both of you and Mr S. as to be sure that the largest fortune if you had it would be expended to the Glory of God and for the benefit of your fellow creatures.
>
> I have seen much of life – I have read much – and I can truly declare to you, that my own observations confirm the truth of the opinion which has been laid down by all writers of eminence, that a moderate sufficiency and the middle station of life, are most favourable to happiness. . . . From the uniform account I have received from those who know Mr S. best I have not the smallest doubt, that he is a man of good understanding, of warm affections, of extraordinary proficiency as a Christian, and eminently formed for domestic life.[5]

This was no exaggerated statement of John Sargent's qualities. He soon acquired the reputation of a model country pastor and came to be regarded by his Evangelical friends rather as Keble came to be venerated by High Churchmen. 'He walked in the low valley where the pastures of God's presence are often the greenest', Samuel wrote of him.[6] Simeon was a frequent visitor to his home; Henry Martyn sought strength from his friendship. Was a man of such talent wasted in a tiny parish? Sargent knew that this was not so. 'My parishes are small', he would say, 'but I find that a small parish will produce ample occupation for a minister, if he is inclined to seek for it. The generality of my parishioners . . . are

* 'She was almost my daughter', he once wrote of her. Wilberforce MSS. E. 12 January 1831.

very ignorant of the true foundation on which to build.'[7] He was a true Evangelical to the very last, but of that number which saw the necessity of combating fanatics and respecting the principle of order in the Church. As Samuel put it:

> Deep and reverent was his affection for that branch of Christ's Church from which in infancy he had received the sacred mystery of baptism, and with whose holy orders he was now invested. There was a marked difference on this point between his judgment and feelings and those of some, whose ardent piety he most highly esteemed, and with whom he was constantly connected in active efforts for the spread of God's word and kingdom. Never in this age of various and unbounded religious excitement was he led astray from the path of Christian sobriety. The dazzling light of novelty had no charms for him. In the province of religion, the suggestions of the imagination were at once and unhesitatingly submitted to the scrutiny of a sober and searching judgment. He was strong in the irresistible strength of an humble simplicity.[8]

John Sargent's marriage was a supremely happy one – his family circle, from all accounts, a joy to enter. He had seven children in all – the two boys, John Garton and Henry Martyn (Harry), and the five girls, Charlotte (who died in 1818), Emily, Caroline, Mary and Sophia – 'as fair as the light around them', as William described them to James Stephen in 1817.[9] A fuller description of the girls may be found in a memoir of George Dudley Ryder, written for private circulation by one of his sons:

> The beauty of these sisters was of no ordinary kind. Bishop Wilberforce used to say the most perfect likeness of his wife was the face of St Catharine of Alexandria in the beautiful picture representing her as borne by angels after her martyrdom for burial on Mount Sinai. As to my mother [Sophia] by far the most perfect likeness of her was Our Lady in Leonardo da Vinci's beautiful picture *La Madonna del lago*. Shortly after her death my father was told of the picture by one of his brothers and purchased it at considerable expense. When it was first put up in the drawing room at the Warren I was but a child of about six, but the moment I saw it I cried out how like it was to my mother. I well remember my father saying 'Hush! Hush!' for his heart was still bleeding from the terrible loss he had sustained.[10]

Thomas Mozley met the four of them in 1829 at a breakfast party at Oriel given by Robert Wilberforce, looking at them 'with a strong mixture of curiosity and admiration'. 'Mrs S. Wilberforce was a bride in her first year. The brighter constellation must have eclipsed the brothers from my memory, for all I remember of Samuel was his springing up to remind the party they had a great deal to do and must set about it.'[11] They went for a tour round the college, and were taken to see the holy of holies, the Fellows' Common Room; the ladies were charmed at the dingy masculinity of its furnishings and effects and vouchsafed the opinion that it must be a very happy place. The next day Mozley discussed the sisters with Henry Wilberforce, describing Mary as 'cool', meaning calm and self-collected, at which Henry rather took offence. 'The youngest,' Mozley writes, 'seemed a mere child, indeed she hardly looked more when I saw her at Hanbury, in Staffordshire, seven years later, as Mrs George Ryder, a very sylph in form and in feature. Mrs S. Wilberforce I met again, not two years before her death . . . at Winchester. She was still beautiful, but her strength was evidently declining'.[12] All the Sargent offspring, he noted – even the boys – had about them a strange delicacy of complexion, 'a peach bloom' on the cheeks, which enhanced their attractiveness; it could also be taken as a disturbing sign of a frailty of constitution, giving warning of the tragic succession of tubercular infections which were to ravage the family in the next two decades.*

The beauty of the Sargent daughters was matched by their surroundings. Though sheltered by the beech-covered downs, Lavington House commanded a superb view to the north. You could see Petworth Church spire in the distance, and – on a clear day – the Hog's Back beyond. The garden was walled, enclosing sloping lawns, terraced walks, an old kitchen garden designed in Elizabethan times with long lines of espalier apple-trees, interspersed with standard pears, borders of hollyhocks, roses and Japanese anemones, grassy paths flanked by lilies of the valley; against the three-hundred-year-old wall grew peaches, nectarines and figs, with at one corner an enormous fig-tree reckoned by H. P. Liddon to be the second oldest in England. All about the house lay a country ideal for riding; a chalk road just beyond the outer wall led straight to the top of the downs. When Samuel was master of Lavington he would always take his visitors up this road – to the gazebo in Tegleaze Wood – and there he would read to them from the *Christian Year*. He would then inscribe all their names on a piece of paper and place this in a bottle which was hidden there under a stone. There were many other walks too: 'down to Dominion Wood to hear the nightingales, to the Tumbling Bay at Maine, through "Botany Bay", full of rare ferns, to the Common, to Pot Brook to lunch with the shooters, and the shortest to the trout ponds to catch a fish'.[13]

As the years have passed, the descendants of the sinister Garton Orme

---

* T. Mozley, *op. cit.*, I. 132. This complexion was probably inherited from the Smiths (their mother's side). See Mozley's description of Mosley Smith, a first cousin of Mary Sargent, who at Charterhouse was noted for his 'pinkness' of expression. Also his elder brother in the Derby Bank, frequently teased as 'Sweet pea Smith'.

have severed their connection with Lavington. Perhaps his ghost no longer walks the garden; the willow-tree, under which the famous curse was uttered, has been burnt down; but the house remains, and the church, and the family graves; and, in the words of the last of the Lavington squires, 'the glory of the hillside .... changing only with the seasons; the beech trees, golden in the autumn, deep red and blue in the winter, a radiant green in the spring'.[14]

II. *Life at Checkenden*

Samuel Wilberforce and Emily Sargent were married at Lavington Church on 10 June 1828, Charles Simeon officiating. Shortly before the wedding Samuel had written to Emily on her birthday:

> My prayers indeed my sweetest love are earnestly offered for you to Him who can grant it, that *many* successive years may still find and leave you happy upon this day. That they may find you every year nearer heaven and more ripe for that unfading inheritance for which you are striving. That His supporting arm may strengthen you my dearest in every trial to which you may be exposed, and that He may lead you through a path as perfectly happy as our frail hearts can bear, and my own Emily may He grant in His infinite mercy that I may still be with you to share your sorrows and your joys. May every year find us more united – more knit together, to each other and to Him. I cannot tell you my darling what I do feel for you. May God Almighty my sweetest dear, bless you and keep you: bless you with every blessing of body and soul; may His grace guide us together through life and at last may He take us to dwell together *for ever*. ... Good bye my own most fondly most tenderly and most excessively beloved Emily.[1]

They took a short honeymoon in Italy (Charles Anderson drew a little sketch of Samuel poring over an Italian grammar before they set off)[2] and, on their return, Samuel settled down to prepare himself for ordination. The search for a suitable curacy now began in earnest. Daniel Wilson, Lord Calthorpe, and C. R. Sumner were all approached and they promised to look out for 'any probable opening'.[3] A curacy at Goring was discussed, but rejected on Robert's advice (the parish was 'large, wild and lately extremely neglected').[4] Newman came forward with the suggestion of Adderbury, a little large but conveniently near Oxford.[5] Then Sumner, who had no suitable vacancies in his own diocese, suggested Checkenden, a small parish near Henley, where Samuel could have sole charge of the church while being conveniently placed for help and advice from J. B. Sumner who was then vicar of the nearby parish of Mapledurham.[6] In fact, shortly before Samuel was ordained, J. B. Sumner left Mapledurham to become Bishop of Chester, and early in the next year came forward with another offer – the living of Ribchester, near Preston. Samuel declined it. He had been only two months at Checkenden, and the move to the north would take him far from his family and friends. William Wilberforce was quite sure that it would have been a false step. The population of the parish was too large, the duties too onerous, and the likelihood of religious controversy (because of its proximity to Stonyhurst) too pressing. It would be especially unfortunate for a young man at the outset of his career to be thrown into a situation 'in which he would necessarily be almost incessantly arguing for Protestant principles – in short, would be occupied in the Religion of the head rather than of the Heart'.[7]

Checkenden, indeed, was a very different proposition. The population was barely three hundred; the village, while within riding distance of the University, was secluded among the low hills and woodland of rural Oxfordshire; the church itself was tiny, although not without interest, since the original Norman chancel and twelfth-century frescoes had both been preserved without injury or alteration. One of the main attractions, however, for Samuel and Emily was the fact that there was a rectory for their sole occupation. The retiring incumbent, William Crabtree, sent a long letter two months before the move to acquaint them with the house, its effects and its servants:

It is well you have a horse and gig [he began], for I am quite sure you could not have been comfortable without one – but I trust it is a strong horse and the lightest gig possible to be sufficiently strong. Our roads are rough – and the distances great – and all against the collar on every side to return – so that no poney could stand the work. I had one at first, but was soon obliged to sell it at a great loss, as it had been overstrained. A good horse is best in every way and it costs no more to keep. . . . In addition to your gig you will want a covered errand cart for luggage etc. – like the baker's carts you see about London. That you can have from me. You will find it desirable, especially to save your gig in the bad weather.

Now with respect to the Man-servant. You can make your own terms with him – I will tell you my opinion of him – what he can do – and what I pay him – then you can make your own calculations. He is strictly honest and sober – rather a prosing talker but not a particle of mischief about him. His work is to clean all the knives and shoes – fetch in wood – draw water – sift cinders – take care of the horse and gig which he does well – and do the main work in the garden. Occasionally I allow him a woman at 7d a day to weed – and a regular gardener to prune the wall-trees. I give him no livery – only he gets my left-off clothes. The wages are £10 per ann. with board and lodging in the house. He belongs to the parish which is an important point as the farmers are frightened at the idea of our making an extra-parishioner.

Your idea is to have your man live out of the house. Now if I may obtrude my advice I should decidedly discountenance such a plan – for two reasons. One is, that a common labourer's pay would not be sufficient – besides you would find probably that you would be keeping him with a great part of his victuals after all. Another great reason is – for the sake of protection. I regret to say that retired as we are, we are too near London to be secure. A short time ago a neighbour's house was broken into and plate and linen to a great amount stolen. Only last Thursday the house at Lane End was attempted – and I have thought it prudent since to have two lamps burning all night in different parts of the house – and the man to sleep down stairs with a gun loaded with ball at his side and a sword-stick. It is lamentable to think what a state the country is in, at least in our neighbourhood, where six or seven years ago a burglary was almost utterly unknown.

With regard to the female servants, if you have trusty ones already by all means keep them. They will be well worth their coach-hire in addition to their wages. But I must request a positive answer early, that if you bring your own, I may give mine warning. My two are – a steady decent woman – a plain cook at 12 guineas a year, and a stout girl, as housemaid, at 7 guineas. I could not particularly recommend the latter, because she is not over bright, but she is very well-behaved. The cook has a violent temper in the kitchen – but she is respectful and I believe honest. Yet if you are fortunate enough to have servants already that you like and approve, you cannot do better than bring them. . . .

I have laid in for you 8 stacks of ash roots, split for use at 5/- per stack. Next week I will order some coals. I shall also brew this week 84 gallons of beer to serve you and myself as a winter stock. What I leave you will pay me for at cost price. I brew 5 bushels at 9/- with 4 lbs hops at 1/4 to make the above quantity. My man brews well. In spite of all your care, you will find beer an article of great consumption. Every bringer of a message or errand expects a pint of beer – but you see home-brewing is not dear. You will find a large store of potatos and onions – and the garden well cropped – and of course you leave it the same. You may have part of our linen – as all our pillows are *Oreillers* as the French call them – a large size. I hope I have touched on everything essential. You will oblige me much by an early reply to the doubtful points. . . .[8]

The hint at increasing lawlessness and violence did not go unheeded. The ugliness of the political scene had made of Samuel, he admitted to his friend Patrick Boyle, 'a very high Tory'.

The state of things seems to forebode some storm, some great and violent convulsion, before equanimity can be restored to the apparently jarring elements of our political constitution. . . . My own belief is that things will grow worse and worse. I think that the Church will fall within fifty years entirely, and the State will not survive it much longer.[9]

Charles Anderson sent him hair-raising accounts of incendiarism in the north;[10] and in 1830 even Lavington had its troubles, one of the many demonstrations among the agricultural workers of southern England, agitating for higher wages with a truculent confidence engendered by rumours of revolutionary events in France. Caroline Sargent sent the news to Emily:

This morning just before breakfast a party of Graffham men headed by the Bridgers and Fleet, came to the kitchen door and Papa went to speak to them. They were tolerably civil and after Papa had given them a lecture they walked off. Stoner had with difficulty escaped from them as he was coming to his work for they threatened to drag everyone through a pond who would not come in with them. Howick the shoemaker who was one of them carried a lanthorn with him which Papa has no doubt was a sign that he meant to burn the stacks if he did not get what he wanted and Mr King said that it was enough to take him up. We heard the other day, that some of the people said they should be contented if they could but have the Parson's head. Whether this is true or not I cannot say but Papa said as he was the Parson he should certainly enquire who wanted his head.

Today has been Petworth fair day, and has turned out rather flat and stupid after the *rumtion* as Stoner calls it, that was expected. The soldiers were armed to defend the Prison when it was beseiged! Only suppose they had all been let loose upon New Grove. Papa is very much laughed at for his fears by all except Grandmama: he would not let Mama or Mary go to the meeting the other night, and he stopped Mama from going with Aunt Rosamund to New Grove this morning to fetch Sophy: we expect soon that he will barricade us into the house for the winter. The barn is still watched every night, and will be so till it is insured, and there seems more reason in it since Howick's lanthorn has appeared. . . .[11]

As things turned out, John Sargent kept his head, and Samuel his property, intact. Actually the sojourn at Checkenden lasted only sixteen months; sufficient time, however, for Samuel to display that ardent evangelical zeal allied to a strong respect for Church principles which remained a consistent feature of his churchmanship throughout his career. Soon after his arrival he instituted Sunday afternoon lectures on the Gospels and introduced special services on Saints' Days. He experienced his first encounter with dissenters and quickly learnt the perilous consequences of teaching tending towards antinomianism. While it would be an exaggeration to say that his short ministry at Checkenden converted Samuel into a High Churchman, it is clear that his frequent meetings and conversations with Oriel friends, combined with his distaste for methodistical enthusiasm and his fears over the threatened position of the Church, led him much nearer to the position occupied by his two brothers than he had hitherto been disposed to adopt. Thus he hotly attacked Grimshaw's biography of Legh Richmond because it gave the entirely false impression that it was possible to repudiate baptismal regeneration by resting on the concurrence of Hooker.[12] His admiration for the Caroline divines became more intense. 'I want', he wrote to Robert in January 1830, 'any old, tidy, not expensive copy of the Eikon Basilike you can procure me. I should hate a new edition, though I suppose there is not one. I want this not merely upon the general principle that it is a shame for an Englishman and above all a clerk to be without this work of the blessed martyr's, but also because I want to read it through'.[13]

His severe denunciation of dissenters in his neighbourhood disturbed his father and caused him to rebuke him. It is interesting to observe that the fault which William especially deprecated was one which was to cause him trouble many times in his later career – his tendency to form his opinions on persons and affairs too quickly and to denounce before he had examined dispassionately both the reasons for his taking offence and the possible consequences of his speaking out.*

> I trust I need not fear your misconstruing me [William wrote on 19 March 1829], and supposing I can be advising you either to be roguish, or shabbily reserved. But really I do think, that you may produce an unfavourable and false impression of your principles and professional character, by talking unguardedly about *Methodistical* persons and opinions. . . . Mrs Reed may report you as *unsound* to the Bishop of Winchester and he imbibe a prejudice against you. Besides my dear Samuel I am sure you will not *fire* when I say that you may see reason, on further reading and reflection and more experience, to change or qualify some of the opinions you may now hold. I owe (I should not be honest if I did not say so) that I think I have myself witnessed occasions which have strengthened with me the impression that you may need this hint against needlessly exciting prejudices.[14]

Samuel did not modify his judgment. Five years later he wrote to

---

* Gladstone was to upbraid him for the same fault forty years later (in 1869), warning him against 'a habit of too free comments or remarks'. Wilberforce MSS. G. 168. The most notorious instances of 'needlessly exciting prejudices' are his conduct of the Hampden case in 1847 and his strictures on *Essays and Reviews* and Darwin's *Origin of Species*.

Newman to complain most bitterly about the conduct of his successor at Checkenden, who was subverting all the principles of Church order for which Samuel had laboured. He asked Newman to have a word with the Bishop of Oxford about him. 'His procuring Mr Sherwin from Reading to preach in his turn, and from the altar,' he observed, 'are I fear parts of a system, and not eccentric deviations from it; and unless his views be materially altered he is likely to be again eminently pernicious.'[15]

In his pastoral work Samuel made a deep impression upon his flock. His father encouraged him to open a lending library, and promised to keep him plentifully supplied with copies of the *Christian Observer* and the *Church Missionary Register*.[16] Emily frequently accompanied him in attending sick-beds. One such visit she described to her father:

> I have been with Sam to-day to the sick bed of a poor girl of 15, who is dying of a consumption. She is a most humble sincere and patient Christian wishing to be at rest with her Lord but quite willing to wait His good pleasure and her only anxiety seems how to comfort her poor heartbroken mother. It is quite a lesson to see her. . . . Sam asked her if she felt to love her Saviour and she answered with the greatest earnestness 'As much as ever I can love, Sir'. What should you be without Him? 'Most miserable.' 'Do you feel very sorry when you grieve this Saviour?' 'I always felt very sorry for my sins, but now I feel *doubly* sorry.' I saw she had her Bible in bed and I asked her what text she felt most comfort in. She said 'There is one I love more than all others, *Jesus Christ came into the World to save sinners* and so He came to save me. No one has sinned so much.'[17]

Robert was a frequent visitor from Oxford to help Samuel out. On one occasion, when asked to preach, he read a sermon written by John Keble.[18] Until Samuel was admitted to priest's orders (in December 1829), he regularly came over to celebrate on 'Sacrament Sunday'. His advice was often sought. How should one address 'nominal' Christians, should one assume the best or the worst?[19] Should one hold out in refusing baptism if the godparents were non-communicants?[20]

One of their most welcome visitors was Louisa Noel, the niece of the celebrated evangelical preacher Baptist Noel. From her childhood she had been Emily's most intimate friend and was always addressed by Samuel and Emily as 'sister'. ('She is a kind of Emily Long', Emily once described her to her father.[21]) They were well furnished with Oxford news, for Oakeley, Froude, Frederic Rogers and George Dudley Ryder all came to stay for short visits. In July 1829 they were called upon to entertain another old Oriel friend, Sir George Prevost, who, having recently married, came to exhibit his wife. Emily reported to her mother:

Lady Prevost is ... very ladylike and pleasing, but her mother – Oh! her mother! – is something quite horrible. She is huge and black with a long, long, grey beard and she was dressed in a short blue common coloured gown *just* like the maid's with black stockings and boots. She called me Madame and would sit the whole evening behind the blind looking at the black night. In short she was so odd, so hideous, so huge and so like an ogress that I expected every moment to be devoured.[22]

They were just beginning to settle down, with the first of their family (a daughter called Emily, 'Arnie' or 'Ella' for short) just a month old, when Bishop Sumner wrote to Samuel to tell him that he was now in a position to offer him a living in his own diocese. This was the rectory of Brighstone on the Isle of Wight, worth £700 a year, with a fine house and a manageable population of some 700.

I may say with the utmost truth [Sumner wrote] that I have selected you for the situation, not without much serious consideration, because I know no one whom I think so likely to justify my choice for a sphere of usefulness which, as I may have an opportunity of explaining to you, is in some respects peculiar. But besides this *first* feeling, I have great pleasure in reflecting that a living on the Isle of Wight will probably be particularly acceptable to you on account of the suitableness of the climate to Mrs S. Wilberforce's health and its vicinity to her own family.

Nor can I refrain from adding that if your Father derives any gratification from this proposal, it will be a compensation for not a few of the anxieties of my office to have had the power of making an offer of the kind to the son of one whom I have so many reasons, public and private, to love and honour.[23]

Samuel acted at once. Within a fortnight he had been inducted and had read himself in, and arrangements were made for the family to leave Checkenden and move into their new rectory at the end of July 1830. He sent an account of his first impressions to Robert in June.

... a very pretty village, the cottages ... neatly built of stone and thatched. They are sprinkled about and interspersed with elm-trees. The church is a very pleasant, pretty edifice. The rectory is a capitally complete house for what it does contain: anything more entirely complete for a bachelor's house you never saw; but for a family house it will not do without some alterations. ... The principal inhabitants are yeomen farmers who have inherited their farms from their ancestors, time without mind. The register goes back as far as 1645, and therefore, of course, bears Bp. Ken's (incumbent from 1667/9 – 1670) handwriting.... I pray God it may be a sphere for useful labour; it is one, I already see, of much more difficulty than Checkenden.[24]

Sumner had written of the 'peculiar' nature of the work at Brighstone.

John Sargent also noted the toughness of the assignment, while delighting in the opportunity which it gave to his son-in-law to evangelise in an area notorious for villainy and loose living.

> In your varied feelings dearest S. I perfectly participate [he wrote], but I must say that it scarcely in my mind would have been possible to have selected from any diocese – had all the bishops given you a carte blanche – a more desirable piece of preferment. I had been thinking of it and wishing that I could fix you there. . . . The smugglers and the Barracks are not the pleasantest soil to cultivate, but who can say what the Gospel-plough may do even there – and may many my dear S. have cause to bless God for your coming amongst them.[25]

On every account the move to Brighstone was a sensible one. In the next few months it became clear that the new preferment, with its higher stipend and larger house, had come not a moment too soon. During the latter part of 1830 and the early months of 1831, the full extent of the disastrous speculations of the spendthrift brother William was revealed, and the crash threatened to be so ruinous that his father was forced to put Highwood to let. He had now to look to his married children to provide him with a home.

III. *The Speculations of an Eldest Son*

What had happened to the traditional business acumen of the Wilber-forces, which had in the eighteenth century gained for the family sufficient wealth to enable them to rise to a position of eminence? It had scarcely shown itself in the great Emancipator who was wholly indifferent to money matters save to thank God for providing him with the where-withal to support religious and philanthropic causes. Samuel commented on this to Robert in 1836, when James Stephen had unfairly accused their father of being in part responsible for the foolish financial operations of his eldest son.

> The truth is [Samuel wrote] that, as my father said I dare say often to you as he did to me, 'William is risking his own fortune and *considering every-thing* I think it is the safest thing to let him do it. It is I think an *innocent* employment and that is a great thing and I trust that the degradation of it may be useful to him, though I own I think William had not a due sense of this as I have made him angry once or twice by hinting it.' Now all this was quite another thing from sharing the blame of poor William's over sanguine ignorance of life.[1]

The only one of the sons who appears to have been able to manage his financial affairs efficiently was Robert. At least by 1852 he had saved £10,000 to buy himself an estate in Connemara to which he could retire into obscurity when the time came for him to resign his Anglican preferments.[2] Henry was, as might be expected, wildly extravagant as a young man (in 1835 Robert upbraided him for spending £55 on a second-hand piano),[3] and Samuel always found it exceedingly difficult to live within his income. He had to borrow £100 from Robert in 1831[4]; he was overdrawn at the bank in 1833,[5] and by 1835 was in debt to the tune of £200.[6] 'It is a melancholy fact how naturally I spend money', he wrote to Robert mournfully after sounding his mother for one of many loans.[7] He found the expense of becoming a bishop so crippling that he had to confess to Robert in 1846 that he could not afford the £40 or £50 necessary to convey the family to Burton Agnes for their summer visit.[8] Shortly before this, however, he had given £1,000 towards the building of a new church at Gosport – an action which prompted the Archbishop to question his sanity. Robert passed the remark on to Samuel, anxiously enquiring about his solvency.[9] On another occasion, Samuel took it into his head to advise Robert about his investments and involved them in a loss of some £500 apiece.[10]

The misfortune of brother William was that he combined a bad business head with a sanguine disposition. 'Oh I sincerely wish that poor William was tired of speculation', Samuel wrote to Charles Anderson in 1831, 'but (most private) he has that unbounded sanguineness of temper that he finds out some good reason why he should not gather experience from every past failure.'[11] In other respects he does not appear to have been particularly endearing. Marianne Thornton said that 'he never was endurable'[12]; he was apparently very fat,[13] but the testimony of Coupland, who suggests that he suffered from poor health,[14] and of Miss Trevor who describes him as a 'semi-invalid',[15] appears to conflict with a description by Robert in a letter to Samuel in September 1840 where he writes of William as being 'always violently well'.[16] In his own letters he complained from time to time of a delicate stomach.[17] When he grew older he indulged in grotesque mannerisms with his dentures, Newman recalled – he 'throws the whole set out of the gums upon his tongue, and chews them, as an infant might a coral. I never saw anything so strange.'[18] Yet for all his eccentric ways he still had something of his father's charm. Agnes Wrangham, who knew him through her friendship with his wife Mary Owen, described him in 1828 to Jane Legard as 'the most attentive and kind of all the married race, his voice and manner are even more charming than formerly and his conversation is delightful even when compared with his father's'.[19]

It had been hoped that his marriage to Mary Owen in 1820 would help him to settle down after his disastrous Cambridge career. He began studying for the bar in London, and his mother thought she discerned a change for the better – he was even becoming faintly 'serious'.[20] This, however, was a transitory phase, for by 1829 the family had cause to deplore his spiritual apathy.[21] There was some reason for William's depressed spirits. Of his two sons, one had died in infancy and the other boy, William, was very delicate. Also it was clear that his hopes of making a fortune were rapidly fading.

In the early 1820's William launched out into agriculture. He had fallen in with a would-be business partner, Major Close, who had presented him with a grandiose scheme for milk-farming on a very large scale, offering his services as manager of the project if William could supply the large share of the capital. In fact the capital was chiefly supplied by William's father. The concern appears to have been managed from properties in the Edgware Road and at St John's Wood with a Mr Cleave as agent at the Edgware Road establishment and Major Close as manager.* From the first the scheme produced poor returns; by 1829 the losses were so considerable that recovery seemed impossible. Nevertheless William held on for another eighteen months while the position steadily deteriorated.

Charles Anderson heard rumours that all was not well in April 1831 and wrote to Samuel for confirmation:

> I use no false delicacy with you, my dear Sam, and state it plainly as I have heard it – it is 'that your brother has had a sudden call for £50,000, that in consequence your father has been put to great inconvenience and that it was feared he would be compelled to part with his books'.[22]

Samuel replied on the following day:

> My dearest Charles, . . . I am sorry to say that there is too much truth in what you have heard, although it is not literally true. There has been no *sudden* loss – the loss was principally before my brother took such an active

---

* St John's Wood in the opening decades of the last century was rather different in character from what it has since become. See the letter of Robert to Samuel (Wrangham MSS. VII. 15. 22 April 1830) where he says that he has advised William not to sell in a hurry: 'St John's Wood, which is the worst part of the business, will clearly become more desirable when there is a road by it. . . . By the way I should like you to ask him (William) whether the increased facilities of communications which railroads and steam carriages will probably open, will not interfere with his business.'

part in it, whilst Major Close managed for him. Altogether I am afraid you have not in the least overstated the loss – indeed I fear it is a few thousand pounds more than you mention.[23] The injury falls upon William. He entered into the vile business contrary to all of *our* wishes at his own risk – and my father does not of course intend that the fortunes of his younger children should be injured. We give up some of our present allowance to increase my father's income. It is, of course, a dreadful blow to the family. . . .

William has made over the business in some way or other and *intends* to return to the bar: but has not just now enough to live upon in London. He is therefore gone abroad for a year. It is of course a melancholy matter that so discreditable and dirty a business should have been paid for at so dear a rate. However, I trust it may ultimately benefit dear William himself. My father does not appear the *least* out of spirits. Mr Sargent upon hearing of the matter kindly went up to him and I quote his account of his visit in a letter to me – 'I found your father quite well and with his heart so set on heaven as to soar above all pecuniary disasters. He could not call it an affliction' etc. . . .[24]

Samuel did not tell Charles the whole of the story. William and Mary and their little boy certainly went abroad. They were in Florence in November 1830, returned to England at the beginning of the new year, and set off again for Geneva in March, taking with them – to the inexplicable dismay of the brothers – a Miss Patty Smith.[25] In the meantime Richard Spooner, William's uncle, stepped in to try to sort out the financial wreckage. From his letters, and also from those written by William and Mary during their exile, it is clear that the reason for their flight was not the expense of living at home but the evasion of possible legal action by a disgruntled creditor called Eyre.

In April 1831 Richard Spooner wrote to Robert to acquaint him with some of the facts.

I proposed to William to let Cleave *buy* the business. I lend him the money for a debt due to your Father in order to prevent future responsibility, but William urged that the loss in that case would be *eventually* wholly his . . . I think Cleave can have no motive to cheat and no ground for self-deception. . . . As to William being set free from future responsibility, it would be desirable, but till St John's Wood lease and Melbourne lease can be disposed of, that cannot be. Eyre asked me £5000 to release William from the former; and if William is answerable for the dilapidations of the latter £600 or more will be required there. . . . St John's Wood I am in treaty about, not without hopes of settling it by a payment which his Father might make without injury, but all this uncertain. William ought to stay abroad till all is arranged.[26]

Two years later, the situation was still grim. William wrote to Robert from Naples:

> When I left England there was a memorandum written down and left with my uncle which specified what was the arrangement which my Father sanctioned, with respect to all the property at Edgware Road and elsewhere. If I recollect right, my father undertook to pay the mortgage interest, and all the proceeds of rent and yard interest etc. and profits were to be applied to paying off the various debts incurred and raising the capital which was invested in that business. ... About St John's Wood, I am extremely anxious to be freed from the responsibility, a responsibility so great that I dare not return till by some arrangement I am freed from the danger of a bill in Chancery which Eyre (who has behaved to me like a rogue) would certainly file against me did he know of my return to England. ... I am indeed so anxious to be out of his clutches that I feel myself incapable of judging of the price which as a matter of business I ought to be content to have paid to effect it. I therefore have left it in R. Sp.'s hands.[27]

These were hard and anxious years for William and his family. It was impossible to find suitable schooling for their son in Switzerland, because of the wide extent of onanistic practices among the children in the neighbouring schools,[28] so that the expense of securing a private tutor had to be met. Mary's health was bad. There were repeated scares of cholera outbreaks nearby. Money was running short.

> We rarely go out [William wrote to his father], all our spare money when food, house, clothing and education is paid, we spend on books, excepting what we think it prudent to lay by, in case we have to move from necessity.[29]

The prospects looked very gloomy.

> As to coming home [William told Robert], if Uncle Richard can only manage what he seemed to have some hopes of, I shall be delighted to get home: and then you must find me a nice place, very small, close to you, only I must get a garden. I have no hopes of employment, and therefore with the little we have to live on I wish to be close to you that I may be able to have some society both for myself and Mary such as we like.[30]

Actually things turned out not too badly, thanks mainly to Richard Spooner's management of affairs and William Wilberforce's readiness to shoulder the greater part of his son's debts. Robert reported to Samuel in October 1833 that there were hopes that William and Mary might still be able to count on an income of about £800 per annum.[31] They were able to return to England in 1834.

The family fortune, however, had suffered seriously. Throughout his life William Wilberforce had poured large sums every year into charity and had never added to his capital. As soon as he moved into Highwood he reduced the return on his capital by dropping the rent of his tenants by thirty or forty per cent. At the same time he embarked upon the costly project of building a chapel for the use of his tenants and the nearby hamlet of Mill Hill. The collapse of his son's business came therefore at a particularly unfortunate time. There were friends, of course, who offered him assistance – six of them, indeed, assuring him of their readiness to make good the whole of the loss.[32] He would not accept. The only help which he permitted was donations towards the cost of his new chapel.

This was a little hard on Barbara who felt her privations keenly. Here was a fresh anxiety to be added to the many others. In 1837 she wrote to Samuel to remind him of her circumstances and to rebuke him for his extravagance:

> How little your Father conceived that the whole his widow should receive annually from the Wilberforce fortune should be six hundred pounds without house or home or legacy to set her out – but blessed be God for kind sons who are willing to have one under their roof. . . . I must leave some space for Robert. Yet I must say 3 words –
>
> Do find some way dearest Sam of living within your income, otherwise your mind will be distracted and your attention too much taken up with worldly things and your own peace and your usefulness be impaired. Allow me to say that you and Emily have such talents for spending, and would both grace a very handsome income, but while you have only what you have, tho' you have no occasion to save, you should live within your means and some self-denial is needed. I wish you would have at all times only two horses and one should be what Emily can *ride* with safety and comfort, if indeed she does ride, and one that could draw a little low pony chair if she is to drive and not ride. *I* should be content with a good strong ass, fed with corn now and then, to draw me about, if I had courage to drive it – such a one as I rode at Malvern – belonging I believe to Lady Harrowby who rode it about those hills. Pray forgive me for meddling with such matters – only do live within your income, your affectionate mother, B. A. Wilberforce.

(Barbara's 'three words' left only a tiny space at the corner of the letter for Robert to comment tersely on 'this very characteristic letter of my *poor* dear mother'.[33])

At this time Barbara was living with Robert, who had set up house at East Farleigh in Kent. The worsening financial situation had been the decisive factor in persuading him to leave Oxford and follow Samuel's example in finding himself a wife.

IV. *New Links and Losses*

First of all, however, Robert went to Germany to learn the language and to sit at the feet of the leading theologians and orientalists. This was in the summer and autumn of 1831. He was not very happy. A letter to Samuel from Bonn in July shows him very homesick and wholly out of sympathy with German ways and manners.[1] He was lodging with an Englishman of German extraction who was 'honest and obliging, tho' silly, talkative, intrusive, shallow and conceited'. The rooms were cheap enough – twenty-four shillings a month, with board at a shilling a day. He always took his dinner *table d'hôte* at one of the nearby inns, usually thronged with students, where meals of varying quality could be had from three-pence-three-farthings to two shillings and twopence (wine thrown in). There he would sit, solitary and diffident, looking with fastidious distaste at his student neighbours 'indulging themselves to excess in all the luxuries of vulgarity – *exempli gratia* spitting at dinner – running their knives into the salt, having before and after run them into their monstrous Westphalian mouths – for which reason, never eat salt at dinner in Germany, except indeed you carry a private stock in a snuff box'.

He conscientiously avoided English society, so that he could try out his German on every possible occasion. Staying with him in his lodgings was another Englishman, a nephew of the Bishop of Salisbury, apparently as deaf as a post. 'I told him when I came', Robert wrote, 'that I should not associate with him. I nearly shouted myself hoarse to tell him, the poor fellow – and he being a very sensible fellow quite understands the grounds for it. He . . . does not belong to the University, only is here to hear the language spoken that he may talk it the sooner – which, poor fellow, he won't do before the Greek Calends.'

Robert did not fare much better – he too was slightly deaf.[2] He took daily lessons and paid a man to come regularly to converse with him. 'It is really no joke to a slow and modest man like me to commence talking so outlandish a tongue as German. . . . I am getting on a little in the reading, but the speaking I find exceedingly difficult. I have to mould my notions into such a strange form to get out a sentence.'

He had been attending some of the University lectures:

> I never had before so full a conviction of the excusableness of sleep in poor people during a learned sermon, for the sitting still hearing a monotonous sound not one syllable of which I could comprehend produced every time such irresistible drowsiness that I could scarce hold myself up. At present

I don't go to the lectures, but hope in a week's time to be able to make out some of them. Schlegel is now the most celebrated professor since Niebuhr's death, and is certainly a man of great powers. Pusey gave me letters to 3 professors – Sach – Freytag – and Brandis. I have besides a circular from Mrs Latrobe to the Moravians, and a letter from a person in the bible society's house to many of their agents. . . . Of the Professors here Freytag is a man very learned in the oriental tongues, and I should think a cleverish man, but not anything very remarkable. Sach is a most excellent man, but he does not strike one as a man of very surpassing ability. Brandis is a very superior and I should think a very good man. Professor Sach inquired very much after my father, he had been at his house many years ago when in England.[3]

An approaching cholera epidemic cast a shadow over his sojourn at Bonn and provoked some frantic letters from his mother who was prompt in dispatching a series of injunctions on remedies to resist infection. Chlorate of lime was not to be trusted, on the family doctor's advice; she had heard good reports of C. Smith's remedy of purified nitre and vitriolic acid[4]; James Stephen favoured the taking of 'Emetic Tartar immediately. . . . I suspect could the Bile be made to flow into the stomach the people would be likely to recover.'[5]

Receiving news from Samuel that their father's health was declining, Robert decided to return home in December. He was 'as sick as a dog' on the boat,[6] partly induced – one cannot help feeling – by a long and fearsome account by his mother of a frightful sea accident which she had heard of and passed on to Robert to assure him of her deep anxiety 'for those of my children "who go down to the sea in ships" '.[7]

Within a month of his return Robert had proposed to Agnes Wrangham, the daughter of Francis Wrangham, Archdeacon of Cleveland and of the East Riding. They had first met at Highwood in April 1828, and Agnes (then aged 28) described the occasion in a letter to her cousin Jane Legard with such delight that clearly her heart had been stirred.

Messrs. Robert and Henry (are) delightful, clever as their eldest brother, attentive and civil as all men ought to be, with voices, manners and conversation worthy of angels, and in short quite indescribable. Robert has just been ordained and read prayers at Hendon beautifully. He only came home on Saturday so we saw too little of him.

. . . How we passed all the days I can hardly say. I only know that I never knew what o'clock it was, was too much excited to eat anything, and hardly slept, for we went to bed horribly late, and got up very early. The days begin and end with prayers and a hymn, played on the organ and sung by all the party, and a chapter read and explained by Mr Wilberforce as chapters are very seldom explained. We had a good deal of reading aloud – Bp. Heber's Journal, which appears delightful, as much walking about the place as the variable weather permitted and I played at battledore with Henry and at chess, about 6 or 7 games. . . . I hope you will study and learn really to admire *The Christian Year* which they all rave about.[8]

Two years later Robert met Agnes again while staying in Yorkshire just before Christmas and hinted to Samuel that he liked her 'most exceedingly'.[9] He acted very speedily on his return from Germany. On 27 January 1832 he wrote to Archdeacon Wrangham and received a reply by return of post.

My dear Sir, It gives me great pleasure . . . to say that from my long-cherished and most respected regard for your father, and my very high opinion of yourself, I most *readily* and *heartily* assent to the application which it [Robert's letter] conveys. I think you have both made an admirable choice in selecting each other and I earnestly pray to God to give you His blessings. As to pecuniary matters, I believe Agnes will be a good manager of a household. Of a most generous temper, she has got the very necessary virtue of discretion to regulate her liberalities. Her present income is, I think, about £120 per annum. Of the £2000 which I received with her mother, I gave to her £1000 at her grandfather's death, when it accrued – and of the other I propose in the present instance to consign to her the interest, hoping at my death to give her £1000 at *least* in addition. But I trust that still more may be in my power.[10]

Robert wrote immediately to Samuel to tell him the news – as diffident and self-effacing as ever:

I fear you will be disappointed at her first appearance. However I am sure you will like her when you come to know her, even besides that you would of course like her for my sake. I am too old to feel desperately in love like young gentlemen at school, but I feel a firm conviction that to live with her will greatly increase my happiness. I hope I shall get rid of some of that rust, which E.* used to consider adhered to me. It is a thing I should be very thankful of that I have found a person who really likes me, which from the uncouthness of my manners is so very unusual.[11]

The engagement was not made public at first. During February Robert went to stay with Agnes at the house of one of the Wrangham aunts – a Mrs Creighe – at Rawcliffe Snaith. In a long letter to Samuel he described the bliss of these weeks, giving occasional details of the progress of this sedate romance:

My dearest Sam, . . . I am so happy here in the society of Agnes that tho' idle enough I scarce find time to write. We read together always in a morn-

* This is probably his sister Elizabeth ('Lizzy'); it may of course be Emily.

ing before luncheon, and then we walk or ride for some hours, and I often read, or at all events sit, with them in the evening. . . . There is no one here but Mrs Creighe and her daughter and their governess, so that we could not have a better opportunity of getting nicely acquainted with one another. As I said before, I wish you knew Agnes a little, for tho' I have no fear of you not liking her as you ought when you know her, yet you may perhaps be disappointed by her first appearance. I believe it always happens so in respect to persons whom you like very much, but I find that the more I see of her the more handsome I think her. I wish we could marry without waiting for a house, indeed I hope we may, for I don't at all like the waiting plan. At present, however, I know nothing determinate, for I suppose it must depend on what my Father's income, and what his plans, are. . . .

I have been reading Miss Austen's novels since I came here. They are certainly prodigiously clever. *Mansfield Park*, by far the best of them, is I think a most useful book to read. It illustrates so the infinite superiority of affection over all other goods which this world can give, that I think it might be very useful to persons who think God has not placed them in a favourable enough situation, because they are not rich, clever, or powerful. For one reason it is fortunate for me that I never read the books of Miss Austen till I was engaged, for they make all young ladies so dreadfully wicked (or at least many) that I should have been quite afraid to have addressed myself to any one. Like most observers of character she sees all the worst parts, but she can also describe some most enchanting characters. I shall be surprised if you can read thro' it without finding Fanny Sargent there in places, but there is also a Fanny in *Mansfield Park*, who is I do think about the most delightful person I ever knew. There is also, of which we have all seen the horror, a mother whose one ambition is to marry her daughters. In short they are a melancholy but I fear too correct a copy of human life. . . .

By the way we find two sober persons like Agnes and myself cannot walk about together every day, sit next each other whenever they can, talk to one another all day . . . without it being reported that they are going to be married. Now since we don't intend to deny ourselves these gratifications, whenever we can have them, and don't think it worth while to humbug on the matter, the result is that if anybody is curious about it, we intend to confess without any scruple our engagement, and therefore . . . you need not make any point of concealing it. . . . Agnes is making great progress in German, so that we shall soon be able to talk secrets in company. I am happy to say she is a very good walker and rider, and not frightened, tho' she well might be having had a bad accident (i.e. broken a rib) some three years ago. Good-bye, dearest Sam. . . .[12]

Robert and Agnes were married in June 1832. Samuel had hoped to officiate himself,[13] but the approaching confinement of Emily meant that they could not face a coach journey to Yorkshire. They met Agnes for the first time in August that year. Both Keble and Newman wrote to Robert to congratulate him, Keble very warmly, Newman manifestly less so.

> Rickards and your brother Sam [he wrote] have told me news at which I am more sorry than surprised: yet it is so selfish to say so, that I must add, still more glad than sorry. I sincerely trust and hope that, though we love you, you will gain a great addition to your happiness, and blessings now and for ever. And this you will account very liberal in me, who walk by a different rule of life.[14]

In the meantime great activity had taken place to find for Robert a suitable living. In February the rumour was abroad that he had been offered the bishopric of Calcutta, and Samuel wrote to him in high delight: 'I have heard from every quarter, from Oxford ... from Cambridge (in a rejoicing mention of it by Simeon), from London ... that you have been offered Calcutta. I do not know whether it be true, or whether if true your wanting nine months would be sufficient objection. Otherwise I suppose you would hardly dare refuse it.'[15] Robert assured Samuel that he had heard less about the proposal than anyone else, 'having merely been told by W. Spooner that such a thing was talked of in Oxford, but not knowing that it had gone further. I am glad to be saved from any necessity of thinking what I should do by being too young, and by not being asked. I imagine the report arose only from C. Grant being supposed a friend of my father's. I am told now Daniel Wilson is talked of.'[16] Robert's information was more accurate than Samuel's; no approach was ever made to him.

Offers were to come – a curacy at Whippingham, the living of Kenilworth (where the father of C. R. and J. B. Sumner had been incumbent) and the living of Denbury.[17] William Wilberforce sounded Lord Clarendon, and John Sargent approached Lord Grey, the Prime Minister, through Charles Grant. In fact it was Lord Brougham, the Whig Lord Chancellor, who came to the family's aid. Hearing from James Stephen of the decline in the family fortune, he was so horrified at the prospect of William Wilberforce becoming 'a wanderer without any certain dwelling-place'[18] that he promised to exercise his official patronage at the first suitable opportunity. He offered the living of Rawmarsh to William's son-in-law (a young Evangelical called James, who had married 'Lizzy' in January 1831), and for Robert he selected the substantial living of East Farleigh, near Maidstone, in Kent.

Robert was tempted to accept immediately. One anxiety, however, held him back. If he accepted preferment from Brougham he might appear to be politically sympathetic to the party in power, and he would, at the very

least, feel obliged to conceal his Tory distaste for the policy of parliamentary reform to which the Whigs were committed. Newman was
certainly of this opinion: 'If I were known', he wrote, 'as holding and
expressing opinions strongly opposed to those which Ld. B. has ever been
active in propagating, and for which he is deeply responsible – and I had
habitually expressed them very strongly (and such it strikes me is your case)
I should dread to do aught which should seem to throw suspicion upon
the sincerity and good faith in which my former feelings were uttered.'[19]

On the other hand, Brougham's offer had been made out of love for
Robert's father, with no suggestion of political bribery; and just at that
moment Robert felt that his need was too pressing for him to let principle
stand in his way. After some hesitation he decided to accept. Newman's
reaction was profoundly disconcerting. In a long and searching letter,
thoroughly characteristic of the man who, even at this stage of his life,
was rather inclined to confuse an appeal for friendly counsel with a call
for spiritual direction,[20] he made it plain that he thought that Robert
had acted wrongly, and – with rather less plainness – hinted that their
relationship could never be quite the same again.

> My dear Wilberforce [he wrote], . . . I can say without distrusting myself,
> that, as to your not going by my opinion, it was literally a relief to me. It is
> so annoying to advise others that, first of all I evade being asked if I can
> help – next I wish my counsel to be put by. By doing as you have done,
> you rid me of responsibility, which would have been great, had you,
> partly in consequence of what I said, declined the living. I am speaking of
> my *feelings*, which it is important to show are gratified not hurt by your
> disagreeing with my expressed judgement – tho' my judgement of course
> remains the same, and, when I get myself to consider the matter on *prin-
> ciple*, I am as sorry as possible that you have done as you have.
>
> My notion has been merely this, that a person who speaks so severely
> of Ld. Brougham, as you have done, one day, and the next day takes a living
> from him, exposes himself to the *appearance* of insincerity. I am sure people
> feel this in your case. I happened to hear your preferment mentioned to a
> person you know pretty well, and he at once burst out into a laugh. On
> his informant asking him why he laughed, he could only reply 'he did not
> know – only it seemed odd'. He seemed to feel what I have ever felt about
> Peel 'you were insincere when you spoke against Canning, or you would
> have made a sacrifice now'. I doubt not that such instances make men of the
> world, like Lord Brougham, think, that every man has his price.
>
> But as to yourself individually, I fully give you credit for acting on cons-
> cience, only am sorry that your judgement has gone the way it has. And I
> hope long to have the pleasure and advantage of your friendship, though I
> cannot conceal from myself, that since intimacies depend on opinions, it is

impossible in the nature of things that so great a difference of practical judgement should not necessarily lead to a less eager interest in each other's pursuits than else might have been. I say this by way of being open – for I fully feel a man is a great fool who casts away his friends, which are hard treasures to get and whatever is lost is *my* real loss. . . .

Nor are these times, when those who are anxious for the good of religion can afford to give up others who are honest and zealous in the good cause, merely because they do not happen to agree with themselves on one or two points. So that you might be quite sure that nothing will happen on my part as far as my wishes and efforts are concerned, to interfere with that intimacy which at present exists between us. And considering every man, when he marries, is *bound* to give up (in one sense) all for his wife, perhaps I have said as much, as *practically* is necessary, as to intimacy.

I am amused at your apology for marrying. I always thought you would, when you got abroad from the College Tuition – and heartily pray it may be for your happiness, now and for ever.[21]

The family did not share Newman's view. Samuel was especially relieved, because he was finding the responsibility of looking after his ageing parents something of a trial. His first plan had been to persuade his father to buy a small house near Brighstone. 'I think', he explained to Robert, 'that many reasons will occur to your mind why it would not be comfortable to have them positively *live* with us. My dear mother is not of a disposition in temper to be very long happy where she is not mistress. She would take offence at things which Emily would say and do in perfect innocence of giving it – and once having the feeling of suspicion roused in her mind she would be unhappy.'[22]

He thought of every possible excuse to avert the contingency – his drawing room was to be decorated in the spring and his parents would therefore be sadly inconvenienced.[23] In March 1831, after giving way, he told Robert that 'I fear *entre nous* that two angels would not make my dear mother comfortable where she was to be a *living visitor*.'[24] Once Robert and Agnes were settled at East Farleigh, the parents moved to Kent, and – from incidental remarks in the family letters – it appears that Barbara was no less difficult as a lodger than she had been at Brighstone.[25]

Their father never complained. East Farleigh vicarage was only a mile from the great estate of Barham Court where he had often stayed with his close friend Sir Charles Middleton. Both the house and garden delighted him, and Robert, shortly after moving in, constructed a special gravel walk about forty yards long, entirely sheltered from the north and east winds, for William to take regular fresh air and exercise without discomfort. The only initial drawback, they discovered, was an inquisitive neighbour – the local grocer, who had a disconcerting habit of peering at the newly-weds through the hedge.[26]

Financially the living was an excellent one. Robert reported to Samuel on the negotiations over his tithes in December 1832:

> I have compounded for six years at £940, but I am to pay the deductions on £250. That is to say I am only rated at half what I should be, for we are rented here at half the rental. The Parish therefore in fact pays half my rates, which will be I suppose about £70 a year. I have only £10 land tax to pay so that my living will be a clear £860 a year. Tho' I might perhaps have got more than this, yet I think it questionable. In the case of hops, if I was to demand too much, persons would grub them up and sow corn. Now I have everything settled for 6 years, and a very sufficient income, I ought to be very thankful for it, and am perfectly contented. I managed it by myself without employing any agent, so that I had no expenses about it. In the same way I received my tithes without any expense of agency. I took the Schoolmaster with me, and he and I wrote all the receipts. I think I shall employ him to do it for me for the future.
>
> The Composition I managed by having a general meeting of the 64 payers. I then got a gentleman to propose that the 4 principal persons should come up and make me a proposal. This they did. I required something more than they at first offered. Then they went back and agreed on the matter as I wanted. I am sorry to say that I cannot get the hop ground, at least at present. The owner says he does not choose to divide his property. I suspect that he thinks I shall make him a high offer. But I confess that now our garden is in order I hardly think I want more land.[27]

As Robert did not resign his Oriel fellowship until April 1833[28] and was still receiving his fellowship dividend (of £240 a year) in November of that year,[29] he was clearly well provided for. The parish itself was in hop-growing country, only a few miles from Maidstone. Apart from a few wealthy landowners and hop-growers, the parishioners were mainly poor folk.

> I am sorry to say [Robert wrote to Samuel after six months in his new living] I don't know yet what our rates and Parish expenditure are. I think however that our Workhouse saves us something, for many troublesome persons who should otherwise come upon us keep away for fear of being put into it. We pay I think 3/6 for each person in the house. After this Spring I think I shall be one of the Inspectors of the Workhouse, and shall look into the Parish accounts. My own wish about poor laws is that when a poor man applies for work the Parish should be allowed to say, supposing him below a certain age, that they will find him work abroad. After having paid the passage money the Parish ought not to be called on further.
>
> One thing I want to do for our poor. I find they always have a dislike to the Parish Doctor. I want them to subscribe to some sort of Dispensary,

to which the rich also should give something; by which means they might have what doctor they like. I think you have some sort of dispensary in your parish.

I am just beginning with my Lending Library. I had some shelves put up in the Bathroom for the purpose of holding it. I am also enquiring about a place for a second schoolhouse.[30]

In all these hopes and plans William Wilberforce took an active interest in so far as his health permitted. The departure from Highwood and the affliction almost immediately afterwards, in February 1832, of the sudden death of his surviving daughter Elizabeth shortly after her marriage,[31] aged him considerably. His eyesight was failing fast. In the early summer of 1833 he went to Bath to take the waters in the hope of throwing off the lingering effects of a severe attack of influenza which he had contracted in Kent. Henry, who was with him at Bath, sent a series of alarming bulletins to his brothers. On 25 June he noted that his father was suffering from severe swellings in the knees and thighs.[32] A fortnight later he had to report: 'the swelling of his legs made his breeches so unpleasant to him that he has had a pair of large very loose trousers made. This makes a great alteration in his appearance and he is so much more infirm. The infirmity too which you know he has long had – the protusion a posteriori is aggravated of late and greatly prevents him taking exercise.'[33]

On 17 July he decided to go to London to consult his specialist, Dr Chambers, and was lodged with his cousin Lucy Smith at 44 Cadogan Place. It happened that Parliament was in session at that time, debating the second reading of the Bill for the Abolition of Slavery; and on Friday (July 26), when all hope of his recovery had been abandoned, the news was brought to William that his great life-work had been fulfilled – abolition had been triumphantly carried. Three days later he was dead.

His sons had known that death was imminent, but actually only Henry was with him when the end came. It was therefore to Henry that the petition was addressed from both Houses of Parliament that his father should be buried in Westminster Abbey. On the day of the funeral – August 5 – all public business was suspended in Parliament. 'You will like to know', S. F. Wood wrote to Robert afterwards, 'that as I passed down the Strand to the Abbey on Saturday morning, every third person I met (going about their daily business) was in mourning.'[34]

The family were barely recovering from another grievous shock. Within the space of four years three generations of John Sargents had been borne to the grave – the eldest son of the family in 1829, his grandfather

(John Sargent the elder) in 1831 and, in May 1833, following a short and sudden illness, the Rector of Lavington himself. Samuel wrote to Robert from Lavington on 5 May:

> Our beloved Mr Sargent is no more. I am perfectly stunned by the suddenness and violence of the blow. It has come like an overwhelming whirlwind. God grant that it may perform its intention of mercy to our souls. You knew him. You knew how entirely formed he was to attract the fondest love of all. You know how his family hung upon him – and you can form some idea of the wrench which has torn him from us. I could not have conceived suffering as I have done – and what then must it be for all – for his beloved widow and his fatherless daughters. Harry is perfectly overwhelmed. With him it is the loss of Father, friend, guide, companion and playfellow. Mrs S. is calm and composed as she always is and with a crushed and bleeding heart bows in unfeigned submission to the will of God. . . . Emily has borne it all wonderfully. She is perfectly crushed by the blow for she most dearly loved him. I never saw such affection as hers was for him. . . . The last days of the beloved Saint were such as you might anticipate from his life. He was almost incessantly delirious – but the stream of his thoughts had been so long and so fully purified that the mind could revert to nothing unholy. All his exclamations were those of humiliation, of faith, of gratitude and of joy.[35]

The male line of the Sargents did indeed seem blighted. Only Harry remained – and he perilously delicate. His father had thought to lose him earlier in the year. In the next eighteen months, however, the family circle was to be reinforced by the marriages of Caroline, Mary and Sophia.

v. *Husbands and Wives*

When John Sargent died, Henry Manning and Henry Wilberforce were both at Lavington. Manning was acting as curate, officiating chiefly at Graffham and Upwaltham, having agreed to fill the post until Henry was ready to succeed him. The fears, however, which Newman had entertained for Henry's vulnerability, as a bachelor living in close proximity to three very pretty and very eligible girls, proved to be real enough. Manning was just as likely as Henry to succumb to their charms, perhaps more so since he had recently emerged from an abortive love affair with the younger sister of one of his Harrow friends (a Miss Deffell), which had been frustrated, E. S. Purcell suggests,[1] by the girl's father who had no high opinion of Manning's ultimate prospects. At any rate he appears to have fallen in love with Caroline Sargent within weeks of his arrival at Lavington; and by Easter 1833 they were engaged to be married.

This event – together with John Sargent's sudden death – led to a complete alteration in the original plans. Henry Wilberforce, though adversely affected by the change, took it all in good part and reported on the new situation to Robert on 11 May 1833:

> It seems that my engagement here is likely to be terminated by this breaking up of all our ties here. Manning as you probably know is to have the living here and to marry Caroline and they [the rest of the Sargent family] mean to leave this house and live with him at the Parsonage, continuing to let Graffham parsonage from the rent of which indeed they get almost as much as from the two livings together. Mrs Sar. seems to think that it would be hardly the thing for me to live with them now that there is no father with them. Under our circumstances I cannot say that *I* feel this but of course we must be guided by *her* wishes. Poor dear, she has indeed the highest claim to consideration from all. She is the very character for whom GOD himself cares. Under these circumstances I am likely to be at sea (I say likely because when she comes to consider it, she *may* wish me to stay, and could I be of any use to her I would gladly do it).[2]

Only Henry – of the brothers – knew Manning at all well. The first reference to him in Samuel's papers occurs in March 1833 with the diary entry 'Much talk with Manning'.[3] In fact, as has been seen earlier, the Mannings, the Sargents and the Wilberforces were all distantly related through marriages into the family of the Abel Smiths, and William Wilberforce had corresponded with William Manning (Henry's father) on two or three occasions.[4]

In 1831, when the news of the crash of the firm of Manning and Anderdon,* West India merchants, reached the ears of the Wilberforce family, they found time, amidst their own financial worries, to express their commiseration.

> I am sure you will be grieved [Barbara Wilberforce wrote to Robert in August 1831], particularly for the sake of that young Mr Manning who was at Oxford last year that his Father's affairs are got into a very bad way – I understand he has failed and he seems to bear it in a very pleasing manner, but I fear nothing is yet known as to what will remain to him and Mrs Manning and some of the children – those who were in business with him and those unprovided for – the eldest son† and one of the

---

* John Anderdon, the friend to whom Manning confided most openly during his early years, later married Manning's eldest sister, Anna Maria.

† Frederick, the eldest surviving son. William, the first born, died in 1812 when Henry Edward was aged five. A third brother, Charles, married later.

daughters* will be provided for by marriage and I hope Mrs Carey†
will not suffer in pocket.[5]

Henry Manning was still at Oxford when he first learnt of the financial
difficulties of his father. He at once abandoned a life of leisured elegance
(for apart from his celebrated appearances at the Union he had devoted
much of his time to cricket, rowing and boxing) and directed all his
energies to reading for a First Class. His ultimate objective was a distinguished political career. As he had told his father, soon after arriving at
Oxford, 'the thought of being a clergyman had utterly passed from me.
. . . It is impossible.'[6] His Oxford associates would have seen the wisdom
of this. They recognised in him a great statesman in the making. The one
of their number who appeared an embryonic archbishop or a future
theologian – certainly *anima naturaliter Christiana* – was Gladstone.
Yet when, in 1832, Manning proceeded to orders, the incongruity was
immediately forgotten. Between leaving Oxford in the winter of 1830 and
returning as Fellow of Merton in Easter 1832, he underwent an experience
which was to transform his life. Henceforth it was his intense spirituality
which was the dominant feature of his character, so that others, seeing
him, never wondered at his calling. 'The words rise unbidden to my
lips', wrote G. W. E. Russell. '*Ecce, Sacerdos magnus*. Here was a man
who was a priest in every fibre of his being.'[7]

Manning's fifteen months away from Oxford were spent in London as a
clerk in the Colonial Office; his prospects of a great political career
seemed bleak indeed. During that time, however, he had become very
attached to some friends of the Anderdons – the Bevans, who lived at
Trent Park, a banking family of ardent Evangelical piety. The most
impressive member of that family was the saintly Miss Bevan, who became the first of three women in Manning's life to whom he felt he
could confide his innermost thoughts.‡ In the autumn of 1831 she saw
Manning regularly and corresponded with him voluminously; together
they attended open-air religious meetings; under her guidance he
became aware of the first glimmerings of 'illumination' which was later
to suffuse his soul. Miss Bevan was a discerning spiritual director. Her
notes on their meetings and discussions plot the course of Manning's

---

* Caroline, who married a Colonel Austen.

† Henry Edward's half-sister, Mary, who married Major-General Thomas Carey.
Mrs Carey was a cousin of Mary Sargent and lived at Graffham.

‡ The others were Caroline, his wife, and, after her death, Mary Wilberforce,
Caroline's sister.

conversion, while assessing his qualities and failings with remarkable insight.

> Mr Manning dined with us [she recorded on one occasion]. I think a work of grace is going on in his heart. He is deeply convinced of the vanity of the world and the sinfulness of sin. He is much interested in the Scriptures, from which he has formed a very high standard of religion. It is delightful to see him so much humbled and sanctified, but he does not for a moment think himself religious: he looks very poorly, and is not happy. He remains at the gate knocking; reflecting on his conversation, I perceive he is in bondage to the law.

By November he had received the call. The gate had been opened. 'H. M. is in the hands of One who can guide by His counsel and fit for His own work by His Spirit.'[8]

Later Manning described his sense of conversion thus:

> All this made a new thought spring up in me – not to be a clergyman in the sense of my old destiny, but to give up the world and to live for God and for souls. . . . I had long been praying much and going habitually to churches. It was a turning point in my life. . . . It was as surely a call from God as all that He has given me since. . . . It was a call *ad veritatem et ad seipsum*. As such I listed it and followed it.[9]

In this conviction he entered for the Merton Fellowship and began studying for orders. A month before his election to Merton was announced, Miss Bevan made her final assessment of her pupil's character. She read his character with uncanny accuracy and prophesied the storms that were to come: 'I know of no power in which he is deficient. His imagination is warm, his taste refined, his memory retentive and accurate in no common degree. . . . He is fond of reasoning rather than of argument.'

And yet how proud he was!

> This is the ruling passion of H.E.M. One characteristic, however, of a truly great mind is also his – namely, an ardent love of truth, which leads him to pursue investigations, and not to remain content with knowledge that has no ultimate purpose. . . . It gives a peculiar colouring to his proud, ambitious desires. He seeks not only praise, but *deserved* praise, praise doubly deserved because hardly earned. He seeks rather merit than praise, a merit of the highest order. . . .
>
> Know that he struggles with a temperament of a most susceptible, excitable, I may say morbid, kind. He would find it difficult *indeed* to carry into effect the suggestions of his ambition, or the resolutions dictated by his upright, noble intentions. He has courage sufficient to enable him to face the world in arms against him. His pride would spur him on,

but his nature is incapable of seconding his inward impulses. . . . He has bullock's horns, but not the bullock's hide. . . .

With the regard to the qualities of his heart, I own *they* are the most difficult rightly to estimate. But I am mistaken if his heart is not tender, kind, and constant. His sensitive disposition calls for the consolation of friendship. He cannot readily dissolve a tie once formed, nor harbour a suspicion of anyone who had given him proof of amity. . . . He is easily won by kindness and deceived by flattery. . . . The want of candour in another is the fault that irritates him the most. . . .

If I called him great and daring you would not believe in his sensitive points and fits of despondency. Well, I do declare him capable of braving public opinion. . . . He is a complicated creature, and calculated to disappoint expectations in some respects and at some seasons. Yet he may take a flight beyond the warmest hopes of those who wish him well. I fear he will occasion his friends to live an unquiet life.[10]

This was the man who came to Lavington in the winter of 1832 to serve as John Sargent's curate: grave, upright and handsome, with sharp, refined features, high forehead and dark receding hair. The Sargents were delighted with him, especially Mrs Sargent who grew to love him as a son.

The marriage between Henry Manning and Caroline Sargent took place at Lavington Church on 7 November 1833, Samuel Wilberforce officiating. The following day found the couple in London, at 23 Chester Street,* and Manning wrote to Mrs Sargent to tell her of their first hours of married life. It appears that even then Caroline's health was very delicate.

My dearest Mrs Sargent, I can send you an account of dearest Caroline, which you will hardly believe. She is at the moment playing and singing, without a single evidence of fatigue, or indisposition. We reached London at a little past six. She bore the journey surprisingly well, and has been more like herself, with the vigour, and activity she used to show, than I have seen for many, many months. It really seems as if a weight of uncertainty and depression had been removed, and her mind had reassumed a perfectly natural tone. All this is as unexpected to me, as it is comforting. How I would you could see her. What peace it would give you now you are distant from us. We found everything in this house most kindly, and comfortably prepared. Indeed there is all we can desire. Caroline was much pleased by a tribe of little notes, and presents from the Anderdons. She found a table covered with them, and enjoyed them far more than all her other valuables.

* The house, near Belgrave Square, belonged to one of Manning's brothers. The remainder of their honeymoon was spent at the house of a married sister near Sevenoaks. They returned to Lavington for Christmas. Henry, as usual, unearthed all the details (Sandwith MSS. B. I. 27).

Indeed we have to thank God most unfeignedly; and the more so because I do not think her present activity of body and mind at all results from excitement, or any temporary cause, but she seems to find her strength when demanded equal to the call. I have thought of you all – an affectionate recollection in all I would express, for I do not feel any separation to have arisen between you and her you so love. May it please Him to unite us in one family: and give you the comfort and support of Caroline's affection.

There is much I would say to you, but had rather you should gather it from your future observation. I cannot forget the intimate relation that was sealed between us yesterday, and I believe you will never want an evidence of this conviction hereafter.

I know we have your constant prayers. Ask for us that our union may comprehend both time and eternity and that our sincere, our single, aim in all things may be the glory of God in our holy and devoted life. You shall hear frequently from me – but I beg of you to write me word how you are yourself. *Once* you were so good a correspondent to me that I am sure you will not fail me *now*. Caroline sends her affectionate love, and a promise to write soon to you. Pray give mine to my sister Mary, and tell her I regret I did not see her to kiss her for all her kindnesses to me, before I left Lavington. Give my love or rather our love to all. Believe me, my dearest Mrs Sargent, your affectionate Son, H. E. Manning.[11]

Samuel Wilberforce again officiated at the next family wedding to be held at Lavington – the marriage of Sophia Sargent to George Dudley Ryder in July 1834. Ryder was three years younger than Henry Manning and, although he had known Henry Wilberforce, Gladstone and Manning well at Oxford, he did not in fact leave Oriel until 1833. He proceeded to orders in the same year. Already he had met Sophia Sargent and fallen deeply in love. He had proposed to her just before John Sargent fell ill in May 1833, but he had to wait until August before consent was given to the match. His son has described how he walked over the Sussex Downs to Lavington to attend John Sargent's funeral, and watched the ceremony from the woods above Lavington House, unknown to the family. His eyes were on Sophia, then only nineteen, dressed in mourning and looking indescribably lovely. He walked back alone for 'his delicacy of feeling forbade his intruding upon so great a sorrow'.[12]

The match was a very natural one, for the Ryders, the Wilberforces and the Sargents were all intimately bound together in the Evangelical cause. Henry Ryder, George's father, was then Bishop of Lichfield and Coventry, having previously been Bishop of Gloucester. His uncle was the Earl of Harrowby, who had shared with William Wilberforce a close friendship with William Pitt, serving under him as Foreign Secretary in 1804. The

Ryders were also related by marriage to the family of March Phillipps (whose daughter Henry Ryder had married in 1802) and thus George Dudley Ryder was a cousin of Ambrose Lisle Phillipps who later, on his conversion to the Roman Church, changed his name to Ambrose Phillipps de Lisle and offered a haven to others in the same predicament as himself at his great estate, Grace Dieu, in Leicestershire.

In 1833 Ryder's Evangelicalism was fast waning. Unlike Manning, who had found 'true' religion after leaving Oxford, he had been drawn into the Newman circle at Oriel and shared Henry Wilberforce's enthusiasm for apostolical views. In common with all the others, however, he maintained something of that moral earnestness which had inspired him from early childhood. Indeed the sense of the duty of self-discipline and the need to practise holy living had been brought home more sharply to him by his acquaintance with Newman. As a young man, just before his marriage, he resolved never to allow himself the luxury of lying in bed late of a morning, and cured himself of this indulgence by fining himself ten shillings for every offence (the money to be cast into a nearby stream lest he should – by giving it to charity – persuade himself that self-indulgence could be profitable to others). He was, he later told his son, at the same stage of his life much troubled by sexual fantasies during the night, when the urge to sin 'against the Holy Virtue of Purity' was so strong that he would fling himself out of bed and fall on his knees, begging God to cast him into Hell rather than let him give way to his desires. 'Shortly after came my marriage and all such troubles ceased.'[13]

Both the Bishop of Lichfield and Mrs Sargent gave their consent to the marriage to Sophia in August 1833. The Bishop wrote first, Mrs Sargent replying on 29 August. Her letter is as charming a period piece as one can hope to find:

> My dear Lord, Upon my return to the Isle of Wight [she was staying with Samuel and Emily at the time] . . . I found your lordship's very kind letter for which I beg to express my sincere thanks. The manner in which you speak of Mr George Ryder's connexion with my daughter is peculiarly gratifying to me; it evinces your esteem for my beloved Husband's memory and I well know there were very few upon Earth for whom he had a higher regard than for your lordship. I do trust if it please God to bring about the union to which we are looking forward, my dear Sophia will prove worthy of the affectionate feelings with which Mrs Ryder and yourself seem disposed to receive her into your family.
>
> I think I can answer for her being affectionate and docile and I hope it will be the study of her life not only to make your Son happy but to secure

the good opinion and attachment of all who are most dear to him. As to their income being small I cannot consider that as altogether a disadvantage. I hope they will be desirous to keep their expenses within very moderate bounds, and habits of economy early learned are very valuable in after life. The drawback to me is the distance to which my child is to be removed from her former home but I think with much comfort that she will be near Eccleshall Castle and from Mrs Ryder I doubt not she will receive that natural guidance and protection which I shall no longer be able to afford her. In committing my dear Sophia to the care of your Son I feel that I am as far as possible securing both her temporal and eternal happiness; his excellent principles and very sweet disposition leave me without a fear that she will enjoy as large a share of domestic felicity as is compatible with the dangers and trials of the World of sin and sorrow.

I beg to present my very kind regards to Mrs Ryder and I remain your lordship's sincere and obliged

Mary Sargent.[14]

The distance to which Sophia was to be removed was from Lavington to Hanbury in Staffordshire – a living in the gift of the bishop – a beautiful country parish, although its income was slight. In 1836, after his father's death, Ryder was presented to the wealthier living of Easton, three miles from Winchester.

Rumour had it that Newman was excessively displeased at Ryder's desertion from the dwindling number of his celibate companions. The rot had set in with Pusey's marriage in 1828; then Robert Wilberforce had fallen, followed by Ryder – and even Keble himself in 1835. Henry Wilberforce, who had a taste for gossip, spread the news round Oxford that Newman had actually 'cut Ryder for marrying'[15] – an exaggeration which understandably upset Newman intensely. He had merely told Ryder that he was at liberty to marry because 'the generality of men ought. . . . The celibate is a high state of life to which the multitude of men cannot aspire.'[16] But when George Ryder and Sophia came to Oxford shortly after their marriage, he commented rather sourly, 'G. Ryder and bride passed through Oxford yesterday – he seems proud of showing her off; which I suppose is proper.'

The event which really pained him was Henry Wilberforce's engagement to Mary Sargent in December 1833. He received news of this months later – not from Henry himself, but from Harriett Newman, to whom Henry had confided without his knowledge. The supposed grounds for Henry's bad manners were that Newman might be likely – did he know of the engagement – to treat him as he had treated George Ryder. Newman wrote in great impatience to Froude in June 1834:

'H. W. engaged to marry Miss S. last December, was afraid to tell me and left Oxford without – spread abroad I had cut Ryder for marrying. He now wishes to go into orders but *cannot get a title, because* he wants one with a house and £100 a year. Precious nonsense and foolery – it makes one half beside oneself. Yet he has not ratted and will not (so be it). Marriage is a sin which it is sinful to repent of.'[17]

He then wrote to Henry very severely; but, having written the letter, decided it was too severe to send.

> My poor dear foolish Henry – dear, for auld lang syne, – foolish for being suspicious of me, – poor, because I suppose you have been pained at your own suspicions.

Henry had misjudged him in supposing that he would put adherence to a principle above the claims of friendship:

> You surely are inconsiderate – you ask me to give you my heart, when you give yours to another – and because I will not promise to do so, then you augur all sorts of ill treatment towards you from me. Now I do not like to speak of myself, but in self-defence I must say, it is a little hard for a friend to separate himself from familiarity with me (which he has a perfect right and perhaps lies under a duty to do) and then to say, 'Love me as closely, give me your familiar heart as you did, though I have parted with mine'. Be quite sure that I shall be free to love you, far more than you will me – but I cannot, as a prudent man, forget what is due to my own comfort and independence as not to look to my own resources, make my own mind my wife, and anticipate and provide against that loss of friends which the fashion of the age makes inevitable. This is all I have done and said with respect to you – I have done it to all my friends, as expecting they will part from me, except to one who is at Barbados [Hurrell Froude]. . . . My dear H. – you really have hurt me – you have *made* a difficulty in the very beginning of our separation. You should have reflected that to remove it, you would not only have to justify it to yourself but explain it to me. . . .[18]

For the next twelve months Henry and Newman were estranged. Since this letter was never sent, Henry was not aware of the offence which he had caused, and Newman's long silence led him to suppose that he was no longer to be reckoned a member of the Tractarian inner circle. He only made matters worse by confiding yet again in Harriett Newman. In June 1835 came a very sharp letter from Newman, accusing him of unkindness and lack of consideration, warning him brusquely that 'he wanted to have nothing to do with their intimacy and was going to bind himself to a definite line of conduct towards Henry for three years, dating from the offence'.[19] By this time Henry was thoroughly perplexed. After another exchange of letters (in which Henry took Newman to task for being 'stern and rigid in his attitude to people as well as to principles'), Newman offered him the chance of forgiveness. The change of tone melted Henry's heart and he replied by asking Newman to become the godfather of his first-born son. 'Thus', writes Miss Trevor, 'the only serious misunderstanding of their long friendship was closed'.[20]

It is difficult to read these letters without a feeling of impatience; if their language is that of grown men, the tone exhibits something of the petulance of adolescence. But neither contestant was quite himself. As Dean Church recalled, the ethos of Oxford in the thirties was such as to lead men into extremes of love and hate; and in the early years of the Oxford Movement, while the first number of the *Tracts* was being launched, Newman was fierce in his demand that everyone must choose his side. Prevarication and the very suggestion of disloyalty were, in that over-charged atmosphere, apt to be magnified in the minds of the members of a closely-knit group – too bound up with one another, too dedicated to the common cause, for comfort – into faithlessness and double dealing. Henry was seriously off balance during this time. Always impulsive, usually tactless, he was then more restless and on edge than he had ever been before. His future was uncertain; he had no settled home; and he somehow contrived to find fault with every offer of a title for orders which came his way. Also he was head-over-heels in love. In the winter of 1833 Mary Sargent accepted his proposal of marriage, and thereafter Henry was like a man in a dream. Even after their marriage, he was constrained to pinch himself to see if it were really true: he would make faces at himself in the mirror and marvel 'how the most beautiful woman in the world could have loved and married such an ugly fellow as I am'.[21]

In seeking a living, Henry had thought that it would be good for him to have Samuel or Robert near at hand to keep him in order and to make him read. Thus West Farleigh was a possibility, but proved after investigation to be unsuitable. He considered Newport, on the Isle of Wight, then West Cowes, and toyed for some time with the idea of applying for Godshill or Shalfleet.[22] At last, C. R. Sumner, in whose diocese he had expressed a wish to serve, came to the assistance of the Wilberforce family yet again with the offer to Henry of the perpetual curacy of Bransgore, a small village near Christchurch on the outskirts of the New Forest. It was not a wealthy post,* but it would do; and to this title Henry was ordained deacon by Sumner at Midsummer 1834.

---

* In a letter to Gladstone, dated 20 May 1839, Henry described the benefice as worth only £72 *per annum*. B. M. Add. MSS. 44356 (Gladstone Papers, Vol. 271), f. 258.

The marriage to Mary Sargent took place at Lavington on 24 July. Sumner officiated. 'The Samuel Wilberforces were there,' the bishop wrote subsequently in his diary, 'old Mrs Sargent, a most magnificent old lady of eighty, in full possession of all her faculties and full of life and vigour, the very picture of a venerable and happy old age – Mrs John Sargent, cheerful and full of sweetness in her widow's dress, and evidently never forgetting her loss for a moment, but entirely acquiescent and not incapable of entering into the happiness of others – Mr and Mrs Henry Manning, the youngest daughter, looking quite like a child, extremely pleasing, and said to have much talent.'[23]

Henry kept his spirits in check and behaved with decorum. He had been taken by Robert beforehand to Dowdrey's, the tailor, to be measured for his suit, 'the tailor evidently supposing him a runaway lunatic and me his keeper', Robert afterwards told Samuel. 'I could see when Henry made sharp speeches to him if he asked whether the coat should be shorter etc. that the man watched him and made preparations for jumping aside in case Henry should bite or stab at him.'[24]

It was hoped that at last Henry would settle down.

VI. *At Brighstone and East Farleigh*

Brighstone Rectory was an imposing house, built of local stone, heavily creepered, standing close to the parish church. The countryside was not unlike Lavington, chalk downs interspersed with little hamlets; Brookside, Atterfield and Sutton were all outlying hamlets within Samuel's parish. Half a mile from the house was the sea. Compared with Checkenden, the house seemed palatial – the main block being three-storeyed, with attic rooms for the servants, and an additional one-storeyed wing to the side. Through french windows from the drawing-room, one passed to a verandah looking out on a walled garden with the sea beyond. A covered walk led to a quaintly domed summer-house with a view of a large lawn broken irregularly by circular flower beds. So Emily saw it in May 1832, when she was brought down from her bedroom for the first time after a period of enforced confinement because of a threatened miscarriage. She was writing to Louisa Noel:

> I am much better though very weak with being kept in bed. Sam was determined on Monday to bring me downstairs so, contrary to Mr Bloxam's orders, he carried me down to the Drawing-room sofa, and never shall I

forget the kind of intense delight I felt to look out into [our] dear little garden once more full of flowers, with all the young green leaves just come out, the grass just mown and swept up into heaps, the sea looking very blue and making a great noise, Sam's tulip bed in the fullest and brightest bloom, and that loveliest flower that ever bloomed, that sweet Arnie skipping about the grass after her cat! And to see all this instead of my curtains! Well, Sam was right, it did not hurt me, and I have been down again to-day and have had a small walk too in the room. . . .

Dear little grand William, or Edith! I should be *so* sorry! Will you remember that I have *only* told my sister – And so you are coming once more to see your brother and sister and child. How very nice it will be, my dearest, you shall help me to teach Arnie her letters and her hymns.[1]

Emily lost the baby. After the miscarriage, she and Samuel visited East Farleigh for the first time, and – in spite of Robert's foolish, though typical, fears – Emily and Agnes became firm friends from the start. Emily especially admired Agnes's good taste in the furnishings of her house and told Samuel that he must obtain specimens of them to be used for the décor at Brighstone. The chintz must be green and lilac with a white stripe marked with black spots. It would do nicely for both chairs and curtains. Samuel wanted to copy Robert's bookshelves. They considered putting up mahogany heads for the pelmets, just as they had seen them at East Farleigh. Emily plied Agnes with questions about their carpets. 'I am sure you will laugh at this list of questions which I have sent you as if I thought you were an old established upholsterer yourself. . . . You will be a most kind and charitable dear if you will answer these questions by return of post and at length.'[2]

East Farleigh might have superior furnishings, but a countryside of hop-fields had few glories to compare with the downs, the beaches, and the rocks of Brighstone. Samuel's diaries tell of morning bathing in the sea; crisp, exhilarating rides on the sands; and drives to Freshwater to take a boat to the caves, where the water was so clear that you could see down some thirty feet. On one expedition to Blackgang Chine (in 1838), with Bishop Sumner and his chaplain, the party were all nearly drowned. They had descended the Chine on a day of high wind and a furious sea, and, rounding the point at the bottom, they paused to watch a magnificent tall wave rolling in upon them only to discover too late that they were standing within its reach. The chaplain dug his stick into the ground and hung on to it for dear life; Samuel, in foul-weather hat and waterproofs, and the bishop, who had made no concessions to the weather save to attach strings to his hat, scrabbled up the bank and plunged together into a cavity so that the water swept right over them. They squelched home drenched to the skin.[3]

Bishop Sumner was a frequent visitor to Brighstone. ('There is some truth in what Woodrooffe says of him', wrote Samuel to Robert in 1834 after the bishop had been staying with him for a week, 'that he goes about with a hum; like a bumble bee.')[4] He formed such a high opinion of Samuel's qualities that within a few months of his induction to Brighstone he was consulting him about the character and efficiency of the local clergy.[5] The bishop was charmed by Samuel's hospitality. 'The Wilberforces are very dear persons,' he wrote to his wife in 1832, '. . . they are exactly what you would like, and really among the very nicest people in spirit and agreeableness, and amiabilities as well as in talent, etc., that I know.'[6]

When possible they would take brief holidays at Lavington. The two horses, Minna and Brenda, would be harnessed and Wheeler the coachman with another servant, James, on the box beside him (to jump down at Sherwell Hill to put on the drag) would take them to catch the Portsmouth packet which left on the hour throughout the day. From Portsmouth they would take the stage to Chichester, disembark at the Dolphin, and make the rest of the journey by pony gig to Lavington. More usually, however, Mrs Sargent or Louisa Noel (the two most frequent guests at Brighstone) would spare Emily the journey and cross to the Island themselves. There was hardly a moment in these early years when Emily was not either bearing children or nursing babies; and because she was prone to miscarry, travelling was always something of a hazard. After the misfortune of 1832 she was soon pregnant again, and she and Agnes (who was bearing Robert's first child) had a little friendly – if anxious – race to see who would be the first to give birth. Agnes won by three days. Her son (William, usually called 'Wilfranc') was born a little before 11 p.m. on 26 June 1833. Robert wrote to Samuel immediately – a little philosophically, perhaps, for his mind had turned at once to Lucretius and a poem in *The Christian Year*: 'How striking it is to hear the newly-born one issue with lamentations into the world, – *vagituque locum lugubri complet ut aequum est, cui tantum in vita restat transire malorum*.* How strikingly does Keble's Poem on the subject come in to qualify the melancholy impressions which such thoughts would otherwise excite. It is an anxious thing to be a Parent however, even a Xtian parent'.[7]

---

* Lucretius. *De Rerum Natura*, V. 226–7. 'He fills the place with woful wailing, as is but right for one for whom it remains in life to pass through so much trouble.' (Cyril Bailey's translation.)

The most immediate anxiety of Samuel and Emily ended on 29 June. Samuel wrote that very evening to Louisa Noel:

> My dearest sister, Oh magnify the Lord with me and let us exalt his name together. Our beloved Emily was very ill from 4 o'clock this morning till at ½ past one she gave Arnie a fine and promising brother – oh indeed it is an inconceivable weight off my mind; after all she has lately gone through I was *unusually* anxious about her – and *ordinary* anxiety about one so dear at such a hazard would not be slight. But God has generously been pleased to hear our prayers. ... Our dearest Emily was kept in great patience. She is going on well – *very* well till just now when she has been seized with a violent headache, which we feel sure is only nervous.[8]

Actually she was ill for a week thereafter with an obstruction which the doctor deemed it necessary to remove 'by violent means', prescribing twelve leeches.[9] The infant was christened Herbert William, his godfathers being Robert Wilberforce and Bishop Sumner.

There were many more letters about babies. Some twenty months after the birth of Herbert, Emily was again confined only to deliver herself of a pretty baby girl, stillborn. 'A day of intense anxiety and evening of deep pain', Samuel wrote in his diary. 'All the possible combinations of her disappointment and sorrow before my eyes.'[10] He took consolation in reading Henry Martyn's *Journals*. To Louisa he wrote: 'She whispered to me last night "I have been thinking that God who took my baby from me 'delighteth in mercy', then he would not have taken it unless it was good for me. How much more than 'being merciful' – how nice to think it is not being punished 'in anger'." ... Henry and Mary are in the house but do not allude to it in any letter. We have not been able to tell her that they are here.'[11]

The few surviving letters of Agnes are mainly concerned with babies too. Occasionally she writes of their family life at East Farleigh – the tedium of repaying hospitality by formal dinner parties, descriptions of visits to neighbours to play chess, teasing references to Robert's delight in Newman's book on the Arians ('I am so glad', she wrote to Samuel, 'that you will point out his friend's errors, and not let him incline too much like some of the Oxford Tracts to our aunt the Roman Catholic Church.')[12] In April 1834 Agnes wrote to Emily to tell her that another baby was expected.

> And now, Mrs Emily, please to take notice (both you and Sam) that if you put it into Robert's head, or the dear Mother's, that there can be any harm in going into Yorkshire in June because people expect to be confined at the end of November, I never can speak to either of you again, and that

not from any spirit of malice, but merely to shew a proper disapprobation of such unchristian-like behaviour. .... I cannot tell you exactly when to expect your new niece, as nursing rather interferes with the power of reckoning, and I did not shew much ability of calculating last time, so if it should be a month before or a month after the time I mentioned, you need not think it surprising. Do not scold me for having the same nurse (which I hope to do) instead of sending an immense distance for yours, for if she never does worse by the baby than putting pins in the clothes I can get over that in consideration of her other excellencies. .... Wilfranc is as bluff and bonny as ever, brays very like a donkey, eats minced meat and grows every day.[13]

Agnes's second child – a son, Eddy – was born on Sunday, 9 November 1834. Tragedy followed. Agnes was taken with a violent fever. After it had raged for four days, the full seriousness of the infection became plain. Robert was able to talk with her a little, and told Samuel of what passed between them.

At this time, looking at me, as tho' she felt the pain of separation, she said in the most angelic manner 'I do love you very tenderly' but she added on my asking her in what state of mind she had been 'I thank God I am en-abled to be quite calm. I feel no disquietude.' On Friday she became much worse and again suffered great pain. This she concealed in the most sur-prising manner and told the women about her, not to tell me of it, lest it should grieve me.[14]

At the week-end the rest of the family were warned that the end was near. On the Sunday Agnes made no longer any attempt to hide from Robert that she knew that she was dying. She told him not to mourn.

She went on [Robert later recorded]: 'Why dear one, a man is but a lonely being in the world without a wife, so do marry again.' I answered, 'it is of no use to make resolutions about such matters, but I feel sure that I never can think of such a thing.' ... 'I should like', she said, 'to kiss my dear children once more.' William was brought to her first, he was frightened dear boy and sobbed when taken up in the midst of his sleep. When he was brought she kissed him and said, 'My dear boy, may you be like your grand-father.' Then came the baby whom she kissed and said, 'May you grow up like your Father.'

My mother came in, she kissed her and said 'Good-bye, and forgive me if I have ever —' My mother was quite overpowered and said 'Oh what have I to forgive in you?' Then she said she wished to take leave of the servants. She shook hands with all who were present. To Hannah she said, 'Good-bye and thank you for all your kindness to me.' To the nurse she said nearly the same. To Jane, she said 'Thank you for being so kind to me and take care of my dear boy.' She shook hands with the physician and said

'Good-bye Dr Welsh. I thank you for all your attention. May we meet in Heaven'.

Kneeling by her bedside I said, 'My dear one, we don't part in sorrow and our meeting will be in joy'. 'Yes', she said, 'I am very happy – all my trust is in my Saviour and I hope soon to be with Him.' I quoted a line of the *Christian Year* 'For one short life we part'. . . . She went on and said 'I don't wish to stay, I had rather depart, I don't wish to stay', she repeated turning to me, 'even to be with you'. The last words were scarcely uttered, but I could not mistake their purport. God enabled me to answer (I hope from the bottom of my heart) 'I would not keep you'. . . . From this time she lay quite still, till about twenty minutes before six on Monday morning, she fell asleep in Christ – no groan or sigh gave intimation of the exact moment when she became a glorified saint.

'May I die the death of the righteous and may my last end be like her's.'[15]

Grief was freely indulged in those days. To weep was not unmanly; to brood over the last hours of a loved one, to collect and record the sayings from the death-bed, were not thought morbid occupations. When Robert had finished writing this account, Samuel made a copy to send round to members of the family.

Oh they *are* indeed encouraging [he wrote to Emily], and should lead both of us firmly to trust our souls to him who can renew them with righteousness here – and hold them up in the troublous time. My sweetest wife, may we both take courage and determine that we will live more near to God.

Poor Robert seems more low to-day, I think, than I have yet seen him. Though still calm and peaceful. . . . Each hour comes more charged with its peculiar load of remembered sorrow. We have been reading the Service here. Henry read the prayers and I read that most beautiful sermon of Hooker's, 'On the Remedy of Sorrow and Fear'. There was not a dry eye I believe in the room. May God bless these scenes truly to our souls.

I am now writing in the drawing-room. Henry is writing on the other side of the table to Mary. Nurse has just brought in the poor little infant. Dr Welsh has taken it entirely from the wet nurse hoping to get rid of its illness – and it has mended rapidly. To-day its little countenance looks placid and easy and its hands are open. It is taking constant medicine. Fed on gruel. . . .[16]

When Emily, after the sadness of the stillborn infant in March 1835, next gave birth to a child, a little girl born on 4 January 1837, she called her after Robert's wife – Agnes Everilda. The baby died that same day. Robert wrote to Samuel when he heard the news:

How singular that when you were giving a short-lived renewal to the association of those two names with our hereditary one, I should be putting up the memorial to her by whom they were originally conjoined. Who knows

161

my dear Samuel what intercourse of the same blood may hold in a better state.

As I wrote the thought came to me of those many objects of affection of whom a few years have deprived us: a few more – and we must follow; may our deaths be equally blessed and to that end our lives equally hallowed.[17]

Chapter 4

QUESTIONS OF CHURCHMANSHIP

I. *Apostolical Enthusiasms*

In the meantime affairs at Oxford had begun to make something of a stir in the outside world. John Henry Newman had returned from Sicily a changed man, filled 'with such exuberant confidence and energy that his friends at Oxford actually failed to recognise him'.[1] John Keble had preached a forthright Assize Sermon (14 July 1833) on the text 'I will teach you the good and the right way'[2] which, though not intended to be a call to arms, was a public expression of the alarm felt by High Church-men at the determination of the Whigs to reform the scandalously un-reformed Irish Church. A conference had been held at the parsonage of H. J. Rose at Hadleigh where the more staid of the High Churchmen, with the firebrand Hurrell Froude in their midst, had noted with concern the tyrannical pretensions of secular authority, signs of subversion within the Church and 'worst of all – no principle in the public mind to which we could appeal'.[3] Newman, Keble and Froude had gone their own way and launched a series of pithy exhortations – to the clergy to magnify their office, exalt the bishops and choose their side, and *ad populum* to teach them to regard their pastor as 'the Deputy of Christ, for reducing men to the obedience of God'.[4] E. B. Pusey, Professor of Hebrew, had joined them in 1834* – a man of little pith but weighty learning – and the *Tracts for the Times* were beginning to swell into theological treatises, studded with patristic citations and supported by *catenae* of the writings of the Caroline divines.

The Wilberforces and their most intimate circle were not at first greatly affected by these happenings. Henry Wilberforce and George Dudley Ryder were the best informed on the course of events and most sanguine in their expectation of enduring results. Robert, too, received bulletins from time to time from Newman and passed the information on to Samuel and to Henry Manning who, because of their strong Evangelical

---

* Pusey's first contribution – the first also to appear over the initials of the author – was *Tract 18* in 1834.

sympathies, were rather less likely than the others to be overpowered by these draughts of heady wine.

As early as October 1833, Newman had written to Robert to secure his help in circulating numbers of the *Tracts* and in forming a local association of sympathetic clergy to carry out judicious proselytism.[5] The next letter from Newman amongst Robert's papers, dated 30 August 1835, has the tone of a man who has rather lost contact with his correspondent and must therefore give a résumé of general news. One passage, however, both in style and content, has the authentic Newman touch. Having apologised for his long silence and given an account of Keble's latest work (he was busy on his edition of Hooker), he wrote:

> For myself, I am prosecuting my reading of the Fathers, which is very slow work. There is so much to digest, that it is quite dispiriting to find how little I get through, though I suppose one moves on imperceptibly. I am editing Dionysius Alexandrinus – there is not much left of him, but it gives me an object for reading. Also I am engaged in a controversy with a chattering French Abbé,* who says three words when one would do – but this is a stimulus for reading. It is so difficult to read without an object. I may almost add so unprofitable – but I rather mean this – that nothing at all is done, if a man begins to read the Fathers without a previous knowledge of controversies which are built upon them. Till then their writings are blank paper – controversy is like the heat administered to sympathetic ink. Thus I read Justin very carefully in 1828 – and made copious notes – but I conceive most of my time was thrown away. I was like a sailor landed at Athens or Grand Cairo, who stares about – does not know what to admire, what to examine – makes random remarks, and forgets all about it when he has gone.[6]

The best source of Oxford gossip, as might be expected, was Henry. Any story which might add to the discomfiture of their foes he retold with gleeful hyperbole. Thomas Arnold, always suspect because of his liberal inclinations, was thought to have gone out of his mind when his sweeping indictment of sectarianism and ecclesiastical conservatism – the *Principles of Church Reform* – was published in 1833. He represented everything that the Tractarians most detested – a 'low' view of the Church, a sympathy towards dissenters, a contempt for dogma and a willingness to advocate radical reform in order to bring the Church into effective contact with the industrial masses whose lives were spiritually starved.[7] Fierce things were therefore said about him at Oxford,

* This was the Abbé Jager with whom Newman was in correspondence from 1834 to 1836.

and Henry saw to it that his brothers were kept up to date. He first of all recounted the 'inside story' of Newman's famous query (which understandably hurt Arnold keenly) 'But is Dr Arnold a Christian?'

An amusing private correspondence is going on between Arnold and Neander. N. at Rome sitting with the Froudes, Neale and Grant (New Coll.), on Neale's remarking that Arnold says Niebuhr is a Christian replied 'and who answers for Arnold?' or some such words. Hare of Cambridge ... noises it about and it gets to Arnold's ears. A. writes to Hare and Hare to Grant for the exact circumstances. Grant writes begging that A. will let it pass. It was a hasty and quite private expression and with 500 apologies for having repeated it. A. writes to Grant a very severe letter on N. demanding apologies. ... So comes the whole to N. who writes a *very* stiff answer explaining the sense in which he used the words and I imagine by no means likely to allay the ire of the Heresiarch or the wrath of the Paedagogue. ... I reckon that A. expected a very different answer from N. more like Grant's.

I have been very much surprised at the very strong manner in which A. expresses his contempt for 'the party with which N. has connected himself', their intellectual power etc. tho' he allows him to be a 'good' man. All this as well as the language of his Postscript to the Principles of Ch. Reform where he speaks in the most insulting way 'of these extraordinary men who gravely maintain that primitive Episcopacy and episcopacy as it exists are essentially the same'[8] combine to show a most diabolical pride in one who has known Keble as well as A. has. But I have heard that in conversation he expresses *a very low opinion of K's power*!!! Ha Ha Ha.

Private

By the way there is one good trait in his character which I have heard reported, did not and could not believe and by enquiry have so confirmed that I cannot help (strange as it is) believing it. This is that he sends his children, a boy of 13 and a girl of 12 (of whom the eldest has been taken away from a school where he was for bad conduct and is quite a precocious rip) to bathe together in a bath house with no dressing rooms whatever except the room in which the bath is, every morning – and that he actually goes himself with them *both* to bathe all three together in the river both in Cumberland and at Rugby. This I think a *very* good point because (as no man wishes his own daughter to be a scortum) it shows that his mind cannot connect cause and effect and therefore he is less responsible for his Ch. plans. I heard this first from Froude, and thought he had invented it but I have enquired from young Ryder who tells me not only that all the school believes it but that he has had it confirmed by more than one person very intimate with and fond of A. and who had been stopping with him in Cumberland, and as to Rugby *many* whom he well knew and who were exceedingly fond of A. have told him that they have seen the whole family of young ones go into the Bath house together and come out bathed. The boy he knows has heard him swear etc. Also he himself heard A. regretting that he could not get Mrs A. to bathe at Rugby, whether with him or the school or her son or in the River or where he did not say.[9]

No doubt Henry's brothers were vastly amused by all this. While they could still speak of Evangelicals with profound respect (except Calvinists and 'ranters'), latitudinarians were regarded with utter contempt. All the members of their circle agreed in the condemnation of the unfortunate Dr Hampden, appointed Regius Professor of Divinity by Lord Melbourne in 1836. This indeed was the first issue in which they all became involved in the affairs at Oxford, taking the Tractarian side.

The circumstances are well known. Renn Dickson Hampden, one of the milder but most learned of the 'Noetics' at Oriel, had become a marked man in Tractarian Oxford ever since his publication of a pamphlet in 1834 in which he had advocated the abolition of subscription to the Thirty-nine Articles before matriculation so that dissenters might be admitted to the University. The suspicion of heterodoxy led his opponents to examine his previous writings, most particularly his Bampton Lectures of 1832 on 'Scholastic Philosophy considered in its relation to Christian Theology'. The lectures had caused little stir at the time; they were very dull; the study of the medieval schoolmen was *terra incognita* in Oxford at that time. An interested reading of the text of the lectures, however, provided disturbing discoveries, not least the appalling revelation that Dr Hampden seemed to be saying that there should be a distinction between the divine facts of scripture, which were binding on all Christians, and all human interpretations of these facts (in formularies, creeds, theological writings etc.) which, because they were products of human intelligence, were therefore fallible and open to differences of opinion. When Melbourne chose this man to be Dr Burton's successor as Regius Professor of Divinity, Oxford churchmen were immediately up in arms against what they deemed to be at the best an egregious insult and, at the worst, a calculated act of subversion, whereby the Whigs planned to undermine the Church from within.

Robert Wilberforce had described Hampden to Samuel as 'a paradoxical prig and a heartless heretic' as early as April 1835.[10] Manning agreed with him. He wrote to Samuel in February 1836:

> Perhaps it is as well that we should be fully advised to what extent party spirit can carry our present rulers. Hampden seems to be from the parts I have read in his B. lectures to be a cold, audacious Speculator. He writes

with perfect impartiality on Sabellianism, Arianism, and Orthodoxy, so that except from an incidental expression as to the greater excellence, or more philosophical precision of some orthodox definition, he would hardly seem to be hampered by any of the unhappy prejudices (which have so long distracted the charity of Xtians in controversies) touching the Godhead, and Incarnation, of the Son and Personality of the Holy Ghost. There is an odd principle of gregariousness combining Whately, Hinds, Arnold, Blanco White, and Hampden. They are all cold, audacious and speculative.[11]

What troubled Samuel was the effect of Hampden's appointment on the Church. The notion 'that man is irresponsible for his belief . . . is very shocking in a divinity professor, who ought to be one to nail his colours to the mast and uphold orthodoxy to the very utmost; to be a sort of *rule*; knowing that other men's *lines* will be a little less straight than the rule'.[12]

As usual, it was Henry who kept them all informed of Oxford gossip. In an undated letter to Samuel (which, from the events described, must have been written in February 1836), he gave a racy chronicle of the proceedings as seen by a member of Newman's circle:

Things here are lulled again after the storm. The history of what has happened is this – Newman was in London the week before last – and there heard all the various reports as they arose. Many names were discussed, among others I believe his own. However when he came home his opinion was that some moderate neither here nor there man would be appointed. Well, on Monday morning it was offered to Hampden and he talked about intending to accept it. It is believed here that Arnold had previously refused it on thinking it would not do. N. tried to get up some protest but it was reported there would be one from authority and he thought it important not to put himself forward. . . . Wednesday morning was come and nothing done. N. resolved that he and his friends would lay aside shame and act. So they called a meeting at an hour's warning at Corpus Common Room. Many came. Pusey, the Archdeacon etc. – and after long talks made a Petition to the King which 176 signed, beginning with Martin Routh. This was sent off to the Abp. of Cant. That night N. sat up all night to write a pamphlet which he finished before morning showing by quotation Hampden's views on all subjects. This was sent off to be printed but owing to Baxter's delay it did not come out till late on Saturday evening. Well, in consequence of this meeting, the Heads had a meeting on Thursday evening to consider whether they should prepare a petition to Convocation. They sat at Vice's and had hardly begun talking when in came Hampden.

Long silence, each looking at one another.

Dean of Christ Church: 'Um – it's very strange of you to come, seeing we are met to discuss you.'

This Jenkyns repeated. Hampden attacks him. Then the Dean says,

'It was I that said it.' So they went on fighting. . . . Shuttleworth who was against him asked, 'Do you mean to vote on the question?' He said 'no' – Then he said, 'Well, Mr Vice-Chancellor, or the President of this Inquisition, I demand of you copies of Mr Newman's, Mr Pusey's, and Mr Hook's late sermons and I can show *them* to be contrary to the articles.'

The Dean: 'That is a very insolent speech' etc. etc.

After some time and a particular discussion of his heresies, they came to the vote and were 9 one way and 9 the other, Vice who has casting vote being against him. 'Oh', says he, 'If it comes to this *I* will vote' and so gave his casting vote for himself. Then the business of the meeting being over, the party against him wanted to talk over matters without him – and he would not go. So the Dean goes and pokes the fire and turning to H., says 'How long do you mean to stay?' When he was gone, the party against him stayed and sent off a memorial to the Archbp. . . .[13]

In March 1836 there was a great gathering of the Oxonians of the family to attend the vote against Hampden in Convocation. Melbourne had proved obdurate and the anti-Hampden party in the University was determined to strike at the new professor in the only way left open to them – to deprive him by vote of Convocation of his right as Regius Professor to have a voice in the appointment of Select Preachers before the University. Their first effort was thwarted by the proctors who vetoed the proceedings; a second attempt in May, when new proctors came into office, succeeded by the considerable majority of 474 votes to 94. The whole affair was carried out in high spirits and with sanguine expectations. Samuel suggested that they should propose a motion to compel Dr Hampden to preach in Hebrew[14]; it had been noticed, on an earlier occasion, by Francis Doyle that there was a colt named Hampden, owned by the Duke of Grafton, which was fancied as a Derby winner, and the story went round that Gladstone, when apprised of this fact, consulted a racing list and commented: 'Well, Hampden, at any rate, I see, is in his proper place, between *Zeal* and *Lunacy*.'[15]

In May they attended Hampden's Inaugural *en masse*: differences and disagreements were for the moment forgotten in the excitement of going to war. The only cloud in that Oxford sky was the absence of the most high-spirited and tempestuous of them all – Hurrell Froude, who, more than anyone else, would have relished this occasion to confound the latitudinarians. He had died, after a long illness, on 28 February 1836 at his home in Dartington at the age of thirty-three. 'As to our present loss', Newman had written to Robert, 'I cannot speak of it – as you may well understand. I never on the whole can have a greater.'[16] Samuel passed on the news to Louisa Noel: 'Did you hear anything of Froude's death – of the quietness and peace with which that mighty intellect left its tabernacle, as if it had been the departing breath of a fainting child, on a Sunday, when his father had read the liturgical service with him, and had just finished a sermon. He was, I think, upon the whole, possessed of the most original powers of thought of any man I have ever known intimately. He has left MSS behind him enough to make 2 or 3 volumes, all unfinished but which will be published.'[17]

During the earlier visit in March, the Wilberforce party took the opportunity of having a long talk with Newman into the night. Robert and Samuel were there; and Henry Manning and G. D. Ryder.

> We got Newman upon several of the most mysterious parts of the Christian revelation [Samuel wrote later to Louisa Noel], as well as upon some of the greatest practical difficulties to faith arising from the present torn state of Christendom, and it was really most sublime, as an exhibition of human intellect, when in parts of our discussion, Newman kindled and poured forth a sort of magisterial announcement of truth in which Scripture, Christian antiquity, deeply studied and thoroughly imbibed, humility, veneration, love of truth and the highest glow of poetical beliefs, all impressed their own pictures upon his conversation.[18]

Indeed Samuel was very much more impressed by Newman and his friends than he had been on a previous visit in November 1835. On this last occasion he had had some sour remarks to make to Robert about the Oriel Common Room. He was staying with G. D. Ryder at the time, and was a little anxious about Newman's influence over his host:

> I have passed a very pleasant week here with G.D.R. [he wrote]. He is a very good fellow. I am sorry to see that his health is so weak as it evidently is – and that it so much affects his spirits. I have not heard him preach. He has read me one of his sermons which is very sensible but too much 'whole duty of mannish', I think. I fear that Newman makes such preachers contented out of all mind which [*sic*] have less internal heat and volcanic heat than is always boiling in his own mind. . . . I spent a day very pleasantly at Oxford. Newman was very kind indeed – stayed at our inn till 11 o'clock with us. I dined in common room where the sights and sounds were curious: the cantankerous conceit of Denison's pettishness; the vulgar priggishness of Neate's jokes; the loud ungentlemanliness of Eden's cutlip arguments; the grunt of Ben Harrison; the disinterred liveliness of Golly and the silence of Newman: contemplating the actively employed fish mouth of that quondumbial Christie were all *surprenant*, nay *épouvantable*.[19]

Samuel Wilberforce's churchmanship, during the middle years of the 1830's, is not easy to define. There was so much in the Evangelicalism of his father's generation that he had cause to love, so many of the 'Peculiar' tendencies of his own generation that made him wince. The worst features of the 'Peculiars' were their unscriptural emphasis on 'illumination' together with the spiritual pride which so often accompanied such 'Calvinistic' teaching,[20] and their correspondingly 'low' conception of the role and authority of the Church. For this reason both he and Robert felt that they could no longer tolerate the ranting histrionics and undisguised undenominationalism of the Bible Society. When Robert, as early as 1831, wrote to tell Samuel that he was intending to sever all connections with it, his brother agreed: 'I feel all you say about the Bible Society. . . . If the Sackville St. junta had established a *Church* Bible Society, I should have joined it.'[21]

Robert and Samuel did not always see eye to eye in their estimate of the Evangelicals. In 1831 Samuel admitted that he was liable to be more indulgent than his brother to their peculiarities and that he would infinitely prefer a sermon from an 'X' (an Evangelical) to one from a 'Z' (a 'High and Dry'). He was writing about a visit to Ryde and his encounter with the curate there:

> He seems to me to be a sincere and humble Christian, but very slow indeed, and his sermons from all accounts are of just the lunar rainbow sort of inefficiency and generalization, which you would expect to find from an X superstructure upon so foggy a foundation. I am to preach there the next Thursday evening Lecture, and what the good people will say to me I know not. There is a great deal, I fear, of want of charity, great judging of one another – and a great deal of that sort of summer lightning religion which the muggy atmosphere of a little town full of old maids etc. is apt to excite. There is with it I really hope much true religion – and I am by habit and constitution less offended by the evil and ill taste – and catch more readily something I hope of good warmth from such society – than you do, but when they get to evil speaking, faugh! . . . The more I see the more I am convinced of the evil of general preaching, of the evil of cold preaching, and of the infinite superiority of the X's over the Z's.[22]

Robert was certainly less respectful than Samuel to the inherited tradition. He did not share his brother's deep and enduring regard for C. R. Sumner, and on one occasion in 1837 incurred a firm rebuke for speaking scornfully of the Bishop's qualities. 'I must say one or two of your expressions about the dear Bishop', wrote Samuel, 'gave me a good deal of pain. e.g. "Throw him overboard" and "as your Bishop I will not speak" etc. I dare say you meant nothing – but it looks disagreeable in writing. You must remember that affection and respect are both *very strong* in me towards my Bishop.'[23]

A month later, however, Samuel confessed in his diary that he was drawing further away from his Bishop in his approval of the resuscitation of Church principles at Oxford: 'I am in a false position with him', he wrote. 'I do not hold what he truly dislikes in Pusey and Newman etc., and I hardly know how to disavow this without seeming to disavow what I do hold – being more High Church in feeling than he is. Lord keep me humble and free from the fear of man.'[24]

On Daniel Wilson, Bishop of Calcutta, the brothers were similarly divided in opinion. Samuel always held him in high esteem, especially admiring his sermons and theological writings.[25] In all his letters he would write of him with real affection.*

To Robert, on the other hand, Daniel Wilson seemed to bear the ineradicable imprint of the brashness and vulgarity of St Edmund Hall.

> Did you hear Daniel's demonstration at 79 Pall Mall? [he wrote to Samuel in July 1845] My dear Father used always to remark on Law's (of Bath and Wells) charge to Middleton, in that he was sent to India 'to stop the progress of Enthusiasm – Fanaticism'. I should have thought that Daniel might have thought that he had as much to do in India in opposing Paganism as in withstanding Church Principles. I wonder whether he still stops while he is expounding at prayer, and asking of any persons who are present what they think about it. The truth is the man is no gentleman – and therefore his exaltation to a position of honour brings out all the violence and overbearing traits of his character.[26]

He wrote of him in rather more kindly vein a few months later, after he had been staying at Bishopthorpe with Archbishop Harcourt when Daniel Wilson was a fellow guest:

> We had a very singular scene at Bishopthorpe the other day with Dan: Calcutta. While the servants were moving breakfast in the great dining-room, up he comes to His Grace, and falls down upon his knees to ask a blessing. The Archbp. was quite taken by surprise – and did not get out of it as he ought and might have done. However, after a sort of blessing, up springs Daniel and embraces him. Then he went on to tell us that when he came back from India, Inglis fell on his knees to him for a blessing. One cannot but feel that in all this there is a feeling after a reality in the Church's offices, which the other acts of the parties fail to vindicate. . . . At a meeting

---

* E.g. Wrangham MSS. VI. 300. 1 September 1846. 'I saw Daniel Wilson at Portsmouth, just re-embarking for India. Strong and vigorous; and full of heart and hope.' He did not show such respect towards the younger Daniel Wilson who succeeded his father as Vicar of Islington. On being asked to find a headmaster for Islington Proprietary Grammar School in 1836, he wrote to Newman 'Can you suggest anyone who will creep into the midst of the bee-hive and poison the Islingtonians?' (Oratory. Miscellaneous Letters, 1829–1836, no. 99.)

which he [D.W.] attended at York, he spoke strongly of the importance of supporting the Prop. Soc. [S.P.G.], but with a kind of reservation which greatly took off the force of all he said. It is obvious that there are people about him who get him to modify his tone, while at the same time he wishes to give satisfaction to Church people.[27]

If Daniel Wilson was prepared to defend the principles of Church order, this – in Samuel's eyes – would atone for his occasional unseemly Evangelical exuberance. Samuel had a horror of the evil effects which might arise from defiance of the canons and formularies of the Church and from a lukewarm attitude towards episcopal authority. 'Gospel-preaching' Christianity, on the other hand, was wholly admirable. The true genius of Evangelicalism was its Christocentric emphasis, its soteriology, and its compulsive sense of mission. It is no surprise, therefore, to find him in 1833 singing the praises of the Church Missionary Society for the benefit of Charles Anderson.

We have been busy setting up Church Missionary Associations hereabouts [he wrote] with much prospect of usefulness. It is my favourite society – so thoroughly Church of England, so eminently active and spiritual, so important for a maritime nation, whose eminence has led her to carry the devil's missionaries everywhere. I often think that the way to keep up the honour of our flag is to use our naval supremacy more by far for the promotion of God's glory – or we shall be thrown aside as Tyre and Carthage have been before us. I hope you are a good friend to it. Have you any associations about you? That and the Church building society are my especial favourites. You must be looking round you now for openings to use your influence, station, etc., wisely for GOD's glory. The time is short, my dearest Charles – and if he come at the *first* watch and find them watching, 'blessed be those servants'.[28]

It was quite possible for a man to be as firmly wedded to the Evangelical cause as this while counting himself an active supporter of the Newman party at Oxford. The Tractarians seemed to be supplying the deficiencies of the Evangelicals and correcting their excesses. This is clearly shown in a letter, dated 6 November 1835, in which Samuel described to Robert his impressions of a visit to Birmingham with G. D. Ryder to see an Evangelical friend called Shirley and to hear Richard Spooner address a large public meeting on Church affairs:

George Ryder and I went over to see Shirley, whom we found very kind and hospitable, very little changed from old days, but much improved I should think in clerical character by practical acquaintance with parochial work; in some degree too 'X', which I attribute very much to his wife's influence – evidently a strong minded and somewhat vulgar woman who has been supposed to be the more 'illuminated' of the two and therefore competent to instruct him. I plied him with the duty of enforcing Church principles and he answered by the plausible arguments of expediency. . . .

I was pleased at the Birmingham meeting with the evidently strong Church spirit which is rising there. The meeting was not much less than 3,000 strong – more than half men – and all cheering all 'the most offensive parts' of the church system – e.g. tithe collecting etc. Richard Spooner was in the Chair and spoke at the beginning and ending of the meeting. He impressed me very much. I had expected a good speech, as far as power and words go; but he was 'dignified' also. . . . There was nothing approaching to vulgarity in his appearance, words or thoughts, and he was evidently highly appreciated by the people present.[29]

Samuel respected the Tractarians for two qualities above all others: their magnification of Episcopal authority and their call to holy living. In April 1835 he wrote quite crossly to Charles Anderson for joking about the Church of Ireland and for suggesting that it would benefit from a dose of presbyterianism. This was no subject for jest. Presbyterianism could never withstand popery; worse than that, it was unscriptural. 'I believe that the Episcopal form of government is the appointment of God through his inspired apostles; and that the *assurance* we have of the validity of "sacraments generally necessary to salvation" comes from our adhering to "the apostles' fellowship as well as doctrine".'[30]

It is interesting, too, to observe that Samuel's first encounter with the writings of Pusey (*Tract 18* on 'The Benefits of the System of Fasting' stirred him deeply. His comments in his diary (Good Friday 1835) are worth recording:

Read Pusey's tractate on Fasting. Am convinced by it – if not of the duty, yet certainly of the expediency of conforming to the rules of the Church on this point. I think it likely to be especially useful to me in 3 ways:—
First in enabling me to *realize* unseen things: one of my especial difficulties.
2, as likely to help me in prayer in which I am greatly interrupted by an unbridled indolence.
3, in helping me to subdue the body to the spirit which I think very needful for me – being naturally more prone than many to like eating etc.
I have also been brought to this conclusion both by seeing in my dearest Father's private journals his difficulties on this very point when he set himself to serve God in earnest – comparing it with the mortified and unself-indulgent life he led afterwards; and also by Mr Martyn's experience recorded in his journals on the same point. I have therefore determined with GOD's help to make a conscience of observing the fasts of the Church. I set myself no exact limit of abstinence – intending only to practice on those days with a view to self-conquest and humiliation such self-denial –

especially in meat, drink and the like – as I can do *secretly* and without injury to my health or present exertion.[31]

Moved as he was by the power of Pusey's words, he looked for the exemplars of disciplined self-denial amid the ranks of the rival tradition. Henry Martyn had proved the efficacy of such discipline by the manner of his life and death. Samuel was reminded yet again of his father's teaching.

II. *Filial Duties and Dilemmas*

That Samuel should have felt this so strongly at this time is not in the least surprising. He was engaged in editing Martyn's letters and journals for publication and had been working, together with Robert, for two years on the compilation of the five-volume biography of his father. Both undertakings were labours of love. The charge – recently made by Mr Ford K. Brown – that the two 'High Church' sons of the Emancipator were so embarrassed by the militant Evangelicalism of their father that they deliberately suppressed certain facts about his career and manipulated their evidence in such a way as 'to minimise, or even to conceal so far as they could, their father's adherence to the Evangelical party'[1] is an opinion hardly supported by the facts.[2]

There are grounds perhaps for supposing that, had Robert been left to himself, he might have tried to tone down some of the more ardent and intimate expressions of his father's Evangelical zeal. But neither Samuel nor James Stephen (to whom the book was read before publication) would allow this. When Robert objected to the frequent and lengthy extracts from William's religious journals ('these . . . quite grate upon the ear'),[3] Samuel protested that 'I really believe striking out such notice will do more to abolish the living interest of the *Life* than almost any similar alteration which could be suggested'.[4] Four months later, Robert admitted that Samuel had been right. 'In the years I send', he wrote, 'you will probably want more detailed extracts from the Diary. I have rather shrunk from thus exposing him too much, but I confess the more I have seen of such extracts, the more reconciled do I become to their publication.'[5]

The finished work can hardly be described as a great biography. It is prolix and dull.* Some of the dullness may be explained by the refusal

---

* 'Not a model biography', Leslie Stephen commented in his article on William Wilberforce in *D.N.B.* LXI. 217.

of the authors to intrude their own personality into the narrative. This they conceived to be their duty. Not only were they anxious to abstain from using phrases which might betray the filial connection; they even sought to refrain in their daily lives from entering any religious controversy which might expose their 'apostolical' sympathies, lest their opponents should seek their revenge by attacking the biography when it appeared. This, at least, is how Robert felt. He wrote to Samuel in November 1835: 'I am not as you know one of those prudent people who will run no risks, but I think it is quite our duty to keep in the background till our work is out. ... It would greatly injure us if we were to get violently attacked as Apostolicals – and tho' it is our duty to run this risk for ourselves, yet not till we have launched My Father.'[6]

It was this quality of withdrawal which most appealed to James Stephen and which he singled out for special praise in his review of the book for the *Edinburgh Review*: 'It is impossible to deny the praise of fidelity and diligence, and unaffected modesty', he wrote. 'Studiously withdrawing themselves from the notice of their readers, they have made no display of their own theological, scientific and literary wealth. Their work has been executed with ability, and with deep affection.'[7]

Not all the reviewers were so kind. *John Bull* and the *Literary Gazette* praised the book; the *Record* was non-committal, considering it 'interesting and useful'.[8] But the *Quarterly* and the *Christian Observer* came out against it. Exception was taken to the lukewarm treatment of Clarkson, whose work as a pioneer of the cause of emancipation had hardly been recognised. The *Christian Observer* made specific charges of misrepresentation, mainly on the grounds that the authors had presented their father as an upholder of the doctrine of baptismal regeneration. The reply, sketched out by Robert, was simply this – that their father's view on baptism, however much it may have resembled 'Oxford-tract doctrine', was defined accurately in the book; the view objected to 'was taught me by my father himself'.[9]

The treatment of their father's religious views in the biography provides no reliable evidence that Samuel and Robert had proceeded far into the Oxford camp. In fact, from other evidence available, we may be quite sure that Samuel was lagging some way behind his brother on this journey. While Robert was following Newman in his researches into the early Fathers, Samuel was lost in the hagiography of Evangelicalism. Not satisfied with presenting his father and Henry Martyn to the world, he threw in for good measure a *Sketch of the Life of the Rev. John Sargent,* to form an introduction to his edition of Henry Martyn's journals, and his *Note Book of a Country Clergyman*, dedicated to C. R. Sumner, and published anonymously in 1833. These works have a single theme: the portrayal of Evangelical sanctity, the working out of dedicated lives, illumined and enriched by the gift of God's grace. For all Samuel's respect for Newman and his increasing admiration for the Caroline divines, he was still very much his father's son.

His mother, the good, garrulous Barbara, who outlived her husband by thirteen years, was somewhat perplexed by the eager interest which all her children took in affairs at Oxford in the 1830's. But she tried to follow their enthusiasms, reading portions of Newman's works with knitted brow and calling for their help when she found his arguments beyond her. She was not at first hostile to the Oxford teaching, only curious, since the doctrinal emphasis was different from what she had been brought up to understand as all-important. Alarm was shown only when rumours of popery came to her ears, or when any of her sons were attacked for apparent disloyalty to the teaching of their father. In 1835 she took counsel of Samuel to discover how sympathetic he really was to the Oxford school, whose praises Robert and Henry were always singing in her ear, and which was beginning to attract hostile attention in the Evangelical press. Samuel replied:

> My dearest mother, I well know that we must expect to be calumniated. All persons must, who do not fall in with the fashion of the day; and above all those who offend that most irritable class, the self-contented religionists of small attainments, are sure to be maligned. ... I do not understand the Articles in a Calvinistic sense. But I do maintain that I understand them in their true sense. For though written in great part by Calvinists, they were not intended to maintain Calvinistic opinions. The errors they were aimed at were the errors of the Scholastic Philosophy, and it is only ignorance which makes many think that they refer to Calvinism where they really are aiming at quite another mark.
>
> ... I belong to no school. In many things I do not agree with the few Oxford Tracts I have read. But I do agree as far as I can with all these great lights which God has from time to time given to his Church; with Hooker and Bramhall and Taylor, with Beveridge and Stillingfleet, and with the primitive Church of the first three centuries. It may be called Popery by an ignorant or a malicious latitudinarian; but, if I do not greatly mistake, it will one day be found that he was far nearer to Socinian heresy than I to the Romish inventions.[10]

Barbara's fears were allayed for the while. A letter written three years later to Samuel, however, reveals that she was feeling keenly the tension between her love and respect for her sons and her allegiance to the group with whom she regularly attended Bible readings, amongst whom were many Calvinists very hostile to the tenor of Newman's preaching.

I am little read in Mr Newman's works [she wrote], but the want of the Saviour's being held forth – the want of comfort to the penitent and contrite being dwelt on always strikes me and when I have read his Sermons could feel with Mrs Neale who said 'If I had no better hopes than Mr Newman's views afford me I should be very wretched.' . .'. Surely the reading of Scripture by the laity is not enough encouraged – and Preaching is undervalued. Yet whatever I have seen of his, or heard read, has a weight in it which I wish I could find in other authors. I am thankful to say that neither Robert nor Henry teach like him . . . on these points I have mentioned. Henry's sermons are exceedingly good and interest *me* he does very greatly; as the countenances of his congregation shew they do them – and it was only yesterday morning dear Robert delighted me, in reading in course in his family, the History of Jacob and Esau, in speaking most delightfully of the Promises made in Xt. *to every penitent*. You could not have done it more strongly or more to the comfort of my soul.

. . . I am afraid that the first part of this letter appears as if I took more against Mr Newman's views than I do – yet I think the wants I have mentioned do exist. I have heard much against other points and the dangers of popery but I *know nothing* and am thrown into such different Circles holding such opposite opinions and maintaining them with much warmth and apparent reason sometimes that my poor mind is greatly moithered and often sadly wavering. Yet I think on the Sacraments and on Calvinism I feel *perhaps* more with them than on any other points – yet I must lament the many divisions in the professing Xtian Church. Have you read Newman on Anti-Christ? It struck me much and I think agreed considerably with your view of the Man of Sin.

. . . I think however that the Papal power must be in some degree Anti-Christ and I see Robert does not *quite* agree with Mr Newman's views on this subject. It is an awful thing to look forward to such a Time as these sermons speak of. Oh that any I love may be on the right side in such a dreadful struggle and that for the Elect's sake the Time may be shortened. I perhaps may have passed out of this world before it comes and if I can but stand before the Son of Man – be admitted into the Paradise of God, happy will it be to be gone hence: for, alas how could I stand against a fiery Persecution? . . . I must say Mr Manning's views in conversation affected my mind exceedingly, especially with regard to the Union, in this world, between Christ and His People. May he be one with us and we with him. St John 14 Chap. I must conclude. . . .[11]

She had already taxed Robert (in April 1837) about a report in the *Record* which had described him as a disciple of Pusey and a secret proselytiser on behalf of the Church of Rome. Robert wrote to rebut these charges in a vein very similar to Samuel's letter to his mother in 1835:

> I have not seen the *Record*. I am sorry they should slander me, tho' it seems to be their habit about everybody – so I need not be surprised. As to my adopting Pusey's opinions, all I can say is I have read little that he has written and in that little seen much which I disapproved. Therefore tho' he is, I doubt not, a good and able man, I should be sorry to adopt all his opinions. As to Newman's becoming a Papist, it is very likely his enemies will charge him with it, for he is certainly not a Socinian – and men's opponents I observe always charge them with being inclined to one or the other. His book lately published on *Romanism and Popular Protestantism* contains much of his controversy with the French priest and I think gives some of the most convincing refutations of Romanism I have seen. But, my dear mother, we must not distress ourselves about what may be said by hard and prejudiced men about us. We can but do our duty and avoid all needless misconceptions and we may be sure that, do and say what we will, we shall not avoid them altogether.[12]

Neither Samuel nor Robert was insincere. They both wished to avoid committing themselves at a time of mounting party strife, largely because they perceived both the virtues and the excesses of the two chief contestants. They knew well enough what they abhorred – Calvinism and Socinianism, and anything which might tend to lead towards these heresies. If they both held no high opinion of the Church of Rome, Robert – because of the great influence which Keble had wielded over his spiritual development – was more disposed than Samuel to enter fearlessly into the work of unearthing those pure and ancient Catholic principles which the first generation of Reformers, in a fit of wanton destruction, had tended to confuse with Roman perversions. He had communicated to Samuel his love for the Caroline divines and his respect for the Fathers, but there was a limit in this work of resuscitation of the teaching of the primitive Church beyond which Samuel was not prepared to go.

Deep down inside him, two convictions always held Samuel in check: his absolute certainty that his father had not been in error on the fundamentals of the Christian faith, and his belief that the Reformers, for all their mistakes, had none the less been guided by the will of God. Samuel believed, as passionately as Newman did in the 1830's, that the rôle of the Church of England was to demonstrate the *via media* between Protestant heresy and Romish corruption. Unlike Newman, throughout his life he maintained a remarkable, perhaps a unique, consistency, in his understanding of what this *via media* should be. Some may call this pigheaded; others may see it as typifying Samuel's refusal ever to face problems fairly and squarely, a sort of intellectual coldness-of-feet. Many of his contemporaries tried in later years to disfigure his public image with the epithet of 'soapy' or 'slippery', passing to posterity the picture of a man who was adroit and elusive, 'who sniffed the way the Court winds blow',[13] and who deserted friends and befriended foes as circumstances dictated. On the other hand, what some have seen as weakness may also be represented as his strength. The Church of England would have cause to be grateful in the years that lay ahead to a man whose convictions stood the test of calumny and the extremity of private grief, who, while abandoned by all whom he held most dear, could still insist unflinchingly on a *ne plus ultra* – and plot exactly where that limit should be – as the necessary safeguard of that doctrinal synthesis, that admixture of Catholic and Protestant elements, which was the true essence of Anglicanism.

This, however, is to anticipate. In the early 1830's, Samuel was uneasy about the attitude of the Evangelicals towards the Church. He welcomed the first numbers of the *Tracts*. By the winter of 1834, however, he came to feel uncertain about the influence of John Henry Newman, and resolved to hold back. It was the first sign of the parting of the ways.

III. *The Law and the Gospel*

Samuel Wilberforce was frightened by the theological implications of Tractarianism. It may be said that to separate the theology of the Oxford Movement from its programme as outlined in the first *Tracts* (the resuscitation of Church principles and the elevation of episcopal authority and the priestly office) or from its moral vocation (the call to holy living) is to detach the soul from the body and thus to nullify both parts. They are interdependent, the one needing shape and expression, the other requiring that animating principle which could convert a desire for institutional and moral reform into a real spiritual movement. This Samuel would not have conceded. He was fond, in later years, of speaking about the 'peculiarities' of the Tract system, by which he meant its unacceptable doctrinal accretions to the pure body of High Church theology as taught by Richard Hooker and Bishop Beveridge.* The doctrine of Reserve

---

* See especially his letter on the alleged Tractarianism of his two books for children (*Agathos* and *The Rocky Island*) in A. R. Ashwell, *op. cit.*, I. 217–18.

was one such; the over-emphasis of sanctification to the exclusion of justification was another; a third was the Tractarian teaching on the enormities of post-baptismal sin. He believed that if these items were rejected – as being, as it were, accidental excesses, brought to the fore by that tendency to extremism which must always accompany theological conflict – then Tractarianism would be entirely acceptable and the Oxford apostolicals and sober-minded Evangelical churchmen could meet on common ground.

So they might. But Tractarianism without its peculiarities would no longer have been Tractarianism; and what Samuel thought to be its accidents were to Keble, Newman and Pusey the very essence of the system which they were striving to recover. Each of the three peculiarities to which Samuel took exception was none other than the individual theological contribution of each of the acknowledged leaders of the movement. Keble had supplied Tractarianism with its distinctive ethos, its yearning for sacramentalism and its understanding of the nature of worship by his teaching on the doctrine of Reserve.[1] It might be unfair to Pusey to say that his chief individual contribution to Tractarian theology was his teaching on post-baptismal sin; nevertheless his understanding of the central position of the Eucharistic Sacrifice, and the supreme importance of its mediatory role, was so closely related to his baptismal teaching that to have challenged the one must have entailed at least a partial repudiation of the other.

The same could be said of Newman's teaching. So convinced was he of the iniquity in appealing to the privileges of the Gospel without recognising the obligations of the Law, that he came to stress with a vehemence truly horrifying to the faint-hearted the pitfalls and uncertainties in the Christian's quest for sanctification. Christians too often deluded themselves into thinking that the way to salvation was easy; that the claims of obedience were light; that even if the flesh was notoriously weak, God's mercy was boundless, and He would be indulgent at the last to good intentions. Beware of false hopes!

There may be found in the writings of all the Tractarians an undercurrent of pessimism and gloom. With Newman, however, the severity of the message is inescapable. It was as if he conceived it his duty to bring all professing Christians to their senses, to undo the harm wrought by generations of Evangelical preachers who had profaned the Holy Mysteries by speaking of them in a vulgar and familiar tone, and who had implanted in their hearers a perilous over-confidence. There are two sides to every coin. All gifts must be paid for. The Christian religion itself can bring comfort to the weary soul; but it also induces a holy fear. This is the recurrent theme of Newman's Anglican sermons.

It may be illustrated by a passage from a sermon preached early in his Anglican ministry and by another from a sermon delivered at its close. At Whitsun 1831, on the subject 'Christian Nobleness', Newman had this to say:

> Does not this Scripture imply thus much, whatever else it implies, – that our ascended Saviour, who is on God's right hand, and sends down from thence God's Spirit, is to be feared greatly, even amid His gracious consolations? Hence St Paul says, 'Work out your own salvation with fear and trembling;' . . . This great truth is impressed upon the whole course of that sacred fellowship with Christ, which the Church provides for her children; in proportion as it is more high and gracious than that first intercourse, which the Apostles enjoyed, so is it also more awful. When He had once ascended, henceforth for unstudied speech there were solemn rites; for familiar attendance there were mysterious ministerings; for questioning at will there was silent obedience; for sitting at table there was bowing in adoration; for eating and drinking there was fasting and watching. He who had taken his Lord and rebuked Him, dared not speak to Him after His resurrection, when He saw and knew Him. . . . And as the manner of His coming was new, so was His gift. It was peace, but a new peace, 'not as the world giveth;' not the exultation of the young, light-hearted, and simple, easily created, easily lost: but a serious, sober, lasting comfort, full of reverence, deep in contemplation.[2]

On 22 September 1842, he preached his greatest sermon of all on this same theme – 'Feasting in Captivity'.

> One danger there is – that of attempting one of these aspects or constituent portions of the Christian character while we neglect the other. To attempt Apostolical Christianity at all, we must attempt it all. It is a whole, and cannot be divided; and to attempt one aspect of it only, is to attempt something else which looks like it, instead of it. 'All is not gold that glitters', as the proverb goes; and all is not Catholic and Apostolic, which affects what is high and beautiful, and speaks to the imagination.
>
> Religion has two sides, a severe side, and a beautiful; and we shall be sure to swerve from the narrow way which leads to life, if we indulge ourselves in what is beautiful, while we put aside what is severe. . . .
>
> Let us recollect this for our own profit; that, if it is our ambition to follow the Christians of the first ages, as they followed the Apostles, and the Apostles followed Christ, they had the discomfort of this world without its compensating gifts. . . . If we have only the enjoyment and none of the pain, and they only the pain and none of the enjoyment, in what does our Christianity resemble theirs?[3]

Samuel felt the force of this – as all Christians must. But the proportions were somehow all wrong. He felt this on reading Newman's first published volume of sermons, a presentation copy of which he received in November 1834. He at once took Newman to task, complaining of the unscriptural tone, most particularly in the way in which the author appeared to deny the free working of the Holy Spirit in bringing sinners to repentance: 'God's spirit acts as a free agent: . . . there are unnumbered passages of Scripture which use *this* language; but I remember none which urge instant repentance on the ground of a certain time being necessary for God's spirit to work in.'

He felt that Newman's injunctions on a change of heart as necessary to salvation were unduly severe, taking exception to the passage in the sermon on 'Sins of Ignorance and Weakness', where Christians are warned to guard against spiritual vanity in these terms: 'Let us then approach God, all of us, confessing that we do not know ourselves; that we are more guilty than we can possibly understand and can but timidly hope, not confidently determine, that we have true faith.'[4]

He concluded by informing Newman that he had sought the opinion of James Stephen, who had agreed in deploring that a man of such evident gifts 'should contrive to invest Christianity with an aspect so harsh and repulsive'. Stephen had added that, from the point of view 'of touching other men's hearts and influencing their conduct . . . Charles Simeon is worth a legion of Newmans'.[5]

Newman replied at length in two separate letters. The essential point was this: his commission was to preach the scriptural norm, not to indicate exceptional instances of God's mercy.

> In truth there is much that is unknown. Infants are saved without a formed character of holiness; God has other ways of saving. He has *many* mansions in His house. This is my private comfort, but I dare not *preach* so, lest I should be wise above that is written, lest I should depart from the letter of my commission. The whole of Scripture speaks of holiness being indispensable, and a change of heart – the whole of Scripture speaks of our being judged by our works. Must I not boldly preach this? and then leave particulars to the time and place as they come?[6]

He turned to James Stephen's comments in his second letter:

> I allow that my sermons are not adapted to *influence*; first I have selected them on purpose on a different principle, next the Xtian preacher, using his own words cannot dare hope to be more than a Baptist preparing the way for the Gospel. Doubtless Mr Simeon is ten thousand times more attractive than I, but not than the Church I serve. The Baptist is but the

friend of the bridegroom – and hath not the bride, and speaketh (so to say) of the earth. It is as a Priest that I should have influence – i.e. in the sacraments, ordinances etc. of the Church – and since the divinely ordered system is (alas!) but poorly developed among us, no wonder I seem cold and uninfluential. The single ordinance of the Lord's Supper, rightly taught and administered, is full of persuasion. But that is a large subject.

Why did he preach so much on the subject of sanctification? The times demanded it:

My reason for dwelling on the ... subject was my conviction that *we required the law* not the Gospel in this age. We want rousing – we want the claims of duty and the details of obedience set before us strongly. And this is what has led me to enlarge on our part of the work not on the Spirit's.[7]

Samuel did not find this explanation satisfactory, and wrote rather brusquely to say so.

I cannot think we are at liberty to reason out what should be the exact tone of our preaching without testing our conclusion by the modes of address exhibited in S.S. It seems to me (if I may so speak) spiritual Quixotism to trust to the results of reasoning on this subject rather than to the example of Scripture.
    ... The Scripture modulus places no limit on the Spirit's power of renovation, but teaches them [sc. lapsed Christians] to doubt his *willingness* if they refuse to listen *in the day of grace*. I might add that this is the tone of our Lord's teaching in the parable of the Virgins – the wedding garment – the Servant whose lord was absent etc. ... Here then, as it appears to me, is an *evident* difference between your mode of address and that of Scripture which of itself suffices to prove you wrong even though in the slippery subtlety of argument I cannot detect your particular errors.[8]

A further exchange of letters ensued.[9] But Newman soon lost patience. On 23 April he dispatched a letter of ominous stiffness:

My dear Wilberforce, As I see that I cannot by letter sufficiently explain to you my views ... so as to profit by your remarks upon them, I write this to save both of us ... the trouble of writing more. ... I do not feel that you allow your mind swing enough to put yourself into my views.[10]

In the meantime, Samuel had been having further correspondence with James Stephen. He had clearly exceeded the bounds of propriety in passing on to Newman Stephen's comments which had been made in a private letter. It is interesting to see that Stephen, in letters both to Samuel and to Newman, was very anxious to correct the former impression of hostility. Evangelical though he was, Stephen was quick to perceive that Newman had exposed the fatal weaknesses in the system of the

'Peculiars'. On the whole he was prepared to take Newman's part. 'No man,' he assured Samuel 'has exhibited the Gospel in a holier and more dignified aspect. . . . It is in no irreverent spirit that I am disposed to compare him to the Baptist in an age of Herodians, Sadducees and Pharisees, greeting his disciples as a generation of vipers, and asking, with much more of sternness than compassion, "who has warned them to flee" etc.'[11]

This did not mean that he was wholly convinced by Newman's arguments, or that he was prepared to renounce the tradition in which he had himself been reared. He explained himself more fully to Newman.

> That this [sc. Evangelical] mode of instruction is capable of great improvement, I cannot doubt. But it seems to me to possess the inestimable advantage of being right in the great fundamentals. . . . I can scarcely bring myself to doubt, that a preaching replete with these subjects, is the mode of administering sacred truth which is most in accordance with divine will, and with our very weak and puerile condition.
>
> Thus my acquiescence in that which is usually called Evangelical preaching, for myself, and my deliberate selection of it for my children,[12] is certainly not founded on any delight in the mere intellectual accompaniment – nor in any belief that it takes possession of the whole ground which ought to be occupied: but rather in my persuasion that the world being what it is, and I and mine partaking to our full proportion of the common infirmities, it is that discipline which is the best calculated for our improvement. Besides, I have no manner of doubt that defective as this so called Evangelical system is, they who addict themselves to it surpass those who reject it, comparing the two Bodies collectively, in almost all the other requisites of good preaching. We are living at a time when it is difficult to form a fair estimate of what this scheme of theology really is or might become – this being a degenerate age, to which one might apply what someone says of Fanaticism in the second generation – that it then invariably runs to seed. Simeon is one of the last survivors of the race in whom were exhibited the genuine characteristics of this doctrine, before it had become diluted by fashion and by being the symbol of a Party.[13]

Now Newman really did open his heart – he could hardly fail to in response to this challenge. He was obliged to discuss with Stephen the fundamentals of the Christian ministry, as he conceived them, and to explain the errors in emphasis which he discerned in other acknowledged and revered teachers. Above all, he had to show that there was a better way. In a letter of extraordinary power and insight, he began by suggesting that the test of good or bad preaching was an improper one to apply; and because the Evangelicals were wont to apply it, they thereby revealed a weakness in their system. Sermons were not the principal ministry under

the gospel. He agreed that Christian teaching must be based on fundamentals and that the Evangelicals in concentrating upon the doctrine
of the Atonement were 'but natural witnesses to our need and its remedy'.
He continued:

> In this spirit I would receive the Incarnation as the great doctrine of the
> Gospel – and certainly we cannot and need not get beyond it and its
> developments. Now the (so called) Evangelicals feel this by a natural instinct
> – the instinct of spiritual life, which all of them (I would trust) have in a
> measure, and some in high measure. While I say this, I must not forget
> to state my most entire agreement with you, according to my limited know-
> ledge of them, in what you say about the difference between the last and
> present generation of them. Schools of men seldom outlive their founders
> without declension, and they tend to corruption. The Church alone has
> the principle of reproduction and renovation lodged within it – and though
> for years it may seem a dry and sapless stock, yet at length has a fresh
> spring. I am told that the school of Neander in Prussia is already degenera-
> ting. In like manner, while lamenting the present state of their followers,
> one cannot but look with the greatest respect on the integrity and zeal of
> such men as Scott, Joseph Milner and Venn; and on the fidelity with
> which they brought out certain great lines of gospel Truth; especially the
> Incarnation, as including the two great doctrines of the Divinity of Christ
> and the Atonement.

Even the best of them, however, were not above rudeness and irreverence in dealing with holy subjects.

> The poorest and humblest ought to shrink from the irreverence necessarily
> involved in pulpit addresses, which speak of the adorable works and suffer-
> ings of Christ, with the familiarity and absence of awe with which we speak
> about our friends. Zaccheus did not intrude himself on our Lord – the
> woman that was a sinner silently bedewed His feet. Which of us is less
> refined than 'a tax-gatherer or a harlot'?

What was needed, above all else, was the reverential spirit and a finer
appreciation of the sacramental system as the guardian of the fundamentals of the Christian faith. Bishop Butler was almost alone amongst
his contemporaries in perceiving this truth.

> No mode of inculcating doctrine upon Christians can be imagined so
> constant, public, universal, permanent and at the same time reverential
> than that which makes the form of devotion, the memorial and declaration of
> doctrine, reverential, because the very posture of the mind in worship
> is necessarily such. In this way Christians receive the gospel literally on
> their knees, and in a different frame of mind from the critical and argu-
> mentative temper which sitting and listening engender.
> Hence the supreme importance of sacraments, as demonstrated by the

history of the Primitive Church. What indeed can so well supply the very desideratum you speak of ... as that ordinance in which we bring back (as it were) the solemn event on Mount Calvary, and 'shew forth', reiterate and continue on 'the Lord's death' day by day? In no way perhaps has the Church of Rome inflicted more injury upon us, than in making us afraid of this most blessed and gracious privilege, in consequence of its own abuse of it. ... I am persuaded that the only way to stop fanaticism, irreverence, and (on the other hand) Popish supersitition is to return to this primitive Catholicism on which happily our Services are constructed. ... The Sacraments with their accompaniment are the permanent presence of Christ and His Gospel.[14]

Stephen was delighted by this and arranged for Newman to come and visit him at his home. He then wrote to Samuel in high enthusiasm: 'It would be difficult without seeming absurd to express the veneration I feel for his understanding and for the use he makes of it. He has established an alliance between the two apparently antagonistic principles of quietism and shrewd common sense – a sort of Benjamin Franklin graft upon a Fénélon stem. There is nothing more elevating, more pure, and more thoroughly to the purpose, than his printed sermons.'[15]

Samuel was not so sure. He felt, on the whole, that the salutary elements in Newman's teaching outweighed the perilous, and joined with his brothers in deploring the first attacks upon the Tractarians in the Evangelical press. All his friends seemed to be falling victim to 'Newmania' – even Charles Anderson, who was bubbling with fury at the 'stupid, wishy-washy' emotionalism and 'dirty pride' of the *Christian Observer* in venturing to criticise his idol.[16] In October 1836, Anderson wrote to Samuel to tell him that he intended to establish a depot at Lincoln for the distribution of the Oxford Tracts,[17] and, in January 1838 he described the progress of his Tractarian sympathies in terms which caused Samuel some disquiet:

I am more and more convinced of the importance of those views of Apostolical Succession and the Sacraments which the Oxford men enforce. The safety of Christ's Church seems to depend upon them. My only danger is the dislike I feel to those who do not agree with them and the hazard one has in consequence of forgetting that all the clergy are equally to be considered as Ministers sent by God. ... I think Herbert says, God preaches patience when you hear a bad sermon. ... I think the Oxford men are more self-denying than any I know, which after all is the great Test.[18]

There was nothing in this letter to which Samuel could really take exception, but he felt it necessary to issue a word of warning:

I agree with all you say about the Oxford school. *But I have some fears.* When did the mind of men not move into extremes? My principal fears are: that they will lead to the depression of true individual spirituality of mind, in the rebound of their minds from the *self-idolizing* tendency of the late leading religious party*; by leading others to elevate solely the *systematic* and communion parts of Christianity – that they will disgust some well intentioned churchmen by a fanciful imitation of antiquity and drive them into lower depths of Peculiarity.

I cannot use all their language about the Eucharist. I cannot bear Pusey's view of Sin after baptism. They hold up a glorious standard of Holiness, and for *us*, my dear Charles, who know well the riches of the Gospel and can supply all they leave deficient it is the very thing needful – but there are ignorant and bowed-down souls who need I think a more welcoming treatment than their view of penitence will allow.[19]

Charles Anderson took the point, and admitted that he was inclined to let his enthusiasms run away with him. He had such an innate hatred of puritanism that the new *penchant* for 'observances' was particularly attractive to him. 'I think I see clearly the truth of the middle course you are taking.'[20]

James Stephen was having second thoughts, too. He could never remain any man's disciple for long. He began to feel irritated by Newman's insistence on obedience and horror of private judgment and suspected that he was trying to turn himself into a kind of Pope. Also – ironically – he began to turn Newman's own arguments on the inevitable declension of 'schools of men' into a strong case for repudiating the ominous dependence of the Oxford churchmen on the personal qualities of their leaders. He wrote to Samuel in May 1837:

> I think you may as well keep . . . Messrs Newman and Pusey for *occasional* associates only; for if not they will infallibly teach you to talk about 'sacramentals', to bow towards the altar, and to start at the look of the consecrated wine. . . . Pray do not allow your Oxford friends to subjugate your understanding to their dreams which are very distinguishable from their genuine inspiration. They are only taking a new road to very old conclusions, and proving once again how the pain and impatience of doubt drive men to repose on human authority. What is humility and poetry in the founders of these schools degenerates rapidly into arrogance and downright nonsense in their disciples.[21]

In view of the consistency with which Samuel had cautioned his own

* Spiritual pride was to Samuel the worst characteristic of the 'Peculiars'. See his description of one of Louisa Noel's relatives in a letter to Charles Anderson (Bodleian. c. 191. 14 April 1836) – her 'miserable, whining, canting drawl: creeping on like a broken-backed spider and seeming all the time to say "how good I am".'

friends against an uncritical acceptance of the Oxford teaching, and his refusal to echo the former eulogies of his correspondent, it looks rather as if James Stephen had committed the unpardonable sin of trying to teach Minerva wisdom.

IV. *The 'Renversement des Alliances'*

Although Newman and Samuel Wilberforce had agreed to differ on the subject of justification and sanctification in the spring of 1835, their relations remained fairly amicable in the months that followed. Samuel expressed his admiration for the third volume of Newman's sermons,[1] and ventured – in the winter of 1835 – to send him a little collection of religious poems in the hope that he might think them fit for publication. The response was not encouraging – Newman thought the poems 'too Byronian' for a clergyman to publish[2] – but at least the gesture was repaid by Newman who, having ascertained that Samuel shared his views on the nature of sacred poetry,[3] offered him the *Lyra Apostolica* for review in the *British Critic*.

This, as things turned out, was rash. Both Henry and Robert could have told Newman that Samuel was unlikely to give the volume unqualified praise, since, when the verses had first appeared in separate numbers of the *British Magazine*, he had then expressed the opinion that many of them were 'very poor'.[4] It rather added to the embarrassment of both parties that the poems, which made up the *Lyra*, were by six different contributors (by far the most prolific being Newman himself), who were identified in the volume by a letter of the Greek alphabet,[5] so that the reviewer, while respecting their anonymity in his article, was clearly perfectly well aware of the authorship of each poem which he singled out for praise or blame. He might appear impersonal, while giving vent to his spleen. To be fair, Samuel had tried to excuse himself from undertaking a task which, if he was to be strictly honest in its discharge, would almost certainly involve treading on someone's corns. Unfortunately, they had to be Newman's.

The two letters, however, which Newman wrote to Samuel when he had received the review (before transmitting it to the editor, Boone) do not suggest that he was in any way put out. Indeed in both letters he expressed his warm thanks for the article, adjudging it 'very valuable' and looking forward 'with great satisfaction to its appearing in print'.

In the letter dated 'Monday evening', he added 'the only fault I find with it, is that . . . the letter δ is brought rather too prominently forward: and makes one feel modest or sheepish'.[6] Newman's was indeed the only single contribution actually assessed at any length in the review – not surprisingly, since it comprised about three-quarters of the volume; and if Samuel was able to recognise the exceptional beauty of certain of his poems – four were singled out for praise (numbers 23, 25, 36 and 132) as well as three of Keble's (numbers 17, 163 and 164) and two of Froude's (numbers 16 and 79)* – he was not noticeably reticent when it came to finding fault.

The volume was reviewed in conjunction with three others in an article entitled 'Sacred Poetry'. For the general tone of the work, Samuel had nothing but praise.

> It is a book of a thoroughly Catholic spirit. There is nothing of that sickly sentiment which so often infests devotional poetry – but all is *real* and wholesome in its tone – it is full of the objective truths of our holy religion – it duly exalts the sacraments; and it is rich in those high and ennobling associations which are the heritage of the one true Catholic Church.[7]

He then turned to the major contributor:

> The compositions of one of these writers are marked by a peculiar grandeur of thought, high poetic powers, a certain severity of feeling . . . and remarkable truthfulness of view. The main defect, we think, is in the mechanical construction of the language. It is very often to our ears constrained and inharmonious. He is a writer of whom it would probably be true as it is of Jeremy Taylor, that his prose writings would be much fuller of poetry than those in which he is fettered, and the true movement therefore of his thoughts impeded, by the arbitrary restraints of verse. We should indeed decidedly say at once, that their author, though possessing every other qualification of a poet, was radically wanting in a metrical ear, if it were not that the beautiful flow of some of his pieces seem rather to mark the harshness of the others to be the effect of haste or carelessness.[8]

In a later passage he regretted also what others had sometimes taken exception to in Keble's verses – 'obscurity of language, or studied quaintness of expression.'[9]

According to Isaac Williams, Newman was intensely annoyed. 'This was the cause, I believe, of his never writing a verse afterwards.'[10] (Williams wrote these words before the composition of the *Dream of Gerontius* in 1865.) Nevertheless Samuel, while maintaining that independence of

---

* *British Critic.* XXI. no. XLI (January 1837), 180–4. It is interesting to see that 'Lead kindly light' was one of the four praised.

judgment which sometimes earned him the reputation of being a doubtful friend, had made no secret of his admiration of the Catholic tone and temper which the authors of the *Lyra* had done so much to engender; and this, together with the University Sermon which he preached during Lent 1837, marks the highest public expression of his sympathy for the Tractarians that he was ever to exhibit in the course of his ecclesiastical career.

Samuel chose to preach from the pulpit of St Mary's a sermon on a Newmanian theme, *Receive not the grace of God in vain* (2 Cor. VI. 1). The influence of his earlier correspondence with Newman on the relationship between justification and sanctification is very plain to see; and Samuel appeared to be taking Newman's part. He pointed to the dangers of building up rash hopes 'of future amendment'; how the falling into a course of sinfulness after the purification of baptism may forfeit all hopes of a second chance. 'You may reclaim the sinner from open vice; you cannot renew him to holiness.'[11] There are some things which cannot be restored after corruption. Samuel then turned to an argument which Newman had himself employed in the letter written to him on 29 January 1835, reminding his congregation – in almost precisely the same words which Newman had used: 'that it is the ordinary mode of the Holy Spirit's working upon man, as revealed to us in Scripture, and seen in life, with which we have to do. For who shall dare to stake his salvation upon an unwarranted hope, that God will, in some unusual way, interfere in his behalf? The Holy Spirit, then, we are taught, acts upon the minds of the regenerate members of Christ's Church, in suggesting good and restraining evil, not by an irresistible constraint, but as on reasonable beings in a state of trial and discipline.'[12]

The two sermons which Samuel was to deliver as Select Preacher to the University in the following year were very different in tone. They could be taken as a blunt denunciation of the preacher's right to lay undue stress upon the fearfulness of post-baptismal sin – to remind his congregation of one truth without tempering the severity of his message by pointing to the scriptural testimony of God's unbounded mercy to fallen man. As early as January 1838, Samuel decided to switch to the attack, writing to Robert at the end of that month: 'Advise me: I think of anti-Pusey sermon on the Prodigal Son.'[13] Certainly the sermon which he preached from the University pulpit in February on the text from St Luke (XV. 31–2), *He was lost and is found*, was an extraordinary change from the harsh tone of the previous year. When his sermons came to be printed, Samuel sought to explain the apparent contradiction in the *Advertisement*: 'The first two sermons only of this set,' he wrote, 'have any direct connexion with each other; and it is important that they should be read together: for some expressions of the first, taken by itself, might seem to favour that view which the second is specifically intended to counteract. The Author is deeply convinced that the combination of these two views is an especial feature of Christ's Gospel.'[14]

He began the 'anti-Pusey' sermon by referring to the text of his previous sermon. He then demonstrated the scriptural testimony of the occasions on which sinners had been restored 'to a state once enjoyed, and lost'. These occasions of God's mercy were not 'chilled by a cold delay of pardon'. The loss of baptismal grace is not a final withdrawal of all assurance. For the sinner, 'if he comes in sincerity and faith, the seal is still sure, and is for him; his baptism is on him, fresh as when its waters glistened upon his infant brow; he is received into his Father's house; and there the words of gracious promise, the blessed seals of holy eucharists, and the fresh-springing fountain of the Saviour's blood, these are sure and for him; and they are meant to carry to his soul the same certain consolation which the holy waters of baptism would be the outward means of bringing, if he came as a catechumen, instead of coming as a penitent.'[15] It was a powerful sermon, strenuously bolstered by scriptural and patristic evidence (largely Cyprian and Augustine) and by the writings of Jeremy Taylor.*

He preached again in Oxford in November of that year. On this occasion he spoke of 'the temper of mind in which to receive the Christian Mysteries', preaching on the text of Exodus III. 5, *Put off thy shoes from off thy feet, for the place whereon thou standest is holy ground*. Again he had chosen a subject on which he could scarce forbear comment on Tractarian doctrines, for the first part of Isaac Williams's tract 'On Reserve in Communicating Religious Knowledge' (*Tract 80*) had only recently been published.

Samuel's contradiction of Oxford teaching was much less direct than in his treatment of post-baptismal sin, but towards the end of the sermon he issued a warning against those whose researches into patristic literature led them to undervalue the teaching of holy scripture, and to turn to 'man's authority and secondary fountains ... to quench that thirst of

---

* S. Wilberforce, *Six Sermons*, 53. 'Hear the words of Bishop Taylor: "it is an uneasy pusillanimity and fond suspicion of God's goodness, to fear that our repentance shall be rejected, even although we have committed the greatest or the most of evils".'

the spirit which should be slaked only at the living waters of God's word'.[16]
This led into a peroration of great beauty and eloquence:

> Seek, we charge you, as you love your souls, thus to use that sacred deposit
> which . . . the Church brings out before your eyes: turn not from it idly,
> as from some ineffectual dogma of the schools; gaze not on it curiously,
> as on some fitting thesis for skilful argument; but receive it with earnest
> reverence; lay hold on it with your affections, as the very pith and kernel
> of that blessed revelation which from it unfolds itself in every part into a
> pervading principle of life, and peace, and joy.[17]

What had happened to bring about this change of tactics? There can be no
doubt that it was the publication of Froude's *Remains*, in the opening
months of 1838, with the disturbing revelation (which the editors,
Newman and Keble, had allowed to break upon a largely unsuspecting
public) of Froude's profound contempt for the early Protestant Reformers.
Samuel had been growing restless at the tone and content of recent
Tractarian publications – Pusey's three *Tracts* (67, 68, 69) on Baptism in
1836, Newman's *Lectures on Justification* early in 1838, with its onslaught
on the doctrine of justification by faith alone. A reading of Froude's
Remains compelled him to speak out. He wrote to Robert in December
1837 when news of what was in the wind reached him: 'Henry's account
of Froude's *Remains* truly grieves me. They will I fear do irreparable
injury. He says "He seems to *hate* the Reformers"!!'[18] In January he
noticed that High Churchmen everywhere were receiving a bad press –
'It is all the fruit of the wretched folly of Froude's *Remains*.'[19] In his
diary he described the work as 'Henry Martyn unchristianised'[20] and
lamented to Charles Anderson that the effect must be to '*put back* numbers
who were beginning to imbibe better Church views'.[21]

Just as Manning, in November 1843, was to take the opportunity of the
November 5th sermon at Oxford to demonstrate that the cause of the
Church was not lost by the publication of *Tract 90* and by the Romanist
leanings of Newman, who had recently resigned the living of St Mary's,
so Samuel in 1838 felt that it was his duty to warn all those who were
boarding the Tractarian vessel that – once they slipped their scriptural
moorings – they would be likely to drift into stormy seas and maybe at the
last end up in an alien port. He had no intention of attacking Newman or
Pusey individually. Manning, who was in Oxford at the time, assured
him that the sermon had aroused no personal resentment:

> The sum, I have heard, is this. I heard that some of Pusey's friends
> thought parts of it unguarded, but did not seem to think it directed

against him. On the other side, the Champneys school thought it *was* directed against him, and were pleased with it. ... I derive ... much satisfaction in this respect, that those who would be likely to be sensitively alien to anything like attack on Pusey did not seem to feel it, and therefore it had not the effect I had apprehended. I should indeed have been most unfeignedly sorry if it had been so, and it is a relief to my mind to find it otherwise, and you must ascribe my fears to the sensitiveness I feel about every overt and important step you take.[22]

He could not, of course, speak for Newman, who seems to have been much displeased. In one of his notebooks in which he recorded from time to time his opinions of his friends and acquaintances, he wrote in 1862 a very frigid account of his relations with Samuel: 'Whatever alliance there was between us was brought to an end by his preaching against Pusey's view of Baptism in the University pulpit; I forget the year.'[23]

At the time, however, he felt the snub sufficiently deeply to take a reprisal; and in July 1838 the opportunity came. He was then editing the *British Critic* and received a letter from Samuel with the offer of an article. He replied as follows:

My dear Wilberforce, – I felt the kindness of your offer, and certainly it seems folly to hesitate about accepting it, considering who offers it; yet, on the whole, I think it best to do so. ...

To say frankly what I feel – I am not confident enough in your general approval of the body of opinions which Pusey and myself hold, to consider it advisable that we should co-operate very closely. The land is before us, and each in our own way may, through God's blessing, be useful; but a difference of view, which, whether you meant it or not, has shown itself to others in your sermon before the University may show itself in your writings also; and, though I feel we ought to bear differences of opinion in matters of detail, and work together in spite of them, it does not seem to me possible at once to *oppose* and to co-operate; and the less intentional your opposition to Pusey on a late occasion the more impracticable does co-operation appear. While I feel, then, what I lose, and not the least on the particular subject you have selected, I think it best to conclude as I have expressed above. With kindest thoughts, I am, my dear Wilberforce, yours very truly, John H. Newman.[24]

At the time, Samuel was not greatly perturbed. Robert showed the most vexation, branding Newman's action as 'foolish'.[25] Samuel sent the news to Charles Anderson.

Newman has just, very kindly towards me but as I think very unwisely, declined receiving any more articles from me in the *British Critic* because my sentiments 'do not sufficiently accord with those of Dr Pusey and himself'. This is to me another mark of Party Spirit which I greatly lament seeing amongst such great and good men. He knows well that I am a strong and dutiful Church man – and to refuse co-operation from such – because the *colour* of their opinions is not exactly the same as his, is to prefer party to truth: and to seek rather to attach to himself a body-guard of men than to disseminate through the existing Church a higher measure of Church sentiments. However they are great and good men – and have a great vocation.[26]

Who was right? In a sense, they both were. The storm which the publication of the *Remains* had raised was such that the Tractarians were being attacked from all sides. In Oxford there had been a *renversement des alliances*. In 1836 High Churchmen and Evangelicals had joined together to bring about the discomfiture of Dr Hampden; now the Evangelicals and latitudinarians came together to embarrass the Tractarians. Newman had no time for waverers and doubtful friends. Samuel, on the other hand, felt that the Church party needed every ally it could find, and that to raise the party banner was to exacerbate ill-feeling and to convert potential friends into open foes. They had only themselves to blame for the fuss over the Martyrs' Memorial affair in the winter of 1838–9.

This project, devised by the astute and scheming mind of C. P. Golightly (now a bitter enemy of the Oxford party), had at least the implicit intention of embarrassing the admirers of Froude's *Remains*. Could they conscientiously subscribe to a monument to the Protestant martyrs? More to the point, were they so hostile to the work of the Reformers that they would be prepared to risk the triumphant charges of disloyalty and Romanism to which refusal to subscribe would inevitably give rise? As a scheme to detach the waverers and moderates from the extremists it was perfect. Samuel was quite clear as to what should be done. He wrote to Robert on 29 November 1838:

> The proposal for putting up a memorial to the martyrs and Bishops now fills men's mouths: some say it is a slap at Froude's *Remains* and so at Newman and Pusey. It is exceedingly desirable surely that they should turn under such an imputation by at once subscribing as the inscription (I will put in a prospectus in case you have not seen it) is most entirely unobjectionable *me judice*. Indeed I believe Pusey originally suggested part of it. Party division runs high at Oxford, and numbers are sent to Cambridge instead of Oxford even by parents not X's through fear of Popery etc. e.g. even some of the Phillimore set are so doing. This presses most heavily on Oriel, and McBride told me the Provost felt from it that he could not at once choose the best to admit but must take such as he can get. Surely this is the necessary consequence of publishing such a book as Froude's.[27]

From this point onwards, in almost every issue which divided the Tractarians from the main body of English churchmen, Samuel Wilberforce and Newman found themselves on opposite sides. As events turned out, this estrangement was to prove more serious to the cause of Newman and Pusey than either might have anticipated in the 1830's. It so happened that all of them were in firm agreement on one point: the entire respect and complete obedience due to the episcopal office, and Samuel in 1845 was to succeed the sympathetic, if somewhat perplexed, Bishop Bagot in the diocese of Oxford. The new bishop was neither very sympathetic nor very greatly perplexed. In fact his views and criticisms of the Oxford party had changed not at all. He hated party spirit as keenly as ever, and the horror of Romanism had intensified rather than abated. Pusey, left with Keble to rally the Tractarian ranks – severely reduced and dispirited after the news of Newman's secession – thought to find in Samuel a powerful ally; hoped that memories of early friendship and common battles would prove stronger than the differences and misunderstandings of later years. This indeed was wishful thinking. Before Pusey had made any overtures to his new bishop, Samuel had written privately to Louisa Noel deploring his 'great want of humility', his 'sophistical and false' writings and his 'egotistic assumptions'. 'There must be *some cause*', he had written, 'why so good a man should fall into such fearful errors and do such deep mischief.'[28] It was a sad anticipation of the later parting of friends that Samuel should – as early as 1842 – have begun to speak of Pusey's party as 'that bad word beginning with T'.[29]

v. *The Brothers and Henry Manning*

On the whole his brothers had been spared these misgivings. Henry had no qualms whatever, at least until 1839. While Samuel sighed anxiously over indiscreet expressions in the introduction to the *Lectures on the Prophetical Office of the Church*, Henry crowed to Robert 'the X's will gnaw their tongues for rage. Poor creatures, they are to be pitied.'[1] He had the highest praise for both the *Lyra Apostolica* and the *Lectures on Justification*,[2] and took delight in conforming to Catholic custom in his ministry.

> Now about bowing at the Holy Name [he wrote to Robert in November 1838], I have one rule: whenever it is spoken and I am standing or sitting I bow e.g. Creeds (Athanasian when it is pronounced by the *people*),

Lessons, Gospels, Epistles, Sermons, prayers at the altar. Of course not when I am *kneeling* as in the desk prayers, nor at any other name than Jesus as Christ. The reason – that this is ordered by the canon and the Catholic custom. The rationale, I suppose, because as Jesus is the human name (answering to John, Peter etc.) by paying Divine honour to that name we profess the *reality* of the incarnation etc. against Nestorius and his modern fry.[3]

As usual Henry kept the others posted of events in Oxford. In March 1837 he sent Robert a bulletin which he had recently received from Newman:

Apostolicity is growing so fast in Oxford that I trust it is not too fast. Do not say all that I am going to say *from me*. At Magdalen two men have taken to wear the stole. Oakeley is growing prodigiously and is Whitehall Preacher. Sewell's article in the *Quarterly* is reckoned in London the greatest triumph our principles have had. At Exeter right opinions are strong. At Magdalen, Trinity, University and Oriel nucleuses are forming. Marriott goes the whole hog. Browell is much stronger. Ch. Ch. alone is immobile. Archdeacon Hodson's son . . . has taken up apostolic views.

Henry added his own comments:

It is very remarkable. I fear we must make up our mind to reverses. I mean the most painful of all – wrongheadedness or falling away in one direction or other, when light spreads so fast, but the LORD will provide.[4]

Two years later – in April 1839 – Henry was even more sanguine.

Newman has now morning and afternoon prayers at St Mary's as well as afternoon at Littlemore. The whole interior of the latter is really something beyond description – so solemn and Catholic. Church views in Oxford spread in a degree which astonishes all men. Men like Hamilton 'desiring to sit at the feet of such men as Pusey and Newman' – daily service at St Peter's etc. etc. – and what *I* feel more, the very men who now revile them assume as their axioms the very principles for which they themselves reviled Newman etc. six years ago.[5]

In the summer of that year – at a great gathering of the Tractarian clan to attend the dedication of Keble's new church at Otterbourne – Henry was to get a painful shock. Newman first intimated to him that his conviction in the *via media* was weakening.[6] Looking in his mirror, he had seen for a moment the face of a Monophysite. Shortly after the Otterbourne rally, Newman read Wiseman's article on the Donatists in the *Dublin Review* and was again tormented by doubts – the words of St Augustine ringing in his ears, *securus judicat orbis terrarum*, a phrase which seemed to demonstrate that catholicity was a more essential requirement than apostolicity. Newman and Henry met again in October that year, and during a walk in the New Forest, Henry heard a more disturbing confirmation of these early doubts. 'For the first time since I began the study of theology', Newman said to him, 'a vista has been opened before me to the end of which I do not see.' Henry's appalled response was that he would wish to see his companion dead rather than become a Papist, to which the other rejoined that if serious danger were to come, his petition would be that his friends should deliver up just such a prayer.[7]

The clouds lifted for a season. But Henry was never again to know complete peace of mind. He did not, however, communicate his fears to the others; nor indeed did he see any the less of his mentor. To Samuel, who was now being branded as an apostate, Henry's antics and enthusiasms seemed wayward and irresponsible. While Henry was feeding Robert with up-to-the-minute reports of party manœuvres at Oxford, Samuel was writing to him in a very different vein: 'Do you know that Henry was at the conclave of Newmanians at Oxford?' he wrote in April 1839. 'Two things were voted: one to christen Henry's new boy Hurrell Froude (he tells me so), the other to prosecute my mother for heresy on grounds given in by Henry – *inter alia* – saying Newman resembled the "worst parts of Clement of Alexandria". Henry touched the clouds with applause for having "given up his mother".'[8]

In his religious opinions, Robert occupied a position mid-way between his two younger brothers. Although his relations with Newman had been a little strained after his acceptance of Brougham's offer of the living of East Farleigh, he was able to resume a fairly intimate correspondence with him from about 1835. In 1837 Newman had consulted him about materials for Froude's *Remains* and had sought his services as a contributor to the *British Critic*. He began to report directly to him accounts of the progress of apostolic views at Oxford.[9] In June 1838 they corresponded about the value of the theological writings of Alexander Knox, whose views on the Apostolical Succession as preserved in the Anglican Church have been represented as a significant anticipation of the stress which the Tractarians themselves were to lay on this doctrine.[10] Newman had no very high opinion of Knox. Indeed he had read very little of him: 'I do not know enough of Knox to speak [he wrote]. He seems to say dangerous things, but then his works are private letters, and his words can hardly fairly be taken by the inch. I should be unwilling to think him more than an eclectic, though that is bad enough. Froude did not like him. I think his works on the Eucharist have done much good'.[11]

Robert was not drawn into the controversy between Samuel and Newman on the alleged unscriptural tone of the first volume of *Parochial Sermons*, but he corresponded at length with his brother on the *Lectures on Justification*. He described his first impressions of the book in May 1838: 'Much of it is quite capital. The subject is one, which I feel I have never understood and have been very uneasy at: for while its importance and prominent station make it essential to speak of it in general terms, I felt I was not going to the bottom of it.'[12]

Robert's perplexity may surprise us to-day, especially in view of the immense respect which his own theological powers commanded amongst his contemporaries. But this bewilderment was by no means singular. The first three decades of the century had witnessed a spate of polemical writing on the subject of *sola fide*, most of it little more than the ephemera of party conflict. What was lacking was a systematic exposition of the Anglican position. For this reason, Newman could state with some truth that the doctrine was '*terra incognita* in our Church'.[13]

Robert explained his difficulty further:

> I confess I have found it hard to steer between one of these alternatives – either pure solifidianism, of which one feels all the falsehood and evil at once – or else the assertion that faith is moral not intellectual – of the heart, not the head, and then is not our salvation the result of works not of faith? St James seems to agree with me and say it is: but Daniel Wilson used to tell us the contrary. Newman's book has not as yet enabled me to see my way, but I trust by the aid of what he suggests I may get towards it.[14]

Two years later, when he was beginning work on his first book (*The Five Empires*, published in 1841), he found himself forced to master the doctrinal teaching of the Reformers, and came to the conclusion that Newman's criticisms of Luther had been just, if his hostility to the Reformers generally had been somewhat misdirected.

> I have been much struck in Maurice's books [he wrote to Samuel in 1840] with his remarks upon Luther's position as wanting something to satisfy the mind. I now see the meaning of what Maurice said when we dined there, which was then a sealed book. . . . I should like to see that subject treated by some man who had not only head like Maurice but as much learning as would fill the square in Guy's Hospital. I cannot believe Luther right in his views – on the contrary the more I read the more entirely do I agree with that profound book of Newman's about Justification (his view is very much Maurice's with one exception) – but I admire and value Luther as Newman does not.
>
> Now my feeling is that the Reformation satisfied a longing of men's souls for some want i.e. of the means of pardon which Popery had staved

off by its 'rags of saints and purging fire'. Where men of earnest and thoughtful mind were found they accepted its solution. But the Reformation did not meet men's longing for another thing – the unity of the outward Church. Hence these two principles have ever since been in conflict, and the one cannot master the other. But during the first heat of the Reformation men hoped the whole Church would go with them, so that then this want was not perceived.[15]

Robert was near to Newman's position in the late 1830's, and was especially respectful of his bold attempt to find the doctrinal mean between the two extremes of Romanism and popular Protestantism, and to introduce system where no order or clarity had been. But he shared Samuel's misgivings about Froude's *Remains*, felt profoundly uneasy at Pusey's tract on Baptism,[16] and showed his disapproval of the Tractarian onslaught on the Reformers by subscribing a guinea to the Martyrs' Memorial Fund.[17]

It would be nearer the truth to say that Robert was drawing closer to Manning than to Newman; but in fact their close intimacy did not begin until 1843, when Manning came to stay at Burton Agnes while conducting a preaching tour. In 1836 Samuel described Manning to Robert in terms which suggest that the two men had met but rarely: 'H. Manning is a very pleasant as well as profitable companion. He reads and thinks a great deal especially upon Church subjects and is really become not only a thoroughly sound but a very well informed Churchman. He is likely I think to be very useful here – in the clerical meeting etc., though several of the old X's, especially Bliss, are jealous of his influence and set themselves to thwart him and to lessen it.'[18]

Henry's intimacy with Manning was of earlier date, through the circumstances of their being brothers-in-law, but their regular intimate correspondence did not begin until 1837, when Henry and Mary came to stay with Manning after Caroline's death.[19] Of the brothers, Samuel was the nearest to Manning during the ten years immediately following his marriage; he, W. E. Gladstone and S. F. Wood were Manning's closest friends.

Newman he hardly knew in these early years; but potential supporters and distributors of the *Tracts* were soon brought to Newman's notice, and by 1835 Manning was, as it were, on the mailing list. Newman wrote to him in 1835 to ask him to find a bookseller to handle the sale of the *Tracts* in and about Chichester.[20] In the same year he was invited to participate in a study of the Fathers with a view to contributing to the *Tracts*.

Manning suggested St Vincent of Lérins as a suitable subject, offering to prepare a *Catena Patrum* on Catholic Tradition. 'It is curious you should mention the subject', Newman replied. '[It was] the very next subject I meant to have taken.'[21] This catena was published in February 1837, with additions by Charles Marriott, as *Tract 78*.

At the time of his marriage in November 1833, Manning was accounted an Evangelical. His passage, therefore, into the Oxford camp was effected very speedily – almost as quickly, indeed, as his first conversion through the offices of Miss Bevan. Fortunately Manning has put on record a statement of his religious opinions in the 1830's, and from his own recollections, letters, and published writings, it is possible to reconstruct the development of his views up to the point of his receiving as an acknowledged High Churchman the preferment of the Archdeaconry of Chichester at the age of thirty-two in 1840. The sources show not only the remarkable individuality and independence of judgment of Manning as a young man but also the futility of reducing the discussion of ecclesiastical and theological history into terms of Church parties. No party label could have been meaningfully applied to Manning in 1833. This is clear from his own description of his views at that time, written some fifty years afterwards:

> The state of my religious belief in 1833 was profound faith in the Holy Trinity and the Incarnation, in the Redemption by the Passion of our Lord, and in the work of the Holy Spirit, and the conversion of the soul. I believed in baptismal regeneration, and in a spiritual, but real, receiving of our Lord in Holy Communion. As to the Church, I had no definite conception. I had rejected the whole idea of the Established Church. Erastianism was hateful to me. The royal supremacy was, in my mind, an invasion of the Headship of our Lord. In truth, I had thought and read myself out of content with every system known to me. Anglicanism was formal and dry, Evangelicalism illogical, and at variance with the New Testament, Nonconformity was to me mere disorder. Of the Catholic Church I knew nothing. I was completely isolated. But I held intensely to the 'Word of God', and the work of souls. In this state I began preaching to the poor in church, and in their homes.[22]

A letter written some thirty years earlier, when his memory was fresher, to Samuel Wilberforce, describing the sad story of their gradual estrangement, on the whole confirms this analysis, with the single exception of the development of his views on the nature of the presence in the Eucharist. 'When I came to Lavington in 1833 I believed, as I always did, in baptismal regeneration: I had no view on the sacrament of the Body and Blood of Christ; and no idea of the Church. You sent me in the year 1834 to Hooker to learn the doctrine of the Real Presence.'[23]

Other evidence enables us to test the truth of this statement. Gladstone recalled that the young Henry Manning was quite out of sympathy with Henry Wilberforce's early flirtation with High Church doctrines and that he recommended a course of work amongst the poor and the sick to 'knock such High Church nonsense out of his head'.[24] Manning's earliest letters to Samuel reveal a growing understanding of the sacramental principle. In 1835 he was writing strongly on the essential link between baptism and confirmation, between regeneration and renewal. 'I am convinced that neglect of confirmation is one of the great and efficient causes of our present low state of religion in the Church. Regeneration without renewal is as a withered seed, and renewal without repentance and faith i.e. the personal appropriation of God's mercies in Christ, is impossible.'

There were two perilous errors – 'the one in preaching baptismal regeneration but neglecting . . . confirmation and renewal, the other in preaching personal appropriation of God's mercy to the adult, and denying regeneration in Baptism – *which involves necessarily Pelagianism or Calvinism*'.[25] He had been reading Jeremy Taylor on Confirmation and Bull's *Condition of Man before the Fall*.

That these views – and his course of reading – were leading him towards an open sympathy for the Oxford school and the *Tracts* is clear. He became friendly during 1835 and 1836 with William Dodsworth, one of the few Cambridge supporters of the *Tracts* and at that time minister of Margaret Street Chapel in Cavendish Square: 'Dodsworth I see often and like very much', he wrote to Samuel in November 1836. 'Did I tell you . . . that Carr has been here? . . . You will be glad to hear that he is righting wonderfully in his views. He is very strong on Baptism, and on all other points shows a good Catholic temper.'[26]

Two months later he was writing to Samuel again with a pronounced apostolical tone:

> Does not the mystery of our weakness lie in our neglect of apostolical censures, and absolution? I hear that Jones's parish is in a state very unsatisfactory to himself, that out of about 1200 he has 40 or 50 communicants. The whole is solved when you hear that he never preaches on the Eucharist, and expresses, I believe, a wish that his curate shd. also be silent about it. This seems to me like trying to build Stonehenge singlehanded, and without any mechanical power. And is not this very wilful when Christ has appointed the apparatus . . . ?[27]

Up to this point, Manning appears to have developed along very similar lines to those of his brother-in-law. In December 1834, Samuel had consulted him about Newman's sermons, before writing his lengthy critique of his treatment of the doctrine of justification. Manning's letter in reply shows him in general agreement with Samuel's views:

> As for Newman's sermons [he wrote], I have had no time to do what I promised – and the more I read them, the more I feel that it is the hardest book to criticise I ever met with ... because it contains so much truth, and because its fault is rather defect than disease. ... It exhibits religion most fully and pointedly as a system of *requisitions*, but seems to cramp the attractive, encouraging and cheering spirit of our 'better hope'. ... I believe this general appearance results from omission rather than positive assertions. And moreover the omission of the agency of the Holy Ghost, as a person continually present, helping, teaching, strengthening, guiding, and enabling us to use God's appointed means of renewal, is especially unfortunate when the general tone of the Sermons is that of requisition.[28]

Again like Samuel, during 1835 and 1836 he sometimes gives the appearance of being fickle in his allegiances, now defending the catholicity of the Anglican Church with the Tractarians (as he did in a brief controversy with Dr Wiseman in the pages of the *British Magazine*, signing himself 'A Catholic Priest'),[29] now representing himself to Gladstone as the defender of the Evangelical cause in the dispute over the management of the S.P.C.K.[30] It may be true, as E. S. Purcell has written, that Manning was still accorded the mild benedictions of *The Record* (the organ of the extremist wing of the Evangelicals) up to 1838, but it is clearly an over-simplification to maintain that it was not until his wife's death that Manning 'passed out of the slough of Evangelicalism'.[31]

The first five years of his ministry were of immense significance to Manning's religious development. It was during this time that he came to concern himself with – and to perceive the germs of his later answer to – several fundamental problems which were to become the great preoccupation of his life: wherein lay the authority of the priesthood to be a witness for Christ? How could one determine whether one's teaching had the stamp of authority? Were there *rules* which one could take as an infallible guide? If the essence of the Church were its unity, how could the sin of schism be uprooted? In Manning, as in Samuel Wilberforce, we are confronted with a person of extraordinary single-mindedness and, despite apparent tergiversations, remarkable consistency. At the close of his very long life, men looked back – not always very kindly – on a momentous career which had embraced the prosecution of a series of dramatic causes: infallibility and authority; the enduring power of tradition; the exalted character of the priesthood; the unity of the Church; the depression of secular pretensions; the championship of the fundamental rights of labour and the conquest of poverty. Every one of these issues became real to him and were impressed upon his mind in varying degrees of urgency during the years immediately following his ordination.

Manning wrote in the late 1870's: 'The first question that rose in my mind was, What right have you to be teaching, admonishing, reforming, rebuking others? By what authority do you lift the latch of a poor man's door and enter and sit down and begin to instruct or to correct him? This train of thought forced me to see that no culture or knowledge of Greek and Latin would suffice for this. That if I was not a messenger sent from God, I was an intruder and impertinent.'[32]

It may be no unusual occurrence for the newly-ordained to suffer occasional doubts about their vocation; but Manning, it may be noted, is describing the dilemma in a far from normal way. And it is especially significant, in view of the strain of social radicalism which was sometimes exhibited even in his Anglican career, that he should have raised the question of his right to force his instruction upon the poor at a time when nine-tenths of his contemporaries of his social class would have failed to recognise that there *was* any dilemma, considering themselves, as gentlemen, to be naturally endowed with the privilege and responsibility of lifting the latch of a poor man's door whenever the spirit moved them. Manning's anxiety was not for his personal vocation but for the order to which he had been called. What made a priest different from a layman? What exactly did ordination mean and on what authority did it rest? His final answer is well known, for it is the subject of his most enduring literary work, *The Eternal Priesthood*, published in 1883. His first attempt at answering this question was in July 1835 when he was called upon to preach the Visitation Sermon in Chichester Cathedral, his chosen title being *The English Church, its succession and witness for Christ.*

The sermon did not at the time excite general interest; much of it, indeed, was devoted to a brief survey of the historical evidence for the retention of the apostolic succession within the Anglican Church. Nevertheless the theme was closely akin to the first of the *Tracts for the Times*, the major precept of the sermon being 'magnify your office'. The office of the priest is great, almost too great for any man to bear; it is 'invested with a dignity of unequalled brightness'[33]; through the peculiarity of its direct link with Christ's apostles, it is raised incomparably above any 'other office of moral teacher or labourer in God's service'.[34] This, however, is no badge of honour or rank to be proudly flaunted; it is rather a burden to be borne with humility and awe. 'We magnify our office, not to exalt ourselves, but to abase; for it is ever seen that they who lay the least stress on the commission, lay the most on the person; and they that esteem lightly of the derived authority of Christ's ministers, exalt personal qualifications, intellectual or spiritual, into credentials of their ministerial office. "But we have this treasure in earthen vessels", fragile, and vile, formed of the dust, and to the dust returning, "that the excellency of the power may be of God, and not of us".'[35]

This aweful awareness of the nature of the sacerdotal commission and the vivid sense of the historical continuity of the commission from the apostolic era were – as early as 1835 – so keenly impressed upon Manning's mind that he was already exposing his detestation of the two elements which most threatened to frustrate that witness for Christ with which the Church was charged, although as yet his tone lacked the stridency and vehemence which were to mark his later writings. The poisonous elements were schism and subordination to secular power. 'For these three hundred years, men have seemed to sicken at the very name of unity; and to contemplate the unhealthy self-production of sects and divisions within the bosom of the Church with a spurious charity, a cold indifference, and even a misguided satisfaction. . . . Our hearts' desire, and prayer to God for his Church is, that its scattered parts may be again fused, and recast into a perfect and indissoluble unity.'[36]

Then, while recognising that it was 'the providential design of God to his Church' that it should throw out branches, and that these branches should be '*national*, . . . *endowed* and, . . . *established*', he was quick to point out that these features are only 'accidental adjuncts, and perishable dignities, separable altogether from its indestructible essence, against which alone the gates of hell shall not prevail'.[37] What the world gave, the world may take away. The Church in England could be disestablished. This could not, however, render it any less the witness for Christ. 'The invisible spiritualities of our apostolical descent, and our ministerial power in the Word and Sacraments, no prince, no potentate, no apostate nation, can sully with a breath of harm.'[38]

The closing pages of the sermon must rank as one of the most eloquent passages which ever came from Manning's pen. As witnesses of Christ, 'we must continually seek a growing conformity to the mind and conduct of our Master'.

The mind of Christ must be transfused into our own. There must be somewhat of the same intense love of perishing sinners, of the same patient endurance of moral evil, and unwearied striving to bring the impenitent to God: a portion of the same holy boldness and fearless inflexibility of purpose: a measure of that perpetual self-denial and self-sacrifice to the service and glory of His Father: of that acute, affectionate, and universal sympathy with the sick, the suffering, the tempted, and without partaking of their contamination, even with the sinful; and somewhat also of that intuitive penetration of heart and character, which His omniscience apprehended at a glance, but we can gather only by keen observation, strict analysis, and rigid search, under the guidance of the Holy Ghost, into all the depths and windings of our own. What a mission, Brethren, is ours![39]

Anyone who would hope to understand Henry Manning, and to perceive the principles which underlay his life and work, would do well to study this sermon closely. He will cease to puzzle over Manning's intensity and effectiveness as a spiritual director, or wonder at his awareness that the Church of England would prove itself in schism if it repudiated private confession. Manning allowed his principles to develop; he sometimes changed his mind (as he did – after fearful conflict – on the question of the validity of Anglican orders); but his understanding of the fundamental character of the priesthood and of the nature of the Church – its unity and its independence of secular control – was never shaken. It was because he would not abandon these principles that he found himself obliged, in the end, to join the Church of Rome; and to fight on the side of the ultramontanists from the moment that he took this step. He, who was ever a priest, knew something of the sacrifices which that office entailed. He was conscious also of its privileges and would never allow either its character or its exclusiveness to be impugned.

Such confidence could only be engendered if there was some infallible authority to protect Christ's witness from error. The most frightening text for any minister were the words addressed by St Paul to the Galatians, *If any man preach any other Gospel unto you than that ye have received, let him be accursed* (*Gal.* I. 8–9); and it was on this text that Manning chose to preach in Chichester Cathedral on 13 June 1838, when he was called upon to deliver a second Visitation Sermon. The sermon was published under the title *The Rule of Faith*. From the point of view of Manning's theological development it is less interesting than the earlier sermon, although it provoked a far greater volume of criticism, chiefly because Manning drew his hearers' attention to the inadequacy of Scripture

as a sure and unquestionable repository of doctrinal truths. Much of
the argument of the sermon, impressively substantiated by a wide variety
of patristic sources, is drawn from his researches on St Vincent of Lérins
and his particular controversy with Wiseman, which had switched from
the pages of the *British Magazine* to those of the *Dublin Review*, concerned
with the claim of the Anglican Church to catholicity.

The substance of the argument was as follows. While every Christian
should accept that the Holy Scripture is 'the one sole foundation and proof
of the faith'[40] – as laid down in Article VI of the Thirty-nine Articles,
it 'containeth all things necessary to salvation' – it has to be admitted that
the meaning of Scripture is not always so clear that individual Christians
can be protected from error in interpreting them. 'Churches both may err
and have erred, and private Christians, by the repugnancy of their interpretation, daily convict themselves of error.'[41] There must therefore be
'some further rule for our common guidance'.[42] The first rule must be the
creeds, which were intended to act as summaries of teaching or interpretation for particular churches. 'Scripture . . . being the proof of the
creed, and the creed the interpreter of Scripture, the harmony of these is
the first rule of interpretation.'[43] After the creeds, one must look for those
'depositions of evidence' which the Church gives to her members to guide
them in faith. In the Anglican Church, the Thirty-nine Articles are such
a deposition of evidence, 'exhibiting interpretations that have obtained
from the beginning'.[44] It is, indeed, their apostolic character which renders
them authoritative. The remainder of the sermon is concerned with the
witness of antiquity, to proclaim which – it is clear – is the preacher's
main purport. He quotes at length the testimony of Archbishop Cranmer
at his trial, when he declared his veneration for 'the most holy Fathers
of old', who were the sure guide of the mind and understanding of the
early Church and whose writings therefore exposed the corruption of
Romish innovations.[45]

Much of this was good Tractarianism – and as such was rather frowned
upon by Samuel Wilberforce[46] – although Manning appears to have
worked out his position irrespective of Tractarian influence. The tone of
the peroration – like that of his previous Visitation Sermon – is fiercely
apocalyptic. As God would protect His Church against any incursion of
secular power, so He would protect her revelation against those who, with
'an insatiate lust of ever-progressing discovery . . . and a loathing of fixed
and measured knowledge', should attempt to assail the teaching of tradition. 'The first axiom of apostolic truth is, whatsoever is new is not of

Christ. God has set up the landmarks of Revelation, and no man may remove them.'[47] Against all foes and false prophets – 'Let us calmly answer, We have no power over ourselves. We testify what we have received. We may not be won over by men's allurements – of their wrath we dare not be afraid. The presence of our Master besets us behind and before; the ministry He hath laid on us is guarded by a curse. . . . We dare not yield, lest He that walketh in the midst of the golden candlesticks remove our candlestick out of his place, and ourselves be accursed in the day of the Lord's coming.'[48]

In view of the offence which the sermon caused, especially to Evangelicals, Manning published a lengthy appendix, largely devoted to a catena of authorities to support his claims. The main interest of this work lies in his attempt to rest his argument on the testimony of Scripture and the writings of the English Reformers, in the hope that his references to Cranmer and Ridley would both confound his opponents and help to allay the fears of Romanism aroused by the publication of Froude's *Remains*. He certainly failed to appease the editor of the *Record*, who accused Manning of apostasy and declared that 'the Sermon was bad enough. The Appendix was abominable.'[49] A further point of interest is that Manning, in his attempt to demonstrate the corruption of Rome, began studying Berington and Kirk's *The Faith of Catholics* – 'a work in great repute among the Roman Catholics in this country'[50] – which in the years to come was to form the basis of his own study of post-Tridentine doctrine, a subject virtually unknown to his Anglican contemporaries.

Manning's parochial sermons, published in four volumes between the years 1845 and 1850, are a valuable source for a study of his religious views, but it is difficult to plot from them the course of his development since, unlike Newman, he left all of them undated. The affinity, both in tone and content, with the more famous parochial sermons of Newman is very remarkable (as Dr Brilioth was the first to note)[51] and makes the more surprising Manning's approval of Samuel Wilberforce's strictures on Newman's severity and gloom. Manning's sermons were hardly more cheering. Neither Newman nor Pusey could have produced a more severe admonition on the perils of post-baptismal sin than his sermon 'On falling from the Grace of Baptism', based on the lugubrious text of St Luke – *Remember Lot's wife* – solemnly reiterated by the preacher to the discomfiture of his congregation. 'Let him that thinketh he standeth take heed lest he fall. Lot's wife is an example of those who fall from baptismal grace.'[52] In the same volume are contained sermons on 'Salvation a difficult work' and 'A severe Life necessary for Christ's followers'. Such a subject was one to raise the preacher to the heights of eloquence:

> To all mankind, as fallen men, the way of life is not more blessed than it is arduous. . . . There must pass on each a deep and searching change. And this change, though it be wrought *in* us of God, is wrought through our striving. It is no easy task to gird up the energies of our moral nature to a perpetual struggle. The most watchful feels as one that strives against the half-conscious drowsiness of an oppressive poison; the purest, as he that leaves upon driven snow a dark and sullying touch; the most aspiring, as a man that aims his shafts from a strained and slackened bow; the most hopeful of eternal life, as one that toils for a far shore in a rolling and stormy sea. It is a hard thing to be a Christian. It is a hard thing to keep ourselves unspotted from the world.[53]

Manning shared with Newman a horror of religious complacency. With the other, he was always saying 'we can never be sure'.

> People who are really religious sometimes trust in God's keeping, without considering the limits and conditions under which the keeping is promised to them. It is not promised absolutely, as if they should be safe anywhere, or in anything, go where they may, do what they will. . . . They know very clearly that they have no warrant to look for this keeping, if they should go out of the path of duty, or run themselves into temptation. All deliberate courting of the temptor they know does at once cancel God's promise of protection.[54]

With Newman also, he warned against procrastination. No folly could be greater than that of a man who looked for a deathbed repentance.

> Next to sin, death is the most terrible of all realities: the very instincts of nature shudder at it; the soul of all men, except great saints, must shrink from it. And even they, though filled with the love of God, are fullest of the consciousness of our fallen state at that last and fearful hour. . . . I will not say repent; because, alas for us at such a time, if we have not repented long ago.[55]

Sometimes one feels that both Manning and Newman worked out for themselves an impossible position; that the Anglican period of their lives was an essentially transitional time, when they were groping for a way of salvation which at the last they had to abandon as men without hope. They had both been touched by Calvinism; both were feeling the pull of Catholic sacramentalism. They therefore tried to reconcile the two. They were conscious of personal election (Newman had known it since the age of fifteen, Manning since the age of twenty-three) and this sense of an immediate vocation never left them to the end. Often in their sermons they spoke of predestination, *Many are called, but few are chosen.* They reminded their congregations and penitents to look for the marks of election.

> Ask yourselves, therefore [Manning wrote in his sermon 'The Sealing of the Elect'], whether or no you are one of this secret number? whether or no you have received this seal of God? ... By what tokens shall we discern the hope of our election? Not by any external signs, nor by any supernatural intimations, nor by resting upon absolute decrees and the like; but by the deep inward marks of the work of God in us, by the correspondence of our spirit with the will and working of the spirit of God.[56]

And again, in an earlier sermon:

> If we can find ... no seal, or countersign, of that service which has left its visible impression on all the fellowship of saints – ours must be a fearful self-deceit. Surely, if we have no mark upon us which He will own, when 'the sign of the Son of Man' shall be revealed – no imprinted tokens of His sharp crown, or of His sharper cross – how then shall they know us for His, who shall be sent to gather His elect from the four winds of Heaven?[57]

They believed in election, but they could not accept the comfort of final perseverance, the assurance that God would protect them through further trials. There must be striving, which may be fruitless in the end. They saw the power of sacramental grace, the nourishment to the soul through the infusion of Christ's presence in the Eucharist, but as Anglicans they felt the dangers of Pelagianism from accounting good works (which they knew to be necessary for salvation) meritorious. They came, therefore, to unite the severer elements of two different systems – the notion of election and the necessity of attaining sanctification – while rejecting the comforts (*perseverantia* and the ascription of merit to good works) which made the Cross more possible for sinful man to bear.

This may be an over-simplification of their dilemma. Newman privately took solace in his faith in the superabundant mercy of God to sinners – but he rarely preached on this theme. Manning frequently exhorted his parishioners and fellow-clergy to have compassion for those labouring in the toils of sin. At the same time, they were both men of superhuman spiritual power who steadfastly set themselves to scale the highest peaks. They thought that all men were, through baptism – to use Manning's phrase – 'saints *in posse*. Even those whose lives are openly profane and evil ... are of the nature of saints'.[58] Sometimes, in their anxiety to bring others with them, they forgot that the mass of men might be incapable of climbing further than the lower reaches. They might need to be directed to the gentler slopes; or to be equipped with a rope so strong that it could never break.

Chapter 5

CHURCH, STATE AND COUNTRY PARISH

1. *Conservatives and Reformers*

The history of the early nineteenth century abounds in contradictions. The Church of England before the Reform Bill and during the decade thereafter, which saw the successful establishment of the Ecclesiastical Commission, has been labelled both by contemporaries and historians as 'unreformed'. It is pictured often enough as blind to the forces of change, rife with abuses such as nepotism, non-residence and pluralism, hampered at every turn by an outmoded machinery, wedded to privilege, zealous only in obscurantism, and tied, partly through its own pastoral sluggishness, to an old and dying order. On the other hand, the same decades witnessed an extraordinary vitality which seems to have stimulated every limb of the supposedly sickly body – national societies were founded by the score, and proliferated in hundreds of associations throughout the land, monster meetings were held in huge public halls, tracts were published by the thousands – a frenzy of activity which cannot entirely be explained in terms of radical attack and conservative reaction, of Reformers demanding drastic change and of Tories, stung by a sudden panic, hotly defending the *status quo*. It may be conceded that the strident tone of angry polemic sometimes suggests this. But it would be a strange negation of historical law (or historiographical experience) if positive and negative could be so neatly divided, and if enlightenment could really be shown to have been the exclusive property of the progressives. The truth is rarely so simple.

Something akin to panic certainly gripped the Church at the time of the Reform Bill crisis. As Peel himself had said, once the door was opened it could never again be shut,[1] and churchmen, not unreasonably, felt acutely nervous at what a government might do which had for its allies those who crowed triumphantly 'Down with the Church'. 'Never', Dr Best has written, 'since the seventeen-thirties, had the clergy been subjected to such general scorn and dislike.'[2] In the summer of 1832 there was published what appeared to be a blue-print of the immediate

measures to refurbish the Church – *The Plan of Church Reform*, by Lord
Henley, the Evangelical brother-in-law of Sir Robert Peel – promising,
inter alia, a redistribution of ecclesiastical revenues, by reducing the
establishments of cathedrals and colleges so that the poorer clergy might
profit; a fairer deal for the dissenters who were still suffering under irk-
some disabilities; and, finally, the establishment of an Ecclesiastical Commission which should take over the management of Church property and
superintend the redeployment of its resources. We can see the sense of
all these proposals, most particularly in the eventual judicious implemen-
tation of them by Blomfield and Peel, who perceived the expediency of
acting quickly and the folly of holding back until elements less friendly
to the Church gained control and reformed the Establishment root and
branch. At the time, however, the fearful demonstration of parliamentary
control of the Establishment – the wilful flouting of conventional susceptibilities in the tampering with ecclesiastical endowments, and the evident
readiness of those in power to make further concessions to dissenters so
soon after the repeal of the Test and Corporation Acts – appalled those
whose answer to the manifest abuses in the Church was hardly less positive than that of their opponents, while being more in conformity,
as they thought, with the divinely ordained polity of the Church.

All the leading figures of this narrative fell into this last category.
They had no sympathy whatever with those who were prepared to make
concessions to popular feelings; to the argument of expediency they
stopped their ears. None of the sons of William Wilberforce had inherited
their father's respect for dissenters. Samuel commonly referred to
them as schismatics. ('Alas for England!' he wrote to Robert in April
1833. 'Her politicians are radicals and her religionists schismatics: and
the people love to have it so. And what shall we do in the end thereof?'[3])
As for politics, with the exception of Manning who eschewed all party
connections, they were all of them fierce Tories. Samuel wrote to Charles
Anderson in April 1835 in that tone of vehement hyperbole which he
delighted in using in his private letters:

> I am sure a fortnight's residence in London will convince you that you are
> really what I have always known you to be – a tory; not a nasty-jobbing-
> unimproving-slaving-partisan of loaves and fishes – but one who for con-
> science towards God obeys those above himself, and is kind to those below
> him – who hates the march of mind and of railroads – and would keep up
> the Reformed Episcopal Church of England *and Ireland* as by law estab-
> lished. I think if the so-called Whigs do knuckle down to O'Connell after
> all they said of him last year – and overthrow the Irish Church to please

him – 'I would beg just to insinuate, just to hint in the most delicate way in the world' that they are a set of as shabby, word-eating, pocket-picking, halter-earning sacrilegious villains as ever poisoned fresh air.[4]

But above all they detested any assertion of parliamentary control of the Church, especially since Parliament, through the removal of the political disabilities hitherto imposed on Catholics and dissenters, contained elements hostile to the Establishment – heretics and even atheists. Samuel fumed to Charles Anderson when he heard rumours of intentions to legislate over church rates: 'What right has Parliament to touch my chancel – or to say that because a few empty-headed and strong-hearted babblers make a great outcry – and say that they are half of the Population when they are not one 10th of it: the country shall be taxed to pay for the ancient liabilities of their Property. It is shocking to see men like Stanley giving in to such delusions.'[5]

He favoured some measures of Church reform, so he told Robert in January 1835, but he deplored the Erastianism implicit in the method by which reform was to be effected. 'I do not much like the sound of equalizing Bishoprics. I am quite sure that taking away from the rich ones will be really spoliation in its working. If it is meant to attach permanently London stalls etc. to the poor Bishoprics I think that it will be an excellent measure.'[6]

He and Manning were in complete agreement here. Manning was moving heaven and earth in 1837 to challenge the right of an infidel parliament to legislate on Church affairs. He had been prominent at a clerical meeting at Chichester in April of that year, which had agreed, he told Samuel, to correspond with the clergy of the diocese on the following subject – 'That all Church matters ought to be administered by the Church alone, i.e. by Bishops and clergy, and King and *laity in communion* with the Church.'
He added privately to Samuel:

> The omnipotence of Parliament is a gross, secular, wordly, infidel boast. *It is limited*, having no power in spiritualia i.e. creeds and sacraments. It has omnipotence over secularities as Nero had. . . . There remain Ecclesiastical, or mixed matters – and in this there are two functions – to *secure* and to *administer*. To *secure endowments, glebes*, is a pure secular matter for the common law of the land. *To administer* e.g. division and revenue of bishoprics etc. – is rightfully the authority of the Church alone, sanctioned by the King as Eccles. Head – which he can only be as a *communicant*. I proposed the resolution at Chichester . . . and nearly everybody fully agreed.[7]

Later in the same year Manning turned his attention to the Ecclesiastical Commission, which had been set up – very much on Henley's model – initially as the Ecclesiastical Duties and Revenues Committee during Peel's short ministry (December 1834 to April 1835), acquiring its more familiar title and permanency under Lord Melbourne in 1836. In its first form the Commission was composed of five bishops and eight laymen. In 1840 its composition was revised to include all the members of the bishops' bench, with three deans. It is difficult at first to see why this body should have attracted so much opposition from both High Churchmen and Evangelicals. (Manning wrote in 1838: 'I cannot remember having met any one, who has not expressed his regret and alarm at the very existence of the Ecclesiastical Commission.'[8]) It was thought to be the creature of Parliament; the predominant lay element of the original commission was declared offensive; many of the lower clergy resented the exclusion of the lesser dignitaries as members of the board.* More disturbing perhaps, was the terrifying efficiency and speed with which the Commission produced its reports, advocating a reconstruction of the diocesan geography, a revision of episcopal incomes and – most revolutionary of all – the suppression of non-residentiary canonries and the reduction in size of many of the cathedral chapters, the revenue secured therefrom to be used for augmenting the stipends of the less favoured beneficed clergy.

Manning's severest indictment of the Commission appeared in his *The Principles of the Ecclesiastical Commission examined, in a letter to the . . . Bishop of Chichester*, published in January 1838. It contained little, the germ of which had not been perceived in earlier writings or letters, the main argument resting on the independent spiritual jurisdiction of the Church as vested in the bishops through the apostolic succession. The institution was condemned as '*a virtual extinction of the polity of the Church*, and an open assumption of the principle that all legislative authority, ecclesiastical as well as civil, is derived from the secular power'.[9] More positively, Manning advocated an increase in the episcopate and an infusion of a new vitality into cathedral chapters, so that they should become centres of theological learning in which the canons might serve as instructors to candidates for ordination, as Thorndike had hoped.[10] He looked forward to the day when the cathedrals would once again be the spiritual heart of the dioceses, in which the chapter's main duty would

---

* G. F. A. Best, *op. cit.*, 316–17. This was because of Blomfield's autocratic temper.

be 'to pray without ceasing, and, by the frequent ministrations of the Eucharist, to keep up a standing memory and witness of Christ's holy sacrifice'.[11]

Dr Olive Brose has pointed out the similarity between Manning's proposals and those of Pusey in his lengthy article on the Commission and the proposed 'rifled canonries' which he contributed to the *British Critic* in 1838.[12] Certainly Manning scored a success with his open letter, brought his name to the public notice and acted rather as the leader of the anti-Blomfield party. He had private discussions with his bishop,[13] drew up a scheme which he submitted to the archdeacons for petitions to be presented in every diocese, and sent copies of his *Letter* to all church dignitaries and members of both Houses of Parliament.[14] 'Something may now be done,' he wrote in November 1837 to Samuel, 'but one more Act of Parliament and the principle of absolute Erastianism or Hobbism even in doctrine is covertly established.'[15]

Writing of the 'hard-hitting high churchmen' and their organ of anti-Blomfieldism, the *British Magazine*, Dr Best uses the happy phrase – they 'combined keen contemporaneity with unblenching conservatism'.[16] It is true that Manning and all the Wilberforce brothers tended to equate concession with timidity, but it would be mistaken to suppose that this attitude denoted either complacency in the condition of the Church as it then was or apathy in reforming zeal. Many of the opponents of the Commission were as eager to bring about a transformation in the work and effectiveness of the Church of England as the Commissioners themselves – especially those who, like the Wilberforces, had been brought up in the ardent pietism of an Evangelical household. They differed mainly on the question of the means by which this transformation was to be wrought. Even here they were not entirely divided. They would have agreed that the first duty of the Church was evangelisation: the Word must be spread to all the corners of the earth, and it was the Church's task to ensure that the facilities were provided for the Gospel to be preached. There must be a supply of suitable men and adequate buildings.

Samuel Wilberforce felt this so keenly that he assured Charles Anderson in 1833 that the first responsibility of churchmen must be to support the two greatest societies of the time – the C.M.S. and the Church Building Society. This was not just an idle aspiration. In 1831 he preached the missionary sermon on behalf of C.M.S. at Chichester, performing the same task again in 1836.[17] His chief concern in the missionary field, however, was the achievement of episcopal organisation of missions –

the establishment of colonial bishoprics and the introduction of missionary bishops (a work in which he was joined by his brother Robert and
Henry Manning, who found themselves, at least in this instance, in alliance
with Bishop Blomfield). The best expression of Samuel's understanding
of missionary work and the organisation of a mission church may be found
in his *History of the Protestant Episcopal Church in America*, published
in 1844, on which he had been working in the few spare moments which
an active life could afford over the preceding seven years. The Gospel must
not only be spread, it must be maintained faithfully and with due order
in the areas where initial triumphs had been won. The banner of the
mission church must be: 'Evangelical truth with apostolical order – the
Gospel in the Church. There must be no paring down, on the one side,
of the great doctrine of grace; no attempt, on the other, to win the good
will of men by changing, according to their wandering fancies, that form
of Church-order which Christ has appointed.'[18]

In the 1830's, therefore, he was working primarily for two ends – the
rapprochement between the C.M.S. and the episcopate in England, in the
hope that this would lead in time to a union with the S.P.G., the society
which more nearly approached his ideal of missionary endeavour; and,
secondly, the establishment of colonial dioceses and missionary bishops.
The first aim was at least partially achieved in 1841 through the endeavours
of Henry Venn, J. B. Sumner and Francis Close (as Society members)
and of Blomfield, representing the episcopate, when as a result of a
concordat the two archbishops and seven other bishops became members
of the C.M.S.[19] Samuel did not himself take a leading part in these
manœuvres – he was not yet in a powerful enough position to do so –
but that he actively canvassed on behalf of the *rapprochement* as early
as 1838 is clear from two letters from Manning approving his efforts.

As to the Ch. Miss. [Manning wrote in July 1838], as you know, I am
altogether of one mind with you about it, and should rejoice and be most
thankful to see it effected. It is a plain and overwhelming duty and the
neglect of it [i.e. episcopal control] is not only *wrong*, but foolish, and disastrous. I dare not foster any sanguine hope of our success till we grow orderly,
teachable, and faithful enough to set about God's work in His own way. . . .
As to the proposal itself there are many difficulties. . . . If there are Bishops
sent out, there must be sees and dioceses and a perpetual succession. In
our colonies this, alas, will require the consent of Parliament otherwise the
Abp. will do nothing. The Bishop of *Australia* is Bishop of *nothing*. He has
no see. This is a fatal mistake of which the R.C.'s will take due advantage.
He ought to be Bishop of Sidney with metropolitical right over the whole.

He suggested a form of wording for Samuel's proposed memorial to the Archbishop of Canterbury:

> Episcopacy is the universal rule of the Church of England both at home, and in the Churches planted by her in our colonial possessions; ... all our labours in Colonies must be under the same, and ... Episcopacy is the absolute, indispensable condition to the future communion of the Church of England and the Churches we may hope with God's blessing to plant among the heathen.[20]

In October of the following year he wrote further:

> Let me say how my heart has been with you in your work. The two papers you sent me gave me extreme pleasure, more than I can say, in every way, for yourself personally and the promise of good hereafter, for the immediate object of your mission, but most of all for the indirect strengthening of right principles in our Mother at home. ... Perhaps nothing is more likely to form a central principle of union, which shall imperceptibly unite men in England, than the Church Missions abroad.[21]

As early as 1837, Samuel had consulted Newman about the possibility of consecrating a bishop to be sent out amongst the heathen – possibly inspired by the sermon of the Bishop of New Jersey (George Washington Doane) in September 1835 at the consecration of Jackson Kemper as 'missionary bishop' for Missouri and Indiana. That Samuel knew of this sermon, entitled 'The Missionary Bishop', is clear from his admiring references to it in his own history of the American Episcopal Church.[22] A 'missionary bishop' was 'a new office in the Church', Doane had declared, '– a bishop *sent forth* by the Church, *not sought for of* the Church – going *before*, to organise the Church, not waiting till the Church has partially been organised – a leader, not a follower'.[23]

Newman was interested by Samuel's enthusiasm at this idea.

> Doubtless [he replied], the only right way of missionary-izing is by bishops and the agitation of the question must do good. Perhaps you are hardly called upon ever to say *how* it is to be done in the case of a given society, as the Ch.Miss. – it being at once a sufficient object at first to make out the *duty*, and, when it is made out, to fulfil it being other persons' concern quite as much as yours. If you prove your point, others are bound to co-operate with you in acting upon it. . . . Is there any precedent in the English Church of a Bp. being sent among the heathen? Could not the difficulty be met by getting Daniel Wilson and his colleagues to consecrate. . . . One should like to try the powers of at least *colonial* bishops to do without the State. . . . I am exceedingly glad you are stirring the question, and think it a very happy thought. The very stirring it will be of great use.[24]

Three years later Blomfield was writing to Archbishop Howley to make a similar representation: 'Let every band of settlers which goes forth from Christian England, with authority to occupy a distinct territory, and to form a separate community, take with it not only its civil rulers and functionaries, but its Bishop and clergy.'[25]

Blomfield's pioneering endeavours in encouraging the establishment and spread of missionary dioceses cannot be challenged. What, perhaps, is sometimes overlooked is that in this work he was giving official backing to a movement whose leading representatives were those very churchmen who were most vehement in their strictures against the principle and projects of the Ecclesiastical Commission. No one could have made a more trenchant attack upon tampering with cathedral endowments than did George Augustus Selwyn in 1838.[26] Nevertheless Manning and Blomfield together supplied Selwyn with his life's work – Manning in calling him to the missionary field,* Blomfield in causing him to be sent out as first bishop of the diocese of New Zealand.[27] Again, if in the 1830's and early forties Blomfield stands out as the most active of all the bishops in the support which he gave to the S.P.G., his most effective ally at that time amongst the lower clergy was Samuel Wilberforce, whose preaching tour for the Society in the autumn of 1839 through the vast diocese of Exeter was little short of sensational, both in its immediate impact and in its ultimate effect upon the personal career of the preacher.†

The first half of the nineteenth century was the golden age of religious societies. Most of them were Evangelical in origin; many, which had been initiated as instruments to disseminate gospel Christianity had, through

* Selwyn admitted this himself in a letter to Manning, dated 1 June 1847 (Manning Archives, bound volume of miscellaneous letters, no. 347). The occasion was Manning's speech at the opening of the Colonial Bishops' Fund, which impressed both Selwyn and his mother so deeply that 'it involved no less a consideration than the whole question of my coming to New Zealand'. The speech was so powerful 'as scarcely to have lost any portion of its effect even now'. I am deeply indebted to the Abbé A. Chapeau for showing me this letter. It is also clear from another letter (Wilberforce MSS. D. 27) that Manning was actively canvassing for a bishop to be sent to New Zealand as early as 1837.

† This interest lasted a lifetime. See the Minute adopted by the Society on the news of Wilberforce's death: 'He had preached for the Society in nearly every cathedral in the kingdom, and there was scarcely a town where his voice had not been heard in its behalf. . . . Whenever the annals of the Colonial Church, and of the Society in its relations to it, during the eventful middle years of the nineteenth century come to be compiled, there will not be recorded in them one individual to whom both are under more lasting obligation.' C. F. Pascoe, *Two Hundred Years of the S.P.G. 1701–1900* (1901), 718 n.

their popularity or through the confusion of Church parties in the opening decades of the century, become less exclusive and less militantly partisan. Because their father had been himself the pioneer and sponsor of so many of these societies, the Wilberforces could hardly avoid being personally embroiled in their later development. Seldom did a letter pass between them without some reference to society business – Robert lamenting his difficulties as Secretary of the C.M.S. auxiliary or Samuel excusing himself for absence from home or tardy correspondence because of the pressure of public engagements. But the society which made most claim upon their time and affections was one which the Evangelicals had played no part in founding – no less evangelistic for all that, but rather more concerned with the exclusiveness of the Establishment and the maintenance of its liturgy and doctrinal teaching than most Evangelicals were wont to display – the National Society for the Education of the Poor in the Principles of the Established Church.

The Society had been founded in 1811 largely through the efforts of the so-called Hackney Phalanx in order to promote a national system of education for the poor, the basis of which was orthodox Anglican religious instruction which might protect the lower classes from the influence of dissent and imbue them with a firm respect for Church principles. By providing schools with teachers, trained on the monitorial principle ('The Madras System') of Dr Bell at the Society's central school in Baldwin's Garden, and by paying grants to establish and maintain new schools, the National Society grew within twenty years of its foundation into the largest and most significant educational organisation in the country. In 1832 it had no fewer than 3,678 schools 'in union', educating 346,000 children, and in 1833 the State made friendly advances in the shape of an annual grant of £20,000.

The early thirties, as Mr H. J. Burgess has shown,[28] were a period of calm before the storm. As the relations between Church and State became more strained, so the churchmanship of the National Society became more Tractarian in tone, and the Committee of the Society came to be increasingly influenced by a militant *avant-garde*, younger men highly suspicious of the State's pretensions and religious indifference and therefore eager both to extend the field of the Society's activities and to resist tooth-and-nail any attempt by the State to use its annual grant as an instrument to impose its own conditions on how the money was to be spent. The most prominent members of this 'ginger group' were Manning, S. F. Wood and Gladstone, who were not slow to canvass for support among like-minded friends. Samuel, Robert and Henry Wilberforce were all brought into the deliberations and projects of this inner circle, an event not without significance in their lives since it was through this joint interest in extending the sphere of the Church's control over education that Manning's friendship with Gladstone ripened into intimacy, and that the Wilberforces themselves first became conscious of a new and powerful ally.

Manning, indeed, saw the early successes of the National Society as but the first step towards the fulfilment of a national educational system which would transform the spiritual life of the nation; and he revealed his vision to the world in a great sermon preached in Chichester Cathedral on 31 May 1838. He confronted his audience with one incontestable fact and one highly disputable premiss. The fact which none could gainsay was that the need for a national educational system was grievous, especially in view of a growing population – 'a new population of millions'[29] – for which no educational provision existed. His premiss was that the supplying of such a system was the responsibility of the Church, not of the State. 'For all men of all ranks, characters and destinies, there is one, and only one great idea running through all, the first aim, and groundwork of education, the vital element, and perfecter of the whole work; and that is the right determination of the will, confirmed by the formation of christian habits for God's service here, and for salvation hereafter.'[30]

The responsibility lay at the door of the Church. She alone had the means. Between the parochial schools at the foot of the ladder and the universities at the top, new intermediate schools could be founded by reviving and expanding the teaching function of the cathedrals and cathedral institutions, training ordinands and teachers for the secondary schools, the whole gamut of religious education up to university level being contained within the existing diocesan framework.* It was an exciting prospect, and with S. F. Wood and Gladstone the details were more fully worked out. Every diocese was to have a diocesan board of education, a seminary and a central college. There were to be 'middle schools', to which promising pupils from the parochial schools were to be promoted, lists of suitable books (to engender wholesome Church principles) would be drawn up for the use of such establishments, and a system of inspection should be devised.[31]

* Manning hoped to use the 'unendowed canonries' in this work. See H. E. Manning, *The Presentation of the Unendowed Canonries. A Letter to William, Lord Bishop of Chichester* (1840), esp. 14-15.

These proposals were certainly ventilated within the circle of Manning's friends some time before the preaching of the Chichester sermon. Samuel Wilberforce favoured the scheme, but was a little frightened at the sanguine disposition of the extremists. He wrote to Robert in January 1838, after a conference at Winchester at which Keble had been present:

> We have been again very busy at Winchester and I hope things promise well. It is of great moment I think not to make the terms of union strict as to Middle Schools at first. For, as they are now independent, they will not join us if we at first threaten them with very severe rules. . . . It is very desirable that ultimately we should get the middle schools to as much uniformity as possible in the books they use; but at present, all I think possible is to get them to send in the lists of those now used for our inspection. New schools of course we can start with our books. In all such points as these I find that I and Keble are practically opposed at Winchester and hitherto we have essentially modified his plan in spite of the Warden (dear man!) being his cypher.[32]

For a while the future looked rosy. Manning and Wood were asked in 1838 to become members of a Committee of Inquiry and Correspondence set up to advise the Committee of the National Society on the details of future development and to implement the scheme for the establishment of diocesan boards. Wood reported to Manning in February 1839:

> There have been great meetings at Lichfield and Warrington, to form boards for Lichfield and Chester dioceses; at the former, Peel, at the latter, Stanley, spoke; the last with brilliant eloquence. Chichester meets to form a board tomorrow. We have issued our appeal for funds for the central establishment, and in a few days have got about £300 in donations, and £200 annual: the nobility have not as yet been applied to, and I am sanguine of our getting enough to begin. The Archbishop of Canterbury has given a donation of £200 and £100 annual to his own diocesan board.[33]

In 1839 the Committee of Council on Education was set up by Lord John Russell with Dr Kay (later Sir James Kay-Shuttleworth) as Secretary — a clear indication that the government intended to abandon 'the role of mere paymaster'.[34] Largely through the efforts of Blomfield and Peel, Russell's plan to establish 'Normal Schools' in which religious instruction should be confined to the Bible only was defeated, but a fierce struggle ensued over the Council Minute of 3 June 1839 which laid down that all future government grants should carry with them the right of inspection. The contest was settled by an uneasy compromise (government inspectors were to be approved by the archbishop in each province) in 1840. The alarm, however, had been sounded. It was clear that Kay-Shuttleworth and Russell regarded the Manning faction as 'medieval' in outlook and that the avowed purpose of the Committee of Council was to thwart the realisation of the project which Manning had looked forward to in his Chichester sermon of 1838. In a letter to Russell in April 1843, Kay-Shuttleworth stated their aim to be 'to prevent the successful assertion on the part of the Church of the claim they put forth for a purely ecclesiastical system of education'. He described the practice of 'founding a central Normal School and a Diocesan Normal and Model School in every cathedral town' as 'the first steps towards the accomplishment of this design'.[35] It was equally clear that their opponents were not likely to give way easily. Robert Wilberforce let off steam to Samuel, when he heard that Sir James Graham had been defending undenominational religious teaching in schools: 'This is the most monstrous of all fallacies. It will lead to the teaching of falsehood under the name of indifference.'[36]

Enraged by the reforming zeal of a parliament seemingly conducting its legislation on utilitarian principles, and frightened by the prospect of the thwarting of the Church's own efforts to discharge its responsibilities, the enemies of Erastianism were bound sooner or later to press for the restoration of the traditional rights of the Church to deliberate on spiritual subjects in their own assembly. After all, Parliament had now ceased to be representative of the Church; it had become a mixed assembly. Furthermore, the Church had itself become intensely 'assembly-conscious' at this time: the first step of any potential reformer was to promote an association; all the best bishops were achieving informed control of their dioceses by encouraging clerical meetings – a lesson which Samuel Wilberforce was to learn from C. R. Sumner. The logical culmination of this movement to knit the Church together by means of deliberate assemblies was to regain the lost powers of the Church to meet in Convocation for more than purely formal purposes.

Not even Samuel Wilberforce, who played a leading part in the eventual restoration of the Canterbury Convocation in 1852, was wholeheartedly enthusiastic about claiming these powers in the 1830's. He was mindful of the circumstances which had led to the suspension of the right to conduct public business in 1717 – the warfare between the Upper and Lower Houses. In April 1836, he admitted to W. F. Hook that to agitate for a restoration of the old powers would be premature. 'The great bulk of our clergy are still so ignorant of Church principles that we have no sufficient bond of union to resist the necessary divisions which must always spring from the shades of individual opinions, and we should fight in the presence of our enemies.'[37]

Manning agreed. He was very uncertain whether Convocation could ever fulfil the needs of the Church, being a royal instrument, usurping what once had belonged to 'the ancient Diocesan Synods and Provincial Counsels'[38] of pre-Reformation England. He consulted H. J. Rose on the subject and reported the conversation to Samuel:

> Rose says it is incorrect to argue that Convocation should give assent to such bills as the Irish Bprks, or any tithe bill etc., that the Convocation called by the king is wholly distinct from a Ch. Synod which should be called by the Abp., and that this could do nothing except with ... internal matters. This, he says, is historical fact. It seems to leave us like a lodge in a garden of cucumbers. But we may contend that times when Church and State were coincident, and times when they are – as at present – separate, and, except so far as the remainder of churchmen in the country and parliament go, repugnant, are very different, and call for different treatment. The clergy might then be confiding and supine – now they must watch, and vindicate their office and authority.[39]

Samuel was to change his mind after becoming a bishop, when he saw how far the State was prepared to go in the defence of heterodoxy and when he realised with alarm what steps his friends were contemplating in view of the powerlessness of the Church to protect itself from being governed by seemingly heretical bishops. A state of emergency had arisen.

No one would accuse this group of zealous churchmen of being complacent or unresponsive to the general cry to rid the Church of abuses. Yet the fact remains that they opposed the Ecclesiastical Commission; and for that reason it would be fashionable to represent them as doggedly conservative – at best, unrealistic; at the worst, ostrich-like and intransigent. Nevertheless one may find perception and prophetic insight in the most unlikely places. And one such repository of unlooked-for wisdom is a little book which Henry Wilberforce published in 1838 – a prize essay awarded by the Christian Influence Society – entitled *The Parochial System. An Appeal to English Churchmen.*

At least Henry did not bury his head in the sand. He knew – even as did Arnold, whom he disliked so much – that England was changing from a predominantly rural to a predominantly urban nation. 'From an agricultural, we have become, in great measure, a commercial and manufacturing people.... Villages have swelled into towns, and towns into mighty cities.'[40] The first chapter of his work is devoted to a survey of the rocketing increase of population in urban parishes (the statistics mainly relating to towns in Yorkshire and Lancashire and the more populous district of London) compared with the static supply of clergy to minister to this ever-increasing flock: 'Taking an average of thirty-four parishes (in London), we find the proportion of pastors to their flocks to be one to 15,100. . . . Our parochial system is little more than a delusion. . . . There are thousands, nay hundreds of thousands, who, although baptised with us into the same body, are not only . . . without any parochial ministry, and so are not invited to the house of God . . .; but for whom, moreover, there is no room, should they desire to come. . . . They are aliens of necessity from His Church.'[41]

The author then makes a brief, and necessarily superficial, sociological analysis of the congregations of churches in populous areas, coming to the conclusion that 'they are almost exclusively confined to the higher and middle ranks of society, whom, by a most unchristian abuse of language, we have learned to call "the respectable classes"', reminding his readers of Christ's injunction that 'to the poor the Gospel is preached'.[42]

Something had been done to meet 'this monstrous evil', he admitted, in his second chapter. Laymen had been active in district visiting and through societies like the City Mission. But such efforts were not enough. They did not remedy the deficiency of a permanent and ready supply of clergy.[43] One might acknowledge the achievements of the Church Building Society, but the unhappy truth remained (as the Bishop of Middleton, in our own day, has seen in chronicling the religious history of Sheffield) that even in the periods of boom the Church, while providing places of worship to serve the estimated increase in population, could not make up for past deficiencies.[44] The problem was not to be solved – again as E. R. Wickham observed – by 'periodic spurts of so-called "aggressive evangelicalism"', but rather by planning on a hitherto undreamed-of scale.[45]

> Let an annual report be published in every diocese, stating the number of churches built in the year past, and of those which we still required; and under the latter head, specifying by name every existing parish which exceeds the due measure of population, and every hamlet in which a church is requisite. We should then stand pledged to supply the wants of our whole people. If men neglected them, they would do it with their eyes open, and every Christian (instead of feeling something of surprise at the number of churches erected, and the frequent calls for aid), being continually reminded of those which were still required, would rather be ready to wonder and regret that so few are annually undertaken. Now he measures the work done; then he could not withdraw his eye from that which remains.[46]

As for the pressing need for resident clergy, Henry echoed the aspirations of Pusey and Froude that houses for a collegiate establishment of priests should be provided in areas which had been spiritually starved. This would be both economical to the Church and immensely rewarding to those who participated, for they would be 'drawn closer by daily social prayers and all the blessed intercourse of religious fellowship'; and in their work they would gain opportunity for theological study and discussion as well as practical experience in pastoral care.[47]

Then again, the laity must be brought in to share in the actual internal administration of the parishes. 'The pastor, in general, stands too much alone.'[48] Hitherto the services of willing laymen had been too unsystematic. They should now be encouraged to obtain the bishop's licence to undertake regular visitation of the poor, to instruct in Sunday schools and to give guidance to the more ignorant of the adult parishioners. This would not only take a load off the shoulders of the parish priest, but would also enable the laity to appreciate that their diocesan 'was their own spiritual ruler, and, under God, the source of every order of religious ministration'.[49]

Finally, the Church needed money. Manifestly, charity was not enough; it bred self-satisfaction and a miserably low conception of Christian obligation. 'It has become a common argument, in behalf of our religious societies, that they ask of each a sum so small that he will never miss it.' Worse still was the habit of extracting money painlessly by bazaars or sales-of-work – 'devices to effect the great results which are the natural fruit of genuine self-denying Christian beneficence, by means of our meagre and niggard rule of giving that which we shall never miss. . . . We must be bribed to give to God even that which we do not want.'[50]

What was the answer of the Ecclesiastical Commissioners? Not for them the satisfaction of making bricks without straw! They were taking bricks from one part of the foundation to use in another. 'The only reason for the confiscation of the cathedral property, for instance, is that we may gain about £120,000 per annum, to extend the parochial system, i.e. that we may save the necessity of spending so much.'[51] Perhaps the most perilous consequence of such a measure would be to engender in people's minds the notion that the Church's financial needs can be supplied from its own resources and that their liberality is no longer called for. For fresh sources of money, the Church would have to rely on underhand means which make a mockery of the Christian duty to count one's worldly treasure as a gift from God – 'a trust committed to our stewardship'.[52]

The remainder of the work is really a development of this theme of Christian stewardship.

> The rule of charity proposed by our Lord is opposed to that commonly adopted: it regards the giver, and demands of him something, whether great or small, which shall be to him a real sacrifice and self-denial; and this it demands for the love of Christ, and for the benefit of our own souls, and that we may not deceive ourselves with idle professions, and trust in our worldly goods, while we say and think that we trust in God through Christ.[53]

The answer lies in *planned* giving:

> First let every man, instead of giving one large sum merely, and then suffering himself to remain contented, deliberately dedicate to God a certain measure of each year's income, to be set apart as soon as he receives it, and no longer accounted as his own. The exact proportion to be thus consecrated each must determine for himself, after a solemn consideration of his own circumstances and duties, in the sight of God Almighty. ... Almost every one may begin by a tenth part, a measure recommended to us by a divine precedent.[54]

The book has more to say than this, but its gist and significance may be gathered from this digest. Much of it – the desire to see the establishment of collegiate houses for priests, the abhorrence at tampering with ecclesiastical endowments – is conventional Tractarianism. On the other hand, the perception of the importance of the role of the laity in diocesan administration, the need for mission to industrial areas, the futility of supposing that the needs of the Church can be met by the proceeds of jumble-sales, and the stress upon the primary duty of Christian stewardship, are all lessons which the Anglican Church has come to learn only in recent years. The Tractarians were not always backward-looking; not wholly devoid of the gift of prophecy.

The bulk of the English clergy were agitated, more or less, by these and kindred issues. The Wilberforces and their circle seem, however, to have been exceptional in their readiness to play an active role in the prosecution of public causes – to serve on committees, to take the platform, to produce a timely tract. Robert, who took least kindly to this type of work, admitted to Samuel that within the Maidstone area 'we have few spouters of froth among the surrounding clergy but myself'.[55] Keble could write teasingly to Samuel, addressing him as 'the agitator general of the Diocese of Wight'.[56] And James Stephen, with characteristic candour, was wont to warn Samuel of the perils of becoming too absorbed in the petty problems of one's little world:

It is indeed desirable [he wrote in 1837] that we should all be kept out of much conversation with any one small section of the world to which we may happen especially to belong; and this is the more needful for such of us as stand at the centers of our miniature circles. . . . For is it desirable that you should attend a great many clerical meetings in the Isle of Wight; lest you should find yourself growing in superfluous indignation against Spring-Rice* and his abettors . . . ? To keep our thoughts from collapsing, and from converging constantly upon the same point, we should invite some friendly voice to disturb our established trains of thinking; and that service I am at all times most happy to render to you and to receive at your hand. . . . When the Southampton railway is finished, I will take a cup of tea with you in the evening, between business hours and bedtime, and we will try to explore each other's errors. Mine indeed are innoxious except to myself and to the Colonists for whom of course you care as much as for the people of Timbuctoo – but your errors are a public concern, and require to have a vigorous war made on them.[57]

It would have profited Samuel if he had taken all this to heart. But it is unlikely that he was discountenanced. Much as he liked James Stephen personally, he thought his judgment rather frivolous and eccentric. As he told Robert, he was a good man, if incurably prolix, but 'most uncertain in all his conclusions'.[58] He failed to see that James Stephen's greatest gift was shrewd common sense.

II. *The Cure of Souls*

When they were not 'spouting froth' they were discharging their duties as conscientious parish priests. In *country* parishes, it may be observed; indeed, it was customary in the early nineteenth century for the newly ordained to seek a living which allowed some time for study in order to supply the want of a specific theological training. Such parishes could be lucrative or miserably poor, depending largely upon the nature of the advowson and the disposition of the patron. From what has been seen already, it is clear that the Wilberforce-Sargent circle was influential enough to ensure that none of its members should be subjected to undue hardship on this score. Henry Manning enjoyed the family living at Lavington; George Dudley Ryder profited from the patronage of his own father

* Chancellor of the Exchequer at that time. He had moved a petition in the House of Commons to abolish religious tests at the universities, and was also a fierce opponent of church rates.

as Bishop of Lichfield; Robert Wilberforce's patron was the Lord Chancellor and the living a wealthy one; Samuel accepted the patronage of his cousin, the Bishop of Winchester, with whom he was on terms of the closest friendship. Henry, too, had C. R. Sumner as his patron, although his position as perpetual curate* was less enviable than that of his brothers.

Henry, indeed, was rather an anxiety to his brothers in the 1830's. Like Samuel he was generous and improvident, and consequently was always short of money. His prize of 200 guineas for the essay on *The Parochial System* was immediately handed over *in toto* as a subscription to the new church which he was building at Burley, the neighbouring village to Bransgore.[1] Samuel wrote to Robert in September 1837: 'It is important to get Henry some increase of income *soon*. He is pressed. Our Bishop has a good will I doubt not towards him – but he has been long without patronage and this suffers pressing claims to grow up.'[2] His chief worry was that Henry should too plainly reveal his Tractarian sympathies and thereby estrange his main hope of future patronage. The living of Tunbridge Wells was shortly to become vacant, and Samuel considered the ethics of actively canvassing on Henry's behalf. 'I would not *force* or even *humour* the leadings of God's providence', he assured Robert, 'but it is a part of them to use natural openings.'[3] Three months later, Manning suggested that Henry might be offered the living of Graffham, but it was found that the value of the living – £120 a year with a house – was insufficient to see him out of his difficulties.[4] The situation deteriorated in the course of the next year, and Samuel began to fear that Henry could hope for nothing from Sumner. He asked Robert to use any influence he might have with the Archbishop (Howley). 'I do not think asking can do any harm. . . . I think it would be the making of H. – only it were a great loss to us to have him live in Kent.'[5]

Evidently Robert made an approach to Howley which was not immediately fruitful. After some abortive negotiations with Hook to secure Huddersfield for Henry, an offer at last came from the Archbishop in 1841 – the living of Walmer in Kent. It was not a wealthy position – there was not even a parsonage there – but it sufficed for two years, during which time Henry was able, by pressing his legal rights, to recover the lost glebe lands and a house erected on them which he duly occupied. In 1843 his fortunes changed. East Farleigh, which had been vacated by Robert three years earlier, was now vacant again and – thanks to

---

* An incumbent whose tithes – both rectorial and vicarial – have been impropriated by the patron, who pays in lieu a fixed stipend.

Samuel's efforts with Prince Albert – the living was offered to Henry. For the first, and only, time in his life he was free from financial cares.

If only Henry would learn the virtues of tact, Samuel would sigh. It was rash in the extreme to invite his bishop to stay with him at Bransgore (in 1835) with Newman as his fellow guest, although it appealed to Henry's sense of fun.* If only he would show a little more circumspection in his admiration for Catholic principles. There was much in Henry's ministry which his brothers found to admire – his utter disregard of self, his passion for church building, his unwearied work among the rustic poor at Bransgore and among the even coarser inmates of the naval establishments at Deal, his firm discipline, his determination to engender strong Church principles. He could be a powerful preacher and was mastering his early faults. He preached a sermon before his bishop in October 1835, after his elevation to priest's orders at Farnham, and Samuel passed on Sumner's account to Robert: 'He says they "all liked Henry *extremely*, that 3/5ths of his sermon was very good – but that his manner was very bad". I suppose that he was nervous and shall take some opportunity of talking to him about it. I have heard a nice account of his sermon from one who was ordained with him also.'[6]

A few months later he and Samuel appeared on the same platform to speak at a meeting of the Newport District Visiting Society on behalf of Church principles and Samuel was delighted at the improvement in oratorical style: 'H. made a very beautiful speech of about 7 or 8 minutes – very quiet, hardly perhaps kindly enough: but perfectly free from hesitation – and very much like Newman's sermons a little enriched.'[7]

From what we can gather of his ministry at Bransgore and at Walmer, his services were, from the very beginning, Tractarian in tone, also 'a little enriched'. Although it is true to say that Catholic forms of worship and ritualism belong to a later stage of Tractarianism, many of those who had been influenced by Newman at Oxford and who departed early for parochial duties, at once sought to realise a more Catholic ethos in their system of worship, and did so mainly by reviving liturgical practices, authorised by the canons or rubrics, which had in the course of the preceding century become practically obsolete. One such revival, which because it became standard practice among Tractarian sympathisers developed into a handy test of churchmanship in the 1830's and 1840's, was the daily observation of morning and evening prayer. The Anglican

---

* Actually the encounter was by no means disastrous, for the bishop took great pleasure in Newman's company. See G. H. Sumner, *op. cit.*, 244.

authority for this was incontestable, but – as Dr Wickham Legg has pointed out – 'in 1824 the daily services had fallen almost as low as they could without being extinct.'[8] Other practices were the special observance of Saint's Days (which, when introduced by Dodsworth at Margaret Street Chapel in 1835, was considered by S. F. Wood so exciting an innovation that he wrote enthusiastically to Robert Wilberforce to describe the first of such services held on St Andrew's Day)[9]; the separation of the Litany from the Morning Service (strongly advocated by Newman and followed by his disciples)[10]; bowing at the Holy Name; the chanting of the Psalms, and the holding of weekly Communion.

Henry was convinced of the propriety of all these revived practices; and indeed was prepared to go further. As early as May 1833, while staying with his father in Bath, he first experienced the seductive power of the Roman liturgy and felt slightly dizzy:

> I *did* go last Sunday [he wrote to Robert] to the Vespers at the Chapel just by here and very delightful it was. There was very *little* objectionable. When I came in they were chanting the Psalms in Latin to a common Cathedral Chant very beautifully; then they sang Magnificat, Veni Creator etc. – and then a little about the virgin of an objectionable nature. I wish they had our own cathedral service here and could not wonder if those who delight in music and know little of doctrinal differences were perverted in numbers by the delight of their music which wonderfully affected me. . . . If I were a dissenter I should I think certainly become a Papist.[11]

A year after he had settled at Bransgore, Samuel and Emily came to stay with him. They were much impressed by the influence which Henry clearly wielded over his congregation. Samuel wrote to Robert: 'The Church was very well attended in point of number and the people appeared to me to be particularly attentive. It is a curious thing that it should be so; for the place is a neglected common upon which a group of mud cottages have been crowded together there; the refuge for the most part of those who have been chased from more civilised places – but so it is. Not having had a church they now value as a *new* blessing what use has taught so many to despise.' He was a little nonplussed by Henry's garb: 'I never saw him look so well as when he was mounted in his pulpit clothed in his Romanist cassock which he imported from Antwerp.'[12]

Henry introduced daily service during 1838, beginning cautiously in Holy Week, and was pleasantly surprised to find that his evening congregation averaged forty members.[13] He assured Robert that he was all for wearing stoles, and commissioned Mary to make a fine surplice for

Newman. It was to be of the best Irish linen 'worked round the collar with crosses'.[14] There is little doubt that had Henry remained within the Anglican Church he would have become a ritualist. Certainly he was well in advance of his brothers and brothers-in-law in his appreciation of the importance of externals.

The nearest to him in sympathy during these years was George Dudley Ryder, whose active Tractarianism really dates from his becoming Rector of Easton in the diocese of Winchester in 1836. Easton, like Bransgore, was a small parish of about five hundred souls, but it was a great deal wealthier, the glebe lands amounting to five acres and the tithes being commuted at £620 per annum.[15] From the first Ryder introduced daily service, although his efforts were met initially by an attitude of cold indifference. He proceeded to effect the restoration of the church, decorated the altar with an ornate frontal and – as his confidence increased and the apathy of his congregation waned – began the practice of offering daily prayers for the union of the Anglican and Roman Churches. He became convinced of the salutary effects of private confession, although there is no evidence that he encouraged the practice among his parishioners until 1843, the year in which he asked Keble to become his own spiritual director.[16]

Samuel, Robert, and Henry Manning were rather less *avant-garde*, if their notion of their calling was no less high. Samuel was exchanging letters regularly throughout this time with the other two, discussing common parochial problems, comparing ways and means of exercising that combination of pastoral care, moral surveillance and educational supervision for the provision of which in the early nineteenth century the parish was generally and officially regarded as the primary and essential unit. Rarely did they differ in their views; perhaps at no other period of their lives was their intimacy so close. 'I trust we may be spared to be drawn nearer and nearer together,' Manning wrote to Samuel in July 1835. '. . . It is a very great privilege to have in the close relation of brothers, those, with whom we have an unity of affection, feelings, tastes, and where these things are found, above all profession. I enjoy the thought, if it so please God, that we may grow old, and mellow, and wise together.'[17]

A few months later, he suggested that they should write regularly to each other on subjects of mutual interest, emulating the correspondence of Bishop Jebb and Alexander Knox.[18] This was a friendship which was in no way soured or rendered the less free and open by the fact of Samuel becoming Manning's squire and patron in 1841 – the Lavington estate being appointed to Emily and her heirs by Mrs Sargent in 1836, and therefore passing to Samuel on Emily's death.*

Manning seems, from the beginning of his ministry, to have perceived the prime importance of engendering a strong Church feeling among his parishioners. In his first surviving letter to Samuel, dated 12 January 1834, he writes: 'I am now beginning a course of sermons upon the Liturgy, the ministerial office, and the doctrine, and discipline of our Church. I do not know whether you have ever done the same. I have always found the people much interested by any discussion of the prayer book; and at the time of confirmation was struck by their attention to some remarks on that and the Baptismal service.'[19]

Possibly because of the pertinacity with which he impressed Church principles upon his flock, or maybe just through good fortune, he was hardly troubled at all by the menace of dissent. 'My church Rates returns were scantily signed,' he informed Samuel in 1837, 'because we did not make much stir about them – No refusal as I know. If we had dissenters – or any 2nd opinion, I should have tried the question, but being of one mind, until the question is begged, I thought it best to leave it.'[20]

Whatever doubts he may have had after his ordination as to his right to intrude into other peoples' houses to deliver spiritual admonitions, these were speedily resolved. On one occasion, in 1836, he appears to have incurred the displeasure of a gentleman called Holford for entering his house unbidden to rebuke two of his servants for unseemly behaviour in church. He wrote to Samuel to explain the circumstances:

> I am provoked with myself, that I should not have had more forethought and discretion than to enter Holford's house. I was betrayed into it by the needless advances, and expressions of friendship etc. etc. that he has by word and letter used towards me. . . . I certainly say that I did it in the wish to spare his two servants the annoyance of coming thro' our household and thereby exciting curiosity and notice, which often irritates the parties against the adviser. I was very incautious in doing so and am truly sorry that I did give a goose a plea for misrepresentation, especially as I have always found that exaggeration is one of the prerogatives of a fool. As to the *interference*, I feel that my obligations to all my people make it my duty to admonish etc.; that I do not require the leave or sanction of anybody to exercise that office so long as I confine myself to my commission, and meddle with nothing beyond. Had Holford been at home I should not [for]

---

* In time this arrangement was to cause some ill-feeling between Samuel and Henry Wilberforce and George Dudley Ryder, the full details of which may be found in two lengthy memoranda among the Ryder papers. The bare details of the original settlement are set out in Ryder MSS. B. 3. 19 July 1836.

a moment have thought of asking his permission to reprove any member of his household for gross irreverence in one of my churches. It is a doctrine wholly unXtian and unecclesiastical that anyone can draw a circle round his household and forbid the ministry of Christ to reprove, and admonish. He and all his are under our ministry.[21]

This deep sense of the priestly duty to discipline his flock and to superintend their moral behaviour led Manning gradually to perceive the efficacy of the sacrament of penance and the need to encourage private confession. As early as 1837 he was corresponding with Samuel on the desirability of making the body of the regular communicants conscious of the fact that they formed the moral and spiritual core of the parish:

> We had an early service [at Graffham] on Sunday at 7 o'clock he [wrote]. There were abt 60 or 70 present, at the Communion and afterwards 47 which with Lavington makes about 80 communicants this Xtmas. I hope I do not deceive myself in thinking that for the most part they are consistent according to their several measures of knowledge. I do not think there are many of a very high reach of faith, but I hope there is a healthy religion. I have thought much lately on this question, whether we may not exercise a great influence upon a parish by endeavouring to raise the standard and state of such among our people as show the best disposition of mind; whether they may not be made among their families, and neighbours, a sort of reflector to report and spread abroad the light of the Church. Are not the communicants a body marked out for this – or at least the first fruits of them? And if so how are we to bear upon them in a way which shall be at once effectual and safe?[22]

The answer, Manning came to see, was confession. Samuel could not admit this. It would be playing with fire. Newman agreed with him up to a point, but for different reasons. In 1839, Manning consulted Newman about one of his first penitents – a lady who yearned to join the Church of Rome. Newman's reply explains the dilemma precisely:

> Our blanket is too small for our bed. . . . We are raising longings and tastes which we are not allowed to supply – and till our bishops and others give scope to the development of Catholicism externally and wisely, we *do* tend to make impatient minds seek it where it has ever been, in Rome. I think that, whenever the time comes that secession to Rome takes place, for which we must not be unprepared, we must boldly say to the Protestant section of our Church – '*You* are the cause of this: you must concede; you must conciliate; you must meet the age; you must make the Church more efficient, more suitable to the needs of the heart, more equal to the external. Give us more services, more vestments and decorations in worship; give us monasteries; give us the signs of an apostle, the pledges that the

Spouse of Christ is among us. Till then you will have continual secessions to Rome.'[23]

Samuel and Robert encountered different problems from Manning's – especially the incursions of dissent. Samuel put it down to the extreme degree of poverty in the Isle of Wight, the extensive unemployment and the influence of radicals.* He took the platform on several occasions on behalf of the Friends of the Church, noting with satisfaction in 1834 (after a speech at Newport) that he had been able to crush a determined body of dissenting hecklers. He wrote in high spirits to Charles Anderson: 'I spoke for an hour; and never spoke with so much comfort to myself or effect upon others, before. In short it was a glorious day for the Friends of the Church: and Hawkins and Ord [two radical M.P.'s] sneaked out of the town discomfited.'[24]

Sometimes he had 'ranters' to deal with – the disciples of Edward Irving who had received the gift of 'the tongues'. On returning from a visit to the mainland, he discovered that one of his parishioners had been driven mad by them and was declaring himself to be 'bodily possessed by the Devil'.[25] On another occasion two Irvingites were rash enough to confront Samuel himself. He listened to them politely, occasionally interjecting a probing question:

> We discussed for an hour [he told Robert later]. At last he [a Captain Gambier] quoted for the 50th time 'the tongues', and being driven to it quoted them as a sign to unbelievers. Upon this I answered that I had examined them upon the testimony of most able and impartial witnesses, and was convinced that they were not superhuman. On this he rose, declaring that I had blasphemed the Holy Ghost; and he denounced woe. I said, 'And before you leave my room I must deliver to you *my* message, and I do it most solemnly and in the name of God. You have come to me claiming to be a messenger from God, speaking in His name by direct commission; and I have tried your claim and found it false. I tell you, therefore that you are under a dreadful delusion, and are guilty of a dreadful sin. You are one of those false prophets mentioned in Jeremiah XIV who say *the Lord sent me*, when the Lord hath not sent you, and you have much reason to fear the burning fire of His offended jealousy.'[26]

He was troubled no further.

Any insult or challenge to the sacerdotal commission touched Samuel to the raw. It was ever so. He had despised at Oxford the unsolicited sermonising of the pious undergraduates of St Edmund Hall; in his own

---

* Wrangham MSS. V. 76. 'The leaven of dissent is working furiously in the Isle of Wight.'

ministry he could never endure the gauche or loud-mouthed effusions of the lowly born. Soon after his arrival at Brighstone he encountered just such a vexation on visiting a parishioner called Gordon, who was at home at the time with his wife. 'The former asked me to pray with them.' he recorded in his diary, 'and before I could begin – began. Then his wife prayed. A good deal too much of "God I thank thee" . . . phraseology. As soon as I got upon my feet I told them very plainly my entire disapprobation of things of the sort – that I disliked it – that I never could allow of another leading when the Minister of God was present etc. etc. etc. She apologised and he took the rebuke humbly.'[27]

Robert, too, had his troubles. One of his parishioners was a tiresome Socinian farmer, whom he sought to appease by accepting an invitation to dine with him. Samuel and Henry chuckled together at the thought of Robert's 'unimpassioned endurance' which he would surely display throughout the evening.[28] Then there was an importunate lunatic by the name of Mortlock who tried to persecute Robert through the post, begging him to desist from his life of self-indulgence and assuring him of his prayers that he might be set free from the thralldom of Satan.[29] As the hop-picking season approached, so hordes of Irish Catholics descended on the parish to earn what they could. Robert did his duty by them as far as he was able – without conspicuous success.

> I have had down a reader of the Irish society to teach them in their own tongue [he reported to Samuel in September 1836]. . . . Mr Ellis has supplied me with a very grand room for the purpose, and an additional motive has been to draw off the people on Sunday afternoons, when they commonly crowd the streets. Yesterday the men came, but he seems not to have made much progress. They abused and pelted him with old shoes and dirt. However he got about 50 to come to him in his room and read and talked to them. I attribute his bad success in part to his being known by the St Giles's Romanists as a bitter protestant, and I suppose it is impossible to get a man of this kind not to enter at once into questionable points, and in truth to blaspheme sacred things. For in truth I found my man had no notion at all of the real nature of the Eucharist, and I doubt not he is full of irreverence towards it. He has much impressed me with a sense of thankfulness that at our Reformation the hatred of transubstantiation did not lead to a similar tone of blasphemy in our articles and liturgy.[30]

Robert was never very sanguine about his own endeavours in his letters to his brothers. He deplored his inability to get to know his flock well, blaming his short-sightedness – ' a sad impediment to my usefulness'.[31] He felt profoundly dissatisfied with his own preaching. 'From preaching

to a set of villagers I seem to have got into such a ranting way, and I am
not hardened in it yet. In time I suppose I shall get used to it, and then
it will seem sensible enough.'[32] He procured himself an Evangelical
curate called Davey, and had mixed feelings when the parish went into
raptures over him and seemed to like his pompous, heavy approach.
He kept him for two years.[33]

In this, as in other respects, Robert underrated his own powers and his
unflagging conscientiousness. Before he engaged a curate, he found the
strain very taxing. In 1833 he complained to Samuel that he was getting
stale. He had over fifty candidates to prepare for confirmation and he had
for ten months without intermission preached two new sermons every
Sunday.[34] In the same year he sought permission from the Archbishop
to begin Cottage Lectures, writing to J. B. Sumner (Bishop of Chester)
for support in this infringement of the Conventicle Act.[35] He opened a
boys' school in Cox Heath and built in his own garden a new school for
girls in 1838, following this up with a visitation of the parish to discover
defaulters. 'The age . . . at which boys leave school is very early here', he
complained to Samuel. 'I have very few above 10 and scarce any above
11. They are then taken by their parents to work, and this is especially
the case now in consequence of the distress which is occasioned by the
high price of flour. Were this a very severe winter, I scarce know what
should be done, but thank God as yet our people have not been much out
of work.'[36]

He was cautious in his introduction of unfamiliar services. After he
had made extensive alterations to the church in 1836 – involving a new
aisle and the restoration of the chancel – he began special services on
Saints' Days, and an evening service on Fridays when there was no Saint's
Day. He sent his first impressions of the experiment to Samuel in December 1837:

> I am thankful to say my communicants are increasing and we have more
> attendance at Church than I remember, tho' still very few for so large a
> parish. I began last week to have evening service in my chancel . . . It was
> very well attended last night, but perhaps this was its novelty.
>
> I have got a couple of old wooden candles from some church abroad,
> and a chandelier of the same: the latter my clerk who is a natural took
> up by one of the branches, and broke. It was rather a scene. The chandelier
> had just arrived before our service; all the people were there, when this
> man to hang it up laid hold of it, lifted it up and tumbled it down. The
> people gave such a groan. Master Scars looked more stupid and foolish
> than usual.[37]

Samuel had been spared the gaucheries of a ham-fisted clerk; otherwise his problems were very much the same. He had quarrels with the local farmers about tithe and decided to employ a tithe factor[38]; he gradually installed all the necessary apparatus to supply the needs of the parish poor. There was a lending library (replete with S.P.C.K. tracts – Basil Wood's *The Day of Adversity* and Hannah More's *The Faith and Duty of a Christian Man* were especially recommended)[39]; a dispensary and infirmary; Sunday schools and day schools. 'Samuel does not eat the bread of idleness,' Barbara Wilberforce had informed Robert in August 1831. 'We are rather afraid of his overdoing himself on Sundays by going twice a day to the School, besides his two services, and his examining the children after evening service and he *talks* of an adult school of Boys and young men if he can get it together in the evening in order to occupy their evening leisure a little. His sermons are excellent.'[40]

Samuel appears to have shown sternness to defaulters from the start. In January 1832 his diary records: 'At the boys' school expelled Wm. Chambers for obstinately going Sunday afternoon to play instead of to Church.'[41] He turned to the problems of the day school in 1834:

> I want you [he wrote to Charles Anderson in September of that year] to send me some help towards a school I am about building in this Parish. Send me some plans which shall be pretty and cheap – for I have great difficulty about means as I cannot apply to my farmers for subscriptions. Some of my friends have helped me; and I have applied to the National Society. I want to get two rooms of not less than 30 ft. by 20 ft. each and very high – which will open into one by folding doors – doubled. I want the entrances to be some distance apart – that the boys and girls may not quarrel.[42]

The proposed class for boys and adults turned into a regular Bible Class, described by Samuel to Robert in November 1833 in very Evangelical terms: 'I have just had my Bible Class – 8 men and a very nice spirit and indeed I trust promise of usefulness. It draws them out, attaches them to me, and tonight we got upon *separation* and I think had a very useful conversation.'[43] It is interesting also to observe that in the same year he sent details to his brother of his mode of instructing confirmation candidates, and that among the tracts which he recommended for use were one by Daniel Wilson (to be read by the candidates) and another by Richard Baxter (to assist in the minister's own preparation).

> I have just had the candidates for an hour on Sunday afternoon in the Church [he continued], marking their attendance on a prepared muster

roll. I began by *inviting*, went on to *explaining, enforcing* and *warning*. Many drew back. More persevered. As the time came on I had them in the house weekday evenings in classes – and latterly individually. For a long time it seemed as hopeless a work as I ever took in hand, but before the day of Confirmation* I had more to encourage my labours, by far, than I had ever seen in this Parish and I humbly hope there remains much permanent good from the affection, resolution and prayer to which it gave rise. May a far more abundant blessing be vouchsafed to you. I am convinced that a *good deal* of strictness is of essential service. You know our readiness to do boldly what we are afraid of, if we can blame another tho' we shall suffer ourselves (e.g. men idling with a private tutor, paying him and being plucked). They will come boldly to confirmation with your *ticket* and conscious unfitness – unless you can fix strongly upon them their own sole personal responsibility and risk. I found it in this way very useful to represent it to them as qualifying for the Lord's Supper because their unreasonable dread for the most part of receiving that made them cautious. Of the other, I do not mean that I *refused* tickets to those who would not communicate. Indeed I refused tickets to none but 2 or 3 who held back till the morning of confirmation, disliking the preparation.[44]

From time to time Samuel felt the pressure of his work exacting too great a strain, most particularly in 1835 when he was so troubled with rheumatism that he was sent to Dr Jephson at Leamington to undergo 'violent' treatment.[45] On one occasion in that year, when he bent down from a chair to pick up a paper which had slipped from his knees, he stuck in that position and lay gasping and groaning on the floor 'like one in a fit'.[46] In 1837 he was stricken with severe inflammation of the lungs and, as he himself thought, was brought 'very near to the grave'.[47] The year before had been especially heavy. Although he had taken on a curate early in 1835 (a man called Ramsey), he kept him for only a short while and was without assistance for most of the year.

Much of the time was devoted to attending society meetings and outside engagements of a varied sort. In April 1837, surveying the current week, he excused himself to Robert for doing little work on their father's biography because of a Church Building Society at Winchester, a dinner engagement with his archdeacon, a meeting at Southampton, and four Church meetings at Newport.[48] Then there were always the harrowing occasions – attendance at deathbeds, the conducting of funerals – which, when they occur, must take precedence over everything else. Perhaps few could have been so harrowing as the terrible grief which accompanied

* Not – it seems – at this stage an annual event at Brighstone. See Wrangham MSS. V. 64. 'We are to have a confirmation this summer.'

the funeral at St Leonard's in 1840 of young Ella Raffles, whose family the Wilberforces had grown to know intimately while they were living at Highwood.* Samuel attended with the bishop, and wrote to Emily directly after the proceedings:

> My own love, We are just returned from the Church. The prayers of the Holy Bride of Christ have been breathed over the earthly form of the young virgin bride whom Christ hath taken to himself. It has been a heart-rending scene from first to last. God grant it may have been useful: deeply useful to my heart.
>
> We got here a little before 8. . . . To Ella's room. There were the two beds with the bedding gone: the smooth cold whiteness which one knows so well and which seems to say that it could give no rest – and that now rest is found elsewhere. . . . We met at ½ past 8 for breakfast – a sad, silent, solemn time. The sudden swell of the sea only a few yards off sounding as a deep bass to our sighing spirits – and coming in again and again as there was a still pause in our party. Hardly anyone spoke. Hardly any efforts were made to speak. We were not afraid of being silent: of looking into each other's faces and seeing the full tear in the red eye. . . .
>
> After breakfast we met in the drawing room – and were there to go into the room for Common Prayer. Our beloved Bishop came to me and asked me if I could trust my voice: that he could not nor could he trust Mr Page: that nothing would so soothe Lady Raffles. I could hardly assent: not so much that I doubted my power of self-command as that I felt so utterly unworthy to lead the thoughts of such mourners and was afraid of . . . in any degree forcing my own feelings. However it was clearly right and so after a moment I consented and we all assembled in the dark stillness of that room. It was an awful time: I trust that I prayed: I am sure many did and the deep sobbing of poor Lady Raffles and John was most affecting. Then Lady Raffles had to be removed: and it was almost too much. She clung to the coffin and kissed its repulsive blackness: saying in a sort of thrilling whisper of agony 'My child, my child, my babe. Must I leave thee. Cannot I keep even this. My child, my babe.' The Bishop took her hand: and bid her for love to her who was gone bear this one more struggle: and she rose and left the room with her brother.[49]

It must be admitted that Samuel had rather a flair for writing such descriptions: the solemnity of death could never be left to speak for itself; there was no grief so dreadful, no dying utterance so exquisite, that it could not be improved by expatiation. And of all his writings during these years, three books afforded him more pleasure and satisfaction – perhaps because of their direct pastoral significance – than any other. These are, indeed, the three of his writings which would least attract a

* Her father – Sir Thomas Stamford Raffles – had died in 1826.

modern reading public, save in the opportunities which they give of unearthing the grotesque and misconceived in the didactic literature of a former age. The *Note Book of a Country Clergyman* has very little to recommend it. The atmosphere is gloomy, the providences and judgments are hardly less absurd and far-fetched than those favoured 'Authentic Anecdotes' which gained notoriety for such spiritual penny-dreadfuls as the *Evangelical Magazine* or the *Cottage Magazine*, or *Plain Christian's Library*. The piety, the torments, the villainy, the sticky ends are all rendered the more repulsive to modern minds by their stark hyperbole; the descriptions, which set the scene, at once reduce the stories to melodrama by the guileless recourse to cliché and amateurish repetition. Even the demonstrations of pastoral solace to the afflicted (one of the alleged purposes of the book) are unconvincing – sometimes, indeed, disastrously inept. The story entitled 'Confession', for instance, points no obvious moral, save to demonstrate – unintentionally – how an inexperienced spiritual director can mismanage the problems of his penitent.

The other two works, written for children – *Agathos and other Sunday Stories*, published in 1839, and *The Rocky Island*, published in 1840 – were far more successful, and deservedly so. They are not entirely free from the mawkish and the grisly. Each tale concludes with an edifying catechism on the moral of the story, a duologue between Father and Child, displaying something of that tone of self-righteous didacticism and wide-eyed filial reverence which seems as little real to us to-day as do the infants portrayed in the sombre illustrations – gaunt, unearthly creatures, draped in shrouds, or chubby saints, rapt in pious contemplation. But the author's heart was clearly in the right place; and the unreality arises partly from the archaisms and pedantries of the style, and partly from the fact that the twentieth century has lost its nerve for the didactic and its confidence in parental authority. For these stories were actually told by Samuel to his children (aged then between five and nine); some of the illustrations were executed, very beautifully, by Emily herself; and one of the reasons for their publication was to deliver children from the oppression of unimaginative religious instruction which could cause them 'insensibly to feel the Lord's day a weariness'. 'If on other days they are used to amusing employments, if they love . . . the times of relaxation in which they see their parents as friends, and in some sort companions, what else can happen if on this day all amusement be banished?'[50] One needs only to read the first story about Agathos himself – a simple, felicitous and exciting allegory illustrating the meaning of taking upon onself 'the whole armour of God' – to see what a powerful, and painlessly wholesome, impression the book must have made upon the young.

The Rocky Island, a collection of eight skilful allegories, is in its way equally entrancing. At the time, it aroused criticism from Evangelical quarters because of its strong emphasis on the authority of the Church and on sacramental grace. The *Record* accused the author of offering 'the *soupe maigre* of Popery instead of the sincere milk of God's word',[51] taking exception to passages such as this:

> *Father* [catechising the child on the meaning of the allegory of the children warned to flee from the perils of 'The Rocky Island'] What are the boats by which they are to escape?
> *Child* The 'Ark of Christ's Church', into which we are admitted by baptism.
> *F.* What is the compass, and the musical instrument, and the bread, and the water?
> *C.* God's Word, and the privilege of prayer and holy sacraments, and the other gifts of God to His Church.
> *F.* What is the gentle wind which the musical instrument awoke?
> *C.* The grace of God's Holy Spirit, promised to the members of His Church, to be sought by earnest prayer, and in all the means of grace.[52]

Samuel wrote in reply to these charges what he always maintained against his critics: his High Churchmanship sprang from the writings of Richard Hooker and Bishop Beveridge; his opinions had been formed not by Newman or Pusey, but 'in a far different school. They are those of my beloved father, as I could prove, were it needful, from many written records of his judgment as to the tenor of my ministry, of which, during his late years, he was a most kind, but a close observer.'[53] It was an assertion yet again of his own individual *via media* which neither his contemporaries nor posterity seem properly to have understood.

III. *Bidding for Power*

They all had their moments of depression. Samuel would worry at times over his inability to stir himself into serious study: 'My parish is not nearly so pressing of course as yours,' he wrote to Robert in July 1833, 'but time is sadly poached by life's minutiae. The locusts are small but many and they eat up every green thing in the land. I never begin my sermons until Friday or they would take me all the week.'[1]

Then there were moments when all his work seemed to have come to naught, when he despaired of ever doing any lasting good. He would pour out his troubles to Louisa Noel:

> My dearest sister, ... I *never* come home to my parish without a saddened spirit: saddened with myself and with the state of things round me. The *prospect* of work and exertion promises more than the reality performs: and the new forms of sin and of suffering which have accumulated in a few weeks' absence, come with a force while the daily load progresses at no one time. I have been low-spirited all day; and am so to-night.[2]

The real truth of the matter is that Samuel was often restless; he wanted recognition and sometimes felt that he had failed to get it. There were moments when he thought himself stuck in an ecclesiastical backwater from which he would never be summoned to do the things which he knew he was capable of doing. He was torn between his ambition to occupy a great position and his love of quiet domestic bliss. When he was absent on society business, his letters to Emily were full of remorse at the tiresomeness of the responsibility which called him away from home. Writing from East Farleigh to Emily, he lamented that public business called him to London and therefore he could not return on the expected date – 'This is a fresh disappointment to me and not a little one as it puts off again my return to you. ... I never loved you or grieved over you as I have done to-day. I have read your sweet letter over and delighted in it. ... How I long to be with you. *Far* more than ever before. Goodbye most beloved creature.'[3]

Often enough, however, once he was settled at home, the fidgets began. He had a special yearning for a cathedral appointment. As early as 1831 he had heard whispers that he might be offered a prebend: 'I do not affect to dislike what I perfectly well know I should very much like', he admitted to Robert. 'My love of form – of cathedrals – of dignity – an occasional town residence – above all chanting of my own – would make it a great pleasure to me.'[4]

As the son of his father and a ready and brilliant speaker on behalf of Church societies, Samuel expected offers to come. When they did, however, there was always some drawback which compelled him to decline. The first offer, made in January 1834, was a preachership to the Tunbridge Wells Chapel – an influential Evangelical post, but not especially rewarding (£350 per annum) and he was only prepared to take it if he could retain Brighstone. His bishop, however, disapproved – 'the two livings are not tenable simultaneously', he wrote.[5] A few months later, he had the chance of taking an influential London living, when Charles Simeon put him forward for St Dunstan's, Temple Bar. He thought it over seriously, trying honestly to set aside all worldly concerns. 'As to ambitious feelings,' he wrote to Robert, 'I trust I should not act from them. . . . Looking at it so, I should say it was a lottery in which I staked certain comfort against the chance of rising to an uncomfortable eminence. But I earnestly desire and pray *constantly* to be able to put these thoughts altogether aside.'[6]

It was not very wealthy by London standards – possibly £700 to £800 a year – but James Stephen assured him that he could live quite comfortably in the City on £650.[7] In communicating this fact to his bishop, Samuel earned a mild and rare rebuke. James Stephen had written very pretentiously. 'The question is not whether you can bear to live on mutton and beer, instead of champagne and turtle, but whether you can afford to give 8d a pound instead of 6d for the meat you must provide for your family.'[8] In the end it was the question of residence within the parish which decided Samuel. Sumner warned him of the insalubrious atmosphere of Fetter Lane and Chancery Lane,[9] and therefore Samuel came to the conclusion that he could not 'risk Emily's and the children's health'.[10]

A still more important post came his way in February 1837 – the offer, through Sir Robert Inglis (a close family friend since he had become the guardian of the Thornton children) of the post of Vicar of Leeds. Again Samuel consulted his bishop who felt bound to tell him that he had already determined on making the offer to him (when the living fell vacant) of St Mary's, Southampton, but that Leeds was clearly a post of superior importance. In the end, Samuel's doctors decided for him. He had two medical opinions; Emily and the children were passed as fit to live there, but Samuel was advised against it in the interests of his own health.[11] Reluctantly, Samuel acquiesced. He then at once urged Robert to let his name go forward as a possible candidate: 'You would govern Yorkshire. . . . It is a *grand* situation, much grander upon close inspection than I at first thought; neither do I see why it should be so contentious. Coventry was as bad, and Hook has managed that. Either *write* or *come* in answer to this as speedily as you possibly can.'[12]

Robert – cautious and unambitious as ever – could not give a decision at once. He wanted time to pray for guidance.[13] He was afraid lest his studies should suffer. He pondered the matter earnestly and eventually wrote to Samuel to tell him that he was no longer interested.[14] In his next letter he reported that Hook was now 'high in the stakes' for the position[15]; and in gaining it, as is well known, Hook himself was to make history for the effectiveness with which he dominated and transformed the religious life of a great city.

It is not surprising that Samuel's name was often coming up as a candidate for substantial preferment, even though at the time when he received the offer of Leeds he was only thirty-one. In 1836 he had become a rural dean. There was little doubt that his bishop looked upon him as the outstanding clergyman in his diocese, and frequently invited him to stay at Farnham Castle and to take the platform at important diocesan meetings. At one such meeting – the Diocesan Church Building Society meeting held in Winchester in March 1837 – when Lord Palmerston and the Duke of Wellington were present, Samuel ventured to criticise Palmerston's speech with extraordinary vehemence. Some eyebrows were raised at this presumption and the Duke of Wellington was asked why he permitted so junior a clergyman to steal Palmerston's thunder. He replied that he had thought of intervening, until it occurred to him that this might divert the speaker's 'indignant eloquence' to himself. 'I assure you', he added, 'that I would have faced a battery sooner.'[16]

Rumours, therefore, frequently circulated about Samuel's elevation; and it is interesting to note that as late as December 1837 his name was still being connected with Evangelical preferment. 'Have you heard', Samuel wrote to Robert during that month, 'that I am Rector of Bath and Henry Rector of Brighstone? This is Newport news. . . . I do not believe it because I think I should have known if it was so.'[17]

It was all rather unsettling. Fame was coming Samuel's way, but he still had had no offer of a cathedral appointment. He and Robert discussed jokingly the names of possible recipients of presentation copies of their father's *Life* with a view to gaining the friendship of the mighty. The Archbishop should certainly have a copy. 'He may perhaps give you a stall for it', Samuel suggested to Robert. A copy must go to the Athenaeum 'which you ought to give as a member', Samuel added, 'and I as an aspirant and so in which we both have an interest'.[18] Samuel was also in favour of sending a copy to the Duke of Wellington. 'My only reason for wishing to do it was, as I told you, that being my Lord Lieutenant, I sometimes meet him on public occasions and it might then be an advantage to me to have had even that claim to acquaintance.'[19] A copy was sent to Peel, who apparently liked it. 'From Peel's remarks', Robert observed to

Samuel, 'I think that if he comes in, he will at least make you a Dean.'*

Some of this was jest; but not all. Samuel was certainly piqued at not being a member of the Athenaeum, and he privately blamed John Wilson Croker, whom he suspected of having written a hostile review of the Wilberforce biography in the *Quarterly*, for this rebuff. On 6 July 1838 Samuel wrote to Robert to convey the news of his failure. 'I was *not* elected – Dr Hodgson told me. They must be unanimous. Any one voice postponed, put off the election. . . . No question is asked or reason given. 15 out of the whole 25 who could have been present signed my recommendation – the feeling for me was strong.' Surely Croker was to blame. He 'is a man who has raised himself by doing the dirty work of others – he is clever; but he owes far more to being a clever dung feeder than a clever man; few men would carry talents to *his* Master and therefore he found little competition'.[20] He was subsequently to change his mind about Croker, but this is an interesting – and not untypical – example of Samuel's quickness of temper and hasty judgment, which were in later life often to land him in trouble. In December 1839 he was still bent on securing election and discussed with Robert the best way of 'silencing Croker'.[21] He wrote to Gladstone to ask his advice and received a friendly reply: 'I do not know Croker well enough to write to him: but I have written to Mahon who I think is better acquainted and asked him if he could do it, as well as named you to him. I have also written to Lord Braybrooke, and when I get to Town I should hope to see Lord Aberdeen and perhaps to have some other means of reaching Croker. I cannot however think that you are in danger from him. I trust we may meet in town.'[22]

The approach must have been successful, for Samuel was elected to the Athenaeum within a few months.

Robert tried to soothe his brother from time to time, singing the praises of obscurity. He would have liked to have seen him in a great place – at the centre of things – 'yet I hate the vile, crowded London, full of sin and misery, where every man is destroying himself and plotting against his neighbours. I am glad to live in a calmer region. It is sometimes provoking to people who feel – as you may – that they have talents which are fit *res gerere terra marique* to lie unknown in a corner, – yet when I look even at the glorious actions of my Father I cannot but feel that at times he was led into courses, which in the long run were of dubious advantage,

* Wrangham MSS. VII. 86. 20 April 1838. Gladstone was also sent a copy – by Robert Wilberforce, his first of many letters to Gladstone. B. M. Add. Mss. 44356 (Gladstone Papers Vol. 271) f. 62.

and that there is a blessing in having a simple, unostentatious inevitable duty prescribed as the path-way for one's feet.'[23]

He rather agreed with Samuel, however, that the advantage which they enjoyed of having had a celebrated father was somewhat offset by the unhappy circumstance of a highly unsatisfactory eldest brother. Brother William was tainting the family name. The *débâcle* of the farming business had been bad enough; unfortunately William had not learnt from experience, and although *he* had every reason to sing the praises of obscurity, he was constantly pushing himself forward where his presence could only lead to embarrassment. Having settled at Markington after his return from exile on the Continent, he decided at last to enter Parliament. He thought of standing in the Conservative interest for Newport I.O.W., so that he could be near Samuel (a proposal which evoked the most subdued rapture from Brighstone)[24]; and he appears to have committed a gaffe by allowing himself to be put forward as a candidate at Hull at the same time.[25] The matter was resolved and he successfully contested Hull in 1837, only to be unseated on petition in the following year. Thereafter his career is shrouded in mystery, although incidental references to his doings in the family letters suggest the less said the better. He was insolent to John Murray in the Athenaeum ('There are inconveniences having relations in your club', sighed Robert)[26]; in September 1839 Robert alluded to some scandal involving William 'in James St' which necessitated his going to town to sort it out. 'I am most unwilling to do so', he wrote to Samuel from Yorkshire, 'because to go away in the midst of my mission here would be to proclaim some family disaster which if possible I would conceal.'[27] A month later Robert expressed the wish that William were '4,000 miles off' and deplored the fact that poor Mary, his wife, did not dare to be seen in public.[28] William then took himself off to Paris.

In 1841 he was back again with plans to stand for Parliament, on this occasion unsuccessfully contesting Taunton. Somehow or other he managed to bungle this, as a letter from Samuel to Robert indicates: 'Now William is here: having come down for consultation on his Taunton case. Poor Fellow! I see in my own mind that he lost that entirely through bribery. He now he says sees that is wrong and will never do it again. But!! All his present correspondence turns on this – and I feel little doubt that had his hands been clean, some case would have been found out on the other side.'[29]

Undeterred, William went on to contest Bradford – not surprisingly with equal lack of success. It was hardly unnatural for Samuel to resent his brother's irresponsibility and to try – as he did later in 1846 – to get him safely tucked away in some comfortable berth, such as a Governorship in the Ionian Islands.* Indeed, with these facts before us, it is clear whose name should fill the blank which Samuel discreetly inserted in an interesting letter written to Robert in June 1840, in reply to the suggestion that Peel, who had been heard to praise Samuel, would be likely to raise him to the episcopal bench:

> Many thanks for your truly affectionate letter. It is your affection which makes you partial in judgement of me and sanguine in anticipation. There is an infinite distance between paying such a passing compliment and the first beginning of a thought of preferring. However all such thoughts I utterly dismiss. If we had the natural political allies whom our Father's sons might naturally have had, if poor ——— had been other than he is, it would not be an unnatural termination for any of us. But ———.[30]

Is it a sin to count one's chances of future preferment? If Samuel seems at times to have thought so, it must be admitted that he often transgressed. He was aware of his own powers; he wished to employ them to the full where they would have most effect. Robert and Henry had learned from Keble and Newman that (as Robert himself put it) 'the trees which grow in the valley have greener leaves than those upon the hill tops'.[31] Newman had also observed to Henry that the best men must not expect any reward in this life. 'A world where people rise according to *real* merit may be a very good world, but it is not *this* in which Providence has put us.'[32] Was this to be accepted without challenge? If the mediocre were to rise to the top and the really able men were to languish in obscurity, how would the Church's mission be served, how – in times of crisis – could the defence of the Church be effectively maintained? And just how passive was this injunction to put oneself into the hands of Providence intended to be? Should one not use 'natural openings', as Samuel had expressed it?

This may be special pleading. Two things, at least, are certain. In the first place, when Samuel's fortunes had turned and the recognition which he had sought so keenly came to him in great abundance, he was to be chastened by sorrow almost to the limit of human endurance. Thereafter he was never quite the same. Secondly, the use of the power he acquired may be said to have justified his longing to acquire it. Robert, with all

---

* He applied on William's behalf to Sir James Graham and to Lord Aberdeen. Robert tackled Gladstone. Wrangham MSS. VI. 284, 308.

his humility, would not have made a great bishop; Samuel became one of the greatest bishops in the history of the Anglican Church.

IV. *Jane Legard and Burton Agnes*

They were so unlike each other, these two brothers; yet utterly devoted. Robert confided to Samuel all his anxieties. After Agnes's death, East Farleigh never seemed the same. He wanted to return to Yorkshire to be within reach of their friends. Two of Agnes's most intimate friends, however – her Aunt Jane (Legard) and her cousin, also named Jane Legard – came to live with Robert in order to look after his children. They coped well, but for many months Robert felt deeply the pangs of separation.

> This last has been to me a mournful week [he wrote to Samuel on the first anniversary of Agnes's death], and I feel very thankful that I have now passed the time in which every day is loaded with its peculiar burden of sorrow. I have the greatest possible comfort in the health and never-ceasing vivacity of my dear William. I greatly wish that you could see him, who have had experience, for I have never expected that the charge of guiding him would devolve on me. Aunt Jane, I must say, seems to manage him very well, and he is perfectly obedient to me, but I am afraid he is headstrong and insubordinate in the nursery. Jane has let him have too much his own way. Now I don't know how to teach her to enforce any obedience, and is it better to let him grow up looking upon her as a sort of playmate, and regarding Aunt Jane and myself as the people to be attended to. I have never yet had to punish him. . . . Dear little Edward increases in sense every day and seems sweet-tempered and lively also. Alas how hard do I find it not to feel towards them an immoderate affection. What trial or trouble can one feel to be burthensome which is undertaken for their sake. But I am running on as I am apt to do to Jane Legard and my aunt, talking about nothing but these dear boys.[1]

Agnes had told Robert that he must marry again; and since Jane Legard was looking for a husband, it was quite natural that she and Robert should draw closer together. By January 1837 they were engaged,[2] and in April Samuel officiated at their wedding. 'All went off very well' he told Charles Anderson, 'though it was quite impossible not to have very *peculiar* feelings about the wedding. Digby Wrangham gave her away.'[3]

They took their summer holidays in Yorkshire – as a sort of second honeymoon. But Robert was soon called away; he returned to Kent at the beginning of July, making the journey by sea (more comfortable than the three-day journey by stage). Jane sent him the family news:

> I fear the house will feel very lonely to you, not having the children or anything, but now you can read to your heart's content with no interruptions from impertinent people who are apt to look with a jealous eye on the absorbing qualities of those deep folios.
>
> . . . Now my love do you want to know what we have been doing since you went, if so I will describe and take my chance of your reading my letter through; at all events I shall not be there to see you if you thrust it behind the picture on the chimney piece unread. Thursday was very bright and beautiful and if the day did seem long, it was not its fault. I sauntered down in the evening to take a look at the sea and pray for your prosperous voyage. Friday, we took the children down to bathe. Eddie was in exstasies beforehand and screamed with delight when we got into the machine, 'Oh it is like a little omnibus'. He kicked a little when he was popped into the sea, but upon the whole liked it very well, better than his brother, who made a sad uproar – but I hope he will get over it in time. It appears to agree with him beautifully. . . . I want to know how the garden looks. The roses must be in high beauty, I should think and I dare say many annuals in bloom. I wish I could see them. Moreover if I were there I might just peep into the window and see what the master was about. I quite pine to see thee my love and hardly know how to enjoy the company of so many friends as I have around me here, separated as I am from my best and dearest. . . .[4]

After the marriage to Jane Legard, the move from East Farleigh to a living in Yorkshire became even more desirable. Robert began making serious enquiries in 1838, looking carefully at advertisements for exchanges of preferments in the *Record* and the *Ecclesiastical Gazette*. Samuel sent him details when he heard of anything likely, at the same time expressing his regret that Robert should wish to remove himself from the neighbourhood of London as this would lead to 'a diminution of your opportunities of usefulness, which I very much doubt whether any peculiar features of Yorkshire society . . . would at all counterbalance'.[5]

In April 1840 Robert at last found what he wanted: the living of Burton Agnes near Beverley in the East Riding of Yorkshire. It was advertised for exchange by the vicar, a man called Lutwidge, whose brother-in-law was the patron and therefore amenable to the arrangement. Robert was less certain about securing the permission of the Lord Chancellor.[6] By August 1840 the necessary sanction had been obtained and the exchange was effected without delay. Robert described the move and his first impressions of Burton Agnes in a long letter to Samuel, dated 1 September.

We got down on Thursday evening. The next two days I passed in superintending the disembarkation of my goods. I am thankful to say they suffered no injury, but what they must needs receive from being packed into the hold of a vessel, and from being run upon and stamped on as such things always are by sailors and watermen. They have managed I believe to break a good many small things in this way. But Lutwidge's things had got as far as off Cromer in their way south, when his vessel was run down and nearly sunk by a steamer. It was brought back here, and will have to be unloaded and refitted before it can proceed. . . . The sailors at Bridlington were greatly astonished at my having so many books, and told me 'I could not possibly look thro' so many!'

I got every thing carried into my house by Saturday night, and now the difficulty is to put them all away. I have been over to unpack the glass and china, which has come quite safely. Jane is going over with me to spend some days tomorrow, when we hope to get things into some order. The place is certainly a very desirable one – a good house, and gentlemanlike, and a pleasant, tho' not a pretty country. I have two very nice churches about a mile from one another. The real question is what degree of annoyance I shall receive from the Dissenters, but then I have to take into account that the hopping which is now just beginning at Farleigh is an evil from which I am delivered. Here are conflicting afflictions – just as I am now considering whether to employ a drunken churchman as my bookseller or a sober anabaptist. . . .[7]

Gradually the good and bad points revealed themselves. The parish was smaller than East Farleigh, the total population being barely six hundred[8]; but with the two churches it was necessary (after he became archdeacon) to employ a curate. Burton Agnes church was an ecclesiologist's nightmare – the walls had been plastered, the roof underdrawn and the squire's pew was a capacious and cosy chamber complete with fireplace.[9] Robert made a mental note to restore a proper ethos when the time was ripe. He looked in vain at first for the magnificent Norman font which he had expected to find in the church – it eventually turned up in the vicarage garden, where it had been used as a flower bowl. The tower, however, was very handsome. There was a glebe farm, very near the vicarage, from which on a clear day one could enjoy a distant view of Beverley Minster; the garden was overcrowded with trees, greatly favoured by some tiresome rooks. As for the vicarage, 'its great fault', Robert wrote to Samuel, 'is the want of dressing rooms. I fancy old Raikes who built it was wont to dress like the Yankees at the Pump.'[10]

He was soon to have his hands full. The rural clergy of the barbarous north were very much more difficult to organise and discipline than his brethren in the south, apathetic though they had often seemed. Within a year of his move he was to find himself their immediate master.

250

v. *The Death of Caroline Manning*

In the meantime, tragedy had befallen the Mannings at Lavington. Caroline had always been delicate, suffering periodic attacks of violent coughing which would greatly weaken her. During the early months of 1837 she had fallen victim to influenza. By May, however, it appeared that she was on the mend. 'Her cough is less, and though she gets well lingeringly', Manning wrote to Samuel, 'I hope the weather will soon relieve the remains of her attack.'[1] A week or so later there was a relapse. Not until 22 June was there any cause for alarm. Samuel had been with Manning on that day, and – as he subsequently recalled in his diary – the look on his brother-in-law's face told him at once that something was seriously amiss.[2] A few days later he sent a full report to Robert:

> Dear Caroline is in a very alarming state. . . . Last week she had apparently a fresh attack and has been very unwell ever since. On Sunday it was thought necessary to put on leeches – and she is so exceedingly reduced that her state is most alarming.

Emily and Samuel had thought it best to remain at Lavington so that Henry Manning would not be left to suffer alone.

> Yesterday we had *all* given up hope; and poor Manning was in a most distressed though . . . resigned condition. To-day the symptoms are alleviated and we are buoyed up with hope; yet we cannot conceal from ourselves that in this most invidious of all maladies (for it is Consumption that we dread) there is no real reliance to be put upon these occasional improvements. We cannot tell dearest Mrs J. Sargent of the amount of this our new alarm because as Mary is not well enough to be left we do not like to *distract* her when she cannot come.[3]

Mrs Sargent was summoned to Lavington a few days later. Yet Caroline rallied again. The watch by the bedside carried on into the third week of July. On Sunday, 23 July, Mrs Sargent wrote to Sophia, knowing that the end was near:

> My dearest Sophia, Our beloved Caroline is not in a suffering state. She is perfectly tranquil, her pain all past and sinking most gradually. The cough is rather better last night and to-day. There is no delirium but a great weakening of her mind and no power of attending to anything but the present bodily wants. She is not aware she is worse.[4]

On Monday, 24 July, Caroline died. She was only twenty-five years old. She was buried in Lavington churchyard on 28 July. 'We are just returned from the funeral of our dear sister,' Samuel wrote to Robert that day, 'having laid all that was mortal of her by the side of the beloved ones who have been earlier called, in the beautiful shadow of the peaceful church-yard. She is at rest – and works do follow her. Many good works; humbly and patiently performed. Manning is calm and quiet and I trust will not sink when this strain is over.'5

Indeed Manning's self-possession seemed a miracle. There had been no children. He was alone in the world. Mrs Sargent came at once to live with him and stayed there until 1841 when another dreadful bereavement visited her family and she was called away to take charge of another stricken household. For nearly four years, then, Mrs Sargent kept Manning's house, loving him as her own son, attending to his every need. It had been Caroline's wish. Something of what passed between the mother and her dying child was recalled by Mrs Sargent a year later when she wrote to Emily to describe her ministrations to Henry Manning during an illness caused by an obstruction:

> All Tuesday night he was in dreadful pain ... and we sent off in the night again for Mr Ingram. Henry bore his pain like a martyr as you know he would do, but it was very severe. ... By the blessing of God the obstruction gave way to the remedies tried and inflammation has not come on. ... I stood by him and had the comfort of seeing him sleep quietly like an infant. ... Mr Ingram went to bed in my room and I lay down upon the sofa in Henry's room.
>
> But my dearest Emily to find myself sitting up in *that* room – you can imagine, but I cannot describe what I felt – and then he was obliged to take from his neck the chain that has hung there the last year, and I saw her locket and the two dear rings he himself took from her fingers and I almost fancied she was there herself. As I was watching him sleeping I saw her lovely smile when she looked at me and said 'I am sure Mama you will do all you can to take care of Henry'. I felt fulfilling her wishes and was comforted.6

It would not be too much to say that this catastrophe changed the course of Henry Manning's life. It was not that his character was changed: perhaps the intense spirituality, which was always there since his first calling to the ministry, was deepened. Nor were his principles and ideals changed; rather were they now made the goals of a wholly dedicated life. For Manning, when Caroline died, turned his back on the world, doing so because his worldly happiness was inseparable from the person of the wife whom he had loved with such devotion. Men marvelled at his self-control when he preached at Caroline's funeral – an address of exquisite simplicity and tenderness – to offer consolation to those that mourn. The greatest proof of that consolation was the demeanour of him who was most afflicted. Yet the grief which he suffered inwardly was intense – so great that he spoke of it only to those who were closest to him, and then only rarely. He could, in later years, speak freely of Caroline and all that she meant to him to one person alone, and that was her sister Mary, Henry's wife, his penitent, who aroused in his heart something of the love which he had known in the early days.

Two months after Caroline's death, Manning tried to explain his state of mind to Samuel:

> I find the difficulty of speaking daily grow upon me – so that I shrink even from those who with the kindest interest, would refer to the past. Do you remember our conversation as we rode to Milland this time year? You ask me whether I can keep my mind *simple* – do you mean as opposed to self-deception, or to excitement? There are kinds of employment which to you and to myself would minister temptations to self-deception; and we should be liable to lay ourselves out in them with too little simplicity of heart. But you probably mean as opposed to excitement – and although it might only be the deceitfulness of excitement that would lead me to say 'no' – I think I may say that, to the best of my judgement and belief, I am not. I feel that I cannot trust myself to dwell upon the past except in direct acts of devotion – at these times, in church, but especially day by day at home – I both can, and do, fully and fixedly – and these are the most blessed moments of my present life. At all other times I feel the absolute need of full employment, and to the best of my powers I maintain a habit of fixed attention, and suffer as few intervals of disengaged time as I can – but I do not overwork myself in any way by late hours, or anything of the kind – and my work does not excite but only weary me in a wholesome way, and the last hour or so before going to bed is a deep and calm refreshment, and I sleep, I thank God, almost always very quickly. I cannot therefore feel that I am excited, which, if I thought, I should be uneasy lest I should be doing myself harm in body and mind, and losing the sad, but sanctifying benefit of my affliction.[7]

Everything we know of Manning's actions after his bereavement supports this analysis of his emotions and of the effects of Caroline's death upon his subsequent life. He would compose his sermons sitting by her grave; he would pray and meditate daily from her own book of prayers. Nothing can be further from the truth than to say that he tried to cast Caroline out of his mind. But he refused to live in the past. His daily energies became more intense; and, in the course of the following year, the strain, which he had made light of in his letter to Samuel, began to tell. During 1838 he suffered badly from asthma, and in August was obliged to take to his bed. His doctor insisted that he should take a holiday – preferably in southern Europe, where the warmer climate would do him good. He knew that Gladstone was in Rome and that Charles Marriott was also going. He decided therefore to follow his doctor's advice. He would join the party in Rome, enjoy a rest-cure, and take the opportunity of studying at first hand the actual workings of the Roman Church. He set off for the Eternal City, the first of many such visits in the course of his long life.

Chapter 6

THE THREE ARCHDEACONS

1. *Triumph and Tribulations*

On 19 November 1839 Samuel Wilberforce received the offer from his bishop of the archdeaconry of Surrey and was installed at Winchester a week later. The turning point in his fortunes, however, had really been the invitation, earlier in the same year, to undertake a preaching tour in the diocese of Exeter on behalf of the S.P.G. The tour coincided with Bishop Phillpotts's triennial visitation, and the redoubtable Henry of Exeter (a pugnacious and inflexible High Churchman) had – it is said – shuddered at the prospect. 'I shall scream', he said; one mission sermon was bad enough; a whole string of them from the same preacher would be unendurable.[1] To have made an ally of the most feared controversialist in the Anglican Church was not the least of Samuel's triumphs. Phillpotts was utterly won over by his charm, eloquence and inventiveness, and wrote at the end of an exhausting tour, in which Samuel had travelled fifteen hundred miles and preached or spoken daily (occasionally three times in the course of one day) for the best part of ten weeks, that he felt nothing but praise for his 'extraordinary efforts', signing himself 'with warm regard, your faithful friend'.[2] It was clearly an unqualified success, and memories of his sermons were still vivid forty years afterwards. 'My tour has been very interesting', Samuel wrote to Manning. 'The zeal raised for the S.P.G. considerable and the sound Church principle evidently spreading: and I hope quickened much by the exhibition of the Church in a living and actively aggressive character and position.'[3]

Future preferment was now assured. Samuel had behind him not only the superlative opinion of the most considerable Evangelical influence on the Bishops' Bench (C. R. Sumner) but also the rare privilege of Philpotts's active support.

Robert was overjoyed. When he heard the news of the archdeaconry, he wrote at once to send his congratulations:

I hope you will coerce some of the troublesome spirits, particularly the

Parson of Godstone, of whom I heard as exposing himself shamefully at (sic) the Archbishop about ten days ago by talking the most low-church and almost infidel slang. The Archbishop I am told rather put him down. . . . May God abundantly bless you, my beloved brother, both here and hereafter. May this advancement make you the instrument of usefulness and enhance your reward. So prays your truly attached brother.[4]

The next few months were hectic. Engagements and fresh honours came in, as it seemed, by every post. Samuel was elected to the Stirling Club; secured, at last, election to the Athenaeum. Hawkins wrote to ask him if he would accept nomination as Bampton Lecturer for 1841 ('I have trembled and assented', Samuel wrote to Robert. 'I shall if appointed want your help. I hope it will fix me to a year's hard reading of Theology').* Above all, he was inundated with requests to preach or to take the platform. A particularly significant invitation came to him on 24 March 1840, which he at once reported to Robert:

> I have just got a hateful business: a letter from Bp. of London in name of Archbishop of Canterbury, requesting me to take a resolution at a public meeting for S.P.G. to be held in Egyptian Hall, April 8th, Wednesday, Lord Mayor in chair, a requisition of between 3 and 4 hundred leading bankers, merchants etc. The 2 Archbishops and all London are to be there. It is most absurd having me. I cannot speak without facts and a position, and there I shall have none. However I have clearly no choice, as it has come unsought, so I have assented.[5]

Samuel need not have worried. This event was second in importance only to the great S.P.G. tour in bringing his name before the public and in gaining the estimation of those who were in a position to offer rewards. He described the triumph to Robert shortly afterwards:

> Our meeting went off very well. It appears I gave satisfaction to all but myself. I spoke not nearly so well as in the West, and infinitely below my own perception of excellence. Yet I trust it answered its purpose in stirring up the meeting. The Bp. of London spoke most kindly to me about my speech yesterday and to-day only saying, 'I do not quite like hearing you, for you make me cry.' Our Bishop said 'you spoke admirably'. Dearest R. I do not tell you this with a feeling of vanity. I am sure I do not, but because I know you, from affection, will wish to know *just all*. I greatly fell below my own standard, and the opinion of others somehow does not alter that.[6]

A month or so later he took the platform at Exeter Hall, speaking at an anti-slavery rally to launch the Niger expedition of Captain Trotter,

* Wrangham MSS. VI. 208. 31 March 1840. This acceptance was later withdrawn, because of the death of his wife.

at which Prince Albert was present to give his first public speech. The accounts of eye-witnesses represent the occasion as being flat and lifeless until the proceedings were electrified by a speech of immense fire and originality by the least known of all the celebrities on the platform, earning Samuel a thunderous response from the grateful audience. The Prince asked his name; Peel revealed the secret of Samuel's power by reminding the assembly of his paternity.[7]

And so fresh honours were heaped upon him. In August 1840 he became a Canon of Winchester, and in October he received the offer of the Rectory of Alverstoke, the parish in the Portsmouth area which stood in eminence and significance at this period rather in the position which Portsea was to occupy in the later years of the century. The population of the parish was estimated at 12,637, including Gosport (6,798) and Forten (2,256), with the tithes commuted for £1,250.[8] 'My ministry', Samuel informed Robert, 'will be brought to bear upon a much more educated as well as numerous class. I shall also be at the head of the Gosport and Forten clergy. In short, here is a great opening for usefulness, if it please God to give me a single eye, a zealous heart, and a clear head.'[9]

Alverstoke had the added advantage of being a town parish with a country residence. 'I have always thought', Robert wrote to Samuel, 'that nothing could be more eligible than a parish, where you yourself enjoyed a country retirement, while there was a Town at hand to supply a more educated audience. Perhaps it is scarce a right feeling to entertain, but it is difficult to escape altogether from the sentiment of Aristagoras when he told the Spartans that in petty quarrels with their rivals at Tegea they were wasting the might which might subdue the world.'[10]

The move from Brighstone took place just before Christmas in that year. Samuel preached his farewell sermon on 20 December, and then – while the rest of the family were at Lavington – he stayed at Alverstoke at the house of a General Burrows, whose son had been his curate in the Isle of Wight and who now accompanied him to help him in his new work. The rectory was not occupied until the spring. Indeed, apart from his short visit to the parish over Christmas and during the opening days of the new year, Samuel's work lay chiefly in Winchester. During October and November 1840 he held his primary archidiaconal visitation and for the early part of the next year he was bound to Winchester by his canonical residence. While he was there he heard in January 1841 that Prince Albert had nominated him to be one of his chaplains, clearly moved to do so by the impression which he had formed of Samuel's powers at the Exeter Hall meeting some six months before. In February, at their house in the Close, Emily gave birth to their fourth son – Basil Orme. Every happiness and satisfaction seemed to be coming at once. The future had never looked so full of boundless promise. God indeed had blessed them abundantly.

Then, at the moment when everything Samuel had ever wanted was his or seemed to be within his grasp, his whole life was suddenly blighted. He too, like Henry Manning and Robert before him, was to pass through the fire.

For him it burned more terribly. Much as they suffered, he must needs have suffered more. To begin with, his nature was intensely passionate, his emotions far less disciplined. All men may be the better for intimate companionship and that understanding of individual moods and needs which such companionship can bring – to be encouraged when depressed, to be soothed when embittered and frustrated, to be teased out of solemnity, to enjoy the complete and constant sympathy of another. For Samuel these consolations were his indispensable source of vitality and strength. Above all, he needed love – love such as his own passionate nature was ready to give in overwhelming abundance. And in Emily he had found – as he had known since childhood – all these things: perfect understanding, absolute loyalty, a tenderness and willingness to give, which were themselves the secret of her supremely happy disposition.

The Sargent family had every gift of nature save good health. Young John, Harry, Charlotte and Caroline had all been taken from the circle in their youth. The three surviving girls – Emily, Mary and Sophia – were all delicate; and every illness, and sudden weariness, and confinement were attended by the gravest anxiety. The only shadows which darkened the happiness of Samuel's married life were the occasional stabs of fear that he too might be put to the dreadful test of sudden and early bereavement. In 1838 he had written in his diary: '*I fear being scourged into devotedness*'.[11] What price might be exacted for all his blessings?

Perhaps the intensity of their love was heightened by this sense of living on the edge of a precipice. Emily would make light of her illnesses and her troubles after confinements for Samuel's sake. After just recovering from a fever which had lasted three weeks, her first thoughts were to relieve her husband's anxiety by joking about her condition; she looked in mock horror at her nails and compared them to Nebuchadnezzar's, so that he could go off with an easy mind to attend to some diocesan business in Winchester.[12] Once he had gone, however, the agony of separation seemed very hard to bear.

> My own beloved husband [runs one letter, written while Samuel was away from home], I must only say one word to you in great haste tonight for Mama is urging me to go to bed as it is getting late. I opened the Bp's letter thinking it might want to be forwarded and Charles's [Charles Anderson] to amuse me at my solitary breakfast the other morning. . . . Our treasure is quite well. She smiled when I gave her your kiss. Saml, Saml, you will come back on Tuesday and not help them to stay another day. Henry will come and see us you know, and think how soon you are going, how much we have been separated and how excessively I want you. It is so sad to have half torn away, more especially when it is the precious, precious treasured half I love so warmly. Oh! husband, husband, do come – I got your dear letter and love you for it. I am well. God bless my own and bring you safely back to the arms of your most tenderly and faithfully and warmly attached wife, Emily Wilberforce.
> Sunday night. You have been close in my thoughts all day.[13]

Samuel's letters were no less tender.

> Never my own darling, *never* before did I get such precious letters from you as this time [he wrote on one occasion, on hearing from Emily that she had narrowly escaped a serious accident]. Your last was the dearest I ever had, the most tenderly affectionate, and so I said to myself as I read it over again today in the coach as we came here – but the one I found here is even more darling and precious than that. Oh indeed my beloved we have abundant cause to bless God for his goodness in keeping you from a serious accident. It quite made me hold my breath as I read your account of it though I knew it was quite passed now. Pray be most careful of yourself my darling that Wednesday may be most delicious. You cannot think how much it is in my thoughts.[14]

Shortly before her death, while she was at Lavington, Emily was sitting with old Mrs Wilberforce in the garden, under the apple tree, and they began to talk about *Agathos* and the favourable reception it had gained. What passed between them so affected Barbara that she could not bring herself to tell Samuel until several months after Emily's death.

> Quite thoughtlessly and not expecting anything would follow I said that Charles Kennaway fancied he traced in it [*Agathos*] a great deal of her companionship of mind with you. Little did I think what a spring I had unconsciously touched – her whole soul was roused, her eyes filled with tears as she spoke, and with that look no one else ever had of tender seriousness, she said, 'That shews how very little C.K. can know of Samuel or of me. I have been the receiver in *everything*: and whatever there is of good in me I owe it all through God to him. I always feel it was the crown-

259

ing mercy of my life that I fell into such hands, and my responsibility will be great for the use I shall have made of his example and instruction.'

And then she spoke as if she felt there had been much in her naturally to be subdued, and what a continual blessing your tender guiding had been to her, not only for this world but the next; and dwelt some time upon it, but this is the outline of what I remember. I have half hesitated to touch this tendrest string, but I think it cannot but be comforting to you to dwell on what was eternally abiding, and that God made use of you to train the soul of one so dear to Himself.[15]

Emily died on 10 March 1841 at Winchester. She had been unwell ever since her confinement on 14 February; she had seemed to recover, and then at the beginning of March was stricken with a fever. On 5 March Samuel entered in his diary:

> My mother stayed. Dearest E. very ill this morning. Return of attack. Very low about herself. 'I have seen my face: shocked: it is the stamp of death: it is *the* look all the rest had.' Miserere mei, domine.

On the 8th, Dr Locock, the family doctor, was summoned from London. On the 10th:

> ½ past 9. The end came. She took leave of the children on the Tuesday afternoon. To Ella saying 'Take care of your brother: be a good child – I will give you my trinket box, but mind it does not make you vain.' To Herbert, 'Be a good boy – mind you are obedient to your parents.' A day of unknown agony to me. Every feeling stunned. Paroxysms of convulsive anguish – and no power of looking up through the darkness which had settled on my soul. O Lord have mercy upon me. Henry and G.D.R. very kind and beloved Sophia and Mary also. God bless them and spare them if it be His will this cup of agony.

On the next day:

> May the utter darkness of my life which never can be dispelled kill in me all my ambitious desires and earthly purposes; my love of money and power and place and make me bow meekly to Christ's yoke.[16]

He wrote to Charles Anderson on 13 March:

> The blow is greater than even you can conceive. But even now I feel that it is far less than I have required. May God only give me grace to profit by it. It has after all come upon me like a thunderclap. I had never indeed reckoned upon it. Dark shadows truly had been often of late cast over me and they chilled my soul; but they passed; and in them somehow I always thought that I was to be alarmed lest my heart should cling too fondly to her but that after all she would be spared. You and your dear Emma entered into her rare and lovely character: and I love you better than ever because you did so. The nobleness and purity and affection and

rich feeling. Oh, my dearest Charles, how much less have I valued such a loan than I should have done: and yet God knows I loved her tenderly. But then I had loved her from boyhood: I had thought of her, I am certain, *daily* at school, at College; and now for 13 years almost of married love in which she had grown dearer and dearer to me. Well: I do not repine. I believe not at all. But I long to learn my lesson – and I know calmly and settledly, that a sunless life, as far as earth goes, is before me: and I do not wish it otherwise. I wish to do my work meekly and cheerfully till I also am called.[17]

She lay in Winchester Cathedral and was taken to Lavington for the funeral, where she was buried alongside her sister and her father. 'I, like adamant', Samuel recorded, 'with the sense of being so; an awful state.'[18]

For a while Samuel was quite crushed; and with a heart as heavy, Mary Sargent, Emily's mother, left Henry Manning and Lavington to take charge of Samuel's children and to move with them to Alverstoke. Old Mrs Sargent, the grandmother, survived this fresh disaster by barely three weeks. She had been a fine old lady, always teased by John for her taste for murders and gory stories,[19] wanting little else in her last years save to be read to – particularly from *Peter Simple*.[20] Samuel reported her death to Robert:

It is very affecting to me: brought on as it clearly was by my sorrow. 'And is she too taken' was her continued secret lamentation just overheard by those who sat round her. She never rallied; and the day 3 weeks she herself fell asleep. I cannot tell you how it affected me as I stood over her corpse. The calm gathering of unreluctant age blended and yet contrasted so strangely with the violent breaking of the silver cord in its utmost beauty and loveliness, when other hearts must break with its breaking and the closing of those eyes must darken others for a life. Yet so be it. God's will be done.[21]

From all this tragedy, the figure of Mary Sargent stands out for the courage and patience and the spirit of calm acceptance with which she shouldered the task of rallying the afflicted and comforting the children whose mother had now gone from them. She had gone straight to Henry Manning as soon as she was needed; it was a pain for her to leave Lavington even for a few days. She had now at the age of sixty-two to manage a large family of small children when she had forgotten what such a household was like; and all the time she had her memories. She had been at the bedside of each of her loved ones as they had died, and to her the last confidences had been given. Only to her most intimate friends did she reveal her real feelings. Thus she wrote to Mrs Anderson in April, while still at Winchester with Samuel and the children:

> I ought to have written to you long ago but I cannot tell you how much I have been hurried and how very incapable I have felt of getting on with business. After writing, and looking over things that distress me for a short time, I am quite bewildered and my senses seem nearly gone.
>
> We have fixed to try an elder sister of Sarah's as Nurse – it was my beloved Emily's wish and we cannot bear to omit anything that she desired for the children. We shall secure kindness whatever else is wanting and the youngest child (except the infant) is very backward with his teeth and very irritable so that he will want peculiar tenderness for the next year or two. I cannot say anything about this dreadful crush of the most perfect domestic happiness that was ever witnessed. I can hardly believe that she is really gone. . . .
>
> As to my dear son-in-law I know not what account to give of him, he suffers sadly tho': he goes about as usual and shrinks from no duty. At present life has lost all interest. I hope after a time his dear children will a little fill up the dreadful blank. I think we both feel our loss more than at first when the stunning effects of the blow made us unconscious of its full weight – but I cannot bear to name my share of the affliction with that of dearest Sam. Alas! I know from bitter experience what his sufferings are and how the brightness and colour of every earthly enjoyment is gone. I feel dreadfully useless and inefficient as regards these dear children but if I can be a little comfort to their dear Father that will be something and I feel sure my lovely Emily would have wished me to do everything I could to cheer him. The great concern she felt at dying was on his account. 'My heart bleeds for dearest Sam – no one can comfort him as I can' were words uttered the last day of her life and they still ring in my ears.[22]

They moved to Alverstoke at the end of the month. Mary Sargent again wrote to Mrs Anderson.

> The days slip away without my doing anything as I ought to do it. I could sit for hours gazing out of the window at the lights upon the sea and unwilling to move till I hear one of the children cry or some necessary occupation forces me to exertion. My faculties feel benumbed and I can neither read or work. . . . The example I have in dear Sam is quite striking. All day long he is most busily occupied as if he was afraid of giving himself time to think and his whole life seems altered. We breakfast at $\frac{1}{2}$ past 8 with the elder children, dine at $\frac{1}{2}$ past one with them and dearest Sam spends a great part of every afternoon and evening with his poor or sick parishioners and comes in about nine or later (half dead with fatigue) for some tea and unable to do more than look at a book when he is eating his toast – What a change from the once cheerful happy drawing room at Brighstone.

Sometimes he would break the routine of parish work to ride with the children; there would be frequent callers – well-meaning folk paying their courtesies, but not very welcome to poor Mary Sargent who was finding keeping house a great strain.

> It is beginning life again in old age with broken spirits and a sad and weary heart. I am so unable to bear the darling children's mirth and noise, and altogether I feel so out of my place. . . . I hope all those who loved my sainted Emily will pray for me, that I may be enabled to do my duty by her children. Though I say all this I assure you my dear Mrs Anderson I try to be cheerful before dearest Sam and I would not on any account have him know all I feel. It seems a relief to unburden my mind to her friends and I well know you were of that number. . . . She was so lovely, and seemed so full of life, that I still almost expect to see her enter the room.[23]

For Samuel, like Manning, work was the only relief. Not surprisingly their letters to each other during this year were more intimate than at any other period. Each knew precisely what the other was suffering. Each felt that he had been punished for an undue love of the world and that the pattern of his future life had therefore been revealed through this act of suffering.

> It is a call to a different mode of life [Samuel recorded in his diary]. This is my settled conviction. I have had the best of this world's blessings, the fullest enjoyment of the most faithful and strong affections. Now what [else] *can* the sudden removal of all this mean than that I am to serve Him in a different way: in a more severe, separate, self-mortifying course? I am called as Abraham was to 'come out', to care no more for the things of this world.[24]

Manning wrote to Samuel in April 1841:

> For my own part, I doubt if anything else would have made me so love and yearn for the unseen world as to counterpoise the stifling hold with which the world we see and act in weighs one down. For both of us it has a manifold lure – and I cannot doubt that if anything short of our sorrow would have saved us, that would have been sent, and not this. You are now, I imagine, beginning to unwind slowly the hourly consciousness of the change which has passed upon you. This I know to be hard to bear. I always felt as if my only strength were in silence. Had I ever let words draw feelings I should have broken down.[25]

Samuel had longed for recognition, and loved applause. In the years that were to come he was to have both in plenty; but every year on Emily's birthday and on the anniversary of her death, both meticulously and lovingly observed,[26] he renewed his pledge to withstand the temptations of secularity. Indeed the honours which he acquired during the next five years brought with them a strange flavour of bitter-sweet. It would be too much to say that they were unwanted; but the pleasure of gaining them was constantly soured by the memory of a former happiness never to be restored.

He had become a great favourite at court, paying his first visit to Windsor as the Queen's guest in September 1841.

> I came of course with some nervousness [he later wrote to Robert], not about the service a bit for there one is on high ground: but as to the social intercourse, dinner etc. However all went off most pleasantly. The Queen came and talked with me after dinner; about my Father and his visit: his mention of her in his journals at 2 years old; that she had read it with great interest etc. We sat round a small table all the evening after dinner till 11. The Queen, Prince Albert, Miss Paget, Lord Portman, myself, Miss Lister, Baron Stockmar, Baroness Lehzen, Lady Portman: talking, playing at games etc. in the quietest and easiest manner. This morning I read prayers and preached in the private chapel.* The Queen has lately not been able to stay out a full sermon and only had Prayers, but specially desired a sermon. She was very attentive throughout the service and as well as the Prince said all the Responses etc. most regularly. Afterwards I had a long talk with the Prince; about Church matters etc., etc., etc. and very intelligent and right principled he shewed himself, regretting all the liberal tendency of things etc. undisguisedly. All are very pleasant and kind and my nervousness is now quite gone.[27]

He met the Prince at Windsor again in November, breakfasted with Baron Bunsen and was taken to see the young Duke of Cornwall asleep in his bassinet.[28] In January 1842, he was again at Windsor with Lord Melbourne, spending a large part of the evening discussing etymology with the Duchess of Kent.[29] He was asked to preach at the Brighton Pavilion and at Claremont – and rumours circulated that the royal favour would soon be marked by fresh preferment. As early as January 1842 it was widely believed that he was to be brought on to the episcopal bench. 'These fears are groundless', wrote Samuel to Robert. 'Certainly the Episcopate is now nothing for vulgar counting: though one's heart will stir at hopes of being able to carry out plans of making the adminis-

---

* The subject was 'The Widow of Nain': S. Wilberforce, *Four Sermons preached before . . . Queen Victoria in 1841 and 1842* (1842). The dates and titles of the sermons are as follows: 26 September 1841 ('The Widow of Nain'); 2 January 1842 ('The Character of the Virgin Mary'); 20 February 1842 ('The Canaanitish Woman'); 27 February 1842 ('The Punishment of Jacob's Sin'), the last two being preached at Brighton.

tration of the Church system more efficient. But it would be a fearful thing to choose about. At the same time no see could be to me what Chichester would be: from Manning: Lavington etc.'[30]

There was talk, too, of his becoming tutor to the Prince of Wales, Robert sending him advice on suitable Latin 'beginners' – perhaps Mrs Arnold's *Henry's First Book*.[31] 'Among other excellences,' Robert reported to Samuel from hearsay accounts, 'the Queen mentioned that you only preach 20 minutes. But Mrs Dawson says the Queen does not behave well at Church, but is always looking about and talking to her neighbours. Is this only Tory scandal?'[32]

The royal pleasure was further marked by a Christmas gift of an inscribed silver inkstand in December 1842[33] and by more frequent invitations to Claremont. Although Samuel was not appointed to the office of preceptor to the Prince, he was favoured, in October 1844, with the post of sub-almoner to the Queen, generally considered to be a springboard to the episcopate. In December of that year he was again at Claremont, spending an hour skating with the Prince, while the Queen and the Duchess of Coburg watched admiringly from the bank.[34] Three months later, he was preferred to the Deanery of Westminster.

All these triumphs and favours are recorded in Samuel's diaries; but the prevailing note of the entries during these years is one of despondency, sometimes almost despair. 'A day of deepest dejection', he wrote on the third anniversary of Emily's death. 'I read through my dearest's journal. *Her* last two letters to Louisa – and endeavoured to look at my life in the light of these realities. I trust please God it will not be altogether fruitless. But the agony has been sharp. The bitter waters rolled again over me. I am alone in life. I *cannot* without raising the dead have my old blessed life. Yet God's will be done.'[35]

He drew nearer, of course, to his children for comfort and companionship – especially Herbert, his eldest son. There was a dreadful moment in May 1842 when Herbert was taken gravely ill, but the nightmare passed, leaving Samuel even more conscious 'of the tinsel emptiness of this world'.[36] The following January, Herbert, now aged nearly ten, had to go off to boarding school, a private establishment at Stratton. Father and son arrived for the start of a new term – a lugubrious pair indeed, for Herbert was feeling rather wretched at leaving home and Samuel was sick with grief at losing Herbert's company. The previous night the boy had cried until, at two in the morning, Samuel took him into his own bed, 'and though so very small both – D.G. – slept well'. Then, as the diary relates, 'after breakfast with an almost breaking heart tore myself from my weeping boy. Prayed earnestly.'[37]

Shortly after becoming Dean of Westminster, he and Herbert were together again in Oxford. It ought to have been an occasion of happiness and perhaps a little pride, especially the meeting with Hawkins and others at Oriel, for Samuel was not yet forty and it was his first visit to the University since he had acquired great office. He displayed all his customary charm and brilliance in conversation; but a letter to Robert shows what was really in his mind:

> How strange is the re-visiting under widely altered circumstances old scenes with which feelings and actions have been very greatly identified. Here I am as 'The Dean' with my Herbert with me – and here I am having already lived out all that was the hope and dream of my life as far as its joy and pleasure went from long before the time and all through the time that I was there. The very secretness of the life of hope I was there leading have [sic] impressed its feelings so very deeply upon all things around me. I could fix the very spot in my little bedroom where I prayed daily for her and that She might one day be my own.[38]

These private feelings reveal the true character of Samuel Wilberforce. Fame brought him both praise and abuse. If he was saluted as God's gift to the Church of England, he was also reviled for his ingratiating ways. Few looked beneath the surface. When he was Bishop of Oxford and had just received resounding acclamations for his maiden speech in the House of Lords, he wrote again to Robert in that strain of melancholy which is rarely absent from his intimate letters written during that new life which began in March 1841: 'How little do men see us, see the torn heart under the seeming hilarity. May God bring us safely through.'[39]

II. *Charges, The Church and Confession*

In the meantime both Robert and Manning had become archdeacons. Manning had returned from Rome in the early spring of 1839, his health restored and his spirits raised. Although Blomfield had joked about Manning's heart being in Rome ever since he had written *The Rule of Faith* there is no reason to suppose that his activities there – or indeed the impressions which he had formed of the Roman Church – had been very different from those of his companions, Gladstone, Charles Marriott and Stephen Glynne. It is true that he stayed in Rome rather longer than they did, that he attended Catholic services and that he held several conversations (sometimes accompanied by Gladstone) with Dr Wiseman, then Rector of the English College. There was nothing surprising or unconventional in this. He had returned to England with that mingled feeling of admiration and repugnance, the expression of which may be found in almost every journal of such travels which it was becoming fashionable for English clergymen, especially of a Tractarian inclination, to compile for the edification of their posterity.* Perhaps he felt the seductive attraction rather more keenly than most.

> I abhor and tremble at Romish error [he wrote to Gladstone in 1841] ... but I cannot refuse to sympathise with what is high and true and lovely in their system. And as for the hollow false soulless shapeless no-system of Protestantism I can yield to it neither the homage of reason nor of affection. The English Church is a real substantive Catholic body capable of development and all perfection – able to lick up and absorb all that is true and beautiful in all Christendom into itself – and this is our problem.[1]

He at once resumed all his former labours – attacking the Dean and Chapter Bill in a tract on the *Preservation of Unendowed Canonries*, frequently attending on his bishop as Secretary of the Diocesan Board, speaking on behalf of the National Society within and without the diocese. In January 1840 he was in Sevenoaks speaking on the same platform as Robert Wilberforce. Robert was rather overwhelmed by the sense of his own incompetence. Manning made 'a very good speech', he wrote to Samuel; 'He said all I was going to say, and I made a very sorry speech afterwards out of his relics. We were all greatly pleased at Manning's visit, but I am afraid he is in a delicate state of health. He seems to take scarce any food. He has evidently a great extent of reading, and his opinions seem very well digested.'[2]

The chances of preferment seemed good. In April 1839 he appears to have been offered the headship of Bishop's College, Calcutta,[3] and he was on friendly terms with both archdeacons of his diocese, the senile Webber and – rather more improbably – Julius Hare, Archdeacon of Lewes, a staunch Broad Churchman. His bishop – William Otter – was entirely in sympathy with Manning's strictures on the Ecclesiastical Commission,

---

* Examples are legion; but one of the best descriptions of the typical attitude of a young Anglican in the Eternal City may be found in a letter written by E. W. Benson to Mary Sidgwick (aged 12) in A. C. Benson, *Life of Edward White Benson* (1899), I. 121–3, concluding with the characteristic comment: 'How strangely are good and evil mixed in this complicated earth.'

and was coming to regard him with something of the same esteem which Sumner felt for Samuel Wilberforce.[4] It seemed a disastrous blow to Manning's chances when Otter died suddenly in August 1840 and was succeeded by Dr Shuttleworth, Warden of New College, a convinced opponent of the Tractarians. But the recommendations on his behalf from the Dean of Chichester (G. Chandler) and Archdeacon Hare allayed the new Bishop's suspicions and, braving the storms of his wife's fury and chagrin (for she had ideas of her own and the domineering spirit of a Mrs Proudie),[5] Shuttleworth offered Manning the archdeaconry of Chichester in succession to Webber, whose great age had compelled him at last to resign his office, on Christmas Eve, 1840. The jubilation within the Tractarian ranks was great. It was the first official sign of recognition, and from the least expected quarter. Letters of congratulation poured in to Lavington, among them letters from all his brothers-in-law. 'I am not sure', wrote Henry Wilberforce, 'that the thing which first struck me was not how very peculiarly indeed dearest Mrs John Sargent would feel it. One archdeacon almost turned her head. I think *two* will clean upset it.'[6]

Manning had, as one would expect, an exalted conception of the nature of his office. He was scrupulous and painstaking in the regular visitations which he conducted; in his first charge, in July 1841, he began with a dissertation on the rights and duties of the archdeacon as 'embodied in the unwritten law of England'.[7] He was later to express his strong disapproval to Samuel Wilberforce of the practice which he had introduced as Bishop of Oxford of by-passing the authority of the archdeacon by commissioning the rural deans to act under his immediate authority.

> The Rural Deans [he wrote] are appointed by the Bishop as assistants to the Archdeacon, not as co-ordinates or a parallel system, independent of the Archdeacon. As he came once on a time out of the Bishop, so they come out of him; yet so as to be appointed by the Bishop, and directly responsible to him ultimately tho' not in the first instance. ... In the Bishop's absence they should report to the Archdeacon. You remember what we agreed, of the importance of the Bishop personally working on and thro' the R.D.'s – but that was morally and by influence – and not by changing the ecclesiastical order and relations. This order seems most important for both R.D.'s and Archdeacon – and ... without it the whole system will have an incoherency in it.

He accused Samuel of leaving no place for the archdeacon, especially at chapter meetings. 'In our system the chapters are held "with the *authority* of the Bishop and *consent* of the Archdeacon" which gives him a real place in them. The same remark applies to the Visitation of Parishes etc. It appears to me to be of the first importance to call out all officials into their fullest efficiency, first and before others the Archdeacon, next the R.D.'s and in that way I believe both offices are rendered helpful to each other.'[8]

Manning's early charges were primarily concerned with matters of church administration – how to render the Church more efficient and its ministry more pervasive. In a sermon preached in Chichester Cathedral on Trinity Sunday 1841, he had pleaded eloquently for the cause of peace and humility. There must be an end to the cramping effects of *odium theologicum*. In his first charge, he sounded a stricter note on the subject of ecclesiastical discipline. He deplored the loss of the Church's legislative powers:

> To this overlong suspension of her powers may be ascribed all that is sometimes alleged against her on the score of stiffness, and want of a self-adapting pliancy to meet the yearnings, and changed habits, and multiplied numbers of the people. . . . It is worthy of remark that the only great effort made in the last century to provide churches for the growing population of London and Westminster was made at the instance and petition of Convocation. Had the Church really acted in Synod since that day, it is not to be believed that the 80,000 souls in Bethnal Green, or the million reported by the Commissioners, should have been left destitute of spiritual guides.[9]

Equally injurious had been the decay and disuse of the spiritual courts, most damaging to the maintenance of the penitential office. He recalled how in times past cases of immorality had been regularly brought before the Consistory Court of the Diocese and how gradually the practice of presenting offenders had lapsed through the years. Possibly the courts killed themselves by their unspiritual punishments, 'nevertheless they were the testimonies to the primary obligation of the Church to use a discipline of spiritual chastisement, and to take cognizance of the moral acts and character of her people. . . . Surely, brethren, the sin of the Church, if she only admonish with weak words, and forbear to chastise with a searching discipline, – her sin, in His sight, must be as the sin of Eli.'[10]

Citing the authority of Thorndike, Manning exhorted his clergy to remember the power of the keys, to inform their ordinary of the moral delinquencies of their parishioners, to punish evil-doers by spiritual chastisement and voluntary penances. 'It was by such a voluntary penitential system that the Church chastised her offending members for the first three hundred years: and certainly her spiritual health was never higher nor more vigorous than in those ages.'[11] He concluded with a reminder to churchwardens of their duties in levying church rates and with a plea to the clergy to strive to deliver dissenters 'from the bondage of imperfect Christianity'.[12]

In the following year, Manning dealt mainly with the problem of church restoration, deploring the vandalism and negligence of past generations. 'We are on our way to recover the true theory and practice of Divine worship, and to recognize the symbolical order of our Churches and the emphatic meaning of architecture, and the relation of all that is costly, beautiful, and majestic, in forms and harmonies, with the worship of Almighty God.'[13]

One particular monstrosity remained – pews; exclusive pews, illegal pews, hideously ugly pews, pews which have converted 'a type of the communion of saints and the courts of the heavenly Jerusalem' into 'a very compendium of exclusiveness and a field of jealous litigation'.[14] The first to give up their pews must be the clergy; the laity might then follow. Let the rich give the example to the poor. In the peroration Manning turned to the theme which had been exercising his mind ever since his visit to Rome in 1838 – the subject of his most scholarly and considerable theological treatise, published earlier that same year – the unity of the Church. Privilege, niggardliness, arrogance are the marks of a divided Church. 'It is not the token of a divided Church to be banded in self-denial and self-sacrifice, to act with one common purpose for the extension of one and the same communion. . . . The strength and earnestness of our bearing . . . is an incontrovertible proof of reality and of life. Such a moral temper never yet failed of truth at last. No man ever yet sold all that he had but he won "the pearl of great price" for his reward.'[15]

As one might expect, there was a general exchange of charges between the three new archdeacons – Samuel and Robert Wilberforce and Henry Manning[16] – and since all their addresses could well have appeared under the title 'Thoughts on the causes of our present discontents', the subject matter was very similar. Robert was inclined to introduce more theology into his discourses. In 1841 he dwelt at length on the meaning of baptism and the duties of godparents, and in 1845 touched upon baptismal regeneration and post-baptismal sin, leading up to a consideration of the neglected office of the visitation of the sick.[17] Otherwise they all had a nibble at church restoration, church rates, pew-rents, church schools and spiritual discipline.

Robert and Manning were in general agreement on all these questions, but their affinity was most marked in their desire to see spiritual discipline properly exercised and the Church empowered with the means to excommunicate evil-doers or to withhold the sacraments from those living in open sin. This was the chief subject of Robert's charge at the visitation of 1843 and of a book, published in the same year, entitled *Church Courts and Church Discipline*. In the charge, he had begun by stressing the rôle of the laity in the life and administration of the Church, reminding churchwardens and sidesmen of their duty to report to their ordinary those who were slack or negligent in their attendance at church or at Holy Communion. He admitted that he had no power to impose spiritual sentences against such persons. The State had seen to that by imposing civil penalties to accompany the sentences of spiritual courts. 'I cannot desire to see spiritual sentences pronounced, till we can escape from the odious consequences with which the civil power has loaded them.'[18] Because of this the practical way of enforcing discipline could only be admonition.

In his book, Robert attempted to prove that this state of affairs was in defiance of scriptural injunction (I Cor. v. 1–5) and of tradition as exemplified by the practice both of the early Church and of the Reformers. While he applauded the action of the Long Parliament in rendering illegal the imposition of the *ex officio* oath (the favourite tool of the Court of High Commission), he believed that spiritual jurisdiction since that time had become a perversion, whereby the ecclesiastical courts were permitted to deal with 'mixed or purely civil' causes (testamentary and matrimonial cases) but denied the right to correct spiritual offences.[19] There were two possible remedies: first, the Church must recover her lost legislative power; secondly, she must be allowed to enjoy the right, granted to all other associations recognised as legal by the State, to impose its own binding rules upon its members. 'So much the Church seems to have a right to demand', he wrote, 'that she should have either the advantages of an establishment, or those, which pertain to a voluntary association.'[20] In short, the Church of England, through being the Established Church, was denied the disciplinary liberties of the dissenters while her compensating privileges were being gradually whittled away. This cry was to be raised often enough by High Churchmen in the years that followed, until John Neville Figgis, seventy years later, in deploring the impotence of the Church in face of the great Leviathan, showed that the allegedly Free Churches, as voluntary associations, were really in quite as dangerous

271

a position as the Establishment, since the State regarded them as corporations and could regulate their life through the application of the principle of *ultra vires*.[21]

Samuel differed from his brother on this issue. He believed that the relaxation of ecclesiastical discipline from the necessary restraint of early times was 'providentially intended'. It was God's will that such discipline 'should gradually die out as the Church approached maturity, or rather, turn from a formal and external rule to an inner curb on the spirit – should run into the opening of God's Word, and its application to the individual soul and life'.[22] He suspected that Robert was falling into the Tractarian delusion of 'substituting the Church for Christ'.[23]

In other respects, too, Samuel went his own way. In his charge for 1842, he echoed Manning's reproach on the disfigurement of churches by the building of large, luxurious pews and expressed his indignation at the shocking repudiation of the Christian spirit implicit in the claims to exercise private rights and special privileges within the house of God.[24] But, in the following year, he defended the lawfulness and even the expediency of the pew system.

> When pews are nothing more than fixed or settled seats, duly apportioned to habitual worshippers or their families, I believe them to be beneficial, if not needful. . . . Diversities of rank and station do exist among us: they are evidently part of God's appointment for maintaining quick and real the mutual charity of all. Yet these are but transient and external; and under them there is in Him a true spiritual equality amongst all the members of Christ's body mystical. . . . But as the distinctions of our daily life may coexist with the true equality which lies beneath them, so in the house of God may this equality combine with the convenient separation of worshippers of different stations. To insist on intermixing all, as necessary to it, is to aim at an artificial equality which we do not feel, and which would not be maintained, by its most strenuous advocates, in dress and manners. To attempt it in this single instance would only be to bring affectation into the house and worship of the Lord.[25]

The charges which each of the three archdeacons delivered in 1845 exhibit well certain significant differences in their understanding of the problems of the time. Robert's charge was concerned mainly with the need to effect church restoration, to realise the beauty of holiness, to enhance the sacramental character of the priesthood and to inspire his clergy with George Herbert's profoundest truth – 'The Parson's Library is a holy life.'[26] Manning's charge was almost entirely given over to social questions – the parochial responsibility for educating and nourishing the

poor, the iniquity of child labour, the godless nature of the numerous
Provident Societies, which, when divorced from parochial control, became associations for immorality, meeting in public houses.[27]

Samuel considered both the need for church restoration and the importance of preserving the parochial system intact. But his tone was different. On the parochial system, the appeal to conservative instincts and
love of country is almost Baldwinesque: 'Our national character, and therefore all our most valued institutions are, under God's blessing, eminently
due to the pervading influence of our parochial system. . . . It has done
more, perhaps, than anything else, through its indirect influence, to mould
and fashion the English mind.'

The instrument of direct religious training, the school of self-government, the sphere in which social responsibility has been allowed to develop from earliest times – these have been its blessings.

> Thus does the English peasant differ from the Sclavonic serf: to make
> him what he is, brave men have bled, good men have toiled, great men
> have dared, and wise men have thought: in what they leave behind they
> breathe into him, unconscious as he is, a noble spirit – for though he knows
> not their names, he feels that he is himself an Englishman, and thus, he
> too is formed by that which they have made England to be.
> Now, of this whole system, the key-stone is the parish church.[28]

And when Samuel turned to the great work of church restoration, he felt
obliged to issue warnings. Beware of externals, lest the interior life should
suffer. Beware of symbols, lest the love of forms and objects should pervert the true spirit. What was needful in an early age of the Church's life –
what, indeed, might suit other nations with different racial temperaments
– was not necessarily beneficial at all times and in all places.

> At the reformation of religion our forefathers threw off a multitude of
> such outward forms, some the produce of error almost unmingled with
> the truth; some the symbols doubtless, at their first production, of love
> and faith, but which, having since become the withered leaves of a dead
> formality, they freely shed amongst the searching winds of truth which
> waited on their healthier season.[29]

Samuel stood staunchly by the Reformers. So, apparently, in his first
charge, did Henry Manning, describing the Reformation as 'this gracious
act of God's providence towards His Church . . . the purging of the intellectual sight of Western Europe prepared for the restoration of Apostolic
truth'.[30] It is possible that he said rather more than he meant, by way of
appeasement or to demonstrate his quite genuine concern at the direction

273

in which affairs in Oxford seemed to be tending. But a closer examination of his words shows that he was really defending Anglicanism, a phenomenon very different, in Manning's estimation, from its continental counterpart.

To Manning this must have been so, or he would have left the Church then and there. In these years he was seeking to clarify the position of the Anglican Church as a portion of the Church Catholic, the fruits of his labours being published in 1842 as *The Unity of the Church*. It is a book of weighty learning and was generally received with delight by High Churchmen, especially by Gladstone to whom it had been dedicated. Samuel, however, found it over-subtle, and was not too happy at Manning's firm assertion of *nulla salus extra ecclesiam* and what appeared to him to be the recognition that a revealed doctrine might have to be modified to suit historical fact.

Manning replied as follows:

> The Revelation that there is salvation in the Church alone is a *doctrine of Faith not a judgement on individual souls*,
> 1. God has revealed *affirmatively* that there is Salvation in the Church.
> 2. He has revealed no other way.
> 3. He has not revealed that no soul out of the Church can be saved.
> 4. He does sanctify souls out of the Visible Ch. as a *fact*. Therefore the *doctrine* and the *fact* are not inconsistent. . . . The *fact* is a quasi revelation as to individuals, as the *doctrine* is to the fixed economy of salvation. . . . Again the *doctrine* is a dogma revealed *positively*. The *fact* is provided for implicitly by the rule of vincible and invincible ignorance.[31]

Five years later (in 1850), Manning told Samuel more explicitly what had been in his mind when he wrote the book.

> In 1841 I . . . had learned that unity is a first law of the Church of Christ and that our position was tenable only as an extreme and anomalous case: full of difficulty and fatal if we could be shewn to be at variance with universal Tradition in Faith and Discipline. Here again we diverged. We discussed it also in this room: and we have since been consistent. These three revealed laws, Succession, Tradition and Unity plainly convinced me of two things.
> First, that Protestantism is both a schism and a heresy.
> Secondly, that the Church of England is alone tenable as a portion of the Universal Church and bound by its traditions of Faith and Discipline. From which it further became manifest to me (and that on the plainest proofs of Holy Scripture) that as the Universal Church is guided and kept in the Faith by the Holy Spirit it is impossible that any authoritative contradictions of Faith should exist in it.[32]

On the question of faith, Manning had really reached this position when he preached his controversial sermon on *The Rule of Faith* in 1838. His understanding of the nature of discipline, however, had matured more slowly during the late 1830's until, by the time he became archdeacon, he had arrived at a position more nearly approaching that of Pusey than of any others of the Tractarians. He had convinced himself that the Church of England must recover what he was wont to call an 'ascetical theology'. If she were a part of the Church of the Saints, she must bear the marks of sanctity upon her body; and he had come to know, through his own personal experience and observation of Catholic practices abroad, something of the power of the penitential system and those aids – chiefly the confessional – which the Church had devised to guide the aspirant to sanctity in his progress towards his goal. To repudiate these aids would be to cripple the pilgrim. Thus Manning came gradually to feel the force of F. W. Faber's sad admission, made shortly before his own secession to the Roman Church: 'I could [do] all things in my parish if I were Roman, and had not my feet in the stocks of our system.'[33]

But was it not presumption to suppose the Anglican system to be so confined? After all, the Church of England *had* produced her saints and divines who had practised and taught what was pre-eminently needed at that time. This was indeed Manning's assurance in the 1840's, his chief source of strength. His views on this were most fully expressed in a letter to Samuel, dated January 1849. Miserably deficient as the Church might be in her ascetical theology, there was at least Jeremy Taylor's *Ductor Dubitantium*:

> In his preface [Manning wrote], he accounts for this 'scarcity of books of cases of conscience' among other reasons by 'the careless and needless neglect of receiving private confessions'.
>
> Our whole Theology is without *order*, We have not one 'Theologia' of any system, unity, or completeness. And that which is true even of dogmatic theology is still more true of all moral, spiritual and ascetical theology. The reasons . . . I suppose are what Jeremy Taylor says – that we were drawn off to controversy, and that the practice of confession was neglected. For I suppose that Spiritual Direction is in fact 'the science of applying to *individual souls* the laws and truths of the Gospel'. And that where the practice of dealing with souls one by one languishes, and is abandoned for preaching to multitudes, then all particular, close, exact, spiritual application declines. This has certainly been the case in the Church of England, for though we know that Hooker, Sanderson etc. had their confessors, and Bp. Morley, Patrick and others received confessions, and no doubt thousands of priests and people both received and made confessions, yet

the practice has died out like daily service, Feasts, Fasts, Frequent Communion etc.

The general tone of our Preachers and spiritual writers is, therefore, didactic, intellectual and vague – for instance Donne, Hammond, Sanderson, South etc.

The only writers I know who have the tone of spiritual directors are Hall (whom J. Taylor names as a single instance in his Preface to the Ductor Dubm.), Taylor – and the Puritanizers Hopkins, Leighton etc.

It is remarkable that J. Taylor names *Lutheran* writers on conscience and direction. And Luther held confession strongly, which accounts for the existence of such writers. On the other hand, we have writers approaching to the same kind among the Puritans, such as *Baxter*, Bunyan etc. They retained the tradition of spiritual direction but when separated from Confession and the Priesthood, it became fanatical. The same we see among Dissenters. What we call enthusiasm, and fanaticism, and experience, is the disembodied soul of Confession; and a testimony of the spiritual necessities of man, and of the Divine wisdom in ordaining a channel and a guidance for souls conscious of their sin. The Wesleyan Class Meetings are an example of the mischief of neglecting to use the keys of the Church. And I suppose that while the spirit of the Confessional went to the Puritans, the Formality remained as a Theory in the Church, so that while they became fanatical, we became lifeless – a miserable divorce which drives one side into unspirituality and the other into unbelief.

Another reason why we have no post-reformation writers on Confession and Direction I believe to be that our controversies with the Roman Church turned not on these subjects *generally* but on the question whether confession be an obligation by *Divine* precept. I am not aware that there is any difference between the Churches of England and Rome but only in this – 'Is confession *generally* necessary by Divine precept to all Xtians?'

They maintain the affirmative – 'that contrition with the Sacrament of Penance or at least the desire (votum) is necessary'.

We the negative: or stated affirmatively – 'that contrition alone is sufficient'.

There being no controversy about the rest, our clergy went on using the old Books, theirs and ours. . . . The sum of all this prose is that we are miserably poor in this matter, and our clergy are left to their own resources and the unwritten system of the Church of England in directing consciences, as in preparing adults for Baptism, or confirmation, or communion and the like. We have nothing *ad Parochos* but Burnet's Pastoral Care, Herbert's Country Parson and such small beer. . . .[34]

At about the same time Pusey was writing to Robert Wilberforce in the same vein.

I am more and more convinced that nothing except an extensive system of confession can remedy our evils. The corruption under the surface is frightful in the extreme. It is a most cruel way thus to boast of our purity etc. while we are utterly ignorant of that deep current of evil which is flowing below. I cannot speak against the Ch. of Rome now that I see that it does apply itself to guard its young against evils which among us fester to an extent quite awful into which they continually fall unawares, while we boast of not applying the only remedy, and attempt to substitute nothing.

These are hastily written lines on a large subject, but may shew why I can no longer sympathise so *far*, with Hook and others who speak, as I used myself, against the Ch. of Rome vaguely, without knowing what she contains or what saints have been formed in her.[35]

Robert himself – even in the late 1840's – was unhappy at the tone of Manning's and Pusey's teaching. Pre-occupied as he was with the problem of Church discipline, he was chiefly concerned with his difficulties in administering a backward and spiritually lethargic archdeaconry. He had hardly turned his mind to the spiritual needs of individual souls. He wrote to Manning in December 1848:

Probably you go further than I do in thinking confession desirable as a general and constant practice. I hardly see how it can be made so, and I am inclined to think that it would be one of those things which when it became a form might be very injurious. I say this without having altered my policy about its great uses, how could I, as an occasional thing: for those who voluntarily seek it. But counsels of perfection don't suit for general use, any more than Folio vols. for ordinary pockets.[36]

As Samuel himself was to say later, when Bishop of Oxford, confession 'is medicine and not food'.[37]

III. *The Clergy of the East Riding and the Curates of Alverstoke*

Robert's problems, as Archdeacon of the East Riding, were clearly more pressing and frustrating than those which bothered Samuel and Manning. Even before he came to Burton Agnes, when preaching for the S.P.G. in Yorkshire in 1839, he had had a foretaste of what was to come. Indifference and spiritual apathy had greeted him almost everywhere. Whitby was the worst place – a parish of 11,000, served by a single clergyman with no curate, only one church and that inaccessible in bad weather, a small proprietary chapel which had no accommodation for the poor, and no Church school of any sort. At Helmsley and Pickering the local clergy would not let him preach; at Redcar he had to hire a room at an inn because of the opposition of the incumbent.[1]

Occasionally he had found himself supported by weird allies. At Halifax he fell in with a wayward genius called Dr Wolf ('dirty, stinking and odd') who had come over from Huddersfield to join Robert on the platform. 'He and Lady Georgina', Robert afterwards reported to Samuel, 'have turned violent Apostolicals. Lady Georgina says "I am an Oxford Tract woman". .... He made a very clever speech but rather intemperate ... saying the Prop. [S.P.G.] was not supported by the Peculiars because they maintained its missionaries were not converted etc. There was a strong Peculiar who got up afterwards and abused the Dr with great violence, but they made it up afterwards and proceeded to hug one another (literally) on the Platform.'[2]

Once he had settled at Burton Agnes, Robert hoped that he might find more time for study; and, indeed, in the first three years of his period in Yorkshire, he published a little volume on ancient history (a survey of the history of man from the Creation to the fall of the Roman Empire in the West, entitled *The Five Empires*) a novel set in the days of Diocletian and Galerius (*Rutilius and Lucius*), consisting of two independent tales of Christian bravery during an era of persecution,[3] and his more weighty treatise on *Church Courts and Church Discipline*. Samuel, however, pressed him to strive for higher things. Francis Wrangham, Robert's father-in-law by his first marriage, who had been Archdeacon of Cleveland and since 1828 Archdeacon of the East Riding, was over seventy and was contemplating retirement. By a little exertion, Robert could very easily become his successor. 'I am deeply convinced', Samuel wrote in June 1840, 'that you ought to keep Archdeacon Wrangham *in until you are well established in the living*. Next year he might probably resign with advantage to your promotion but not now.'[4] Six months later Robert was summoned to Bishopthorpe and the offer was duly made. Robert wrote to Samuel on 15 January 1841: 'James Stephen says the only thing is that one of our Venerables should be changed to Right Revd. and there can be no doubt which it should be.'[5]

If the clergy of his archdeaconry had expected to be ruled by a mild and benevolent recluse, they were soon to be disillusioned. For all his humility, caution and distaste for unpleasantness, Robert was – as his dogged determination throughout his S.P.G. tour had shown – almost painfully conscientious. Within a fortnight of his appointment he was at loggerheads with the Dean and Chapter at York over the disposal of

Chapter funds, gradually prevailing over the other two archdeacons, after he had given them a little lecture on canonical dress.* His reports to Samuel during the next few weeks were gloomy in the extreme.

> You can hardly fancy such louts as many of the clergy here [he wrote in February 1841][6]
>
> I am preparing next week for a commission on two drunken clergymen in this neighbourhood who have been the scandal of the Church about here for years [he reported a month later]. This very shocking, but I have heard of two men, in the very next Parish to my own, who I fear are habitual offenders in the same way. We cannot wonder at the Church's weakness in these parts. . . . I understand that the Dean openly crows and defends his practice of selling livings. I cannot help hoping that we shall get him deprived.[7]

The conduct of confirmations was wretchedly irreverent. At Beverley the clergy disgraced themselves by gossiping to each other throughout the service and actually laughing during the laying-on of hands. After this spectacle Robert made a point of standing in a conspicuous place during confirmations and exhibiting his displeasure very noticeably when any cleric misbehaved.[8]

By the end of his first year he had made his mark, although – with characteristic modesty – he disclaimed any personal credit. His letters tell rather of his wonderment at the ubiquity and tirelessness of Samuel. 'I don't know how you find time for your sayings and doings', he wrote in October 1841. 'I find it hard to write to you because from your great occupations there is no reciprocity in our correspondence.'[9]

> Tho' I am tired [he wrote in December 1841], having had 3 sermons to preach, yet I must send you a short reply. I know how occupied you are. I don't think I am half so beset with business, but then it must be satisfactory to feel that you make way, which I hardly do as yet. However I have no reason to be discontented: it is slow work getting under weigh in the Dead Sea, and such certainly is this part of the country. I observed the other day that the Judge of the Spiritual Court at York deposed lately that he had never known a case of suspension: I have already ejected or suspended 5 persons within the year, besides 2 others who are gone into temporary exile.[10]

One of Robert's chief handicaps was an indulgent Archbishop who was practically senile. Harcourt was ninety when he died in 1847, having

---

* Wrangham MSS. VII. 126. 'I am excellently well off for colleagues – Corbett – Todd – Archdns of York and Cleveland. I have already got them to agree to dress canonically wh. they have not done before.'

been at Bishopthorpe for forty years. Time and again Robert appealed to him to no avail.

> We have several mad clergymen in the Wolds [he observed to Samuel in April 1845], and because they are needy he will not take any steps to punish their defalcations. There is one who has three churches which he has repeatedly left unserved for weeks. This Spring he had no service for 2 Sundays, saying he was ill. On the 3rd Sunday he set off from home a little before service time and went to York. But I can't get the Archbishop to take any steps to cure it. It is the most painful thing to me, for I constantly hear complaints which I cannot deny are well founded. In the Wolds, a very large district of above 18 parishes, there are but 2 resident incumbents of respectability.[11]

Not surprisingly, dissent seemed to be winning the battle to capture souls. The chief curse of the area was the extreme poverty of the clergy: very rarely could there be found a clergyman who had money to spare to put to the foundation of a school or to the restoration of his church. Now and again Robert discovered 'an oasis of excellence in the midst of this desert land' – such as the parish of one of his rural deans at Holderness[12] – but these occasions were very rare. He took what measures he could to encourage a more spiritual tone in the services, to promote evangelisation and a strong Church feeling. He began at home with his own church, rebuilding the chancel and removing the plaster from the walls; his somewhat Puseyite curate, Skinner, persuaded him to introduce chanting, the effect of which was entirely lost on Robert since he was – as he admitted sadly to Samuel – quite tone deaf.[13] He inaugurated a clerical meeting at Beverley, held regularly in the vestry of St Mary's Church, although he found that as often as not the intended speaker would arrive without a paper, so that he was compelled to deliver the address himself. Alone he strove to extend the activities of the National Society in his area, opening a school for yeomen, establishing a training college for male teachers at York (which was nearly wrecked by an overenthusiastic Puseyite principal in 1845)* and another for women at Ripon.

As early as January 1842 he was himself charged with Puseyite leanings – by his own squire, with whom on the whole he seems to have kept on good terms. The excesses of the young and ardent Skinner were the occasion of the tiff. 'The outcry against Puseyism is gradually spreading into

---

* Wrangham MSS. VII. 169. 'Our Training School is almost the only thing which is going on well in the diocese and if it was knocked up we should be quite ruined.'

this corner, assuming a strange type', Robert wrote sadly to Samuel. 'My curate lately desired the sexton not to *ring* but *toll* for a funeral. On this my squire came to me to say that this had never been done except for *Quality*, and he complained of the innovation, saying he understood the Bishops intended to take measures against this Puseyism. So much for names. . . .'[14]

It was all very disheartening: no support from the top; no appreciation.

In 1848 Robert conformed with the order for a National Day of Humiliation by requiring its observance throughout the archdeaconry, and was encouraged by the response in his own and adjoining parishes. 'My church was crammed from end to end. . . . It was the same in all the adjoining villages. I am very sorry that the Archbishop did not order the day through the whole diocese. It was only done in this Riding: certainly a most irregular thing that I should be left to give the order. But it is the misfortune in this county that people who choose to step out of their spheres do all the work.'[15]

At least he had Hook at Leeds for an enthusiastic ally – for a while – although he came under another jurisdiction. Hook knew something of the trials which Robert would have to face when he wrote to congratulate him in 1841 on his preferment: 'I only wish with all my heart you were *my* Archdeacon: under your command what a glorious battle we might fight. But this is a Blessing which is denied me. It has been one of my trials to labour under leaders who have differed from me in opinion and disliked me personally. All is for the best: but one cannot help thinking of what might be done if one were well supported.'[16]

Samuel also was a tower of strength, writing as frequently as he could, praising his charges, encouraging him to persevere. During these years they met but rarely. Even had they been nearer to each other, their crowded programmes permitted hardly a moment's relaxation.

Quite apart from all his engagements at Court, his canonical residence at Winchester and his visitations, Samuel was now in charge of a parish whose demands were limitless. Alverstoke was the leading Portsmouth parish, with a large and rapidly increasing population which comprised all classes and conditions, ranging from the nobility and gentry who came to Stokes Bay as a watering place (Lord Ashburton, the Marchioness of Bath and John Wilson Croker) to the naval and military establishments at Haslar and the sprawling poverty of Gosport. The whole area was served by only two churches and one chapel and was therefore rife with dissent. The parish church itself was hopelessly inadequate in size and wretchedly drab in its atmosphere and decoration. One of the first of Samuel's tasks was to launch a great building scheme. In the four and a half years of his incumbency he was able to build two new churches (St Thomas's, Elson, and St Matthew's, Gosport) and to provide two national schools, one at Alverstoke and the other a vast establishment to serve the slum area of Gosport. He himself headed the subscription list with a donation of £1,000.[17]

He gathered round him a body of devoted curates – an interesting anticipation of the 'Portsea experiment' many years later[18] – and these all lived with him at Alverstoke on terms of great intimacy. In addition, a small clergy house in the most squalid part of Gosport served as a base for the operations among the poor. With one of these curates, R. C. Trench, who gave up the perpetual curacy of Curdridge in 1841 for the challenge of ministering in a vast urban parish under a vicar as inspiring and venturesome as Samuel, he came from the first to enjoy a special intimacy, heightened perhaps by the mutual sense of agonised bereavement (Trench having lost both his eldest son and two baby daughters[19]). On 3 May 1845, Samuel wrote in his diary: 'Dear Trench as always earnest, holy, high-minded. My best male friend. May God give me grace to profit from being with him.'[20]

The experience which Samuel himself gained at Alverstoke, surrounded by his curates – holding regular prayers with them, conducting readings from the Fathers, organising discussions of pastoral problems, especially on the preparation of individual candidates for confirmation – led him to appreciate more keenly than ever before the benefits of close association in the ministry and the value of constant guidance and encouragement. Something of this he had learnt from the close contact which he had always enjoyed with Bishop Sumner at Farnham. As Bishop of Oxford, he was himself to conduct his ordinations on this same pattern, collecting the candidates together at Cuddesdon to live with him over the Embertides, personally examining and guiding them, and establishing thereby a relationship which might endure throughout their ministry. It is interesting to see that while at Alverstoke he liked to bring in groups of young ordinands, who would live for a short period in the parish, observing the problems which they themselves would encounter, and gaining from the vicar and his curates both instruction and first-hand advice which, in the days when theological colleges were in their infancy, was a rare privilege.[21]

Samuel welded his curates into a strong and purposeful team. House to house visiting; combined operations with laymen helpers; meetings to discuss progress and ways and means of surmounting difficulties; regular visits to the parish workhouse, the naval hospital and the Royal Clarence Victualling Yard – by such efforts the large parish was gradually made to feel his impact. The arrangements for public worship were revised: daily prayers were introduced, public catechising of the children was held twice weekly, and there were evening services every Thursday and most Saturdays. The Sunday services were matins and evensong, with an afternoon service at 3 p.m., after which public baptisms were conducted. There were three celebrations of Holy Communion during the month, two at the parish church and one at St Mark's, Anglesey.

Robert Wilberforce and Henry Manning, active as they were, had never known this sort of life – the day-to-day worries and problems of an urban parish, the immediate responsibility for the guidance and training of a band of curates, the additional strain of frequent attendances at Court and constant engagements to speak before eminent and influential audiences. Robert watched from afar with admiration, tinged with a little sadness. The old days had gone. Now it was all new responsibilities, grievous decisions, differences and misunderstandings arising from the storms raging in Oxford. It had all been so different when Agnes and Emily had been alive. He wrote to Samuel in March 1842:

> How strangely, my dearest brother, have our lives been marked out by those events which have separated us from our former selves. How do we seem by the Disposition of God to be cut off from affections and re-gards, which were once so near to us. The length of man's life affords opportunity for so many pictures into which his being is divided. I can never think of you, oppressed as you are with public cares, but as a dif-ferent being from what you were, when I used to visit you in the days of your early happiness at Checkenden and Brighstone. But it is in the hands of a wise and gracious ruler that all the destiny of our being is held. ...
>
> And amidst all the trials and difficulties of life, it is a great comfort that we have been able to keep up such unity of feeling, and even of opinion (and the first more than the last even) so that we can tell what effect the same event or statement will produce on one another. May we ever be able, my dear brother, to keep up this unity of heart, and may we leave something of the same even to our children.[22]

What were these 'affections and regards' which had once been so near? There can be little doubt that Robert was thinking about their mutual friends at Oxford.

IV. *New Issues at Oxford*

Strictly speaking, the history of Tractarianism comes to an end on 27 February 1841 with the publication of *Tract 90*, the most considerable of the Tracts from Newman's pen. Thereafter the series was discontinued (by agreement between Newman and Bagot, Bishop of Oxford), and new forces began to make themselves felt. Golightly had thought to split the Oxford party by his project for the Martyrs' Memorial and had – in a measure – done so; both James Stephen and Newman himself had unwittingly, in discussing the declension of the Evangelicals, foretold its sad destiny – 'fanaticism in the second generation . . . invariably runs to seed'.

It need not have done so had the control from the top been tighter. Newman was still full of fight when *Tract 90* misfired. He had intended to demonstrate that the Thirty-nine Articles would admit a Catholic interpretation, to prove that latitudinarianism could, so to speak, be stretched both ways. He had genuinely not foreseen the storm which the experiment would raise. But when it came, from the protest of the 'Four Tutors' and the censure of the University, he was ready to retaliate with reasoned exposition where his opponents had remonstrated in venomous frenzy. What crippled Newman was a broadside from the Bench of Bishops – a succession of hostile charges, which threw him into a position from which not even the most skilful casuistry could rescue him. Like Lamennais, rejected by the one authority which he had striven to enhance, Newman had exalted the apostolical authority of the bishops only to discover that the logic of his argument compelled him to submit to their injunctions to retract his errors. While he searched for an escape from this quandary he could effectively lead no more.

The sentence of silence was imposed – more outrageously and on far flimsier grounds – on E. B. Pusey. Since the death of his wife in 1839, he had withdrawn himself utterly from public life. He would write, and counsel and preach; otherwise he wished for the solitude and simplicity of a hermit. Yet when he emerged to offer a salve to those who had been disquieted by his teaching on post-baptismal sin, by preaching on the Eucharist as a comfort to the penitent, his sermon was delated to the Vice-Chancellor by the Lady Margaret Professor of Divinity, Dr Faussett, a man whose egregious gift for trouble-making could be challenged only by C. P. Golightly. In consequence, by a questionable judicial act, Pusey was suspended for two years from preaching *intra praecinctum universitatis*.

John Keble was certainly not silent. With typical unconcern for self, he rushed to Newman's and Pusey's defence as readily as he sought to take upon his own shoulders the unnamed doctrinal excesses of his curate Peter Young, whom the Bishop of Winchester repeatedly refused to elevate to priest's orders. But periodic fits of depression, the feeling that he was regarded as a marked man, the frequent illness of his wife – all served to blunt the edge of Keble's polemical sword. What had he to say to the new and younger men who had flocked round Newman at St Mary's in the late 1830's? He knew them hardly at all; and they, in their turn, had been practically untouched by that personal demonstration of humility and reserve which to an earlier generation had been an enduring inspiration. Besides, Keble's sanguine period was now at an end. It had died with Hurrell Froude. The younger generation wished for triumphs, not for homilies on the futility of success. Keble is best understood by a remark he once made to Isaac Williams, later in life, looking back on the militant years of the 1830's. He called those years 'a sort of parenthesis in my life' and rejoiced that he had now returned 'to my old views such as I had before'. 'At the time of the great Oxford Movement, when I used to go up to you at Oxford, Pusey and Newman were full of the wonderful progress and success of the movement, whereas I had always been taught that the truth *must* be unpopular and despised, and to make confession of it was all that one could do; but I see that I was fairly carried off my legs by the sanguine views they held, and the effects that were showing themselves in all quarters.'[1]

Maybe this gave to Keble the touch of fatalism, the impression of indolence, which some have seen in his character. On the other hand, here lay the strength of his teaching, which, if he failed to communicate it to Newman when he most needed the reminder, still served to bolster the faith of other supporters of the Tracts. Pusey, if shaken, was not shattered by adversity; nor were Isaac Williams, Charles Marriott, Frederic Rogers or R. W. Church.

This feeling, and a deep love of the Anglican Church and an unflinching conviction in the apostolic nature of the *via media*, served to protect them from an undue veneration for the Church of Rome. They did not revile her. But they did not flatter her virtues with the deliberate intention of embarrassing their co-religionists. There was forming in Oxford, however, a group who had no such respect for the Church of their baptism, the most prominent members of which were W. G. Ward and Frederic Oakeley, who from the moment that Tom Mozley took over the editorship of the *British Critic* began to use that organ as the chief medium for the expression of views entirely out of tune with the sentiments and arguments of the *Tracts for the Times*. The Romeward movement properly begins in 1842, the year when Ward and Oakeley became publicly articulate and when John Henry Newman practically disappeared from the Oxford scene by retiring to Littlemore.

To express briefly the standpoint of this new 'Romanising' party is not easy, since to over-simplify is to obscure the differences which separated them from a nascent Anglo-Catholic group which was beginning to form itself round the person of Henry Manning; and much of what Ward and Oakeley were presenting was perfectly acceptable to Pusey and Newman, who had hitherto been reluctant to express themselves quite as boldly as these two *enfants terribles*. Roughly, their position was this: they were concerned far less with apostolicity than with catholicity, caring more for the living voice of the Church than for the frozen authority of the ancient Fathers, more for the unceasing guidance of the Holy Spirit, preserving the Church from error, than for the test of the Vincentian canon. Steeped in Möhler, both the romanticism of *Die Einheit der Kirche* and the dogmatism of the *Symbolik*, Ward saw that Protestantism was chaos – it lacked beauty, order, holiness, authority, dogma, all these being the essential marks of the organic, infallible Church. Logician though he was, he was governed far more by conscience (the moral sense of certainty) and by emotion (the sensation of the right *ethos*) than by cold, remorseless reason. He came to see – as Professor Chadwick has expressed it – that 'obedience to conscience . . . is not one method of attaining metaphysical truth; it is the only method'.[2] By obeying the dictates of conscience, one discovers by experience what is true and what is false. Or, to put it another way, one cannot test the truth of Catholic teaching until one has lived it; then the moral experience eliminates all doubts. In the end, this comes to mean (as Manning, and to some extent Newman too, believed) that the final proof of the authority of the true Church is the possession of an 'inner holiness', made manifest by certain irrefutable signs – a discipline unto holiness, an unending succession of acknowledged saints. Once one accepted this, it was less difficult to swallow the dogmatic assumptions. If a certain type of sanctity could be found only among those who subscribed to a particular set of dogmas, then that was sufficient proof that subscription to those dogmas was the *sine qua non* of the sanctity to which Christian men must aspire.

And when did Ward experience this moment of truth? Certainly, some years before he wrote *The Ideal of a Christian Church* (1844). The first sure indication that he was beginning to feel the power of the Catholic *ethos* was his visit to St Mary's, Oscott, with Frederic Oakeley in July 1841, and his visit to Grace Dieu in the autumn of the same year. What could an Anglican public school, even Arnold's Rugby, show to compare with the ordered sanctity of a Catholic college?[3] This was a question which he raised in a passage in *The Ideal*.[4] Ward, whose chief defect was an inability to recognise that different temperaments react to such scenes in different ways, and to perceive that one man's heaven might be another (equally good) man's hell, had tasted Catholic sanctity for the first time and had found the flavour irresistible.*

It may be a mistake to suppose that this appetite for all things Catholic and this urge to apply the test of 'inner holiness' were peculiar to Ward and Oakeley. After all, in a sense, these had at least been implicit in Tractarianism from the start and may explain in part the difference between the churchmanship of Newman's party and that of the friends and supporters of William Palmer. When Ward and Oakeley became fanatical in their adulation of Rome in the 1840's they were indeed accelerating or accentuating a process which was carrying many of their senior and less impetuous colleagues into a changed relationship towards the Roman Church. Newman in January 1843 made a formal retraction of everything he had previously written or said against her; and Pusey made it quite plain that he was prepared to stand by him.

All this was to provoke the ultra-Protestant element and the firm Establishment men into retaliation; and it was ironical that the first main battle should have been fought over the body of poor Isaac Williams. No friend of Ward's, in controversy and polemical temperament relatively ineffectual, he was chosen to be the scapegoat. The occasion was Keble's retirement from the Professorship of Poetry in the autumn of 1841, to which post in normal times Isaac Williams might reasonably have expected to succeed. Williams, however, was now a marked man; and the appointment, an election in Convocation, was to be determined by the theological merits of the candidates, not by their literary scholarship or their poetical accomplishments – a circumstance for which Pusey was

---

* Robert believed that Sibthorp, a convert to Rome in 1841, had fallen in the same way. He wrote to Samuel: 'I suppose at Oscott Sibthorpe saw a show of Catholicity, just in the particulars which among us have been so sadly neglected, and was taken with a bauble, tho' the reality of Primitive truth and order were alike wanting.' Wrangham MSS. VII. 134.

largely to blame by making the tactical error of issuing a circular on behalf of Williams in which attention was drawn to his sound religious principles. The opponents of the Tractarians replied by rallying round the other candidate, a Mr Garbett of Brasenose, whose poetical abilities were as yet undiscovered but whose religious sympathies were deemed by Low Churchmen unimpeachable. At once, principle was at stake and the contest raged furiously into January 1842.

Among others, the Wilberforces and Henry Manning were eagerly canvassed. Newman wrote to Robert to beg him to vote for Williams, fearing that victory for Garbett would be the prelude to 'some measure which will have the effect of driving us out of the university'.[5] Gladstone, after consultation with Manning, tried another tack. Determined to prevent the issue becoming a *cause célèbre*, he wrote to Samuel to try to persuade him to sign a circular advocating the retirement of both the candidates in the hope that the appointment might go to an uncontested *tertium gaudens*. 'All sensible persons not of Oxford with whom I have conversed are entirely of the same mind. . . . Your name will be of great value and I look very confidently to your approbation and aid. . . . Manning is most anxiously with me.'[6]

Robert, too, believed that this was the best way out of an embarrassing situation,[7] but warned Samuel that if he had to vote between the two existing candidates he would certainly choose Williams. 'He is clearly the better candidate in himself as a poet.'[8] If censures were to be applied to the 'Tract Party', the effect might well be 'like the ejection of the Methodists last century'.[9] Samuel was adamant in his support of the other side, despite vehement efforts by Gladstone to detach him from the inappropriate alliance. As he explained to Robert, the time had come for a firm stand against 'the extravagances and party feelings' of the Oxford school, and a vote against them on this occasion would be the safest way of ensuring the maintenance of Church principles.[10] A letter to Samuel from Sumner suggests that he was acting very much under his bishop's instructions.[11] As things turned out, a preliminary assessment of the votes persuaded Isaac Williams that he had insufficient support and he decided to withdraw from the contest rather than face a public defeat in Convocation. Samuel's defection was duly noted by Williams in his *Autobiography*. He accused him of cautious prevarication until it was clear which way the wind was blowing. And so, 'no sooner did it become the unpopular side, then he took part against me'.[12]

At the same time the affair of the Jerusalem bishopric was causing a division within the ranks of the Church. The project – seemingly even to Pusey an innocuous one at first – was the brain child of the Chevalier Bunsen, warmly approved by Prince Albert and supported by both Archbishop Howley and Blomfield: to found in Jerusalem a Protestant bishopric, to be held in turn by a nominee of England and Prussia, who would be duly consecrated by English bishops and who would exercise jurisdiction over both English and German Protestants in the Holy Land. Newman was the first to perceive the enormity of this scheme, which was carried into effect by Act of Parliament in October 1841. Not only did it demonstrate the kinship between Anglicanism and Lutheranism,* which the Tractarians hotly repudiated, but it also had the appearance of an impudent and mischievous gesture against the Eastern Church – for the bishop appeared to be empowered (despite official assurances to the contrary) to indulge in Protestant proselytism by taking under his wing any who cared to submit to his jurisdiction. Robert Wilberforce and Henry Manning clearly viewed the whole matter with acute suspicion, Robert accusing the Archbishop of having acted with 'reckless neglect of the feelings of the Church', and suspecting 'that Bunsen means to make Alexander [the first bishop] a sort of channel for introducing Episcopacy into Prussia'.[13] Again Samuel found himself on the opposite side. He was, in truth, in a very embarrassing position, having been taken into Bunsen's confidence[14] and being obliged, through his close relations with Prince Albert, to echo the sentiments of the Court. He did his best to dilute the noxious elements in the scheme in a letter to Robert in February 1842, but he had to admit, in the strongest terms, that he found the attitude of the Tractarians utterly unreasonable: 'I confess I feel furious', he wrote, 'at the craving of men for union with idolatrous, material, sensual, domineering Rome and their squeamish anathematizing hatred of Protestant Reformed men.'[15] In an earlier letter he had recommended the scheme to Robert as 'a truly noble plan by which, I trust, on a back current, Episcopacy will flow into Prussia'.[16]

Samuel did not know that for Newman the announcement of this bond with heresy marked the beginning of the end. It was the third of the three calls which scriptural precedent demanded for the evidence of a clear directive from God.[17] The four years' agony of Newman's Anglican deathbed now began. Henry Wilberforce had realised how dangerous the position was as early as 1839. Now Robert was to be let into the secret. In

---

* The bishop was given power to ordain Germans who subscribed to the Thirty-nine Articles and the Confession of Augsburg.

December 1841 he wrote in great anxiety to Newman to gain confirmation of disturbing rumours which had reached him through S. F. Wood:

> Knowing you, my dear Newman, as I do, being aware of your extraordinary powers and deep seriousness, I know that it would be hopeless for me to turn you from any course which you had resolved upon. But I cannot and will not believe that in the bottom of your heart you have more idea of an union with Rome than you had when we used to take our quiet walks together on the banks of the Isis. What change is it then which has come over your spirit, which has made men venture to speak of you as inclining towards this schismatical and idolatrous author of so many divisions in the Church of GOD? My belief and hope is that you will say . . . – 'how absurd'. It is not merely Golly's [Golightly's] foolish interference which has alarmed me but the tone in which such a man as Wood seems to be writing.[18]

Newman's reply, undated, was a full statement of his doubts since 1839; how in his study of both the Monophysites and the Donatists, he had come to 'see as in a glass reflected our own Church in the heretical party, and the Roman Church in the Catholic'.

> This [he continued] is an appalling fact – which, do what I will, I cannot shake off.
>
> One special test of the heretical party is absence of *stay* or *consistence*, ever shifting, ever new forming – ever consumed by internal strife. Our present state . . . is a most miserable and continual fulfilment of this Note of error. . . .
>
> Another is a constant effort to make alliances with other heresies and schisms, though different itself from them. Thus the semi-arians attempted the Donatists, and the Arians, the Meletians, and the Nestorians (I think) the Pelagians etc. Now, I confess, miserable as this Prussian business is to my mind in itself, it is rendered still more stumbling and unsettling by its apparent fulfilment of this Note of error. . . .
>
> This has led me to look out for *grounds* of remaining where Providence has placed me. . . . It has also forced me back upon the *internal or personal Notes of the Church*: and with thankfulness I say that I have received great comfort there. . . .
>
> *P.S.* Of course the painful thought comes in to my mind – whether, if Rome is the true Church, the divinely appointed method of raising her from her present degradation be not *to join* her. Whether either she or we *can* correct our mutual errors while separated from each other.[19]

Robert was dumbfounded. He could see no logic in abandoning one defective communion in order to embrace another, equally if not more deficient. He would rather have seen Newman retire into lay communion or join the Scottish Church than contemplate 'joining a communion which is stained by image-worship, saint-worship, the denial of the cup,

John Henry Newman

William Wilberforce, Junior

the Pope's supremacy *de jure divino*'.[20] When a second letter seemed to confirm this last intention, Robert wrote in desperation:

> I don't think that I ever was so shocked by any communication, which was ever made to me, as by your letter of this morning. It has quite unnerved me. And what adds to its effect upon me, is that in justice to you, I cannot communicate what occupies my thoughts even to the natural partner of all my feelings. . . . Knowing your superiority to myself both in learning and ability I despair of saying anything which can be of use to you. . . .
>
> What is Rome's position at present but that of a slight numerical superiority? Were the East and West united it were different. Then for 3 centuries I see no trace of the Papal supremacy. After our own Reformation I know of no act by which we have disowned ourselves from the communion of the Church universal. And what is the meaning of the Apostolical Succession if the evil acts of individual Bishops can be taken as a denial of the Church's gifts? What can be worse than the Roman Popes of the 10th century? Why do they not destroy her claim as much as Whately and Sumner ours?[21]

Robert saw that he had undertaken a hopeless task. Newman replied on 2 February:

> I grieve indeed at the pain I am causing you, but in self defence I must say you have brought it on yourself. Why did you ask me? It was impossible I could shuffle with one whom I have known so long and loved so much.

The only comfort which he could offer was that he was not contemplating any immediate decisive step:

> I have said *not a word* of anything practical following as regards individuals from even a *conviction* that our Church were without the pole of Catholicity. If I believe that Christ has been gracious to me, that He is present with me *in* my own communion, *how can I leave him?*
>
> . . . Recollect that I wish to be guided not by controversy but by $\mathring{\eta}\theta o s$ – so that (please God) nothing would seem to me a reason for so very awful and dreadful a step as you point out, but the quiet growth of a feeling through many years.[22]

There must be quiet – an escape from controversy. Hence Newman retired to Littlemore and, in September 1843, resigned St Mary's. What were his followers to do now, as he drifted slowly towards the Roman Church? Some followed him to Littlemore: others looked in near despair to Keble and Pusey. The chief fears of those who had sympathised with the ideals of the Oxford Movement were that Newman's defection would drive a large number of his supporters into the arms of Rome and that the original cause would be irreparably shattered. Someone had to speak out –

to rally the loyal Anglican elements in the party by demonstrating that Romanism was not the inevitable outcome of Tractarian principles. Chance – in the form of an invitation to preach the November 5th sermon at Oxford in 1843 – put that burden upon the shoulders of Henry Manning. From Newman's own pulpit, Manning launched into a fierce invective against Popery, predicting the advent of troublous times when all Christendom would be put to the test, the outcome of which would be the perfecting of 'our highly favoured Church' to act as 'a principle of reconciliation between East and West, and a law of unity and peace to mankind'. And for that providential task, 'the energetic acts of the sixteenth century may have been the stern but necessary preparation'.[23]

It was not – it could hardly have been expected to be – an unqualified success. J. B. Mozley took exception to its tone.[24] Keble thought its violence would provoke a nemesis.[25] Newman was, not unnaturally, offended, although his letters in reply to Manning's personal apologies convey an air of serene indifference to the substance of Manning's attack, showing clearly that the ties of his first loyalty were loosening alarmingly quickly.[26] There is no doubt that Manning found the task distasteful, and – despite E. S. Purcell's innuendoes of time-serving and boot-licking – believed that it was his duty to put his loyalty to the Church before his obligations to a friend whose errors were threatening to frustrate all the efforts of those who had once fought with him. Nor is there any reason to suppose that Manning was insincere. As he explained to Pusey in a letter written shortly after the sermon,

> I can no longer deny that a tendency against which my whole soul turns has shown itself. It is an imperative duty for me to be plainly true to myself at all cost and hazard. . . . I feel to have been for four years on the brink of I know not what; all the while persuading myself and others that all was well; and more – that none were [sic] so true and steadfast to the English Church; none so safe as guides. I feel as if I had been a deceiver speaking lies (God knows, not in hypocrisy), and this has caused a sort of shock in my mind that makes me tremble. Day after day I have been pledging myself to clergymen and laymen all about me that all was safe and sure. I have been using his books, defending and endeavouring to spread the system which carried this dreadful secret at its heart. There remains for me nothing but to be plain henceforward on points which hitherto I have almost resented, or ridiculed the suspicion. I did so because I knew myself to be heartily true to the English Church, both affirmatively in her positive teachings and negatively in her rejection of the Roman system and its differential points. I can do this no more. I am reduced to the painful, saddening, sickening necessity of saying what I feel about Rome.[27]

Doubtless this repudiation of the Romanising influences would have come better from Pusey. But Pusey – in Manning's opinion – was not in these years quite as rock-like as Liddon and those who have followed Liddon have cared to portray him. When Pusey upbraided Manning for his harsh words against Rome in his charge of 1845, Manning retorted with some truth, 'We owe the Church of Rome a pure Christian charity as to a member of the Catholic body; we owe the same also to the churches of the East. I do not find your expressing the latter feeling, and that seems to me the cause why you are misunderstood to have not a charity to the whole Body of Christ, but a partial fondness and leaning to the Roman Church.'[28]

The trouble was that almost every decision involved a clash between the claims of duty and the bonds of friendship; a tension painfully revealed in the last great issue which preceded the secession of Newman – the condemnation and degradation of W. G. Ward in February 1845. This event marked the climax of anti-Tractarian hysteria in Oxford and, through the public exhibition of the unseemly lengths to which *odium theologicum* could go, served to bring to an end an internecine war which had really begun with the attempt by the Tractarians themselves to prevent Dr Hampden's elevation to the Regius Chair of Divinity nine years earlier. Ironically, as A. P. Stanley pointed out, 'the victors of 1836 are the victims of 1845'.[29] The wheel had come full circle.

Three propositions were to be submitted to Convocation: the condemnation of Ward's *Ideal of a Christian Church*, the degradation of its author from his degrees, and a change in the University statutes whereby all those subscribing to the Thirty-nine Articles should be required to understand them in the sense in which they were both first published and at that present time imposed by the University. The absurdity of this last requirement was so manifest that pressure from spokesmen of all the parties in the Church compelled its withdrawal before Convocation was summoned. In its place, however, was substituted a proposition to censure Newman's interpretations of the Articles as contained in *Tract 90*. What followed is well known. At the meeting of Convocation, attended by an unprecedented number of M.A.'s, the first two propositions against Ward and his book were carried, and the condemnation of *Tract 90* was prevented by the *non placet* of the proctors, one of whom was R. W. Church. Throughout the whole proceedings the least put out was Ward himself. Chuckling at the prospect of a Fellow of Balliol dressed in an undergraduate gown, he decided to relieve his colleagues – who had all been loyal to him at the vote – of this embarrassment. He resigned his fellowship and his orders: took a wife; and in September 1845 was received into the Roman Church.

On this issue there was a great deal of preliminary canvassing. Pusey, who had little sympathy with Ward's outrageous indiscretions, could never take the part of the Heads of Houses. Their worst sin, he wrote to Robert, was to make a declaration of war at a time when everyone was sighing for an eirenicon. 'In a "crisis", physicians stand still and leave all to God. Mariners do not shift the ballast when the vessel can hardly hold up. It does seem to me utter madness.'[30]

Gladstone tackled Samuel who was showing disconcerting signs of going the whole way with the Evangelicals. To censure Ward was to choose as allies men who were far more worthy of punishment for heterodox teaching; and, he continued, 'I have a further difficulty in declaring Ward guilty of a breach of faith. I think his interpretation of the last clause of Art. XIX utterly untenable; but certainly not more so than Simeon and Scott's interpretation of Articles, Catechism and Prayer-Book alike with respect to baptism.'[31]

Both Samuel and Gladstone wrote to Manning to put their different points of view. Manning decided in the end to follow Gladstone, but he felt profoundly sick at heart. In a letter to Pusey, he accused Ward of indulging in 'the recklessness and wilfulness of a schoolboy'. The whole tone of his writings was 'raw, headlong and unreal', and would have a bad effect on 'our younger men': 'I would a thousandfold rather that they should sign the 39 articles "renouncing no one Roman doctrine", than throw off the modesty, delicate sensitiveness, and keen perception of what is due to great moral truths, relations and fitnesses, which appear to me to be the foundation not only of a saintly, but of a manly character. This is as distasteful a letter as I ever wrote; but I was resolved not to leave my meaning in any ambiguity.'[32]

In the meantime Samuel and Robert had come to the sad conclusion that they must vote on opposite sides. Samuel had been unhappy at the original third proposition and had suggested that at subscription a declaration should be added that the Articles were to be understood as a condemnation of the 'formal teaching of the Church of Rome, as defined at the Council of Trent'[33]; but, as Robert pointed out to him, this would oblige all subscribers to study the Tridentine decrees beforehand, which he supposed could hardly have been Samuel's intention.[34] They eventually agreed to vote together in censuring Ward's book, but to take opposite sides on the remaining two issues. Henry, of course, was entirely with Ward and wrote (anonymously) a heated pamphlet to condemn the illegality of Convocation's proceedings. Samuel thought this singularly injudicious:

> No call of duty can require the Vicar of East Farleigh to volunteer for the office of disemboweller of the University [he observed to Robert], and there being no such call of duty I am quite sure
>
> 1st that it is very bad for his own mind: far too much given to abuse and dissection.
>
> 2nd that it is most injurious to his future and abiding influence. It is always known who wrote such an article; and that *who* is *never* forgiven.[35]

Perhaps Samuel, at this period of his life, was a little inclined to let considerations of 'his future and abiding influence' weigh too much in his mind.

v. *Episcopal Ambitions: Samuel Wilberforce and Henry Manning*

Some unfriendly spirits certainly thought so. Isaac Williams had said as much in his chagrin at Samuel's defection in the contest over the Poetry Professorship. J. B. Mozley's letters are full of acid comments. In 1842 he observed to his sister that Samuel had played a game of see-saw for so long that he needed a bishopric if only for the sake of his health.[1] Jealousy and bitterness were bound to be engendered amongst the members of a persecuted party, victimised by their bishops, when they saw favours lavished upon those who had once been – or had seemed to be – their companions. Manning suffered from the same imputations. Nevertheless Samuel's persistent avoidance of party ties and his acknowledged influence in Court circles were earning for him the popular reputation of being evasive and adroit. Not until his mishandling of the Hampden affair of 1847/8 did the sobriquet of 'Soapy Sam' gain general currency, but earlier versions such as 'Sly Sam'[2] or 'Slippery Sam'[3] were being savoured by his critics before he became a bishop, until that phrase was found which seemed most euphoniously satisfying and most cruelly apt.[4]

In one respect, as has been seen already – the imputation of shifty churchmanship – this epithet was monstrously unjust. On the other hand, it must be admitted that Samuel loved power and position and was blessed with a superabundance of those gifts which might help him to attain them. When grievous personal tragedy in 1841 threw him into self-examination, he saw his temptations clearly enough. But knowing one's weaknesses is not the same thing as conquering them; and for all his remorse and increasing sense of the hollowness of public honours, Samuel was not noticeably less ambitious until 1845 when his immediate ambition had been fulfilled. Thereafter even his sourest critics of the early 1840's had to admit that they had misjudged their man.* Isaac Williams noted a 'wonderful' improvement in his character[5]; James Mozley discovered far less 'artificialness' of manner than he had been led to expect[6]; and William Palmer who had written Samuel off as too concerned in becoming 'all things to all men' changed his opinion entirely. He was 'angelic'; his life was 'an astonishing example of what Christianity is capable when it is influenced by right and enlightened views of duty'.[7]

They were not wrong when they thought that Samuel had been over-anxious to please. Now and again we find a trace of studious affability, which becomes on occasions presumptuous intimacy. Greville, for instance, who had met Samuel for the first time while staying with Lord Ashburton in January 1845, had been greatly taken with his 'quick, lively and agreeable' manner[8]; but he was much shocked a year later when, after recovering from a serious illness, he received from Samuel a wholly unsolicited letter tendering him spiritual advice and aid. 'In the whole course of my life, I never was so astonished,' exclaimed that impenitent gentleman, 'for he was about the last clergyman from whom I should have expected such an overture, and my acquaintance with him was so slight, that I could not conceive why he had selected me as the subject of a spiritual experiment.' He replied politely, pointing out, however, 'that his proposal was extraordinary and uncalled-for'.[9]

More to the point, perhaps, was Samuel's changed attitude towards John Wilson Croker. In the late 1830's, when Croker seemed to be barring his election to the Athenaeum he was described in private letters as a 'clever dung-feeder'.[10] When Samuel went to Alverstoke, however, he found Croker to be one of his most influential parishioners, and his opinion rapidly changed. In November 1841, in a letter to Robert, he described him as 'very kind and amusing. . . . I really think that I have never heard him make an unkind remark on any one. He is very attentive at Church.'[11] Samuel had clearly been mistaken in his first opinion, and it was only proper to say so. On the other hand, Croker was a man of considerable influence – a Privy Councillor who had the ear of Sir Robert

* Matthew Arnold was an exception. See G. W. E. Russell (editor), *Letters of Matthew Arnold 1848–1880* (1901), I. 216.

Peel. It would have been nothing short of folly for Samuel to nurse an unreasonable grievance against such a man, especially since there was now no longer any cause for resentment. His letters to Croker during 1842 and 1843 are, indeed, intimate and confiding. He was at pains in January 1842 to demonstrate his lack of sympathy for the Tractarians. He described them as 'essentially non-Anglican' and stated that he had suspected this almost from the beginning. His own adhesion to the Oxford cause had been very limited.

> I could not find rest in the narrow views of the so-called strict Evangelicals, and clung to the Church of England, and so far fought with them [i.e. the Tractarians], and was often classed by the low Church with them; but their hatred of the Reformation, their leaning to a visible centre of unity for the Church, the essence of Popery, their unnationality, for they can have no notion of a national life; their cramped and formal dogmatism; their fearful doctrine of sin after baptism, and many other things of the same sort, revolted me long since.[12]

Having presented his credentials as a middle-of-the-road Churchman, Samuel kept Croker informed of his opinions and desires in a series of letters, steadily decreasing in their formality.[13] In April 1843 he attempted to clear the indiscreet Henry from a charge of Romanism, and inveighed against Mariolatry.[14] He sent Croker a review of various episcopal charges, pointing out the 'essentially un-Church' standpoint of J. B. Sumner.[15] He also made it clear that Sir Robert Peel could count upon his political support: 'I trust that Sir Robert will not yield an inch to the Dissenting clamour as to his Education Bill. It seems to me the very crisis of the moral power of his government, and deeply anxious as I am for its stability and renown *hereafter*, I watch every step with the keenest anxiety.'[16]

Doubtless all this could be interpreted by a hostile critic as a calculated measure to smooth the path to a bishopric. On the other hand, Samuel was being perfectly sincere; and the sentiments expressed accord well enough with the tone of his letters to other, and less influential, personal friends.

The truth is that Samuel was now moving in an exalted circle, a fact hardly surprising in view of his reputation at Court. His diary records a growing affection for W. E. Gladstone; they went for walks together while Samuel was staying at Windsor in October 1841; they took breakfast together at Gladstone's house in the next month.[17] Samuel regularly sent him complimentary copies of his charges. These were appreciated on the whole, although in 1843 Gladstone felt obliged to admonish him gently for a tendency to pontificate before he was a pontiff. 'I doubted in one or two places', he wrote to Samuel, 'whether you allow the members of the Church all the liberty they have a right to claim: and what is I admit still more beyond my province I am apprehensive of the increase of trouble and diversity among us . . . from the extension of the practice of delivering (even partially) doctrinal charges beyond the Bench of Bishops.'[18]

In the most tactful way possible, Gladstone sought to rescue his new friend from the fault which had earned him rebukes before: the inclination to impatient censoriousness. Had he taken the lesson to heart he might have checked himself from plunging into the disagreeable Hampden affair of 1847/8 and might have softened the reproaches of T. W. Allies, the most turbulent priest of the Oxford diocese. As it was, he failed to take the hint.

In March 1844 we find him at his most censorious in dealing with the excesses of his brother Henry who, in asking Samuel for advice, received in return a severe drubbing. Not without cause. For Samuel had used his influence with the Prince Consort to obtain the living of East Farleigh for Henry in January 1843 (Lutwidge, with whom Robert had exchanged livings, having resigned through ill health)[19]; and Henry had repaid him in poor coin. Indeed, even Robert was beginning to find Henry's Tractarian enthusiasms somewhat ill-judged. 'I am sorry dear H. does not exactly move in feeling with you', he had written to Samuel in May 1843. 'I can enter into many of his feelings, but the main difference between us is that he does not enter into mine. He does not seem to feel the evils of the medieval Church nor the advantages of the present. He estimates its bad parts only: which I join with him in lamenting.'[20]

From the moment that Henry arrived at East Farleigh he was faced with trouble in the person of Lutwidge's curate, a man called Jenner, whom he was rash enough to permit to serve him in the same capacity. Within a few months it became apparent that this arrangement would not do. Jenner turned out to be a violent anti-Puseyite, who rejoiced in denouncing from his vicar's pulpit the very innovations, both in ritual and devotions, which Henry was hoping speedily to introduce. Samuel had begged Henry to take care and – if he insisted on changing the system of worship to accord more with Oxford views – to do so very gradually, changing nothing for the first two years. This was not Henry's way. He must have daily service; he liked the services to be intoned; he intended to restore the chancel in the proper Catholic manner – to remove the gallery and get rid of all the pews. Although Samuel advised him to keep Jenner, on the grounds that breaking with him would 'effectually bar your usefulness in your parish, it may be for years, it may be for life',[21] Henry decided to give him the sack, hoping to persuade Ambrose St John, his curate at Walmer, to take his place. Unfortunately St John had joined Newman at Littlemore in the summer of 1843 and clearly wanted to stay.[22] Henry was able to secure a new curate – a man of advanced Tractarian leanings – and was immediately confronted with a plot, hatched by the disgruntled Jenner and one of his parishioners (called Kennard)* who organised a memorial to the Archbishop to complain of the introduction of offensive Popish practices. Howley, who had previously turned a blind eye to Henry's peccadilloes, having had his assurance that they were agreeable to his parishioners, insisted, on receipt of the memorial, that everything objectionable should be discontinued. The chief cause of offence was the intoning of the services.

Henry's instinct was to fight back. Samuel then intervened with a long and frank letter to persuade Henry that he had not a leg to stand on. He admitted that Jenner had acted unfairly – that he had 'stirred up strife; and found weak material to work with. But still if you had made no changes Jenner could not have succeeded. Your changes *are* therefore the cause of the movement; and I cannot think the ArchB. to blame in treating them as being so.'

Henry had denied the charge of intoning. Samuel brushed this aside:

> It is clear that there *is* something very surprising about your way of reading.
> . . . Only yesterday Chandler not having heard of the memorial at all said:
> 'do you think it right for clergymen to introduce a new way of reading – a
> sort of ½ chanting the service: because Mr Butler says your brother has
> adopted a very striking and peculiar way of doing so: 'very solemn indeed',
> he says to him; 'quite new etc. etc.' Now this shews *how remarkable* the
> intonation is; whether it is good or bad is another point.

Samuel suggested that Henry should have replied in this vein:

> 'I will follow St Paul's example: become all things etc. etc., I will give
> up anything which is not a principle rather than become a cause of offence.
> It is true I like these things and I am sure there can no evil come from them:
> I think you should not have suspected them: and should not have thus

---

* 'A mere puppet', Henry wrote to Gladstone. 'Not an ill meaning man, but wonderfully conceited and very ignorant – a small farmer of some 30 acres who delights in the notoriety of appearing before the world as author of learned letters and I doubt not also he has been persuaded by Jenner that in gratifying this vanity he is doing GOD's Service.' B. M. Add. Mss. 44361 (Gladstone Papers, Vol. 276), f. 321.

addressed me, but ... I will give up every one of them rather than lead one of you into sin. ...'

Two things make me uncomfortable in giving you advice. 1st, the consciousness that, after all, you do, I fear, hold extreme opinions on some points: that you do sympathise with a great deal of the Tract movement wh. I think very dangerous, and therefore (1) that what would be in me no sacrifice of principle may seem such to you and (2) that after all these memorialists are pointing at some truth in your doctrines which these things will not reach. And 2ndly, the fact that you have already so committed yourself to certain things that I hardly know what you are now at liberty to do.

Meanwhile will you do this – with the Memorial before you will you write to me; as *short* and as *temperate* an answer to it as you can – pointing out clearly and shortly: the untruth in it, what is e.g. the real thing you have done in lighting your chancel – and taking the trouble to put the contradictions etc. in order and clearness. If you will do this, I may be able to make use of it, and if you could let me receive it on Saturday at the Athenaeum by the afternoon post I shall be *particularly* glad.[23]

Henry's troubles were not over. A month later his new curate was in hot water again, this time for taking to the bedside of a dying parishioner a cross, bidding 'him fix his dying thoughts on Him who hung upon it'. Samuel wrote at once to Croker to tell him the true story, in case he should come to hear exaggerated versions. 'My brother (my youngest brother) is more tolerant of such ineptiae than I can be in so serious a subject matter: and the curate, being a very good and a very zealous man, he as far as possible defends him.'[24]

The storm died down; and, in the end, Henry got his way.* All the internal improvements to East Farleigh church were carried out by 1850,[25] and his services gradually assumed the Catholic tone which he had wished to see. He sent Robert details of his Holy Week services in 1848:

I asked leave last year to have a separate penitential service in Holy Week and was *refused*. This year I asked and got the inclosed. What I did was to have late Evening Prayer, begun with the Litany, then a short sermon, then the Commination Prayers beginning with the 51 Ps. It was dark save one *compline* lamp quite in the roof of the chancel which gave a most religious light on the altar piece and all over the church. We knelt in silence and then began the Litany in a low deep note – and staid in silence a while when all was over. All together it was the most solemn service I have ever had in our Church.

* The Archbishop cleared Henry of the charges against him, according to a letter from Henry to Gladstone, dated 23 July 1844. B.M. Add. Nos. 44361 (Gladstone Papers Vol. 276), f. 195.

Henry was in a specially good humour because he had just returned from J. B. Sumner's enthronement at Canterbury, where he had rejoiced in the spectacle of the Evangelical Archbishop's bemused submission to the elaborate ritual. 'It was ... important as a precedent to have J.B.C. walk in *procession, chanting* the *Psalms* from the Chapter nave through the cloisters, in at the North door, then down the N. aisle to the West end, then up the Nave into the Choir. Outside stood a man with a huge playbill – and on the other side opposite one with a great placard "Ridiculous Farce – Carrying the Pope in Procession". Only think of poor Chester after 68 or 69 years turning into the Pope!'[26]

Henry and Samuel were now clearly drifting apart, and what once had been a tightly knit circle was during the 1840's – partly through its inevitable enlargement and also through the changes in circumstances of its members – splitting up into separate groups. Manning and Henry were coming very much closer to each other, an intimacy marked by Mary Wilberforce becoming Manning's penitent. Soon Manning found in Mary the confidante to whom he could communicate his most private thoughts, rather in the same way as Samuel leant for solace and support on Louisa Noel.

> My dearest Mary [Manning wrote to her from Lavington in October 1845], You do not know what I felt in reading your letter this morning. Neither do you know how I love you. Such words as yours are now almost more than I can understand: they seem to wake up something which I have dreamt, and cannot remember. The other night I was full of all sad thoughts of things past and to come; and the past and the future jarred harshly together, and I could not talk of what I felt most. But it was a heartfelt pleasure to see you, my most dear Sister. I trust you do love me for I feel that I should grow worse if people left off loving me as I desire they should. May God bless you: and will you always believe me to be your loving brother, H.E.M.[27]

Manning and Henry often exchanged letters. After all the fuss about intoning, Henry asked Manning his opinion of chanting.

> My dearest Henry [Manning replied], ... Chanting needs to be carefully kept up as it is frightful work. I really feel still at a loss about the manner of dividing. And hardly know what to say. I have a feeling that we are all wrong hitherto: and that confirms a feeling I never can get rid of about the unreal and almost irreverent effect of making the Psalms light and musical, which I always have when they are sung in harmony and somewhat fast. The genuine Roman chants are extremely slow and monotonous, as we hear them abroad, and certainly they are more like worship.[28]

While Henry was applying to Manning for his learned assistance on Catholic devotional practice, Robert was more and more seeking the opportunity for theological discussion with him. In the years after Newman's secession it became difficult for Robert to communicate his doubts and difficulties to Samuel with the openness and instinctive understanding which had marked their earlier correspondence. From 1843, however, Manning sought Robert's confidence, beginning to write to him 'under the seal' and welcoming the same treatment in return. Both felt acutely the need for greater system in Anglican theology, Manning especially discerning in the other the ability to supply what was deficient. He wrote to him in October 1845:

> Everything, my dear Robert, has conspired to draw us together in brotherly love. ... Our meetings have been so few and hurried, and I long for a time when we can, without interruption and alone, really weigh some of the matters which are now forced upon us. ... Nothing can shake my belief of the presence of Christ in our Church and sacraments. I feel incapable of doubting it: again the saints who have ripened round our altars for 300 years make it impossible for me to feel it a question of safety.
>
> But it seems to me that our theology is a chaos, we have no principles, no form, no order, or structure, or science. It seems to me inevitable that there must be a true and exact *intellectual* tradition of the Gospel, and that the scholastic theology is (more or less) such a tradition. We have rejected it and substituted nothing in its room. Surely divine truth is susceptible, within the limits of revelation, of an expression and a proof as exact as the inductive sciences. Theology must be equally capable of a 'history and philosophy' if we had a Master of Trinity to write them.
>
> This is what I want to see either done or shown to be impossible or needless.[29]

Could Robert be the William Whewell of theology? Manning thought so. Gladstone looked rather to Manning himself to do this work. During these years his intimacy with Manning was at its height. He loved him as a friend, venerated him as a spiritual counsellor and – after the publication of *The Unity of the Church* (which had been in part inspired, according to its author, by a reading of Gladstone's own work on *Church and State*)[30] saluted him as the first theologian of his day. If Samuel Wilberforce was gaining ground in Gladstone's affections, he never enjoyed such a close personal *rapport* as existed at that time between the trio of Gladstone, Manning and James Hope.

This is how the personal relationships stood in the middle years of the 1840's. Each of the three archdeacons was engaged in a great work, and saw in the others the potential of greater work to come. Both Manning and Samuel were clearly on the way to becoming bishops. The question was, who would get there first? Samuel had Court favour and a greater popular reputation; Manning's strength lay in the respect which his abilities and sincerity were earning from both High Church extremists and the moderate party in the Church. Only the Low Church supporters – notably the *Record* – regarded him as their implacable enemy. One of his most significant conquests was Henry Phillpotts, Bishop of Exeter. Their correspondence (in the Spencer MSS), beginning in 1842, has been recently analysed by Mr G. C. B. Davies, who has shown how – in their discussions of surplice riots, diocesan seminaries and the revival of convocation – the natural barrier of a wide disparity of age was surmounted almost on their first exchange of letters.[31] Phillpotts showed not the least resentment at Manning's criticisms of his actions; indeed, he asked for more; an attitude which, as Mr Davies has written, 'argues an unusual depth of mutual regard and understanding at a period which saw a vigorous onslaught preparing against the Tractarian clergy'.[32]

It was Phillpotts' conviction that 'no power on earth can keep Manning from the Bench of Bishops',[33] and the younger Anglo-Catholic element yearned for some such mark of favour. Men such as William Dodsworth of Christ Church, St Pancras, W. J. E. Bennett of St Paul's, Knightsbridge, T. W. Allies in the country living of Launton in Oxfordshire, and Maskell (chaplain to the Bishop of Exeter) were as little afraid of incurring official displeasure as Henry Wilberforce had been, but they were finding the cumulative effect of hostile episcopal appointments frustrating and deadening. After Newman's defection in October 1845, they came to see in Manning the prospect of better times.

This view was shared by many of the moderates. One of the most remarkable achievements of Manning was his maintainance of amicable relations with his fellow archdeacon, Julius Hare. They had virtually nothing in common; on many issues they found themselves on opposite sides. Nevertheless their letters were refreshingly free from rancour and they retained for each other an abiding respect.[34] Hare's brother-in-law, F. D. Maurice, marvelled at the ability and potentiality of both Manning and Samuel Wilberforce. In 1843 he wrote in a letter to a close friend (Sir E. Strachey) a description of a visit to Alverstoke and a journey to Lavington, during which he met both men:

> I have had much pleasant refreshment, both bodily and spiritual, and, so far as the sight of men in zealous action, and the conversation of men full

of thought and love of truth can impart hopes, to one not over hopeful respecting the Church, I have had much to encourage me.

Manning is one of the completest, perhaps the completest man I ever met with; there are doubtless deficiencies, which completeness itself implies, seeing that the incomplete is that which is ever seeking the infinite and eternal to fill up its hollows; and in him there is a logical rotundity which I should not wish for. But it is united with so much appreciation of everything good, such great refinement, tolerance and kindliness, that I know not where one would look rather, for a wise and true bishop in these times. Wilberforce is far less finished, but therefore more suitable to me, of the greatest geniality and cordiality, open to receive any truths, and with singular capacities for imparting all he has received. I have seen little of Manning, but all our intercourse has been friendly and unconstrained.[35]

If Manning wished for high office – and the evidence would suggest that at this period of his life the prospect was not unattractive to him – there were certain acknowledged 'spring-boards' into the episcopate which influential friends might be able to obtain for him. One such was the preachership at Lincoln's Inn which became vacant in November 1843. Gladstone pressed him to apply and he duly did so. His failure to secure this post – a bitter disappointment to his friends – may be explained by the anti-Tractarian fever which succeeded the news of Newman's resignation of St Mary's, Oxford, and the determined efforts of the *Record* to block Manning's further advancement. As it turned out, this was to be one of those small fortuitous events which change the course of a man's life.

So Samuel won the race to the episcopal bench, being sent by Sir Robert Peel to Oxford only six months after he had been installed as Dean of Westminster. It was, of course, an appointment of the utmost significance. The diocese was – on Bagot's translation to the see of Bath and Wells – greatly enlarged, following the decision of the Ecclesiastical Commissioners to add the counties of Berkshire and Buckinghamshire to the Oxford diocese at the next vacancy. To add to the difficulties of administering what was virtually a new unit, the successor to Bishop Bagot was appointed only one week after the news of John Henry Newman's secession to the Roman Church. That Peel chose Samuel for this assignment may have been due to pressure from the Court. Certainly Blomfield, whom Peel was wont to consult on all appointments, favoured the nomination of Edward Cardwell, Principal of St Alban Hall, a Low Churchman who would exercise 'a more salutary control over the young divines of Oxford'[36]; and when Peel informed him of his choice, he admitted that he had taken 'a hazardous measure'.[37] Croker, also, appears to have been left in the dark until Peel's mind was made up. On 13 October 1845, Peel wrote to Croker:

> I have this day had the satisfaction of proposing to place Wilberforce on the Bench. I entrust to him a See of special importance, that of Oxford. He is a distinguished Oxford man, and I have confidence that his high moral character and varied learning, and the soundness and moderation of his Opinions – religious and political – will give him an influence in his Diocese and the University which he may render most beneficial to the cause of Religion and of sound academical instruction.

Croker replied enthusiastically:

> You could not have made a better choice – the only personal defect that I can detect in Wilberforce, will help him in the business both of his Diocese and the Church at large, namely that he inclines to be overactive and rather too adroit. He is, and deservedly, the most popular person that I have ever known – his zeal is great, but his prudence rides it in a tight bit. I think he will do you honour, and great service to the Church at large both in Oxford and in the House of Lords.[38]

Samuel received the news on 14 October. He wrote immediately to Robert:

> My dearest Robert, I received today in a letter of most unusual cordiality an offer from Sir Robert Peel of the See of Oxford: and unworthy as I feel myself of such a charge I have not ventured when so presented to me to decline it. I feel more than ever before, my beloved Brother, to need your prayers that I may have wisdom and faithfulness: that this new responsibility may not lead to my damnation or to any injury to Christ's Holy Church: but to its edifying and to my salvation. It is ½ past 12 at night and I must write a few lines to Henry and Manning so I will not say more. Pray for me: write to me: do not mention it till it comes out from other quarters. The Bishop of Oxford only *yesterday* accepted Bath and Wells and Peel says he had previously ventured to suggest to Her Majesty my name as fitted for the post if he did. I am ever, my dearest Robert, your most affectionate brother, S. Wilberforce.[39]

Robert was stunned; utterly overwhelmed. He could think only of the 'indescribable awfulness of the charge'.

> I was thinking as I came back by the coach this afternoon [he wrote to Samuel], how happy it was that we two, who had been so much brought up together, were so united as we are in all matters of feeling and in so many matters of practice. Among all the necessary confusion of the world I cling to the feeling of concord and unity with one, to whom I am bound by a tie which cannot be divided. And now when I have seen you pass . . . thro' all the lower offices of the most respectable of professions to see you

preferred to its highest rank is of course a thing which looking at it in a worldly view is unspeakably gratifying to me. But then comes back the thought of life's uncertainty – of the many contemporaries whom I have already seen sink by me into the grave – of the great account which we must all render at God's tribunal – and I am unable to disentangle the conflicting emotions which excited me to joy and anxiety. I must now go to bed and sleep upon it, before I can sufficiently recover myself to feel exactly what you are and what awaits you. May GOD only bless you in your new work, may He guide you in the uncertainty, and guard you against the dangers which await your path.[40]

Samuel was in his fortieth year; he was to return to Oxford, where only twenty years before he had been an undergraduate. As his father's voice had moved and charmed the House of Commons, his voice was now to be heard in the House of Lords. Would he be equal to the task? Prince Albert, within a few days of Samuel's appointment, wrote a long letter to him to state what was expected of him. He was 'to abstain *completely* from mixing himself up with the politics of the day, and beyond giving a general support to the *Queen's Government*, and occasionally voting for it should take no part in the discussion of State affairs'. Only when the interests of humanity were at stake should he come forward boldly in the House of Lords to give his advice. He should never allow himself to take the part of a 'mere *Churchman*', but always that of 'a *Christian*'. He must be 'meek, and liberal, and tolerant to other confessions; but let him never forget that he is the representative of the Church of the Land, the main-tenance of which is as important to the country as that of its Constitution or its Throne'. He must be a peacemaker, not over-anxious in pressing for 'new rights, privileges, grants etc.'. He must be 'a guardian of public morality, not, like the Press, by tediously interfering with every man's private affairs, speaking for applause, or trampling on those that are fallen, but by watching over the morality of the State in acts which expediency or hope for profit may tempt it to commit, as well in home and colonial as in foreign affairs'.[41]

Such was his political role. As for the Church and his troubled diocese, the thoughts of what confronted him gradually cast out the first feelings of joy and gratification and pride. On 13 November, as the day of his consecration approached, he wrote to Charles Anderson:

My desire, dear Friend, will be in God's help to be in the position of Father in God to all my Clergy: to sympathize with their trials: to help, love, pray for, work with them: to be the same to all who love Christ: whether they verge to Tract or Low Church errors; to allow the full

Henry and Mary Wilberforce

W. F. Hook

licence the Church allows, without ever compromising what seems to me wrong.

I see the difficulty of being at all what I want to be. I pray to God I may say hourly to make me this:

My soul often sinks within me. I know I shall be mistaken by those I love, on the one side and on the other; perhaps by you: but if through all my weakness and errors I can save my soul and bring me to Christ's Church I am content.[42]

Chapter 7

DEFEATS AND DEFECTIONS

1. *The Defection of the Ryders*

Samuel Wilberforce was consecrated Bishop of Oxford in Lambeth Chapel on 30 November 1845. The previous day had been spent quietly with his closest friends – Robert, Trench, George Prevost and Henry Manning. Of these, his brother Robert was chosen to preach the consecration sermon. Samuel gave him explicit instructions. Fearful that Robert might choose a favourite Tractarian theme or sound an incautious Catholic note, he particularly begged him to preach on the 'more spiritual' aspects of the ministry – 'its one work to testify of Christ, and converting souls through the might of His Name'. He should also take the opportunity to demonstrate 'the full and undoubting allegiance of your own mind to our Church; your no sympathy with the morbid leer towards Rome; your no absolute damning foreign Protestants etc.'[1] Robert agreed. He would preach on the episcopate and its responsibilities: 'I will write something and put into it as much as I can of the topics you suggest. As far as I can tell we do not differ much in what we aim at and dream, but I think you take a different view of the persons who have moved towards the medieval Church.'[2]

The enthronement took place on 13 December; and, a week later, Samuel conducted his first ordination. He did not, however, take up residence at Cuddesdon until the last day of the old year. He was laid low in the deanery over Christmas with an inflamed windpipe, which required the services of a surgeon, and then, taking Mrs Sargent and Herbert with him, he drove off through the dark and violence of a stormy winter's evening to see in the New Year at the Palace.[3] He felt about as low as he had ever been before: 'It is inexpressibly depressing to me entering on a new year and coming to a new place. Old days of new year happiness rise with all their bitterness upon me. But it is best as it is. I can hardly keep from weeping.'[4]

Also fighting against his tears, John Henry Newman was saying good-bye to Littlemore. He saw in the New Year at St Mary's, Oscott, returned to

Oxford to pack up his effects, and on 23 February he left Littlemore for good, 'kissing my bed, and mantelpiece, and other parts of the house' before tearing himself away to join his fellow converts at Maryvale.[5] Samuel was pleased to see him go. The diocese would be healthier without the presence of the great 'pervert'[6]; it was all the fearful consequence of unbridled self-will 'which has ever driven heretics and schismatics to the accomplishment of their lamentable end. May God give him the grace of repentance before he falls through Rome into infidelity.'[7] They were never to exchange words again. Once in February 1848, Samuel was obliged to ride by Maryvale and on seeing one of the brothers out walking felt his heart miss a beat[8]; and at Sophia Ryder's funeral in March 1850 he saw Newman for a moment and turned away: 'I heard the unmistakeable voice like a volcano's roar tamed to the softness of a flute-stop, and got a glimpse . . . of a serpentine form through an open door – "The Father Superior".'*

Of the brothers, Henry Wilberforce was the one most personally affected. The bond of love could not so easily be severed. Newman had kept him informed of developments at every stage of his *anfechtung* in letters of tenderest affection. He was the first to receive word of the intended reception at the hands of Father Dominic the Passionist,[9] and he wrote to Robert directly:

> My dearest Brother, I grieve to say that our beloved Newman writes me word he is going *immediately*. . . . I cannot say how bewildered I feel by this awful event, tho' I have contemplated it (more or less) for 6 years. . . . Only think of the man who admits Newman! What will he dare to do afterwards?[10]

Naturally enough, Newman fished for Henry's soul; sometimes tenderly and carefully; at other times, petulantly and impatiently, accusing him of 'nauseous humbug' in his confessed dread of succumbing to his influence on the grounds that Catholic proselytism had the effect of increasing his own perplexity. 'I doubt whether you *have* a creed now', Newman objected. 'I don't know *what* you believe. I don't think you can say. Is this a right state? . . . Is it a state to live and die in?'[11] Robert did his best to blunt these attacks. He had warned Samuel that as soon as Newman jumped into the ditch they would all be dirtied with the splash[12]; and, as soon as the news of Newman's reception reached him, Robert invited Henry to come and stay with him at Burton Agnes. They had a furious argument over the question of the advisability of suspension of all inter-

---

* Wrangham MSS. VI. 401. 26 March 1850. Compare Newman's account (Oratory. Notebook A. 7. 36) when he saw Samuel and noted his turning away.

course with the renegade, and Robert prided himself on having had the better of the exchange.[13]

George Ryder was equally perturbed. In July 1845, realising the inevitability of Newman's secession, he wrote in great perplexity to Manning. Where did the Anglo-Catholics stand now?

> Men have been following Newman, to speak generally, and not Bramhall and Andrewes, just as an army follows its leader and not the men who have made his armour. . . . The nearest approach to an answer is the counterbalancing fact that Pusey, K., you and others do not decide – but that by itself is very insufficient, for who knows that you won't go in time also? What grounds are there for our feeling more certain about you than about Newman five years ago? N.'s going is a fact of a very different kind and much more weight against Anglo-Catholicism than Pusey and others staying, just as Pusey's would be, if Newman stayed. My conviction is that either Newman's going throws the whole Catholic fabric amongst us to the ground . . . or it must be based on a theory which shall embrace and account for our present ecclesiastical state – which is so very different from, and so much at variance with the Caroline theory of Bramhall, Taylor etc.[14]

He had made a similar approach to Keble in the previous month, but had received no satisfactory reply. 'The *onus probandi* lies on those who go, not on those who stay', Keble had told him. 'We are in a state of appeal, to the next general council, and . . . *ordinarily speaking* it can scarce be the duty of an individual to decide in such an appeal for himself.'[15]

George Ryder then really began to play with fire. He went abroad in the autumn of 1845, following the advice of the family doctor who was seriously worried about the state of Sophia's health.[16] He obtained two years' leave of absence from his bishop, and departed for Paris, on the first stage of a journey to Italy, with Sophia, his three eldest children (Harry, Lisle and Alice) and his sister Sophy, full of the best intentions to write a book comparing the Anglican and Roman systems. First-hand experience of Romish corruptions would strengthen his waning faith in the English Church. So he thought. But men tend to see only what they want to see; and George Ryder's heart was firmly in the Roman Church before he embarked on his continental tour. His vision of Christian sanctity in all its fullness, his yearning for order, interior discipline and total surrender to a systematised and unambiguous sacramentalism dominated every spiritual impulse, blinded him to anything suggestive of decadence or corruption. The Ryders were lost to the Church of their baptism from the first moment they entered a Catholic church.

Keble awoke to the dangers too late. Even so he would not send Ryder the informed and detailed apologetic which his friends believed him capable of supplying. Not only was he too humble to accede to such a request but he was also unusually incensed at the want of humility in others who would suppose that the Church of England was one 'cause' among many which ought to be maintained against the claims of her rivals. He accused Ryder of betraying 'intellectual restlessness' – a sort of perverse arrogance which would demand of his spiritual mother that she should supply 'sufficient answers' to what the Roman Catholics urge. 'I am sure', he wrote to Ryder, 'it is long since I dreamed of "maintaining the cause" of all the truths I firmly believe, or of "finding sufficient answers" to all objections. In such matters I should have made shipwreck long ago, had I not accepted, and tried to act upon the theory of Bishop Butler – that theory which seems now to be so sadly despised and forsaken by so many of our friends.'[17]

This was all very well, but it was hardly the medicine to suit Ryder's particular malaise. Like Ward and Oakeley before him, he felt compelled to search for signs and proofs of catholicity just because all the signs seemed at that time to be pointing the other way. The Church Catholic must possess the marks of 'inner holiness'; it must also possess the means to guide its members in this quest for the sanctified life. When those who had inspired them with this vision of catholicity were themselves obliged by jealous authority to stand all the day idle, and when all attempts to demonstrate the possession of the Catholic ethos within the Anglican Church were frustrated, if not explicitly denied, by the episcopate, to whose authority they had themselves appealed, they felt – not unnaturally – that they must either abandon the Catholic principle or look for it elsewhere. Give a banquet to a starving man, a fortune to a pauper, and you invite indulgence. Everything is palatable; even the dross may seem as gold.

The Ryder party went first to Paris, where they met Manning and William Dodsworth on their way back to England; they bought rosaries and crucifixes; Sophy Ryder, as she was saying good-bye to Henry Manning, accepted thankfully a gift from him of a book of devotions to the Virgin Mary. She had long wished to use such prayers, but feared to do so without Manning's sanction. He was no longer prepared to stand in her way. From Paris they went to Italy. They attended midnight Mass in Naples, following the service in the missal. Sophy Ryder obtained permission to attend a Lenten retreat at the Convent of the Sacred Heart. Then, at the end of April, George Ryder fell dangerously ill.

Timor mortis was to force the issue. Ryder came to see that if death approached he should feel bound to send for a priest and to plead for reception. The call was so clear that he was received into the Roman Church, with his sister Sophy and his children, as soon as he recovered. Sophia could not so easily commit herself. Her decision to follow her husband came two days later, while receiving the blessing of the Holy Relic of the True Cross in the Church of Sancta Croce.[18]

It all happened very quickly; and their friends and relations in England were stunned. Bishop Sumner, Henry Ryder's close friend and colleague, was one of the first to receive the news.

> I do not remember any occurrence [he replied, in accepting Ryder's resignation], which has occasioned me so much concern, as well on Diocesan grounds, as for private reasons. But you have taken the irrevocable step, and it is useless for me to comment upon it, and it would be an unkindness most foreign to my heart to harass you with unavailing personal regrets. And the expression of them, after all, would but faintly describe the reality of my feelings. . . . I cannot close this last official communication without adding that although my diocesan connexion with you is terminated you and your family will not cease to have a place in my prayers.[19]

For Mrs Sargent this was yet another cross for her to bear. Two of George's brothers were speedily despatched to Rome to try to bring the renegade to his senses. Of Sophia's family, Mary was at first the most bitter. She had had charge of Sophia's two youngest children while the rest of the family was abroad, and now had to surrender them to be received into the Catholic Church. She felt as if she had been exploited and tricked; her own unsettlement of mind may have made her resentment the more intense. Henry, who wrote to Newman to tell him of Mary's distress, was reminded that 'the loss or alienation of friends by their conversion may be the divinely sent trial of others'.[20]

The Ryders were the first of the Wilberforce family circle to secede; they were the first to discover the price that had to be paid: social ostracism, alienation of friends, loss of money, position and employment. For a while they could not face the awful prospect of their return, spending the summer quietly at Frascati, making fortnightly visits to Rome. The journey home was made in June 1847 – to London for a year in lodgings, and thence to Grace Dieu, where Ryder's cousin, Ambrose Phillipps de Lisle, offered him the tenancy of a house on his estate. There, in Holy Week three years later, Sophia Ryder died, the sixth of Mary Sargent's seven children to predecease their mother.

Henry Manning sent the news to Samuel, who had seen nothing of the family since with great bitterness of heart he had accused George Ryder of acting in Rome 'with the utmost precipitation and wilfulness'.[21]

> Twelve years ago [Manning wrote] I remember writing in a private book 'Of four brothers I am called to go first through this fire.' You soon followed, and now a third. Only our dearest Henry tarries outside the furnace. God knows for how long: or how soon he may be with us. But *anima justorum in manu Dei sunt.* . . . Somehow this last sorrow has set all my memories at work. All are there together now except the Mother and one alone. All that I saw at Lavington but two are in Paradise. I do not know why I write all this but it seems to flow and to flow towards you. Forgive me all my faults towards you and give me not as much love as I deserve but as much as your loving heart will bestow. I need not, I believe, tell you that in all and through all I feel my heart knit with ever greater closeness to yours. Ever your loving brother, H.E.M.[22]

II. *Manning and Anglo-Catholicism*

Newman had gone from Oxford to the obscurity of Maryvale and thence to Rome, but his pen was not long inactive. In the summer of 1847 there was a mild twittering in ecclesiastical circles at the publication of his novel *Loss and Gain*, with Oxford as its setting, and its theme the spiritual pilgrimage of the hero, Charles Reding, into the Roman Church. Henry Wilberforce read it avidly, and fairly hugged himself with delight. Not so Robert, who thought the characterisation tasteless. Jennings, the Vice-principal of St Saviour's, was plainly meant to be Edward Hawkins. Henry countered by praising Newman for his restraint: 'If he had pleased, armed with his immense power of satire, he could have pounded Hawkins in a mortar like Solomon's fool. I have a vision before me of that picture in the old edition of Foxe's martyrs – of the monk preparing the poison for King John. Our J.H.N. being the monk and Hawkins of course the toad who is in the mortar. If I could execute my conception like Punch or Anderson I could send you a picture of it.'[1] Samuel condemned the book out of hand: 'I think *Loss and Gain*', he wrote to Robert, '. . . about the most mischievous book I ever read; so suggestive of scepticism. Newman all over.'[2]

Newman had certainly not intended to malign his former friends and enemies; to hint as much, he once assured James Stephen, would be to take the part 'of the good lady in the Spectator, who turned the *Whole*

Duty of Man into a manual of personal slander'. He mocked at certain types of the religious character, one of which might have given Henry Wilberforce and George Ryder food for thought.

> In the tale [Newman wrote to James Stephen], I hit at young men professing celibacy and then marrying. Yet, I confess it with pain, when a Protestant, I actually quarrelled with two friends, for marrying after tacitly concurring with those who were advocates of a single life.

He had not intended to be spiteful.

> I have laughed at nothing in my Tale, which I did not laugh at when a Protestant. I have laughed at antiquarian foppery, at affectation of dress, at unreality and inconsistency of conduct. But as to my 'Bateman', who is the pseudo-Puseyite (so to speak) introduced, not only do I not know *whom* people take him to be, not only is he drawn from no one at all, but I have spoken as a Protestant quite savagely of his type of man, in a passage in the *British Critic*, though my words are primarily and directly aimed at Catholic controversialists: 'We see its agents', I said, speaking of Catholicism, 'smiling and nodding and ducking to attract attention, as gipseys make up to truant boys, holding out tales for the nursery, and pretty pictures, and gold gingerbreads, – and physic concealed in jam, and sugarplums for good children. Who can but feel shame when the religion of Ximenes, Borromeo, and Pascal is so overlaid? . . . We Englishmen like manliness.' The Bateman of my Tale is essentially an unmanly, unreal character. In like manner, I never could relish the Cambridge Camden Society, and never augured well of it; though I should now be the first to confess that various excellent Catholics have come out of it.[3]

Loss and Gain, however, was little more than a joke compared to the weighty apologetic of the *Essay on the Development of Christian Doctrine*, completed two days before Newman's reception into the Roman Church. It was – it must be admitted – strange apologetic, less impressive to his new co-religionists than it was to the party whom Newman had abandoned. Newman was putting the case for Rome by arguing from the very materials and in the particular terminology which the Tractarians thoroughly understood but which his Jesuit instructors at Rome – Perrone, Passaglia and Mazio – found unconventional and muddling.[4] Whereas the Tractarians had stoutly maintained that the history of the Catholic Church revealed a movement away from the pure teaching of the apostolic fathers, a movement into corruption against which the Anglican Church stood as the preserver and guardian of the original deposit, Newman began his thesis with the claim that history proved the very opposite. 'One thing at least is certain: . . . the Christianity of history is not Protestantism. If ever there were a safe truth, it is this. . . . To be deep in history is to cease to be a Protestant.'[5] Whereas the Oxford Movement had been, from the point of view of its theological significance, a great concerted effort to recover the spirit and teaching of the early Church, Newman strove to prove the principle of doctrinal development – of gradual elucidation from the implicit towards the explicit[6] – from precisely the same sources. As Professor Chadwick has written: 'He was not reading Möhler, nor Wiseman, nor Perrone, or even Petau. He was reading Justin Martyr, Athanasius, Tertullian, Lactantius, Cyril.'[7]

There had to be some sort of answer. Even Samuel conceded that the book was powerful – though not 'calculated to overthrow the faith of many'. The argument had no force whatever, he assured Gladstone, 'for those who believe that the first Divine afflatus conveyed to the Church in the person of the Apostles all truth concerning God which man could know, and that the inspired Word of God is the written transcript of that entire knowledge which it was but given to the Church afterwards to draw out and define with logical accuracy as heresy created the necessity.'[8]

Gladstone was not so confident.

> I am not able to convince myself that 'to draw out with logical accuracy' what is actually in Scripture, constitutes the whole expository gift of the Church. It is long since I read Vincentius; but I have always taken it for granted that there is necessarily in the Church some power of 'development'; and he gives certain limits of that power. I feel that the Church of England has effectually confined this power from extravagating by the terms of the sixth Article; that explanation and definition founded thereon constitute its principal elements; and I have never felt that in matters *de fide* the Church had exercised anything more.

He wished to find someone capable of drawing out 'with precision against Newman the limits of this power; but it would be a noble work, and I am sure Bishop Butler could do it if he were among us'.[9]

There was no Bishop Butler; but there was Manning – in those days, to Gladstone, perhaps the next best man. And Manning admired Newman's book without being in the least convinced by it. In a letter to Robert in December 1845, he compared it with Trench's Hulsean Lectures on a similar subject, and came to the conclusion that Newman was immeasurably better 'by a thousand to one'. Nevertheless Newman was over subtle and tended to scepticism.[10]

In November Gladstone suggested that Manning should 'entertain the idea of answering Newman's book', a proposal which did not go amiss, for Manning evidently started work at once.[11] Gladstone was delighted;

and when, a month later, Manning wrote to say that he was losing confidence in his ability to produce a reply, Gladstone swept his objections aside. 'I am more sanguine than you about the ultimate issue; ... I augur that you will find your confidence grow as you proceed.'[12]

A critical stage had now been reached in Manning's religious development. Between October 1845 and August 1846 he himself experienced the first pangs of unsettlement. The news of Newman's secession had saddened him but he had not been shaken. His state of mind is most fully expressed in a letter, dated 28 October 1845, written to Edward Coleridge, the Eton master whose Tractarian sympathies had made him the life-long friend and counsellor of G. A. Selwyn, T. W. Allies and James Hope Scott.[13]

My dear Friend, Our dear friend Newman has, at last, taken the step we have so long feared. Long as we have looked for it, I can hardly realize it as an event done and over. It is a heavy sorrow, which will stand alone having nothing like it.

How can we be surprised if it should affect many minds? And yet it seems to me that it ought not. Natural as it is, that one to whom we owe so much, should powerfully affect us by every step he takes, yet our probation before God is so severely distinct and personal that I dare not look anywhere but to my own conscience. Being unable to find there the dictates on which he has acted, I feel that the case is closed: 'to our own Master we stand or fall'. To me it would be as clear a disobedience, as to him it is obedience, to the Light within, to do what he has done. To rely on individual minds has been a strong temptation to many of late, and one design of the Head of the Church may be to correct this dangerous inclination. We have perhaps all been too intellectual, too much related to persons, or to a school of opinions: too little to the Church and to the Person and Presence of our only true Master. I trust that this sorrow may humble us, and turn us back to Him with a firm and fervent attachment.

Certainly there has never been in my memory, any movement when the Church of England has put forth such tokens of life and power. It is almost incredible that a body which 15 years ago was elated at being an Establishment should now be conscious of being a Church. The work that has been done in and by the Church at home and through its Episcopate and Missions abroad seem to me overwhelming signs of Christ's love and power. What may not be hoped from a body that has even conceived such works of Faith? It is not the nature of severed or barren branches to blossom after 300 years, except 'an Aaron's rod that budded'.

But all this you know as well as any one. Certainly I would as soon disbelieve my own waking and living consciousness as doubt of the Presence of Christ with us; and of the boundless tendencies and powers of development which are thereby bestowed upon the English Church. ...

Most earnestly do I desire and pray that we may have, as all other graces, so that of patience. Half a generation has not passed since we were what I will not venture to describe. What do people want or expect? It will be impossible for any man to pronounce against the Church of England, until a new race of pastors and a catechized people have been suffered to grow up, without manifest haste and rashness. Who knows what GOD, in His tender mercy and long suffering, may bring out of our present disordered and turbulent beginnings? ...

I do wish people would talk less or more wisely, i.e. more seriously and guardedly. It is certainly 'the tongue that causeth many to fall' by the mere unsettling of themselves and others, by rash judgements and superficial contrasts and ungrounded fears. I cannot doubt that GOD is nearer and more gracious to us than our weak Faith allows us to believe.[14]

In the autumn of 1845 Manning's future never looked brighter. Gladstone had committed to him a task which would enable him to prove himself as a theologian of consequence. He had already revealed something of his consummate statesmanship. Would he now rally the broken forces of the Oxford party and bring victory in the hour of defeat? He did not wish this rôle upon himself. In his diary in November 1845, he recorded: 'I feel I have taken my last act in concert with those who are moving in Oxford. Henceforward I shall endeavour, by God's help, to act by myself, as I have done hitherto, without any alliance.'[15] Others decided for him. Time and time again his name was linked with those of Pusey and Keble. He was known to be 'safe'. And, indeed, it was seen that he was capable of supplying a type of leadership quite beyond the powers of the other two. Pusey was venerated for his resilience and courageous refusal to accept defeat. But his reputation suffered from his inability to restrain the excesses of the clergy at St Saviour's, Leeds, and he came himself to see that his voice was more often resented than acclaimed.

All confidence in me is gone [he explained to Gladstone in February 1847]. I do not mean that it has not been by own doing; still it is gone, except among some who love me, and shaken among some of those. Everything seems then to withdraw me from attempting to do anything for the Church – I mean to act upon her – as a whole. I feel myself a suspected person, go to no meetings, take part in no Societies (though I continue to subscribe). I should only make a thing suspected by taking part in it. . . . So you see I am not a physician for these days; and my medicine is stronger than people would take, so I had best keep it to myself.[16]

Manning's medicine was not, in fact, very different: confession, dogmatic firmness, love of system and authority, an ardent, compulsive yearning for sanctity. But he was more gentle and tender as a physician; he tried to keep the peace with his fellow practitioners; he did not thrust his cures upon a reluctant patient; he sometimes kept his physic hidden in his bag. It is often the way that a man who conscientiously eschews all party ties – F. D. Maurice was one, for instance – is obliged, in spite of himself, to become the spokesman of a recognisable group. This was Manning's fate. Not only did he stand out for his temperate opinions and seem capable, therefore, of achieving a reconciliation between Hook and Pusey, of keeping the Bishop of Exeter on an even keel, and of stuffing sense into the heads of the die-hards in the National Society, like George Anthony Denison; he was also regarded by many of the Anglo-Catholic clergy as the one man theologically equipped to supply them with an informed account and explanation of Roman doctrine and practice.

'Anglo-Catholic' – we use the term for want of anything better. The deeper one delves into the history of the nineteenth-century Church, the more inadequate the traditional labels appear. If the use of the word 'Evangelical' in a party sense can lead to serious misconceptions about the religious history of the first three decades of the century, then the designation of 'High Church' must be similarly understood as a loose and general description covering a conglomeration of various groups which differed greatly in their interpretation of the needs of the Church. It must embrace the robust Protestantism of Samuel Wilberforce and W. F. Hook; the indigenous and fiercely conservative Anglicanism of the Wordsworth brothers and G. A. Denison; those – like Gladstone and G. A. Selwyn – who seem to have had a foot in both camps, staunchly Anglican but intensely sympathetic to the new trends and temper; and finally the various gradations of advanced High Churchmanship which all, at some stage or another, were discredited with the misnomer of 'Puseyite': the remnant of the original Tractarians, the ecclesiologists whom Newman had mocked in *Loss and Gain*, the Anglo-Catholic element who worked to restore confession and religious orders (consciously copying the devotional methods of Rome), and, at the far end of the scale, the ritualists, who were, on the whole, a later manifestation, syncretising the Catholic enthusiasms of the other three groups, becoming more flamboyant and assured in their adoption of Catholic practices and less prone to capitulate by secession to Rome, possibly because they were beginning to witness those signs of enduring success which their predecessors, stunned by the seemingly catastrophic setback of the Gorham Judgment, had sought in vain.*

The precursors of the ritualists – those who came to the fore between 1845 and 1851 – still await their historian. The years which immediately follow the secession of Newman are too often regarded as a sort of hang-over after the feast. On the contrary, this was a period of peculiar richness, more faithful in its representation of the essence of Puseyism than were the post-Gorham decades, in which Puseyism came to be misconceived as synonymous with ritualism. Mr C. P. S. Clarke has described the years 1845 to 1857 as the period of 'Dispersion', the main object of the leaders of the movement being evangelistic. 'To attain this object', he writes, 'they put the sacramental system of the Church, including the sacrament of Penance, in a prominent place, instead of relegating it to the background, and used such Catholic adjuncts to worship as they could command.'[17]

This puts the position well. Their ideal of parochial evangelism is seen at St Saviour's, Leeds; their theological assumptions can be found in the systematic exposition of sacramental theology by Robert Wilberforce; their belief in disciplined asceticism found expression in the efforts to encourage regular confession, to gain acceptance of the right to take religious vows, to introduce a more spiritual ethos in the training of the clergy (by clerical retreats and coenobitic settlements for the clergy in urban parishes), and to promote sisterhoods – religious communities for women devoted to works of mercy – as the first stage in the revival of corporate religious life in England. In all these things, Pusey was deeply concerned. He was, through his heroism and refusal to compromise, the inspiration of this movement to infuse the Anglican Church with the Catholic spirit.

Manning's rôle was different, if no less important. His ultimate decision to seek refuge in the Roman Church may have exposed to the Puseyites who remained behind that his understanding of the organic nature of Anglicanism had fallen somewhat short of the constructive genius of

---

* After 1850, syncretism between religious groups takes three forms: (a) the synthesis of Evangelicalism and High Churchmanship as exemplified in Samuel Wilberforce; (b) the phenomenon called 'Catholic Evangelicalism', i.e. G. H. Wilkinson, Stanton, Dolling and others, recently described in Dieter Voll, *Catholic Evangelicalism* (1963); (c) the synthesis of Tractarian and Mauricean elements in both the Cambridge trio (Lightfoot, Westcott and Hort) and the *Lux Mundi* group.

Pusey and Charles Marriott.* Nevertheless he seemed to his contemporaries to have the authority and the temperament to translate theory into fact. William Dodsworth, for instance, who mistrusted Pusey's judgment on the extent to which Roman practices might be introduced into the religious life and observances of the sisterhood which he had founded with Bishop Blomfield's permission,[18] regularly resorted to Manning for practical advice. W. J. Butler allowed himself to be guided by Manning – sometimes against his better judgment[19] – in the formation of his Community of St Mary the Virgin at Wantage. Both his ecclesiastical superiors, like Phillpotts of Exeter, and his more intimate contemporaries, like Robert and Henry Wilberforce, T. W. Allies, Maskell, Upton Richards and W. J. E. Bennett, corresponded with him, or came to converse with him, on questions of policy, on theological difficulties or, most especially, on all matters relating to the *regimen animarum*.

Only those who were on terms of closest intimacy with Manning – his confessor, Laprimaudaye (curate at Lavington from 1847), Robert, Henry and Mary Wilberforce – appreciated what personal anxiety and inner conflict these constant references to his judgment involved. Not even Gladstone guessed this. The truth is that, by the summer of 1846, Manning was beginning to have doubts. This loss of confidence is marked by three events, which may be simply stated. In the first place, he decided, at the end of December 1845, not to accept the post of sub-almoner to the Queen. This was not because he had already come to suspect that the Anglican Church might be in schism, but because he feared that if he allowed himself to occupy a position which would render his elevation to the episcopate virtually inevitable, he would be succumbing to the sin of ambition and thereby preventing himself from making a cool and un-prejudiced appraisal of the claims of the Anglican Church to catholicity. He was still working on an answer to Newman's *Essay on Development*. To accept further preferment at that time, to take a step which would commit him irrevocably to the Anglican cause, would be to prejudge the issue. He wrote to Robert at considerable length on 30 December:

> I owe to you more reasons for not taking the sub-almonry than I need give to others, and therefore under the seal of the relation existing between us I will tell you. The reason I assigned is a true, real and sufficient reason. I feel that I owe it to my Flock and to my own soul to avoid absence and

* This is a view argued at length by Dr R. H. Greenfield in his unpublished D. Phil. thesis (Bodleian Library, Oxford), 'The Attitude of the Tractarians to the Roman Catholic Church 1833–1850' (1956), 494–509.

distraction at the season of Passion week and Easter. Also I feel it would be no good example among those with whom I am working to sit so loose to the Easter Communion. But beyond this.

It is no *unsettlement*, I thank God, which makes me wish to avoid new bonds. But I feel it safest for my own soul, both in regard to a clearer perception of the truth of our position,* and to a simpler line of practice to keep myself just as I am. The Lincoln's Inn affair convinced me that my duty is to have only one field and one work. And besides, I am aware that others wished me to be in a more prominent place, with kind thoughts. A word or two in your letter looked that way. This taken alone would decide me. I know myself and am afraid of secularity. In my past life I have great causes of self-reproach: and, with God's help, I propose to keep myself from all ways which are not within the compass of the Altar.[20]

The second event was Manning's realisation that he could not proceed with his refutation of Newman's theory of development. He wrote in August 1846 to tell Gladstone that he was abandoning the project, confessing that he was so shaken by recent secessions, most particularly that of the Ryder family *en masse*, that 'I have a fear, amounting to a belief, that the Church of England must split asunder.'[21] Gladstone dismissed Manning's fears by reminding him of his early confidence. He could not conceive that on a matter of magnitude he could ever differ from Manning, and 'nothing can be more firm in my mind than ... that the Church of England ... will live through her struggles, and that she has a *great* providential destiny before her'.[22]

Manning may not have been as open with Gladstone as their intimate correspondence up to this time would lead one to expect. To Laprimaudaye, two years later, he admitted that he had abandoned the task of replying to Newman because the arguments and factual details of the *Essay* had caused him to question his own earlier assumptions, as presented in his *Unity of the Church*.[23] His journals confirm this. In May 1846 he could write: 'I am conscious to myself of an extensively changed feeling towards the Church of Rome. It seems to me nearer to the truth, and the Church of England in greater peril. Our divisions seem to me to be fatal as a token, and as a disease. ... I am conscious to be less and less able to preach dogmatically. ... Though not Roman, I cease to be Anglican.'[24]

Gladstone had no notion of the extent to which the third event of significance – Manning's serious illness of February and March 1847 –

---

* Compare also the diary entry for 8 December 1845, when among the reasons for refusing the post he includes this: 'That everything which complicated my thoughts and position may affect the indifference with which I wish to resolve my mind on the great issue. Visions of a future certainly would.' E. S. Purcell, *op. cit.*, I. 279.

contributed to the loosening of the ties. *Timor mortis*, as it had with G. D. Ryder, forced him to be honest with himself. His diary during this period speaks frequently of a new conversion, in which the sins of his former life were revealed to him for his humiliation and remorse – vanity, secularity, jealousy (he had resented Laprimaudaye's more successful efforts in drawing Easter communicants). 'I have prayed that all pride, vanity, envy, jealousy, rivalry and ambition may be crucified in me; and I accept this as a nail driven into me, and desire to be wholly crucified. I had rather suffer any humiliation and disappointment than harbour the accursed shame of jealousy.'[25]

He recovered. By May he was nearly well again. It had been, it seems, a tubercular attack, with symptoms similar to those which had accompanied the last illness of his wife. The effect of this chastening was not, at least immediately, to force him to accept that his soul was in danger by remaining in the Anglican Church. Indeed, shortly after his illness, he celebrated Communion in Lavington Church and wrote in his diary: 'I never felt the power of love more: nor so much bound to my flock. It is the strongest bond I have. I believe it to be of the reality of the Catholic Church. And yet it will bear no theological argument except a denial of visible unity altogether – which is self-evidently false.'[26]

Recovery from the jaws of death impressed upon him that he had been providentially spared to effect some great work; and that the accomplishment of this work must involve a complete repudiation of all the ties of friendship, memories and comforts and all hopes of temporal rewards. Whether this meant that he was to embrace the Roman faith or not he could not say. The only answer he could make was this: 'For some time past I have been conscious of one thought enlarging itself in my mind, and one feeling expanding in my heart; that thought has been the reality of the Roman and negatively the unreality of the English Church: that feeling has been a longing to rest in the Church of Rome, and a cessation of rest in the Church of England.'[27]

This might be delusion. All he could do was to wait upon events – to listen for the voice of God. It was imperative, for the sake of his own health, that he should travel abroad, and he chose to go where he could best imbibe the spirit of Catholic piety and devotion. He would go to Belgium, Germany and France and thence to Italy for the winter months. On 5 July 1847, he wrote in his diary: 'Tomorrow by the will of God I go forth, it may be for a year, it may be for ever. I feel to be in His hands. I know not what is good for myself.'[28]

Manning's second long continental tour has been well chronicled. Much of the journal which he compiled has been reproduced by E. S. Purcell. He left as planned, was taken ill on Lake Lucerne, and returned to England in a panic lest he should die away from his friends. He set off again in October and arrived in Rome on 28 November. There was now a greater intensity, a more direct purpose, in his conversations with ecclesiastics and theologians, notably with the Abbé Gerbert, and in his visits to ceremonies, services and shrines. Everything was carefully noted. Much sunk deep into his heart. Perhaps more than anything else, more enduring in its effect than his audience with Pio Nono, was the last visit he recorded before returning home – to Milan, to the shrine of St Charles Borromeo. 'In Milan happened what I have always felt like a call from St Charles. . . . I was thinking in prayer, "if only I could know that St Charles who represents the Council of Trent was right and we wrong". The Deacon was singing the Gospel and the last words, *et erit unum ovile et unus pastor*, came upon me as if I had never heard them before.'[29]

III. *Conflicts of Heart and Head*

From 1847 until 1851, he spoke, we are told, with a 'double voice'. E. S. Purcell expressed it thus: 'Manning had, to put it broadly, two sets of people to deal with: the one set those who put their trust in him – the ecclesiastical authorities and his own penitents; the other set, those in whom he put his trust – his intimate friends and confessors. He dealt with each set from different standpoints; from the one he considered it his duty to conceal his religious doubts and difficulties; to the other he laid bare, as in conscience bound, the secrets of his soul.'[1]

This is true. But it must be remembered that during these years, Manning was going through a prolonged and bitter *anfechtung*, the outcome of which he could not foresee. Whereas Newman, in a similar state of transition and hesitation, retired to the seclusion of Littlemore, Manning felt that it would be disloyal to his calling if he made public his private misgivings before his mind was fully made up. J. E. C. Bodley has recalled how Bishop Moberly feared that when Manning visited Rome in 1847, he would return a Catholic. A letter from Manning confirmed these suspicions. He was therefore immensely relieved, on his return, to read his new archidiaconal charge in which the position of the Anglican Church was stoutly defended. 'I was so moved', Moberly wrote, 'that I wrote at once to Manning to express my relief and thankfulness on reading the charge, and the reply was "My opinions are what they were when I wrote to you from Rome. My charge is the case for the Church of England."[2]

Some may say that this was dishonest or insincere. But his attitude can be expressed differently. 'If an officer in time of warfare', Bodley writes, 'or an advocate in the course of litigation, comes to feel in his heart and conscience that the cause for which he is fighting is not the righteous one, he has no right to help the other side until he has changed his uniform, or sent back his brief.'[3] This provides an important clue to the nature of Manning's *anfechtung*. He felt 'in his heart and conscience' that he was committed to serving an unrighteous cause. Manning's heart – Bodley is suggesting – was moving Romeward more quickly than his head. With Newman it may have been otherwise. According to Newman's own testimony, he received the three calls to abandon the Church of his baptism in 1841 – appeals to his reason to lead him to suppose that the Anglican Church was in schism. He had not, however, experienced a 'change of heart'. This, indeed, seems to be the meaning of his famous denunciation of paper-logic in the *Apologia*, when he sought to explain the delay between his act of reason and his act of faith: 'It was not logic that carried me on. . . . All the logic in the world would not have made me move faster towards Rome than I did; as well might you say that I have arrived at the end of my journey, because I see the village church before me, as venture to assert that the miles, over which my soul had to pass before it got to Rome, could be annihilated, even though I had had some far clearer view than I then had, that Rome was my ultimate destination. . . . Great acts take time.'[4]

That Newman's mind was in Rome is manifest in the whole scheme of the *Essay on Development*. He set out to prove something that he knew to be true. But the length of time he actually took to make the decisive move was the measure of the emotional struggle which must be involved in that 'preparation of heart', without which no man can be a judge of religious truth.[5] How should a hearer – he once asked – judge the evidence which is offered to him? 'That the evidence is something, and not every thing; that it tells a certain way, yet might be more; he will hold, in either case: but then follows the question, what is to come of the evidence, being what it is, and this he decides according to (what is called) the state of his heart.'[6]

There were those who knew Newman well who had little doubt that his heart must sooner or later find itself in Rome. Dean Church, for instance, was familiar with the emotional appeal of Roman Catholicism, most particularly its ethos of devotion and self-sacrifice. In time it must loosen the emotional bonds which tied Newman to the Church of England. 'It was the reproduction, partial, as it might be, yet real and characteristic, in the Roman Church of the life and ways of the New Testament, which was the irresistible attraction that tore him from the associations and the affections of half a lifetime.'[7]

Manning seems to have felt the emotional pull before he was intellectually convinced. But it is not quite as simple as that. In the first place, emotional and intellectual convictions are not easily separable. Both emotionally and intellectually Manning yearned for unity, discipline and system. To him the Catholic Church must bear the marks of holiness, high sacramentalism and a true priesthood (with all the elevated connotations that word can supply). From his earliest acquaintance with Rome he satisfied himself that she bore all these marks. The question remained, did the Anglican Church bear them also? If not, did she potentially bear them? Were her manifest deficiencies more or less malignant than the known corruptions which he at first believed to exist in Rome? In August 1846 he gave the answer that wherever Anglicanism 'seems healthy it approximates the system of Rome, e.g. Roman Catholic Catechism, Confession, Guidance, Discipline'.[8] Where these things were everywhere visible in the Roman Church, they had to be sought in odd corners and out-of-the-way places in the English Church. The general picture denied the crucial test of catholicity. 'There seems about the Church of England a want of antiquity, system, fulness, intelligence, order, strength, unity; we have dogmas on paper; a ritual almost universally abandoned; no discipline, a divided episcopate, priesthood, and laity.'[9]

Secondly, although a part of Manning reached out longingly for the Catholic ethos of Rome, there was always a lingering emotional attachment to Anglicanism which nothing could eradicate. This comes out clearly in a letter to Henry Wilberforce written from Rome on Easter Tuesday 1848:

> Holy Week is just over – and I have been at all the services in the Pope's chapel. Of course I felt Easter to be very unlike Easter away from Lavington. Everything there is old and familiar and excites nothing intellectual, is no tax on one's eyes or ears. Everything there turned my mind inwardly on things seen only by Faith. Here of course intellect, attention, eyes and ears were all excited and all my thoughts were drawn outwardly upon sensible objects. I am making no comparison or judgment, but only stating the fact. Our own system is . . . unconscious to *us*, and theirs to them, but

to us it is at first a distraction. Now having said this, I must say that for majesty and beauty, simplicity and severity, I have seen and heard nothing like it. Yet in the midst of all I could have almost wept to be in Lavington Church.[10]

To Mary Wilberforce, a year later, he sent similar impressions formed during the course of his continental tour:

On Monday coming from Nice to Genoa we saw the sun rise out of the Mediterranean. We were on the heights above Monaco. It came up round, liquid and blazing – not a cloud – and the edges of the disc seemed to burn with a twofold brightness. When it rested with its full orb on the waters, I thought of the perpetual Exposition of the B.S. and the moment of breathless and awful silence, when the Monstrance is lifted at the Benediction, as I saw it in S. Luigi dei Francesi at Rome or at Aix on All Saints Night.

The hymn tunes at Nice brought back the Lavington tunes of 15 years ago, the hill-side, and the Spring evenings, the dusk and the stillness, the Evening Lecture at Graffham and at Norwood, and the world of inner thoughts, hopes, faith and happiness without a doubt or cloud. All this is now like a page in Undine.

Then as I came inside the gates of Rome on Advent Eve and said the 1st Collect I felt myself in Lavington Church with all the thoughts of Advent, and a Lavington Xtmas, the dressings of Holly, and the Altar, the Charity and Xtmas communion, alms and kindliness, bright hearths and loving faces, and the homely plain open Xtmas joy of the Church of England.

Then I thought of the severe majesty and awful near reality of the Roman Church, with its claims and its denials.[11]

The strain upon Manning during these years was terrible. Time and time again his spiritual counsel was sought. Was a soul safe within the Anglican Church?

My dearest daughter in Christ [he wrote to Mary Wilberforce, coming to him as a penitent, in Holy Week 1849], ... Nothing has ever moved me in the point of not fearing to die where I am. I feel that but for my sins I could commend my soul without a fear into the loving hands of my Redeemer.

Even though I be blind as to matters of controversy, 'I will fear no evil'. I should speak falsely if I said that anything except the fear of contradicting His will could sway me in this great choice. The world and life has [sic] too little for me to make the forsaking of the few things I have about me any great sacrifice. I am ready at an hour to go or to stay as God reveals His will.

My deep belief is that He wills me to be where I am; and all those whom He has submitted to me. Having said this I need not say what I have said before. There are points in the R.C. which I could never do more than accept as from a divine authority before which all my own belief must give place. I mean for instance the whole subject of invocations which I am persuaded is of a purely human origin. I could instance more which are to me difficulties as great as some on our side. But all this is needless. My own foundation is a belief of the Presence of our Blessed Lord in the midst of us, and that all coldness, darkness, doubt, weariness, inconstancy are my own personal faults.

If with my heart, such as it is, I were before the Altar in any church in Christendom, or at the foot of St Peter himself in Rome or Antioch I should be but what I am. The cure is from within. External changes are but on the outside. The faintest mark will not give force or aim to a slack or swerving bow. What I feel to need is energy, intensity, perseverence, zeal and love. Be our outward system as imperfect as it may these would bring 'oil out of the flinty rock'. . . . .[12]

Was it right to say prayers to the Virgin?

I feel it hard to answer [Manning wrote again to Mary in November 1848]. Certainly she is an object of our Love and Veneration. I know of no affection of heart which is not due to her. 'Son, behold thy Mother' is enough to make us her children in spirit. . . . At least I cannot think that they will lose her prayers who do not invoke her out of a loving fear of doing amiss.[13]

In an agony of mind, when memories of Caroline were pressing upon him, Manning wrote to Mary to explain that his difficulties were largely intellectual.

My most dear Mary. Your few words were very pleasant to me. And they did not seem to me to be only yours. They seemed to speak for two: as two could speak now who never thought or felt unlike each other. How often I have said 'What would she have thought of what I am doing, feeling and believing?' If it is a delusion perhaps she would have saved me. . . .

I sometimes feel as I have always said no fear to die where I am: because I cannot doubt great spiritual realities and laws. My difficulties are *intellectual and somehow impersonal*. But I see what may be said to all this. There is, I believe, one only thing I seek in life, not home, happiness, honor, power or wealth but to be daily and hourly united with God and with our Lord. If in drawing nearer to Him I am drawn or driven away from anything else, so be it. May God be with you. Pray for me; and love me still. Ever your loving brother, H.E.M.[14]

Manning was a master at concealing his emotions. The only outward signs he gave of these trials was the greater intensity of his austerity in his style of living. Slim he always was, but not yet had he developed the emaciated look which years of self-denial[15] were to stamp upon him. He

327

lived frugally – often enough a single chop was his meat for the day; he indulged himself only in the excellence of his horses (he was a superb rider) and in his delight in cats and dogs. He contemplated giving up his carriage during his illness of 1847, but decided against it. Travel was a necessity; so he redeemed the time spent, and the comfort enjoyed, in carriage journeys by having a lamp fixed inside so that he could occupy his mind in serious study.[16] There was always about him a great dignity – *gravitas*; nothing sombre or chilling. 'The trait in him which made, I think, most impression on me', wrote Captain Laprimaudaye, the father of Manning's curate, 'was a sort of quiet merriment, as though he enjoyed and appreciated anything humorous or laughable, without the hearty and boisterous accompaniment seen in others, less reserved.'[17] No one who heard him in the pulpit or on the platform could have guessed that the speaker was a man tormented by an inner conflict. What stuck in the mind was the firm, beautiful voice, the authoritative assurance, the lucidity of a speaker who had complete command over his material.

This, indeed, was so. Purcell seriously underrated Manning's intellectual powers. Doubtless Aubrey de Vere erred in the opposite direction when he described him in a sonnet as combining 'the intellect of Aquinas with the imagination of Dante'.[18] Nevertheless Robert and Henry Wilberforce both constantly referred to him for explanations of Catholic writings and assistance in dogmatic exposition. During the last five years of his Anglican life, Manning was employing every spare minute in study. If his difficulties were intellectual, it was not through any laxity in his determination to penetrate to their roots.

His writings of the 1830's revealed a very thorough understanding of patristic sources and of the Caroline divines. Henry, congratulated by Robert in 1838 for a particularly scholarly review of a theological work, wrote back to say – 'As for the learning it is chiefly H. Manning's. I read the review to him and he said there is a passage of Hammond and J. Taylor etc. However Austin and some others were my own thunder.'[19] In the 1840's he was studying Catholic writings – the Tridentine decrees, Suarez, Vasquez, Melchior Cano, Möhler, De Maistre. He was able to send Robert a detailed exposition of Perrone's lectures on Transubstantiation.[20] He never aspired to the profundity and originality of Newman, being primarily an objective thinker. But there is no doubt that he had acquired by the time of his secession a far greater knowledge of Catholic teaching and contemporary theology than Newman possessed in 1845.

At the same time, his researches into the Anglican position were taking him into a study of the nature and origin of the Royal Supremacy, into Bramhall and historical interpretations of the Constitutions of Clarendon. But where did it all lead to ? What did it all mean ? He knew that the Church of Rome was truly Catholic; he suspected that the Anglican Church was not. He, like Newman, must ask for signs: the three calls, that he might answer even as Samuel had done – 'Speak, Lord for thy servant heareth'.* And since the head interprets as the heart dictates, the end was now clearly in sight.

IV. *Samuel Wilberforce and the 'Via Media'*

Samuel Wilberforce knew little of Manning's fears and doubts. Affectionate letters passed between them from time to time, but not until April 1849 did Manning hint at any fundamental difference of opinion or give the slightest indication that there might be cause for alarm. They met fairly often, since Samuel came to Lavington whenever he could. These were the moments which Mary Sargent loved. She was still keeping house for Samuel at Cuddesdon, but her heart bled for Lavington and all its associations. Barbara Wilberforce felt the same about East Farleigh. She never came to Cuddesdon. In her old age she was very infirm and for the last few months before her death in April 1847, she clung to a few treasured memories while her reason rapidly declined.

She could hardly have been aware of Samuel's changed circumstances, that he was fast becoming a national figure. He made a triumphant maiden speech in the House of Lords in March 1846, on the transportation of convicts,[1] and found himself on a Lords' Committee to deal with Irish railroads. Again in June he was in full voice on the Corn Laws, his conscience pricking him a little that he had adopted 'too *lay*' a tone. It 'did not come up to my own estimate of the long-suffering gentleness of the Bishop', he subsequently confided to Robert. 'However we serve a gracious Lord; and I trust he will not forsake me.'[2] He was immediately swept up in the higher deliberations of the National Society in their collision with the Committee of Privy Council over the disputed management clauses, whereby Kay-Shuttleworth strove to vindicate the rights of

---

* Common practice among those on the brink of Rome. See Mary Allies, *Thomas William Allies*, 62.

conscience against those who sought to preserve the clerical domination of the National Schools.

In his diocese, Samuel's impact was immediate and highly personal. From the very first he determined to avoid all appearance of partial treatment. For this reason he dealt very stiffly with Pusey who had written to him to solicit his sympathy for the Oxford party in their trials of the moment, reproving him so sharply that their relations were upset for the next ten years. Samuel's letter was ominously pontifical. Pusey had been guilty of self-will. 'This seems to me to lead you to judge the Church which you ought to obey; sometimes to blame, sometimes almost to patronise her; and hence to fall into the further error of undervaluing the One inspired Revelation of God's will given to us in His perfect Word.' He must therefore 'watch most earnestly against self-dependence and the spirit or acts of party'; this – and a proper sense of the 'obedient reverence due to our Church' – should be 'at this moment your especial duty'.[3]

Samuel had judged Pusey rather harshly; and the rebuke may seem misconceived when one recalls that they were not writing as strangers. Perhaps each of them should have known better. The finest example, however, of Samuel's pastoral ideals and his aspirations for the diocese may be found in his primary charge delivered in the autumn of 1848. Much of this was devoted to questions of the hour: the duty of the Church to superintend any national system of education (with a splendidly chauvinistic passage on the superiority of sound English principles to the showy efficiency of Prussia 'where every rustic labourer was rapidly becoming a philosopher'[4]); the necessity of introducing legislation to provide for the speedy punishment of criminous clerks; matters relating to church rates and pew rents. But the chief message of the charge was simply this: if the Church were to fulfil her mission she must be united; and the only way to achieve this unity was to practise it first at the diocesan level, by the bishop maintaining close and regular contact with his clergy, by the clergy readily co-operating with each other, and by every member of the diocese, from the bishop downwards, widening his sympathies, trusting his fellow-workers, and prosecuting his own particular cause in a proper spirit of moderation.

Firstly the bishop, who has 'the care of all the churches':

> It is as holding, however unworthily, such an office, that I come to-day amongst you; desiring greatly to be amongst you, through the aid of God, as a partner of your labours, a sharer of your griefs, a lightener of your anxieties, a helper of your joy; earnestly entreating your prayers that

I may have grace so to fulfil the duties of my office, that, at the great day, I may give up my account with joy; and bespeaking, my reverend brethren, your forbearance towards the infirmities and errors which may attend my administration, your candid interpretation of much which, as years pass on, suspicion might distrust, or maliciousness pervert; your confidence in the singleness and simplicity of my desire to discharge its duties, as in God's sight, and your full and cheerful co-operation with me in the due fulfilment of our great common task.[5]

To secure this sense of co-operation and understanding, Samuel had introduced regular annual meetings of the rural deans at Cuddesdon 'for common prayer and common counsel', and he hoped to go even further by bringing all the diocesan clergy to annual retreats at the Palace where, after mutual counsel and prayer, their unity would be sealed by 'partaking together of the Holy Eucharist'.[6] For the clergy themselves, their chief temptation was for each incumbent to become 'a little sovereign in his own realm'.[7] Too often we 'introduce discord in maintaining truth'. 'Our duty surely is, whilst we maintain our own view to be as tolerant as possible of that of other men; to accustom ourselves, where-ever it is possible, to the charitable hope that even with their different statement of it they do hold with us the common truth; to see that certain and often very considerable discrepancies of statement are the necessary consequence of presenting a great truth to different minds.'[8]

He chose as his example the most topical issue of baptismal regeneration. Perhaps no other doctrinal controversy better illustrated the truth of the text, *knowledge puffeth up, but charity edifieth.** Pride will lead men in controversy, on the one hand into dead formalism, on the other into a gross undervaluing of sacramental power, so that both parties will blind themselves as to the truth which their adversaries apprehend, by supposing that the acknowledgement of that truth must betoken a readiness to abuse it by pushing it to extremes. Hence anger, unreasoning and uncharitable dogmatism; hence division and loss of souls.

It would be a rash man who would challenge Samuel on this score; or who would claim that he failed to practise what he preached. By virtue of his position, he was bound himself to deliver doctrinal judgments and sometimes to castigate others for false teaching. But whether these offenders were latitudinarians or Romanisers (whom he whipped soundly in his second charge in 1851),[9] they were all, on his showing, extremists who

---

* The text (1 Cor. VIII. 1.) which Samuel chose for his University Sermon of June 1847, entitled 'Pride a hindrance to true knowledge'.

were so obstinate in the prosecution of their own particular views that their influence was tending to separate rather than to bind. He may have been wrong, along with all other conventional and orthodox churchmen, in his understanding of what teaching might or might not be in the long run beneficial to the Church, but he certainly was never untrue to his principles or inconsistent in his application of them.

Gladstone, then, seems to have been in error when – in an injudicious moment – he let slip in the hearing of E. S. Purcell, the remark that 'it was not until after he became bishop that Sam Wilberforce developed his High Church views'[10]; a misunderstanding which may be explained by the facts that Gladstone knew little of Samuel's views prior to 1845 and a great deal about them thereafter, and that he came to regard Samuel as one of the few members of the episcopal bench to whom he could confide his chagrin at Lord John Russell's miserable policy of elevating fierce Low Churchmen or latitudinarian nonentities to the chief offices in the Church. When Archbishop Howley died in February 1848, having lingered at death's door to the wonderment of his doctors and the frustration of the speculators with his pulse beating only five strokes a minute,[11] Gladstone was deeply pained by the choice of J. B. Sumner as his successor. He drew nearer and nearer to Samuel, expressing his fears and hopes quite openly, building him up, at least in his own mind, as the one man with the courage and circumspection to rouse the other bishops into a true understanding of the duties of their office. It is little wonder that sometimes his sanguine hopes of Samuel's achievements led him to suppose that their ultimate objectives, and their views as to the best means to attain them, were the same.

The truth is that Samuel, as a bishop, favoured no single party, and championed no party cause. If he appealed for moderation and tolerance, this did not mean that he was timid in permitting innovations or that he discouraged men of zeal. As Owen Chadwick has written, 'Wilberforce was not in the habit of picking nonentities. . . . When he selected his men he placed an unceasing confidence in them.'[12] Recognising the deep spirituality of H. P. Liddon, he overcame his distaste for his manifest Puseyite leanings and appointed him Vice-principal of Cuddesdon. W. J. Butler, the founder of the Community of St Mary the Virgin at Wantage, was taken completely into his confidence and was appointed one of his rural deans. Samuel showed the same understanding towards T. T. Carter and R. M. Benson. He made clear the limits which he must impose on their first experiments in the revival of sisterhoods and religious communities

– to the end he objected to the imposition of vows – but once his views had been expressed, he allowed his subordinates considerable discretion, supported them when they were impugned and intervened directly in their affairs as rarely as possible.[13]

It may be that as the fears of Romanism gradually subsided and the number of secessions decreased, he was more disposed to make concessions than he had been in the late forties when confronted with the Puseyite excesses of the prickly and stubborn T. W. Allies; but he was never one-sided in his willingness to support and trust those whose views differed considerably from his own. F. W. Robertson recalled that in 1847, when he was offered the Oxford living of St Ebbe's, he felt compelled to inform the bishop that 'he did not hold, and therefore could not preach, the doctrine of baptismal regeneration'. Samuel replied by assuring him: 'I give my clergy a large circle to work in, and if they do not step beyond that, I do not interfere.' He asked Robertson to explain his difficulties and discussed the subject with him for an hour. At the close, he conceded that the other's position had been well maintained and renewed the offer of the living.[14]

Another clergyman, new to the diocese, whose religious sympathies inclined to Puseyism, received a similar reassurance from the bishop:

> I do not wish to dogmatize within the wide circle of (the Church's) formularies. All who can honestly subscribe *them* seem to me to have as much right to their views as I have to mine. . . . I had far rather see working under me a true, earnest, self-denying, loving follower of my Lord, though he differed from me on many such points, yet did in his life and doctrine set before sinners the living power of the Cross of our only Saviour, than one with whom I far more agreed in dogma, but whose devotion and love and zeal and readiness to bear and do, were languid and poor.[15]

This must not be pressed too far. At his ordinations, Samuel probed deeply in his personal examination of the candidates. He wrote to Robert in December 1846: 'I had a very satisfactory ordination – a remarkable serious earnestness, and high standard almost universal. No tractarianism – only one verging decidedly to it and he within lawful limits: only *one* loose on Baptism and he also within lawful limits. It quite cheered me.'[16] Five years later, he commented joyfully, 'not one low churchman in the set'.[17]

In prescribing the course of study for ordinands, Samuel did his best to ensure that they would be right-minded. They must study their Bible and the Greek Testament; they must know the great orthodox classics like

333

Hooker, Pearson on the Creed and Wall on Infant Baptism; they must have a good grounding in early Church history, with a sprinkling of Tertullian and St Augustine thrown in; they must receive an informed statement of popish errors through Blunt's *English Reformation*. Later, candidates for priest's orders were also examined on the bishop's own ordination addresses which ousted St Augustine's *De Doctrina Christiana* from the syllabus.[18] His examining chaplain for sixteen years, J. R. Woodford, later Bishop of Ely, has testified to the nature of Samuel's churchmanship during his years at Oxford in terms which suggest that he had changed hardly at all since the days when he chose to cross swords with Newman on the doctrine of justification.

> Upon the doctrines of Justification and Sanctification, he was in harmony with the Evangelical School rather than with Bishop Bull; in regard to the Sacramental system, he was in accord with Andrewes, Ken, Brevint; whilst the intense activity of his own mind gave the speculations of the Broad Church party an interest in his eyes, which, joined to the affectionateness of his nature, held him in the bond of sincere friendship with some of its leaders. From this character of his theology, it followed as a necessary consequence that he should be exposed to the charge of inconsistency from all sides; the fact being, that when to one school he appeared to be compromising a truth, he really so spoke and taught respecting it, because upon that special point he was in accord with the opposite school.[19]

The only change which Woodford could discern in the direction of a more advanced churchmanship, was his gradual understanding of the Eucharist as a commemorative sacrifice, counterbalanced by the more emphatically expressed conviction of the identity in effect between public and private absolution, and a greater insistence, against the contributors to *Essays and Reviews*, on the verbal inerrancy of the scriptures.

The chief aims of this scrupulous personal supervision of the ordinations were twofold. In the first place, he wished to establish from the beginning a close relationship between all his diocesan clergy and himself, in the hope that the confidences which he both invited and gave would be maintained throughout their ministry. Secondly, like his own former diocesan, C. R. Sumner, he tried to stress in every way possible the spiritual nature of the Embertides, to convert them from formal examinations in the cathedral city into retreats held at the bishop's palace. Sometimes the ordinations would be held in a large town in the diocese, perhaps in an area where one of the bishop's Lenten missions had been held (an unusual practice in those days) to try to bring home to congregations

334

who had never witnessed such an event the solemnity and inner significance of the ceremony.[20]

The project dearest to Samuel's heart, however, was the establishment of a diocesan theological college. The idea was pressed upon him originally by Robert, who wrote to him within a week of hearing the news of Samuel's elevation to the episcopate: 'I see that you will have a very large Diocese. I wish that you would establish a Theological seminary in it, where all your young men should be for two years to learn Theology and to acquire devotional habits. But the existence of the University in your Diocese is rather an impediment to such a design.'[21]

The story of the foundation of Cuddesdon, in the year 1854, really lies outside the scope of this study, and it has already found a gifted and sympathetic historian. Two points, however, may be observed. The college was to be under episcopal control and management, and was near enough to the palace for the bishop to maintain the close personal contact with the ordinands which Samuel so eagerly sought. On the other hand, the students were no part of the bishop's *familia*. He set out his aim most plainly: to 'rear therein ripened clergymen with the spirit of Richard Hooker and the temper of Lancelot Andrewes'.[22] His principal and vice-principal were given wide discretion in the means they chose to realise this aim. Sometimes they offended Samuel in their inculcation of an unmanly and un-English seminary tone,[23] but although he might remonstrate privately, and occasionally exact conditions,[24] he boldly and willingly took their part against the mischievous and strident accusations of G. P. Golightly, the erstwhile champion of the Martyrs' Memorial.

The transformation of the Oxford diocese, the deeper spirituality discernible in every aspect of religious life within a few years of Samuel's arrival, must be one of the most remarkable examples of what a single man can achieve through tenacity of purpose, high principles and unrelenting physical and mental effort. For those who were prepared to respond and co-operate with him, the experience was electrifying. Christopher Wordsworth, later Bishop of Lincoln, was one such. His daughter described the effect thus:

> No one who recalls those days will ever forget the magical effect of his presence – like the coming of spring to a winter landscape – in the little nooks and corners of that agricultural county, his thrilling confirmation addresses, his cordial appreciation of what was done by others, the brilliant wit of his conversation, the inimitable force of his wonderfully-modulated voice, and the fascination of his look and manner.[25] How much of the poetry,

life and enthusiasm of Church work is due to Bishop Wilberforce; how much also of its organisation and practical development! And it was a happy thing for the future bishop of an agricultural diocese like Lincoln that his work at Stanford brought him not only into contact with a poor and neglected country population, but with that kindling and stimulating spirit, so far in advance of his age in his conception of the duties of an English bishop, and so marvellously endowed with the power of carrying those conceptions out in active life.[26]

The pressure of work and engagements upon him was intense. He was no less ready than he had been before to preach for the S.P.G., to attend committee meetings and rallies; and now were added his extra-diocesan duties – attendance at the Ecclesiastical Commission, frequent appearances at the House of Lords and – from the middle fifties onwards – at Convocation, in which he became the acknowledged leader of the Upper House. His correspondence was immense. Burgon has left a vivid picture of how Samuel would press-gang any clergy who might be visiting him to assist him and his chaplains with the mass of letters which poured in by every post, sometimes dealing with 'forty, fifty, sixty letters' between an afternoon conference and the time for changing for dinner.[27] Many letters he wrote in his own hand – often in the train, bumping and jostling from one engagement to another. In December 1859 Gladstone wrote to him teasingly to enquire 'what state your fingers are in during this cold weather after you have written your average of 40 letters'.[28]

One example will suffice: in huge letters scrawled across three sheets, this terse communication to one of his closest friends among the Oxford clergy, T. V. Fosbery, who had ventured to suggest that the bishop might like to speak at the opening of an industrial exhibition.

> My dearest Fosbery, I quite approve – I must return. I have *no conception* what to speak about – I do not know what an Industrial Exhibition is. Pray tell me all about what I am to say unless what would be far better you would run down here (Lavington) Monday and come back with me Wednesday. I am most truly your very affectionate S. Oxon.[29]

So much of Samuel's character is captured in this one brief letter: his assurance, his geniality, his gift of spontaneity, his great heart. It also reveals his tendency – occasionally catastrophic – to speak or declaim on public issues just as the spirit moved him, to commit himself to a course of action before he had thought out the possible consequences. In short, what was his greatest gift was also sometimes his bane. It was exactly this impulsiveness and restless impatience to solve a dilemma in an instant, which led him into the two major collisions of the early years of his episcopate, when he clashed successively with R. D. Hampden and T. W. Allies. Both episodes have a significant bearing on this narrative.

v. *R. D. Hampden and T. W. Allies*

In the years since the storm over his Regius professorship, R. D. Hampden had not materially added to his stock of heterodox views and had kept reasonably clear of controversy, save for his willingness to vote in Convocation against his former foes. If, however, he had not made himself more offensive to orthodox minds in these intervening years, he had certainly not made himself less so. He had retracted not a word. That he had a second time to face the fury of affronted churchmen was thanks to the monumental tactlessness – or subtle malevolence – of the Prime Minister, Lord John Russell.

The facts, in brief, are these. In November 1847 Russell nominated Dr Hampden to the bishopric of Hereford, on receipt of which 'appalling intelligence' (as Phillpotts put it), the Church reeled, fumed in the persons of its most articulate members of both the High and the Low persuasion, and prepared to fight to the last ditch. That Samuel should have fumed along with the many is not surprising. He had joined the Tractarians in their battle over the Regius professorship. As Bishop of Oxford, he was obliged to play a leading part in this second contest since Hampden was in his diocese (although, as professor, exempt from his jurisdiction) and the move to compel him to retract his alleged Socinian views was initiated by a group of Oxfordshire clergy. The matter was further complicated by Samuel's awareness that his most intimate friends and relations were all looking to him to save the Church from the most terrible humiliation through the wayward exercise of the Royal Supremacy which, if he did nothing to avert, might increase the doubts, which he knew Henry to possess and feared that Manning and Robert might share also, of the Church of England's claim to catholicity.

Manning put the point exactly in a long letter written from Rome in December of that year:

> This Hampden affair is a grave one, involving the highest relations of the Church and Civil Power and the most vital principles of the Church. Of all the questions I can remember it is the most decisive. Others, as National Education etc., are more extensive, but this is the most critical. The last 12 years have been preparing for it, and I trust that it may be so

treated as to lay a more Christian basis for the future action of the Spiritual and Civil powers. Though not the best mode of selecting Bishops, the recommendation of the Crown is in England not a point to be contested, but the compulsory election and consecration under pain of praemunire, for such it is in effect, is unrighteous and fatal to the Church. The moral force of their law is now put to the test. I am rejoiced to see that you and so many have taken a decisive step. Had Hampden been received and consecrated with acquiescence, I believe it would have either caused a schism, or a secession of the gravest character. It is monstrous and unspeakably irreverent towards Him who is the Head of the Body that the Bishops of the Church should be chosen by any layman who may chance to lead the House of Commons. It is worthy of the age when courtesans made Popes.[1]

Samuel's first efforts were made in concert with twelve other bishops who addressed a remonstrance to the Prime Minister. Russell replied by denying the justice of their protest and refusing to withdraw his nomination. Samuel then wrote to him personally, asking him to allow Hampden to clear himself of the charges of heterodox teaching before some competent tribunal, citing as a precedent the recent case of James Prince Lee, Bishop of Manchester, who before accepting nomination to the newly-created see appeared before a court to clear himself of charges of immorality which had been mischievously alleged against him.[2] This again was refused. What next? Intentions were expressed to refuse the Queen's *congé d'élire*; to oppose the confirmation of the election (if forced upon the chapter) at Bow Church. Proceedings might be taken against Hampden under the Church Discipline Act of 1840, by obtaining Letters of Request from Hampden's diocesan, which would initiate a trial before the Court of Arches. It was at this stage that Samuel began to blunder.

In the first place, he signed – on 16 December 1847 – the Letters of Request. It seemed doubtful at the time whether he could do otherwise, for the original promoters might have used the weapon of *mandamus* to put compulsion upon him. In the meantime he decided to tackle Hampden himself by writing privately to exhort him to make a voluntary retraction of the errors alleged against him, asking him also to withdraw from circulation his Bampton Lectures and his *Observations on Dissent*, the two works on which the charges of heterodoxy had been grounded. He asked Hampden to do this 'for the peace of the Church and in deference to the expressed opinion of your Bishop and others', not thereby admitting that they contained false doctrine.[3]

Samuel was taking a risk, of course. If Hampden had agreed, then the

338

suit in the Court of Arches could have been terminated, and affronted consciences would have been soothed. Unfortunately Hampden thought the letter was an insult, an opinion shared by Russell, and replied in masterly fashion, evading all the particular questions asked, so that Samuel was back where he started.

He then made three disquieting discoveries. He heard from Hawkins, Provost of Oriel, that Hampden had some time earlier attempted to withdraw his obnoxious pamphlet on Dissent (the *Observations*), and that any copies then circulating were doing so without his sanction. This meant that the charges of heterodoxy could be based only on the Bampton Lectures, a much less provocative work and one from which it would be exceedingly difficult to prove Socinian leanings. Samuel then turned to a serious study of the Bampton Lectures, which apparently he had not previously read, and made his second – more alarming – discovery. He found no heresy in them. Thirdly, on consulting his legal advisor, he was told that he had no right to issue Letters of Request unless he himself believed that there was a *prima facie* case for supposing the teaching of Hampden to be heretical, whereas he had previously regarded the issuing of the Letters as involving no judgment of any kind on his own part, but merely the fulfilment of a ministerial duty, which he could be compelled to discharge by writ of *mandamus*.

Faced with these revelations, he was bound to withdraw the Letters of Request, and – using Hawkins as his go-between – he tried to make his peace with Hampden on the best possible terms, by persuading him to issue some sort of eirenicon which might assure his opponents that he never had intended to deny the fundamental formularies of the Church. But Hampden had now taken legal advice and was determined to say nothing. When Samuel addressed a letter of enormous length to him on 28 December, in which he made the fatal admission that, having examined the Bampton Lectures, 'I am bound to declare . . . that they do not justly warrant those suspicions of unsoundness to which they have given rise,'[4] then Hampden had victory in his hands. On the publication in *The Times* of this letter, the storm of abuse broke out anew and was directed against Samuel. High Churchmen – like Phillpotts – were appalled at his concessions and by his presumption in judging the case himself; the friends of Hampden accused him of trying to extract concessions only in order to save his own face. The popular opinion was expressed succinctly by Greville in his *Memoirs*:

Sly Sam of Oxford (my would-be director and confessor) has covered himself with ridicule and disgrace. The disgrace is the greater because everybody sees through his motives: he has got into a scrape at Court and is trying to scramble out of it; there, however, he is found out, and his favour seems to have been long waning. The Duke of Bedford tells me the Queen and Prince are in a state of hot zeal in this matter.[5]

This was ungenerous in the extreme. Samuel's only fault had been to allow himself to be advised by others without first checking for himself the validity of their charges against Hampden and the actual legal significance of the Letters of Request which he should never have issued. A more cautious man would not have tried to solve the whole question himself by making a direct approach to the other party; a less honest man would not have publicly admitted his errors when he discovered the rashness of what he had done. Nevertheless Greville seems to have been right when he wrote that Samuel lost his intimate connection with the Court through the mishandling of this affair. He may too have put his chances of further preferment in jeopardy. He himself confessed to Robert, when the public execration against him was at its height: 'I believe myself to have given up all that men call worldly promotion when I signed the Remonstrance against Hampden; and now, I fear, many suppose me, when I was afraid of acting unjustly, to have acted from low cunning or cowardice.'[6]

One of Samuel's chaplains, by name Bayley, writing many years after the event to Woodford, Bishop of Ely, confirmed this impression.

> During this time I was continually at the Palace and was in the habit of seeing the Bishop 3 times a day when he was there. The Bishop was very free and open in his communications with his curates upon things grave and gay. My first recollection of him in connexion with the Hampden affair was after a large breakfast party at the Palace. The Bishop was standing on the hearth rug with his back to the fire ... expounding his views of Hampden's heresy and his unfitness to be a Bishop. I think that some one asked him whether he meant to proceed against him, and that his answer was that he did not proceed against him directly, but that he had sanctioned the commencement of proceedings against him. At all events the impression left upon my mind is that Bp. Wilberforce *strongly* advocated its being the duty of *all* to use every means to stay the appointment.
>
> A declaration in support of this view was got up in the Rural Deaneries. I think that only 2 persons refused to sign in my Deanery, of whom I was one. The Bishop asked me soon after the breakfast if I had signed – and I told him that I did not like to sign, as I knew so little of the question and particularly (this I distinctly remember) because I had not read Hampden's book. I think the Bishop advised me to read Newman's pamphlet.
>
> A few evenings afterwards I went up as usual to read Prayers at the

Palace. The Bishop met me in the passage with the words 'I have changed my mind about Hampden' and on my expressing surprise he said 'For 3 days I have been most carefully studying his book which I had not read through before – and I am now convinced that although he is unsound in his views there are not sufficient grounds for proceeding against him.' I said, 'What does your Lordship mean to do!' He answered, 'I have written to the Times – the letter will appear tomorrow' – I went on to say – 'What will the public say to this?' His reply was, 'I must expect to be abused, but anything the World may say is as nothing to having a good conscience.'

I remember that during the whole period he was very much depressed and preoccupied – and at the next ordination his addresses lacked their usual life and power. I have no recollection of any further details until a year or two later.... In a long ride I had with the Bishop he talked freely about the Hampden business – and complained that so many had misunderstood him. He said, 'men charge me with being a time-server when I changed my front and say that in abandoning the proceedings I was only acting with a view to regain favour at Court. My dear Bayley', he said, '*I knew that I had everything before me*, and when I went against Hampden *I knew that I had forfeited all*. How can they charge me with selfish motives when I had already sacrificed everything to what I felt to be a duty. I made a mistake, I admit – but my motives were pure all through.'[7]

Samuel was heartened by the love and sympathy shown to him by his friends. Manning wrote from Rome as soon as he heard the news.

My dearest Bishop, . . . You will believe me that I had thought much of you. . . . I may say that with a very affectionate sympathy I felt with and for you. Knowing how hard it is to determine with all evidence before one, and on the spot, I felt assured that I could form no real estimate of the case you had to decide. I can of course have no sufficient idea of such responsibilities as yours, but every one can imagine from their lesser experience how harassing are the weighings of a case pregnant, either way, with public and future consequences. One thing I am sure of, that what you have done, you believe to be just, and right. And I can see how the points on which in our brotherly conferences we have varied in judgement make the line you have taken consistent with previous views. It is great joy to me, parted as we are by lands and seas, to know that howsoever we have thought differently we have always loved and trusted each other. I feel to need this at your hands so much that it is not more my duty than my interest to give you this pledge in the fullest, largest and most loving way I can. May He who alone is wise ever guide you, as I ask, though too feebly, day and night. . . . Believe me, my dearest Bishop, your loving brother, H.E.M.[8]

Rarely can a fundamental difference of viewpoint have been expressed so tenderly and affectionately. What Samuel could not have known, however, was that Manning, as he expressed himself to Robert, was 'grieved beyond measure about our brother's share in the Hampden matter'[9]; that for him the whole episcopate had partaken in Hampden's heterodoxy by acquiescing in his consecration, and that this accordingly marked 'the separation of the English episcopate from the whole episcopate under heaven'. This affair 'brought out a miserable truth, namely, that the civil power is the ultimate judge of doctrine in England, a principle which is not more heretical than atheistical'.[10] He interpreted the catastrophe as the first clear call for which he had been waiting.

Robert could not go the whole way with Samuel over this. He would not concede that Hampden was not heterodox in his views, especially in his notion that 'tho' we might talk about the Xtian religion with perfect propriety, yet that we must not suppose that there was any objective truth in it, for that it was only an accommodation to our views and very likely the reality was something very different from anything which we expected'.[11] He conceded that Hampden was not guilty of 'intentional Socinianism', and thought Newman had been unfair in his original attack, but he thought it vicious of Hampden to refuse to make some public statement which might soothe troubled consciences.[12] As for the public outcry against Samuel, Robert deplored the meanness and unfairness of those who condemned without true knowledge. He sent Samuel a riddle to try to cheer him up. ('Why are walnuts like Protectionists? They are so troublesome to Peel.'[13])

The affair of T. W. Allies received less public notice and in no way injured Samuel's position and prospects; but it revealed the width of the gulf between Samuel and his brothers and therefore did more to lead to the rupture of the family circle. Allies was, indeed, a very tiresome man. He had proved a sore trial to Blomfield, as his chaplain, and had been despatched to the rustic obscurity of Launton in the diocese of Oxford in the hope that seclusion and an ignorant, bucolic congregation would help him to see sense. All it achieved was to increase his frustration and provide a genuine grievance to a man of peevish and querulous disposition. A considerable scholar, he was denied an appreciative audience; an advanced High Churchman, largely through the influence of Dodsworth and the writings of Newman and Ward, he found himself in the position of F. W. Faber – confronted with an unruly flock, but prevented from supplying a remedial spiritual discipline because the instruments which he had come to accept as efficacious were repudiated and condemned by ecclesiastical authority. In a state of impotent fury he had taken a fortnight's holiday in France in August 1847 and had been completely over-whelmed by his first encounter with a truly Catholic ethos. On his return he had already overcome the traditional prejudices against the Virgin Mary, the Mass and Catholic ritual and was sickened by the inherent puritanism of the Anglican Church. It would not be long before he gave vent to his pique. He studied the Fathers, published a volume of advanced Tractarian sermons and sought Newman as his spiritual director. By 1844 he had reached the conclusion 'that post-baptismal sin required sacramental confession and absolution'.[14] A reading of Ward's *Ideal* convinced him that the Church of England was not merely 'a machine out of order' but was rather 'a monster with two heads and no feet'.[15]

The Church of England must be put to the test. His first experiment was patristic. Could the Anglican Church be said to possess the faith as transmitted by the Fathers? In 1846 he thought it could, and wrote *The Church of England Cleared from the Charge of Schism* to demonstrate this. When he turned to prepare a more detailed second edition, his heart began to pull decisively in the opposite direction. Anglicanism was a sham; its ethos was stifling.[16] He now drew nearer to Manning and was bidden by him to await 'the three calls'.[17] He began studying Catholic theologians and conversing with Catholics during further travels abroad. In 1848 he resolved to issue a challenge such as Ward had done when he published the *Ideal*. After consultation with various friends – including Manning and Henry Wilberforce* – he decided to go ahead. Early in 1849 his *Journal of the Tour in France*, compiled during a visit in 1845, was given to the public, and Allies then awaited the storm which Manning, Henry Wilberforce and Upton Richards had all predicted.[18]

Samuel unleashed it. He was bound to do so. He had taken note of Allies as early as 1847 when he had received from his pen what he adjudged to be a haughty complaint against the Vicar of Bicester for unsound teaching on baptism. He had retaliated smartly by pointing out to Allies that it was not his place to judge his brothers, or to require explanations from his spiritual superiors. 'Surely this is scarcely, even in your estimate of yourself, the fitting relative position for a Bishop and one of the youngest of his presbyters.'[19] Allies did not know, however, that Samuel had followed up his complaint and privately admonished the Vicar of Bicester, pointing out 'I cannot effectually guard the purity of the faith, in that portion of the Church committed to me, from

---

* Manning was against publication.

dishonesty of subscription on the side of Romanizers, if I wink at a like sin on the side of Puritanizers.'[20]

Now Samuel was to maintain – very reasonably – that Allies's *Journal in France* amounted 'to a categorical denial of our dogmatic formularies' and demanded an unqualified retraction. A very lengthy correspondence ensued in which Allies refused to submit to the bishop's demands, which he alleged were beyond the scope of his office, and Samuel's tone became more menacing.[21] In April 1849 Samuel resolved to take the case into the Court of Arches, but was restrained at the last minute by the intervention of Lord Alderson, a mutual friend of the two contestants, who, after urgent discussions with Manning, Pusey, Edward Coleridge and Upton Richards, pleaded with Samuel to agree to a compromise whereby schism within the Church might be averted. Allies agreed to publish a guarded apology for incurring the censure of his bishop and to pledge himself to the teaching of the Thirty-nine Articles 'in their plain, literal and grammatical sense'. He also undertook not to publish a second edition of the offending book.[22] Samuel accepted this submission. In fact, it meant little. Within four months Allies had resigned his living and three days later was received – at Newman's hands – into the Roman Church. He, with many others, had found in the humiliation of the Gorham Judgment the final witness against the Church of England.

There could have been no other outcome. Samuel had seen in Allies the same temper of mind which Ward had displayed, and for Ward he had nourished – and continued to nourish – the profoundest contempt.* Sincere doubts, anxious enquiries – these he could meet and try to allay tenderly and solicitously; but arrogance and the disposition to matricide were unforgivable. Keble, on the whole, agreed with him, though expressing his feelings more gently. 'I cannot see', he wrote to Allies, after reading the *Journal in France*, 'why we may not acknowledge God's good gifts to another portion of His Church, without in any degree disparaging what He has done, and we trust is doing, for ourselves.'[23]

Samuel failed to appreciate that a hit at Allies would bruise both Henry

---

* See his description of Ward, whom he saw in August 1846, in a letter to Robert (Wrangham MSS. VI. 299): 'As I came away just now who should I meet in the station but WARD with Dr Cox, the Principal of a R.C. St Edmund's Coll: at Old Hall near here. Ward has grown fatter than ever: he has a chin and a dew lap like a bull's and looks as if he could be melted down into a whole shipload of grease – Certainly he begins his (pretended) ascetic life with an almost unlimited accumulation of Protestant fat to sacrifice in the cause of non-naturalism. I heard him state to Dr Cox that Oakeley was well read in the Father's Fudge.'

and Manning. At the consecration of St Saviour's, Leeds, in 1845, Allies and Henry had met and discovered much of mutual concern. Allies recorded in his diary:

> Henry Wilberforce ... said: 'I am fairly vexed – done in my parish. I feel we can do nothing in the Church of England without confession, but how we are to get it I see not.' He expressed the highest opinion of J.H.N. 'I consider N. the greatest blessing God ever gave to any Church.' Considered Manning the best spiritual guide we have; superior to Pusey as having more judgement. I said I could not understand Manning's inordinate opinion of the Anglican Church. He replied that M. had, however, a very deep sense of her corruption. . . . H. Wilberforce is one of the most thorough and decided persons I have met with. It was a comfort to find his experience and his opinion so exactly coincided with my own.[24]

In 1848 Allies consulted Manning and Henry together on the state of the Church. Having agreed on the lack of theology and effective spiritual discipline, they turned to the general situation. Allies recorded:

> As far as I can judge, M. and H.W. are as little satisfied with the present state of things among us, as little able to see their way, as much embarrassed to give a *rationale* of the phenomena on both sides which will completely satisfy their hearts and consciences, as myself. M. is cautious, and H.W. impetuous, but I think there is not much difference of view in them at bottom, or with myself.[25]

All this had been withheld from Samuel. The publication of the *Journal in France* and Samuel's decision to prosecute its author, therefore, caused acute embarrassment. In the first place, Allies was acting towards Manning rather in the way in which Ward had acted towards Newman; he was forcing his leader to accept the ultimate logic of his teaching. Secondly, once Samuel attacked Allies, Manning was bound to come to his friend's defence and reveal to Samuel more than he wished to disclose.

He first wrote to Samuel on this issue in April 1849, linking the proposed proceedings against Allies to the crisis brought upon the Church by the action of the Bishop of Exeter in allowing his refusal to institute G. C. Gorham to the living of Bramford Speke (on the grounds of his Calvinistic understanding of baptismal regeneration) to develop into a *cause célèbre*.

> About Allies' book. There is much in it I wish both out, and otherwise. But I look with grave apprehension at any opening of such questions, the deepest, highest, most sacred, most critically vital by a Legal Tribunal especially such as ours, and above all at this time. The state of our ecclesi-

astical law, and lawyers, and emphatically in the presence of Sir H. J. Fust,* is such as to cause just alarm at the thought of questions of doctrine, and Faith, being brought to issue. One Gorham case is enough for one day.[26]

Manning took Allies's part more plainly in a letter written on 16 May, turning to a discussion of the *Journal in France*:

I am convinced –
1. That it contains no Roman doctrine properly so called.
2. That it contains no proposition or word contrary to the Catholic Faith.
3. That it contains no doctrinal statement at variance with the 39 Articles.

In language, sentiment, and opinion there may be parts which in the present state of feeling, in the present disorder of our Ecclesiastical courts, and in the present confusion of our Theological interpretations, might give occasion to an adverse judgment.

But I believe that such a judgment would put not so much Allies' book in opposition to the 39 Articles as the 39 Articles, and the living Church of England, in opposition to the Faith of the whole Church, both East and West, according to Bishop Ken's rule, before the division and from the beginning.

It is not therefore Allies' book nor Allies himself that is alone at stake. I have his expressed repeated declaration both by word and writing that he does not hold any doctrine in which the Roman Church differs from the East and from ourselves; but that his agreements with Rome are in points of faith, where Rome agrees with all alike. His statements on the Royal Supremacy, and on Transubstantiation are full evidence on these two points.

Indeed the whole book in defence of the Church of England against the charge of schism is one direct and continuous proof throughout. And it is a work which, so far as I know, stands alone, for completeness, honesty, and truth.

Any judgment, therefore, against Allies upon the language of his journal, these facts standing, would be a manifest injustice.[27]

Foremost in Manning's mind was the dread lest Samuel's action against Allies should lead to further secessions. If Allies were driven into Rome, what would his own position be? Tortured by doubts as he was, Manning counselled caution. He instructed his penitents to wait for a clearer revelation of God's will.

* Dean of the Arches, who was presiding over the initial hearing of Gorham's case, in the action brought by Gorham against Phillpotts to compel him to show just cause for withholding institution. Fust gave judgment for Phillpotts. The case then went, on appeal, to the Judicial Committee of the Privy Council.

VI. *The Crisis of the Gorham Judgment*

By 1849 the Wilberforce circle was on the point of disintegration. Henry and Mary were looking to Manning for guidance, and Samuel feared that the regular correspondence with Newman which Henry maintained was beginning to have its effect. He persuaded them both to come to Cuddesdon to stay with him in November and sent a report on their state to Robert.

> Henry and Mary are still here i.e. the latter having been at E. Farleigh since Wednesday. He has been very kind with me this time; but there is a manifestly increased holding back of opinions, more than there was, which is both painful for the present and I fear ominous for the future. I had one conversation with him. *The* point is 'Are we in schism?' the Eastern Church in schism; all but Rome in schism. The influence I take it is still Newman's and that correspondence which I think he ought to have given up as a matter of duty. He is manifestly less sensitive than he was about mariolatry and he and Mary both talk great nonsense about the awful neglect of the blessed virgin – and Mary last night told me she did not the least believe she had ever died. . . . How grievous is dear H.'s perversion of mind. May God still keep him right.[1]

For several years Samuel had felt that he and Henry were beginning to speak a different language.[2] He was also beginning to have fears about Manning's influence over Robert, knowing that it was his brother's way to underrate his own intellectual powers, thereby exposing himself to the danger of being 'led away by Manning's subtleties'.[3]

During the late 1840's Robert was giving more and more of his time to theological study, the demands of which to some extent preserved him from the frustration and instability which were tormenting Henry. This is not to say that he was free from anxiety and doubt. After the fiasco of the Hampden controversy, he felt so low and dispirited that Samuel had to write to persuade him that the contest was really a victory after all.

> My dearest brother, there is an expression in your letter which fills me with sadness. You must not say your 'hopes and purposes are frustrated'. Surely you have been let to do already more than most men do in a whole life: and if in the evil days we are fallen on we cannot *restore* all the breaches for which we moan, we ought not therefore to let even a sad thought whisper evacuating the citadel. After all *the* question I suppose is: not is there great evil amongst us? Where is there not? but have we the presence of Christ through His Holy Sacraments: if so we may not leave our place whatever goes wrong. On the whole I think . . . that so much *life* has been shown in the Church as to be very encouraging. Surely it is plain that if anything

heretical could have been brought home to Hampden legally ... the minister could *not* have caused his appointment. It is I think clear that the monarchy and with it all our institutions are in the utmost peril. Now anything which leads the Church to weaken the Crown instead of strengthening it, is helping on that evil and *therefore* I feel that anything we can do to *stay* an increase of separation of Church and State it is our duty to do. ... It is I think clear that in this last struggle we have gained not lost; Lord John is universally condemned and if anyone were ready to take his place he would have lost his premiership in this affair. This will not be forgotten or ineffectual.[4]

This was hopelessly sanguine on Samuel's part. A little over a year later the Church had to swallow the elevation of Samuel Hinds, chaplain to Archbishop Whately and a suspected Sabellian, to the bishopric of Norwich; and as the Gorham case worked its weary way from the Court of Arches into the Judicial Committee of the Privy Council, it became increasingly clear that the Royal Supremacy could exercise powers even more obnoxious than the appointment of heterodox bishops. In addition to this, Robert's personal loyalties were being severely tried. He was torn between his love for Samuel and his profound respect for Manning's learning. His wife Jane had such a horror of Romanism that he dared not communicate his troubles to her. William Henn, the curate with whom he had enjoyed the closest *rapport*, had left him in order to convalesce on the Continent after a serious illness, and was himself hovering on the brink of the Roman Church, writing regularly to persuade Robert that he must abandon a sinking ship. His new archbishop – Musgrave – was hostile to him and attacked his teaching in his primary charge of 1849. His own advance into Anglo-Catholicism had led to strained relations with W. F. Hook, who poured out all his fury at Puseyism and its vicious effects in Leeds on the nearest eminent adherent whom he could find. No wonder Robert took refuge in his books.

Both Robert and Manning dreaded the advent of another Hampden crisis which might force the one to come out into the open and the other to concede that God had called him yet again. The Gorham controversy turned out to be just such an event. The full horror of its implications was pressed upon the Anglo-Catholics at the moment when Gorham, defeated in the Court of Arches in August 1849, appealed to the Judicial Committee of the Privy Council. At once a case, which had since its beginnings in December 1847 always been fraught with significant consequences, became – as Gladstone described it to Manning – 'a stupendous issue'.[5] For every party in the Church the decision, and the mode of arriving at it, involved a fundamental principle. A decision favourable to the Bishop of Exeter would have condemned a Calvinistic interpretation of the Thirty-nine Articles and might have led to a disruption from the Establishment comparable to that of the Presbyterians in 1662 or to the Methodists a century later. It would also have been the death-blow to latitudinarianism, since it would have repudiated the first principle of the Broad Church party – that the Church of England was essentially undogmatic, permitting the widest possible latitude in the interpretation of its formularies.

For the High Church party, the Gorham case presented two major problems. In the first place, there was the original doctrinal issue raised by Phillpotts himself. If the Privy Council were to uphold Gorham's claim that a bishop had no right to insist upon a particular interpretation of article XXVII (on baptism) and hence on articles XXV to XXIX (all referring to the reception of sacraments), then the Church of England's claim to be the guardian of apostolic teaching would be even more questionable than it had been before. Secondly, the very fact that the point at issue was brought before a secular tribunal demonstrated that the Royal Supremacy – irrespective of what judgment might be pronounced by virtue of its authority – could violate the divine office of the Church by determining the limits of its teaching.[6] Thus in two respects the Gorham case brought to a head the most contentious issues of the preceding decades – in the realm of doctrine, the meaning of baptismal regeneration and the function of the sacraments; in the realm of authority, the precise relationship between the Royal Supremacy and the teaching office of the Church.

Those who felt that the crux of the issue was the doctrinal question waited anxiously for the judgment. From a sermon which he preached at St Barnabas, Pimlico, early in 1850, it appears that Henry Wilberforce put the doctrinal consideration first. He exhorted the bishops to 'defend the sacrament of baptism against attack, and to preserve the unity of the faith'.[7] But in fact, he – like Manning – fully appreciated that the Anglo-Catholic position would be completely undermined if the Church were to accept the Privy Council's judgment, whether favourable to Phillpotts or not. In December 1849 he observed to Robert: 'I can't for the life of me feel that it makes personally *to me* much difference which way it goes. The fact that such a cause is to be decided by such a court is the one great symptom which seems far to outweigh the consideration *which way they may* decide it. How long, Lord, how long.'[8] He adhered to the same opinion two months later when the unofficial news of the adverse judgment leaked out.[9]

Manning was the most forthright in expressing this view. On 24 January 1850 he tried to explain his convictions to Samuel. He began by defining the principles on which he based his submission to the Anglican Church. Until that time he had believed that the Church in England, by being a member of Christ's kingdom, possessed the 'full and supreme custody of doctrine and power of discipline, under the same guarantee and guidance with the whole Church at large', and also 'that the Church in England being thus an integral whole has the fountain of doctrine and discipline within itself; and has no need to go beyond itself for succession, orders, mission, jurisdiction, and custody of Catholic Tradition'. Where did the Royal Supremacy fit in?

> The office and relation of the Civil Power towards the Church in England is to protect, uphold, affirm, and further this sole, supreme and absolute Character and office in all matters of doctrine, and of discipline. In this sense I have accepted and interpreted expressly or implicitly our whole ecclesiastical law: and I can accept it in no other sense either expressly or by silence. . . . The Royal Supremacy is therefore strictly and simply *civil*. And in no sense spiritual or *ecclesiastical*, understanding that word to mean concurrent or mixed spiritual jurisdiction.
>
> It seems to me
>
> (1) That the claim of the Crown in the confirmation of Dr Hampden to the see of Hereford is a violation of the divine office of the Church in respect to its discipline.
>
> (2) That the pending appeal to the Judicial Committee of the Privy Council is a violation of the divine office of the Church in respect to its doctrine.
>
> I say the *appeal* – because it is indifferent which way the judgment may go. Indeed a decision in favour of the true doctrine of Baptism would mislead many. A judgment right in matter cannot heal a wrong in the principle of the Appeal. And the wrong is this: 'The Appeal removes the final decision of a question involving both doctrine and discipline out of the Church to another centre and that a Civil Court.'[10]

He posed the same question to many others, and received different answers. James Hope told him that he had been deluded by a wrong understanding of the history of the Supremacy. The circumstances of both the Hampden and the Gorham cases had been implicit in the Royal Supremacy *ab initio*. 'If you have not hitherto read Erastianism in the history of the Church of England since the Reformation, then I fear you and I have much to discuss before we can meet on common ground.'[11]

Samuel and Robert both thought Manning was displaying an unnecessary alarm. He was prejudging the issue.

> I cannot suppose [Robert wrote] that any lawyer or court would say that the Oath of Supremacy gave the Crown a right to settle points of doctrine. This seems precluded by the preamble of 24 H. VIII c. 12, and by the Royal Declaration prefixed to the Articles. The Crown can only act for a time on what the Church has decided. And it is the fault of our heads if they let the legislative powers be virtually superseded by the judicial.
>
> Now it is only in this way that your difficulties can arise –
>
> If the decision in the present case is for us, I don't see that anyone is committed, unless the Bishop is who pleaded. It is just the case of the Donatists. After having been judged by the Church they appealed to Constantine. He heard the case, confirmed the Church's judgment. S. Austin refers to this with approval. . . . Had the Emperor given it against the Church, I conclude he would have objected to his decision. But to confirm a judgment is to leave the old one standing. So that in this case, we shall act on the decision of our own eccles. court.
>
> But if they alter Fust's Judgment, it will be the time to call on the Church to object to the interference, and to demand Convocation. And if this is not done, *I am ready.*[12]

In a later letter he observed to Manning that the Judicial Committee might well decide that they had been confronted with a theological question beyond their competence and, in consequence, refer the case to Convocation. 'How can we tell they will not do so?'[13]

Judgment was given on 8 March 1850, reversing the previous decision of the Court of Arches. Gorham had won his case. There had been a gathering of the most prominent clergy and laity of the Anglo-Catholic party in London during the preceding week to take counsel with Manning, Hope and Gladstone on a possible course of action should their worst fears be confirmed. Robert and Henry Wilberforce were there, along with Dodsworth, W. H. Mill (Regius Professor of Hebrew at Cambridge), Bennett, Pusey and Keble. Sidney Herbert, Richard Cavendish and Edward Badeley (counsel for Phillpotts) were among the laity who attended. When the judgment was known, meetings were held, with Manning in the chair, in the vestry of St Paul's, Knightsbridge, and finally at Gladstone's house. The first question was to decide the form of a Declaration against the judgment, exhorting the Church in general and the episcopate in particular to defy the Privy Council's ruling by issuing an authoritative re-affirmation of the doctrine of Holy Baptism.[14] After this, the course was not so clear. James Hope had been talking wildly about a mass secession to

Rome if their efforts failed. Gladstone proposed a covenant whereby all those disturbed by the judgment promised to do nothing of the kind – at least for a given space of time. Manning could not agree to this. Keble's answer was to ignore the judgment altogether. If the Establishment meant the perversion of the true faith, then the Establishment must go. He explained his views to Robert: 'Whatever be the details, our principle must be to agitate for having no Church Establishment with whatever sacrifice of endowment. But we must make up our minds to wait an indefinite time, working of course incessantly.'[15]

Two months later, the thought of separation began to alarm him.

> I myself feel more deeply every day that it would be a deadly sin to separate from the present Church of England, but how to support her and serve her best is hard to judge; and it may be that the right course is one which would lead to one's being forcibly separated from her visible communion. You seem to me to attribute too much force to judicial decisions as expressing the mind of the Church.

He advised Robert to ignore general and abstract principles and to stick to scripture and primitive antiquity.[16]

This was all very well. But the unhappy facts remained. As William Henn pointed out to Robert, the recent events did not suddenly make the Church of England assume a Protestant guise. They merely rendered explicit what had always been implicit in Anglicanism. And what good would disruption do? Henn put the point precisely:

> How can you think of setting up a *Free Church*, of troubling the nation with a new sect? ... Right the Church of England if you can: I wait to hear that it is hopeless – on (which) I abandon her. But if she cannot be righted, let us not furnish *new* scandal by new divisions, nor thereby weaken the only institution in the Western world at least which while she will not recoil from combatting the fearful evils which run riot throughout Europe and our own lands, has a solid ground for believing that she shall not be annihilated by them. 'Out of a ship into a boat, out of a boat into a tub' are Manning's words. I go further. The tub is leaking. It will sink of itself ere it is well launched.[17]

So then, the choice was simply this – reform at once (if it could be done) or secede. There must be a new court of appeal and the nature of the Royal Supremacy must be redefined in a form acceptable to Catholic minds. Robert and Manning now turned to these objectives, hoping that Samuel's influence might be brought to bear on the episcopate as a whole, so that the Church could speak with a single voice (preferably Samuel's) in the House of Lords. In July 1850 Manning published his opinions in an

open letter to the Bishop of Chichester, declaring that 'the whole jurisdiction of the Episcopate over the oral teaching of the Church, after orders
once given, and the whole power of giving mission, the most sacred and
vital in the discipline of the Church, are. . . prostrate at the foot of the
Civil Power'.[18] In collaboration with Robert and W. H. Mill, he compiled
a declaration to be circulated over their joint signatures to every beneficed
clergyman and to every layman who had subscribed to the oath of supremacy, denying the Crown's right to determine 'spiritual questions touching
doctrine or discipline'[19] and inviting support.

Their hopes were vain. Samuel did his best in the House of Lords,
supporting a bill introduced by Blomfield, which provided that all spiritual causes should be determined by the Upper House of Convocation and
not by the Judicial Committee. There was no unanimity on the Bench,
however, and the bill was rejected in June 1850. There was little more
that he could do at that stage. He was not himself unduly discountenanced
by the Gorham Judgment (it was a 'mere state decision', he assured W. J.
Butler, and practically 'leaves the matter where it found it'),[20] and felt
that the Declaration against the Royal Supremacy was both intemperate
and ill-advised.

He wrote to Manning shortly after the rejection of Blomfield's bill to
assure him that it was his duty to continue to hold office in the Church:

> Your oath is of obedience to the law as it is whilst it is the law. You
> are at perfect liberty to seek to obtain an alteration in the law. Now the
> profession and object of our *law* is to leave spiritualities wholly to the
> Church: if in the infirmity of legislating upon difficult mixed questions,
> the State, contrary to her interest, has invaded the rights of the Church,
> the fitting remedy would be not to quit office but to strive for the practical
> redress of the unintended evil.
>   e.g. if the language of the Church is held by the lay court not so explicit
> as to exclude from office some maintainer of false doctrine, it is the Church's
> duty to struggle for a restoration of her synod in which she can amend her
> declaration.[21]

To Samuel, then, the answer lay in the restoration of Convocation.
Manning might have replied that he was already taking steps to strive for
'practical redress' in his circular repudiating the recent interpretation of
the Royal Supremacy. If the clergy backed him in sufficient number,
he might then reasonably hope that the Church would be powerful enough
to force the State to recognise her rights. In fact he was not sanguine of
any substantial support. By September, shortly after the circular had been
despatched, he was gripped by a terrible depression. 'My dear Robert', he

wrote on 19 September, 'I feel as if my time were drawing near, and that, like death, it will be, if it must be, alone. But I shrink with all the love and fear of my soul. Pray for me.'[22]

Robert begged him to wait a little longer. 'Your letter is very affecting to me, for it makes me feel that we may be possibly divided, and with no one have I more accorded in judgment than with you. But I cannot bring myself to wind up such a mighty argument without having more weighed the case both one side and the other.'

> It is idle to enter upon reasons with you, with whom I have so often discussed them. I will only say therefore that I think you should at all events allow some delay as your late address to the clergy with Mill and myself renders natural. You have appealed to the whole body of the clergy. To act before you get their answer would be to imply that you had a foregone conclusion, and had somewhat hastily changed your mind. . . . I do not speak about myself on this. I am very indifferent what people say about me. My own hope and wish has been that some prosecution might be commenced which might decide our position.[23]

The response to Manning's circular was only lukewarm. Yet he waited; waited, while every day, it seemed, news came to him of first one and then another of his friends and penitents who had given up the struggle and sought refuge in the Roman Church. He waited as a man without hope; not knowing what he waited for. A third call? He had half expected the heavens to open and the divine wrath to be visited upon them all on the fateful day in August when all Phillpotts' fulminations against the archbishop had proved to be in vain, and Gorham was instituted at last to the living of Bramford Speke. Nothing had happened. As Robert observed to him, a week later: 'One can hardly fancy that all would see that day just as usual: the sun shining, the birds singing, just as usual.'[24] Yet so it was.

VII. *Henry and Mary Wilberforce*

Henry and Mary Wilberforce were now to take the plunge. For them the closing years of the 1840's had been a time of bitter trial. In successive years – 1847 and 1848 – they had lost a son in early childhood.[1] Indeed four of their nine children died between the years 1841 and 1853.[2] In the autumn of 1849, cholera broke out amongst the Irish hop-pickers working at East Farleigh, imposing the severest strain and anxiety upon Henry and his family who stayed throughout the epidemic to minister to the sick and dying. It may well be that this event was the turning point in their lives.

For years, as has already been observed, both Henry and Mary had felt a deep attraction towards the Roman Church and had resisted the blandishments of Newman largely through Manning's insistence that the Anglican Church possessed the means of grace and was, albeit slowly, recovering the Catholic devotional ethos and discipline which would prove it to be a living portion of the one true Church. Mary, indeed, as early as December 1835, had indicated that the traditional English prejudices against Rome were no impediment to her,[3] and to the very end she was always a little in advance of her husband in her readiness to submit. In 1846 Henry reported to Robert that he trusted that Mary 'from the manner of her discourse . . . thinks of Rome less than she did. Indeed I hope, tho' she has not told me so, that she is settling down in mind.'[4] In January 1850 he wrote to Manning, lamenting that 'the poor dear Aziola* coughs a great deal more than I like, and is sadly Popish. I wish you would come and indoctrinate her.'[5]

Both Henry and Mary, however, felt that Rome held the key to the sanctified life. A visit to Grace-Dieu at the close of 1847 – 'my first adventure among Papists'[6] Henry told Robert – made his head swim. He read the life of St Ignatius in a fever of excitement, and pointed out to Robert, who had shown some annoyance at his enthusiasm, that this was a record of 'the work of the Blessed Spirit. I am as sure as it is in my nature to be of anything. To doubt it would be like giving up my belief in revelation. You had better buy Ignatius. He is only 4/- a volume.'[7] He even fell for Faber's hymns: 'They are *ultra* as to all Roman doctrine, B.V.M. etc. and some are too familiar, but many of them appear to me *most beautiful*. I hardly ever read anything which I so intensely admired as many of them. . . . I dare say Anderson would be disgusted.'[8]

Henry's heart was certainly in Rome at this stage. What had brought him there were his love for the sacramental system and his conviction of the necessity of confession. Manning put it succinctly in a letter to Mary written in Holy Week 1849: 'Surely if anything ever brought us to the Foot of the Cross it is confession, the altar and the Sacrifice.'[9]

How could an Anglican clergyman bring others to the foot of the Cross, if all these things had to be said in whispers, effected secretly, and disguised lest worldly bishops or a prejudiced public should find grounds for crying 'scandal'? Before 1849 Henry and Mary had acute misgivings

* Henry often referred to Mary as 'Aziola'.

about the catholicity of a Church which allowed such things to be. The cholera epidemic of 1849, as Newman himself observed, was the occasion of these misgivings 'ripening into convictions'.[10] Do what he could for the dying Irish Catholics, Henry could not bring them the sacraments. A Roman priest came over from Tunbridge Wells; reinforcements were brought in from the London Oratory; also two nuns of the Convent of the Good Shepherd at Hammersmith. Henry and Mary helped them and gave them accommodation and hospitality in their own house. This personal acquaintance with the ministrations of the Roman priesthood made a very deep impression. Samuel, from whom Henry tried to conceal this news, was indignant and dismayed. 'I wrote to Dr Pusey', he informed Robert, 'to tell him the danger. P. wrote in confidence that he would go down yesterday. Today came a letter saying that he had not gone, from finding that the R. priests and one Oratorian he had known . . . were staying in H's house. All this is very sad indeed and I feel dear H. has not been quite honest, for he told me that they were all at the "Bull" etc. etc.'[11]

For several weeks Henry and his family lived under the shadow of *timor mortis*. It had been on what he believed to be his deathbed in 1847 that Manning had been forced to come to terms with his growing unsettlement. Ryder had been in the same position in 1846, just before his reception. W. G. Ward had been given only a year to live by his doctors in 1844.[12] As Henry's reports of the epidemic reached his brothers, the prospect of a sudden decision for the safety of the soul was not far from any of their minds. The first death occurred in the second week of September. 'Humanly speaking, it must spread', Henry wrote to Robert. 'Pray for me that I may be spared – and above all that I may not disgrace my Christian profession either by deserting duty and taking hastily a step which perhaps I ought to have taken deliberately. You may tell the Bishop my state of mind. Oh, that my soul were safe and I could do these duties easily.'[13]

A month later, the roll of dead had reached fifteen or sixteen, the school and two barns were full of cholera victims, Mary working among them like a Sister of Charity. 'I trust by God's help', Henry wrote again, 'I shall take no rash and sudden step, but I do not expect the effect of this scene (in many different ways) will wear out if my life is spared – indeed I hope not.'[14]

Manning was deeply anxious. He knew in his heart that his fate was somehow bound up with that of Henry and Mary. In October 1848 he had written to Henry 'I feel that in the end nothing will ever part us three. Either we shall all die where we are, or thro' much heart breaking we shall all meet elsewhere.'[15] Samuel tried to enlist Manning's aid in warning Mary of the danger of making decisions when the mind was overexcited. The letter was dutifully passed on.

> It is very painful [Manning told Henry]. His great tenderness makes it so. I feel what he says about acting under excitement – and my own belief is that God has given you the faculties and means to act only by conviction. I have no doubt that this you ought to do so as to make up your mind one way or the other hereafter. For the present I feel you are commending yourself to God, 1. by acts of charity, and 2. by mistrusting yourself and yielding to such a warning as your brother's letter. For I am sure God will accept the intention and disposition which makes you listen to him and take time. Great love to you. Nothing, I believe, in God, will part us living or dying.[16]

The crisis passed; but the load – especially on Mary's mind – hardly lightened. The death of her sister, Sophia Ryder, in the spring of 1850, followed by the conviction that an approaching confinement would see her taken also, meant that the fever of anxiety was as intense as before. In the midst of all these worries, Henry was being pressed to stand in line with Manning, Robert and others who had resolved to work for the undoing of the Gorham Judgment, and the instrument which had brought it about, before taking any decisive step on their own account. But how could Henry promise anything?

> My beloved brother [he wrote to Robert in May 1850], I quite feel all you say of the fitness of waiting to see what is done – and were I in your situation I should do it quite cheerfully. But here is my difficulty. I see my beloved Mary's mind is uneasy – that she feels if she died without taking a step she would be neglecting a *Divine Call* – and then her confinement is coming on and who can doubt that this impression makes that even physically more dangerous – besides which I feel that were I in her situation I should feel the same. This so presses on me that I think I *must* have her received before the time of her confinement – and if she is, my position is as much gone as if *I* were. The truth is tho' the Gorham case brought my feelings and hers to a head, it was *not* the cause of them.[17]

Robert made one desperate effort to restrain them: 'As to dear Mary I could not urge her one way or other. But for myself, if I were about to be taken away, I should feel unable to take so serious a step as to say adieu to my former dependences. I daily pray God that He would rather remove me than allow me to do anything which may be contrary to His will or my brethren's welfare.'[18]

At least Henry promised that if Mary succumbed in a moment of danger, everything would be kept as quiet as possible until he had made up his own mind. On the other hand, he would not attempt to dissuade her if she felt that she had received a direct call. They were moving to London for the confinement, but he expressed the hope that 'nothing will be done unless it is done quite privately at East Farleigh'.[19]

The secret appears to have been well kept. On 22nd June, Mary was received into the Roman Church by Father Brownbill, S.J., at 44 Cadogan Place in the early hours of the morning, just after giving birth to a son, Wilfrid, whom Brownbill immediately baptised.[20] For obvious reasons no one was told immediately. Henry called on Archbishop Sumner to explain his own difficulties and asked permission to take his family abroad.

> He quite approved [Henry informed Robert]. ... I was much impressed first by his extreme kindness, which really *nothing* could exceed. I spoke very plainly to him about the Gorham case etc. – but at the same time, I was equally struck with his entire unconcern of anything above Quaker principles ... declaring there is no means of approaching Christ but 'by the action of our own hearts'. This, as you show, is a virtual denial of the Incarnation. ... I was at E. F. yesterday for some things we needed. It was like seeing a dead friend and never was the place half so lovely. All seemed so calm and redolent after London. Eheu![21]

They crossed to Belgium. In August they were in Malines.

> We have been interested with some of the services here [Henry wrote to Robert], but it is very difficult to understand the Mass. They do not usually try *here*, I think, to make the people accompany the words as they do in Normandy. They seem merely to accompany the sacrifice and follow it with their own private devotions.[22]

For the next month Henry struggled in great agony of mind to find the answer to his own personal problem. The news of Mary's reception had now reached England[23]; he was not conscious of receiving any clear call. For a desperate moment he thought he was lapsing into complete scepticism. In this state of mind, he decided to attend a retreat at the Jesuit house in Brussels. He took Manning into his confidence.

> I am where I am [he wrote on 10 September] having fully resolved not to act on any impulse. This you advise by the way in your letter which I found here on my return. But in truth there was little to excite me at Brussels. I only saw one of the fathers who spoke no English and with whom I had hardly any talk on the subject. ... I was almost wholly alone. This was what I sought. There was no one else there. I ate by myself, prayed and meditated by myself – no public services, no sermons etc. The father ministre Van de Meere visited me twice a day.

... I feel less *drawn* than I did to Rome. Much less impulse any way – much less desire of gain – much more sense of loss. Yet, on the other side, my convictions are not lessened and I feel the effects of unsettlement to such a degree that I *really* and seriously feel myself in real danger of universal unbelief. I much incline to believe that if I stay as I am I shall lose my faith altogether. Also I do not think I *could* either celebrate or receive in our Church. I have now not communicated since I left London a month ago. How long is this to continue?[24]

By the time that Manning received this letter, Henry had made up his mind – acting, for all his protestations to the contrary – on a sudden impulse. On 12 September he wrote to Manning to tell him that the die was cast: he was to be received into the Roman Church on the following Sunday.[25] Two days later he wrote to Robert.

My beloved brother. You will hardly be surprised to hear that I can wait no longer. Tomorrow morning D.V. I am to be received by Father Van de Meere, a very pleasing Jesuit. I have been staying at the college since Thursday on purpose. I cannot doubt that I am doing right, but I do it with fear and trembling. Pray for me that my faith may not fail, and that I may have grace to adorn it by a holy life. I feel it an awful thing to be a Catholic and I so unworthy, but truly it is His pleasure to lift the poor out of the mire that He may set him with Princes even with the Princes of His people.[26]

Henry wrote also to Archbishop Sumner to ask him to accept his resignation. 'In taking this step I feel so many heartstrings breaking that I dare not allow myself to think of the consequences or the cost on earth, either to myself, or to those I love. I have put my hand to the plough, and I must not look back.' He thanked Sumner for all his many kindnesses and grieved at the pain which he must be causing him, concluding with the hope – albeit somewhat improbable – that 'He, who has been pleased to call *me*, so deeply unworthy of His grace, may extend the same favour to one so much more meet for it as yourself'.[27]

The deed was done. According to Cyril Ryder, Mary knew nothing of the event until, at the Communion on the last day of the retreat, she found her husband kneeling beside her.* Whether this be true or not, it is certain that the final decision was made in great haste and took his brothers at home completely by surprise. The last to learn the news – for indeed

---

* Ryder MSS. 'A Son's Reminiscence', 57. The accuracy of this account is questionable. For instance, the author writes that Henry was received on the Saturday evening before the communion. In fact he was received at 8 a.m. on Sunday, 15 September (Manning archives. Wilberforce letters, IV. 116).

Henry dreaded writing to him and left it to the others to perform this distasteful task – was Samuel. He was told on 23 September, over a week after the event. He dashed off a letter at once to Robert, addressed from Bletchley.

> The blow came when it could not but be very heavy at last and so I feel it. I suppose it *is* so: though I have not heard from H. However it draws me nearer and closer than ever to you and God forbid that we should ever be parted. I love dearest H. just as much as ever but I feel that our *lives* are parted in their purpose, aim and association. I heartily wish he might settle abroad: but having him here after this dreadful fall seems to me beyond measure miserable: and his broken vows and violated faith weigh heavily on my soul. May God forgive him.[28]

Chapter 8

THE FINAL PARTING

1. *The Secession of Henry Manning*

The conversion of Henry Wilberforce may have saved his soul from perdition, but it certainly did nothing to sweeten his temper or to improve his manners. The humility of the honest doubter was replaced, almost overnight, by the arrogant assurance of the zealot; and where conscience should have dictated, and circumstances clearly required, moderation, a temperate spirit and an abundance of charity, Henry rushed hotly into a campaign of furious proselytism, quite heedless of the susceptibilities of others, mindful of nothing save the satisfaction of proclaiming his newly-found orthodoxy and of adding to the discomfiture of the Church which he had so lately renounced.

Within months of his reception, he published a bitter attack on the Anglican Church in his *Farewell Letter to his late Parishioners*, full of sour invective against the futility of the sectarian spirit implicit in the Anglican claim to possess catholicity while remaining separated from the one true Church.[1] Samuel, who had not written to Henry since the news of his reception, now broke his silence.

> The deep and unchanging love I bear you learned when we knelt as little children together in our early prayers forces me to speak. . . . We should I am sure agree that so to state a proposition as to make it suggest what was untrue to the party to whom it was addressed, even if in a certain way the absolute truth of the statement can be defended, is still untruth in the sight of God.
>
> Now my beloved Henry, try your letter . . . by that rule and remember that you are not writing a clever review of some unimportant subject, but dealing with God's Truth, and Souls for which Christ died, and I think you can hardly avoid feeling what I mean.

He took Henry to task for glib and false taunts at the Anglican Establishment, and for bad history in his remarks on the sustained persecution of Catholics in England until recent times. His disregard for truth was so blatant 'that I quite tremble to read your letter'.

He concluded thus:

I earnestly entreat you to try yourself on this matter before God. I cannot forget the awful threatening of His sending on men strong delusions that they should believe a lie – and knowing what follows, and being ready to bear anything rather than that our separation which now embitters my life should be eternal, I must break all restraints and set this plainly before you.*

In his letters to Robert, Henry fairly crowed with triumph at the embarrassment of the Anglican clergy, forced to rush to the defence of an Establishment which many of them had lately impugned, in their fear of the papal aggression, visited upon them in the shape of the restoration of the Roman Catholic hierarchy. 'I can hardly say how much I feel cause for thankfulness that I am clear of it all.' He was full of plans, among them an approach to 'the Holy Father [to] license married converts to *preach*', so that those who had once held Anglican orders could, with the assistance of a priest to administer the sacraments, conduct missions in their former parishes and thereby capture a multitude of souls. 'Bennett, I am convinced, might do wonders in Pimlico, and I think and believe that if I had a chapel somewhere near Rocky Hill, on the walking way from Maidstone to E.F. with my priest (being with me) to say Mass, I could do much toll in Maidstone and dear E.F. There is no mission in Maidstone with all its 25,000 and its Irish, its depot, gaols, hoppers etc. etc.'[2]

Not even Mrs Sargent could find a good word to say about Henry's conduct in these months. She wrote to Mary as usual, sadly but lovingly. In one letter, shortly after the publication of Henry's address to his late parishioners, she vouchsafed a P.S. on the subject of her intemperate son-in-law: 'My love to Henry. I could *talk* volumes about his "letter", but cannot write. It is so very unfair. All the great R.C. families in Yorkshire have always been received and have we not R.C. members of Parliament?' She could not approve of the opprobrium which Catholics generally had incurred through the recent papal aggression. '*But a clergyman* who forsakes us is a very different matter.'[3]

Who would be the next to follow Henry's example? This was the dreadful question which pressed upon Samuel. He prayed daily that Robert should be given strength to resist 'this most fearful sin', marvelling – as he confessed to Robert himself – that the other who was 'so much better a man than I am' should be 'ensnared by such a painted hag as that Roman

* Wilberforce MSS. K. 31 March 1851. He was particularly objecting to the closing section of Henry's *Letter*, in which he claimed that the Catholic Church had been kept down in England by 'sheer persecution'. H. W. Wilberforce, *op. cit.*, 43–5.

Jezebel'.[4] During the late summer of 1850 he spent as much time as he could spare at Lavington so that he could be near Manning in the hope that he could bring him to his senses. Throughout the year he had sought the confidence of Gladstone, believing that the two of them together might diagnose the true nature of Manning's *malaise* and somehow discover a cure. In April they discussed his case in the committee room at the House of Lords, and Gladstone then was fairly sanguine. He confessed to Samuel that he had been worried about Manning's state ever since his illness in 1847, noticing for the first time his dangerous inclination to let his mind be 'coloured a good deal by external events'. Nevertheless he could assure Samuel that the whole spirit of Manning's recent letters 'negatived the idea of a formed intention'.[5]

In September Gladstone wrote a long letter, recalling their earlier conversation. He was growing less confident now.

> It seems to me likely that if he shall go, he will do it upon broad grounds reaching far back into history as well as forward into the future: upon these grounds avowedly, but really, though less consciously, in consequence of the equivocal and hesitating attitude of the Church of England during these past months of crisis with respect to the maintenance of the faith. If you yourself, if a few other Bishops have declared that the doctrine of Baptism will be by them maintained as the doctrine of the Church, such has not been the will of the English Episcopate at large.
> ... Not that I at all despair. His mind has it seems to me fluctuated much: his almost unrivalled intellect giving to each momentary phase all the semblance of completeness and solidity. Even now I believe he would be secure – and with him many more, of such men as are not to be numbered but weighed – were there a hope of a resolute movement, if not corporate, yet at least combined.[6]

Samuel replied on 14 September, having had several talks with Manning since he received Gladstone's letter.

> My stay here has let me see much of Manning. Never has he been so affectionate, so open, so fully trusting with me. We have been together through all his difficulties. But alas it has left on my mind the full conviction that he *is* lost to us. It is, as you say, the broad ground of historical inquiry where our paths part. He seems to me to have followed singly, exactly the course which the Roman Church has followed as a body. He has gone back into those early times when, what afterwards became their corruptions, were only the germ buds of Catholic usages: he has fully accustomed his mind to them: until a system which wants them seems to him incomplete and uncatholic and one which has them is the wiser and holier and more catholic for having them, until he can excuse to a great

degree their practical corruptions and justify altogether their doctrinal rightness. All this has been stirred up and rendered practical in his mind by our own troubles but the result of all leaves me very hopeless of the issue. Few can at all understand what his and my brother's present state are to me. I believe you can; the broken sleep, the heavy waking, before the sorrow has shaped itself with returning consciousness into a definite form; the vast and spreading dimensions of the fear for others which it excites; the clouding over of all the future. It has quite pressed upon me and I owe, I believe, to it as much as to anything else a sharp attack of fever which has pulled me down a good deal.[7]

Gladstone still clutched at the only remaining straw: the repudiation by the episcopate of the Gorham Judgment. A wrong would have been righted and Manning's inherent sense of loyalty – always far stronger than that of Newman – would do the rest. Although his heart might be in Rome, this emotional pull had – until the Gorham case – been 'effectually neutralised by a sense of duty, not abstract or cold, but strong, commanding, and warm with life and action'.[8]

Manning's own letters to Samuel suggest that the whole fiasco of the Gorham Judgment had been to him symptomatic of a disease within the Anglican body, diagnosed some years before the event but now shown to be uncurable. He wrote tenderly and guardedly. But in October Samuel went too far in his attempt to persuade his brother-in-law that he was in error. In describing Manning's attitude to Rome, he let slip the word 'dishonesty', and provoked a blunt and forceful response.

I have never [Manning replied] assumed a posture or tone of hostility to the Church of Rome. God being my helper I had rather die.

... The subjects I have pressed are, as you know, besides the great mysteries of Faith, such points as repentance, obedience, and devotion, and as related to these the Christian priesthood, the power of absolution, the Real Presence, the Christian Sacrifice, the authority of Divine Tradition and the unity of the Church: points, every one of which is either broadly and literally taught by the offices and Ordinal of the Church of England or by its chief writers. How then, my beloved brother, did your heart endure to write the word dishonesty?

You know that there does not exist in any of the 7 or 8 volumes I have published a doctrine which is not to be found in Andrewes.

But I admit at once that my teaching has been and is nearer to the Roman Church than to the Church of England as it teaches now. And why? Forgive me if I speak without reserve. It is because the Church of England is betrayed by the majority of its pastors to the public opinion of the day. Its voice contradicts its formularies. The manifest faithlessness of the living Church of England to its own recorded Faith, even more than its miserable contradictions is driving multitudes into mistrust, unbelief or secession. Fears and doubts which men do not dare to speak before Bishops are freely spoken before us. And I do not believe that the Bishops of the Church of England are aware of the fearful unsettlement of faith, and relaxation of affection which is spreading at this moment.

My very dear Brother, the word dishonesty shall be laid up for judgment at that day when our common Lord will take account of His servants. I thank you for it with all sincere affection. . . . It seems to me that as I have steadfastly pressed on in the convictions of 1835, 1838, 1841 I have found myself more and more removed from the living Church of England. These convictions prohibited all sympathy with protestantism, and the compromises of the Reformation. But every year has brought out fresh proofs that what I believed to be the Theology of the English Church is only the opinion of a school, early, learned, and devout, beginning with the end of Q. Elizabeth and neutralized at the Revolution. I am as fully persuaded as I can be that your opinions are and that mine are not tenable now in the Church of England.

I could as soon doubt of the Holy Trinity as that the Church of Christ is One, Visible and Infallible. Holy Scripture seems to me clear as the Sun.

He then proceeded to summarise his conclusions:

In the Church of England there exists a protestant and a catholic element. Between these an unintelligible and as it seems to me false hearted compromise.

The protestant element I have believed to be the disease of the English Church: the catholic to be its only life and substance.

In that catholic element I have lived and laboured with an unchanging and uniform perseverance: as I believe both our agreements and our opposition will prove.

If therefore, by dishonesty you mean that I have lived in and for this alone and have thereby contravened the protestant element or destroyed the balance of the compromise; and that by consequence I and others with me are in a position more nearly allied to the Roman Church than to any other communion I am ready to say the same. But my inference could be the reverse of yours.

If you mean by dishonesty that I have knowingly and intentionally used my place and office in the Church of England to advance ends of the Church of Rome as such, I 'answer nothing'. I should be too deeply wounded by a sense of unutterable wrong: and turn to Him who will judge us both.

But in saying this, believe me, dearest Brother, I will cherish the truest, warmest love for you. And will wait in sorrow and in silence till we shall both give up to the same Master the reckoning of our life and work.[9]

How could Henry Manning hold back any longer? He had promised Henry and Mary that in the end the three of them would never be parted.

If he was still awaiting a third and decisive call, the events of November 1850 – the storm provoked in England by the restoration of the Roman Catholic hierarchy – was a further sign of the Protestant spirit of the Anglican Church which he could not ignore. In fact, this event was made decisive for him by the fact that as Archdeacon of Chichester he was required by the diocesan clergy to convene a meeting of protest against the Papal Aggression. On 23 November 1850 he wrote to James Hope that 'events have driven me to a decision'. Rather than associate himself with the outcry against Rome, he would resign his office. 'I went to the Bishop and said this, and tendered my resignation. He was very kind, and wished me to take time, but I have written and made it final.'[10]

Thereafter it was only a question of time. Manning ceased to officiate as a priest after the beginning of the new year. In December he left Lavington to stay with his sister, Mrs Carey, at 44 Cadogan Place. In January 1851 he wrote to his confessor, Laprimaudaye, who was himself about to seek reception, that 'I cannot think to be long as I am now'.[11] In the last months before his own reception he was in constant correspondence with both Robert Wilberforce and James Hope; and in the latter, at least, he found a companion to travel with him over the last stage of the journey. In December he had written to Hope that 'it would be to me a very great happiness if we could act together, and our names go together in the first publication of the fact'.[12] They were received together into the Roman Church on Passion Sunday, 6 April 1851, by the Jesuit Father Brownbill, after a terrible and prolonged struggle in which Manning had been compelled to make the final act of abjuration – the agonising admission of the invalidity of his Anglican orders.

The news had been expected any day; yet those whose counsels Manning had sought right up to the last moment and who had been privy to his inmost thoughts found when the irrevocable step was taken that the blow was no less numbing for its being long anticipated. Gladstone lost in a single day the two most intimate friends of his life. Hope's action was intelligible to him. Manning's was not. Despite the understanding and sympathy which he had shown, when discussing Manning's dilemma with Samuel some months before, his letters written just after the news of the secession reveal a tragic perplexity. Grief, resentment and incredulity combined to throw him into just that state which he had experienced when he had first received the news of Newman's unsettlement: 'I stagger to and fro like a drunken man, and am at my wit's end.'[13] He wrote to Robert Wilberforce on 11 April 1851:

I do indeed feel the loss of Manning, if and as far as I am capable of feeling anything. It comes to me cumulated, and doubled, with that of James Hope. Nothing like it can ever happen to me again. Arrived now at middle life, I never *can* form I suppose with any other two men the habits of communication, counsel, and dependence, in which I have now for from fifteen to eighteen years lived with them both. But I will not pursue this subject. . . . My intellect does deliberately reject the grounds on which Manning has proceeded. Indeed they are such as go far to destroy my confidence, which was once and for so long at the highest point, in the healthiness and soundness of his. To show that, at any rate, this is not from the mere change he has made, I may add, that my conversations with Hope have not left any corresponding impression upon my mind with regard to him.[14]

As the years passed, Gladstone's rejection of the logic of Manning's action remained firm. In 1854 he warned Robert to steer clear of polemics. 'Nor can I forget our dear Manning's state when he made his plunge; fever of the mind really brought to him blindness of the eye.'[15]

Of the happy circle which had gathered at Lavington at the house of John Sargent in the early 1830's, only two of the womenfolk had survived (Mary Wilberforce and Mary Sargent) and they were divided in their faith. Of the men, only Samuel remained securely within the Anglican Church. For them all, Lavington was a store of precious memories; an evocation of happier times, to recall which was inexpressibly painful, with all the thoughts of what might have been and what now was – the blighted hopes, the bleak reality of separation and mistrust. In June that year Samuel was at Lavington. The sense of loss was overpowering. He wrote to Richard Cavendish:

We came here yesterday and return (D.V.) tomorrow. It is a sad visit. The glory of our beloved little church is departed. The heavens weeping over us, and the trees dropping round us, seem acted parables of our thoughts. Twenty-three years ago tomorrow, and the sun shone on me as I came out of the church the most blessed of bridegrooms, having won her whom I had loved, as few love so young, ever since the vision of her beauty enchanted my early boyhood. How has wave followed wave from that day to this![16]

To Robert he recalled the effect of Manning's parting:

Our last time here was with dear Manning for the last time – and the coming back having lost him is very, very painful. The Laprimaudayes too are here. She in extreme danger from sudden illness. He worse than dead to me.*

* Charles Laprimaudaye was already a Roman Catholic; his wife did not follow him until a few months later.

He was to communicate in Lavington Church on the following morning, 'with my dear Ella, Mrs Sargent and one or two more – and you shall not be forgotten, dear, dear Brother – one of the very last left me of all the mighty wreck which has left me so alone'.[17]

What Mary Sargent felt that morning may be imagined. She had suffered so much already, and suppressed her sorrow time and time again by thinking always of those whose loss was greater than her own. On this occasion, none could have felt Manning's desertion more profoundly than Caroline's mother, mindful as she had ever been of the promises she had made at her daughter's deathbed, ready as she always was to try to fulfil them at whatever cost to herself. She passed something of her feelings on to Mary; soberly, as was her wont.

> My dearest Mary, I have felt too much depressed lately to be able to write to you, but now that beloved H.E.M. is gone from me quite, I have nothing to do but to bear his loss as I have done other sorrows only I hope with increased patience. I am now stripped very bare, but no doubt it was necessary for me who have been always ready when one idol was removed to cling to another.[18]

Henry Manning suffered cruelly at times during the first months of his new life. As the world knows, he was groomed from the beginning by Cardinal Wiseman to undertake the conversion of his brethren, and he was admitted to priest's orders within ten weeks of his reception. None of this, however, could have been immediately foreseen. Manning could not have known of the great responsibilities which lay in store for him. His first impressions of his changed state were the shedding of a crippling burden which he seemed to have been carrying for countless wasted years, an elation in part offset by the consciousness that his active life was over and that the future offered only loneliness and obscurity. When the opportunity for valuable work came so quickly he readily accepted it; he knew that he must never look back. But that was more easily said than done.

In September 1851 he was obliged to return to Lavington to pack up all his goods before setting off for Rome to study at the Accademia Ecclesiastica. Present hopes and past memories jostled each other in his mind, and he described his feelings to Mary Wilberforce shortly after his return to London:

> My beloved sister, I did not write from Lavington for I was so much engaged as to have no time. Every day was taken up by packing and by seeing people – so that I went for two days and stayed four.

It was a strange time. I had shrunk from it as if I dared not go there – but when the time came I longed for it. And when I got there I had the sort of happiness and sadness which I suppose I should have if I had died and come back again. Everything seemed even more beautiful because new and fresh to me – but I had no desire to go back again and would not bring up the past if I could. I was in my own house and rooms – and the kind people who are there were kindness itself.

The mornings I spent in looking over and destroying papers. The afternoons in walking to and fro among my people, for somehow I felt that they belong to me more than to anybody else, and more than ever now – and that I have a certain and divine message and mission to them. In the evening people came to see me.

Now I wish you not to mention *names* except to dearest H. Certainly 8 or 10 people would come at once if I were there – and the people evidently are not estranged from me. Two of the best families in the place were the first to come to me – Edward Hedge and Osborne. I left them books. Mary Marshall I hope has been received. Maria Kelsy is on the brink. Could you receive her if need be into your house for a time?

... It was so wonderful to walk about thro' the woods and garden as a stranger. Nothing ever brought back 1833 so vividly. But would I have it back? As Henry says 'Track home' is best and we shall go no more out. Little Ann was full of the deepest affection and talked to me of that summer when all broke up, and you all went to Brighstone – in a way that seemed as if it were this year.[19]

There was to be no looking back; but when the moment came to pack his things for the journey to Rome, Manning bundled all Caroline's letters up and slipped them into a small black bag which carried his money for the journey. When he and his companion (Aubrey de Vere) reached Avignon and sought their hotel, the bag was stolen from the coach. It was never recovered. 'At the first moment after the discovery of his loss the expression of grief in his face and voice was such as I have seldom witnessed', Aubrey de Vere recalled. He remembered also how Manning, once they had entered the hotel, sat apart for a short time until he caught sight of a maid-servant, abandoned by her employers for the while, looking lost and nervous. True to his nature, he went over to her to see that she was supplied with whatever she wanted, so that she should know that she was not without friends. Some months later, when de Vere met Manning in Rome, he asked if the stolen bag had ever been recovered. 'No', he replied. 'The loss was probably necessary – necessary to sever all bonds to earth.'[20]

II. *Robert Wilberforce and the Theological Synthesis*

Robert would sometimes let his mind wander into the territory of what might have been. He was sleeping badly in the early part of 1850, when the Gorham crisis was at its height. On one particularly restless night just before Easter, he at last fell into a state of half-sleep, his brain still pondering over a letter which he must write the next day to William, his brother. He found himself transported back to childhood days, recalling a particular piece of boyish madness into which William had once led him. He was nine at the time and the family were on holiday at Dungeness. William (aged fourteen) had taken him out to negotiate the dangerous quicksands which lay nearby. They lost their way; night came; they faced the double danger of being trapped in the bog or being swept out to sea by the incoming tide. By luck rather than good management they found a track home, it being then past midnight. If they had not been blessed by good fortune that night, what strange changes might have been wrought in their family history! Samuel, as the eldest son, would have been sent into Parliament, and would have become in time Prime Minister, with Gladstone as his Chancellor of the Exchequer. Henry would have gone to Oxford to enter the Church, but would have been preserved from 'Newmania' through not having an elder brother to lead him astray. Samuel would then have made him Bishop of Oxford. The happy fantasy ended at that moment. Robert woke up.[1]

There were indeed times in that year when Robert thought that his being spared at all was a doubtful mercy. So fearful was he of error, of taking a step or expressing an opinion which might endanger the salvation of his brethren, that he prayed that he should rather die than unwittingly lead others to perdition.[2] He had reached a stage in his life when whatever step he took was certain to cause bitterness and estrangement. Henry and Manning, with whom in doctrine he was in far greater agreement than with Samuel, expected him to go with them into the Roman Church. On the other hand, the thought of differing from Samuel on any subject was sufficient to make him doubt the conclusions of his own reasoning. His love for Samuel was a real love; far stronger, far more intense, than the bond which is naturally and conventionally reckoned to exist between brother and brother. For years, Robert had gone to Samuel when his spirits were low, or taken up his pen to unburden himself to one whom he described as 'my dearest friend and the sympathiser in all my distresses'.[3] And then there was Jane. She had never quite taken the place in Robert's

Robert Isaac Wilberforce

Henry Phillpotts, Bishop of Exeter

heart which Agnes held,* but during these years when she was practically bed-ridden, Robert could not add to her distress by confiding in her his own doubts about the Anglican position. As early as 1842 he had told Newman that he was unable to confide in 'the natural partner of all my feelings'.⁴ By 1850 he had come to the unhappy conclusion that if Jane discovered the extent of his sympathies for Manning's predicament she might go out of her mind.†

There were therefore personal reasons to explain why Robert Wilberforce failed to follow Manning and James Hope in the spring of 1851. The explanation may, however, go deeper than this. After all, even in the late 1840's, Robert was still unconvinced by the argument of Manning, Allies and Henry Wilberforce that the most grievous deficiency of the Anglican Church was its low view of ascetical theology and its neglect of sacramental confession. He was certainly far more subdued in his enthusiasm for Roman Catholic devotional methods and remained so to the end. He did not, like Ryder and Henry Wilberforce, succumb to the seductive attractions of Romanism. He studied Roman theology, but interested himself hardly at all in its pastoral system. Whereas most of the Anglo-Catholic converts were detached from the Church of their baptism because they looked for and found the marks of the true Church elsewhere, Robert gradually discovered that the Anglican system was untenable – mainly through the operation of the Royal Supremacy – and was prepared to consider a 'half-way house' between England and Rome. In February 1850 he suggested to Manning that he should do the same, after finding a handy colonial bishop to be the head of the new Free Church.⁵

It is clear also that Robert was more sanguine than Manning as to the power and will of the episcopate and the clergy at large to repudiate the decision of the Judicial Committee of the Privy Council in the Gorham Judgement. In his charge for 1850 he held out hopes that the Church would soon cease to be ruled by the judiciary and would recover her proper legislative voice. He encouraged his clergy confidently to expect that 'among our many Bishops at home and in the colonies, there will not be wanting surely some Athanasius in the hour of the Church's danger'.⁶

* In November 1853, Robert was still pining for Agnes. He wrote to Samuel: 'At this time of year also I always feel much from the recollection of what befell me 19 years ago – and from which I have a scar which will go with me to the grave.'

† There are many references in the letters to this, e.g. Manning archives, Wilberforce letters, IV. 93 (24 May 1850), 98 (17 June 1850), 141 (17 December 1850). Sandwith MSS. B. III. 12. 25 August 1850.

If challenged to be more particular, Robert would have cast Samuel for that rôle. In May 1850 he warned his brother that his own fate really lay in his hands. 'It is for you, my dearest brother, to give us something to trust to, by showing that the Church claims divine teaching – supernatural guidance, and does not depend either upon the strength of a Maskell, or the imbecility of a Sumner. I feel that it is wholly dependent (under God's blessing) upon you, whether I, and such as I, have any standing ground left.'[7]

Personal ties, a less eager confidence in the superiority of the Roman system, a deep trust in the abilities and resolution of his brother, to-gether – it must be admitted – with a natural timidity which made him acutely nervous of the prospect of slipping all his moorings and beginning life again at the age of fifty* – all these factors helped to bind Robert more securely to the Anglican Church. One further consideration, however, has to be taken into account – perhaps the most important of all. At the moment when the storm of the Gorham Judgment broke, Robert was deeply engaged in a massive theological study which it was to be his life's work to fulfil. In 1850 this work was incomplete. Until the task had been accomplished, he could not surrender his claims to teach; could not perhaps allow himself seriously to question those claims and thereby risk the frustration of what he had come to feel to be his appointed task.

If Robert Wilberforce's contemporaries erred in their estimation of the value of his theological writings by an over-generous reckoning of their originality and by an extravagant assumption of the needs which they fulfilled, posterity has tended to fall into the opposite error of neglecting to accord them any recognition at all.† There are two possible explanations. In the first place, the greatest deficiency in Tractarian historiography has been the tendency to concentrate upon the figures of Newman, Pusey, Keble and Froude, and to suppose that the Oxford Movement can

---

* William Henn chided Robert on this score. 'It was what most of the first con-verts had to do: it was Nicodemus' difficulty; it is for you the shape in which you are tested as to "becoming as a little child".' Wrangham MSS. Henn letters, 16. 10 May 1851.

† This neglect is now being remedied. There is a long section on Robert Wilber-force's writings in the recent compilation by the Canadian scholar, E. R. Fairweather, entitled *The Oxford Movement* (New York 1964), 283–367. I have derived great profit from conversations with Dr A. Härdelin, Librarian of Uppsala University, who has been working on the Eucharistical doctrine of the Tractarians, now published under the title *The Tractarian Understanding of the Eucharist* (Uppsala, 1965). This is the most learned study of Robert Wilberforce's theological writings which has appeared to date.

be fully understood by studying only the most notable of its pioneers and leaders. This has led to a neglect of the period which lies between the secession of Newman and the collapse of the Anglo-Catholic party after the Gorham Judgment, with the result that insufficient attention has been paid to the movement, in which Manning played a leading rôle, to supply the Anglican Church with an effective ascetical theology. In the same way, the thought of the Oxford Movement has suffered constriction, as if the seed, the blossom and the fruit of Tractarian theology were all to be found in the writings, albeit prolific, of the four acknowledged leaders.

Secondly, conservative theologians have been, perhaps for fifty years and more, rather out of fashion. Mid-Victorian theology is studied primarily through the writings of F. D. Maurice, partly because he was unusually forward-looking, partly also because of the supposition that the works of this elusive theologian, so ripe in their subtle repudiation of conventional notions, might contain somewhere a crock of gold, might conceal within the mass of difficult constructions and eccentric terminology, the answer to theological questions which still sorely exercise the minds of churchmen today.

It was Robert Wilberforce's misfortune to produce his great doctrinal synthesis in the three years which lie each side of 1850. He was attempting to answer questions which had been posed in the first half of the century, knowing little of the storms which were to come – the impact of Darwinism and the fierce clash over *Essays and Reviews*. His writings, therefore, became out of date before they had had a chance to make the impact which they deserved. His task was to look back and to sum up. Maurice, by contrast, looked forward and enquired. This may, indeed, supply the clue to the proper significance of Robert Wilberforce's theological writings. Firstly, he systematised where system was desperately needed. Manning and Gladstone had both cried out for this, deploring the poverty of the dogmatic theology of their time. Where was a Tübingen school in England? Where was their Möhler to produce a work comparable to the *Symbolik*? Robert accepted this challenge, in a spirit of great humility, although manifestly he was peculiarly qualified to make the attempt. Only Pusey could command a greater linguistic apparatus. Robert had gained a working knowledge of Hebrew[8] and had become a very competent German scholar, being familiar with works which the mass of his informed contemporaries had barely heard of.[9] He had also acquired an immense knowledge of patristic sources, and – in his efforts to keep pace with Manning – a fair grasp of Catholic theological writings.

373

In his three great works, *The Doctrine of the Incarnation* (1848), *The Doctrine of Holy Baptism* (1849) and *The Doctrine of the Holy Eucharist* (1853), he drew together the various strands of sacramental teaching, as it had been variously understood and communicated both in past ages and in recent times, to form a single corpus of theology. In the early nineteenth century, as is well known, theological conflict had tended to centre on the issue of baptismal regeneration, in which may be included the great Justification controversy which reached a climax in the late 1830's and early forties.[10] By a natural process, accelerated perhaps by Newman's *Lectures on Justification*, with their stress on the *imparted* righteousness of Christ through the medium of the Eucharist, and also by Pusey's controversial University Sermon of 1843, the conflict gradually shifted away from baptism towards an interest in the nature of the presence in the Eucharist and in the dispute over the sacrificial interpretation of the sacrament. Inevitably, too, this intense exaltation of the mediatory rôle of Christ through the sacraments became inseparable from a fresh appreciation of the supreme importance of the doctrine of the Incarnation; so that a change of emphasis in their doctrinal teaching can be discerned in the theological writings of all the Tractarians – the Atonement (the central doctrine of the Evangelicals) becomes subordinate to the Incarnation[11]; *Christus Redemptor* gives way to *Christus Consummator*.[12]

This is seen most particularly in Pusey, as Professor Chadwick has reminded us: 'He loved to contemplate the presence of Christ in the soul; he conceived obedience, less as action than as a quiet resting in the will of God; he thought of the Eucharist as the gate through which the Lord came to take up His habitation in the soul. In this aspect of Tractarian thought is to be found the chief source of that greater emphasis upon the Incarnation in its relation to the Atonement, which has often been noticed as a characteristic.'[13]

It should be observed that the Tractarians, and those most influenced by them, did not arrive at this change of emphasis unconsciously. Manning admitted to Samuel in 1849 that he had come to the conclusion that the cause of the misunderstandings which their brethren were time and again having to face was the unhappy fact of 'practical unbelief of the Incarnation and its consequences'.[14] Robert Wilberforce felt the same. His writings mark the climax of the movement to exalt the doctrine of the Incarnation 'as the great objective fact of Christianity',[15] before at least the revolutionary re-interpretation of incarnational theology brought about by the fusion of Tractarian and Mauricean teaching in the work of the *Lux Mundi* group, and most notably Charles Gore.

He set out to demonstrate that the two sacraments of Baptism and the Eucharist are subsumed, as it were, in the central doctrine of the Incarnation, so completely related to it that it was impossible to speak of any one of these three doctrines without attaching a significant interpretation to the other two. This comes out in all his theological writings of these years. The least important, for our purpose, was the exceedingly learned treatise on baptism, published in 1849 to refute the Calvinistic assertions of Goode's *Effects of Infant Baptism*. This was much more of a *livre de circonstance* than his other works, a weighty compendium of scripture, patristic, and Reformation treatises on baptism, aimed at proving the false Augustinianism of Calvin and the inadmissibility of attributing the Calvinist denial of the sacramental system, 'by which the blessings of Mediation are distributed through the Body of Christ',[16] to those who framed the formularies of the Church of England.[17]

The other two works are rather massive syntheses of Anglo-Catholic doctrine, as illuminated by an examination in the first instance of the supreme mediatory act of the Son Incarnate, the Second Adam, who 'became the head of man's race, that in Him we might recover the likeness of God, which in Adam we had lost',[18] and, in the second instance, of the supreme mediatory sacrament whereby a channel was ordained to extend to each individual 'those gifts which were bestowed in the Incarnation upon humanity at large'.[19]

The grand design is outlined most lucidly in the sermons preached between 1847 and 1850, published under the title *Sermons on the New Birth of Man's Nature*.[20] Every one of these sermons deals with some aspect of the Incarnation and the sacramental system, and the whole scheme is summed up in the sermon preached before the University of Oxford on 10 March 1850 ('The Sacramental System'), which – for comprehensiveness and clarity – must rank as one of the most revealing documents of Tractarian history. The sermon was preached on the text from St John's first Epistle General (IV. 2–3) in which those who deny that 'Jesus Christ is come in the flesh' exhibit the spirit of Anti-Christ. The acceptance of the doctrine of the Incarnation, therefore, is represented as the very essence of Christianity, to question which is to pass from Christ to Anti-Christ. Thus does St John 'declare Mediation to be the great law of the Gospel Kingdom, the central fact in the economy of grace'.[21] The terms Christ and Anti-Christ can be, therefore, applied respectively to the sacramental and anti-sacramental systems of religion.

> For since the doctrine of Our Lord's Mediation is founded upon His taking our flesh; since its primary law is the re-creation in His person of our common nature, the entrance of divine graces into humanity in its Head and Chief; – therefore some medium is required, by which those things, which were stored up in Him, may be distributed to His brethren. To speak of the Head as the fountain of grace, is to assume the existence of streams, by which it may be transmitted to His members. Now this function is so plainly assigned to Sacraments, that nothing else can be alleged to supply their place. If union with Christ be union with His manhood, it is clearly through these means, whereby we become members of His Body that we are united to Himself. . . . On these means of union are built all those affections and sympathies, which ripen into the fulness of the divine life. Prayer, praise, the converse of the thoughts; public worship or private meditation – all these are means of intercourse with Christ, which have their origin in the Christian's oneness with the Church's head. Not that communion with Christ is confined to the occasions of sacramental approach; but they supply the principle, on which all the other ordinances of grace are dependent. For that real union must underlie them all, whereby men are truly, and not only in name united to Christ. And this union has its being through that Sacramental relation, whereby we are members of His Body, of His flesh, and of His bones. And as this is the Sacramental, so that which is opposed to it may be called the Anti-Sacramental system.[22]

He then turns to a question made famous by the later controversy between H. L. Mansel and F. D. Maurice. How may the finite reach forth to the infinite? Certainly, it is quite beyond man's intellect to serve as a bridge.

> The answer is given in one word, through the Incarnation of Christ. . . . [Thus did God] become capable, in the human nature of the Word, of sympathizing with human sorrows; and manhood become capable of being the seed of grace, through its being taken into God. The one was able to participate through its inferior nature in the weakness of limited humanity; the other through its alliance with a superior nature was endowed with heavenly efficacy.[23]

In another sermon (entitled 'The Mediation of Christ'), he puts the same point with different imagery: 'The manhood of Our Lord . . . is the bridge whereby the gulf between heaven and earth has been spanned over. Thus have men become comrades with God's higher servants; the true Jacob's Ladder is set up; and "the angels of God" ascend and descend on the Son of Man.'[24]

Following from this, the sacraments are represented as 'the natural

376

outworks of the Doctrine of the Incarnation'; through our understanding of the true presence of Christ working through his sacramental ordinances, the truth of the Incarnation is regularly demonstrated to us. In this way 'are we carried on to a genuine belief, that two natures are really united in His adorable Person. For if Godhead and Manhood are truly united in Christ, both must co-operate in those offices which He discharges towards mankind.'[25]

If man had never fallen – if he were still 'the perfect image of his Maker' – then the sacramental channels would be unnecessary. The dream of the gnostics and the rationalists would have some substance. Man and his maker might communicate one with another through 'the mere natural intercourse of mind with mind'. But since Adam sinned, the means of man's recovery has lain in the hope – and in Christ, the fulfilment of that hope – of mediation.

> In the mere intercourse of mind with mind, Sacraments would be an unnatural interruption: but they are exactly suited to effect that union whereby the Divine Head of man's race is bound to His fellows. Since this union is itself foreign to the course of nature, so must the media be by which it is effected; the work cannot depend on their natural influence, but on that influence with which they are super-naturally endowed. And that those outward means which we call Sacraments are truly attended by an inward effect, that what is done on earth in holy mysteries effects a real change in the whole nature of those who are acted upon, is known to us by the distinct declaration of God's Word.[26]

Thus regeneration takes place in baptism; thus man is spiritually nourished in feeding on the flesh and blood of Christ in the Holy Communion.

It is for the playing down of the mediatory rôle of sacraments and for a correspondingly low estimate of the spiritual nature of the Church that Robert Wilberforce takes Schleiermacher to task. He falls into the common Protestant error of representing the Church as the Catholic substitute for the person of Christ. This Robert believed to be – as he once told Samuel very sharply* – either a meaningless form of words or, if it was sincerely maintained with all its implications fully appreciated, dangerous heresy. When Schleiermacher writes thus he is supposing the Church to be some mere human institution, forgetting that it is the

---

* Wrangham MSS. VII. 152. 29 November 1843. 'A very common form of words, but I really do not understand what it means. It seems like saying that you ought not to go into the warmth of the sunshine lest you should mistake the sunshine for the sun. For really all that can be meant by the Church is the truth of Christ's presence with His collective people. How far this can be substituted for Christ I cannot say.'

mystical body of Christ, wherein 'the presence of Christ's manhood' acts 'spiritually on all who are engrafted into Himself'. 'How is it', he continues, 'that a writer who enters so deeply into some parts of the Christian system, and is regarded as their chief authority by a large portion of what are considered the more orthodox Germans, should have adopted a principle, which implies a complete denial of the spiritual life of the Church?'

He puts it down to a false understanding of the doctrine of the Incarnation and of the nature of the Trinity. To Schleiermacher, the medium by which the Holy Spirit works is 'the Christian's inward consciousness', and he supposes that this *modus operandi* can take the place of those mediatory channels which Christ himself had defined, promised and ordained, namely 'the presence of the Holy Ghost within the body of the Church'.[27]

To sum up: the sacramental and anti-sacramental systems are, in reality, 'two different religions'. 'If we adopt one, must we not discard the other? Can we confess Christ's Mediation, and also deny it? Allow the one, and the Sacramental system is a groundless superstition; allow the other, and the Anti-Sacramental system is a presumptuous unbelief.'[28] This notion – that the Incarnation and the two sacraments of Baptism and the Eucharist are really different manifestations of a single phenomenon – is not an original one. If it had been so, it would hardly have appealed to Robert Wilberforce's mind. St Athanasius had claimed that 'a denial of the Personality of God the Son, of necessity involves a denial of the grace of Baptism'[29]; St Irenaeus had declared a similar connection between Incarnation and the real presence in the Eucharist[30]; Bishop Jeremy Taylor had given his authority to the conception that the sacraments are 'the extension of the Incarnation'.[31] What Robert Wilberforce was seeking to do was not only to demonstrate the catholicity of Anglican doctrines on the sacraments, with the supporting testimony of both scripture and the Fathers, but also to examine the origin and recent growth of contrary doctrines so that teaching, which was in essence Sabellian or Gnostic, might be recognised as such in modern guise.

That he would excite controversy, he anticipated without qualms. Indeed, by the time he came to publish his work on the *Doctrine of the Holy Eucharist*, he believed that his relations with his archbishop were so sour that he would certainly be prosecuted.* He rather welcomed an eventuality which would at least force a decision on the personal issue –

* As early as 1849 he had pronounced Archbishop Musgrave's charge of that year heretical (Manning archives. Wilberforce letters, IV. 53).

the question of whether he ought to seek reception into the Roman Church – which was haunting him day and night during these years. His treatment of eucharistic doctrine, with its clear affirmation of the Real Presence and its unequivocal representation of the sacrificial nature of the sacrament, was, after all, little less incautious than the sermons of George Anthony Denison, preached during 1853 and 1854, which provoked almost instant retaliation in the form of legal proceedings.*

The Doctrine of the Holy Eucharist was designed, as the author tells us,[32] to be the sequel to *The Doctrine of the Incarnation*. From the 'grand objective fact of Christianity' he passed to the fulfilment of that act within the Church – 'the crown of public worship; the bond, whereby men are attached to Christ; the focus, in which all Church ordinances culminate'.[33] His definitition of the Real Presence is rooted in the words of Christ, as recorded by St John, 'I am the Bread of Life'; and the significance of this allegory is explored through the writings of the Fathers, chiefly St Augustine, St Chrysostom and St Cyril. Thence he comes to the traditional variations of the teaching on the Presence, illustrated in the following way:

> The Emperor Charlemagne might be said to be present *figuratively*, or *symbolically*, throughout his vast empire, because justice was everywhere administered in his name. He was present throughout it *virtually*, for such was the energy of his character, that his influence was everywhere felt; but *really* he was only present in his palace at Aix-la-Chapelle. If our Blessed Lord's Humanity had no other than that *natural* presence which belongs to common men, His *Real* Presence would in like manner be confined to that one place which he occupies in heaven. But by reason of those attributes which His Manhood possesses through its oneness with God, He has likewise a *supernatural* presence; the operations of which are restricted only by His own will. And His will is to be present in the Holy Eucharist; not indeed as an object to the senses of the receiver, but through the intervention of consecrated elements. So that His Presence does not depend upon the thought and imaginations of men, but upon His own supernatural power, and upon the agency of the Holy Ghost. He is present *Himself*, and not merely by His influence, effects, and operation; by that *essence*, and in that *substance*, which belongs to him as the true Head of mankind. And therefore he is *really* present; and gives His Body to be the *res sacramenti*, or thing signified.[34]

* Denison, too, was inviting prosecution, although rather more bluntly, as was his wont. He described the sermons as 'challenging, and eventually compelling, the public enquiry which I had demanded'. G. A. Denison, *Notes of My Life 1805–1878* (1878), 231.

Just because there is in the Eucharist an 'inward reality' – the Body and Blood of Christ – the sacrament is supplied with an element which may be sacrificially offered; an element missing from both the Zwinglian and Calvinist conceptions of the Eucharist, which because of the absence of any *res sacramenti* cannot allow a sacrificial interpretation.[35] The institution and purpose of this sacrifice spring from, and may be explained by, the nature of Christ's priesthood – of the order of Melchisadek, king and priest. As priest for ever, He perpetually intercedes for us so that there may always be a bridge between the Father in heaven and 'the lower sphere of our earthly service'.[36] While there is no repetition of the sacrifice of the cross, nor any substitution of another victim, the sacrifice which Christ Himself once made is continually and perpetually working within the Eucharist. We say the words 'O Lord God, Lamb of God, Son of the Father, that *takest* away the sins of the world'. We do not put it in the past tense – 'that *tookest* away' – for 'that acceptance, which He purchased through the sacrifice of the Cross, He applies through the sacrifice of the Altar'.[37]

> He who has been consecrated a Priest for ever after the order of Melchisadek [he concludes], chooses this medium for giving effect to His perpetual intercession. . . . He himself it is, who through the voice of His ministers consecrates these earthly gifts, and thus bestows the mystery of His Real Presence. By himself, again, is the precious Victim presented before the Father's throne; and the intervention of their Heavenly Head gives reality to the actions of His earthly ministers.[38]

All this might be very strong and unwholesome fare for an Evangelical to swallow, but to Manning, Gladstone, Phillpotts and others like them it came as manna in the wilderness. Robert did not always carry Samuel with him – certainly not on the Real Presence, for Samuel believed that the disposition of the recipient was an essential factor in the reality of the Presence and was therefore opposed to eucharistical adoration[39] – and sometimes found that he could not satisfy Henry's ardent craving for Romanist excesses. Those who preceded him into the Roman Church were a little uneasy about his unsoundness as an interpreter of Catholic doctrine. Newman felt that certain phrases on the Virgin Mary in *The Doctrine of the Incarnation* betrayed an ignorance of Catholic teaching,*

---

* Kensington MSS. A. 43. 3 April 1850. Also Oratory. Box 137. 17. 9 December 1860, letter to William Wilberforce (junior): 'Protestants don't know what our doctrine is. Dear Robert did not, when he wrote his book on the Incarnation, as I pointed out to him.'

and Samuel, rather gleefully, reported to the author in 1853: 'I hear that the perverts in their secret communications regard your work as the most dangerous entire denial of the great doctrine of Transubstantiation ever put forth.'[40]

Manning, who had been his closest partner in his theological researches, remained convinced that Robert was the most powerful theologian of his generation and dearly sought to harness that intellect to the service of Rome. Such talents, he thought, were wasted in the Anglican Church; Phillpotts and Gladstone, on the other hand, believed that their continued dedication to the cause of the recovery of Catholic truth would do more to check the spread of heresy and infidelity than the writings of any other churchman of their times. Phillpotts came more and more to refer difficult questions to his judgment, especially after April 1851 when he could no longer rely on Manning's help. In March of that year he asked Robert to assist him in the preparation of his charge, admitting with rare magnanimity, that 'there is hardly one other man whose concurrence I so much value'.[41]

Gladstone, too, was rarely given to extremes of praise. On the appearance of *The Doctrine of the Holy Eucharist*, however, he cast aside all restraint. He wrote to Robert at the end of October 1853:

> I cannot remember the appearance of any work of Theology from which I should expect anything like the same amount of real revival and progress, both in doctrine and in the habits of thought by which doctrine is embraced and assimilated, that yours I trust is destined to produce.
>
> If there is an especial feature of the book which beyond all others gives it strength, it seems to me to be this, that you have maintained so faithfully the historical and traditional character in it, and have theorised so little; except in those parts where theory was appropriate and even necessary, viz. the *rationale* you have given of the Lutheran and Calvinian opinions, and of the tendency of various schools in the Church from particular circumstances to derange the equilibrium of the true doctrine.[42]

It is evident that at this stage Gladstone had little idea of how tenuous were the bonds which tied Robert to the Anglican Church.

By March 1854, however, he realised the truth and launched into a series of long letters to persuade Robert to come to his senses. In his letter dated 26th March while the country was seething with excitement over the news from the Crimea, he wrote from Downing Street a long treatise to show that the tide had turned and that with W. K. Hamilton's appointment to the bishopric of Salisbury a new era of progress in Catholic principles had begun.[43] Robert could not resist, in his reply, pointing to the incongruity of Gladstone writing on such a subject at such a time: 'Your letter perfectly amuses me', he wrote, 'by its entire abstinence from all topics which one would suppose were rife last Sunday in Downing Street. If it is preserved hereafter people will think the date a mistake – and hold it impossible such a letter could have been written from Downing Street the day after the last Courier returned from St Petersburg before the Russian War.'[44]

In September that year Gladstone opened his mind more fully in a letter which, when its full implications are considered, must rank as one of the most remarkable judgments on the work and achievements of a contemporary to which Gladstone ever gave expression. He began by asking Robert to stay with him at Hawarden. He continued:

Under an impulse as one had hoped of Almighty God, you have for many years past brought your whole time and strength to bear upon the vital and central truth of Christianity, have resuscitated in many souls a faith which had sunk to the condition of dry bones, and have by the sheer force and merit of your labours established an association between your own name and the living tradition of the Catholic faith in the Church of England respecting the Incarnation, which I can only compare, in our smaller sphere, and on a lower level, to what the association was between the name of St Augustine and the doctrine of original sin, or the name of St Athanasius and that of the Trinity. I am not as I trust a flatterer, and I am not speaking of degree but of kind when I venture to affirm so remarkable a parallelism. It is at any rate not invented for the occasion; for I have long seen or seemed to see, and said to others, that the care and charge of this great dogma and of its consequences had in the Providence of God devolved for our day and generation upon you.

You may conceive what the feelings of an individual believer would have been if St Athanasius had said, on account of such and such language, that I find in such and such Fathers, or on any other account, I find that my doctrine, the true doctrine, is not the doctrine of the existing Church and I must leave it: or to draw my analogy closer if St Augustine thinking himself unable to prove the identity of his system from the Greek Fathers had taken refuge among the Donatists. Of course I do not say that by such a course either of these great champions would have destroyed that true profession of the Faith for which they previously had fought: but I say they would have done more towards destroying it than by any other possible combination they could have devised, and that surely they had far better never have opened their mouths than after opening them have brought their course to such an ending.

I do not mean to raise or beg the question whether the Church of Rome is fairly compared to the Donatists: my meaning is to point your view, if I only could, to the fearful position in which so far as depends on man, you in a contingency I cannot bring myself to name will leave those great doctrines with which as a responsible teacher in the Church of England you have identified your name.[45]

Whatever may be the qualities for which Gladstone is remembered by posterity, one of them is certainly not levity. He always meant what he said. And if Robert Wilberforce was to him the Athanasius or Augustine of his generation, then a motive clearly existed – over and above the normal charity which one may feel towards an individual soul – for fighting with unmatched vigour to restrain him from desertion. But when this opinion of his qualities was shared by those who had already gone over – and notably by Manning, whose esteem for Robert's learning was heightened by the closest personal affection* – the arena was all prepared for a battle royal. The champions assembled to contest for the possession of Robert's soul.

III. *The Battle of Burton Agnes*

Perhaps never in the history of man have two such formidable teams of contestants arrayed themselves on rival sides to dispute for the prize of an individual soul. On the Catholic side, working independently, though with the force of a combined operation, were Manning, Newman, Henry Wilberforce and last – but through the prolixity of his representations and the vehemency of his emotional claims, certainly not least – William Henn, the convert who had once been Robert's curate. On the Anglican side, the list comprised Gladstone, Keble, Pusey, Hook and Samuel Wilberforce, Bishop of Oxford, fighting – it must be admitted – with less than his usual vigour through the disability of a breaking heart. Every available weapon was used. Every conceivable appeal to the interests, both in this world and the next, of the perplexed victim was offered, temptingly, subtly, emotionally, menacingly. No possible argument in favour of this Church or that was neglected; no corruption on the other side, no wayward extravagance of the human spirit, no significant and revealing failing escaped the discernment of eager and interested eyes. It was all committed to paper, all dispatched to the rectory at

---

* It is significant, for instance, that Manning wished Robert to become a Roman Catholic not only for the the sake of his soul but also so that he could serve *under* him. In June 1853 he suggested a scheme for a community of priests, devoting themselves to 'study, writing, and preaching', of which he should be a member, serving under Robert as Warden, E. S. Purcell, *op. cit.*, II. 33.

Burton Agnes. And what has survived from a subsequent dispersion would itself fill a volume of daunting dimensions, as fascinating in its revelation of all that the word 'catholic' can embrace, as it would be chastening in its portrayal of the myopia which can inflict pious people who, while working for the same end, will cut each other's throats in order to attain it. No wonder, we may feel, that Robert Wilberforce was the last eminent Anglican convert of this decade. Both sides were exhausted. Indeed, there was nothing left to be said.

Some of the polemic had been solicited. Robert took the initiative in approaching Newman, with whom he had scarcely corresponded at all since the events of autumn 1845. He had been reading again the *Essay on Development*, especially the opening discussion of the inconsistencies in patristic writings.[1] Could Newman give him further guidance? How, for instance, could papal headship be reconciled with the testimony of the early Fathers? Newman replied in a letter of great length.

> It is long since I read my 'Development', and I dare say, did I read it, there are things which would stumble me in it. I did not know at the time the Catholic doctrine in detail, and I applied the theory to details in which it ought not to be applied. Indeed, I was conscious when I was writing it, that I was making a very bold and needless application of it with reference to the *facts* of the case – but I said, 'Well, it is all a fortiori'. If facts are more clearly in the first age in favour of the present received Catholic faith than I have said, then we need not apply the theory so fully or we *might* not at all. However, so far as I know, I do not depart from the principle of the book at all. . . . The principle I hold to be this:– that, till a point of the once delivered doctrines was canvassed, analyzed and digested by the minds of the divines etc. of the Church, you could not answer for individuals, however able and holy, not speaking *inconsistently* about it, contradicting themselves etc.

He referred to differences of viewpoint in the understanding of the authority of the Bishop of Rome, the Real Presence and the nature of the Trinity:

> In matters of thought it is a very difficult thing indeed, not to be inconsistent in our words, especially when party feeling (as in the case of St Cyprian) comes in. . . . St Cyprian is claimed by Protestants as denying the Pope's Supremacy. . . . I think if any one had asked St Cyprian in a cooler moment, he would have acknowledged he had spoken to [sic] strongly – and if any one had said to St Gregory 'Do you really mean so and so', he would have indignantly disclaimed it – St Dionysius *did* explain.
> And to whom? to the Pope. It is to me wonderful that you should think

the case of St Clement, St Victor, St Dionysius, St Stephen, Aurelian's reference to the Pope in the matter of Paul of Samosata, and the like, not *good evidence*, considering the paucity of evidence in those times. As to the Canons of Sardica, I am not at all certain that they were not originally passed at Nicea – or at least not done up in one volume with them – and called by one name, as Nehemias is 'the 2nd book of Esdras'. But I cannot argue the point.

He then turned to the question of accommodation and the *disciplina arcani*.

The two points of Ultramontane supremacy are universal jurisdiction and infallibility. As to the first, *we* know even now how difficult it is for the Pope to enforce jurisdiction with the state of a particular country against him, and how he is forced to temporize lest he should throw a country, which is disposed to resist him (*though it receives the doctrine*) into temptation of schism. This would be strikingly the case in early times – especially, if the Holy See, or rather the Holy Ghost, saw, that one truth must *sink into the mind*, i.e. be developed, before another; e.g. first the being of God (against Gnosticism etc.) then the Divinity of the Son (against Arianism), then the Incarnation etc. etc. – *not as if the truths were not given from the first*, but they had to be worked out historically over long periods, in order to be realized in the hearts of the millions and of the teaching body etc.

. . . What I felt for some years before I became a Catholic, was 'It is *more* probable that the Roman communion is the Catholic Church, than that *these* are not true developments of primitive doctrine'. I saw overpowering reasons for the first point – I saw great difficulties in believing the second, that they *were* developments – but the question was whether these difficulties outweighed, neutralized, or invalidated these reasons. The one was a positive, categorical, substantive conclusion – the other was no positive statement, fact, or the like, but a difficulty in the way of a fact. Truth is something positive – either there is a Church, or there is not – difficulties decide nothing. I want (or, rather I am *bound* in this matter) to find a conclusion. If God has given a revelation, he has given it organ and seat. These difficulties do not decide for me *where* that organ and seat is – or that [there] is none – or that there is no revelation.

There is a note on one of Bishop Butler's Sermons which I have intended, if now I wrote on the subject, to quote. I think it is about house building. If in a huge chaos of iron bars, pillars etc. etc. I clearly see on a large scale the materials of a house, I can come to a pretty clear conclusion. 'This is one of the iron houses intended to be sent out to the colonies', though there are portions of which *I can make nothing*. It is not as if those outlying bits made up anything whatever. In like manner, if the facts of early history build up something very like the present Roman communion, it is vain to say 'Where does *this* fact go? What am I to do with *that*?' This piece

385

of iron looks like part of a waggon, that like part of a steam engine –
Won't the best way be to make a fancy building of my own, which will
comprise every fact whatever, and turn out neither waggon, nor wind mill,
nor ship, nor house, nor wheelbarrow, but something the world never
saw and never will see, but which *according to my idea* satisfies all the primitive phenomena of the case.[2]

Robert was impressed by this letter (as well he might be for it is one of
Newman's finest), but not convinced. He wrote to ask Newman if he
could visit him in January to take the discussion further. Newman replied
that he would be in Ireland. At any rate he could not, and would not, do
for Robert what he could only do for himself. Robert's bane was his own
enquiring mind which conjured up so many objections against every position that truth became obscured in a fog of argument. He was immobilised
by the weight of his intellectual equipment 'while many a David, who
eschews Saul's armour, hits the giant in the very forehead'. 'I have,
some little time since', he continued, 'been saying Mass for you – and I
heartily do wish that prayers and Masses would make you move faster.
You are in the *way* – you are *coming* – why don't you trot on a bit – I
don't ask you, with Froude of old, to go across country but do put your
spurs into your horse – my dear Robert Wilberforce.'[3]

Robert did not consult Newman personally; and indeed felt nervous
at the prospect of showing himself at the Birmingham Oratory. Newman
assured him in August 1854 that he need not worry. No one would
recognise him. There would be no scandal. He might bump into one or
two 'brummagem snobs and factory girls, who know nothing of the
theological world whatever'. Dressed in his archidiaconal attire, he would
be taken for Faber or one of the London Oratorians, coming to pay their
respects.[4] When this letter reached Robert, however, the end was very
near. He was past the stage of needing advice; he wanted only love and
understanding.

Manning had shown him this. As early as March 1852 he had written
to Robert from Rome:

> Well do I know what you are passing through. And what would I not do
> to help you? I well remember how 'the sight of my eye went from me', and
> I seemed to taste nothing. . . . I never venture to press you, greatly as I
> long for you. But I respect you and your trials as I desired to be treated
> myself. All I fear for you is chronic doubt, and the dimness which delay
> spreads over the clearest evidence. I believe nothing will, because nothing
> can, go beyond the revelations of the last three years to prove that the
> Church of England is a human society, out of the sphere and guidance of

Henry Manning, Archbishop of Westminster

Samuel Wilberforce, Bishop of Oxford

the Divine Spirit. It has not in it the essential form of the Catholic Church. Just as the kirk in Scotland. If it were to accept the whole Council of Trent at the next Assembly, it would be a human society. Nothing short of submission to the visible unity of the One Kingdom could make it to be a Church.

Farewell, dear Robert. I hope to be in England at the end of June for some months, and to see you on some island or boat in a neutral river, as great powers are wont to meet.[5]

From time to time Robert would send Manning a list of questions, asking for guidance over his intellectual difficulties – the limits of the Church's jurisdiction, the relationship between the Tridentine decrees and patristic teaching, the precise meaning and implications of the doctrine of Transubstantiation. After the publication of his work on the Eucharist, he was inclined to take its good reception – and the fact that no proceedings were started against him – as signs that the Church of England was not entirely lost. Manning would not have it so. 'What would not be accepted in the Church of England?' he wrote. 'Is your book accepted half as widely as Hoadlyism was a hundred years ago? To me it is the sign of death that the Church of England suffers you to write as you do, and Archbishop Sumner to be at Canterbury. It is *barbam vellem mortuo leoni*'.[6]

Perhaps the writing of another great dogmatic treatise would cure his ills. 'Your private judgement has convinced you of the Incarnation, Baptism, the Eucharist. Apply it now to the third and last clause of the Baptismal Creed, "I believe in the Holy Ghost, the Holy Catholic Church". Write a book on this next. To go on with details of doctrine is to wink hard at the point.'

He proceeded to challenge Robert's contention that the Roman Church looked weakest in the light of historical study, and, in his answer, anticipated the notorious aphorism on the decree of Papal infallibility ('the dogma must overcome history') which has rendered the memory of Cardinal Manning unpleasing to many liberal scholars.[7]

> When you say that the Roman Church is not historically the same, is it not to say *my* view of its history differs from its *own*? But may not the Catholic Church know its own history better, and by a lineal knowledge and consciousness, to which no individual can oppose himself without unreasonableness? I am perfectly persuaded that the Catholic Church is historically the same in personal identity and functions. Details are like grey hairs or wrinkles as compared with youth; or the character of the man with that of the child. But the person is the same.[8]

Then Robert was confronted with that traditional stumbling-block –

Liguorianism. St Alphonsus of Liguori, whose works were not deemed worthy of censure by the Catholic Church, had taught that it is not always sinful to lie. What did Manning say to this? The reply came back: St Alphonsus did not say quite what is usually supposed; and anyway the most difficult passages from his writings were to be found in Jeremy Taylor, who treats the subject far less acceptably. 'I can defend St Alphonsus, but I cannot defend all J. Taylor.'9

Robert showed Manning's reply to Richard Cavendish, who was not in the least convinced.

> That Liguori was a saintly man, I do not at all doubt [he replied] – and that he did not *mean* to inculcate lying I am equally sure. But this only makes the matter worse in my opinion, for does it not excite grave doubts as to a system in which the holiest of its teachers can lay down rules of action which *must* and *do* efface all practical distinction between truth and falsehood? And this too with especial reference to the immediate relations between Man and his Creator. It is all very well for Manning and others to say that all these things admit of *explanation*. That is just what I complain of – It is no doubt by a skilful use of words possible to explain away every charge – special pleading can always make a case for every system – but still the common innate sense of mankind rebels against admitting excuses for saying that black is white.10

Robert, in his later letters, passed from intellectual difficulties to the more popular and chauvinist objections to Rome: Italian devotions and the paralysing effects of submission to the Roman system. Manning rather took this as a sign that Robert's resistance was weakening. He refused to take his objections seriously:

> You know how far I am superstitious or a miracle-monger, and therefore you will give to my testimony such weight as you see fit. . . . If you will read any history of the Holy See you will see how absurd it is to take Rome as the representative or creation of the Church. It has been the untamed, half-tamed, untameable world against which the Holy See has been in continual conflict. It is its contrast and antagonist, not itself.

He spoke of the kindness which he had received both from Cardinal Antonelli and the Pope.

> The whole is a silly gossip. Almost as bad as your talking of your being 'required to carry out the system of St Alphonso'. You are an old Yorkshireman, and know that you, and I, are required to carry out the system of no man.11

It was William Henn, Robert's former curate in the mid-1840's, who perhaps disturbed him most of all with his repeated thrusts at the Achilles' heel of the Anglican Church – the Royal Supremacy and the basis of ecclesiastical authority. Henn was an Irishman, of sickly disposition and a sharp and restless mind. He had developed intense Anglo-Catholic enthusiasms while he was at Burton Agnes and had also become deeply attached to all the Wilberforce family, Robert most particularly. In 1847 ill health forced him to leave Yorkshire for a warmer climate. He went to Germany and thence to Italy, suffering from a chronic condition of the throat which was adjudged by his physician so delicate that it suffered injury even from 'the necessary act of swallowing'.[12] From 1848 onwards he was certain that his final refuge would be the Roman Church, and in December 1849 – after a brief visit to England – he left a sealed envelope with Robert to be opened only when he subsequently directed. This envelope contained a letter exonerating his former rector from any influence in disturbing his allegiance to the Anglican Church, and inviting him to reveal its contents to those who would inevitably accuse him of secret and irresponsible proselytism.

> Here then I leave it upon record that should I at any time abandon the Church of England to join the Roman, I shall do so not because of your influence – no, not even remotely, but in opposition to it. Be the step right or wrong, blameworthy or the reverse, you are in no wise responsible for it. I may go further and say that your influence has always steadily told the other way. It has been the existence within the English Church of what is sometimes called the Anglo-Catholic school – it is this with its teaching, its piety, its learning, which has so long prevented me from feeling the doubts which embarrass me, and which even now prevents me from at once and decisively yielding to them. . . . Of this school you, owing to the providential circumstances which brought us together, have long been to me the most effectual and impressive representative.[13]

Henn was actually received into the Roman Church at Rome on 11 November 1850. He wrote to Robert that very day:

> I was received . . . by Cardinal Fransoni in his private chapel at the Propaganda. The rite is a short one, commencing with some prayers, after which follows the profession of faith which consists of the substance of the Creeds (Nicene and Pope Pius, as they are commonly called), then an absolution from the censures of the Church, and a few more prayers. After this I was conditionally baptized, having been previously asked whether I could give any information as to whether the Sacrament had been administered to me in my infancy with the necessary exactness, which I certainly could not. . . . My application for admission into the C.C. was made to the Rector of the Irish College, who arranged all for me that has been done. Nothing could exceed the kindness of all parties, but without a

word of compliment or flattery. Simply I have been made to feel that a great grace has been conferred on me, and that I shall be worse off than ever if I fail to correspond to it.

He promised that he would not press Robert too hard.

Your mind is one which under God must convert itself. It will work out its own conclusions, and will I feel very sure sooner or later arrive at those which are true. I do not mean that it is a mind closed against influences from others – far from it; but whatever it derives from them in the way of suggestion, it must after all sift and examine for itself before it be cordially accepted. . . . *You'll* be a Catholic yet, I feel persuaded; and will be a perplexed, distracted, troubled man until you are one.
. . . Good-bye my darling Robert. Dare I send my love to Mrs. W.? If I may, I do.[14]

Henn hardly kept his word. He wrote so often to sing the praises of Romanism and to expose the follies of the Church of England, that eventually Robert indicated by his silence that he had had enough.* He was told by the importunate Henn that his dilatoriness was almost perverse,[15] that he was labouring under the most dreadful delusion that his writings were helping to restore Catholic doctrine in the Anglican Church.

You may indeed broach within the E.C. [he wrote] principles eminently Catholic, but you cannot logically locate them there. . . . Newman tried this, say, with the spiritual organisation of the Church as opposed to Erastianism; Manning with infallibility, as opposed to opinion; you with Church authority as opposed to private judgment. But it is all in vain: none of these will work in your system; it won't hold them: it is like pouring new wine into old bottles, and in fact *your* bottle seems already bursting. But why wait for it to burst in your face? Why postpone a conversion till it loses its merit?

He should close his ears to the blandishments of Gladstone.

It does seem to me the veriest stuff talking as you suppose Mr G. does, of appealing to a future General Council. But (as *you* know) it was ever the way with heretics. And if there was one, the E.C. has taken good care to leave herself a loop-hole to escape from deferring to it – 'General Councils *may* err, and have erred'.
My darling fellow, you see how in spite of myself I get back to discussion with you; and rush on as if I were walking up and down your library or your garden. I can't help it. I do so yearn for you, and so wish I could be worthy to move so much as a pebble out of your way that so you might

---

* In a letter dated 1 October 1851 (Henn letters, no 18), Henn promised to keep off subjects concerning his correspondent's soul, but to write merely to exchange domestic news.

the sooner be one with us. Don't mistake my eagerness for arrogance or rudeness. It is nothing of the sort. I love you, honour you, as much as ever; and would do anything, except stifle my heart's wishes for your conversion, to serve you.[16]

Henn was never himself to see his prayers answered. He had been fighting illness all his life. In July 1853 he contracted typhus fever at Marseilles and died before the month was out.*

Robert's Anglican friends knew something of the pressures to which he was being subjected from the ranks of the converts. Their own efforts were scarcely less importunate. Gladstone fastened upon every occasion for optimism – the appointment of W. K. Hamilton as Bishop of Salisbury in March 1854, the passing of the Colonial Church Bill through Parliament, the gradual ascendancy which Samuel was gaining on the episcopal bench – to show that the troublous times were passing. W. F. Hook was always ready to inject Robert with his own special serum for those who should ever show signs of succumbing to the Romish contagion. Hook's head had been turned – not without reason – by the disastrous course of events at St Saviour's, Leeds. He suspected secret machinations and dark conspiracies at work around him, all controlled and engineered by the sinister figure of Cardinal Wiseman, who had somehow contrived to secure the services of Keble and Pusey as popish agents. Robert must be warned in time.

The occasion of Henry's secession provoked Hook's first letter of admonition.

> I have mourned over the loss of your Brother Henry. But from all I had heard of him I was not surprised. If men take Romish Facts, and Romish influences away; if they indulge in sarcastic fault finding as regards the Church of England; if they make black on one side appear white, and white in the other, because a little soiled, appear black; if they read Romish books of devotions, and for Romish follies desert the Bible; if for the practical manliness of English Piety, they adopt the childish sentimentalism of Romish folly and affectation; if they give their Heart to Rome, even before their intellects are perverted – what are we to think or expect? Oh! My dear Wilberforce, how I wish you would reconsider your Principles so as to form them anew – Yes, let us be a band of faithful Church of England men, – and then we may defy the Pope and the Devil, – and really stay the progress of that infidelity of which Popery is the dry nurse, if Rationalism is the Father.†

* E. S. Purcell, *op. cit.*, II. 33. Manning passed the news to Robert: 'Dear William Henn is gone. . . . It is a great sorrow, in which you and I know how to share.'

† Kensington MSS. G. 5. 7 September 1850. In the same letter Hook described Pusey and Manning as heretics and Keble as a 'deeply empassioned Romanizer'.

Two years later Hook was so convinced that Pusey and Wiseman were in league and that somehow Robert had been seduced into joining their company, that he refused to allow him to accept an invitation to preach at St Saviour's.[17] When Robert objected, Hook duly apologised for his extravagances and offered to set down on paper what he conceived to be the *fons et origo* of Robert's errors.

> We both of us regard the Church as the Depository of Grace: and there-fore I can understand how the Church, in its most corrupt state, administered Grace through her sacraments. . . . But I believe the Depository of *Truth*, to be the Bible: and the Church to be only so far the Depository of the Truth, as it is the keeper and witness of Holy Writ. The Church is to be tried by the Bible; and in interpreting the Bible, the voice of the Church has only that influence upon me, which an opinion very generally expressed must have upon any modest enquirer. The creeds themselves are thus in my opinion only helps.[18]

Robert, much as he loved and respected Hook, saw that they could never be reconciled. He was hurt, however, to find that Pusey seemed to have little sympathy with him in his trials. When, in September 1854, Robert had reached the conclusion that conscience compelled him to renounce his subscription to the Royal Supremacy, and sought Pusey's support, he received a rather peevish letter in reply.

> I cannot but think [Pusey wrote] that you have taken a technical view of the Royal Supremacy. I cannot see that it means anything more than was put forth in those declarations*; and the very fact that yours which was the strongest, passed uncensured established the legality of subscription in that meaning. On the negative side, appeals (as you so well know) were disallowed in the African Canons, as decidedly as in our own. On the positive side, I cannot see what ground there can be, why the Sovereign should not see that justice should be done to all his subjects.
>
> But as to your subscription you have decided. . . . I suppose that actually it does not make a very great difference to you, since I understand that your parochial duties, on account of your deafness, devolved chiefly on your curates. But there seems such a tendency now to make this or that a test of the validity of the Church, as though even wrong things might not be done or mistakes be made which did not separate from Christ. They are very grievous things which cut off either the individual or the body from the Body of Christ.[19]

Robert replied that the deed was done and that he felt it advisable to go abroad for a period to consider his next step. Pusey, knowing that this would inevitably lead to his secession, wrote again with far more feeling.

* The declarations, referred to above, which were drawn up by Manning, Wilber-force and others after the Gorham Judgment, protesting against the Oath of Supremacy.

My dear Friend, I must write to ask you earnestly to reconsider your plan of going abroad. I do not know in what position you consider yourself. For although you have withdrawn your subscription to the Crown, I know not that you have thereby hindered yourself from exercising any priestly function. . . . But, abroad, you are not giving yourself a fair chance. I know not how or where you would communicate, unless you consecrated yourself. Isolated, alone, outward circumstances would press upon you – and inward loneliness. Do reconsider this, and see whether you cannot again give yourself to some work which may benefit souls and advance God's truth. It makes one's heart bleed anew.[20]

This was exactly how Samuel felt. Once Robert abandoned an active, pastoral life, he would be lost. He was very nervous when he received news that Robert had decided to buy an estate in Ireland (in Connemara) to which he could retire in solitude when need arose. He would see there 'the worst forms of Protestantism'; also he would be perilously close to Henry, who was working at that time in Dublin.[21] Besides, 'logic cannot settle the many nice points which must bear on the final decision', Samuel pointed out to him in November 1853. 'What *is* wanted is a *right* judgment – the special guiding of God's spirit. Now then, how can *that* be most certainly sought? – Not, as it seems to me, by one in your position, retiring from the activity of work into his study – but by doing with all his powers the work appertaining to his station.'[22] He might have reminded Robert of what happened to Newman once he retired to the solitude of Littlemore.

According to Samuel, Robert's troubles were threefold. He was too much enamoured of system. His mind strove for the ordered and the logical. Everything must fit into place.[23] Secondly, he was too impatient – or at least, too easily discouraged; and this blinded him to the real progress which might be discerned in the spirituality of the Anglican Church.[24] Finally, he was too easily talked over; too ready to listen to Henry's 'eager snapping',[25] too humble to argue his own view against clever opponents.[26] All these deficiencies Samuel brought to Robert's notice; but above all he appealed to his heart. It was impossible for Robert to plead in return that Samuel should try to keep his personal feelings and his spiritual work in separate compartments. 'My love for you overflows all my work', Samuel replied. 'And if ever – which may God in His great mercy forbid – you were seduced from us, I think all my work would be at an end and I should hang down my head to my life's end.'[27]

In desperation Robert turned to John Keble. Thirty years ago he had learnt of Catholic tradition, and the treasures which might be found in the early Fathers, from Keble's lips. This had been the turning-point of his life. As many had done before him, he now laid bare all the perplexities of his troubled soul in the hope that his former master might convey something of his own resolute assurance to one whose faith in Anglicanism was near collapse. Keble felt the sense of obligation. Whereas to others his reply had meant little more than 'I feel no doubt. Why should you?', he roused himself to a serious and prolonged examination of the mistakes which had dimmed the vision of his most learned disciple.

The lengthiest treatment of Robert's problems comes in a letter written from Torquay, dated 8 July 1851. He first turned to the question of the Church's 'living voice' which must guide the faithful to the end of time.

I wonder whether you have really grappled with the thought which our old friend Aristotle (in his *Politics* I think) makes so much of, that there is a danger of mistaking the well-being of a state (or Church) for its being. To get very wrong by counting something essential which is only very desirable. If the Fathers do speak as you say of the necessity of 'a living voice' at all times, we ought to look well into their words and see whether they are not speaking of this secondary sort of necessity. As far as I can now call to mind, I should not say that their writings would lead one to expect that doctrinal matters should always be so clear and plain in the Church as some lately have maintained. e.g. St Basil speaks of the sad, unsettled state of things, and the need of some authority to settle them, over and over again, in words which we might well borrow. Yet he had no doubt nor unsettlement about his own faith. Why? Because he kept to what had been once for all delivered by the whole Church. It was a great grief to him, but no difference to his faith, if all the Bishops round him swerved from the Nicene verities. I cannot but think that it would have appeared very strange to him, to be told that the faith of the Church was most doubtful, though her services and formularies were unaltered, because a certain number, or even all, of her children were hypocritical or false or unreal in their way of taking those formularies. I should expect him still to say, that God be true, but every man a liar – and not only in his time, but continually in Church history, the 'judging power' i.e. the discipline necessary to guard doctrine, was in abeyance for different causes – tyranny of emperors – unfaithfulness or infrequency of councils or what not – yet the Church continued in being; and good Catholics submitted their minds, not always to the decrees of present councils, but to those of *past* councils, as far as they went; to Scripture and antiquity, when these two were undoubted, or when the balance of testimony was clear; and to a future council 'in the preparation of their minds' when a real and great question arose. But no living voice, we may be sure, would have made Athanasius an Arian or Cyril a Nestorian. Neither did those who determined the great questions do it as of a sort of inspired authority, as the

Pope now seems to do, but always as grounding what they said on Scripture and tradition.

Here, then, more clearly than he ever expressed elsewhere, may be found the meaning of Keble's alleged assertion, after the Gorham Judgment, that 'if the Church of England were to fail, it would be found in my parish'. He would, like St Basil, say 'that God be true, but every man a liar'.

> You say [he continued] we are two provinces against the whole Church – but is not this assuming the point in question? When did the whole Church affirm that it was absolutely necessary for a Christian explicitly to believe the Eucharistic sacrifice, to pray for the dead, or to believe in any kind of purgatory? That the two first of these are most necessary and desirable (perhaps) to the entire well-being of the Church, I may well believe; but it is another thing to put them on a footing with articles of the Creed. To the third, as more than a probable opinion, I should entirely demur. For how can that be the judgment of the whole Church, and part of the foundation, on which St Augustine (to go no further) could say no more than he has said on this subject? The whole Church, with me, means 'semper' as well as 'ubique'.

He then took Robert to task for applying the word *patriarch* to the Bishop of Rome and for using the term 'objective presence' as opposed to ' a real *sacramental* presence' when describing the nature of the Eucharist. There is 'a presence for all the purposes of the sacrament', but not otherwise, and he confessed that 'there is more to me by a great deal in the quiet veneration which I see in our devout old people – in some e.g. whom you have known at Fairford – than in the prostrations etc. which I saw at St Saviour's.'

As to difficulties in the Anglican position, one should not lose sight of the fact that there were other, and possibly greater, difficulties in the Roman or the Greek systems.

> Modern Rome avowedly claims a power to add new articles to the faith without any *consensus patrum*: as in the matter of the immaculate conception ... to say nothing of the refusal of the cup, purgatory with indulgences added to it, and other points which to my eyes at least have not a shadow of appearances in antiquity or in Scripture either. To accept this, I must pin my faith on the full doctrine of development – i.e. I must believe a constant stream of fresh revelation, prophecy literally inspired, but without the credentials of which I know to have been true prophecy. I do not see my way in this, but I see too clearly, and Scripture seems to warn me, what infinite mischief may result from it.[23]

It seems – from Keble's pleasure at Robert's reply – that for a moment his mind was eased. But two years later, Keble had cause to write several more letters to him, rather more sharply expressed. In these we may find two very characteristic attitudes which go far to explain why Keble could never fully enter the minds of men like Ward and Oakeley, or Anglo-Catholics like Allies and Henry Wilberforce, who took their lead from Manning in the years after 1845. In the first place, his natural humility – or his inherited faith which had never in his formative years been assailed by doubts – refused to allow him to draw invidious comparisons between the Church of his baptism and other communions. And he was horrified when he discovered that Robert Wilberforce, whose temperament he had supposed to be very similar to his own, was falling victim to this sin. As early as August 1851 he had warned Robert of the dangers. 'I trust, dear friend, that you are not allowing yourself to look out for the worst possible construction on what is said and done in our Church: *that* would be very unlike the R.W. whom I used to know.'[29] In September 1854 he reproved him bitterly for paying so little heed to that warning. 'The truth is (excuse plain speaking from an old friend, whose conscience is even now wringing him that he has not practised it more towards you long since) that you have for some time been drawing towards that mind, so palpable in many others of our old friends, of taking up with the very slightest evidence when it tells in favour of Rome, while in a hard and almost supercilious way you make much of every blemish on the other side.'[30]

Secondly, Keble had been brought up always to understand that those who fight for the truth are always punished for their pains in this world. The folly of the younger generation was that it allowed itself to be upset and discountenanced by failure. This had been Newman's undoing. The hostile charges of the episcopal bench in 1841 should have confirmed the fact that truth was on his side and that he was paying the expected price. Now Robert Wilberforce was going the same way. God had raised him up to teach; the results of that teaching were in God's hands. It was not for him to turn his back on those who were apparently stupid or blind. 'Surely', Keble wrote to him, 'if, as it seems to me, God has vouchsafed to give you before many others the gift of discerning and expressing sacred truth, you and we all, I trust, shall feel bound to pray as well as we can that you may have the gift of patience also, of humility and candour . . . which some alas! have so sadly forgotten. You will not at once think the truth rejected, if you find many who perhaps ought to know better but do not, suspending their judgment for the present.'[31]

IV. *The Last Capitulation*

So what was Robert to do? One charged him with being over-cautious, another with being impulsive. Some thought he had too much humility; others too little. Henn accused him of being too much under the influence of his brother; Samuel accused him of being too easily influenced by the converts. Why had he to suffer so? Why was it ordained that he should cause so much suffering to others?

The situation at Burton Agnes was intolerable in the three years after Manning's secession. Jane had an invalid brother on his death-bed, and Robert had fearful doubts about the propriety of concealing his own fears of the unsafety of dying separated from the true Church.[1] Jane herself died in January 1853, after months of illness, in which Robert had had to delude her about his own thoughts and miseries. He was worried, too, about Eddy, his younger son. Willy and Eddy had gone to Eton, along with their cousin Herbert (Samuel's eldest boy). Willy went up to Balliol, where he was highly successful, but Eddy, who was unhappy at Eton, pleaded with his father to let him join the navy as a cadet. For a while he and Herbert Wilberforce had been together on the same ship.[2] He abandoned this after four years, tried unsuccessfully to follow his brother to Balliol, and then – after travelling on the continent for some months – began to have visions of becoming a great writer. Robert sternly disapproved. 'It is a mere matter of vanity', he confided to Samuel. He found it impossible to understand how one who bore the Wilberforce name could choose to waste his talents on frivolities which were 'of no use to any living creature'.[3] It distressed him, too, that neither of his sons had very strong religious feelings and could not therefore offer their father any sympathy in his predicament. He knew that if he went over to Rome, he would take none of his family with him.

In the end – as Manning and Henn had prophesied – it was the question of Church authority and the inadmissibility of the Royal Supremacy, that tipped the scales. It had agitated Robert's mind since the Gorham Judgment.[4] When his trilogy on sacramental doctrine had been completed, he felt that he could no longer afford to thrust the crucial issue aside, and he turned, therefore, to a study of the origins of the Petrine commission and its development into the papal supremacy. His findings were published in the last book which he was ever to write – *An Inquiry into the Principles of Church-Authority.*

Samuel was unjust when he told Gladstone that he thought that Robert's last book marked a sorry declension in his intellectual powers.[5] It is a masterly work; clear, learned and eloquent. The subject matter – and, indeed, the frame of mind in which it was written – may be compared to Newman's *Essay on Development*. Both men had set out to answer a question which would determine their own spiritual problems, but in fact the final outcome of their inquiries became obvious before they ever put pen to paper. In the opening chapters of his book, Robert reveals this by a direct onslaught on those who elevate Scripture above the Church and who deny the perpetual presence of the Holy Spirit, guiding the Church in the interpretation of divine truth. Having dealt with the dependence of the Canon of Scripture upon ecclesiastical authority, and having proved to his own satisfaction that the original apostles chose to leave this and many other vital questions to be answered by those who succeeded them (they being similarly guided by the inspiration of the Holy Ghost), he puts the question thus:

> If the Church was possessed of a specific commission, when St Ignatius taught at Antioch, why not when St Chrysostom taught there at the end of three centuries? So that if the authority of the Christian Society continued at all after the departure of the Apostles, there was no reason why it should ever cease: if the Holy Ghost remained with it as the guiding principle for a year, the same Spirit might be expected to abide with it for ever.[6]

And again, later:

> These great lights of the Church went out one by one, but no sudden darkness overspread the hemisphere, because the true 'light which lighteth every man' was still present by His Spirit in the world. One generation passeth away and another cometh, but the Church abideth for ever.[7]

The inquiry proceeds to an historical study of the origin of the episcopate and the primacy of St Peter, witnessed in the Gospels, the Acts and the Epistles; thence to the primacy of the Bishop of Rome in the period before the Council of Nicaea and the recognition of this authority by subsequent councils. The second part of the work consists of a study of the break with Rome in the sixteenth century and the establishment of the Royal Supremacy, in which the notion of the existence of an *Ecclesia Anglicana*, independent of Rome, in the Middle Ages is as decisively rejected as it was to be by a less interested and greater historian many years later.[8] The Supremacy, which originated in force and fraud, was initially royal and despotic; it became – under the Hanoverians – the property of Parliament; and, ever since that time with the single exception of a futile oath which presupposes a uniformity which in fact is mere sham, 'private judgment has ... been the real system which has prevailed in England'.[9]

Robert Wilberforce concludes thus:

> The Church's authority ... depends on that presence of the Spirit, which gives it life. This authority had resided first in its completeness in the Person of Our Lord, when He was manifest in the Flesh. He was pleased to bestow it in a plenary manner on the College of His Apostles. From them it has descended to their successors, the Bishops throughout the world. But to preserve the unity of this wide-spread commission, Our Lord was pleased to give an especial promise to one of His Apostles, and to bestow upon him a name and office derived from Himself. ... The Primacy of St Peter ripened into the Supremacy of the Pope.
>
> But then comes a change. There arises a powerful monarch in a remote land, who resolves to separate the Church of his nation from the unity of Christendom. He effects his purpose by force or fraud, and bids it recognise a new principle of unity in himself. He passes to his account, and his children rule after him. But this new principle of unity is found in time to be insufficient. No sooner is the grasp of the civil ruler relaxed, than a host of parties divide the land. The very thought of unity, and hope of concord, is gradually lost. The national Church is surrounded by sects, and torn by dissensions. Intra muros peccatur ab extra. And can it be doubted what advice would be given to its children by the great Saint, who looked forth upon a somewhat similar spectacle in his native land; and whose life was expended in winning back his brethren one by one to the unity of Christendom? He did not think that the national unity of Africa was any pledge of safety to the Donatists; or that the number and succession of their Bishops entitled them to respect. 'Come, brethren, if you wish to be inserted in the vine; for we grieve, when we see you lie thus cut off from it. Number the Bishops from the very seat of Peter, and in that list of Fathers see what has been the succession; this is the rock, against which the proud gates of Hell do not prevail.'[10]

So it had come to this, after all. By the summer of 1854, Robert's mind was made up. One thing delayed him – the spread of certain rumours that the uneasy quiet which had greeted his work on the Eucharist had at last been broken, and that representations had been made to his Archbishop to prosecute him for false teaching. On 30 August he wrote to Archbishop Musgrave to say that since he had had no formal word of an impending prosecution (and therefore felt no obligation to stand his ground and answer the charges) he wished to withdraw his subscription to the Oath of Supremacy and to resign all his preferments. The resignation was accepted. Six days later the *Yorkshire Gazette* announced that legal proceedings against the Archdeacon of the East Riding had already been initiated. Robert immediately wrote to the Archbishop to say that if the report were true, he would stay his resignation in order to defend his views. Musgrave's reply was as frigid a communication as ever prelate addressed to priest:

> My dear Sir, I saw in the *Yorkshire Gazette* the paragraph to which your letter of this morning alludes. By whom, or at whose suggestion that paragraph was inserted, I have no knowledge whatever, any more than you have. On the receipt of your resignation, dated August 30th, I gave orders to discontinue all further enquiry on the subject of the 'complaint' which had been laid before me. To that I adhere, as well as to my acceptance of your resignation. I am, my dear Sir, your faithful servant, T. Ebor.[11]

Now Robert needed the comfort of friends, for none was to be found at home. Manning came up to Yorkshire to be with him over the worst period. Newman wrote, as soon as he heard the news: 'I can enter into your special pain, better than any one else except Manning. In my own case, the separation from friends was the one thing which weighed on me for two years before I became a Catholic – and it affected my health most seriously. It is the price we pay for a great good.'

Robert had offered him the large part of his library, as a gift to the Catholic University at Dublin. Newman thanked him: 'Bear your agony, which is but a little while. The last death-bed I attended some time ago, the poor sufferer kept saying "Will it soon be over?" It is a terrible stress to pass – but you will be soon through it. We have been praying for you here some time. So has Miss Ryder at the Good Shepherd – and my dear child Mary-Anne Bowden at the Visitation – and Fr. Burden and his Trappists at St Edmund's.'[12]

The storm broke immediately, and raged for the next month. Samuel was informed on the same day as Newman, but heard the news later because he was staying at the time with the Bishop of Chichester. He wrote at once to beg Robert to take no further step than the resignation of his preferments, and pleaded with him to come to stay with him at Lavington. He broke off abruptly – 'I cannot write – my eyes are too full of tears and my heart of anguish. God bless you.'[13] Four days later he wrote again to suggest that Robert should join the Scottish Church – he had not yet read his book (it was not published until October) and did not realise that his brother's only refuge could be the Church of Rome.[14] When

Robert told him the true situation, Samuel at last gave full vent to his feelings in a letter of desperate grief:

> My beloved brother, ... I know not how to write about the terrible announcement of your last letter. It seems to strike me to the earth – and I am debating whether contemporaneously with the announcement of your fall I ought not to resign my Bishopric in order that without the reproach of remaining in the English Communion for the sake of my preferments I may testify with what little strength is given me for the rest of my life against the accursed abominations of the Papacy. All seems dark as yet before me. Without taking this step, the increased clearness of my own declarations against Rome which must be forced on me may seem insincere.

Hopelessly, Samuel tried to persuade his brother to hold back.

> Have you weighed all the consequences of such an act? Have you thought how many zealous young hearts you will make cold in Christ's Service, probably for their whole ministry? How many infidels you will create? How great an 'offence' you will make to come? *Can* it be needful for your salvation and can anything less justify such a step, that you should quit a communion in which after weighing every part of the controversy such men as Andrewes and Cosin and Hooker and Bramhall were content to minister and to die?
>
> My beloved brother, *I* as a bystander seem to myself to see the whole case with a clearness which the cloud of personal interest denies to you. I see that *originally* J. Newman obtained a great power over your mind: that since, through your great humility Manning by his great subtlety of intellect and Henry by his unceasing repetition of argument have over-mastered your own far superior understanding, whilst your late unhappy Archbishop has been all along exhibiting to you the Church of England as few but himself could exhibit it. ...
>
> Now my beloved brother – if my solution only *may* be the true one, ought you not to wait till what you have to urge has been thoroughly weighed by such men as Keble, Gladstone, and you have weighed their answer. You mention those who are grasping for you – but you did not tell me that Manning was at Burton Agnes trying to land his prey. My dear, dear brother, I beseech you, before the step is taken, weigh all this well. Delay must in such a matter be safe: precipitation *must* be dangerous.[15]

It was no good, of course. They had now come to the parting of their ways. Robert had steeled himself for letters such as this, and for the anguished cry of John Keble – 'I pray God that I and all who are near and dear to you may sooner die a thousand deaths than do as you seem preparing to do'[16] – but the reality was far worse than all his expectations. 'What a miserable creature am I', he wrote as he witnessed Samuel's agony, 'to cause so much grief. ... I feel ready to wish that I might lie down and die, if it were God's will and I was in a state of Salvation. I have daily prayed for the last four years that I might be taken away rather than come to this.'[17]

In October he sought refuge in Paris, and there he was received into the Roman Church on the eve of All Saints.

It was the end, although he could not know it, of his life's work. It was the end, too – and this his heart told him only too keenly – of what had been a great partnership, which, sealed by the sharing of a great name and quickened by a real bond of trust and love, had achieved much and might yet have achieved far more, to make that name even greater still in the annals of the Anglican Church.

This, at least, was how Gladstone saw the tragedy. He commented in a letter to Samuel as follows:

> It is not only that I look with admiration on your brother Robert's abilities, with affection on his personal and social character, and with reverence on his elevated holiness; but it is that he seemed to me to have had committed to him by God a work of immeasurable moment, the restoration of dogma, and of the very life and heart of dogma, at its most vital point. It may be and would appear to be . . . that you are to show in the service of the Church ecclesiastically how bricks can be made without straw, how the utmost possible events, whether sufficient or not, may be realized in the most embarrassed position and out of the most hopeless materials; and he was, one may almost say, the Church's other hand, for the work of doctrine. I do not pretend to follow him *verbum verbo* or to be bound to all his applications; but he has been a great repairer of what had been sadly impaired and I apprehend he stands at the head of our living divines. His withdrawal from the Church of England could be compared to nothing but that of Newman and of Manning, and I am not sure that the blow would not be as great as either.[18]

EPILOGUE

I. *After the Dispersion*

The lot of a convert could be very wretched. He became, as it were, an exile in his own land. And in addition to the humiliation of social ostracism, the pain of severed friendships and the torment of past memories, there was the inescapable problem of beginning life again within an alien community which could offer few openings outside the field of active, though materially unremunerative, proselytism. Even in this field there was the humbling experience, which all must undergo, of recognising that all one's past distinctions and achievements counted for nothing; the most eminent preacher and the most learned scholar must be reduced to the ranks of recruit or novice. He must go again to school to learn the rudiments of his faith – often enough from instructors far less well equipped than himself in theological learning and breadth of scholarship.

Sometimes, doubtless, our sympathies may be misplaced. Dean Church felt quite overcome when he heard the news of Oakeley's death in 1880 and thought of the mess which the Catholic Church had made of his life.

> He was just the man to pass a happy and useful life, writing elegant and interesting lectures and sermons, and enjoying music and art and good talk without luxury of selfishness, as a distinguished Anglican clergyman. The Romans made nothing of him, but sent him up to Islington to live poorly in a poor house with two Irish colleagues, with just a print or two and a few books remaining of the Oxford wreck, which was the overthrow of his old idea of life. And he was to the last, as far as I saw him, interested in nothing so much as in gossip of the old days; and he was always kindly and patient and gentle, not without touches of amusement when talking of people who did not think with him. It was like a genuine bit of the old Balliol Common-room, set in the frame of this dingy Islington parlour.[1]

We feel the pathos – but was it really so bad? He had work to do, the satisfaction of helping others who could not help themselves, the conviction that he was himself in a state of grace.

For such a man as this, who could take Roman orders, the first years were the worst. Newman felt his early trials very keenly. There seemed something almost cruel in the way he was exhibited by the triumphant Dr Wiseman at Oscott. 'I was made an humiliation at my minor orders and at the examination for them,' Newman later recalled, 'and I had to stand at Dr Wiseman's door waiting for Confession amid the Oscott boys. I did not realize the indignities at the time, though . . . I felt their dreariness.'[2] And he told Allies that it was not only the married men who had their trials.

> Those who are unmarried have their own. They are solitary and thrown among strangers more intimately and intensely than married people can be. You have a house. We have not had one. The very object aimed at has been first, to separate us from each other, secondly to bring us individually under discipline, thirdly to mortify us. I believe all this *in substance* is right, but it may be trying when it is right and it may be done untenderly and rudely when the substance is good. We have been (necessarily) treated as children, being grown men.[3]

The married convert's problem was mainly this: how to find the wherewithal to live and to maintain his family. W. G. Ward, who enjoyed affluence once he had inherited his property on the Isle of Wight, had a few very difficult years at first; so had George Dudley Ryder. Until he inherited a family fortune (large enough to enable him to leave an estate of £21,000),[4] he was in very straitened circumstances. Mrs Sargent, without telling any of his brothers, paid out £70 a year for each of his boys to assist them with their schooling, and often sent drafts to her Catholic son-in-law to tide him over difficult periods.[5] Many of them must have felt as T. W. Allies did, as he looked about desperately for some profitable employment in his early years as a convert:

> I have suffered at times extreme depression of spirits; the root of this is always the same – the utter destitution of my temporal fortunes, and the hopelessness of the prospect, as if the rest of my life was to be heaping up sand hillocks by the sea-shore. The grievance is that I long to study, to produce some work for the glory of God, and I am condemned to the most anxious thoughts as to what I shall eat and what I shall drink, wherewithal I shall be clothed, I and mine, and to the drudgery of teaching dunces. . . . Here is my whole life, as a Catholic, up to the present time summed up.[6]

This was exactly Henry Wilberforce's predicament. He had a little money put by, but this was gradually eaten up as he passed from one temporary employment to another. There were two professions in which he could have excelled – the ministry and the law. He was debarred from both. As a married man, he could not seek Roman orders; since the law of the land adjudged his Anglican orders to be indelible, he was still – technically – an Anglican clergyman and could not therefore practise

404

as a lawyer. As Newman himself put it: he was sentenced to a life of 'dull listless inactivity, and of fitful, precarious employments'.[7]

But Henry's ardent spirit was virtually uncrushable. He was always full of plans. In 1852 he became secretary of the Catholic Defence Association, founded by Cardinal Cullen, with headquarters at Dublin, to resist the anti-popery attacks which raged after the restoration of the hierarchy in England. He bought some land in Ireland, but depleted his meagre fortune by giving away a portion of the estate for the building of a presbytery when he discovered that the tenants had no resident priest.

In 1854 he turned to journalism. He expended more capital in gaining the ownership of the *Catholic Standard*, later called the *Weekly Register*, which came under his editorship to present a rather more *avant-garde* approach to religious issues than could be found in the pages of the notoriously ultramontane *Dublin Review*. This brought Henry into the world of Capes, Simpson and the *Rambler*, and indeed in 1855 Henry won for his paper the distinction of printing the first published writings of Lord Acton – a series of letters defending Döllinger's historical impartiality against his critics in the *Dublin Review*.[8] On the whole, throughout these years, Henry took the part of Newman and Acton in criticising the hierarchy, but always with far more circumspection[9] than he had shown in his strictures on the Anglican bishops in his earlier days. In 1863 he found the pace too hot and sold out. Thereafter he retired from active life, writing occasional reviews and articles for the *Dublin Review*. He was taken ill in 1871 and spent a year in Jamaica with his youngest daughter in the hope that a warmer climate would build up his strength. He died shortly after his return to England in April 1873.

In these last years he was never free from financial anxieties. Shortly after he had abandoned the *Weekly Register*, he went with his family to stay with his eldest brother William, who reported to Newman that 'Henry's affairs turn out worse than I expected. Of course I must keep him and his here till we get them round again.'[10]

William had himself become a Roman Catholic in January 1863. He appears to have settled down, after Samuel's efforts to pack him off to the Ionian Islands, and from the mid-1840's was living as a country gentleman in Yorkshire. His son, also called William or 'Little Willy' – who once as a small boy, seeing a copy of the great five-volume biography of William Wilberforce on his father's shelves, asked his Aunt Jane in all innocence 'Is that me?'[11] – seems to have inherited his father's gift for getting into scrapes. He was tutored for a time by Tom Mozley who found that his chief interest lay in gory crime stories, and Harriett Mozley reported to her sister Jemima that he was 'likely to grow more and more troublesome every day, as he begins to grow into a young man'.[12] When he was older he emigrated to Australia where – according to Samuel – he 'got, as I expected, into scrapes'.[13] His wayward father, who had been responsible for the dissipation of the Wilberforce family fortunes, outlived all his brothers. His nephew, Wilfrid, Henry's son, was touched to see him at Samuel's funeral, sitting in the corner of a room at Lavington House, crying quietly by himself. He processed with all the dignitaries to the little church – 'dear old Uncle Will with his long white beard hanging down'.[14]

Robert Wilberforce's four years as a Roman Catholic were not happy. He had never previously felt the attraction of the Catholic liturgy and devotional exercises which had so excited Manning, Ryder and Henry. Soon he came to feel their spiritual force. Just after his reception he wrote to Ryder:

> There is much as yet which seems new to me. One does not accustom oneself in a hurry to the worship of the Saints. That which I am beginning now to enjoy greatly is the service of the Mass. Its beauty and meaning had been wholly hidden from me. But now that I a little understand it, I don't wonder at the earnestness with which it is attended. Prayer is a perfectly new thing to me and I see that I have been all my life a stranger to God's presence.[15]

After Paris, where he visited the Abbé Gaume and had de Ravignan as his confessor, he returned to his estate in Ireland. His heart still pined for Samuel. He wrote to him in August 1855.

> You are now established I hear at Lavington. I think of the many charming rides, which we have had together on those beautiful Downs, and I pray that you may enjoy yourself there this year with your dear boys. Our years, beloved brother, are fast hastening away: we shall soon be old men. Then there awaits us the Churchyard and what lies beyond it: may God meanwhile give you every blessing, which is compatible with your state and with your welfare. It is among the last solace of my state to think of your tender affection: and to wish and pray for your welfare.[16]

He pressed Samuel to come and spend a holiday with him on the Continent, promising that he had no inclination 'to talk controversies'.[17] He would fall in with any suggestion to prevent any embarrassment to his brother and to avoid any suspicion to which he might feel himself exposed.[18] Samuel came, but only for a short while, for he had soon to return to England on hearing the news of the illness of his eldest son Herbert. Robert had hoped that he might be able to show Samuel some interesting 'Catholic objects', but we may surmise that his brother was little impressed. Just how little he appreciated the magnificence and mystery of Catholic ceremonial may be seen from his diary entries for a continental tour which he made alone in 1851. On that occasion he had attended High Mass at Strasbourg and had been permitted to sit in the choir. He watched it all with grave displeasure:

> The Cathedral full of people who could not hear a word. The officiating priest spitting incessantly: even on the carpet where the moment after his assistant kneeled. The Choir took up the Credo and sung it poorly. The three officiating clergy, sitting and only uncovering their heads at 'and became man'. The priest an elderly man of grave aspect, and from a distance devout manner, must have skipped or hurried through in the most rapid manner all the prayers appointed for him to say in secreto – for I was following him in the Missal and could scarcely read to myself an 8th of the prayers before he had done it. Here is another curse of this most miserable system – its effect in making all functional in the mind of the officiating priest.[19]

Robert hoped that he would come again for the next year, especially when he heard what had befallen Samuel at home. Herbert, recently returned from service in the Crimea as a lieutenant, had died on 28 February 1856 after an illness of four months at the age of twenty-two.[20] This family disaster, which inevitably meant for Samuel yet another visitation of that utter dejection which he had had to endure twice before (in 1841 and 1854), evoked from all the separated members of the family an expression of intense sympathy, especially from Henry Manning. 'It would violate the affection of nearly five and twenty years, and the sacred memory of many common sorrows', he wrote, 'if we were silent to each other at this moment. ... I believe few are more intimately united to your thoughts at this moment than I am; and I am sure that few love you with a more true love: "not in word nor in tongue, but in deed and in truth".'[21]

Samuel, in fact, never saw Robert again. In that same year (1856), Robert decided to prepare for orders. At first he had not wished to; and the only employment he had seriously considered was a post at the Irish University to lecture on geology and mineralogy.[22] On 9 April 1856 he wrote to Newman to say that he was more conscious of having received a call:

I went into retreat ... the beginning of last month, and was amazingly impressed by the exercises. Moreover they chimed in remarkably with the tendency of my own mind, which has been approximating much more towards those feelings towards the Saints – especially towards our Blessed Mother, which prevail among Catholics, than they had done previously. I mean that I felt a greater freedom than I had before done in giving myself up to the service of the Church and that these usages, which I had before looked upon as an impediment, became a positive object of attraction. This is especially the case with the worship of Our Blessed Lady, which I used to feel a sort of drawback to my satisfaction, whereas I have come to regard it as a reward to my faith, in being a Catholic.

This had brought to his mind the possibility of seeking ordination. There was, however, one great obstacle – 'my having been twice married. Some person I imagine mentioned this to the Holy Father – he has lately sent me a message, desiring that I should prepare myself for Holy Orders.' The Pope had also promised to send him to the Accademia Ecclesiastica, where Manning had been – a sign of special favour.[23]

After a holiday in Germany which he spent with his two sons, he began his studies in Rome. All that year he had spoken of bad health – indeed, in a letter to G. D. Ryder at Christmas he had suggested a meeting in England in the following summer 'if I live so long'[24] – but Manning reported to Henry that as soon as Robert came to Rome he had perked up and looked much younger. 'The ecclesiastical habit suited him. He looked grave and very humble in it; and like a man who has been used to it.' In January, however, the wet season really set in and he was much pulled down. He began suffering from acute bilious attacks, not at first taken very seriously because of the commonness of such disorders in Rome at that time. At last Robert insisted on escaping to a healthier climate; and went to Albano where he had to take to his bed.

Manning supplied Henry with further details. Aubrey de Vere came to visit him; he sent word that he wished to be received into the third order of the Franciscans. He seemed content, reading from time to time (St John in Greek, the *Paradiso* and Macaulay's *Lays of Ancient Rome*), but evidently still very weak.[25]

On 4 February 1857 Manning wrote a longer letter to Henry with different news to tell:

Yesterday, Tuesday, at $\frac{1}{4}$ to 6 p.m., it pleased God to take our dear Brother to His Rest; without a sign of pain. On Monday morning he made his confession with full self-possession and received the B. Sacrament in Viaticum, with perfect recollection and calmness, and yesterday morning Extreme

Unction, but his mind was less clear and present. He joined from time to time in words of prayer: and many times kissed the Crucifix with very marked devotion. Through the whole of his illness he has been perfectly free from pain. We have never seen a moment of suffering: nor has he at any moment been distressed in mind. I never saw a death of more perfect peace.

As for the illness, the account given to me by the physician is that it has been for some time coming on in the form of a disturbance of the liver and stomach: it then took the form of Gastric Fever, with diarrhoea. . . . I do not think that anything more could have been done. . . . I expect his boy Edward from Munich. And I wish someone were here. The Funeral Office has just been sung in the Cathedral. But I purpose removing him to Rome and to await the wish of his family.

Send all this to the Bishop of Oxford with my love. It is needless to tell him what I am feeling. . . . In times when his mind wandered, it was always turned to sacred thoughts: and with great desire to be allowed to act as a priest: to be ordained and to say Mass. . . . I never saw such sweetness and patience throughout Tuesday morning when I told him that I was going to say Mass for him, and asked what I should ask for him. He said at once 'Patience' – and the next time 'Submission' – and once he said 'Submission to the will of God in the whole of Religion'. And certainly he fulfilled it. In Rome the one thing remarked in him by every one – especially by the Romans among whom he lived – was his childlike humility. He had in truth entered the kingdom of God as a little child.[26]

II. *Two Ecclesiastical Statesmen*

Both Manning and Samuel Wilberforce had years of active work before them, the details of which lie outside the scope of this story. They corresponded but rarely; met hardly at all. Both were submerged in ceaseless work, and the past was better left unrecalled. When Manning was elevated by Pius IX in 1865 to the Archbishopric of Westminster, in succession to Cardinal Wiseman, Samuel wrote to assure him of his prayers. Manning replied: 'Our life has been indeed no common one. And it is now drawing to its close. I feel this to be the last reach in the river to me. I trust I need not assure you that nothing can change in my mind the memory of our old affection; and that whatsoever the last years have brought between us has left no trace behind. Life is too short for lasting resentments, and I do not think I am tempted much in that way.'[1]

The passage of the years wrought little change either in their characters or their ideals. Manning was at last presented with the opportunity to make real the dreams of twenty years past – the unity of Roman Catholic Christendom on a firm dogmatic basis, expressed by the universal recognition of the infallible authority of the Church which he came more and more as a Roman Catholic to appreciate as residing in the inspired pronouncements of the Holy See; to meet the spread of infidelity and a relaxed spirituality with the example of a dedicated priesthood assured of its commission, unrelenting in its proselytism, united in faith and zeal. In only one respect did he noticeably change. In the course of time he became steadily more hostile to intellectualism. Fearful of the march of mind and of irreverence, he became almost fanatical in his efforts to protect Catholics from the profane philosophy which he suspected to be in the ascendant at Oxford and Cambridge, and came too readily to suppose that liberal thinkers, who championed the cause of free enquiry, betrayed – in spite of their protestations to the contrary – the disposition to put private judgment above the authority of the Church.

But then he had always been at heart a dogmatist; always, too, an Evangelical, conscious that God had called him personally to salvation and was ever guiding him along an appointed path. And the union of these two qualities can easily lead to intransigence. We see it clearly in the letter which he wrote, during his retreat at Highgate, to Mrs W. G. Ward, shortly after he had heard of his appointment to the see of Westminster.

> I have in these last three weeks felt as if Our Lord had called me by name. . . . The firm belief that I have long had that the Holy Father is the most supernatural person I have ever seen has given me this feeling more deeply still. I feel as if I had been brought, contrary to all human wills, by the Divine will into an immediate relation to our Divine Lord. The effect on me is one of awe, not fear, but a conscious nearness to God and the supernatural agencies and sufferings of His Church.[2]

Yet if it seemed that God had directed him far from the point at which he started his spiritual journey, his heart never left Lavington. On his death-bed in 1892 he shocked Herbert Vaughan beyond measure by calling him to the bedside and passing him a well-thumbed little notebook, which he had pulled out from under his pillow. 'With eyes about to close for ever', Vaughan recalled, '. . . [he] said, "I know not to whom else to leave this – I leave it to you. Into this little book my dearest Wife wrote her prayers and meditations. Not a day has passed since her death on which I have not prayed and meditated from this book. All the good

I may have done, all the good I may have been, I owe to her. Take precious care of it".'*

The main lines of Samuel Wilberforce's subsequent achievements have already been drawn. In the years that lay ahead he had still more personal sorrows to undergo – the secession of his eldest daughter Ella and her husband (Henry Pye) to the Roman Church in 1868, and the death of Mary Sargent, his constant companion for twenty years, in 1861. The many letters which passed between Gladstone and himself in the remaining years of his life show that, as each found himself abandoned by those who had been his earliest and dearest friends, they were drawn closer together in intimacy and mutual understanding. Gladstone hoped, and Samuel expected, that this union would mean in time that the one, as Prime Minister, would call the other to a higher and greater responsibility than the bishopric of Oxford could afford. Certainly Samuel was profoundly disappointed at not succeeding Longley as Archbishop of York in 1862, and at the way in which A. C. Tait and Jackson were successively appointed to the bishopric of London in his stead.[3] In 1869, however, Gladstone was at last able to take the opportunity provided by C. R. Sumner's resignation to offer Samuel the bishopric of Winchester. Four years later, still at the height of his powers, he was thrown from his horse while riding with Lord Granville and died instantly.

The scenes at his funeral – he was buried in Lavington churchyard beside the graves of Emily, Herbert, and Caroline Manning – attest the degree of love and respect which he had won from the nation at large. Wilfrid Wilberforce put his impressions on record in a letter to his mother, Mary Wilberforce, who had been too ill to make the journey. He had been amazed at the great number and diverse character of the mourners. Special trains were being run from Victoria to Petworth, the platform thronged with dignitaries of every description – bishops, deans, archdeacons, eminent statesmen, the greatest in the land. 'It was most striking', he wrote, 'to see so many mourning him and truly mourning him. Nothing could give one a better idea of his universally kind and winning ways and of the number of people he came across in his life of ceaseless work.'

The service was overpowering, the Catholic members of the family

---

* F. Von Hugel, *Selected Letters 1896–1924*, edited by Bernard Holland (1927), 256. Sir George Clutton assures me that his grandmother, who knew Herbert Vaughan well, was told that Vaughan placed the book subsequently in Cardinal Manning's coffin.

sitting together, not joining in the prayers, but saying over the *De Profundis* to themselves. When it was all over, Reginald Wilberforce, the new master of Lavington, nearly destroyed the temporary *rapprochement* by ignoring the fact that the day was a Friday and by serving meat cutlets for the funeral lunch, so that the Catholic mourners were forced to go hungry. On the whole, however, resentments and long estrangements were forgotten; the family were united for a moment in their sense of common loss. Wilfrid concluded his description with a reference to the accident itself:

> As soon as the accident had occurred, the owner of the ground sent word to the sons that they might regard that piece of ground where it happened as their own. They are therefore going to have it railed round and on the exact spot is to stand a large stone cross with the Bishop's name and July 19th, 1873. I saw a photo of the place and also of the dear one after he had been placed in the coffin. The face was *perfectly* calm and there was not the least expression of pain upon it.[4]

* * * * *

Both Samuel Wilberforce and Henry Manning were men of unassailable greatness; yet each – curiously – has been remembered by posterity largely for his faults. This is perhaps the fate of successful clergymen, especially of clergymen who cannot easily dissociate success from power. As it happened, both men wielded power to achieve ends which the fashions of a later age have called in question – the assertion of the dignity of the episcopal office and the resuscitation of the dogmatic principle. These things are remembered, while other – perhaps subsidiary – achievements, like Wilberforce's transformation of diocesan organisation or Manning's deep awareness of the Church's rôle in modern society, are recognised as incidental benefits hardly sufficient to counteract the inherent conservatism of the one or the unbecoming intransigence of the other. Then again, public men are inevitably judged by their significant public acts. The profundity of the theologian, the skill of the accomplished writer, are transmitted to posterity in their original form, the printed word, which may – as with a Maurice or a Newman – be recognised as conveying more than their contemporaries could comprehend. Some qualities, however, are not so easily recovered. Both Samuel Wilberforce and Henry Manning possessed extraordinary gifts: above all, an almost irresistible charm of manner, allied to a real and heartfelt tenderness and affection in their relations with their fellows, qualities which enabled them to gain an enduring influence over individuals and a mighty reputation for consummate ecclesiastical statesmanship. These are all talents which must tarnish with the passage of time, when the captivating influence of the man himself can no longer operate to confound the unconvinced. And so it is that ecclesiastical statesmen rarely receive their due. Honoured in their own day, they lose their lustre as the years pass by. Not for them the posthumous accolade. They lived so much in the world that they seem to sit uneasily in heaven. Did not the great Gibbon concede the uniqueness of Eusebius of Nicomedia: the one man in the history of the Church 'who had acquired the reputation of a statesman without forfeiting that of a saint'?[5]

BIOGRAPHICAL DATES

NOTES

BIBLIOGRAPHY

INDEX

BIOGRAPHICAL DATES

Year	Robert Wilberforce	Samuel Wilberforce	Henry Wilberforce	Henry Edward Manning
1820	Oriel College, Oxford	Maisemore School		
1822		Little Bounds School	Little Bounds School	Harrow School
1823	Meets John Keble at Southrop	Oriel College, Oxford		
1824	B.A.			
1826	Fellow of Oriel	B.A.	Oriel College, Oxford	
1827		Continental Tour		Balliol College, Oxford
1828	Tutor of Oriel	Marries Emily Sargent. Accepts living of Checkenden		
1830	Resigns Tutorship	Rector of Brighstone	B.A.	B.A.
1831	Germany			London (Miss Bevan)
1832	Marries Agnes Wrangham Vicar of East Farleigh			Fellow of Merton College, Oxford
1833				Marriage to Caroline Sargent. Rector of Lavington
1834	Death of Agnes		Marries Mary Sargent. Curate of Bransgore	
1837	Marries Jane Legard			Death of Caroline
1839		Archdeacon of Surrey		
1840	Rector of Burton Agnes	Rector of Alverstoke		Archdeacon of Chichester
1841	Archdeacon of East Riding	Death of Emily	Vicar of Walmer	
1843			Vicar of East Farleigh	November 5th Sermon
1845		Dean of Westminster. Bishop of Oxford		
1847		⎱ Hampden		Serious illness
1848	*Doctrine of the Incarnation*	⎰ Crisis		Rome
1850			Received with Mary into R.C. Church	
1851				Received into R.C. Church
1854	Received into R.C. Church			
1857	Death			

NOTES

ABBREVIATIONS USED

Wilberforce MSS   The papers of Samuel Wilberforce, owned by the late Dr Octavia Wilberforce, and kept at Backsettown, Henfield, Sussex.

Wrangham MSS   The collection of Wilberforce papers, owned by Mr C. E. Wrangham, and kept at Rosemary House, Catterick, Yorks.

Kensington MSS   The papers of Robert Wilberforce, owned by Miss Irene Wilberforce, and kept at 2, York House, Church Street, Kensington.

Sandwith MSS   The papers of Henry Wilberforce and William Wilberforce, jnr. owned by Mrs Judith Sandwith, and kept at St Mark's Vicarage, Harrogate, Yorks.

Ryder MSS   The papers of George Dudley Ryder, owned by Sir George Clutton, K.C.M.G., and kept at the British Embassy, Warsaw.

Manning Archives   The correspondence of various members of the Wilberforce family with Henry Edward Manning, kept at St Mary of the Angels, Moorhouse Road, London W.2.

Bodleian   Samuel Wilberforce deposit, lodged at the Bodleian Library, Oxford.

Ushaw MSS   The letters of Manning to Henry and Mary Wilberforce, kept at Ushaw College, Durham.

Oratory   The Newman Papers, preserved at the Oratory, Edgbaston, Birmingham.

Keble College   Letters of John Keble to Robert Wilberforce, kept at Keble College, Oxford.

Oriel College   The letters of Edward Hawkins, kept at Oriel College, Oxford.

Pusey House   Bound volumes of Pusey letters, kept at Pusey House, Oxford.

Lincoln Archives   Papers of Sir Charles Anderson, kept in the Lincoln Archives, The Castle, Lincoln.

B. M. Add. Mss.   British Museum, Additional Manuscripts.

D.N.B.   *Dictionary of National Biography*.

Introduction. THE CRISIS OF EVANGELICALISM

I. *The Beginning and the End*

  1. Ushaw MSS. 18; see also F. Meyrick, *Memories of Life at Oxford and Elsewhere* (1905), 132–3.

  2. Wrangham MSS. VI. 427; see also A. R. Ashwell and R. G. Wilberforce, *Life of Samuel Wilberforce* (1881), ii. 252.

  3. Wilberforce MSS. D. 14.

II. *Evangelicalism and Church Order*

  1. A. M. Wilberforce, *The Private Papers of William Wilberforce* (1897), 272 n.

  2. *Ibid.*, 264–5.

  3. Sandwith MSS. C. 9.

  4. A. Mozley (editor), *Letters and Correspondence of John Henry Newman* (1891), I. 204–5.

  5. Bodleian. c. 191. 17 April 1835.

  6. C. Stephen (editor), *Sir James Stephen. Letters with biographical notes* (privately printed 1906), 24.

  7. Wrangham MSS. V. 99.

  8. Bodleian. c. 191. 21 August 1837.

  9. W. E. Gladstone, *Gleanings of the Past Years* (1879), vii. 209–12.

  10. Oratory. Box 119, no. 133, where Newman and Stephen discuss this particular point.

  11. G. W. E. Russell, *The Household of Faith* (1902), 1.

  12. J. S. Reynolds, *The Evangelicals at Oxford 1757–1871* (1953), 95, argues that their representation was rather stronger than this.

  13. W. E. Gladstone, *op. cit.*, 213.

  14. F. K. Brown, *Fathers of the Victorians. The Age of Wilberforce* (Cambridge 1961), 326–40.

  15. *Ibid.*, 6.

  16. Charles Smyth, *Simeon and Church Order* (Cambridge 1940), 269.

  17. Here I must express my indebtedness to two unpublished works which deal – from different angles – with this rift between the two schools of Evangelicals. The first is Dr J. D. Walsh's Ph.D. thesis, in the Cambridge University Library, entitled 'The Yorkshire Evangelicals in the Eighteenth Century: with especial reference to Methodism' (1956). Chapter One on 'Moderate Calvinism', and the final chapter on the attempt to become a *Church* party are especially relevant. The second is Mr H. Willmer's Hulsean Prize Essay for 1962, also in the Cambridge University Library, entitled 'Evangelicalism 1785–1835', which is especially concerned with the *Christian Observer* school.

  18. M. Hennell, *John Venn and the Clapham Sect* (1958), 263.

  19. E. M. Forster, *Marianne Thornton. A Domestic Biography* (1956), 133.

  20. C. Stephen (editor), *op. cit.*, 87.

  21. H. Willmer, *op. cit.*, 116.

  22. G. Redford and J. A. James (editors), *The Autobiography of William Jay* (second edn. 1855), 317–18.

  23. H. Willmer, *op. cit.*, 127.

  24. See, for instance, C. Dawson, *The Spirit of the Oxford Movement* (1945), 52.

  25. J. D. Walsh, *op. cit.*, 4–5.

  26. J. H. Newman, *Parochial and Plain Sermons* (1868 edn.) I. nos. i and iv. The

dates of these sermons are given in J. H. Newman, *Sermons bearing on subjects of the Day* (1918 edn.) 411–17.

27. J. H. Newman, *Parochial and Plain Sermons*, I. 8.
28. *Ibid.*, 10.
29. J. Bateman, *The Life of Daniel Wilson* (1860), I. 136.
30. J. H. Newman, *op. cit.*, I. 56.
31. F. K. Brown, *op. cit.*, 6, 498–506. For a fuller discussion of these views, see my article 'Father and Sons' in *The Historical Journal*, VI. 2 (1963), pp. 295–310.
32. G. Redford and J. A. James, *op. cit.*, 317–18.
33. A. M. Wilberforce, *op. cit.*, 230.
34. Sandwith MSS. B. 12.
35. W. E. Gladstone, *op. cit.*, 224. Dr Brilioth's views were most fully worked out in *The Anglican Revival. Studies in the Oxford Movement* (1925).
36. There is a recent discussion of this question in Dieter Voll, *Catholic Evangelicalism* (1963), 29–39.
37. R. I. Wilberforce, *A Charge to the Clergy of the East Riding, delivered at the Ordinary Visitation a.d. 1851* (1851), 10–11.
38. Horton Davies, *Worship and Theology in England. From Watts and Wesley to Maurice, 1690–1850* (1961), 223–7.
39. J. H. Newman, *Apologia pro vita sua* (1913 edn.), 108–9.
40. See Dawson's comments in *The Spirit of the Oxford Movement*, 14.
41. In *The Principles of Church Reform* (1833).
42. Y. Brilioth, *Evangelicalism and the Oxford Movement* (1934), 28.
43. This is the closing stanza of the poem for the Second Sunday in Advent in Keble's *The Christian Year*.
44. Sandwith MSS. C. 9.

III. *Dramatis Personae*
1. Maisie Ward, *Young Mr Newman* (1948), 360.
2. *Autobiography of Isaac Williams*, 28.
3. Y. Brilioth, *Evangelicalism and the Oxford Movement*, 23.

1. THE CRADLE OF EVANGELICALISM

I. *Family Alliances and Barbara Spooner*
1. R. Coupland, *Wilberforce. A Narrative* (1923), 25.
2. Caroline Stephen, *Sir James Stephen, Letters*, 16.
3. E. M. Forster, *Marianne Thornton*, 58–9.
4. N. G. Annan, 'The Intellectual Aristocracy' in *Studies in Social History. A Tribute to G. M. Trevelyan*, edited by J. H. Plumb (1955), 244–5.
5. J. A. S. L. Leighton Boyce, *Smiths the Bankers 1658–1958* (1958), 192.
6. Leighton Boyce, *op. cit.*, 185.
7. R. I. and S. Wilberforce, *The Life of William Wilberforce* (1838), V. 166. Letter from Zachary Macauley – 'We are to have a select party tomorrow at Lord Calthorpe's, purposely to talk on slavery.'
8. Wilberforce MSS. A. 17 November 1826.
9. W. Benham (editor), *Catharine and Craufurd Tait. A Memoir.* (1879), especially 30–1. See also R. T. Davidson and W. Benham, *The Life of Archibald Campbell Tait* (1891), I. 122–3.
10. E. M. Forster, *op. cit.*, 42–3.
11. Wilberforce MSS. B. 7 February 1825.

12. Sandwith MSS. A. 8.
13. Wilberforce MSS. A. 3 March 1829.
14. Wilberforce MSS. A. undated.
15. Wilberforce MSS. B. 30 October 1824, 7 February 1825.
16. Wilberforce MSS. B. 30 October 1824.
17. Wrangham MSS. I. 52.
18. R. W. Church, *The Oxford Movement 1833–1845* (1891), 13.
19. Wilberforce MSS. J. 2.

II. *The Wilberforce Household*
   1. E. M. Forster, *op. cit.*, 43.
   2. *Ibid.*, 136.
   3. A. M. Wilberforce, *Private Papers*, 173.
   4. Wilberforce MSS. Notebook entitled 'Fragments', 27–8.
   5. R. I. and S. Wilberforce, *op. cit.*, IV. 140–1.
   6. C. Smyth, *Simeon and Church Order*, 22.
   7. E. M. Forster, *op. cit.*, 137–8.
   8. R. I. and S. Wilberforce, *op. cit.*, IV. 78–9.
   9. A. M. Wilberforce, *Private Papers*, 200.
   10. *Ibid.*, 229.
   11. Wilberforce MSS. 'Fragments', 29–30.
   12. R. I. and S. Wilberforce, *op. cit.*, III. 470.
   13. Wilberforce MSS. 'Fragments', 85.
   14. Wilberforce MSS. 'Fragments', 112–13.
   15. *Ibid.*, 117–18.
   16. See, for instance, the description in G. W. E. Russell's *The Household of Faith, Portraits and Essays* (1902), 231–45.
   17. R. I. and S. Wilberforce, *op. cit.*, IV. 152.
   18. James Stephen, *Essays in Ecclesiastical Biography* (1907 edn.), II. 193–4; R. Coupland, *op. cit.*, 371.
   19. R. I. and S. Wilberforce, *op. cit.*, IV. 208.
   20. *Ibid.*, III. 446.
   21. *Ibid.*, IV. 91–2.
   22. *Ibid.*, IV. 225.
   23. *Ibid.*, IV. 91.
   24. *Ibid.*, IV. 363.
   25. *Ibid.*, IV. 204.
   26. *Ibid.*, III. 423.
   27. Wrangham MSS. V. b.
   28. R. I. and S. Wilberforce, *op. cit.*, III. 416–17.
   29. *Ibid.*, IV. 48–9.
   30. *Ibid.*, IV. 268.
   31. *Ibid.*, IV. 298.
   32. *Ibid.*, V. 71.
   33. *Ibid.*, V. 194.
   34. Wilberforce MSS. I. 7.
   35. R. I. and S. Wilberforce, *op. cit.*, V. 248.
   36. A. M. Wilberforce, *op. cit.*, 206–7.
   37. R. I. and S. Wilberforce, *op. cit.*, V. 287.
   38. *Ibid.*, V. 287.

II. *The Children at School*

1. R. I. and S. Wilberforce, *op. cit.*, III. 348.
2. *Ibid.*, IV. 72–3.
3. *Ibid.*, III. 475–8.
4. Wilberforce MSS C. 1.
5. T. Mozley, *Reminiscences chiefly of Oriel College and the Oxford Movement* (1882), I. 28.
6. E. S. Purcell, *Life of Cardinal Manning*, I. 10–12.
7. T. W. Bamford, *Thomas Arnold* (1960), 108.
8. A. R. Ashwell and R. G. Wilberforce, *Life of Samuel Wilberforce* (1880), I. 4–5.
9. Wilberforce MSS C. 2.
10. This is discussed at length in my *Godliness and Good Learning. Four Studies on a Victorian Ideal* (1961), 80–3, 195–239.
11. Wrangham MSS. V. 1.
12. Wilberforce MSS. B. 14 February 1818.
13. Wilberforce MSS. B. 3 February 1821.
14. Wilberforce MSS. B. 27 May 1818.
15. Wilberforce MSS. B. 15 February 1822.
16. Wrangham MSS. VII. 42.
17. Wrangham MSS. VII. 65.
18. Wilberforce MSS. C. 25 May 1835.
19. Wilberforce MSS. B. undated.
20. Wrangham MSS. V. 8.
21. Wrangham MSS. I. 54.
22. A. M. Wilberforce, *op. cit.*, 199.
23. R. I. and S. Wilberforce, *op. cit.*, III. 497 (Henry is not mentioned by name, but other evidence suggests that William has Henry in mind).
24. Wilberforce MSS. 'Fragments', 34.
25. Wilberforce MSS. B. 7 June 1817.
26. Bodleian. c. 196. 44.

IV. *Joyousness and Seriousness*

1. Wilberforce MSS. E. 8 May 1832.
2. Milner, in his *History of the Church of Christ*, was intending to present a history 'of REAL not merely NOMINAL Christianity', as he himself stated in his Introduction. This is discussed by Dr J. D. Walsh, *op. cit.*, 387.
3. J. D. Walsh, *op. cit.*, 27.
4. Wilberforce MSS. 'Fragments', 92. Compare Wrangham MSS. VII. 10. Writing on a discussion which he, his father and John Sargent had had on Calvinism, Robert Wilberforce observes to Samuel: 'My father very Arminian.' See also Wilberforce MSS A. 17 December 1830, where William Wilberforce writes to Samuel 'You and I who are not Calvinists.'
5. Bodleian. c. 186. Diary 1830–2, 27 September 1830. It is interesting to compare Newman's high regard for Romaine in his *Apologia*, 107–8. He obtained from Romaine the firm conviction in the doctrine of final perseverance. 'I received it at once, and believed that the inward conversion of which I was conscious (and of which I still am more certain than that I have hands and feet) would last into the next life, and that I was elected to eternal glory.' See the interesting comments in Y. Brilioth, *The Anglican Revival*, 32.
6. A. M. Wilberforce, *op. cit.*, 242.

7. *Ibid.*, 196. This is an expression of what Dr Walsh has described as the doctrine of 'Particular Election', the notion that 'Salvation was of God – man's destruction of himself'. See J. D. Walsh, *op. cit.*, 27–32.
8. A. M. Wilberforce, *op. cit.*, 176–7; R. I. and S. Wilberforce, *op. cit.*, IV. 309–10.
9. Wilberforce MSS. 'Fragments', 97–8.
10. R. I. and S. Wilberforce, *op. cit.*, III. 495.
11. *Ibid.*, III. 490.
12. Wilberforce MSS. 'Fragments', 43–4.
13. A. M. Wilberforce, *op. cit.*, 211.
14. Wilberforce MSS. 'Fragments', 9–10. Madan was an itinerant preacher well known to the Venns. See L. Elliott-Binns, *The Early Evangelicals* (1953), 291–2; John Venn, *Annals of a Clerical Family* (Cambridge 1904), 89.
15. R. I. and S. Wilberforce, *op. cit.*, V. 321.
16. G. W. E. Russell, *op. cit.*, 223.
17. A. M. Wilberforce, *op. cit.*, 166, 170, 183–4.
18. Wilberforce MSS, 'Fragments', 104–5.
19. Wilberforce MSS. 'Fragments', 38–40.
20. *Ibid.*, 2–3.
21. *Ibid.*, 87–8.
22. *Ibid.*, 12–13.
23. G. F. A. Best, 'The Evangelicals and the Established Church' in *Journal of Theological Studies*. N.S. Vol. X. April 1959, 64.
24. J. D. Walsh, *op. cit.*, 345.
25. Wilberforce MSS. 'Fragments', 5–6.
26. Wilberforce MSS. A. 26 October 1822.
27. Wilberforce MSS. A. 22 November 1822.
28. Wilberforce MSS. A. 14 June 1823.
29. Ford K. Brown, *op. cit.*, 506.
30. Wilberforce MSS. 'Fragments', 20–21.
31. F. K. Brown, *op. cit.*, 504–5.

2. THE BASTION OF ORTHODOXY

1. *Choosing a University*
   1. Wilberforce MSS. 'Fragments', 128.
   2. R. I. and S. Wilberforce, *op. cit.*, V. 146–7.
   3. *Ibid.*, I. 176–7.
   4. *Ibid.*, I. 223.
   5. W. Rouse Ball, J. H. Venn (editors), *Admissions to Trinity College Cambridge*, IV. 1801–50 (1911), 140–1.
   6. Wilberforce Diary (Hull). 8 January 1819. I owe this reference and the reference to subsequent diary entries to Professor R. W. Smith of the University of Oregon, who kindly sent me details from his notes.
   7. Wilberforce Diary. 15 March 1819.
   8. British Museum. Egerton MSS 1964. undated letter to Lady Sparrow. Again I am indebted to Professor Smith.
   9. Wilberforce Diary, 28 March 1819.
   10. *Ibid.*, 31 March 1819.
   11. *Ibid.*, 8 December 1819.
   12. Wilberforce Diary. 16 March 1817.

13. British Museum. Egerton MSS. 1964. Letter dated 31 July 1817.
14. Wilberforce Diary, 9 February 1816; 21 April 1816.
15. *The Historical Register of the University of Oxford* (Oxford 1900), 829.
16. J. W. Burgon, *Lives of Twelve Good Men* (1888), I. 390–1.
17. Oriel MSS. Hawkins Letters. XII. 1141. 5 February 1828.
18. Oriel MSS. Hawkins Letters. XII. 1142. 19 August 1828.
19. Wilberforce MSS. 'Fragments', 119–20. He especially regretted that at Oxford there was less distinction between those 'who are truly religious and those who are not'.
20. E. M. Forster, *op. cit.*, 78.
21. R. I. and S. Wilberforce, *op. cit.*, V. 91.
22. Wilberforce MSS. 'Fragments', 120.
23. A. M. Wilberforce, *op. cit.*, 157.
24. A. M. Wilberforce, *op. cit.*, 263.

II. *The Oxford Renaissance.*

1. R. H. Froude, *Remains* (1838), I. 433.
2. See Newman's remarks on his debt to Whately in *Apologia*, 111–12.
3. H. Bremond, *A Literary History of Religious Thought in France* (English edition, 1928), I. 8–9.
4. J. H. Newman, *Apologia*, 135.
5. *Ibid.*, 134–5.
6. B. A. Smith, *Dean Church, The Anglican Response to Newman* (1958), 28.
7. Francis Doyle, *Reminiscences and Opinions 1813–1885* (1886), 96–7.
8. William Tuckwell, *Reminiscences of Oxford* (1900), 86.
9. See the brilliant essay by Christopher Hollis, 'Cardinal Newman and Dean Church' in *John Henry Newman Centenary Essays*, edited by H. Tristram (1945), 73.'
10. R. W. Church, *The Oxford Movement*, 141.
11. William Tuckwell, *Reminiscences of Oxford* 3. Compare the beautiful lines of Matthew Arnold in his preface to *Essays in Criticism*, first series (1905), X–XI.
12. *Ibid.*, 6.
13. *Ibid.*, 84–5.
14. Francis Doyle, *op. cit.*, 124.
15. *Ibid.*, 108–113. See also T. Wemyss Reid, *The Life, Letters and Friendships of Richard Monckton Milnes, first Lord Houghton* (1890), I. 77–9.
16. Mary Church, *Life and Letters of Dean Church* (1895), 19; see also H. P. Liddon, *Life of E. B. Pusey* (1895), I. 67. These are Dean Church's words in a letter to Dr. Liddon in 1883.
17. Mark Pattison, *Memoirs* (1883), 125.
18. Maisie Ward, *Young Mr Newman*, 45. This change was not, however, discernible at Christ Church until rather later. Frederick Oakeley, who admittedly fell in with a 'bad set', described the college in the early 1820's as 'addicted to vice and loose conversation'. L. M. Q. Couch (editor), *Reminiscences of Oxford by Oxford Men 1559–1850* (Oxford Historical Society Publications, Vol. 22, Oxford, 1892), 303, 317–18.
19. H. P. Liddon, *Life of Pusey*, I. 360.
20. See especially J. H. Thom (editor), *The Life of Joseph Blanco White written by himself* (1845), III. 360–3.
21. Mark Pattison, *Memoirs*, 67.

22. R. T. Davidson and W. Benham, *Life of A. C. Tait*, I. 107.
23. G. Faber, *Oxford Apostles* (Pelican edition, 1954), 52.
24. C. Wordsworth, *Annals of my early Life. 1806–46* (1891), 95.
25. A. R. Ashwell, *op. cit.*, I. 31.
26. C. Wordsworth, *op. cit.*, 119–21.
27. *Ibid.*, 55–7.
28. E. S. Purcell, *op. cit.*, I. 29–30.
29. M. Pattison, *op. cit.*, 100–101.
30. J. E. Tyler, Dean of Oriel.
31. Bodleian, c. 191. 31 May 1836.
32. Discussed in G. W. E. Russell, *The Household of Faith*, 3–4.
33. See especially G. Kitson Clark, *The Making of Victorian England* (1962), 258–61.
34. Charles Smyth, *The Church and the Nation, Six Studies in the Anglican Tradition* (1962), 160.
35. These remarks of Manning are all taken from J. E. C. Bodley, *Cardinal Manning, and other essays* (1912), 13–14.

III. *Robert Wilberforce and John Keble*

1. T. Mozley, *Reminiscences of Oriel and the Oxford Movement*, I. 98.
2. *Ibid.*, I. 104.
3. *Ibid.*, I. 102.
4. Wrangham MSS. I. 55.
5. Wrangham MSS I. 56. 11 October 1823.
6. T. Mozley, *Reminiscences of Oriel and the Oxford Movement*, I. 31–2.
7. Wilberforce MSS. C. 31 July 1824.
8. Wilberforce MSS. K. 21 June 1823.
9. G. Prevost (editor), *Autobiography of Isaac Williams*, 28.
10. *Ibid.*, 29.
11. G. Battiscombe, *John Keble. A Study in Limitations* (1963), 22.
12. *Autobiography of Isaac Williams*, 22.
13. G. Battiscombe, *op. cit.*, 21.
14. Oratory. Box 119. no. 113. 15 March 1835.
15. The words are Newman's in a letter to Samuel Wilberforce in Wilberforce MSS. F. 5.
16. J. H. Newman, *Apologia*, 120.
17. G. Battiscombe, *op. cit.*, 92.
18. See for instance J. H. Newman, *The Arians of the Fourth Century* (1833), 45–62 for a detailed exposition of this. The importance of 'economy' in revelation, so very dear to the Tractarians and abhorrent to their opponents, is seen by R. D. Middleton in *Newman at Oxford. His Religious Development* (1950), 74.
19. I. Williams, *Tract 80. On Reserve in Communicating Religious Knowledge*. Part One (1838), 61.
20. I. Williams, Tract 87. *On Reserve in Communicating Religious Knowledge*, Part Two (3rd edition, 1843), 12–13.
21. Walter Lock, *John Keble* (3rd edn., 1893), 48. This is expressed most clearly by Keble himself in his own lectures on the nature of poetry, with their oft-repeated theme of 'reverence a sign of love'. E. K. Francis, *Keble's Lectures on Poetry 1832–1841* (1912), I. 74–6. See also his article in the *Quarterly Review*

for 1825 on 'Sacred Poetry' in which he especially admires Spenser's 'shrinking delicacy'. J. Keble, *Occasional Papers and Reviews* (1877), 81–107.

22. Cited in O. Chadwick, *The Mind of the Oxford Movement* (1960), 39.

IV. *Relations with Pusey and Hawkins*

1. *Autobiography of Isaac Williams*, 20.
2. Wilberforce MSS. B. 7 February 1825.
3. Kensington MSS B. 1.
4. H. P. Liddon, *Life of Pusey*, I. 72.
5. Kensington MSS. B. 2. 16 April 1827.
6. Wrangham MSS. VII. 3.
7. Bodleian. c. 193. 16 March 1828.
8. Oratory. Froude Papers, 13 August 1827.
9. The circumstances of Samuel's meeting with Malan are given in A. R. Ashwell, *op. cit.*, I. 36–8. More details may be found in Sir Charles Anderson's diary, where he describes Malan as 'a very apostolic looking man, but a regular Calvinist'. Lincoln Archives, AND. 5/2/2, p. 99.
10. Wrangham MSS. VII. 3. 18 July 1837.
11. Wrangham MSS. VII. 4.
12. Especially verses 23–4 of the same chapter of St John's first Epistle General— 'And this is his commandment, that we should believe on the name of his son Jesus Christ, and love one another as he gave us commandment', etc.
13. Wrangham MSS. VII. 5. 23 October 1827. The quotation from Keble is the last verse of the poem for the 'Second Sunday after Advent'.
14. Wrangham MSS. VII. 3.
15. Oratory. Froude Papers. 13 August 1827.
16. Kensington MSS. B. 3, and A. 1.
17. Oratory. Froude Papers. 27 December 1827.
18. G. Battiscombe, *op. cit.*, 119.
19. *Ibid.*, 58–9; 124–5.
20. Keble College. 69. no. 12.
21. Oratory. Froude Papers. 1 January 1828.
22. Oriel College. Letters, vol. 8. no. 784.
23. R. W. Church, *Occasional Papers* (1896), II. 346.
24. W. Tuckwell, *Pre-Tractarian Oxford*, 154–5.

v. *The Three Oriel Tutors*

1. Oratory. Froude Papers. 8 August 1828.
2. Wilberforce MSS. A. 17 March 1829.
3. Kensington MSS. B. 1.
4. Kensington MSS. B. 4. That William favoured Pusey's candidature is confirmed by the remarks in his letter printed in A. M. Wilberforce, *op. cit.*, 242–3.
5. Wrangham MSS. VII. nos. 8, 13.
6. Wrangham MSS. VII. 14.
7. Wilberforce MSS. E. 26 March 1830.
8. A. Mozley (editor), *Letters and Correspondence of J. H. Newman*, I. 169.
9. Kensington MSS. A. 1. See also Meriol Trevor, *Newman, The Pillar of the Cloud* (1962), 70.
10. Kensington MSS. A. 5.
11. Oratory. Box 137. 1.
12. Oratory. Box 137. 4. 23 March 1840.

13. Kensington MSS. A. 5. 29 July 1828.
14. Kensington MSS. A. 7. 6 September 1829.
15. Kensington MSS. C. 1. 24 February 1828.
16. J. H. Newman, *Fifteen Sermons preached before the University of Oxford* (1918 edn.), 7.
17. *Ibid.*, 191.
18. *Ibid.*, 198.
19. Kensington MSS. C. 2.
20. Kensington MSS. C. 3. 9 March 1828.
21. That this subject was very much on Froude's mind at this time can be seen from his remarks under the heading 'Occasional Thoughts' dated 16 July 1827 in *Remains*, I. 114.
22. S. O'Faolain, *Newman's Way* (1952), 124–30, especially 124, n. 1.
23. Anne Mozley (editor), *op. cit.*, I. 168.
24. M. Trevor, *op. cit.*, 65.
25. Anne Mozley (editor), *op. cit.*, I. 167.
26. *Ibid.*, I. 168.
27. See above p. 77.
28. Dorothea Mozley, *Newman Family Letters* (1962), 22.
29. S. O'Faolain, *op. cit.*, 128.
30. Wrangham MSS. VII. 4.
31. Wilberforce MSS. C. 14 November 1827.
32. S. O'Faolain, *op. cit.*, 134.
33. *Ibid.*, 134–5.
34. D. Mozley, *op. cit.*, 32.
35. M. Trevor, *op. cit.*, 110.
36. S. O'Faolain, *op. cit.*, 139.
37. See Robert's letter on this point in A. Mozley (editor), *op. cit.*, I. 191–2.
38. *Ibid.*, I. 152–3.
39. M. Trevor, *op. cit.*, 84.
40. Oriel College. Hawkins Letters. XIV. 1315.
41. The clash really concerned the position of Sir Robert Peel as University Member. When Peel in 1829, showed his willingness to recognise the claims of O'Connell to the extent of modifying his previous attitude of firm resistance to the removal of the civic disabilities suffered by Roman Catholics, this was interpreted by many of his constituents as a breach of faith. Peel resigned and offered himself for re-election. The election was contested and Sir Robert Inglis was returned in Peel's place.
42. See the last stanza of the poem 'Gunpowder Treason' in *The Christian Year* – 'Speak gently of our sister's fall'. Compare J. H. Newman, *Apologia*, 153.
43. J. H. Newman, *Apologia*, 153.
44. A. Mozley, *op. cit.*, 202–3.
45. Wilberforce MSS. 'Fragments'. 22.
46. Wrangham MSS. VII. 19.
47. Oriel MSS. Hawkins Letters. XIV. no. 1330.
48. W. Ward, *Ten Personal Studies* (1908), 280–1.

VI. *Samuel Wilberforce at Oxford*

1. Wilberforce MSS. C. 27 December 1837: 'Would you be so kind as to spell Keble's name right. Not Keeble. The fewest possible letters!!!'

2. A. M. Wilberforce, *Private Papers*, 222–3.
3. See Isaac Williams's account of his first meeting with Newman at a breakfast party given by William Churton. *Autobiography of Isaac Williams*, 25.
4. Wrangham MSS. V. 187. 29 November 1838.
5. Oratory. Newman Notebook. A. 7. 36.
6. Maisie Ward, *Young Mr Newman*, 247.
7. Oratory. Misc. Letters 1829–36. no. 61.
8. Wilberforce MSS. B. 7 February 1825.
9. Further details may be found in A. R. Ashwell, *op. cit.*, I. 29–31.
10. *Ibid.*, 32 n.
11. Wilberforce MSS. K. 'Friday, 1826'.
12. Wrangham MSS. VII. 29.
13. Wrangham MSS. V. 19.
14. Wrangham MSS. V. 2.
15. Wrangham MSS. V. 16.
16. Wilberforce MSS. K. undated.
17. Bodleian. c. 189. 16 December 1826.
18. Oratory. Froude Papers. 30 July 1827. 'Anderson you know is never very loquacious.'
19. Bodleian. c. 189. 3 March 1826.
20. Wrangham MSS. VI. 283.
21. A. R. Ashwell, *op. cit.*, I. 33.
22. Wilberforce MSS. K. 'Friday, 1826.
23. Oratory. Froude Papers. 20 March 1827.
24. Wilberforce MSS. B. 2 February 1827.
25. G. Battiscombe, *op. cit.*, 102.
26. Oratory. Froude Papers. 20 March 1827.
27. Bodleian. c. 193. 28 March 1827.
28. They were both historical essays – the first on the Reformation, and the second on the Crusades. *Historical Register of the University of Oxford*, 159, 168.
29. Oratory. Froude Papers. 30 July 1827.
30. Oratory, Froude Papers. 9 October 1827, completed 20 November.
31. Bodleian. c. 193. 24 April 1828.
32. A. R. Ashwell, *op. cit.*, I. 32–4.
33. Bodleian. c. 189. 3 May 1827.
34. Bodleian. c. 189. 31 July 1828.
35. Bodleian. c. 189. 29 August 1828.
36. Bodleian. c. 189. 17 February 1829.
37. Bodleian. c. 191. 14 February 1832.
38. Bodleian. c. 191. 31 August 1832.
39. Bodleian. c. 190. 29 January 1838.

VII. *Henry Wilberforce and J. H. Newman*
1. M. Trevor, *Newman. The Pillar of the Cloud*, 79.
2. T. Mozley, *Reminiscences of Oriel*, I. 113–4.
3. J. H. Newman, 'Memoir of Henry Wilberforce' in H. W. Wilberforce, *The Church and the Empires* (1874), 2.
4. Wrangham MSS. VII. 58. 12 November 1836.
5. Sandwith MSS. B. 15.
6. Kensington MSS. A. 9.

7. Sandwith MSS. B. I. 13.
8. Sandwith MSS. B. I. 12.
9. Sandwith MSS. C. 15. 9 September 1830.
10. Wrangham MSS. VII. 27. 28 April 1831.
11. J. H. Newman in H. W. Wilberforce, *op. cit.*, 3.
12. Kensington MSS. A. 6. 23 September 1828.
13. Sandwith MSS. B. 1. no. 2. This is a surprising statement since William in his letters to other members of the family was clearly really delighted at the fact that all three of his sons had secured Firsts at Oxford. See A. M. Wilberforce, *Private Papers*, 263.
14. Sandwith MSS. B. 1. no. 4.
15. Sandwith MSS. B. 1. no. 11.
16. Wilfrid Ward, *W. G. Ward and the Oxford Movement* (1889), 35.
17. T. Mozley, *Reminiscences*, I. 97.
18. Francis Doyle, *Reminiscences and Opinions 1813–1885* (1886), 113.
19. J. H. Newman, *op. cit.*, 3–4.
20. *Autobiography of Isaac Williams*, 69.
21. A. Mozley (editor), *op. cit.*, I. 166.
22. *Ibid.*, I. 187.
23. Kensington MSS. A. 6. 23 September 1828.
24. T. Mozley, *op. cit.*, I. 130.
25. *Ibid.*, I. 134–5.
26. E.g. Sandwith MSS. B. 1. nos. 7, 19. See also E. S. Purcell, *op. cit.*, I. 115 n. 1.
27. Sandwith MSS. B. 1. no. 8.
28. Kensington MSS. A. 7. 26 February 1832. For this aphorism, see especially Sandwith MSS B. 1. nos. 3, 19; also J. H. Newman, *Loss and Gain* (2nd edn. 1848), 19: 'In all collections of men, the straw and rubbish . . . float on the top, while gold and jewels sink and are hidden.'
29. Sandwith MSS. B. 1. no. 21. 18 June 1833.
30. M. Trevor, *Newman, The Pillar of the Cloud*, 235.
31. Wilberforce MSS. C. no. 3. 22 December 1830.
32. Sandwith MSS. A. no. 3. 21 May 1831. His father agreed with this opinion. See A. M. Wilberforce, *op. cit.*, 261.
33. Sandwith MSS. A. no. 5. 9 August 1831.
34. Sandwith MSS. A. no. 6. 5 October 1831.
35. Kensington MSS. A. 12. 26 February 1832.
36. Wilberforce MSS. B. 26 May 1818.
37. Wrangham MSS. V. 46. 27 June 1831.
38. Sean O'Faolain, *Newman's Way*, 161.
39. Sandwith MSS. B. 1. no. 14. St Andrew's Day 1832.

3. FAMILY AFFAIRS

I. *Lavington and the Sargents*
1. Ushaw MSS. 39. 19 December 1852.
2. Ushaw MSS. 55. 28 July 1873.
3. A. M. Wilberforce, *Lavington. The History of a Sussex Family* (privately printed, 1919), 34.
4. S. Wilberforce, *Sketch of the Life of the Rev. John Sargent* (1861 edn.), 15.
5. Wilberforce MSS. E. 4.

6. S. Wilberforce, *op. cit.*, 11.
7. *Ibid.*, 19–20.
8. *Ibid.*, 24–5.
9. R. I. and S. Wilberforce, *op. cit.*, IV. 348.
10. Ryder MSS. 'A Son's Reminiscence', 23–4.
11. T. Mozley, *op. cit.*, I. 131.
12. *Ibid.*, I. 132.
13. A. M. Wilberforce, *op. cit.*, 10.
14. *Ibid.*, 54.

II. *Life at Checkenden*
1. Wilberforce MSS. E. no. 14.
2. Bodleian, c. 189. 10 June 1828.
3. Bodleian. c. 195. 5 April 1828; cf. Wilberforce MSS. A. 20 March 1828.
4. Wrangham MSS. VII. 6. 3 April 1828.
5. Kensington MSS. A. no. 4. 16 July 1828.
6. Bodleian. c. 195. 13 June 1828.
7. Wilberforce MSS. A. 17 March 1829. See K. S. Inglis, *Churches and the Working Classes in Victorian England* (1963), 8, where the author gives the impression that the sole reason for Samuel's refusal was that he would be unable to cultivate 'devotional feelings and spirituality of mind'. This, as the portion of the letter quoted above shows, was not the main reason.
8. Bodleian. c. 196. 44. 11 November 1828.
9. A. R. Ashwell, *op. cit.*, I. 45–6.
10. Bodleian. c. 185, 11 March 1831; Kensington MSS. E. 2.
11. Wilberforce MSS. E. 16.
12. A. R. Ashwell, *op. cit.*, I. 46.
13. Wrangham MSS. V. 21.
14. Wilberforce MSS. A. 19 March 1829.
15. Oratory. Misc. Letters. 1829–36. no. 61. 5 November 1834.
16. Wilberforce MSS. A. 3 April 1829, 19 March 1829.
17. Wilberforce MSS. E. 23 June 1829.
18. Wrangham MSS. VII. 16. 12 May 1830.
19. Wrangham MSS. V. 11. 12 November 1829.
20. A. R. Ashwell, *op. cit.*, I. 47.
21. Wilberforce MSS. E. 23 June 1829.
22. Wilberforce MSS. E. 31 July 1829.
23. Bodleian. c. 195. 3 June 1830.
24. Wrangham MSS. V. 29. 16 June 1830.
25. Wilberforce MSS. E. 7 July 1830.

III. *The Speculations of an Eldest Son*
1. Wrangham MSS. V. 127. 2 November 1836.
2. Kensington MSS. E. 16; Wrangham MSS. VI. 463, 467, 468.
3. Wrangham MSS. VII. 42
4. Wrangham MSS. V. 41. 'Are you in a hurry for the 100 you lent me?'
5. Wrangham MSS. V. 83. 'I am now dry and have overdrawn my account.'
6. Wrangham MSS. V. 135. 8 March 1837.
7. Wrangham MSS. V. 137. 21 March 1837.
8. Wrangham MSS. VI. 297. See also no. 295. 'I am more abjectly poor than ever.'

9. Wrangham MSS. VII. 169.
10. Wrangham MSS. V. 201; VI. 252.
11. Bodleian, c. 191 (b). 19 April 1831.
12. E. M. Forster, *op. cit.*, 139.
13. Wrangham MSS. VII. 118.
14. R. Coupland, *op. cit.*, 505. Cf. R. I. and S. Wilberforce, *op. cit.*, V. 314.
15. M. Trevor, *op. cit.*, 119; also *Newman. Light in Winter*, 279.
16. Wrangham MSS. VII. 118.
17. Sandwith MSS. A. 15. 16 May 1832.
18. M. Trevor, *Newman. Light in Winter*, 279.
19. Kensington MSS. J. 4.
20. Wrangham MSS. I. 54.
21. Wrangham MSS. V. 8.
22. Bodleian. c. 189. 8 April 1831.
23. Compare Wrangham MSS. V. misc. 29 May 1831. Emily to Henry Wilberforce, letter crossed by Samuel: 'Mr Sargent speaks of my father's losses as £65,000.'
24. Bodleian. c. 191. (b). 9 April 1831.
25. See Wrangham MSS. VII. 26. 'I am very sorry Patty S. goes with them. Not that I fear she will do them harm individually but that it will be a scandal and keep them out of the society they should get into.' Also Wrangham MSS. V. misc. Letter of Emily to Henry Wilberforce: 'I am *very much grieved* that Patty Smith is to be Wm. and Mary's companion in their travels.'
26. Sandwith MSS. C. 35. 8 April 1831.
27. Sandwith MSS. A. 18. 6 June 1833.
28. Sandwith MSS. A. 3. 21 May 1831. 'I received intelligence that was perfectly conclusive on the almost universal existence of practices among children of the most dreadful kind. Even long before any feeling of passion can exist among infants from 6 years old upwards, indecencies are taught and practised, which lead with certainty to those wicked practices when they grow older which are called from that son of Judah whose death is recorded in the 38th chapter of Genesis.'
29. Sandwith MSS. A. 14. 16 May 1832.
30. Sandwith MSS. A. 15.
31. Wrangham MSS. VII. 39. 29 October 1833.
32. R. Coupland, *op. cit.*, 506.
33. Wilberforce MSS. B. 14 March 1837.

IV. *New Links and Losses*

1. Wrangham MSS. VII. 28. The quotations which follow about his impressions of Germany are all taken from this letter.
2. See remarks of Pusey in Kensington MSS. B. 14.
3. Wrangham MSS. VII. 28.
4. Wrangham MSS. V. d. 4 August 1831.
5. Wilberforce MSS. B. 6 December 1831.
6. Wrangham MSS. VII. 29.
7. Wrangham MSS. V. 52. Barbara's morbid musings had by this time become something of a family joke. When Henry, in a letter to Robert in 1833 (Sandwith MSS. B. 17), commented on the fact that while Rogers was on his honeymoon in Lyons his wife went down with scarlet fever, he added with a chuckle 'therefore as mother would say, "brides should never go to Lyons"'.

8. Kensington MSS. J. 4.
9. Wilberforce MSS. C. 22 December 1830.
10. Kensington MSS. K. 4.
11. Wrangham MSS. VII. 30.
12. Wilberforce MSS. C. 18 February 1832.
13. Wrangham MSS. V. 56. 'I expect to be asked to marry you.'
14. Sandwith MSS. B. 10. A P.S. by Newman added to a letter from Henry to Robert. Compare the rather cool comments of Newman in a letter to Samuel. Wilberforce MSS. F. 1. 29 February 1832.
15. Wrangham MSS. V. 57.
16. Wilberforce MSS. C. 4.
17. Wrangham MSS. V. 39, 40, 45, 52.
18. A. M. Wilberforce, *op. cit.*, 267.
19. Kensington MSS. A. 8.
20. For a further discussion of this attitude (especially in Newman's relations with W. G. Ward, Manning, Faber, Talbot and Wiseman), see my article 'Newmania' in *Journal of Theological Studies*, N.S. XIV. pt. 2. 1963, 427.
21. Kensington MSS. A. 14.
22. Wrangham MSS. V. 37.
23. Wrangham MSS. V. 40.
24. Wrangham MSS. V. 42.
25. E.g. Wrangham MSS. V. 96, 113.
26. Sandwith MSS. A. 17.
27. Wrangham MSS. VII. 32.
28. Wrangham MSS. VII. 34.
29. Sandwith MSS. B. I. 27.
30. Wrangham MSS. VII. 32.
31. Details of her condition and death are given in Sandwith MSS. B. I. 8–11.
32. Sandwith MSS. B. I. 23.
33. Sandwith MSS. B. I. 24.
34. Kensington MSS. H. 1.
35. Wrangham MSS. V. 77. For details of the illness and death, see Henry's account of the findings of the post-mortem ('gangrene' of the lung) and also his own most moving personal tribute in Sandwith MSS. B. 1. 18. 11 May 1833.

v. *Husbands and Wives*

1. E. S. Purcell, *op. cit.*, I. 81.
2. Sandwith MSS. B. I. 18.
3. Bodleian. c. 186. Diary no. 2.
4. Manning Archives, letters dated 22 January 1820, 1 February 1826, 22 January 1831.
5. Wrangham MSS. V. d. 4 August 1831.
6. J. Fitzsimons (editor), *Manning, Anglican and Catholic* (1951), 3.
7. G. W. E. Russell, *The Household of Faith* (1902), 157. Compare Aubrey de Vere, *Recollections* (1897), 288 – 'I see a word written on the forehead of that man, and the word is *Sacerdos*.'
8. Shane Leslie, *Henry Edward Manning. His Life and Labours* (1921), 37.
9. J. Fitzsimons, *op. cit.*, 4.
10. S. Leslie, *op. cit.*, 39–42.

11. Wilberforce MSS. E. 8 November 1833.
12. Ryder MSS. 'A Son's Reminiscences', 25–6.
13. Ryder MSS. 'A Son's Reminiscences', 27.
14. Ryder MSS. B. 29 August 1833.
15. M. Trevor, *Newman. The Pillar of the Cloud*, 159.
16. *Ibid.*, 159.
17. *Ibid.*, 159.
18. *Ibid.*, 160–1.
19. The words are Miss Trevor's, *ibid.*, 163.
20. *Ibid.*, 164.
21. E. S. Purcell, *op. cit.*, I. 102.
22. Sandwith MSS. B. I. 18, 27.
23. G. H. Sumner, *Life of Sumner*, 231,
24. Wilberforce MSS. C. undated.

VI. *At Brighstone and East Farleigh*
 1. Wilberforce MSS. E. 8 May 1832.
 2. Details taken from two letters in Wrangham MSS. V. 74, 75.
 3. G. H. Sumner, *op. cit.*, 255.
 4. Wrangham MSS. V. 91.
 5. E.g. Bodleian, c. 195. 28 February 1831.
 6. G. H. Sumner, *op. cit.*, 219–20.
 7. Kensington MSS. K. 8.
 8. Wilberforce MSS. E. 29 June 1833.
 9. Wrangham MSS. V. 81. 5 July 1833.
10. Bodleian. c. 186. Diary no. 3. 4 March 1835.
11. Wilberforce MSS. E. 12 March 1835.
12. Kensington MSS. I. 4. 1 February 1834.
13. Kensington MSS. I. 6. 10 April 1834.
14. Kensington MSS. K. 16.
15. Kensington MSS. K. 16.
16. Wilberforce MSS. E. 23 November 1834.
17. Wilberforce MSS. C. undated.

4. QUESTIONS OF CHURCHMANSHIP

I. *Apostolical Enthusiasms*
 1. C. Dawson, *The Spirit of the Oxford Movement*, 55.
 2. I. Samuel 12, v. 23.
 3. W. Palmer, *A Narrative of Events connected with the publication of the Tracts for the Times* (1883), 99.
 4. *Tracts for the Times*, no. 4, 7.
 5. R. D. Middleton, *Newman at Oxford*, 92.
 6. Kensington MSS, A. 15.
 7. See the recent edition of T. Arnold, *Principles of Church Reform* (1962 edn.), with an interesting introduction by M. J. Jackson and J. Rogan, in which the different standpoints of Arnold and the Tractarians are well expressed.
 8. T. Arnold, *op. cit.*, 158. Henry's is not quite an exact quotation.
 9. Sandwith MSS. B. IV. 8.
10. Wrangham MSS. VII. 45.

11. Wilberforce MSS. D. 11.
12. Bodleian. c. 191. 25 February 1836.
13. Wilberforce MSS. K. undated.
14. Wrangham MSS. V. 117.
15. Francis Doyle, *Reminiscences and Opinions*, 47.
16. Kensington MSS. A. 16.
17. Wilberforce MSS. K. 1 April 1836.
18. Wilberforce MSS. K. 1 April 1836.
19. Wrangham MSS. V. 107.
20. E.g. Wrangham MSS. V. 23, where Samuel commented as follows on two polemical tracts: 'The first I think a most offensively Calvinistic patronizing production – the effusion of a rampant – foolish – vainish Xtian . . . The other . . . is foolish, and in a very harsh and bad spirit – and in doctrine appears as unscriptural as the other.'
21. Wrangham MSS V. 55. Cf. also no. 44, where he describes the 'fearful and scandalous scene' at a Bible Society meeting.
22. Wrangham MSS. V. 53.
23. Wrangham MSS. V. 152. For the closeness of his views to those of Sumner, see the letter to the Bishop in G. H. Sumner, *op. cit.*, 246–7, where he expresses his distaste for a 'Popish leaven' amongst some of the diocesan clergy. This was in 1835.
24. Bodleian. c. 186. Diary no. 4. 20 November 1837.
25. E.g. Wrangham MSS. V. 182, where Samuel says that his own understanding of the doctrine of justification differs from the teaching of Newman and 'seems much to agree with D.W.'s'.
26. Wrangham MSS. VII. 167.
27. Wrangham MSS. VII. 176.
28. Bodleian. c. 191. 12 September 1833.
29. Wrangham MSS. V. 109.
30. Bodleian. c. 191. 22 April 1835.
31. Bodleian. c. 186. Diary no. 3, 1834–6.

II. *Filial Duties and Dilemmas*
1. F. K. Brown, *Fathers of the Victorians*, 73 n. 1.
2. For a full discussion of Mr Brown's points and the reasons why they may be challenged, see my article 'Father and Sons' in *Historical Journal*, VI. no. 2 (1963), 295–310.
3. Wrangham MSS. VII. 71.
4. Wrangham MSS. V. 151.
5. Wrangham MSS. VII. 81.
6. Wrangham MSS. VII. 47.
7. James Stephen, *Essays in Ecclesiastical Biography*, II. 186. Greville appears to have thought this a fair review. See *Greville Memoirs*, 2nd part (1883), I. 90.
8. The reviews are discussed in Wrangham MSS. V. 181. The authors expected, however, a later attack from the *Record*. Samuel suggested that the editor was waiting 'for a cue from its leaders'.
9. Wrangham MSS. VII. 85; also V. 185.
10. A. R. Ashwell, *op. cit.*, I. 90.
11. Wilberforce MSS. B. 24 November 1838.
12. Wrangham MSS. VII. 67.

13. A lampoon in the *Morning Chronicle*, December 1847, quoted by G. C. B. Davies, *Henry Phillpotts. Bishop of Exeter 1778–1869* (1954), 210.

III. *The Law and the Gospel*

 1. Discussed *supra*, p. 75.
 2. J. H. Newman, *Sermons bearing on Subjects of the Day* (1918 edn.), 140–1.
 3. J. H. Newman, *op. cit.*, 391–3. See the remarks on this sermon in Alf Härdelin, *The Tractarian Understanding of the Eucharist* (Uppsala, 1965), 9.
 4. J. H. Newman, *Parochial and Plain Sermons* (1868 edn.), I. 96.
 5. Oratory. Miscellaneous Letters 1829–36. no. 66. 23 January 1835. For much fuller citations from this letter and from the whole of the correspondence that follows, see my article 'Justification and Sanctification: Newman and The Evangelicals' in *Journal of Theological Studies* N.S. XV. Pt. 1. April 1964, 32–53.
 6. Wilberforce MSS. F. 4. 29 January 1835.
 7. Wilberforce MSS. F. 5. 4 February 1835.
 8. Oratory. Misc. Letters 1829–36. no. 67. 23 February 1835.
 9. Wilberforce MSS. F. 6. 10 March 1835; Oratory. Misc. Letters 1829–36. no. 69. 16 April 1835.
 10. Wilberforce MSS. F. 7.
 11. Wilberforce MSS. J. 2. 27 February 1835.
 12. The upbringing of the Stephen children is described in N. Annan, *Leslie Stephen. His Thought and Character in relation to his Times* (1951), 15. Leslie Stephen described his father as holding 'the inherited doctrine in a latitudinarian sense'. (F. W. Maitland, *Life and Letters of Leslie Stephen* (1901), 17.)
 13. Oratory. Box 119. no. 133. 5 March 1835.
 14. Oratory. Box 119. no. 133. 15 March 1835. (This is marked in Newman's hand 'sent with many alterations'.)
 15. Wilberforce MSS. J. 3. 4 February 1836.
 16. Bodleian c. 190. 5 April 1837.
 17. Bodleian. c. 190. 28 October 1836.
 18. Bodleian. c. 190. 12 January 1838.
 19. Bodleian. c. 191. 23 January 1838.
 20. Bodleian. c. 190. 29 January 1838.
 21. Wilberforce MSS. J. 4. 10 May 1837.

IV. *The 'Renversement des Alliances'*

 1. Bodleian. c. 191. 31 May 1836.
 2. Wilberforce MSS. F. 8. 4 December 1835.
 3. Wilberforce MSS. F. 11; cf. Oratory. Notebook. A. 7. 36. p.187.
 4. Wrangham MSS. V. 81.
 5. The contributors were J. W. Bowden (α); R. H. Froude (β); John Keble (γ); Newman (δ); Robert Wilberforce (ε); Isaac Williams (ζ). Robert's sole contribution was a poem entitled 'Profaneness', *Lyra Apostolica* (3rd edn., 1838), 172.
 6. Wilberforce MSS. F. 15, 16.
 7. *British Critic*, xxi, 177.
 8. *Ibid.*, 178.
 9. *Ibid.*, 180.
 10. *Autobiography of Isaac Williams.* 67. But compare J. B. Mozley – 'N. was con-

siderably amused with this cut at him when S.W. sent him the critique to read over some little time ago.' *Letters of J. B. Mozley*, edited by his sister (1885), 63.

11. S. Wilberforce, *Six Sermons preached before the University of Oxford* (2nd edn., 1848), 10.

12. *Ibid.*, 11–12. Compare *supra* p. 182. Newman had written: 'The Holy Spirit addresses us thro' our reason. . . . Such is the rule, the ordinary mode . . . of God's dealings with us. And such ordinary mode it is our duty to proclaim. We have little to do with exceptions in preaching His will.'

13. Wrangham MSS. V. 169. 29 January 1838.

14. S. Wilberforce, *Six Sermons*, v.

15. *Ibid.*, 38–40.

16. *Ibid.*, 84–5.

17. *Ibid.*, 90.

18. Wrangham MSS. V. 160. 16 December 1837.

19. Wrangham MSS. V. 167. 11 January 1838.

20. A. R. Ashwell, *op. cit.*, I. 120.

21. Bodleian, c. 191. 13 June 1838.

22. Wilberforce MSS. D. 13 March 1838.

23. Oratory. Newman Notebook. A. 7. 36.

24. A. R. Ashwell, *op. cit.*, I. 125–6.

25. Wilberforce MSS. C. 18 April 1839.

26. Bodleian. c. 191. 31 August 1838.

27. Wrangham MSS. V. 187.

28. H. P. Liddon, *Life of E. B. Pusey*, III. 38.

29. Wrangham MSS. VI. 237. 8 June 1842.

v. *The Brothers and Henry Manning*

1. Sandwith MSS. B. I. 28. 16 March 1837.

2. Sandwith MSS. B. I. 21, 31.

3. Sandwith MSS. B. I. 31.

4. Sandwith MSS. B. I. 28.

5. Sandwith MSS. B. I. 32. 9 April 1839.

6. M. Trevor, *Newman. The Pillar of the Cloud*, 229.

7. *Dublin Review*, April 1869, 327–8; quoted extensively by R. D. Middleton, *Newman at Oxford*, 158–9.

8. Wrangham MSS. V. 194. 10 April 1839.

9. E.g. Kensington MSS. A. 23. 6 October 1837. 'We have the most gratifying news in every direction of the spreading of Church principles. Indeed I think nothing but a Star Chamber or Court of High Commission can (humanly speaking) hinder it – and these expedients are not to be thought of in the 19th century.'

10. E.g. Y. Brilioth, *The Anglican Revival*, 46–55.

11. Kensington MSS. A. 24. 9 June 1838.

12. Wrangham MSS. VII. 87.

13. A. Mozley, *Letters and Correspondence*, II. 249.

14. Wrangham MSS. VII. 87.

15. Wrangham MSS. VII. 112.

16. Wrangham MSS. VII. 55.

17. Wrangham MSS. VII. 95.

18. Wrangham MSS. V. 122. 28 May 1836.

19. Wilberforce MSS. D. 26.
20. Maisie Ward, *Young Mr Newman*, 256; Wilberforce MSS. D. 8.
21. J. Fitzsimons, *op. cit.*, 7.
22. E. S. Purcell, *op. cit.*, I. 112.
23. Wilberforce MSS. D. 89. 20 October 1850.
24. E. S. Purcell, *op. cit.*, I. 107, n. 1.
25. Wilberforce MSS. D. 8. 15 September 1835.
26. Wilberforce MSS. D. 19. 16 November 1836.
27. Wilberforce MSS. D. 21. 3 January 1837.
28. Wilberforce MSS. D. 4. 15 December 1834.
29. Discussed at length, with interesting letters from S. F. Wood, in G. Donald, *Men who left the Movement* (1933), 164–7.
30. *Ibid.*, 164; E. S. Purcell, *op. cit.*, I. 115–16.
31. E. S. Purcell, *op. cit.*, I. 127.
32. E. S. Purcell, *op. cit.*, I. 112.
33. H. E. Manning, *The English Church; its succession and witness for Christ* (1835), 9.
34. *Ibid.*, 5.
35. *Ibid.*, 18.
36. *Ibid.*, 4–5, 'Spurious charity' as applied to the contemplation of sectarianism was a favourite phrase of Manning's. Compare H. E. Manning, *The Unity of the Church* (1842), 5, where he writes of the 'habit of indifference, laxity and a spurious charity, which, like a hidden stream, undermines the steadfastness of principle'.
37. *Ibid.*, 20.
38. *Ibid.*, 21.
39. *Ibid.*, 26.
40. H. E. Manning, *The Rule of Faith* (1838), 14, 23.
41. *Ibid.*, 26–7.
42. *Ibid.*, 27.
43. *Ibid.*, 35.
44. *Ibid.*, 38.
45. *Ibid.*, 48.
46. Wilberforce MSS. D. 89. 'Here began our divergence', Manning reminded Samuel. 'We discussed it over my book in this room: and we have both been consistent in our after career.'
47. H. E. Manning, *The Rule of Faith*, 49–50.
48. *Ibid.*, 55–6. This passage – from Revelation II. 1, 5 (the command to the ministers of the Church of Ephesus) – was a favourite image of Manning's. See also *The Unity of the Church*, 273; *Sermons*, I (1845), 42–3. Robert Wilberforce uses the same image in one of his sermons, R. I. Wilberforce, *Sermons on the New Birth of Man's Nature* (1850), 126.
49. J. Fitzsimons, *op. cit.*, 9.
50. H. E. Manning. *The Rule of Faith*. Appendix (1838).
51. Y. Brilioth, *The Anglican Revival*, 256, 262–3. 81.
52. H. E. Manning, *Sermons* I. 36.
53. *Ibid.*, I. 84–5.
54. *Ibid.*, II (1846), 119–20. This is one of Manning's most moving sermons, entitled 'Spiritual Presumption'.
55. *Ibid.*, III (1847), 314. On 'Preparation for Death a State of Life'.

56. *Ibid.*, IV (1850), 334.
57. *Ibid.*, I. 100.
58. H. E. Manning, *The Unity of the Church*, 306.

5. CHURCH, STATE AND COUNTRY PARISH

I. *Conservatives and Reformers*

1. N. Gash, *Politics in the Age of Peel* (1953), 7–8.
2. G. F. A. Best, *Temporal Pillars, Queen Anne's Bounty, the Ecclesiastical Commissioners and the Church of England* (Cambridge, 1964), 271.
3. Wrangham MSS. V. 76.
4. Bodleian. c. 191. 17 April 1835.
5. Bodleian. c. 191. 2 May 1834.
6. Wrangham MSS. V. 100. 26 January 1835.
7. Wilberforce MSS. D. 25. 2 May 1837.
8. H. E. Manning, *The Principles of the Ecclesiastical Commission examined in a letter to the . . . Bishop of Chichester* (1838), 7.
9. H. E. Manning, *op. cit.*, 9.
10. *Ibid.*, 61–3.
11. *Ibid.*, 31.
12. O. J. Brose, *Church and Parliament. The Reshaping of the Church of England 1826–1860* (1959), 145–7.
13. Wilberforce MSS. D. 23.
14. E. S. Purcell, *op. cit.*, I. 141.
15. Wilberforce MSS. D. 30.
16. G. F. A. Best, *op. cit.*, 274.
17. Wrangham MSS. V. 47, 126.
18. S. Wilberforce, *A History of the Protestant Episcopal Church in America* (3rd edn., 1856), 456.
19. H. Cnattingius, *Bishops and Societies. A Study of Anglican Colonial and Missionary Expansion 1698–1850* (1952), 196–7. Further details of the Concordat and Henry Venn's own prosecution of it, while disliking the projected union with S.P.G., may be found in W. Knight, *The Missionary Secretariat of Henry Venn* (1880), 195–222.
20. Wilberforce MSS. D. 35. 20 July 1838.
21. Wilberforce MSS. D. 38. 18 October 1839.
22. S. Wilberforce, *op. cit.*, 370–1.
23. H. Cnattingius, *op. cit.*, 201.
24. Wilberforce MSS. F. 12.
25. H. Cnattingius, *op. cit.*, 199.
26. H. W. Tucker, *Memoir of the Life and Episcopate of G. A. Selwyn* (1879), I. 30–43.
27. H. W. Tucker, *op. cit.*, 64–6.
28. H. J. Burgess, *Enterprise in Education. The Story of the Work of the Established Church in the Education of the People prior to 1870* (1958), 63–71.
29. H. E. Manning, *National Education. A Sermon . . . in behalf of Chichester Central Schools* (1838), 31.
30. *Ibid.*, 17–18.
31. E. S. Purcell, *op. cit.*, I. 149; H. J. Burgess, *op. cit.*, 68–9.
32. Wrangham MSS. V. 167.
33. E. S. Purcell, *op. cit.*, I. 149–50.

34. H. J. Burgess, *op. cit.*, 76–7.
35. *Ibid.*, 70–71.
36. Wrangham MSS. VII. 148. 4 May 1845.
37. A. R. Ashwell, *op. cit.*, I. 97–8.
38. *The Address of the Clergy of the Archdeaconry of Chichester to His Grace the Archbishop of Canterbury*, concerning Church Synods (1836), drafted by H. E. Manning, 4.
39. Wilberforce MSS. D. 16. 22 October 1836.
40. H. W. Wilberforce, *The Parochial System. An Appeal to English Churchmen* (1838), 9.
41. *Ibid.*, 11–13.
42. *Ibid.*, 15.
43. *Ibid.*, 27.
44. *Ibid.*, 28; E. R. Wickham, *Church and People in an Industrial City* (1957), 149.
45. E. R. Wickham, *op. cit.*, 273.
46. H. W. Wilberforce, *op. cit.*, 31–3.
47. *Ibid.*, 35; compare R. H. Froude, *Remains* (1838), I. 322. For Pusey, see the discussion in W. G. Peck, *The Social Implications of the Oxford Movement* (1938), 66–9.
48. H. W. Wilberforce, *op. cit.*, 35.
49. *Ibid.*, 36–7.
50. *Ibid.*, 52–3.
51. *Ibid.*, 54–5. n.
52. *Ibid.*, 59.
53. *Ibid.*, 75–6.
54. *Ibid.*, 95–6.
55. Wilberforce MSS. C. 21 November 1835.
56. Wilberforce MSS. H. 8 August 1838.
57. Wilberforce MSS. J. 10 May 1837.
58. Wrangham MSS. VI. 211. 17 April 1840.

II. *The Cure of Souls*

1. J. H. Newman, 'Memoir of Henry Wilberforce' in H. W. Wilberforce, *The Church and the Empires* (1874), 6.
2. Wrangham MSS. V. 151. 29 September 1837.
3. Wrangham MSS. V. 152. 4 October 1837.
4. Wilberforce MSS. D. 31. 30 January 1838.
5. Wrangham MSS. V. 200. 9 July 1839.
6. Wrangham MSS. V. 106. 18 October 1835.
7. Wrangham MSS. V. 116. 4 February 1836.
8. J. Wickham Legg, *English Church Life from the Restoration to the Tractarian Movement* (1914), 90; Horton Davies, *Worship and Theology in England from Watts and Wesley to Maurice 1690–1850* (1961), 62; also discussed with reference to T. Keble of Bisley in *Autobiography of Isaac Williams*, 75–6.
9. Kensington MSS. H. 3. 30 November 1835.
10. Kensington MSS. A. 34. 1 March 1841.
11. Sandwith MSS. B. I. 19. 29 May 1833.
12. Wrangham MSS. V. 102. 8 May 1835.
13. Sandwith MSS. B. I. 30. Easter Eve 1838.
14. Sandwith MSS. B. I. 28. 16 March 1837.

15. Ryder MSS. 'A Son's Reminiscence', 28.
16. *Ibid.*, 29; Ryder MSS. Keble letters, no. 6. 16 February 1843.
17. Wilberforce MSS. D. 6. 29 July 1835.
18. Wilberforce MSS. D. 9. 4 January 1836.
19. Wilberforce MSS. D. 1.
20. Wilberforce MSS. D. 24. 20 March 1837.
21. Wilberforce MSS. D. 18. 24 October 1836.
22. Wilberforce MSS. D. 21. 3 January 1837.
23. E. S. Purcell, *op. cit.*, I. 233.
24. Bodleian. c. 191. 3 July 1834.
25. Wrangham MSS. V. 49. 26 July 1831.
26. Wrangham MSS. V. 120. 13 April 1836.
27. Bodleian. c. 186. Diary 1831–2, Monday 25 October.
28. Wrangham MSS. V. 66. 28 May 1832.
29. Wrangham MSS. VII. 58, 59. 12, 19 November 1836.
30. Wrangham MSS. VII. 55. 12 September 1836.
31. Wrangham MSS. VII. 35. 7 May 1833.
32. Wilberforce MSS. C. 28 November 1835.
33. Wrangham MSS. VII. 39, 42.
34. Kensington MSS. 9. 1 July 1833.
35. Wrangham MSS. VII. 40, 41, 55. The illegality was removed by the passing of Shaftesbury's Religious Worship Bill in 1855. G. R. Balleine, *A History of the Evangelical Party in the Church of England* (1933), 246.
36. Wrangham MSS. VII. 7.
37. Wrangham MSS. VII. 79. 29 December 1837.
38. Wrangham MSS. V. 73.
39. Wrangham MSS. V. 66, 73.
40. Wrangham MSS. V. 50. 16 August 1831.
41. Bodleian. c. 186. Diary 1831–2. Sunday, 23 January.
42. Bodleian. c. 191. 15 September 1834.
43. Wrangham MSS. V. 26 November 1833.
44. Wrangham MSS. V. 79. 11 June 1833.
45. Wilberforce MSS. C. 21 November 1835.
46. Wrangham MSS. V. 111. 24 December 1835.
47. A. R. Ashwell, *op. cit.*, I. 80.
48. Wrangham MSS. V. 138. 13 April 1837.
49. Wilberforce MSS. E. 11 May 1840.
50. S. Wilberforce, *Agathos and other Sunday Stories* (1840 edn.), iv–v.
51. A. R. Ashwell, *op. cit.*, I. 215 n.
52. S. Wilberforce, *The Rocky Island* (1852 edn.), 25.
53. A. R. Ashwell, *op. cit.*, I. 217–8.

III. *Bidding for Power*
1. Wrangham MSS. V. 81. 5 July 1833.
2. Wilberforce MSS. E. 5 November 1834.
3. Wilberforce MSS. E. undated.
4. Wrangham MSS. V. 48. 5 June 1831.
5. A. R. Ashwell, *op. cit.*, I. 70; Wrangham MSS. V. 84. 29 January 1834.
6. Wrangham MSS. V. 88, 89. 5 May, 23 May 1834.
7. Wrangham MSS. V. 90. 29 May 1834.

8. Bodleian. c. 195. 23 May 1834.
9. G. H. Sumner, *op. cit.* 230.
10. Wrangham MSS. V. 90. 29 May 1834.
11. Wrangham MSS. V. 136. Ash Wednesday 1837. The living of Leeds was in the gift of Trustees, and therefore an election was necessary. The detailed account of Hook's election may be found in W. R. W. Stephens, *The Life and Letters of Walter Farquhar Hook* (1878), I. 295–319.
12. *Ibid.*
13. Wilberforce MSS. B. 1 March 1837.
14. Wrangham MSS. VII. 62.
15. Wrangham MSS. VII. 63.
16. A. R. Ashwell, *op. cit.*, I. 107–8.
17. Wrangham MSS. V. 160.
18. Wrangham MSS. V. 176. 19 April 1838.
19. Wrangham MSS. V. 177. 22 April 1838.
20. Wrangham MSS. V. 183.
21. Wrangham MSS. V. 202. 31 December 1839.
22. Wilberforce MSS. G. 2. 8 January 1840.
23. Wrangham MSS. VII. 99. 15 June 1839.
24. Wrangham MSS. V. 123. 28 June 1836.
25. Wrangham MSS. V. 121.
26. Wrangham MSS. VII. 64. 23 March 1837.
27. Wrangham MSS. VII. 101. 9 September 1839.
28. Wrangham MSS. VII. 102. 17 October 1839.
29. Wrangham MSS. VI. 231. 30 November 1841.
30. Wrangham MSS. VI. 213. 4 June 1840.
31. Wrangham MSS. VII. 103. 14 November 1839.
32. Sandwith MSS. B. I. 19. 29 May 1833.

IV. *Jane Legard and Burton Agnes*
1. Wilberforce MSS. C. 21 November 1835.
2. Kensington MSS. J. 4. 21 January 1837. Jane complains about George Wrangham letting 'their secret' out.
3. Bodleian. c. 191. 13 April 1837.
4. Kensington MSS. J. 8.
5. Wrangham MSS. V. 175.
6. Wrangham MSS. VII. 116. 3 June 1840.
7. Wrangham MSS. VII. 118.
8. *Victoria History of the County of Yorkshire*, edited W. Page, III (1913), 489.
9. *Church Bells and Illustrated Church News*, 16 June 1905, 589.
10. Wrangham MSS. VII. 119. 8 September 1840.

V. *The Death of Caroline Manning*
1. Wilberforce MSS. D. 25. 2 May 1837.
2. Bodleian. c. 186. Diary no. 4. 24 July 1837.
3. Mrs Sargent was staying at Bransgore with Henry and Mary. Wrangham MSS. V. 143.
4. Ryder MSS. B. 2.
5. Wrangham MSS. V. 145.
6. Wilberforce MSS. E. 3 August 1838.
7. Wilberforce MSS. D. 29. 25 September 1837.

6. THE THREE ARCHDEACONS

I. *Triumph and Tribulations*

1. A. R. Ashwell, *op. cit.*, I. 145.
2. *Ibid.*, I. 148.
3. Manning archives. Wilberforce Letters. II. 5. 4 October 1839.
4. Wrangham MSS. VII. 104. 21 November 1839.
5. Wrangham MSS. VI. 207. 24 March 1840.
6. Wrangham MSS. VI. 210. 9 April 1840.
7. A. R. Ashwell, *op. cit.*, I. 160–1.
8. Bodleian. c. 195. 24 October 1840. Compare somewhat different figures in A. R. Ashwell, *op. cit.*, I. 169.
9. Wrangham MSS. VI. 216. 27 October 1840.
10. Wrangham MSS. VII. 121. All Saints Day. 1840.
11. A. R. Ashwell, *op. cit.*, I. 113.
12. Ryder MSS. B. 19 November (year uncertain), Mrs Sargent to Sophia.
13. Wilberforce MSS. E. Undated.
14. Wilberforce MSS. E. postmark: 10 July 1831.
15. Wilberforce MSS. B. 27 December 1841.
16. All the above extracts are taken from Bodleian. c. 186. Diary no. 4.
17. Bodleian. c. 191.
18. Bodleian. c. 186. Diary no. 4. 17 March.
19. Wilberforce MSS. E. 26 March 1830.
20. Ryder MSS. B. 6.
21. Wrangham MSS. VI. 223.
22. Wilberforce MSS. E. 19 April 1841.
23. Wilberforce MSS. E. 16 June 1841.
24. A. R. Ashwell, *op. cit.*, I. 181.
25. Wilberforce MSS. D. 44. 22 April 1841.
26. See the many extracts from the later diaries in A. R. Ashwell, *op. cit.*, I. 180–188.
27. Wrangham MSS. VI. 227. 26 September 1841.
28. A. R. Ashwell, *op. cit.*, I. 202.
29. *Ibid.*, I. 212.
30. Wrangham MSS. VI. 232. 17 January 1842.
31. Wrangham MSS. VII. 140. 7 March 1842.
32. Wrangham MSS. VII. 143. 28 August 1842.
33. A. R. Ashwell, *op. cit.*, I. 224.
34. Wrangham MSS. VI. 260. 9 December 1844.
35. Bodleian. c. 186. Diary no. 5. 10 March 1844.
36. Wrangham MSS. VI. 236. 26 May 1842.
37. Bodleian. c. 186. Diary no. 5.24/25 January 1843.
38. Wrangham MSS. VI. 270. 22 August 1845.
39. Wrangham MSS. VI. 285. 10 March 1846.

II. *Charges, the Church and Confession*

1. J. Fitzsimons (editor), *op. cit.*, 11.
2. Wrangham MSS. VII. 108. St Paul's Day, 1840.
3. Wrangham MSS. V. 194.
4. E. S. Purcell, *op. cit.*, I. 187.

5. *Ibid.*, 180 n.1.
6. *Ibid.*, I. 184.
7. H. E. Manning, *A Charge delivered at the Ordinary Visitation of the Archdeaconry of Chichester, July 1841* (1841), 9.
8. Wilberforce MSS. D. 52. 27 January 1846. This is a significant letter in view of the stress now rightly laid on Samuel Wilberforce's re-modelling of the diocesan administration. See R. K. Pugh, 'The Episcopate of Samuel Wilberforce' (unpublished Oxford D. Phil. thesis, 1957), 115–29.
9. H. E. Manning, *A Charge . . . July 1841*, 18–19.
10. *Ibid.*, 24–5.
11. *Ibid.*, 31.
12. *Ibid.*, 45–6.
13. H. E. Manning, *A Charge delivered at the Ordinary Visitation of the Archdeaconry of Chichester in July 1842* (1842), 10.
14. *Ibid.*, 16.
15. *Ibid.*, 39–40.
16. See, for instance, Wrangham MSS. VI. 247, 249, 241.
17. R. I. Wilberforce, *A Primary Charge to the Clergy of the Archdeaconry of the East Riding* (1841), 11–17; *A Charge to the Clergy of the Archdeaconry of the East Riding at the Ordinary Visitation, A.D. 1845* (1845), 14–18.
18. R. I. Wilberforce, *A Charge delivered at the Ordinary Visitation . . . 1843* (1843), 11.
19. R. I. Wilberforce, *Church Courts and Church Discipline* (1843), 59–60.
20. *Ibid.*, 70.
21. J. N. Figgis, *Churches in the Modern State* (1913), 11–18; 32–53. Compare R. I. Wilberforce, *op. cit.*, 70–1, 115–16.
22. Wrangham MSS. VI. 248. 10 September 1843.
23. Wrangham MSS. VI. 251. 18 December 1843.
24. S. Wilberforce, *A Charge delivered at the Ordinary Visitation of the Archdeaconry of Surrey, November 1842* (1842), 7–18. Robert also added his voice to the general clamour against pew-rents; see *Church Courts and Church Discipline*, 127–30.
25. S. Wilberforce, *A Charge delivered at the Ordinary Visitation of the Archdeaconry of Surrey, November 1843* (1843), 6–7.
26. R. I. Wilberforce, *A Charge to the Clergy of the Archdeaconry of the East Riding . . . 1845* (1845), 23.
27. H. E. Manning, *A Charge delivered at the Ordinary Visitation of the Archdeaconry of Chichester in July 1845* (1845), 24–5, 28, 30–43.
28. S. Wilberforce, *A Charge delivered at the Ordinary Visitation of the Archdeaconry of Surrey, April 1845* (1845), 10–11.
29. *Ibid.*, 27.
30. H. E. Manning, *A Charge . . . July 1841*, 12–13.
31. Manning archives. Wilberforce Letters. I. 10. 1 February 1845. Manning refers especially to *The Unity of the Church*, 310–11.
32. Wilberforce MSS. D. 89. 20 October 1850.
33. Ronald Chapman, *Father Faber* (1961), 97.
34. Wilberforce MSS. D. 64. 8 January 1849. For a recent discussion of this same point – the Anglican tradition of spiritual direction as illustrated notably by Jeremy Taylor – see Charles Smyth, *The Church and the Nation* (1962), 32–3.
35. Kensington MSS. B. 5. Undated. Keble would have agreed with this. 'We go on

working in the dark, and in the dark it will be, until the rule of systematic Confession is revived in our Church', he wrote to a friend. J. Keble, *Letters of Spiritual Council and Guidance*, edited R. F. Wilson (Oxford 1870), 39–40.
36. Manning archives. Wilberforce Letters. III. 39. 1 December 1848.
37. A. Westcott, *Life and Letters of Brooke Foss Westcott* (1903), II. 305.

III. *The Clergy of the East Riding and the Curates of Alverstoke*
  1. Details from Wrangham MSS. VII. 101. 9 September 1839.
  2. Wrangham MSS. VII. 102. 17 October 1839.
  3. R. I. Wilberforce, *The Five Empires. An outline of ancient history* (1840); *Rutilius and Lucius or Stories of the Third Age* (1842).
  4. Wrangham MSS. VI. 214. 14 June 1840.
  5. Wrangham MSS. VII. 125.
  6. Wrangham MSS. VII. 129.
  7. Wrangham MSS. VII. 130.
  8. Wrangham MSS. VII. 132. 1 October 1841.
  9. Wrangham MSS. VII. 133. 28 October 1841.
  10. Wrangham MSS. VII. 135. 5 December 1841.
  11. Wrangham MSS. VII. 164. 28 April 1845.
  12. Wrangham MSS. VII. 148. 11 May 1843.
  13. Wrangham MSS. VII. 145. 7 December 1842.
  14. Wrangham MSS. VII. 139.
  15. Wrangham MSS. VII. 181. 30 September 1848.
  16. Kensington MSS. G. 2. 2 January 1841.
  17. Wrangham MSS. VII. 169.
  18. Compare the descriptions of the work of Edgar Jacob, C. G. Lang, Bernard Wilson and Cyril Garbett in C. Smyth, *Cyril Forster Garbett, Archbishop of York* (1959), 61–126 and J. G. Lockhart, *Cosmo Gordon Lang* (1949), 116–28.
  19. *Richard Chenevix Trench, Letters and Memorials*, edited by the author of 'Charles Lowder' (1888), I. 251–70.
  20. Bodleian. c. 186. Diary no. 5.
  21. A. R. Ashwell, *op. cit.*, I. 173.
  22. Wrangham MSS. VII. 137. 8 March 1842.

IV. *New Issues at Oxford*
  1. *Autobiography of Isaac Williams*, 118 n.
  2. O. Chadwick, *From Bossuet to Newman. The Idea of Doctrinal Development* (1957), 132. For the whole of this paragraph, I am indebted to the lucid exposition of Möhler, Ward and Newman in chapters V, VI, and VII of Professor Chadwick's book.
  3. Wilfrid Ward, *William George Ward and the Oxford Movement* (1889), 191–2.
  4. W. G. Ward, *The Ideal of a Christian Church* (1844), 359–64.
  5. Kensington MSS. A. 38.
  6. Wilberforce MSS. G. 3. 17 December 1841.
  7. B. M. Add. Mss. 44358 (Gladstone Papers, Vol. 273), ff. 315, 351.
  8. Wrangham MSS. VII. 136.
  9. Wrangham MSS. VII. 135. 5 December 1841.
  10. Wrangham MSS. VI. 221. 2 January 1842. cf. B. M. Add. Mss. 44343 (Gladstone Papers, Vol. 258), f. 29, f. 31.
  11. Bodleian. c. 195. 17 December 1841.

12. *Autobiography of Isaac Williams*, 141–2.
13. Wrangham MSS. VII. 136.
14. Wrangham MSS. VI. 240. 21 August 1841. 'He (Bunsen) has made me privy to his councils.' Also VI. 233.
15. Wrangham MSS. VI. 234. 2 February 1842.
16. Wrangham MSS. VI. 240.
17. J. H. Newman, *Apologia*, 236.
18. Oratory. Box 137. 9 December 1841.
19. Kensington MSS. A. 41. For a learned discussion of the 'Notes of the Church', very influential on Oxford churchmen at that time, see William Palmer, *A Treatise on the Church of Christ* (1838), I. Part I, especially 22–8.
20. Oratory. Box 137. 21 January 1842.
21. Oratory. Box 137. 29 January 1842. In 1841 Robert described J. B. Sumner as a 'Socinian' in a letter to Samuel. Wrangham MSS. VII. 123.
22. Kensington MSS. A. 36.
23. The sermon is printed in the collection of Manning's *University Sermons* under the title of 'Christ our Rest and King' (E. S. Purcell, *op. cit.*, I. 248).
24. *Letters of the Rev. J. B. Mozley, edited by his sister* (1885), 148–9.
25. E. S. Purcell, *op. cit.*, I. 252.
26. The letters are quoted – with severe comments on Manning's conduct – in M. Trevor, *op. cit.*, 309–315.
27. Pusey House. Manning–Pusey volume, no. 13 (a). See the discussion of this episode in Wilfrid Ward's letters to E. S. Purcell in M. Ward, *The Wilfrid Wards and the Transition* (1934), I. 412.
28. Pusey House. Manning–Pusey volume, no. 22.
29. W. Ward, *W. G. Ward and the Oxford Movement*, 305–6.
30. Kensington MSS. B. 7.
31. Wilberforce MSS. G. 9. 29 December 1844.
32. Pusey House. Manning–Pusey volume, no. 19. 5 March 1845.
33. Wrangham MSS. VI. 261. 27 December 1844.
34. Wrangham MSS. VII. 158. 29 December 1844.
35. Wrangham MSS. VI. 263. 14 January 1845.

v. *Episcopal Ambitions: Samuel Wilberforce and Henry Manning*

1. *Letters of J. B. Mozley*, 130–1. The feeling of dislike was mutual. See Wrangham MSS. V. 109.
2. E.g. *Greville Memoirs*, second part (1885), III. 114.
3. E.g. G. C. B. Davies, *Henry Phillpotts, Bishop of Exeter*, 210.
4. For a full discussion of the origin of this sobriquet, see my articles 'How soapy was Sam?' in *History Today*, vol. xiii. no. 9, 624–32.
5. *Autobiography of Isaac Williams*, 69.
6. *Letters of J. B. Mozley*, 188.
7. W. Palmer, *Narrative of Events*, 254–5.
8. *Greville Memoirs*, II. 264.
9. *Ibid.*, II. 412.
10. See *supra* p. 245.
11. Wrangham MSS. VI. 231. Compare 241 – 'I have seen a good deal of Croker lately.'
12. L. S. Jennings (editor), *The Correspondence and Diaries of . . . John Wilson Croker* (1884), II. 410–11.

13. *Ibid.*, II. 413. 'My dear Sir' in January 1842 becomes 'My dear Friend' by October of that year.
14. *Ibid.*, III. 2.
15. *Ibid.*, III. 2–3.
16. *Ibid.*, III. 3.
17. Bodleian. c. 186. Diary no. 5. esp. 3 November 1841.
18. Wilberforce MSS. G. 7. 3 December 1843.
19. Wrangham MSS. VI. 246. 15 January 1843.
20. Wrangham MSS. VII. 149. 31 May 1843.
21. A. R. Ashwell, *op. cit.*, I. 287.
22. M. Trevor, *Newman. The Pillar of the Cloud*, 272.
23. Bodleian. c. 196. 20 March 1844.
24. *Correspondence and Diaries of J. W. Croker*, III. 2.
25. Sandwith MSS. B. II. 59 1 June 1850.
26. Sandwith MSS. B. III. 1.
27. Ushaw MSS. 4. 19 October 1845.
28. Ushaw MSS. 3. 29 July 1844.
29. Manning archives. Wilberforce letters. II. 14.
30. E. S. Purcell, *op. cit.*, I. 271–2.
31. G. C. B. Davies, *Henry Phillpotts, Bishop of Exeter*, 174–8; 191–5, 295–7.
32. *Ibid.*, 195.
33. E. S. Purcell, *op. cit.*, I. ix; 261.
34. These are largely unpublished. Many of them will appear in the biography of Henry Manning written by the Rev. A. Chapeau, who has made fullest use of the material in the Manning archives.
35. Frederick Maurice, *The Life of Frederick Denison Maurice* (1884), I. 351.
36. P. J. Welch, 'Blomfield and Peel: a study in co-operation between Church and State, 1841–1846' in *Journal of Ecclesiastical History*, vol. 12 (1961), 75.
37. *Ibid.*, 75.
38. I have taken the text of both these letters (the originals of which are in the British Museum, Add. Mss. 40575. fol. 331–2; fol. 408) from R. K. Pugh, 'The Episcopate of Samuel Wilberforce', 15.
39. Wrangham MSS. VI. 273. 14 October 1845.
40. Wrangham MSS. VII. 172. 18 October 1845.
41. Wilberforce MSS. K. 19 October 1845.
42. Bodleian, c. 191. 13 November 1845.

7. DEFEATS AND DEFECTIONS

I. *The Defection of the Ryders*
1. Wrangham MSS. VI. 275. 25 October 1845.
2. Wrangham MSS. VII. 174. 27 October 1845.
3. A. R. Ashwell, *op. cit.*, I. 329–30.
4. Wrangham MSS. VI. 281. 1 January 1846.
5. *Letters and Diaries of John Henry Newman*, edited C. S. Dessain (1961), XI. 132.
6. A. R. Ashwell, *op. cit.*, I. 327.
7. M. Trevor, *op. cit.*, 370.
8. Wrangham MSS. VI. 350. 18 February 1848.
9. *Letters and Diaries, op. cit.*, 3.
10. Sandwith MSS. B. 11. 35. 8 October 1845.

11. *Letters and Diaries, op. cit.*, 215–16. For a good selection of Newman's letters to Henry between 1846 and 1850, see W. Ward, *The Life of John Henry Cardinal Newman* (1912), I. 127–31; 618–21.
12. Wrangham MSS. VII. 165.
13. Wrangham MSS. VII. 173–4.
14. Manning archives. Wilberforce letters. II. 13. 12 July 1845. On the notion of Catholicity and the 'experimental' quality of Tractarianism, see G. H. Tavard, *The Quest for Catholicity* (1963), especially 156–7.
15. Ryder MSS. A. 17. 25 June 1845.
16. Ryder MSS. B. 4. 20 June 1845. Medical report of Dr Ferguson.
17. Ryder MSS. A. 19. 22 May 1846.
18. All details from Ryder MSS. 'A Son's Reminiscence', 31–43.
19. Ryder MSS. A. 18. 21 May 1846.
20. *Letters and Diaries, op. cit.*, XI. 167.
21. A. R. Ashwell, *op. cit.*, I. 362.
22. Wilberforce MSS. D. 82. 'Easter Eve 1850'.

II. *Manning and Anglo-Catholicism*
1. Sandwith MSS. B. III. 1.
2. Wrangham MSS. VI. 324, 9 May 1847.
3. All these passages come from a letter to James Stephen, dated 17 July 1853. Oratory. Box 119, 42 (a). Compare J. H. Newman, 'The Catholicity of the Anglican Church' in *Essays Critical and Historical* (2nd edn., 1872), II. 71–2.
4. O. Chadwick, *From Bossuet to Newman*, 168–70.
5. J. H. Newman, *Essay on the Development of Christian Doctrine* (1881 edn.), 7–8.
6. Most concisely put in *ibid.*, 122.
7. O. Chadwick, *op. cit.*, 119.
8. B. M. Add. Mss. 44343. ff. 81–2. Robert told Gladstone that he thought the book 'very sophistical', B. M. Add. Mss. 44363. f. 64.
9. Wilberforce MSS. G. 15. 10 December 1845. Gladstone made a similar expression of Butler's ability to 'tear the whole argument into shreds' in a letter to Manning. E. S. Purcell, *op. cit.*, I. 315.
10. E. S. Purcell, *op. cit.*, I. 311.
11. *Ibid.*, I. 313.
12. *Ibid.*, I. 315.
13. See H. W. Tucker, *Memoir of the Life and Episcopate of G. A. Selwyn*, I. 78–92; Mary Allies, *Thomas William Allies 1813–1907* (1924), 3, 15, 50, 59, 65, 67, 70; R. Ornsby, *Memoir of James Hope Scott* (1884), I. 11–14.
14. Wilberforce MSS. Copy of letter from Manning to Edward Coleridge, marked 'Copy made 1 January 1871 from the original in Washington Rectory'.
15. E. S. Purcell, *op. cit.*, I. 324.
16. H. P. Liddon, *Life of Pusey*, III. 145–6.
17. C. P. S. Clarke, *The Oxford Movement and After* (1932), 134–5.
18. A. M. Allchin, *The Silent Rebellion* (1958), 64–5.
19. *Ibid.*, 85–6.
20. Manning archives. Wilberforce letters, II. 16. 30 December 1845.
21. E. S. Purcell, *op. cit.*, I. 317.
22. *Ibid.*, I. 317.
23. *Ibid.*, I. 318–19.

24. J. Fitzsimons, *op. cit.*, 19–20.
25. E. S. Purcell, *op. cit.*, I. 338.
26. E. S. Purcell, *op. cit.*, I. 342.
27. J. Fitzsimons, *op. cit.*, 23.
28. E. S. Purcell, *op. cit.*, I. 342.
29. J. Fitzsimons, *op. cit.*, 25–6.

III. *Conflicts of Heart and Head*
1. E. S. Purcell, *op. cit.*, I. 465. Compare a rather more sympathetic assessment in G. Donald, *Men who left the Movement* (1933), 218.
2. J. E. C. Bodley, *Cardinal Manning and other Essays*, 27.
3. *Ibid.*, 27–8.
4. J. H. Newman, *Apologia*, 264–5.
5. See the sermon on 'Faith and Reason contrasted as Habits of Mind' in J. H. Newman, *Fifteen Sermons preached before the University of Oxford* (1918 edn.), 198.
6. *Ibid.*, 227. (Sermon on 'Love the Safeguard of Faith against Superstition'.)
7. R. W. Church, *Occasional Papers* (1897), II. 474–5.
8. Diary entry. E. S. Purcell, *op. cit.*, I. 483–4.
9. *Ibid.*, I. 484.
10. Ushaw MSS. 9.
11. Ushaw MSS. 22. 14 July 1849.
12. Manning archives. Wilberforce letters, III. 50. 'Monday in Holy Week, 1849'.
13. Ushaw MSS. 15. 6 November 1848.
14. Ushaw MSS. 17. 26 January 1849.
15. This is discussed by V. A. McClelland in *Cardinal Manning. His Public Life and Influence 1865–1892* (1962), 213–14. Mr McClelland believes that Manning's phenomenal austerities have been exaggerated.
16. E. S. Purcell, *op. cit.*, I. 447.
17. *Ibid.*, I. 448.
18. *Recollections of Aubrey de Vere* (1897), 316. Compare H. D. I. Ryder, *Essays* (1911), 300, where Ignatius Ryder snorts at this judgment ('Grotesquely inappropriate – an Aquinas without the discursive faculty, a Dante without wings!'). See also W. Ward, *Aubrey de Vere. A Memoir* (1904), 170, where Manning is put on a par with de Ravignan and Döllinger.
19. Sandwith MSS. B. I. 29.
20. Manning archives. Wilberforce letters, III. 43.

IV. *Samuel Wilberforce and the 'Via Media'*
1. R. K. Pugh, 'The Episcopate of Samuel Wilberforce', 26.
2. Wrangham MSS. VI. 289. 15 June 1846.
3. Full text of these letters in H. P. Liddon, *op. cit.*, III. 40–8.
4. S. Wilberforce, *A Charge delivered to the Clergy of the Diocese of Oxford at his Primary Visitation, September and October 1848* (1848), 19.
5. *Ibid.*, 10.
6. *Ibid.*, 11.
7. *Ibid.*, 37.
8. *Ibid.*, 40–1.
9. S. Wilberforce, *A Charge to the Clergy of the Diocese of Oxford at his Second Visitation* (1851), 56 *et seq.*

10. E. S. Purcell, *op. cit.*, I. 269.
11. Wrangham MSS. VI. 348. 10 February 1848.
12. O. Chadwick, *The Founding of Cuddesdon* (1954), 51.
13. This is most fully discussed in A. M. Allchin, *The Silent Rebellion* (1958); see especially p. 196 on the unity of purpose of Wilberforce and R. M. Benson.
14. Stopford A. Brooke (editor), *Life and Letters of F. W. Robertson* (1906 edn.), 72.
15. A. R. Ashwell, *op. cit.*, I. 410–11.
16. Wrangham MSS. VI. 313. 27 December 1847.
17. Wrangham MSS. VI. 448. 22 September 1852.
18. R. K. Pugh, *op. cit.*, 256–7.
19. A. R. Ashwell, *op. cit.*, I. 333–4.
20. J. W. Burgon, *Lives of Twelve Good Men*, II. 24.
21. Wrangham MSS. VII. 173. 24 October 1845.
22. O. Chadwick, *op. cit.*, 17.
23. See the superb letter on the 'Peculiar' habits of the ordinands in R. G. Wilberforce, *Life of Samuel Wilberforce*, II. 367–8.
24. For instance, on Liddon's appointment, Samuel was nervous of Pusey's influence and insisted that Pusey should no longer be Liddon's spiritual director. He persuaded him to go to Keble. Chadwick, *op. cit.*, 25–6.
25. There is an interesting description of Samuel's preaching and conduct of confirmations in a letter from Charles Anderson to Robert Wilberforce, written while Anderson was staying at Cuddesdon. This is in Kensington MSS. E. 14.
26. J. H. Overton and E. Wordsworth, *Christopher Wordsworth. Bishop of Lincoln* (1890 edn.), 117–18.
27. J. W. Burgon, *op. cit.*, II. 31–3.
28. Wilberforce MSS. G. 86. 19 December 1859.
29. Wilberforce MSS. K. undated.

v. *R. D. Hampden and T. W. Allies*

1. Wilberforce MSS. D. 62. 27 December 1847.
2. The text of this letter is in A. R. Ashwell, *op. cit.*, I. 442–5. For the proceedings against Prince Lee, see my *Godliness and Good Learning* (1961), 118–26.
3. A. R. Ashwell, *op. cit.*, I. 455–7.
4. *Ibid.*, I. 482–8.
5. Greville, *Memoirs*, III. 114.
6. Wrangham MSS. VI. 342. 6 January 1848.
7. Bodleian. c. 200. Letter to Bishop of Ely, dated 19 May 1879.
8. Wilberforce MSS. D. 63. 14 January 1848.
9. Manning archives. Wilberforce letters, III. 29. 5 February 1848.
10. Manning archives, Wilberforce letters, III. 30. 12 February 1848.
11. Bodleian. c. 200. 31 December 1847.
12. Bodleian. c. 200. 3 January 1848.
13. Bodleian. c. 200. 8 January 1848.
14. T. W. Allies, *A Life's Decision* (1880), 57.
15. *Ibid.*, 60.
16. *Ibid.*, 108–9.
17. *Ibid.*, 113.
18. *Ibid.*, 143.

19. A. R. Ashwell, *op. cit.*, I. 406.
20. *Ibid.*, I. 408.
21. T. W. Allies, *op. cit.*, 178–208.
22. R. G. Wilberforce, *op. cit.*, II. 26–7.
23. T. W. Allies, *op. cit.*, 158–9.
24. Mary Allies, *Thomas William Allies*, 49; compare T. W. Allies, *op. cit.*, 79, where Henry appears to have said 'I am fairly *beat*.'
25. Mary Allies, *op. cit.*, 66.
26. Wilberforce MSS. D. 66. 24 April 1849.
27. Wilberforce MSS. D. 67.

VI. *The Crisis of the Gorham Judgment*
1. Wrangham MSS. VI. 394.
2. E.g. Wrangham MSS. VI. 298. 18 August 1846. Samuel, in discussing holiday plans with Robert, writes: 'Shall Henry go with us? Will he spoil *our* intercourse?'
3. Wrangham MSS. VI. 400. 23 March 1850.
4. Wrangham MSS. VI. 344. 14 January 1848.
5. J. Morley, *Life of Gladstone* (1903), I. 378.
6. This point is put very succinctly in A. O. J. Cockshutt, *Anglican Attitudes* (1959), 41.
7. J. C. S. Nias, *Gorham and the Bishop of Exeter* (1951), 126.
8. Sandwith MSS. B. II. 51. 15 December 1849.
9. Sandwith MSS. B. II. 55.
10. Wilberforce MSS. D. 76.
11. E. S. Purcell, *op. cit.*, I. 527.
12. Manning archives. Wilberforce letters, IV. 69. 19 January 1850.
13. Manning archives. Wilberforce letters, IV. 71. 21 January 1850.
14. Text in E. S. Purcell, I. 532–3.
15. Keble College. 69. no. 33. Copy in Sandwith MSS. E. 12.
16. Keble College, 69. no. 34. Copy in Sandwith MSS. E. 13.
17. Wrangham MSS. Letters of William Henn, no. 7. 23 March 1850.
18. H. E. Manning, *The Appellate Jurisdiction of the Crown in Matters Spiritual. A Letter to the Bishop of Chichester* (1850), 38.
19. Text in E. S. Purcell, *op. cit.*, I. 540–1.
20. R. G. Wilberforce, *op. cit.*, II. 40.
21. Manning archives. Wilberforce letters, IV. 102. 28 June 1850.
22. Manning archives. Wilberforce letters, IV. 118.
23. Manning archives. Wilberforce letters, IV. 119. 23 September 1850.
24. Manning archives. Wilberforce letters, IV. 111. 15 August 1850.

VII. *Henry and Mary Wilberforce*
1. Ushaw MSS. 5, Easter Eve 1847; 11, 23 September 1848 for two very tender letters written by Manning after the news of their bereavement.
2. J. H. Newman in H. W. Wilberforce, *The Church and the Empires*, 16.
3. Maisie Ward, *Young Mr Newman*, 256.
4. Sandwith MSS. B. II. 37.
5. Manning archives, Wilberforce letters, IV. 67.
6. Sandwith MSS. B. III. 6.
7. Sandwith MSS. B. II. 47. 24 January 1849.

8. Sandwith MSS. B. II. 59. 1 June 1850.

9. Ushaw MSS. 21.

10. J. H. Newman, *op. cit.*, 8.

11. Wrangham MSS. VI. 388. 26 September 1849. For a discussion of the effect of cholera epidemics in acquainting Anglican clergymen with Catholic practices, see C. H. Smyth, 'The Evangelical Movement in Perspective' in *Cambridge Historical Journal*, VII. no. 3 (1943), 161–2.

12. W. Ward, *W. G. Ward and the Oxford Movement*, 121. With Newman the *memento mori* of Bowden's deathbed seems to have worked the other way. See *Correspondence of John Henry Newman with John Keble and others 1839–45* (1917), 334. Keble also was strengthened in his faith by seeing his wife on what he believed to be her deathbed. J. T. Coleridge, *Memoir of the Rev. John Keble* (1869), II. 309.

13. Sandwith MSS. B. II. 48. 13 September 1849.

14. Sandwith MSS. B. III. 10.

15. Ushaw MSS. 12. 2 October 1848.

16. Ushaw MSS. 26. 27 September 1849.

17. Sandwith MSS. B. II. 56. 4 May 1850.

18. Manning archives. Wilberforce letters, IV. 101.

19. Sandwith MSS. B. III. 11. 24 May 1850.

20. C. S. Dessain (editor), *The Letters and Diaries of John Henry Newman*, vol. 13 (1963), 477, n. 2. The Memoir of George Dudley Ryder misdates this event as occurring during the first week in July.

21. Sandwith MSS. B. III. 3. 7 July 1850.

22. Sandwith MSS. B. III. 5.

23. Dodsworth knew of it on 17 August 1850. See his letter to Manning in E. S. Purcell, *op. cit.*, I. 563.

24. Manning archives. Wilberforce letters, IV. 115.

25. Manning archives. Wilberforce letters, IV. 116.

26. Sandwith MSS. B. III. 13.

27. J. H. Newman, *op. cit.*, 9–10.

28. Wrangham MSS. VI. 410. 23 September 1850.

8. THE FINAL PARTING

I. *The Secession of Henry Manning*

1. H. W. Wilberforce, *Reasons for submitting to the Catholic Church: A Farewell Letter to his late Parishioners* (1851).

2. Sandwith MSS. B. II. 60. 20 December 1850.

3. Ryder MSS. Letters of Mrs Sargent. 7 April 1851.

4. Wrangham MSS. VI. 408. 5 September 1850.

5. Bodleian. c. 193. 28 April 1850.

6. Bodleian. c. 193. 8 September 1850.

7. Wilberforce MSS. K. 14 September 1850. Also B. M. Add Mss. 44343. ff. 119–121.

8. Bodleian. c. 193. 17 September 1850.

9. Wilberforce MSS. D. 89. 20 October 1850.

10. R. Ornsby, *Memoirs of James Robert Hope-Scott* (1884), II. 81–2.

11. E. S. Purcell, *op. cit.*, I. 597.

12. R. Ormsby, *op. cit.*, II. 83.

13. D. C. Lathbury, *Correspondence on Church and Religion of W. E. Gladstone* (1910), I. 283.
14. Sandwith MSS. Gladstone letters. 11 April 1851.
15. Kensington MSS. D. 18. 13 September 1854.
16. Wilberforce MSS. K. 10 June 1851.
17. Wrangham MSS. VI. 421. 10 June 1851.
18. Ryder MSS. B. 7 April.
19. Ushaw MSS. 36. 18 September 1851.
20. *Recollections of Aubrey de Vere*, 290–1.

II. *Robert Wilberforce and the Theological Synthesis*
1. All details from a letter to Samuel, Wilberforce MSS. C. 'Wednesday before Easter'.
2. Manning archives. Wilberforce letters, IV. 99, 101. 22 and 25 June 1850.
3. Wilberforce MSS. C. 26 November 1853.
4. Oratory. Box 137. no. 10. 29 January 1842.
5. Manning archives. Wilberforce letters, IV. 78. 22 February 1850.
6. R. I. Wilberforce, *The Practical Effect of the Gorham Case. A Charge to the Clergy of the East Riding delivered at his ordinary visitation a.d. 1850* (1850), 35–6.
7. Wilberforce MSS. C. 8 May 1850.
8. This is employed, for instance, in the chapter on 'The Office of Christ as the Pattern Man marked out in Ancient Scripture' in *Doctrine of the Incarnation of our Lord Jesus Christ* (1848), 23, 30.
9. Möhler, both *Die Einheit der Kirche* and *Symbolik*, figure largely in his work on the Incarnation. He himself expressed his indebtedness to Dorner, *Lehre von der Person Christi*, especially on the whole section on the Logos (R. I. Wilberforce, *Incarnation*, 125 n. 9). He also refers frequently to Günther, *Vorschule zur Spekulativen Theologie*, and to the criticism of Möhler by Baur. He had also read, and discussed pertinently, Schleiermacher's *Der Christliche Glaube* (*Incarnation*, 345–7) and Strauss's *Leben Jesu* (*Incarnation*, 465).
10. See, for instance, J. C. S. Nias, *Gorham and the Bishop of Exeter*, 8–9.
11. Expressed very succinctly by Robert Wilberforce in *Doctrine of the Incarnation*, 218–19.
12. See the comments of V. F. Storr, *The Development of English Theology in the Nineteenth Century, 1800–1860* (1813), 73; Horton Davies, *Worship and Theology in England. From Watts and Wesley to Maurice*, 268–9; C. C. J. Webb, *Religious Thought in the Oxford Movement* (1928), 89, Y. Brilioth, *The Anglican Revival*, 289.
13. O. Chadwick, *The Mind of the Oxford Movement* (1960), 49.
14. Wilberforce MSS. D. 72. 17 December 1849.
15. R. I. Wilberforce, *Doctrine of the Incarnation*, 4.
16. R. I. Wilberforce, *The Doctrine of the Holy Baptism* (1849), 179.
17. *Ibid.*, especially chapters V and VI.
18. The words are taken from St Irenaeus, quoted by R. I. Wilberforce, *Doctrine of the Incarnation*, 71.
19. R. I. Wilberforce, *The Doctrine of the Holy Eucharist* (1853), 427.
20. R. I. Wilberforce, *Sermons of the New Birth of Man's Nature* (1850). The earliest sermon (only a few of them are dated) is the Assize Sermon of December 1847 (Sermon VIII).

21. R. I. Wilberforce, *Sermons*, 225. This theme is reiterated very frequently. See especially his criticism of Gnosticism and its modern counterpart in the same sermon – 'a false anthropology finds its complement in a false theology'. *Ibid.*, 231. See also his criticisms of Whately in *Doctrine of the Incarnation*, 422–3.
22. R. I. Wilberforce, *Sermons*, 227–8.
23. *Ibid.*, 231–2. Compare *Doctrine of the Holy Eucharist*, 160.
24. R. I. Wilberforce, *Sermons*, 273. The image of Jacob's Ladder is a favourite one. Compare Sermon XII (*ibid.*, 139), Sermon XVII (*ibid.*, 209); also *Doctrine of the Incarnation*, 185 (where the passage in the text is repeated almost word for word) and 275.
25. R. I. Wilberforce, *Doctrine of the Incarnation*, 195.
26. *Ibid.*, 414.
27. R. I. Wilberforce, *Doctrine of the Incarnation*, 345–7, especially n. 21.
28. R. I. Wilberforce, *Sermons*, 237–8. Compare also his summary of the Catholic notion of the Church and the sacraments in his 1851 charge 'The Evangelical and Tractarian Movements' – *A Charge to the Clergy of the East Riding delivered at the Ordinary Visitation, 1851* (1851), 12–16.
29. R. I. Wilberforce, *Doctrine of the Incarnation*, 422.
30. *Ibid.*, 136–45.
31. *Ibid.*, 410; also 334.
32. R. I. Wilberforce, *The Doctrine of the Holy Eucharist*, 1.
33. *Ibid.*, 348–9.
34. *Ibid.*, 177–8.
35. *Ibid.*, 347.
36. *Ibid.*, 351.
37. *Ibid.*, 351–2.
38. *Ibid.*, 392–3.
39. Robert's views are discussed by Samuel in two letters (Wrangham MSS. VI. 422 and 490), portions of which are printed in R. G. Wilberforce, *op. cit.*, 105, 241.
40. Wrangham MSS. VI. 471. 28 June 1853.
41. Wrangham MSS. Phillpotts letters, 3. 13 March 1851.
42. Sandwith MSS. Gladstone letters, 31 October 1853.
43. Sandwith MSS. Gladstone Letters, 26 March 1854.
44. B. M. Add. Mss. 44379 (Gladstone Papers, Vol. 294), ff. 19–21.
45. Sandwith MSS. Gladstone letters, 24 September 1854.

III. *The Battle of Burton Agnes*
1. J. H. Newman, *An Essay on the Development of Christian Doctrine*, 14–26.
2. Kensington MSS. A. 45. 11 December 1853.
3. Kensington MSS. A. 46. 27 December 1853.
4. Kensington MSS. A. 48. 15 August 1854.
5. E. S. Purcell, *op. cit.*, II. 27–9.
6. *Ibid.*, II. 34.
7. For instance J. S. Whale, *The Protestant Tradition* (1955), 253; A. R. Vidler in *Objections to Christian Belief* (1963), 65–6. The phrase occurs in Manning's Pastoral Letter on the Infallibility of the Roman Pontiff, and is discussed by him at length in (H. E. Manning), *Religio Viatoris* (1887), 76–9.
8. E. S. Purcell, *op. cit.*, II. 35–6.

9. *Ibid.*, II. 38–40.
10. Wrangham MSS. Cavendish letters, no. 6. 27 February 1854.
11. E. S. Purcell, *op. cit.*, 42–3.
12. Wrangham MSS. Henn letters, no. 1. 22 July 1848.
13. Wrangham MSS. Henn letters, no. 4. 24 December 1849.
14. Wrangham MSS. Henn letters, no. 13. 11 November 1850.
15. Wrangham MSS. Henn letters, no. 14. 22 December 1850.
16. Wrangham MSS. Henn letters, no. 16. 10 May 1851.
17. Kensington MSS. G. 7. 13 October 1852.
18. Kensington MSS. G. 8. 3 November 1852.
19. Kensington MSS. B. 14. 11 September (1854).
20. Kensington MSS. B. 15 September (1854).
21. Wrangham MSS. VI. 467. 28 April 1853; also VI. 478, 1 September 1853.
22. Wrangham MSS. VI. 481. 4 November 1853.
23. Wrangham MSS. VI. 478. 1 September 1853.
24. Wrangham MSS. VI. 484. 12 December 1853.
25. Wrangham MSS. VI. 482. 16 November 1853.
26. Wrangham MSS. VI. 478.
27. Wrangham MSS. VI. 484.
28. Keble College. 69. no. 42.
29. Keble College. 69. no. 41. 19 August 1851.
30. Keble College. 69. no. 51. 25 September 1854.
31. Keble College. 69. no. 48. 22 June 1853.

IV. *The Last Capitulation*

1. He sought Keble's advice on this. See the early section of the letter dated 8 July 1851 (Keble College. 69. no. 42).
2. Wrangham MSS. Henn letters, no. 2 11 December 1848. They were only fifteen at the time.
3. Wilberforce MSS. C. 1 April 1854. This somewhat Evangelical trait of despising useless employments was shared by Samuel and Robert as parents and never really left them. They both had serious doubts about letting their boys attend county balls (Wrangham MSS. VI. 339).
4. See his *Sketch of the History of Erastianism* (1851), especially the appended sermons, pp. 99–150.
5. R. G. Wilberforce, *op. cit.*, II. 265.
6. R. I. Wilberforce, *An Inquiry into the Principles of Church Authority, or Reasons for recalling my Subscription to the Royal Supremacy* (1854), 15.
7. *Ibid.*, 18.
8. The self-confessed agnostic, F. W. Maitland, in *Roman Canon Law in the Church of England. Six Essays* (1898).
9. R. I. Wilberforce, *An Inquiry into . . . Church Authority*, 278.
10. *Ibid.*, 283–4.
11. All the letters referred to in this paragraph may be found *in extenso* in the preface to R. I. Wilberforce, *op. cit.*, vii–ix.
12. Kensington MSS. A. 50. 1 September 1854.
13. Wrangham MSS. VI. 503. 3 September 1854.
14. Wrangham MSS. VI. 504. 7 September 1854.
15. Wrangham MSS. VI. 505. 12 September 1854.
16. Keble College. 69. no. 51. 25 September 1854.

17. R. G. Wilberforce, *op. cit.*, II. 263.
18. Wilberforce MSS. G. 53. 4 September 1854.

EPILOGUE

I. *After the Dispersion*

1. B. A. Smith, *Dean Church. The Anglican Response to Newman* (1958), 225.
2. M. Trevor, *Newman. The Pillar of the Cloud*, 383.
3. *Ibid.*, 546.
4. Ryder MSS. 'A Son's Reminiscences', 43.
5. Ryder MSS. B. 12; see also 7 and 13. On one occasion she lent him £250, writing 'Why did you go on so long without telling me? I was afraid of asking about your affairs lest you should think it was an impertinent interference.'
6. Mary Allies, *Thomas William Allies*, 87.
7. H. W. Wilberforce, *The Church and the Empires*, 11.
8. J. L. Altholz, *The Liberal Catholic Movement in England* (1960), 61.
9. *Ibid.*, 104, 136.
10. Oratory. Box 137. no. 23, 29 June 1863.
11. Wrangham MSS. VII. 85. 4 May 1838.
12. D. Mozley, *Newman Family Letters*, 64–5.
13. Wrangham MSS. VI. 495. 10 May 1854.
14. Ushaw MSS. 55. 28 July 1873.
15. Ryder MSS. C. 7. 3 November 1854.
16. Wrangham MSS. VII. 184. 8 August 1855.
17. Wrangham MSS. VII. 187. 1 September 1855.
18. Wrangham MSS. VII. 190. 5 October 1855.
19. Bodleian. c. 186. Diary no. 6. pp. 125–6. He heard a sermon at the cathedral on the next day, and wrote 'It was delightful to feel to be again taking part in united congregational worship.'
20. The symptoms – emaciation and repeated coughing – suggest tuberculosis.
21. Wilberforce MSS. D. 95. 1 March 1856.
22. Oratory. Box 137. 14. 26 March 1855.
23. Oratory. Box 137. 16. 9 April 1856.
24. Ryder MSS. C. 8. Christmas Day 1856.
25. All these details come from a memorandum written by Manning to Henry about Robert's doings in Rome and his move to Albano in Ushaw MSS. 42. 7 March 1857.
26. Ushaw MSS. 41. 4 February 1857.

II. *Two Ecclesiastical Statesmen*

1. Wilberforce MSS. D. 96. 17 May 1865.
2. W. Ward, *Ten Personal Studies* (1908), 270.
3. Wilberforce MSS. G. 117, 119–21.
4. Ushaw MSS. 55. 28 July 1873.
5. E. Gibbon, *The Decline and Fall of the Roman Empire* (edited C. Dawson, Everyman edn. 1961), II. 274.

BIBLIOGRAPHY

A. MANUSCRIPT SOURCES

1. WILBERFORCE MSS

Letters and papers of Samuel Wilberforce, the property of the late Dr Octavia Wilberforce, and kept – at the time of consultation – at Backsettown, Henfield, Sussex. This is a very large and diffuse collection and had been only partially sorted when I came to work on it. I had therefore to make my own working catalogue, and divided the material which I used for the writing of this book into sections under correspondents as follows:

A. William Wilberforce; B. Barbara Wilberforce; C. Robert Isaac Wilberforce; D. Henry Edward Manning; E. Members of the Sargent family; F. John Henry Newman; G. W. E. Gladstone; H. John Keble; J. Sir James Stephen; K. Miscellaneous.

Categories A to J are all sizeable individual collections, containing some letters also from Samuel Wilberforce to the correspondent named. They range in size from the three largest – A (600), G (225) and D (100) – to the two small, but very interesting collections – F (19) and J (18). Correspondents who are represented by fewer than ten letters are all included in section K.

In addition, I have used the Commonplace Book of Samuel Wilberforce and a small MS notebook, labelled 'Samuel Wilberforce MSS. Private. Fragments of his Father's Conversation, 1823'.

This list includes by no means all the Samuel Wilberforce papers collected at Henfield. There are many other papers more relevant to the period after this study ends – e.g. letters of Disraeli, Liddon, Louisa Noel, etc. – and several very interesting large albums of autograph letters from distinguished correspondents.

The diocesan papers, diaries and other personal letters of Samuel Wilberforce were deposited in the Bodleian Library, Oxford, in 1956, and are referred to below.

Dr Octavia Wilberforce died in December 1963, and her will provides that the whole of this collection is to be sold in order to assist the finances of the Backsettown Trust. Since the final arrangements have not yet been settled, enquiries as to the disposal of these letters should be sent to Mrs I. Parsons, Jugg's Corner, Kingston, Lewes, Sussex.

2. WRANGHAM MSS

Letters and papers of the Wilberforce family, owned by Mr C. E. Wrangham, and kept at Rosemary House, Catterick, Yorkshire. The papers which I have used are stored in seven boxes and a large green album labelled 'Scraps'. In addition, the religious journals of William Wilberforce and other papers of the Emancipator are stored in a tin trunk. The contents of the boxes, etc., which I have used are:

Box I. Mainly family letters of William and Barbara Wilberforce to their children.

455

Boxes II, III, IV. Letters of William Wilberforce, many of which are published in the five-volume biography and the two-volume addendum of correspondence.

Box V. (a) Miscellaneous family letters, mainly from Barbara Wilberforce.

    (b) 203 letters of Samuel Wilberforce to Robert Isaac Wilberforce, 1824–1839.

Box VI. (a) 302 letters of Samuel Wilberforce to Robert Isaac Wilberforce, 1840–1854.

    (b) 94 letters relating to material for the biography of William Wilberforce.

Box VII. 198 letters of Robert Isaac Wilberforce to Samuel Wilberforce, 1821–1856.

Green Album: Miscellaneous letters to Robert Isaac Wilberforce, including 18 from William Henn, 9 from Richard Cavendish and 6 from Henry Phillpotts, Bishop of Exeter.

MS Notebook, containing 146 pages of copies of letters in William Wilberforce's hand, and 78 pages of 'Reminiscences of his Father' written by Robert Isaac Wilberforce.

Mr Wrangham also possesses in his library some of Robert Wilberforce's personal copies of his own writings with the author's marginalia, etc.

3. KENSINGTON MSS

Letters and papers of Robert Isaac Wilberforce, collected in one large album, owned by Miss Irene Wilberforce and kept at 2, York House, Church Street, Kensington. This collection is quite small, but contains some particularly valuable letters. The contents (divided for catalogue purposes in lettered sections) are as follows:

A. 51 letters of John Henry Newman, 1827–1854.

B. 17 letters of E. B. Pusey, 1827–1854, and 2 letters of H. P. Liddon.

C. 3 letters of J. H. Newman and J. Blanco White, 1828.

D. 18 letters of W. E. Gladstone, 1838–1854.

E. 20 letters of Charles Anderson, 1832–1853.

F. 3 letters of George Prevost, 1849.

G. 8 letters of W. F. Hook, 1837–1852.

H. 7 letters of S. F. Wood, 1833–1841.

I. 6 letters of Agnes Wrangham, 1833–1834.

J. 8 letters of Jane Legard, 1833–1838.

K. 21 miscellaneous letters and papers, including 3 letters from John Newton of Olney, 3 letters of Archdeacon Francis Wrangham, certain family letters and two copies of Robert Wilberforce's description of the illness and death of his first wife.

4. SANDWITH MSS

Letters and papers of Henry William Wilberforce and William Wilberforce (eldest son of the Emancipator), owned by Mrs Judith Sandwith and kept at St Mark's Vicarage, Harrogate, Yorkshire. These are preserved in bundles as follows:

A. 16 letters of William Wilberforce, jnr., and Mary Wilberforce to Robert Isaac Wilberforce, and 2 letters of Henry Wilberforce, 1830–1833.

B. (i) 32 letters of Henry Wilberforce to Robert Wilberforce, 1830–1839.

    (ii) 33 letters of Henry Wilberforce to Robert Wilberforce, 1842–1854.

    (iii) 17 letters relating to Henry Wilberforce's conversion to the Roman Church.

    (iv) 9 miscellaneous letters of Henry Wilberforce.

C. 35 miscellaneous letters to Robert Isaac Wilberforce.

D. Miscellaneous documents and certificates.

E. Copies of 27 letters of John Keble to Robert Wilberforce.

F. 6 letters of W. E. Gladstone to Robert Wilberforce, 1851–1854.

5. RYDER MSS

Letters and papers of George Dudley Ryder, owned by Sir George Clutton, K.C.M.G., and kept at the British Embassy, Warsaw. These include:

A. Transcripts of letters from John Keble, Bishop C. R. Sumner and R. F. Wilson to George Dudley Ryder.
B. Letters of Mary Sargent to George Dudley Ryder and others.
C. Letters of members of the Wilberforce family to George Dudley Ryder.
D. Miscellaneous family letters, mainly from Sophie Ryder.

Typescript: 'A Son's Reminiscences, or A Sketch of the Ryder family, and specially of the Life and Conversion of George Dudley Ryder.' This was written for private circulation by Cyril Ryder, and is undated.

Two memoranda containing legal opinions on the claims of George Dudley Ryder and Henry Wilberforce to certain portions of the Sargent estate.

6. MANNING ARCHIVES

Letters and papers of Henry Edward Manning, the property of the Oblates of St Charles and preserved at St Mary of the Angels, Moorhouse Road, London W.2. These have been sorted into albums and bundles by the Abbé A. Chapeau. The correspondence with the various members of the Wilberforce family have been arranged into five separate bundles as follows:

1. 3 letters of William Wilberforce to William Manning.
2. 24 letters of Manning and various members of the Wilberforce family, 1839–1847.
3. 38 letters of Manning and various members of the Wilberforce family, 1848–1849.
4. 77 letters of Manning and various members of the Wilberforce family, chiefly Robert Wilberforce, 1850.
5. 26 letters of Manning and various members of the Wilberforce family, chiefly Robert Wilberforce, 1851.

The letters to and from Robert Wilberforce form the major part of this collection. E. S. Purcell, in his original biography of the Cardinal, used the letters of Manning to Robert Wilberforce extensively, but he never saw the other side of this correspondence.

7. BODLEIAN LIBRARY, OXFORD

Letters and papers of Samuel Wilberforce, the property of the late Dr Octavia Wilberforce, deposited in the Bodleian Library in 1956. These have now been catalogued. Of this huge collection, I have made use of the following:

(a) c. 186. 5 volumes of Diaries, 1831–1845, and 1 Diary relating to a holiday in Europe in 1851.
(b) c. 189. 103 letters of Sir Charles Anderson to Samuel Wilberforce, 1825–1833, and 2 additional letters of Anderson to other correspondents.
(c) c. 190. 147 letters of Sir Charles Anderson to Samuel Wilberforce, 1834–1859
(d) c. 191 (b). 231 letters of Samuel Wilberforce to Sir Charles Anderson, 1828–1859.
(e) c. 193. 9 letters of R. H. Froude to Samuel Wilberforce, 1827–1832. 62 letters of W. E. Gladstone to Samuel Wilberforce, 1834–1872.
(f) c. 195. 70 letters of Bishop C. R. Sumner to Samuel Wilberforce, including 2 to William Wilberforce, and various other letters from miscellaneous correspondents.
(g) c. 196. 45 letters from various members of the Wilberforce and Sargent families.
(h) c. 200. 76 letters relating to the Hampden Controversy of 1847–1848.

Bibliography

8. British Museum

Gladstone Papers. The correspondence with Samuel Wilberforce is collected in three volumes (vols. 258, 259, 260), Add. Mss. 44343–5, but only the first of these volumes (containing correspondence up to 1855) relates to the period covered by this book. The letters of Robert Wilberforce (37) and Henry Wilberforce (28) to Gladstone are scattered among the volumes, but they can be located very easily by referring to the separate catalogue volume of the Gladstone Papers.

9. Birmingham Oratory (The Oratory, Hagley Road, Edgbaston, Birmingham)

(a) Newman Papers. I have used letters and papers from the following boxes and bundles:

1. Miscellaneous Letters 1829–1836 (largely correspondence with Samuel Wilberforce).
2. Miscellaneous Letters 1837 (the same).
3. Newman Notebook A.7.36, containing details of Newman's relationship with Samuel Wilberforce, and copies of some letters.
4. Box 119. Correspondence with Sir James Stephen.
5. Box 137. Correspondence with Robert and William Wilberforce.

(b) Froude Papers. This very recent deposit contains several letters which passed between R. H. Froude and Samuel and Robert Wilberforce, mostly during the late 1820's.

10. Pusey House, Oxford

I have consulted the following bound volumes of Pusey letters – chiefly letters to Pusey from the correspondents named:

(a) Letters of Archdeacon Wilberforce to E. B. Pusey, 1833–1854.
(b) Letters of Bishop Wilberforce of Oxford to E. B. Pusey, 1836–1865.
(c) Letters of H. E. Manning to E. B. Pusey, 1838–1864.

11. Keble College, Oxford

John Keble's papers have been recently sorted and catalogued by the late Rev. Charles Linnell. Bundle 69 of this collection has been especially valuable to me, as it contains 51 letters of considerable interest from John Keble to Robert Wilberforce, dating from 4 May 1824 to 25 September 1854.

12. Oriel College, Oxford

The Hawkins Letters, kept in several bound volumes, have been catalogued, and it is therefore easy to locate the correspondence with the Wilberforces. I have used letters to Edward Hawkins from William and Robert Wilberforce in volumes 8, 12 and 14 of this collection.

13. Ushaw College, Durham

Letters and papers of Henry Wilberforce, and of his wife Mary. The most illuminating of these are the 62 letters of Manning to Henry and Mary Wilberforce. Microfilm enlargements of these letters, made at my request, have now been lodged among the Manning archives at St Mary of the Angels (see item 6 above).

14. LINCOLN ARCHIVES (The Castle, Lincoln)

The letters and journal of Sir Charles Anderson of Lea. The journal (AND 5/2/2) contains many references to the early friendship of Samuel Wilberforce and Charles Anderson at Oxford in the 1820's, and details of their foreign tour.

B. UNPUBLISHED THESES

Greenfield, R. H., 'The Attitude of the Tractarians to the Roman Catholic Church 1833–1850' (1956), unpublished D.Phil. thesis in the Bodleian Library, Oxford.

Pugh, R. K., 'The Episcopate of Samuel Wilberforce; with special reference to the administration of the Diocese of Oxford' (1957), unpublished D.Phil. thesis in the Bodleian Library, Oxford.

Walsh, J. D., 'The Yorkshire Evangelicals in the Eighteenth Century: with special reference to Methodism' (1956), unpublished Ph.D. thesis in the Cambridge University Library.

Willmer, H., 'Evangelicalism 1785–1835' (1962), unpublished Hulsean Prize Essay for 1962 in the Cambridge University Library.

C. PUBLISHED WORKS

This list includes only those books to which references are made in the text or in the notes. The place of publication is London unless otherwise stated.

ALLCHIN, A. M., *The Silent Rebellion.* 1958.

ALLIES, MARY H., *Thomas William Allies, 1813–1903.* 1924.

ALLIES, T. W., *A Life's Decision.* 1880.

ALTHOLZ, JOSEF L., *The Liberal Catholic Movement in England. The 'Rambler' and its Contributors 1848–1864.* 1960.

ANNAN, N. G., *Leslie Stephen. His Thought and Character in Relation to his Times.* 1951.

———, 'The Intellectual Aristocracy' in *Studies in Social History. A Tribute to G. M. Trevelyan*, edited by J. H. Plumb. 1955.

ARNOLD, MATTHEW, *Essays in Criticism*, first series. 1905.

———, *Letters*, see Russell, G. W. E.

ARNOLD, THOMAS, *Principles of Church Reform*, edited with an introduction by M. J. Jackson and J. Rogan. 1962.

ASHWELL, A. R. and WILBERFORCE, R. G., *The Life of Samuel Wilberforce*, 3 vols. 1880–2.

BALLEINE, G. R., *A History of the Evangelical Party in the Church of England.* 1933 edition.

BAMFORD, T. W., *Thomas Arnold.* 1960.

BATEMAN, J. *The Life of Daniel Wilson, Bishop of Calcutta.* 2 vols. 1860.

BATTISCOMBE, G., *John Keble. A Study in Limitations.* 1963.

BENHAM, W. (editor), *Catharine and Crauford Tait. A Memoir.* 1879.

———, see also Davidson, R. T.

BENSON, A. C., *The Life of Edward White Benson*, 2 vols. 1899.

BEST, G. F. A., *Temporal Pillars. Queen Anne's Bounty, the Ecclesiastical Commissioners and the Church of England.* Cambridge, 1964.

———, 'The Evangelicals and the Established Church' in *Journal of Theological Studies*, N.S., vol. X. April 1959.

Bibliography

BODLEY, J. E. C., *Cardinal Manning, and other Essays*. 1912.

BOYCE, J. A. S. L. LEIGHTON, *Smiths the Bankers 1658–1958*, privately printed. 1958.

BREMOND, H., *A Literary History of Religious Thought in France*, Vol. 1. 'Devout Humanism'. English edition, 1928.

BRILIOTH, Y., *The Anglican Revival, Studies in the Oxford Movement*. 1925.

——, *Evangelicalism and the Oxford Movement*. 1934.

BROOKE, STOPFORD A., *The Life and Letters of F. W. Robertson*. 1906 edition.

BROSE, O. J., *Church and Parliament. The Reshaping of the Church of England 1826–1860*. Stanford, California, and London, 1959.

BROWN, FORD K., *Fathers of the Victorians. The Age of Wilberforce*. Cambridge, 1961.

BURGON, J. W., *Lives of Twelve Good Men*, 2 vols. 1888.

BURGESS, H. J., *Enterprise in Education. The Story of the Work of the Established Church in the Education of the People prior to 1870*. 1958.

CHADWICK, OWEN, *The Founding of Cuddesdon*. Oxford, 1954.

——, *From Bossuet to Newman. The Idea of Doctrinal Development*. Cambridge, 1957.

——, *The Mind of the Oxford Movement*. 1960.

CHAPEAU, ALPHONSE, 'Manning the Anglican' in *Manning: Anglican and Catholic*, edited by John Fitzsimons. 1951.

CHAPMAN, RONALD, *Father Faber*. 1961.

Church Bells and Illustrated Church News, 16 June 1905.

CHURCH, MARY, *The Life and Letters of Dean Church*. 1895.

CHURCH, R. W., *The Oxford Movement. Twelve Years 1833–1845*. 1891.

——, *Occasional Papers*, 2 vols. 1897.

——, *Life*, see Church, Mary.

CLARKE, C. P. S., *The Oxford Movement and After*. 1932.

CNATTINGIUS, H., *Bishops and Societies. A Study of the Anglican Colonial and Missionary Expansion 1698–1850*. 1952.

COCKSHUTT, A. O. J., *Anglican Attitudes*. 1959.

COLERIDGE, J. T., *A Memoir of the Rev. John Keble*, 2 vols., second edition, 1869.

COUCH, L. M. Q. (editor), *Reminiscences of Oxford by Oxford Men 1559–1850*. Oxford Historical Society Publications, Vol. 22, Oxford, 1892.

COUPLAND, R., *Wilberforce. A Narrative*. 1923.

CROKER, JOHN WILSON, *Correspondence and Diaries*, edited by L. S. Jennings, 3 vols. 1884.

DAVIDSON, R. T. and BENHAM, W., *The Life of Archibald Campbell Tait*, 2 vols. 1891.

DAVIES, G. C. B., *Henry Phillpotts. Bishop of Exeter 1778–1869*. 1954.

DAVIES, HORTON, *Worship and Theology in England. From Watts and Wesley to Maurice, 1690–1850*. 1961.

DAWSON, CHRISTOPHER, *The Spirit of the Oxford Movement*. 1945.

DENISON, G. A., *Notes of my Life 1805–1878*. Oxford and London, 1878.

DESSAIN, C. S. (editor), *Letters and Diaries of John Henry Newman*, Vol. XI. 1961; Vol. XIII. 1963.

Dictionary of National Biography, The, edited by Sidney Lee.

DONALD, G., *Men who left the Movement*. 1933.

DOYLE, FRANCIS, *Reminiscences and Opinions 1813–1885*. 1886.

ELLIOTT-BINNS, L. E., *The Early Evangelicals. A Religious and Social Study*. 1953.

FABER, GEOFFREY, *Oxford Apostles. A Character Study of the Oxford Movement*. Pelican edition, 1954.

FAIRWEATHER, EUGENE R., *The Oxford Movement* (A Library of Protestant Thought). New York, 1964.

FIGGIS, J. N., *Churches in the Modern State*. 1913.

FITZSIMONS, J., see Chapeau, Alphonse.

FORSTER, E. M., *Marianne Thornton. A Domestic Biography*. 1956.

FRANCIS, E. K. (editor and translator), *Keble's Lectures on Poetry 1832–1841*. 1912.

FROUDE, R. HURRELL, *Remains*, edited by J. H. Newman and J. Keble, 4 vols. 1838–9.

GASH, NORMAN, *Politics in the Age of Peel. A Study in the Technique of Parliamentary Representation 1830–1850*. 1953.

GLADSTONE, W. E., 'The Evangelical Movement; its Parentage, Progress and Issue' in *Gleanings of Past Years*, vol. VII. 1879.

——, *Letters*, see Lathbury, D. C.

——, *Life*, see Morley, J.

Greville Memoirs, The. Second part, 3 vols. 1883.

HÄRDELIN, ALF, *The Tractarian Understanding of the Eucharist*. Uppsala, 1965.

HENNELL, M., *John Venn and the Clapham Sect*. 1958.

Historical Register of the University of Oxford 1220–1900, The. Oxford, 1900.

HÜGEL, F. VON, *Selected Letters 1896–1924*, edited by Bernard Holland. 1927.

INGLIS, K. S., *Churches and the Working Classes in Victorian England*. 1963.

KEBLE, JOHN, *The Christian Year*. New edition, 1899.

——, *Letters of Spiritual Counsel and Guidance*, edited by R. F. Wilson. Oxford, 1870.

——, *Occasional Papers and Reviews*, edited by E. B. Pusey. 1877.

——, *Lectures*, see Francis, E. K.

——, *Life*, see Battiscombe, G., Coleridge, J. T., Lock, Walter.

KITSON CLARK, G., *The Making of Victorian England*. 1962.

LATHBURY, D. C., *Correspondence on Church and Religion of W. E. Gladstone*, 2 vols. 1910.

LEGG, J. WICKHAM, *English Church Life from the Restoration to the Tractarian Movement*. 1914.

LESLIE, SHANE, *Henry Edward Manning. His Life and Labours*. 1921.

LIDDON, H. P., *The Life of Edward Bouverie Pusey*. 4 vols. 1894–8.

LOCK, WALTER, *John Keble*. Third edition, 1893.

LOCKHART, J. G., *Cosmo Gordon Lang*. 1949.

Lyra Apostolica. Third editiion, 1838.

MAITLAND, F. W., *Roman Canon Law in the Church of England. Six Essays*. 1898.

——, *The Life and Letters of Leslie Stephen*. 1901.

MANNING, H. E., *The English Church, its Succession and Witness for Christ*. 1835.

——, *The Address of the Clergy of the Archdeaconry of Chichester to ... the Archbishop of Canterbury, concerning Church Synods*. Chichester, 1836.

——, *The Rule of Faith*. 1838.

——, *The Rule of Faith. An Appendix*. 1838.

——, *The Principles of the Ecclesiastical Commission examined in a letter to the ... Bishop of Chichester*. 1838.

——, *National Education. A Sermon ... in behalf of Chichester Central Schools*. 1838.

——, *The Preservation of the Unendowed Canonries. A Letter to William, Lord Bishop of Chichester*. 1840.

——, *A Charge delivered at the Ordinary Visitation of the Archdeaconry of Chichester, July 1841*. 1841.

——, *The Unity of the Church*. 1842.

——, *A Charge delivered at the Ordinary Visitation of the Archdeaconry of Chichester, July 1842*. 1842.

461

Bibliography

MANNING, H. E., *A Charge delivered at the Ordinary Visitation of the Archdeaconry of Chichester, July 1845*. 1845.
——, *Sermons*, 4 vols. 1845–1850.
——, *The Appellate Jurisdiction of the Crown in Matters Spiritual. A Letter to the . . . Bishop of Chichester*. 1850.
——, *Religio Viatoris*, published anonymously, 1887.
——, *Life*, see Bodley, J. E. C.; Chapeau, Alphonse; Fitzsimons, J.; Leslie, Shane; McClelland, V. A.; Purcell, E. S.
MATHIESON, W. L., *English Church Reform 1815–1840*. 1923.
MAURICE, FREDERICK, *The Life of Frederick Denison Maurice*, 2 vols. 1884.
MCCLELLAND, V. A., *Cardinal Manning. His Public Life and Influence 1865–1892*. 1962.
MEYRICK, F., *Memories of Life at Oxford and Elsewhere*. 1905.
MIDDLETON, R. D., *Newman at Oxford. His Religious Development*. 1950.
MORLEY, J., *The Life of W. E. Gladstone*, 3 vols. 1903.
MOZLEY, ANNE (editor), *Letters and Correspondence of John Henry Newman*, 2 vols. 1891.
MOZLEY, DOROTHEA (editor), *Newman Family Letters*. 1962.
MOZLEY, JAMES B., *Letters of J. B. Mozley*, edited by his sister. 1885.
MOZLEY, T., *Reminiscences chiefly of Oriel College and the Oxford Movement*, 2 vols. 1882.
NEWMAN, J. H., *The Arians of the Fourth Century*. 1833.
——, *Lectures on Justification*. 1838.
——, *An Essay on the Development of Christian Doctrine*. 1887 edition.
——, *Loss and Gain. The Story of an Oxford Convert*. Second edition, 1848.
——, *Apologia pro Vita Sua*. Wilfrid Ward's Oxford edition, 1913.
——, *Essays Critical and Historical*, 2 vols. Second edition, 1872.
——, *Parochial and Plain Sermons*, 8 vols. 1868 edition.
——, *Sermons bearing on Subjects of the Day*. Oxford edition, 1918.
——, *Fifteen Sermons preached before the University of Oxford*. Oxford edition, 1918.
——, 'Memoir of Henry Wilberforce' in H. W. Wilberforce, *The Church and the Empires*. 1874.
——, *Correspondence of John Henry Newman with John Keble and others 1839–1845*, edited by members of the Oratory. 1911.
——, *Letters and Diaries*, see Dessain, C. S.; Mozley, Anne.
——, *Life*, see Middleton, R. D.; O'Faolain, Sean; Trevor, Meriol; Tristram, H.; Ward, Maisie; Ward, Wilfrid.
——, *Tracts*, see *Tracts for the Times*.
NEWSOME, DAVID, *Godliness and Good Learning. Four Studies on a Victorian Ideal*. 1961.
——, 'Father and Sons' in *The Historical Journal*, vol. VI. no. 2. Cambridge 1963.
——, 'Newmania' in *Journal of Theological Studies*, N.S., vol. XIV. 1963.
——, 'How Soapy was Sam?' in *History Today*, vol. XIII, no. 9, 1963.
——, 'Justification and Sanctification: Newman and the Evangelicals' in *Journal of Theological Studies*, N.S., Vol. XV. April 1964.
NIAS, J. C. S., *Gorham and the Bishop of Exeter*. 1951.
O'FAOLAIN, SEAN, *Newman's Way*. 1952.
ORNSBY, R., *Memoir of James Robert Hope-Scott*, 2 vols. 1884.
OVERTON, J. H. and WORDSWORTH, E., *Christopher Wordsworth. Bishop of Lincoln*. 1890 edition.
PALMER, WILLIAM, *A Treatise on the Church of Christ*, 2 vols. 1838.
——, *A Narrative of Events connected with the publication of the Tracts for the Times*. 1883.
PASCOE, C. F., *Two Hundred Years of the S.P.G. 1701–1900*. 1900.

PATTISON, MARK, *Memoirs*. 1883.

PECK, W. G., *The Social Implications of the Oxford Movement*. 1933.

PREVOST, GEORGE (editor), *The Autobiography of Isaac Williams*. 1892.

PURCELL, E. S., *The Life of Cardinal Manning*, 2 vols. 1896.

REDFORD, G. and JAMES, J. A. (editors), *The Autobiography of William Jay*. Second edition, 1855.

REID, T. WEMYSS, *The Life, Letters and Friendships of Richard Monckton Milnes, first Lord Houghton*, 2 vols. 1890.

REYNOLDS, J. S., *The Evangelicals at Oxford 1757–1871*. Oxford, 1953.

ROUSE BALL, W. and VENN, J. H. (editors), *Admissions to Trinity College, Cambridge 1801–1850*. 1911.

RUSSELL, G. W. E. (editor), *Letters of Matthew Arnold 1848–1880*. 2 vols. 1901.

——, *The Household of Faith. Portraits and Essays*. 1902.

RYDER, H. D. I., *Essays*. 1911.

SCOTT HOLLAND, HENRY, *A Bundle of Memories*. 1915.

SMITH, B. A., *Dean Church. The Anglican Response to Newman*. 1958.

SMYTH, CHARLES, *Simeon and Church Order. A Study of the Origins of the Evangelical Revival in Cambridge in the Eighteenth Century*. Cambridge, 1940.

——, *Cyril Forster Garbett, Archbishop of York*. 1959.

——, *The Church and the Nation. Six Studies in the Anglican Tradition*. 1962.

——, 'The Evangelical Movement in Perspective' in *Cambridge Historical Journal*, vol. VII, no. 3. 1943.

STEPHEN, CAROLINE (editor), *Sir James Stephen, Letters, with biographical notes*. Privately printed, 1906.

STEPHEN, JAMES, *Essays in Ecclesiastical Biography*, 2 vols. 1907 edition.

——, *Letters*, see Stephen, Caroline.

STEPHENS, W. R. W., *The Life and Letters of Walter Farquhar Hook*, 2 vols. 1878.

STORR, V. R., *The Development of English Theology in the Nineteenth Century, 1800–1860*. 1913.

SUMNER, G. H., *Life of Charles Richard Sumner, Bishop of Winchester*. 1876.

TAVARD, G. H., *The Quest for Catholicity*. 1963.

THOM, J. H. (editor), *The Life of Joseph Blanco White written by himself*, 3 vols. 1845.

Tracts for the Times, by Members of the University of Oxford, 6 vols. Second edition, 1839–41.

TRENCH, RICHARD CHENEVIX, *Letters and Memorials, edited by the author of 'Charles Lowder'*, 2 vols. 1888.

TREVOR, MERIOL, *Newman. The Pillar of the Cloud*. 1962.

——, *Newman, Light in Winter*. 1962.

TRISTRAM, H. (editor), *John Henry Newman Centenary Essays*. 1945.

TUCKER, H. W., *Memoir of the Life and Episcopate of G. A. Selwyn*, 2 vols. 1879.

TUCKWELL, WILLIAM. *Reminiscences of Oxford*. 1900.

——, *Pre-Tractarian Oxford*. 1909.

VERE, AUBREY DE, *Recollections*. 1897.

Victoria History of the County of Yorkshire, edited W. Page. Vol. III. 1913.

VIDLER, ALEC (editor), *Objections to Christian Belief*. 1963.

VOLL, DIETER, *Catholic Evangelicalism*. 1963.

WARD, MAISIE, *The Wilfrid Wards and the Transition. I. The Nineteenth Century*. 1934.

——, *Young Mr. Newman*. 1948.

WARD, WILFRID, *W. G. Ward and the Oxford Movement*. 1889.

WARD, WILFRID, *Aubrey de Vere. A Memoir*. 1904.

——, *Ten Personal Studies*. 1908.

——, *The Life of John Henry Cardinal Newman*, 2 vols. 1912.

WARD, WILLIAM GEORGE, *The Ideal of a Christian Church*. 1844.

——, *Life*, see Ward, Wilfrid.

WEBB, C. C. J., *Religious Thought in the Oxford Movement*. 1928.

WELCH, P. J., 'Blomfield and Peel: a study in co-operation between Church and State' in *Journal of Ecclesiastical History*, vol. 12. 1961.

WESTCOTT, A., *The Life and Letters of Brooke Foss Westcott*, 2 vols. 1903.

WHALE, J. S., *The Protestant Tradition*. Cambridge, 1955.

WICKHAM, E. R., *Church and People in an Industrial City*. 1957.

WILBERFORCE, A. M. (editor), *The Private Papers of William Wilberforce*. 1897.

——, *Lavington. The History of a Sussex Family*. Privately printed, 1919.

WILBERFORCE, H. W., *The Parochial System. An Appeal to English Churchmen*. 1838.

——, *Reasons for submitting to the Catholic Church: A Farewell Letter to his late Parishioners*. 1851.

——, *The Church and the Empires*. 1874.

WILBERFORCE, R. G., see Ashwell, A. R.

WILBERFORCE, ROBERT ISAAC, *The Five Empires. An Outline of Ancient History*. 1840.

——, *A Primary Charge to the Clergy of the Archdeaconry of the East Riding*. 1841.

——, *Rutilius and Lucius, or Stories of the Third Age*. 1842.

——, *Church Courts and Church Discipline*. 1843.

——, *A Charge delivered at the Ordinary Visitation of the Archdeaconry of the East Riding 1843*. 1843.

——, *A Charge to the Clergy of the Archdeaconry of the East Riding at the Ordinary Visitation a.d. 1845*. 1845.

——, *The Doctrine of the Incarnation of our Lord Jesus Christ*. 1848.

——, *The Doctrine of Holy Baptism*. 1849.

——, *The Practical Effects of the Gorham Case. A Charge to the Clergy of the Archdeaconry of the East Riding, delivered at his Ordinary Visitation, a.d. 1850*. 1850,

——, *Sermons on the New Birth of Man's Nature*. 1850.

——, *A Sketch of the History of Erastianism*. 1851.

——, *A Charge to the Clergy of the East Riding, delivered at the Ordinary Visitation a.d. 1851*. 1851.

——, *The Doctrine of the Holy Eucharist*. 1853.

——, *An Inquiry into the Principles of Church-Authority, or Reasons for recalling my Subscription to the Royal Supremacy*. 1854.

—— and WILBERFORCE, SAMUEL, *The Life of William Wilberforce*, 5 vols. 1838.

——, *The Correspondence of William Wilberforce*, 2 vols. 1840.

WILBERFORCE, SAMUEL, *The Note Book of a Country Clergyman*. 1833.

——, *A Sketch of the Life of the Rev. John Sargent*. 1861 edition.

——, 'Sacred Poetry' in *British Critic*, vol. XXI, no. XLI. 1837.

——, *Agathos, and other Sunday Stories*. 1840.

——, *Four Sermons preached before . . . Queen Victoria in 1841 and 1842*. 1842.

——, *The Rocky Island*. 1852 edition.

——, *A Charge delivered at the Ordinary Visitation of the Archdeaconry of Surrey, November 1842*. 1842.

——, *A Charge delivered at the Ordinary Visitation of the Archdeaconry of Surrey, November 1843*. 1843.

——, *A History of the Protestant Episcopal Church in America*. Third edition, 1856.

Bibliography

WILBERFORCE, SAMUEL, *A Charge delivered at the Ordinary Visitation of the Archdeaconry of Surrey, April 1845*. 1845.

——, *Six Sermons preached before the University of Oxford*. Second edition, 1848.

——, *A Charge delivered to the Clergy of the Diocese of Oxford at his Primary Visitation, September and October 1848*. 1848.

——, *A Charge to the Clergy of the Diocese of Oxford at his Second Visitation, 1851*. 1851.

——, *Life*, see Ashwell, A. R. and Wilberforce, R. G.

WILLIAMS, ISAAC, see Prevost, George, and *Tracts for the Times*.

WORDSWORTH, CHARLES, *Annals of my Early Life 1806–1846*. 1891.

INDEX

Index

Bell, Andrew, 219
Bennett, W. J. E., 303, 320, 351, 362
Benson, Edward White, Archbishop of Canterbury, 267 n.
Benson, R. M., 332
Bentham, Jeremy, 6
Best, Dr G. F. A., 53, 211, 215
Bethel Union, The, 68
Bevan, Miss, 148–50, 200
Beveridge, William, Bishop of St Asaph, 176, 179, 241
Beverley, 249, 279–80; Minster at, 250
Bible Society, 8, 28–9, 59; R. and S. Wilberforce sever connection with, 170
Bidborough, 40
Bird, Elizabeth, 22–3, 25
Bird, Hannah, see Sumner, Hannah
Bird, John, 23, 25
Bird, Mary, 22, 24
Birmingham, 26, 172–3, 386
Bishopthorpe, 171, 278
Blachford, Lord, see Rogers, Frederic
Blackgang Chine (I.O.W.), 157–8
Bletchley, 360
Blomfield, C. J., Bishop of London, 256, 266, 289, 304, 320, 353; and church reform, 212, 215; and education, 221; and missionary bishops, 216, 218; and T. W. Allies, 342
Bodley, J. E. C., 70, 323–4
Bonn, 78, 137–8
Boone, S., 188
Bowden, Mary-Anne, 400
Bowdler, John, 36, 38
Boyle, Patrick, 67, 126
Bradford, 246
Bramford Speke, 345, 354
Bramhall, John, Archbishop of Armagh, 176, 310, 329, 401
Brandis, Professor, 138
Bransgore, 231; H. Wilberforce as curate of, 155, 228–30
Brasenose College, Oxford, 288
Braybrooke, 3rd Baron, 245
Bremond, Henri, 63
Brevint, Daniel, 334
Brighstone, 46, 143, 244, 246, 257, 262, 283, 369; description of, 156–7; domestic life of Wilberforces at, 156–9; ministry of S. Wilberforce at, 234–5, 237–8, 241–2; S. Wilberforce offered living of, 130–1
Brighton, Newman at, 86, 90, 92; S. Wilberforce's sermons in Pavilion at, 264 and n.; Wilberforces at, 36
Brilioth, Yngve, 13–14, 19, 207
British Critic, The, 188, 197, 215, 286, 314; Newman ends S. Wilberforce's connection with, 193–4
British Magazine, The, 188, 202, 206, 215
British Museum, 36
Broomfield (Clapham), 20, 33
Brose, Dr Olive, 215
Brougham, Lord, 141–2, 197

Brown, Ford K., 9, 13, 174
Brownbill, Father (S.J.), 358, 366
Brussels, H. Wilberforce received into R.C. Church in, 358–9; S. Wilberforce in, 103
Bull, George, Bishop of St David's, 201, 334
Buller, Sir Charles, 65
Bullingdon Green, 98
Bulteel, H. B., 8
Bunsen, Chevalier, 264, 289
Bunyan, John, 276
Burden, Father, 400
Burgess, H. J., 219
Burgon, J. W., Dean of Chichester, 59–60, 336
Burke, Edmund, 31
Burley, H. Wilberforce's new church at, 228
Burnet, Gilbert, Bishop of Salisbury, 74, 276
Burrows, General, 257
Burton, Edward, 166
Burton, Agnes, 132, 199, 309, 384, 389, 401; description of church at, 250; restoration of church at, 280; R. Wilberforce's move to, 249–50; R. Wilberforce's problems at, 277–81; situation at, on eve of R. Wilberforce's secession, 397
Butler, Joseph, Bishop of Durham, 88, 106, 185–6, 311, 315, 385
Butler, W. J., and S. Wilberforce, 332, 353; his respect for Manning, 320
Byron, Lord, 65

Cadogan Place, no. 44, death of W. Wilberforce at, 145; Manning staying at, 366; Mary Wilberforce received into R.C. Church at, 358
Calcutta, Manning offered headship of College at, 267; rumour of R. Wilberforce becoming Bishop of, 141
Calthorpe, Lord, 26, 79, 124
Calvinism, B. Wilberforce on, 177; its connection with nineteenth-century Evangelicalism, 47–8; Manning on, 201; of G. C. Gorham, 345, 349; of Leighton, 107; of Newman and Manning, 208–9; of Romaine, 421; of the popular preacher Malan, 80–1; R. Wilberforce's understanding of, 375, 380–1; S. Wilberforce's contempt for, 166, 170, 176, 178
Cambridge, University of, 141, 410; era of brilliance at, 64–5; Evangelicalism at, 8, 57, 60; R. Wilberforce's visit to, 79–80; W. Wilberforce jnr. at, 3, 58–9, 133; W. Wilberforce's opinion of, 57–8
Canning, Lord, 64, 67
Canterbury, J. B. Sumner's enthronement at, 301
Cano, Melchior, 328
Capes, F., 405
Cardwell, E., Principal of St Alban Hall, Oxford, 78, 304
Cardwell, Viscount, 69
Carey, Mary (née Manning), 23 n., 148 and n., 366

468

Index

East Riding, *see* Yorkshire
East Waltham, offer of curacy of, 79
Eastbourne, 36
Eastern Orthodox Church, and Jerusalem bishopric, 289; H. Manning on, 293; its relation to R.C. Church, 347; R. Wilberforce on, 291
Easton, G. Ryder as Vicar of, 153, 231
Eccleshall Castle, 153
Ecclesiastical Commission, 211–2, 218, 223, 304, 336; H. Wilberforce's criticism of, 225–6; Manning's attack on, 214–5, 267
Ecclesiastical Gazette, The, 249
Ecclesiology, Manning's views on, 270; Newman mocks enthusiasm over, 314; relation of, to High Churchmanship, 318; S. Wilberforce's views on, 272–3. *See also* Ritualism
Eden, C. P., 114, 169
Edgware Road, W. Wilberforce jnr.'s business in, 133, 135
Edinburgh Review, The, 175
Education, and the National Society, 218–222; in schools at Brighstone, 237; in schools at E. Farleigh, 236; of Herbert Wilberforce, 265; of the Wilberforce family, 38–45
Effects of Infant Baptism, The (W. Goode), 375
Egyptian Hall, S. Wilberforce's speech at, 256
Eikon Basilike, S. Wilberforce on, 128
Elgin, Lord, 64
Emotionalism, at Oxford, 62–4; in religious worship, 49–50, 74–6; over death-beds, 239–40
Emsworth, 40
Episcopacy, Gladstone on weakness of, in England, 363; Keble on divine nature of, 76; Manning on, 214; Newman's and Pusey's respect for, 195; R. Wilberforce's study on origins of, 398; S. Wilberforce on missionary rôle of, 215–8; S. Wilberforce's respect for, 172–3; W. Wilberforce's respect for, 52–3
Erastianism, and church reform, 212–5, 222; implicit in Gorham Judgment, 348–54; implicit in Hampden crisis, 337–8, 342; Keble on, 76; Manning's hatred of, 200, 204, 267, 269; R. Wilberforce on origins of, 398–9; W. Henn on, 390. *See also* Church and State
Essays and Reviews (1860), 70, 128 n., 334, 373
Essay on Development (J. Newman), 324, 398; Manning attempt to answer, 315–6, 320–1; Newman's discussion of, 384–6; opinions of, 314–5
Eternal Priesthood, The (H. Manning), 203
Eton College, 41; Gladstone, Simeon and Sumner at, 8; J. Sargent at, 120; sons of R. and S. Wilberforce at, 397
Eucharist, doctrine of, A. Knox's views on, 197; and S. Wilberforce, 187, 334, 380–1;

as a subject of theological conflict, 374; in Tractarianism, 180; Keble on, 395; Manning's early views on, 200–1, 209; Newman on Evangelical understanding of, 74; Protestant irreverence towards, 235; Pusey's sermon on, 284, 374
Euripides, 99
Eusebius of Nicomedia, 413
Evangelicalism, and opposition to Ecclesiastical Commission, 214; and providences, 106; and religious societies, 9, 218–9; and sacramentalism, 14; and the Established Church, 10–12, 52–3; at Cambridge, 8, 57, 60; at Oxford, 8, 57, 234; characteristics of, 2, 10–12, 35, 47–56, 172, 180, 374; crisis of, in early 19th century, 5–16; in the mission field, 216; in writings of S. Wilberforce, 175–6, 240; its relationship with Tractarianism, 12–16, 194; J. Stephen's estimate of, 184; Keble's abhorrence of, 73–4; Newman's opinion of, 185–6; numerical strength of, 8–9; of Barbara Wilberforce, 27–30, 177; of Daniel Wilson, 171–2; of J. B. Sumner, 301; of J. Sargent, 121–2; of Manning, 148–50, 200, 202, 410; of the Ryders, 151–2; of the Spooners, 26; preaching techniques of, 30, 170; R. Wilberforce on doctrines of, 79–81, 170–1; S. Wilberforce's opinions of, 73, 79–81, 101, 105–7, 127–9, 169–70, 172–4, 234–5, 334; W. Wilberforce's understanding of doctrines of, 47–56, 175
Evangelical Magazine, The, 10, 240
Evangelical Revival, 7–9, 14, 46; its connection with Clapham, 21–2
Exeter, diocese of, S. Wilberforce's tour in, 218, 255
Exeter College, Oxford, 92, 196
Exeter Hall, S. Wilberforce's speech at, 256–8
Eyre, Mr, 134–5

Faber, F. W., 275, 342, 355, 386
Faber, Sir Geoffrey, 68
Faith of Catholics, The (Berington and Kirk), 207
Fairford, 84, 395
Family prayers, 2; of the Wilberforce family, 33–4
Farington Diary, 33
Farish, William, 8
Farnham, 229, 244, 282
Fathers (of the early Church), Allies' study of 343; influence on Tractarianism of, 75–6; Keble on, 394–5; Manning's study of, 199–200, 206, 328; Newman's study of, 112, 164, 175, 384; R. Wilberforce's respect for, 178, 373, 379; S. Wilberforce's disapproval of too much reliance upon, 191–2
Fathers of the Victorians (F. K. Brown), 13
Faussett, G., 284
Figgis, J. N., 271

Index

Index

vert, 403–4; his views on celibacy, 104, 113, 141, 153–5, 314; on A. Knox, 197; on confession, 233; on death of Froude, 168; on Evangelicalism, 8, 14, 74, 185–6; on justification and sanctification, 182–3, 198; on latitudinarianism, 6; on W. Wilberforce jnr., 132; sermons of, 12, 177, 181–3, 188, 202

Newman, Mary, 90–2, 98

Newman, Mrs Jemina, 85, 91–2

Newport (I.O.W.), 155, 229, 234, 238, 244, 246

Newport Pagnell, 36

Newton, John, 7, 13, 48

Nicaea, Council of, 385, 398

Nicoll, A., 85

Niebuhr, Dr, 138, 165

Noel, Baptist, 129

Noel, Louisa, 46, 129, 156, 158, 168–9, 187 n., 195, 242, 265, 301

'Noetics', the, 66, 94, 104, 166; as exemplified by Blanco White, 87

'Nominal' Christianity, Evangelical understanding of, 9, 47–8, 52

Northcote, Sir Stafford, 67

Notebook of a Country Clergyman (S. Wilberforce), 119, 176, 240

Nuneham Courtenay, 39–40, 59–60, 91–2, 110

Oakeley, Frederick, 67, 101, 104, 129, 196, 287, 311, 344 n.; and influence of W. G. Ward, 285–6; Dean Church on, 403; discussed by S. Wilberforce and Froude, 102–3; his letters to S. Wilberforce, 98, 100; Keble's inability to understand, 396

O'Connell, D., 212

O'Faolain, Sean, 90–1

Oratory, at Birmingham, 386; at London, 356

Oriel College, Oxford, 39, 63, 128–9, 151–2, 166; academic prestige of, 65–7, 69; effect upon of Tractarianism, 194, 196; election of Hawkins as Provost of, 82–4; Fellowship examination at, 65; R. Wilberforce as tutor of, 84–6, 90, 92–5; R. Wilberforce resigns Fellowship at, 144; reasons for sending Wilberforce brothers to, 57, 59–61; respect for Church and King at, 57, 61; S. Wilberforce's description of Common Room at, 169; S. Wilberforce's return to, 266; Wilberforces at, 3, 62, 71–3, 77–9, 96–101, 108–15

Origin of Species, The (Darwin), 128 n.

Orme, Charlotte, 120

Orme, Garton, 119–20, 123

Otley, Mr, 99

Otter, William, Bishop of Chichester, 215, 267–8

Otterbourne, consecration of church at, 196

Owen, John, 59

Owen, Mary, *see* Wilberforce, Mrs Mary

Oxford Movement, *see* Tractarianism

Oxford, diocese of, 195; S. Wilberforce appointed Bishop of, 304–7; S. Wilberforce's work as Bishop of, 330–6

Oxford Union, 65, 68–70, 98–9, 111–2, 148

Oxford, University of, 16, 27–8, 54, 56, 125, 129, 141, 147, 151–3, 171–2, 176, 187, 192, 229, 283, 292; academic revolution at, 65–8; anti-Tractarian hysteria in, 284, 293; as pictured in *Loss and Gain*, 313; churchmanship of, 60–2; development of corporate sense in, 68–9; dispute over Catholic Emancipation at, 94–5; early stages of Tractarianism at, 163–9; Evangelicalism at, 8, 57, 234; growth of 'apostolical' views in, 196–7; H. Wilberforce on gossip at, 164–8, 196; its ignorance of German, 78; Manning at, 4, 67–9, 148; Manning's ban on Catholics attending, 410; Newman's sermons before, 88; Poetry Professorship election at, 287–8; R. Wilberforce's sermons before, 375; reasons for sending Wilberforce brothers to, 57–62; reasons for R. Wilberforce leaving, 95–6, 136; renaissance atmosphere in, 62–5, 69, 155; S. Wilberforce's return to, 266; S. Wilberforce's sermons before, 190–2; Wilberforces at, 4, 41, 62, 71–3, 77–115

Paget, Miss, 264

Palmer, Roundell, 69

Palmer, William, 287, 296

Palmerston, Lord, 244

Papacy, Newman on primacy of, 384–5; R. Wilberforce attacks primacy of, 291; R. Wilberforce's study of supremacy of, 397–9; S. Wilberforce on abominations of, 401

'Papal Aggression', the, 366, 405

Paris, R. Wilberforce's distaste for, 72; R. Wilberforce received into R.C. Church in, 402; Ryders in, 310–1; S. Wilberforce in, 101; W. Wilberforce jnr. in, 246

Parochial and Plain Sermons (J. Newman), 198; Evangelical temper of, 12; S. Wilberforce's criticism of, 182–4

Parochial System, The (H. Wilberforce), 223–226, 228

Pascal, B., 104

Passaglia, Carlo, 314

Pastoral Work, of G. Ryder, 231; of H. Wilberforce, 229–30; of J. Sargent, 121–2; of Manning, 232–3; of R. Wilberforce, 235–6; of S. Wilberforce, 129–30, 234–5, 237–9, 281–3

Patrick, Simon, Bishop of Chichester, 276

Pattison, Mark, 65, 67, 69

Paul of Samosata, 385

Pearson, John, Bishop of Chester, 334

'Peculiars', *see* Evangelicalism

Peel, Sir Robert, 94–5, 142, 211–2, 214, 221, 257, 342; S. Wilberforce's hopes for preferment from, 244–5, 247, 297; sends S. Wilberforce to diocese of Oxford, 304–5

477

Index

Index

Sargent, Harry (Henry Martyn), 115, 122, 146, 258
Sargent, John (father of Rector of Lavington), 120, 146
Sargent, John, Rector of Lavington, 3, 23 n., 96, 100–1, 103, 105, 134, 141, 147, 150, 175, 367; death of, 146; early life and character of, 120–2; Emily Wilberforce's letter to, 129; funeral of, 151; H. Wilberforce living with, 40, 112, 115; his encounters with rioters, 127; his offer of a curacy to H. Wilberforce, 115–7; on avoiding a meeting with Keble, 85; on the living of Brighstone, 131
Sargent, John Garton (son of Rector of Lavington), 122, 145, 258
Sargent, Mary (née Smith), 23 n., 123 n., 127, 146–7, 156, 158, 232, 308, 313, 329, 367, 404; and death of Caroline, 251–2; and death of Emily, 261–3; and reception of Ryder family, 312; character of, 261–3; death of, 411; her letter on Sophia's marriage, 152–3; her letters to her children, 251–2, 362, 368; her love for Manning, 150; her marriage, 120–1; letters of John Sargent to, 85; letters of Manning to, 150–1; on H. Wilberforce's secession, 362; on Manning's secession, 368
Sargent, Mary (daughter of Rector of Lavington), see Wilberforce, Mary
Sargent, Sophia, see Ryder, Sophia
Sark, visit of Sumner and S. Wilberforce to, 1
Savonarola, 64
Schlegel, Professor, 138
Schleiermacher, F., 78, 377–8
Scholar-gipsy, The (M. Arnold), 70
Scotland, Church of, 290, 387, 400
Scott, Thomas, 7, 13–14, 185, 294
Scott, Walter, 34
Selwyn, G. A., Bishop of New Zealand, 218 and n., 316, 318
Serious Call to a Devout and Holy Life, A (W. Law), 73
Seriousness, as an Evangelical attribute, 49–52, 74; in G. D. Ryder, 152
Sermons, of Evangelicals compared with 'High and Dry', 170, 184–5; of Manning, 203–10, 220, 292; of Newman, 12, 177, 181–3, 202; of Ryder, 169; of H. Wilberforce, 177, 229, 349; of R. Wilberforce, 48, 235–6, 375–8; of S. Wilberforce, 190–2, 264 and n.
Sermons on the New Birth of Man's Nature (R. Wilberforce), 375–8
Sevenoaks (Kent), 150 n., 267
Sewell, William, 196
Shakespeare, William, 103
Shalfleet, H. Wilberforce offered living of, 155
Shelley, P. B., 65
Shepherd of Salisbury Plain, The, 34
Sheridan, R. B., 34

Shirley, W. A., 172
Shuttleworth, W., Bishop of Chichester, 168, 268, 366
Shuttleworth, Mrs W., 268
Sibthorp, R. W., 287 n.
Sicily, Newman's visit to, 7, 63, 113, 163
Siddons, Mrs, 20
Sierra Leone, 31
Simeon, Charles, 3, 8–10, 48, 57, 105, 124, 141, 184, 243, 294; and John Sargent, 120–1; compared with Newman, 182; his fear of adventism, 11–12
Simpson, Richard, 405
Sisterhoods, and S. Wilberforce, 332–3; and W. Dodsworth, 320; Anglo-catholic interest in, 319
Skinner, Mr, Curate at Burton Agnes, 280
Slave Trade, abolition of, 9, 26
Slavery, abolition of, 145
Smith, Abel, II, 22, 24, 120–1, 147
Smith, B. A., 63
Smith, Elizabeth (Mrs William Manning), 23–4, 120
Smith, Lucy, 145
Smith, Mary, see Sargent, Mary
Smith, Mosley, 123 n.
Smith, Patty, 134
Smith, Payne and Smith (Bankers), 22 n.
Smith, Robert, 1st Baron Carrington, 23–4, 120–1
Smith, Thomas, 22 n.
Smollett, T., 34
Smyth, Canon Charles, 70
Snowdon, 37
Socinianism, 176, 178, 235, 338–9, 342
Sophocles, 99
Southampton, 238, 243
Southrop Rectory, 29, 66, 73, 77, 96
Sparrow, Lady, 58–9
S.P.C.K., 8, 202, 237
Spedding, James, 65
S.P.G., 8, 172, 216, 218, 256, 277–8, 336; S. Wilberforce's tour on behalf of, 255
Spooner, Barbara, see Wilberforce, Barbara
Spooner, Catharine, see Tait, Catharine
Spooner, Isaac, 20, 26
Spooner, Richard, 134–5, 172–3
Spooner, William, Archdeacon of Coventry, 26, 141
Spragge, F. R., 29, 40
Spring-Rice, Thomas, 1st Baron Monteagle, 227
Stanley, A. P., Dean of Westminster, 67, 293
Stanley, Edward, Bishop of Norwich, 213, 221
Stanstead Park (Sussex), 40
Stanton, Arthur, 319 n.
Stephen, St, 385
Stephen, James (Clapham Sect), 26, 41, 122, 138, 141
Stephen, Sir James, 21–2, 26, 131, 174–5, 242, 278, 284; and Newman, 182–8, 313–4; his letters to S. Wilberforce, 30, 182–3,

480

Index

186-7, 226-7; on Evangelicalism, 8, 11, 30, 182-3, 186-7; on the restless spirit of the age, 6; on W. Wilberforce, 35
Stephen, Leslie, 21
Stillingfleet, 176
Stirling Club, 256
Stockmar, Baron, 264
Stokes Bay (Portsmouth), 281
Stonyhurst, 125
Stowe, 36
Strachey, Sir E., 303
Strasbourg, S. Wilberforce at, 407
Streatham, Manning at school at, 40
Suarez, F., 328
Sumner, C. R., Bishop of Winchester, 1, 23, 25, 128, 141, 155-7, 159, 176, 256, 268, 285; and H. Wilberforce, 228-9, 229 n.; and S. Wilberforce, 9, 105, 124-5, 130, 156, 158, 222, 239, 242-4, 282, 288, 334; his letter on Ryder's secession, 312; R. and S. Wilberforce differ in opinion of, 158, 170-1; resignation of, 411
Sumner, Hannah (née Bird), 23, 25
Sumner, J. B., Archbishop of Canterbury, 8, 23, 25, 106, 125, 132, 141, 216, 236, 291, 297, 358, 372, 387; Gladstone's low opinion of, 332; H. Wilberforce's description of enthronement of, 301; H. Wilberforce's letter to, on secession to R.C. Church, 359
Sunderland, Lord, 65
Surrey, S. Wilberforce becomes Archdeacon of, 255
'Swing Riots', 6
Switzerland, H. Wilberforce in, 114; S. Wilberforce in, 101; W. Wilberforce jnr. in, 135
Sykes, Joseph, 23
Sykes, Marianne, 23

Tait, A. C., Archbishop of Canterbury, 26, 67, 69, 411
Tait, Catharine (née Spooner), 26
Taunton, W. Wilberforce jnr. stands as M.P. for, 246
Taylor, Jeremy, 189, 310, 328, 378, 388; Manning's respect for, 201, 275-6; S. Wilberforce's respect for, 176, 191
Teignmouth, Lord, 22
Temple, Frederick, Archbishop of Canterbury, 67
Temple Bar, 8, 243
Tennyson, Alfred Lord, 65
Tertullian, 315, 334
Thirty-nine Articles, 166, 176, 206, 289 n., 344; and subscription to, against W. G. Ward, 293-4; and Tract 90, 284; interpretation of, in Gorham Judgment, 349; Manning on, 346
Tholuck, Professor, 78
Thomason, James, 40
Thorndike, Herbert, 214, 269
Thornton, Henrietta, 33

Thornton, Henry, 2, 20-3, 28
Thornton, Henry, jnr., 60
Thornton, John, 23
Thornton, Marianne, 22, 60; on Barbara Wilberforce, 26-7; on family prayers at Highwood, 33-4; on Edward Irving, 11; on W. Wilberforce jnr., 132; on Wilberforce household, 30-1
Thucydides, 99
Timor Mortis, as an element in conversion, 312, 322, 356
Tithes, at Alverstoke, 257; at Brighstone, 237; at E. Farleigh, 144
Tokat, H. Martyn's death at, 9
Tonbridge, 40
Torquay, 394
Tract 90 (J. Newman), 192, 293-4
Tractarianism, and awareness of reforming needs, 226; and celibacy, 97, 104-5, 153-5; and interest in Catholic devotions, 267; and Jerusalem bishopric, 289; and poetry professorship, 287-8; and R. Wilberforce, 197-9, 372-81; and sacramentalism, 14, 180, 319; apocalyptic note in, 7; attacks against, 194-5, 293-5; beginnings of, 163-9; C. Anderson on, 186; effects on, of Manning's preferment, 268; increasing enthusiasm of Wilberforces for, 195-7; influence of Keble on, 74-6, 285; the Evangelical origins and attributes, 8, 12-15, 106; its relation to Oxford revival of learning, 62-3; J. Stephen on, 186-7; later developments of, 284-7; liturgical marks of, 229-30; Manning's part in, 199-202, 206, 317-20; Manning's defence of, 292-3; Newman's repudiation of, 313-5; of Edward Coleridge, 316; of H. Wilberforce, 229-31; 298-301; pietism in, 14, 106; S. Wilberforce on, 172-4, 179-80, 187, 194-5, 272; severity in theology of, 180-3, 208-10; theological content of, 179-81, 374-81
Tracts for the Times, 4, 62, 155, 159, 163-4, 173, 186, 192, 201, 203, 284, 286; C. R. Sumner's opinion of, 15; Manning's support for, 199-200; S. Wilberforce's opinions of, 176, 179
Tranby (Yorkshire), 23
Trench, R. C., Archbishop of Dublin, 65, 282, 308
Trent, Council of, 294, 323, 328, 387
Trevor, Meriol, 93, 132, 155
Trinity College, Cambridge, W. Wilberforce jnr. at, 58-9
Trinity College, Oxford, 65, 68, 196
Trinity Hall, Cambridge, 57
Trotter, Captain, 256
Tübingen, 373
Tuckwell, William, 63-4, 84
Tunbridge Wells, 228, 242, 356
Tyler, J. E., Dean of Oriel, 69

Ulcombe (Kent), 90-2, 97

Index